PSYCHOLOGY FOR
TEACHERS AND STUDENTS

PSYCHOLOGY
for Teachers and Students

Judith Worell
William E. Stilwell

UNIVERSITY OF KENTUCKY

McGRAW-HILL BOOK COMPANY

New York   St. Louis   San Francisco   Auckland   Bogotá   Hamburg   Johannesburg
London   Madrid   Mexico   Montreal   New Dehli   Panama   Paris   São Paulo
Singapore   Sydney   Tokyo   Toronto

**PSYCHOLOGY FOR
TEACHERS AND STUDENTS**

234567890   RMRM   8987654321

This book was set in Times Roman by Monotype Composition Company, Inc. The editors were William A. Talkington and David Dunham; the designer was Anne Canevari Green; the photo editor was Linda Gutierrez; cover photos were taken by Paul Fusco (back) and Eve Arnold (front); the production supervisor was Dominick Petrellese. The drawings were done by Fine Line Illustrations, Inc.

Library of Congress Cataloging in Publication Data
Worell, Judith, date
    Psychology for teachers and students.
    Bibliography.
    Includes index.
    1.   Teacher-student relationships.
2.   Teachers—Psychology.   3.   Students—
Psychology.   I.   Stilwell, William E., joint
author.   II.   Title.
LB1033.W73   371.1′02   79-21947
ISBN 0-07-071870-9

To the many teachers and students who taught us.
To our children: Amy, Beth, and Wendy Worell;
Belen and Wes Stilwell.
To the teachers of our children's children. . . .

CONTENTS

PREFACE

This book focuses on teachers and students interacting within an effective social learning environment. We wrote the book primarily for undergraduates who are beginning their studies in educational psychology and teacher education. Over time, we have found that more advanced students and in-service teachers will use *Psychology for Teachers and Students* as a reference text throughout their careers in education and in the helping professions.

Our purpose in writing this book is to offer an eclectic and practical behavioral approach to the application of psychology to classroom teaching. The behavioral view here embraces and integrates social learning theories and a cognitive learning skills hierarchy. We call the outcome of this integration "cognitive social learning theory." Throughout, emphasis is given to theory and research which use definable constructs and observable data. Therefore, we remain open to using parts of various theories and applications which fit these criteria. Where appropriate, we present contrasting views which we evaluate for their utility in practical classroom applications. We have tried to place research in a perspective between theory and application. We want the student to be oriented toward evaluating and selecting procedures based upon evidence rather than upon opinion or expediency.

The focus of both theory and research is upon practical applications to real children in natural learning environments. Thus, we describe the interactions of several elementary and secondary students throughout each chapter. In this way, you can become conversant with how theories of development, learning, and instruction provide explanations and guidance for real-life decisions and problem solving. We emphasize a competency-based approach by means of learning objectives, performance-based activities, periodic assessment, and self-evaluation within each chapter. In this way, you will have the opportunity to participate actively in learning and practicing usable skills.

Our style throughout is personal and conversational. We want you to become involved and interested in applying the ideas we discuss to your own behavior. As a teacher, we hope you will find that you can grow creatively and flourish as an individual. We hope you will find that you can be an experimentalist and try out new ideas, that you can relate to students in a meaningful way, and that you can experience joy and challenge in the classroom.

HOW WE ORGANIZED THIS BOOK

You will want to use the organization of the book in two ways: first, by considering the four major content sections, and second, by looking at the pattern of organization within each chapter. Before you use this book, we must introduce you to an important concept that is used throughout the chapters. We have adopted a spiral curriculum approach to the development of concepts and their applications. This spiral curriculum method of presenting content suggests that many advanced ideas are presented early but are not completely developed because their application depends upon further elaboration and more advanced concepts. Thus, you will be introduced early to terms that will be more fully expanded in later chapters. Each chapter builds upon previous ones by integrating key ideas with later explanation, research, and examples. Therefore, we advise careful planning if you decide to reorder the presentation of chapters. You may want to provide some additional background to fill in terms and concepts if chapters later in the book are considered very early in the semester. A look at the number of glossary terms for each chapter will cue you into this procedure. Later chapters have fewer terms, since these were introduced earlier and are integrated in later chapters as we consider new content.

In addition to the key terms and concepts developed sequentially, we have also included some more advanced terms in italics for optional use by the instructor. These terms are relevant to the content being discussed, but are not critical for student understanding of the concepts. Therefore, we have italicized these terms in order to cue instructors. Most of the terms in italics are those which you may wish to ignore and exclude from your curriculum. These terms are not defined in the glossary, and their use is left to your discretion.

There are four major sections. In Part 1, "Introduction to Teaching," we present the basic learning dyad of teacher and students interacting within a social learning environment. Here, you will find a useful teaching model for understanding your role as a teacher. We believe that good teachers do many of the same things in most situations. We also believe that you will apply your knowledge and skills differently as a *facilitator* of individual development, as a *mediator* of interpersonal relations, and as a *manager* of the learning environment. In each of these teaching roles you will find it useful to focus on a basic teaching model. In this model, you will find objectives, assessment of entering behaviors, instructional procedures, evaluation, and feedback. This model for effective teaching is then carried forward throughout all sections of the book.

Part 2 contains three chapters on mediating social and cognitive development. Chapter 2 talks about broad developmental processes and how you can understand each individual child in a unique social learning environment. Chapter 3 focuses on social development, and Chapter 4 gives a broad overview of the development of cognitive skills. In each of these chapters, we emphasize those developmental skills which are potentially teachable by you and manageable by the students. We will introduce you to the concept of self-management and how you can facilitate its mastery by all your students. In Part 2, you will meet some students whom we will talk about throughout the book. We intend to demonstrate how the social and cognitive development of students interacts with their learning and behavior in school.

Part 3, ''Facilitating Learning Experiences,'' contains four chapters on learning, motivation, and problem solving. We talk about several major theories of learning in Chapter 5. In Chapter 6, we discuss alternative approaches to encourage positive motivation for learning and we emphasize the development of self-motivation skills. Chapter 7 focuses on a cognitive learning-skills hierarchy and shows how you can apply this hierarchy in practical situations. Finally, Chapter 8 discusses the application of cognitive skills in problem solving to creativity, affective education, and life-career development. You will find that Part 3 translates the theories of learning, development, and instruction into usable strategies that you can apply to all your teaching activities.

Part 4, ''Managing Teacher and Student Behavior,'' draws upon all the previous chapters. Chapters 9 and 10 discuss how to manage and evaluate learning outcomes. Chapter 11 provides a unique approach to effective classroom management in which we emphasize a shared evolution of management practices in the classroom. Chapter 12, ''Teaching Special Students,'' provides a label-free, individualized approach to meeting the needs of all students.

HOW YOU CAN USE THIS BOOK

Each chapter is organized to demonstrate the principles of the basic teaching model, application of the learning-skills hierarchy, and the development of self-management skills. The student is encouraged to master these chapter goals by means of a self-managed study guide within each chapter. The table below displays the learning aids provided by the study guide. These learning aids focus the student on important ideas, encourage the student to explore and question these ideas, and challenge the student to demonstrate mastery of important concepts and applied skills.

SELF-MANAGED STUDY GUIDE:
CONTENT AND OUTCOMES

LEARNING AID	LEARNING OUTCOME
Chapter Outline	Student maps content of chapter
Learning Objectives (five to ten per chapter)	Student seeks information to meet objectives
Key Terms	Student is prompted to learn important concepts
Probes	Student questions concepts and relates them to personal experiences
Brief Research Studies	Student relates research procedures to theory and practice
Guidelines for Teaching	Students can apply and practice concrete applications to classrooms
Expanded Summary	Student reviews major concepts and terms in context
Glossary	Student rehearses, reviews, and retains important key terms
Self-Test	Student monitors progress toward mastery
Learning Activity	Student applies a selected teaching skill

We have found that the self-managed study guide, as well as the detailed Instructor's Manual which accompanies the text, enables you to use this book in several ways. We intended the text primarily for an instructor-managed course with a lecture-discussion format. However, the book is also adaptable to an instructor-managed course with large lectures and supplementary small-group discussions. Both the Instructor's Manual and the self-managed study guide enable all participants to orient skill development and discussion directly to chapter content. Finally, the text is adaptable to an individually paced course, with students reading the text, answering study guide questions, completing the learning activities, and taking written or oral mastery exams when prepared. Sufficient material is included in the Instructor's Manual to develop several sets of formative and summative mastery exams. Although the text is not specifically designed for a self-paced course, it is easily adapted for this purpose because of the self-managed study guide and the separate Instructor's Manual.

⎧⎩ WHO HELPED US

We would like to express our gratitude and appreciation to the many individuals who helped shape the form and content of this book; to all of the real teachers and students whose lives and experiences appear throughout the book; to our knowledgeable colleagues: Steve Dragin, Anne Graehler, Skip Kifer, Suzanne Martorano, Mike Nelson, and Frances Smith, who provided us with continued encouragement, enthusiasm, and invaluable suggestions; to reviewers of the manuscript who offered us their suggestions for improvement: James J. Van Patten, University of Arkansas; Helen I. Nicklin, California State University, Los Angeles; and Willard H. Nelson, Florida Atlantic University; to Doris Stilwell, with whom one of the authors would like to renew a relationship; and to our efficient and overworked secretaries: Dawanna Hudson, Jill Jensen, and Pam Shelton, who coped with poor spelling, penciled notes, and impossible deadlines. All these persons deserve a large share of the credit for the production of this book.

JUDITH WORELL
WILLIAM E. STILWELL

PSYCHOLOGY FOR
TEACHERS AND STUDENTS

PART 1
Introduction to Teaching

You are invited to join us in a great adventure. As you start toward a career of teaching, consider the road that lies ahead. In this introductory chapter, we hope to show you that there are tested and reliable pathways toward reaching your final goal: to become a good teacher. You can develop a wide range of knowledge, skills, and competencies that will provide you with clear directions for effective teaching. We will introduce you to a teaching model that provides guidelines you may use in mapping your teaching activities for any subject or topic. This teaching model suggests that when you have set up well-defined goals for your students and a structured plan of action to meet these goals, you will be well on your way to becoming an effective teacher.

The excitement and adventure in teaching are provided by the many options—within your broad blueprint for action—from which you can choose. A teacher plays many different roles. Within each role, there are choices and decisions to be made. Each decision involves a challenge to your skills at assessing a new situation and coming up with solutions to new problems. To meet this challenge, you will try to remain open to alternative ways of approaching problems. You will want to be flexible in trying out new methods and strategies. You will have the opportunity to design a learning environment that promotes student growth and achievement.

We will also suggest many possibilities for encouraging your own personal growth and creativity. Each new student you encounter is an individual. For each individual student, you can construct a unique learning environment. You may also choose to develop some meaningful personal relationships. Every teaching situation involves a relationship between two or more people; we call this a behavioral interaction between students and teachers. Your interactions with students can be both instructive and meaningful. Our goal throughout this book is to help you develop your expertise at understanding, managing, and facilitating student behavior. At the same time, you will want to become more aware of your own behavior. You will be looking at the things you say and do that contribute both to student-teacher relationships and to student maturity and achievement. Finally, you may want to consider the opportunities that are offered by a career in the teaching profession. Some of the most important of these are stimulation, involvement, personal growth, and deep satisfaction. To the extent that you find these qualities in your teaching relationships, you may discover that teaching becomes not just a job but a career, a profession, and a life commitment.

CHAPTER 1

Focus on Students and Teachers

<hr>
LEARNING OBJECTIVES
<hr>

After reading Chapter 1, answering the self-monitoring questions, completing the learning activity, and reading any further references of your choice, you will be able to:

1. Define and give examples of key terms.
2. List and describe the three roles of the teacher.
3. Discuss the differences between teaching as a science and as an art.
4. List and explain the four parts of the basic teaching model.
5. Select examples of hypotheses drawn from theories of learning, development, and instruction.
6. Support or disagree with the statement "The teacher should be held accountable for student improvement in learning and behavior."
7. Select behavioral descriptions that are objective and observable.
8. Revise behavioral descriptions so that they meet the criteria for observable behaviors.

⫴ FOCUS ON BEHAVIOR

What do you need to know to become a good teacher? What will you be able to do when you face that classroom of thirty eager and not-so-eager faces each morning? How can psychology help you to develop the knowledge and skills that will be useful and relevant in your teaching career?

LOOKING AT STUDENT BEHAVIOR

Psychology is the study of BEHAVIOR. As a prospective teacher, you will be interested in knowing how to apply psychology to educational settings and to the solution of educational problems. You will want to be a sensitive and knowledgeable observer of student behavior. You will need to know about many facets of behavior: how behavior develops and changes over time; what differences there are in student learning styles and how these differences interact with the learning process; what can be done to stimulate student excitement about learning and curiosity about the world; what conditions within the classroom will promote productive or disruptive student behavior; how unproductive student behavior can be prevented through effective classroom management techniques; and how behavior can be measured and evaluated within the school situation. You will be interested in learning about how students respond in groups and how their group behavior differs from their

individual behavior. You will want to be able to understand your students as individuals. How do their home and family backgrounds affect their learning at school? You will want to understand their hopes, fears, and expectations about school and how these feelings may intrude on their classroom performance. All the behaviors that students bring into the school setting are educationally relevant at one time or another. To the extent that you become skilled at observing, understanding, and managing student behavior, you will find that teaching can be an exciting, challenging, and stimulating career.

Observing student behavior

An important part of psychology's contribution to education is a science for studying student behavior. Consider the following decriptions of students in a typical classroom:

Arnold is writing solutions to math problems on the board.

Janice is reading a book about computer careers.

Millicent raises her hand to answer a discussion question.

Sam reads the instructions in his workbook and fills in the blanks.

Julie laughs out loud and calls to Susan across the room.

Susan pokes her neighbor and asks for the time of day.

Joe passes a note down the row to George.

Sid gets up to sharpen his pencil.

Matthew comes in late to class and slumps down in his chair.

George puts his head on his desk and closes his eyes.

Marilyn sits and stares out of the window.

What do these descriptions have in common? They are all OBSERVA-TIONS of behaviors that occur in one form or another in thousands of classrooms across the country each day of the school year. If you go back and reread the examples above, you will notice that they include varying types of behavior. Some of the student behaviors appear to be ACADEMIC in nature. That is, they are concerned with student-curriculum interaction: reading books, writing solutions to problems, asking and answering questions. Frequently, student behaviors are not academic but can be described as SOCIAL or person-to-person interactions. These interactions involve contact or communications with others: passing notes, talking, laughing, playing, poking. Most of the student behaviors that you will observe in school can be regarded as ACADEMIC or SOCIAL.

Another way to look at student behavior is to classify it as PRODUCTIVE or UNPRODUCTIVE. Productive behaviors—asking questions, answering questions, completing assignments—help students reach their goals. Unproductive behaviors—staring out of the window during class, sleeping at one's desk, coming in late every day—interfere with positive goal attainment. All these behaviors are an important part of the classroom learning situation. However they are expressed in your classroom, these student activities are the raw materials with which you have to work as a teacher. You will want to be an expert in observing and describing student behavior. Your expertise in understanding and dealing with each of these types of behavior will be an essential part of your teaching skill.

LOOKING AT TEACHER BEHAVIOR

A second important application of psychology to education involves the behavior of the teacher. Now you may say, "That's what I'm interested in. How can I become a good teacher? What can you tell me that will be useful to me in my own teaching career?" Given that your goal is to become a good teacher, what does that mean to you? What do good teachers do, anyway? Look back at your own experiences and try to recall some of the "better" and "worse" teachers you have encountered. What did you like about the better ones? Can you describe what they did that led to your positive response to them? One of the authors typically asks this question of prospective teachers in educational psychology classes. Some of the resulting descriptions will not surprise you. Teachers recalled as outstanding were described as tactful; having a good sense of humor; neat in appearance; having a good grasp of the subject matter; being well organized, fair, stimulating, enthusiastic, friendly.

You may notice that students did not state what their teachers did but rather what qualities they had. In this book, we will be talking about what you can do as a teacher that will communicate these positive qualities to your students. Teachers, just like students, display observable, measurable behavior. These teaching behaviors can be learned, taught, modeled, practiced, and evaluated objectively by others. We shall be looking at what you can do to become competent in using a variety of teaching behaviors. We will emphasize teacher strategies to increase your effectiveness in promoting student learning and positive student evaluation of teachers, curricula, and schools. When students evaluate their school experiences in a positive manner, they are telling us that they like and enjoy school. In addition to promoting effective learning of academic subjects, you are also interested in the affective development of your students—their positive responses to themselves and to their environment.

=== **PROBE 1-1** ===

Recall an effective teacher you had in elementary or high school. List three behaviors you observed in this teacher that led to your positive evaluation.

Observing teacher behavior

Let us apply your behavior as a teacher to the classroom described above. If you were the teacher in this class, you might first observe all that student activity. Then, you would ask yourself some questions: "How can I get everyone in my class on target for effective learning? What can I do to motivate Matthew and Marilyn and get them interested in the semester's work? How can I get students like George to work more independently instead of waiting for help all the time? How can I keep Susan and Julie from constantly disrupting the classroom activities?" For each of these questions, you might be planning some action. Your broad goals will be to facilitate student learning and to promote a classroom environment that will be more conducive to the productive development of each student. Your plans will include a variety of teaching alternatives to meet the challenge of differences in individual and group learning and behavior styles. For each of your students, you will match observations of their behavior with some creative solution that will, you hope, get them on their way toward growth and productive change. What kinds of behaviors will you be using here? You will be observing student behavior, asking yourself questions, planning strategies, and implementing some of your plans. Finally, you will evaluate your strategies and adjust them if you find that they are ineffective. This brief sequence of teaching activity resembles the sorts of things we expect you to be doing when you have finished your formal education and are ready to apply everything you have learned and practiced.

STUDENT-TEACHER INTERACTION

You may have noticed that our descriptions of students and teachers in the classroom were examples of DYADIC INTERACTIONS, or interpersonal transactions in which the behavior of each person affects the behavior of one or more other persons. Sam smiles and you smile back. George drops a book and four students look up from their work to see what happened. What Sam and George did affected what you and the other students did. These are dyadic interactions. We want you to focus your attention on how your actions influence what your students do. For our purposes in this book, we shall orient our discussions of teachers' activities to those which directly affect students' behavior: their learning and performance, their attitudes and values, and their interpersonal transactions at school. This approach may appear somewhat narrow to you. It certainly omits important issues of education relevance—school busing for desegregation, for example, or the financing of public education. However, it is appropriate to the goal of this book: to apply the science of psychology to the interpersonal functions of teaching. In one text, we cannot hope to

"Focus your attention on how your actions influence what your students do." (Frank Wing/Stock, Boston)

provide all the skills you will need to become a competent and effective teacher. However, we *can* teach some of the competency skills that will be of use to you when you finally face that class of thirty eager faces. (Now that you are so skilled and competent, they are all eager to learn!)

In the remainder of this chapter, we shall consider your role as a teacher. What is it that teachers do in schools? How can we conceptualize the teacher's roles so that you can begin to familiarize yourself with the kinds of behaviors that will best equip you to fill these roles with competence and pride? Finally, the chapter will conclude with a brief learning activity through which you can begin to practice one basic skill that is essential to all teaching activity—behavior observation.

THREE ROLES FOR TEACHERS

The broad goal of all educational systems is to move the student from here to there or to effect some behavioral change over time. While educators differ on what aspects of student behavior are to be emphasized by the school and how best to accomplish these changes, they do agree on a fundamental goal: that the basic aim of all teaching is to facilitate individual growth and development and to prepare the student to function effectively and independently within a rapidly changing society. Within this framework, the teacher has many choices for action.

DEFINING TEACHER ROLES

Most of your teaching activities can be divided into three broad TEACHER ROLES. These roles describe what you do as a teacher that directly relates to progressive changes in student behavior and development. You can think of roles as sets of related behaviors that you practice in certain situations (McGinnies, 1970; Wrightsman, 1977). At differing times during any teaching day, you may adopt a new set of behaviors that is appropriate to your goals right then. At times, you may decide to be more organized, directive, and planful; here, you can describe your role as that of a MANAGER. At other times, you will want to interact with your students in dyadic relationships that communicate equality, warmth, and concern; we call this the role of the MEDIATOR. Finally, there are many times when you will be using specialized skills to help individual students meet their special learning requirements. This is the role of a FACILITATOR. Figure 1-1 illustrates these three teacher roles and suggests their practical relationship to one another. You can see that the three sets of behaviors overlap. You are at all times the central core of all three roles.

Figure 1-1
Three teacher roles.

=========================== **PROBE 1-2** ===========================

Look at the overlaps in Figure 1-1. Read the text discussion of each role and develop examples of the teacher's participation in each role.

INTEGRATING TEACHER ROLES

These three teacher roles have been separated only for convenience in our discussion. In practice, the three functions merge into a single pattern of teacher performance. At any one time, you may be using components of all three roles in your interactions with students. As you consider these differing roles, you may find that one of them fits your personal style more comfortably than another. Thus, the pattern of behaviors that emerges when you combine these roles into a single teaching style may differ from the pattern that is adopted by someone else. Where you finally end up in terms of a teaching approach will be determined partly by your training and education, your individual interests, your philosophical orientation, and your personal value system. Finally, your personal teaching style will be shaped by the network of skills that develop as you discover how you operate in real situations with students and evaluate what you can do most effectively.

Your individual teaching style indeed remains a personal decision under your control. It is our judgment, however, that you can maximize your potential effectiveness by exploiting the range of skills described under each of the three teacher roles. To limit yourself to one role or another will tend to narrow your flexibility. Some teachers approach their profession with preconceived ideas about their ideal role. One may say, "I want my students to know the subject matter thoroughly and to become involved in it" (manager). Another may decide "I want my students to grow and flourish without artificial constraints; I want them to be free and self-determining human beings" (facilatator). A third may decide "I want my students to love school and to find it a happy place; I want them to see me as a friend and helper" (mediator). We believe that each of these goals, as well as many others, can be realized by the teacher who remains open to varying alternatives for action. You can meet your personal teaching goals by becoming flexible in orientation, competent and skilled in using many possible strategies, and sensitive to the need for continual renewal of your personal growth and creativity. You can become a person who finds joy and satisfaction in teaching.

THE TEACHER AS A MANAGER OF THE LEARNING ENVIRONMENT

As a manager of the learning environment, you will apply your knowledge about the science of learning and instruction. Your major task is to encourage productive student learning and behavior. You will develop your skills within four broad areas. In the role of learning expert, you will become knowledgeable about how to use (1) theories of learning, development, and instruction; (2) research findings that support your daily activities; (3) the scientific process of asking appropriate questions so that you can develop practical answers to these questions; and finally, (4) plans for classroom management according to a structured model of teaching. We shall consider each of these manager functions in turn.

USING THEORIES OF LEARNING, DEVELOPMENT, AND INSTRUCTION

Everyone uses some THEORY every day. A theory starts with some observations about behavior and how it relates to other events. We all observe the behavior of people around us, and we probably have our own theories about what we are observing. These theories lead us to ask questions or state hypotheses about why people behave as they do. In psychology and education, theories make general statements about the lawful and constant relationships between a person's behavior and some other events or factors. When you make a hypothesis about Susan's academic problems, you are probably basing it upon one or more of the theories you will learn about in this book.

Applying theory to classroom behavior

Let us apply these ideas about theories to Susan, who is having some trouble with math. If Susan never finishes her math papers, you might raise some questions about what is going on. Among your guesses might be the following: perhaps Susan is "lazy," or perhaps she is too young for first grade and is not yet ready developmentally. Susan is the youngest of fourteen children, and perhaps she has been given too much attention at home. The problems may be too difficult for Susan. She may not have the necessary skills for math, such as counting to ten. Susan gets tired halfway through her work and probably needs more encouragement. The instructions in the workbook might be too difficult for her reading level. These, and many more, are some common hypotheses about the reasons for Susan's math behavior. Each question about Susan and her math problem is based upon some small theory about the relationship between Susan's behavior and some other event: her home life, her personality, the difficulty of the material, etc. If you conclude that Susan is lazy, your theory may be that learning requires internal motivation; therefore, failure to learn means that little motivation is present. If you conclude that Susan is too young for mathematics instruction, you may be using a kind of developmental theory which says that behavioral skills develop at their individual rates and that the desired behavior will emerge when the child is "ready." Therefore, rather than teach differently, you may decide to assign Susan to a "readiness" class.

It is clear that each type of theory may propose different conditions to explain the behavior you are observing. Each theory may suggest different kinds of teaching strategies to manage the behaviors. Therefore, a knowledge of theories and their application to student behavior is essential for flexible and competent teaching.

Theories for you to use

The three types of theories we shall be considering in this book include theories of learning, theories of development, and theories of instruction. LEARNING THEORIES propose relationships between new behavior and the conditions under which it is acquired. A learning theory proposition might suggest that immediate reinforcement or feedback of information is necessary early in learning. If we give Susan frequent check marks for correct solutions to problems, we might improve her math skills. DEVELOPMENTAL THEORIES consider how behavior changes over periods of time and across many situations. They are generally broader in scope than learning theories and consider more aspects of the individual's life experiences. Hypotheses about Susan's restricted home experiences or her lack of previous exposure to numbers might be relevant here. Finally, INSTRUCTIONAL THEORIES use the concepts and research findings from learning and developmental theory and apply these to the science of managing instruction. For Susan, instructional theory might consider the learning conditions in earlier math classes, the content and difficulty level of her math problems, and the manner in which math is being presented instructionally to Susan as well as the motivating and reinforcing events in her classroom.

When you are ready to assume the role of manager of the learning environment, you will find knowledge of all three types of theories useful. Chapters 2 through 7 will discuss these theories and will consider how the theories can be applied to practical situations.

Using theories to reach your goals: Self-management

Remember that the broad goal of all education is to move students in the direction of independence and effective coping in their personal lives and within their communities. Theories can help you solve everyday classroom problems as they arise (Reigeluth & Merrill, 1978). Theories can also provide useful ideas for encouraging the development of student skills in independent and self-directed behavior. We call this kind of behavior SELF-MANAGEMENT. We view self-management as a complex set of skills for organizing and directing one's own behavior. Probably, some of the students who come to your classroom will have more of these skills than do others. All students can improve their self-management behaviors. Susan will increase her self-management skills by sequencing her work and play times more efficiently. In later chapters, we will discuss specific self-management skills and how you can encourage these behavior patterns in all of your students. The theories we discuss will also include some useful ideas that you can apply in your classroom about how to teach self-management. Self-directed behavior is certainly the final goal in most theories of learning, development, and instruction. The relationship between these three types of theory and self-management is shown

"The broad goal of all education is to move students in the direction of independence and effective coping in their personal lives and within their communities." (Falk/Monkmeyer)

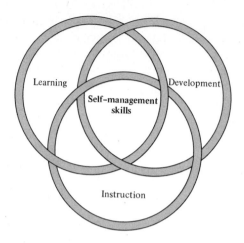

Learning

Development

Self–management
skills

Instruction

Figure 1-2
Self-management is
the product of
learning,
development, and
instruction.

in Figure 1-2. Each type of theory makes a unique contribution. Each type of theory also overlaps in some way with other theories. All three types of theories will provide some valuable suggestions for reaching your goals of preparing self-regulated students who can cope with the world on their own.

USING RESEARCH ON LEARNING AND INSTRUCTION

Theories are only as useful as the research that supports them. When you make use of your own theories, you will have relied on your past experience to determine whether they are true or false. Therefore, the conclusions you develop may have limited value for new situations and for different students. Most of our daily activity is based on our private thinking and generalizations drawn from our experiences. We come to general conclusions from situations similar to the ones we are trying to understand. We call these conclusions common sense, hunch, opinion, feeling, value, or belief. In contrast to the private hunch method, the value of research as a resource for evaluating our theories lies in its reliance on EMPIRICAL EVIDENCE that certain events lead to certain outcomes with certain types of students.

Research uses empirical evidence

Empirical evidence requires that the events in which you are interested be observed and measured in some objective manner. All evidence obtained through research involves a statement about the amount or frequency of the behaviors you wish to understand or predict. This measurement must be objective and unbiased by personal opinion, so that the findings can be repeated in the same manner by others. These measures may be made through careful observation and recording techniques, by using tests or scales that allow you to assign a numerical score, or with actual physical measurements such as those used to assess height, weight, or muscle strength. Most research studies will then apply statistical procedures to compare and evaluate the scores obtained through empirical measurement. Chapter 10 will provide you with some simple statistics for use in reading research reports. You can also use these statistics to evaluate the results you obtain from your own measurements of student behavior and achievement.

Throughout this book, we shall report the findings of research studies. Some of these results will be in summary form; occasionally we will present a brief report of the actual procedures used in the research. Usually, these research studies will be concerned with relationships between teacher behavior and student performance, or between conditions of the learning environment and student achievement. Research studies can provide valuable information about human behavior that can frequently be translated into useful classroom strategy and action.

Applying research to classroom behavior

Our purpose in exposing you to this brief discussion of research is to alert you to the importance of considering research results in your approach to teaching. You may believe passionately in one or another method, but keep in mind the empirical facts and try to guide your teaching behavior accordingly. Bear in mind, however, that experimental studies may be limited by the specific situations in which they are conducted; therefore, the results may not always generalize to all other life situations. Research findings may be limited by the particular students used in the study, by the particular tests or measures used, and by the skill of the researcher in designing an unbiased study. Therefore, research results are conflicting at times. Do not be surprised to find that repeated studies on the same question frequently produce conflicting results. Nevertheless, we hope that you do pay attention to the results of empirical findings. Good research can help you to maintain a rough match between your personal experiences and experimental findings about human interaction.

We will leave this brief discussion of research with a note of caution. The application of research findings to classrooms and students is frequently difficult. You may find that a research study suggests a method that is helpful in working with Susan but not with Joe. Be patient. Researchers usually try to simplify their studies in order to derive principles of behavior. You have a class of thirty very different individuals. A single research finding frequently is not broad enough to deal with thirty sets of behaviors. But perhaps you will find one study we discuss in this book that tells you something important and useful about Susan and her math troubles. Study 1-1 offers one example of the many investigations that show how student learning depends upon both individual characteristics and different teaching methods (Cronbach & Snow, 1977; Soloman & Kendall, 1976; Wittrock, 1978).

STUDY 1-1: STUDENTS LEARN DIFFERENTLY

Grimes and Allinsmith set out to determine whether students with differing personality characteristics would profit from different types of instructional approaches. First they measured some behavioral characteristics by means of parent ratings and self-reports. Two groups of students were selected who showed either high "anxiety" or high "compulsivity." Students who rated themselves as anxious were apprehensive about examinations, fearful of new situations, and generally restless. Children rated by their parents as compulsive were characterized as being orderly, always on time, and requiring rules and structure. These two groups of students were then compared on two reading programs in two different schools. One school tended to be highly structured and used a structured phonics approach to teaching. The other school used a look-see method and was generally less structured in its approach to teaching. Figure 1-3 demonstrates the differences in the performance of the children in the two learning environments. Highly anxious children performed differentially, dependent upon the learning environment. Low-anxious children were less affected by classroom structure or teaching method. In a highly structured setting the high-anxious children did as well as or better than the low-anxious children. In a relatively unstructured situation, highly anxious children performed poorly in comparison with students who were less anxious. This study tended to obscure the difference between teaching method and school structure, so that we do not know exactly what was responsible for the difference. However, it does demonstrate nicely that the same teaching method is not necessarily equally effective for all students. The entering behavior of the student facing a new learning situation may markedly affect that student's response to the teaching procedures.

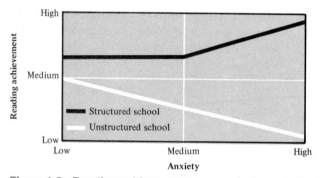

Figure 1-3 Reading achievement among various students in structured and unstructured learning environments. (Source: J. W. Grimes and W. Allinsmith, "Compulsivity, Anxiety, and School Achievement," *Merrill Palmer Quarterly,* **1961, 7, 247–269.**

USING A SCIENTIFIC APPROACH TO ASKING AND ANSWERING QUESTIONS

The third activity of the teacher as manager of the learning environment requires effective skills in how to ask and answer the many questions that arise every day in your school. You will need to develop skills in asking and answering questions before you can plan for effective teaching. We outline here a three-step method which will be useful in all your teaching strategies. In order to answer any question about student behavior or learning, you should be able to:

Observe objectively: What is happening?

Ask a question: If I do A, will B occur?

Answer your question: Did I observe a relationship between A and B?

Did B change when I changed A?

Each of these three component skills is an essential tool in your role as an effective manager of student learning. Throughout this book, we shall be considering how you can use these skills. The learning tasks found both within and at the end of each chapter are concerned mainly with the development and practice of these question-asking and answering skills.

Observation: Learning to look

One of the earliest skills you will develop is that of being an objective and expert observer of behavior. The basic data of all science and of behavior change relevant to education come from OBSERVATIONS of one sort or another. Once you have observed and measured the behavior in which you are interested, you have the raw data upon which to base your interventions or teaching strategies. How does scientific observation differ from just "looking" or "noticing" or "seeing"? There are two major ways to observe behavior: natural and structured.

Natural observation You are using NATURAL OBSERVATION when you take a look at behavior right where it happens. Students are hitting baseballs, completing arithmetic problems, raising their hands, asking questions, talking to friends. A standard way to observe these behaviors can tell you how frequently they occurred and the conditions for their occurrence (where, when, with whom, under what circumstances) as well as the CONSEQUENCES of the behavior, or what occurred afterwards. For example, you might say about Joe: "Joe tears up his composition papers an average of four times every day [frequency]. He tears them up only when I insist on his completing his work independently [condition]. Each time he tears up his paper, the other kids laugh and joke [consequence]. Then Joe grins and looks around the room." This is an objective observation and description of both Joe's behavior and the conditions under which it occurred. Even this brief description gives you information you can use to develop a strategy of intervention for Joe.

Structured observations A second way to describe student behavior objectively is to use STRUCTURED OBSERVATIONS. Here, you will use tests and scales devised by yourself or by professional test developers.

In these structured tests, all students respond to the same test questions. Your observations then consist of the scores on those tests. You can use these scores to measure what students know, believe, feel, or value before you introduce a new learning unit. You can then use these standard observations or test scores afterwards to measure and evaluate what your students have learned and whether or not your teaching efforts were successful. Chapter 10, ''Evaluating Learning Outcomes,'' will offer you some beginning skills in constructing your own tests and in selecting standardized published tests.

PROBE 1-3

Read the passage about Joe. Under what conditions does Joe appear to tear up his papers? List three possible factors to help you observe his behavior in future situations.

Combinations of natural and structured observation   You can obtain additional important information about your students by combining natural and structured observation. Self-report measures are one example of a natural-structured combination. In the self-report method, students volunteer some information about themselves. You may wish to use self-reports on simple questionnaires, published scales, or personal interviews with students. Each method can provide valuable information about your students' interests, motivations, and reactions to your teaching style. You can then use this information to improve the learning environment. Never be reluctant to talk to your students. You will want to hear their points

"Never be reluctant to talk to your students. You will want to hear their points of view. Then, use this information constructively to meet or revise your teaching goals." (Sean Eager/ Magnum)

of view. Then, use this information constructively to meet or revise your teaching goals.

The observation learning task at the end of this chapter was designed to provide the first set of skills in the chain of effective observation techniques. Learning activities in later chapters will help you to build on these skills. All the learning tasks will combine to help you meet your goal: to become an objective and unbiased observer of student behavior.

Asking questions: Looking for antecedents and consequences

Once you have observed the behavior in which you are interested, you are ready to ask some relevant questions. For any behavior you observe, there are an unlimited number of questions you might ask yourself. For example, when Joe tears up his papers, you might ask: "Why is he so impossible? Why does he always do the opposite of what I ask him to do? I wonder what his home life is like? I wonder if he is too slow for this class?" These questions are not relevant for Joe's problem behavior because none of them will help you to change his paper-tearing perform- ance. Some more relevant questions might be: "What kinds of papers does Joe tear? Does he tear up long division or multiplication? Can I change the level of the problem difficulty on his paper? What will happen if I suggest to the other students that they ignore his behavior?" These questions are relevant. They are directly related to the possible ANTE- CEDENTS or CONSEQUENCES of Joe's behavior. Therefore, these questions are relevant for your intervention plans. You will ask questions about relevant *antecedents* when you want to know the conditions under which Joe tears up papers. You will be looking at *consequences* when you try to determine what happens once the papers are torn up. The results of asking the appropriate questions will be a set of possible intervention strategies for you to use. On the basis of your relevant questions, you might decide to look at one antecedent—the specific problems which Joe tears up—and perhaps alter problem length and level of difficulty.

PROBE 1-4

Now look back at your answer to PROBE 1-3. How would you change your answer with the additional information? What else would you like to know? Ask one or more questions that will help you to discover a better strategy for Joe.

Evaluating your questions: Try again

Remember that questions and hypotheses are always tentative. All teaching consists essentially of a series of hypotheses about what works or is effective in any particular situation. What works for one student may not work for another. You will always be evaluating the effectiveness of what you do in terms of the behavior of your students following your interventions and how well these results match your goals. A scientific approach requires that you remain open to change, tentative, and willing to try out new alternatives by asking new questions and making new hypotheses. It requires that you remain open to the possibility that you were wrong on one or more occasions when you did not obtain the results you wished to see. This does not mean that you embrace each new ''educational revolution'' that comes along. Rather, you will want to keep your approach flexible and open to revision. Throughout this book, we will give you samples of situations and the opportunity to make some hypotheses about what might have led up to the problem or what you might do about it. You will see that the process of asking questions and making tentative hypotheses is a primary role of the teacher and underlies all your decision-making activities.

Answering your questions and evaluating your answers

On the basis of the questions you put to yourself, you take some positive action. You then observe the effects of your action and determine whether the results are in line with your objectives. Let us apply these ideas to Joe. Your goal is to have Joe complete his math papers without errors. Suppose you have now adjusted the difficulty level of his work. If this first strategy does not result in behavior that meets your objectives, you have several alternatives. You can call Joe ''a dumb, lazy kid'' and let it go at that. You can have his intelligence tested to find out whether he is too slow for your class. You can yell at him and tell him how exasperated you are with his behavior. No one of these alternatives will get Joe on the road to more effective learning.

On the other hand, you may decide to use observation, tests, or interview data to help identify the problem. For example, using observation, you may watch Joe closely for a few days and determine at what point in his math progress he tears up the paper. While observing Joe, you discover that each time he reaches step four in long division, he sits and stares, looks confused, scratches out one answer after another, and finally tears up his paper. Now you may have ''diagnosed'' the problem. You may ask another question: ''Does Joe become stuck on step four and need additional help at that point?'' Putting this hypothesis to work may be the answer to this situation.

PROBE 1-5

What new information did you gain about Joe here? Was it helpful? Do you need to ask any more questions in order to plan a strategy for Joe?

"Accountability requires that you continually adjust your strategies to help students meet their goals." (Ann Meuer/Photo Researchers)

You can see that the final step of answering your question by putting a strategy into effect and evaluating its outcome is a continuous process. Often, your first strategy is not effective and you move to another solution. The important aspect of this procedure is that you are assuming responsibility or ACCOUNTABILITY in the teaching-learning process. Accountability implies teacher responsibility. If students are not learning, it is your responsibility to observe the behaviors in question, ask relevant questions, and try out varying alternatives. Accountability requires that you continually adjust your strategies to help students meet their goals. In the following section, we shall discuss a model of teaching that can be useful in developing accountability in your teaching.

USING A STRUCTURED MODEL FOR TEACHING

Your fourth activity as a teacher-manager of learning will be to develop an organized plan of approach for all of your teaching activities. We believe that the teaching model discussed below is an effective one for any teaching situation, whether you are covering content in the areas of academic, social, or physical skills.

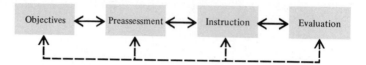

**Figure 1-4
Basic teaching
model.**

**The basic
teaching model**

Many teachers, ourselves included, have found a useful structure for organizing their teaching activities. We call this structure the BASIC TEACHING MODEL (Glaser, 1962). This model provides you with a framework for planning, sequencing, and continually evaluating your teaching activities as you proceed (Popham & Baker, 1970). As you can see in Figure 1-4, the model has four parts: *objectives, preassessment, instruction,* and *evaluation.* Each part of the model includes a set of separate skills for you to master. We will discuss each of these sets of skills briefly here, because you will meet this model many times throughout the book. Chapter 9 will expand this model and will give you more details on how to plan and manage each part.

**Developing
learning
objectives**

Your first task as a teacher is to make some decisions about what you wish your students to learn during the time they are with you. When you use LEARNING OBJECTIVES, you define your goals of instruction in terms of what you want students to be able to do or to demonstrate at the end of an instructional unit. This unit can be for a single task assigned or for a whole day, week, or year. Of course, every teacher has some goals at the beginning of instruction. What is so different about the concept of learning objectives as we will use them here? Let us take a look at Joe Smith, who teaches ninth-grade English. He wants his students to "appreciate" Shakespeare, to "understand" the complexity and beauty of his plays, and to develop "insight" into the motivations of his characters. All these are praiseworthy goals. None of these goals is directly measurable in terms of student behavior. How do you know when Bryan has developed "insight"? What does Bryan have to demonstrate to let you know that he "appreciates" Shakespeare? Instead of using such vague criteria, we shall guide you on how to develop specific, measurable objectives. If objectives are stated in terms of the student's behavior, both you and the student can tell when these objectives have been met. Study 1-2 gives you an example of how objectives were found to be useful in helping inexperienced teachers to be more effective.

**STUDY 1-2: TEACHING
SKILLS UNDER SCRUTINY**

Educational researchers at the University of California compared the skills of experienced and inexperienced teachers in relation to im-provements in student learning. They devised a set of tests that measured specific *learning objectives.* They then gave these *instructional objectives* to a group of fifty-seven experienced teachers in social science, auto mechanics, and electronics. A second group of fifty-seven college students (nonteachers) in social science, practicing auto mechanics, and TV technicians were given the same instructional objectives. These two groups of experienced and inexperienced teachers were then assigned to teach two high school classes each—a total of 2326 students—in any manner they chose for a specified period of time. At the end of their instruction, the students were tested for percentage of correct responses on the performance tests. The results were startling. There were no significant differences in student performance in any of the three areas regardless of who gave the instruction—experienced teachers or inexperienced volunteers. What was the chief factor responsible for the success of the nonteacher? Apparently, it was the specific instructional objectives, which gave these inexperienced teachers clear teaching goals stated in terms of observable student performance.

Adapted from: Popham, W. J. Teaching skills under scrutiny. *Phi Delta Kappan,* 1971, *52,* 199–201.

Preassessing entering behavior

Each student comes to your class with an individual network of learning skills, interests, goals, and aspirations. Each student has a different family background, expectancies about school, attitudes toward your subject, friendship patterns, and social skills; each has had different life experiences. These factors contribute to learning in your class if they are relevant to (1) the capabilities of each student to begin instruction in your class and (2) the probability that each student will profit from the teaching methods you use. We will refer to all skills, behaviors, interests, and attitudes that can be shown to be relevant to effective learning in your class as ENTERING BEHAVIOR. Some of these skills are academic— knowledge of how to attack new problems; discrimination in learning new concepts; skills in addition before starting multiplication. Some of these skills are social-motivational—attitudes toward school, friendship patterns, interest in your subject matter, persistence at difficult tasks. Finally, some skills include life-career goals—career aspirations, extracurricular interests, and leisure-time activities. Before you begin instruction, each of these areas of entering behaviors should be assessed or measured in order to provide the greatest amount of information for developing your teaching strategies. We will see in Chapter 2 that entering behaviors are very similar to the concept of *readiness for learning.*

Preassessment of entering behaviors will require you to be knowledgeable about methods of measuring these skills. Then, your learning objectives can be keyed and adjusted to the needs, interests, capabilities, and limitations of your students. When individual students do not have the entering behaviors necessary for a particular sequence of instruction, we say that they do not have the PREREQUISITE SKILLS. You may wish to consider some remedial activities before continuing with your planning for instruction. If Joe and Susan do not demonstrate the prerequisite skills necessary for effective learning in your class, then you will revise the learning objectives or devise ways to motivate, instruct, or remediate. This step is most often ignored in current teaching because it is time-consuming and most teachers are not trained to accomplish it. In our opinion, failure to pay attention to the preassessment of student skills, motivations, and goals in the teaching procedure accounts for many failures in student progress.

Developing instructional strategy

The third component of our teaching model is a broad one which includes all the methods and approaches in teaching. INSTRUCTIONAL STRATEGIES include all the plans you will implement to help your students meet the learning objectives. These strategies may involve large groups, small groups, individual seat work, peer-to-peer tutoring, teacher lecture, student presentation, audiovisual or other "hardware" aids, programmed learning, field trips, and guest speakers from the community. Here, the teacher is truly a manager of the learning environment. The instructional phase requires prior planning, organization, and decision making in order to move your students toward your jointly determined performance objectives. You will use a variety of activities, materials, motivational devices, and learning resources. You will use your knowledge of learning and development to provide structure, meaning, hierarchical development of ideas, relevance, and motivation. You do not necessarily do all the direct teaching yourself. Instead, you use your knowledge and managerial skills to manage and direct the progress of learning activities (Davies, 1973; Dick & Carey, 1978).

Evaluating your instructional sequence

Once you have developed objectives, measured students' entering behaviors, and developed strategies to enable students to meet your learning objectives, you are ready to evaluate the effectiveness of what you have accomplished. Your initial EVALUATION will always be of student performance: Did your students meet your stated objectives? Can they demonstrate the kinds of information and skills you stated in the objectives? If the student has achieved the objectives, then you may feel satisfied with the previous parts of your teaching procedures.

If the student does not meet the objectives, you may wish to revise any one of the three previous sections. Perhaps the objectives demand too much from this student or group of students, or perhaps students see them as irrelevant or inappropriate. Perhaps you did not preassess students appropriately before instruction, so that they do not possess the prerequisite skills they need to achieve the learning objectives. Perhaps your instructional strategies were inappropriate or inadequate; possibly they did not impart meaning to material, did not include enough examples, or did not provide sufficient practice, etc. The evaluation of teaching procedures is thus continuous. The really nice part of using this type of model is that it does require you to evaluate your procedures continuously. This process of continuous evaluation and revision makes teaching a dynamic and challenging experience for you and a valid one for your students. By the appropriate use of a basic teaching model, you can show accountability in your teaching.

PROBE 1-6

Consider two ways of viewing accountability in teaching: If Sally does not achieve mastery of long division and this is a semester learning objective in your class, are you responsible for helping Sally meet this objective? Why or why not?

Now, let us take Sam. Each time Sam cannot complete a task correctly, he starts to cry. Are you also responsible for helping Sam not to cry in the face of difficult tasks? Why or why not? Is there any difference between Sally's and Sam's behavior as far as accountability is concerned?

THE TEACHER AS A MEDIATOR OF HUMAN RELATIONS

Your second major role in teaching is to become proficient in mediating human relations. In this role, you will use your knowledge of how people interact and communicate with each other. Your broad goal will be to maximize the quality of the social-interactive environment. Here, you will be concerned with three types of activities: (1) encouraging prosocial behaviors in your students, (2) developing a personal style of interaction, and (3) establishing positive relationships with students. Let us look at each activity briefly.

ENCOURAGING PROSOCIAL BEHAVIOR

You may wish to develop interpersonal or personal growth goals for individual students or for your entire class. We call these goals PROSOCIAL because they help people get along cooperatively with each other: sharing ideas and resources, learning to listen to others, waiting to take one's turn, showing tolerance for ideas that conflict with one's own, taking responsibility for task completion, resolving interpersonal conflicts in a productive manner, and assuming effective leadership in a group. These prosocial goals reflect basic values which are generally accepted in our culture as being desirable. You will probably want to encourage many of these behaviors in your classroom. You can demonstrate prosocial values through your own behavior, or you may teach them directly. For example, you might say to your class: "Let's see if everyone can listen carefully while Jim explains his solution to the water-jar problem." Or you might say: "Jack, you really did a good job of leading that discussion; you gave each person a chance to make a contribution, you asked the others for feedback, and you summarized the major points at the end." In the first example, you are giving a verbal model of how to listen respectfully to others. The second example provides a model of how to encourage and reinforce others. You are hoping both to reinforce Jack's effective discussion behaviors and to use his behavior as a model for others to follow. In your role as a mediator of human relations, you will use many opportunities to develop a classroom environment that is helpful for encouraging the growth of mature personal and interpersonal behavior.

DEVELOPING A PERSONAL STYLE

You have probably heard that teaching is an art. The art in teaching will become evident through your personal style in your relationships with students. Many of the things you do when you interact with others fall into the realm of "common sense" or "personal style." Your teaching will go beyond scientific data and methods to integrate your personal style and approach to people with your teaching activities. *What* you do in the classroom can be taught, but to some extent, *how* you do it and *when* you do it remain matters of personal decision and choice. Your individual tempo—speed of action, intensity of voice, amount of movement, degree of organization—reflects your personal style. Your individual characteristics are likely to be in evidence regardless of the particular skills that you develop. As you move along toward your goal of a career in teaching, we hope you will find opportunities to observe your personal style. You may have others observe your teaching style, or you may observe yourself on videotape "microteaching." Later in this book, we will discuss some ways you can observe yourself. In each of these situations, take the opportunity to look objectively at your personal style. Decide whether you like what you are doing and whether or not you wish to change some particular behaviors. You are not stuck with your personal style. The art of teaching involves a continual process of movement toward your goals.

DEVELOPING POSITIVE STUDENT-TEACHER RELATIONSHIPS

The development of positive relationships with your students is an important part of your teaching skills. How you feel about students will come through to them by means of the behaviors you show when you interact with them. We want to assume that everyone who selects teaching

"The development of positive relationships with your students is an important part of your teaching skills." (E. Hamlin/ Stock, Boston)

as a career enjoys the company of young people and wants to establish friendly and comfortable relationships with them. However, if you again look back at teachers you have known, you will no doubt recall many who behaved as though they did not like students at all. What did these teachers do that communicated negative feelings toward others? What do teachers do that communicates positive feelings toward others? We know a great deal about how people interact in dyads and in groups. Chapter 11 will expand this discussion on the interpersonal style of teaching and will suggest ways in which you can be a more effective human relations expert.

Many of the following interpersonal skills can be learned: to communicate warmth, respect, and acceptance toward your students; to encourge cooperative behavior; to establish clear lines of interpersonal communication so that people listen to one another and feel free to talk openly; to establish a system of democratic control so that transactions are contractual and mutually agreeable; and to provide for your students a model of interpersonal behavior in yourself that they can accept, admire, and respect. All these skills and many more are encompassed within your role as human relations expert. Your enjoyment of teaching, your success in establishing a positive classroom environment, and the extent to which your students find school a pleasant place to be may all depend upon the manner in which you play this human relations role.

THE TEACHER AS A FACILITATOR OF INDIVIDUAL DEVELOPMENT

No two students in your class will be identical. Each student comes to you with an individual learning history; individual levels of physical, social, and cognitive development; and particular styles of learning and approaches to new situations. As a facilitator of individual development, you will recognize and adapt to these differences among your students. Donna comes late to class every day and falls asleep. Elton "forgets" his homework and "loses" his workbooks and class assignments. Christine tries to answer every question, often incorrectly. Sally hands in her math papers with half the problems left incomplete. Carla does not follow instructions unless reminded over and over. Alvin counts on his fingers in seventh-grade math. Ike manages to "pick a fight" at least once a week. Paula seldom talks to anyone. Diane completes her assignments early and starts passing notes down the aisle. For every situation that occurs in your classroom, someone is certain to do things differently.

USING SPECIAL SKILLS FOR SPECIAL STUDENTS

When a classroom has a limited range of individual differences, some of your teaching strategies may be equally effective for all students. However, many of your students will deviate in any of a number of ways from the central or average level of behavior. You may require additional teacher competencies in order to observe, evaluate, and accommodate your teaching techniques to these differences. As you plan to meet the particular requirements of individual students, you will need to develop skills in individualizing instruction. These students may demonstrate learning or behavior problems, may be exceptionally fast or slow in adjusting to your classroom routine, or may not respond to the strategies that have been successful with other students. You will need to have information about principles of development, characteristics of special students, individualized learning environments, and diagnostic and prescriptive techniques. It will be your task to determine how each student learns best and how you can adjust the curriculum to meet individual needs.

Many of the skills we shall describe within this teacher role are typically taught to "special-education" teachers. These are teachers who have chosen to work with exceptional children. The exceptional student has learning requirements that deviate from the average sufficiently that regular classroom methods have often been found to be ineffective. In many communities, these children are now being maintained within or integrated into the mainstream of the regular school environment rather than being assigned to special-education classrooms for slow learners, the fast learners, the deaf, the blind, or behaviorally disordered students. Thus, as a regular classroom teacher, you can expect to encounter many students with special learning requirements. You will need to develop additional skills for effective management of these students' learning environments. The arguments for and against regular classroom assignments for students with learning or behavioral differences will be discussed in Chapter 12. Nevertheless, every teacher will encounter some students who fall outside the "average" range of learning characteristics, and these youngsters deserve your fullest attention and concern.

WORKING WITH CONSULTATION: YOU ARE NOT ALONE

Within your role of individualizing instruction, your contact with helping agents outside your classroom becomes particularly important. You will soon discover that you cannot manage the entire task of teaching as the "lone arranger" (Bijou, 1971). You will find it helpful to develop skills in communicating with parents, other teachers, your principal, special consultants, and visiting teachers as well as the school nurse, social worker, counselor, physical education instructor, or reading specialist. Each of these people has skills and information that may be helpful in planning and implementing instruction for any particular student and, at times, for your entire class. Parent conferencing skills are especially critical. You will recognize that the parent has the single most important role in developing readiness for school, providing motivation in academic matters, and offering continued support and encouragement for school progress. Although many teachers are not eager to engage the parent as an ally, we believe that it is in both your own and the student's best interest to maintain continuous contact with each student's home. You will want to use parents as partners rather than making them adversaries. In Chapter 12, we shall consider conferencing skills in working with parents.

PROBE 1-7

Joe's mother comes into your classroom and asks what she can do to help. She has two free days each week and would like to be of use in Joe's school. List three things Joe's mother can do in your classroom or in your school that will facilitate student learning.

ACCEPTING INDIVIDUAL DIFFERENCES

Most importantly, however, your role as a facilitator of learning will take into consideration the observation that we cannot remediate each and every difficulty that appears in a student's development. Despite your best efforts, some students will continue to learn more slowly than their classmates and will require more reinforcement or attention. These students may be more active and troublesome as well as more defiant and insolent; they may fail to keep up with the pace of the rest of your class. While you do not "give up" on these students and cease your efforts to encourage their learning and development, you maintain a patient and tolerant attitude toward them. You accept, to some extent, their individual differences. You recognize that you cannot bring every student up to the highest level of classroom achievement or social behavior. You accept the student's present behavior as a valid and possibly inevitable part of his or her own uniqueness. You are always operating within each child's own scale of development and encouraging each to achieve his or her fullest potential for behavior change. In turn, students with special learning needs will reward you with their best effort when they realize that you support their progress and you accept their limitations.

LEARNING ACTIVITY: OBJECTIVE OBSERVATION

Since you are using this book in order to learn some practical skills, let us begin with some basic observation skills. That way, you can go off the first day and start practicing. Try some of this at home, in your dorm, or with friends. You may be surprised at what you did not observe accurately before.

What do you need to do in order to observe behavior in its natural setting? You will need to be able to do four things:

1 Define the behavior objectively
2 Determine its frequency, or how often it occurs
3 Record or write out its frequency
4 Check (validate) your observations with repeated observations under the same conditions (same time of day, same situation—such as math class—same people around)

When you have completed these four steps for behavior A, you can tell yourself you have been an objective observer of behavior A. We will cover the first step in this learning activity. The remaining three steps will be covered in later chapters.

OBJECTIVE DEFINITIONS: THREE QUESTIONS

Defining a behavior objectively requires that you ask yourself three questions:

1   Is the behavior observable? Can I "see it," "hear it"?

2   Is the behavior definitely different from other behaviors? Do I know when A is occurring and not B? (Are "cussing" and "sassing" different?)

3   Is the behavior measurable? You can measure it by the number of times it occurs (frequency) or by how long it lasts (duration). For example, *frequency* is the number of times Kathy volunteers to answer a question; *duration* is the amount of time she has her head on the desk and her eyes closed.

OBJECTIVE OBSERVATION: SELF-TEST

How do you go about determining whether a particular behavior is observable? Take the following example and answer "yes" or "no" to yourself for observability:

	Yes	No
Mary likes arithmetic.	——	——
Lew prefers girls to boys.	——	——
Alice understands her lessons today.	——	——
Ralph tries hard.	——	——
Jim smiled at me today.	——	——
Amy completed four problems correctly.	——	——
Sue is dumb.	——	——
Sandra is really bright.	——	——
Jill has no motivation.	——	——
John drew an isosceles triangle.	——	——
Rhoda is lazy.	——	——
Bill got up from his chair.	——	——
Dave is shy.	——	——
Millicent is a sweet child.	——	——
Dave talked to Neil.	——	——

Now, meet with a friend and check your answers. You were scoring high if you checked those in which the student was engaging in some observable activity: smiling, talking, completing problems. When students were being described by vague terms such as *shy, bright,* or *lazy*, you were right if you said these were not observable. What are you describing when you tell Dave's parents that he is shy?

OBSERVATIONS AND INFERENCES: WHAT CAN YOU SEE?

What do you mean when you say "Dave is shy"? You may mean that he seldom talks to peers, he turns the other way when you call on him, he stays inside during recess, he eats lunch alone, and he never volunteers an answer. Any or all of these may describe a student who seldom initiates contact with others. Observing Dave frequently in these situations leads you to infer or conclude that he is shy. You did not *observe* the shyness, but you *infer* shyness from Dave's observable behavior. Thus, when you use OBJECTIVE OBSERVATION, you look at behavior as it occurs without interpreting or explaining it.

Let us take another example: "Donna is lazy." What does Donna do to lead you to infer that she is lazy? Consider some of the following descriptions of Donna's behavior:

Donna does not complete her seat work.

Donna comes late to class every day.

Donna stares out of the window while everyone else is working on tasks.

Donna does not start her seat work until half past the hour.

Donna never volunteers for extra tasks.

Donna never offers to help other students.

All of these describe something that Donna is doing that might lead you to infer that she is lazy. On the other hand, all of these behaviors might lead to another hypothesis—that Donna is "unmotivated," does not like school, finds school work too difficult, boring, irrelevant, etc. If you describe students with *inferences* rather than with observable descriptions, you may come to the wrong conclusions. Your intervention strategies might differ depending upon whether you concluded that Donna was "lazy" or "unmotivated." Keeping your observations objective will help you stay on the right track.

TASK 1-1

Now that you have seen the differences between observable and non-observable behaviors, try your hand at correcting the following description of Paula. Decide which sentences contain Paula's observable behaviors and which represent inferences. Revise each sentence that contains an inference so that it describes Paula's observable behavior.

Paula came to class ten minutes late today. She was really upset about something, I could see that. I asked her to take a seat in the back row, since she was late. She didn't even pay any attention to what I said and sat right up in the front row. She really is a willful child. She does what she wants to, regardless of what I say. She just needs to have it her own way all the time. I feel so frustrated with her. When she finally opened her book, it was to the wrong page. I told her we were on page 31. She fiddled around and couldn't seem to concentrate the whole period. Afterwards, I asked her what was troubling her. She looked at the floor and started to cry.

TASK 1-2

Observe one of your friends whom you would characterize as "friendly" and list at least three observable behaviors that lead you to infer friendliness.

TASK 1-3

Select an activity that you "like." List three observable behaviors that would lead your friends to say "Yes, he or she likes to do that" (play tennis, read, etc.).

SUMMARY

1. Psychology applied to teaching involves the BEHAVIOR of the students as well as that of the teacher. The emphasis in this book will be upon the DYADIC INTERACTIONS between students and teachers.

2. In all teaching situations, a teacher plays three major ROLES. These are MANAGER of learning, MEDIATOR of human relations, and individual FACILITATOR. These three roles can be described separately, but in practice they merge into a single pattern of behavior. Each teacher role is developed through specific skills which you can learn and in which you can become proficient. In practice, you will integrate these roles into your own personal style, so that the final result is an individualized and unique teacher.

3. As a MANAGER of learning, you will use scientific methods which include THEORIES of LEARNING, DEVELOPMENT, and INSTRUCTION; research related to teaching; NATURAL and STRUCTURED OBSERVATION; the developing and testing of hypotheses; and the use of a structured TEACHING MODEL for all of your teaching activities.

4. As a MANAGER of learning, you will become proficient at organizing all your teaching activities around a BASIC TEACHING MODEL. This model has four parts: LEARNING OBJECTIVES, PREASSESSMENT of ENTRY BEHAVIOR, implementation of TEACHING STRATEGIES to meet

your objectives, and the EVALUATION of learning outcomes. The model provides for continuous teacher evaluation of each procedure, so that you remain flexible and open to change.

5. As a MEDIATOR of human relations, you will become proficient in dealing with students as individuals as well as in groups. You will be involved in encouraging PROSOCIAL behavior in your students and in considering the values that you hold for the behaviors that students demonstrate in school. You will be concerned with developing a personal style of interaction with students that is most effective for you and is consistent with your teaching goals. You will also develop positive relationships with your students in order to communicate warmth, acceptance, and respect.

6. In establishing positive relations with students, you will develop four sets of interpersonal skills: (*a*) to be a model of appropriate interpersonal behavior for students; (*b*) to provide a reinforcing environment for student learning and behavior; (*c*) to establish a clear and consistent communication system between yourself and your students; and (*d*) to establish a system of fair and democratic control which satisfies both your goals and those of your students.

7. As a FACILITATOR of individual development, you will become proficient in observing, evaluating, and responding with individualized programs to the differences you find among student learning and behavior capabilities. You will develop skills designed to integrate students with special learning characteristics into the regular academic environment. Within this role, you will learn to encourage each student to attain his or her maximum capability. You will also learn to be tolerant of students who are not as competent and do not perform as well as most of your students. In this role, you will have to work cooperatively with consultants in order to meet the special needs of all students.

8. As an expert in OBJECTIVE OBSERVATION, you will be able to distinguish between inference and behavioral decription. You will be able to select behavioral descriptions which are objective and to revise those that contain unobservable inferences. You will be able to observe specific behaviors of yourself or others and describe a target behavior in objective, observable terms.

 KEY
TERMS

ACCOUNTABILITY: Taking responsibility for the outcomes of student learning.
ANTECEDENTS: Prior conditions or events which elicit behavior.
BASIC TEACHING MODEL: A four-part model for planning, organizing, and evaluating instruction. The four parts of the model are (1) learning objectives, (2) preassessment, (3) instructional strategies, and (4) evaluation.

BEHAVIOR: Any activity of an individual that is directly observable or can be measured.

ACADEMIC BEHAVIOR: Student activity concerned with student-curriculum interaction.

ENTERING BEHAVIOR: Skills, behaviors, interests, and attitudes that can be shown to be relevant to effective learning.

PRODUCTIVE BEHAVIOR: Activity that helps students reach their goals.

PROSOCIAL BEHAVIOR: Interpersonal behaviors that promote cooperative interactions.

SOCIAL BEHAVIOR: Activity that is concerned with person-to-person interactions.

UNPRODUCTIVE BEHAVIOR: Activity that interferes with goal attainment.

CONSEQUENCES: Conditions or events following behavior that affect its occurrence.

DYADIC INTERACTION: Interpersonal activity in which the behavior of each person affects the behavior of one or more other persons.

EMPIRICAL EVIDENCE: Evidence derived from objective observation and experience rather than from hunch or opinion.

EVALUATION: Procedures to determine whether students have achieved learning objectives.

INSTRUCTIONAL STRATEGY: Plans and methods implemented by teachers to help students meet objectives.

LEARNING OBJECTIVES: Statements of what the student should be able to do at the end of an instructional unit.

OBSERVATION: The first step in gathering information about behavior.

NATURAL OBSERVATION: Looking at behavior as it occurs in the everyday environment.

OBJECTIVE OBSERVATION: Looking at behavior as it occurs without interpreting or explaining it.

STRUCTURED OBSERVATION: Using tests, scales, or interviews in which all students respond to the same questions.

PREREQUISITE SKILLS: Entering behaviors necessary for a particular sequence of instruction.

SELF-MANAGEMENT: A complex set of skills for organizing and directing one's own behavior.

TEACHER ROLES: Sets of related behaviors used by teachers to reach their goals.

FACILITATOR ROLE: Sets of teacher behaviors to help individual students meet their special learning requirements.

MANAGER ROLE: Sets of teacher behaviors that are organized, planful, and structured to help students meet learning objectives.

MEDIATOR ROLE: Sets of teacher behaviors that facilitate positive interpersonal and group interactions.

THEORY: Sets of hypotheses or propositions about relationships between two or more events.

DEVELOPMENTAL THEORIES: Theories that consider how behavior changes over periods of time and across many situations.

INSTRUCTIONAL THEORIES: Theories that apply the concepts and research findings from learning and developmental theories to the science of managing instruction.

LEARNING THEORIES: Theories that propose relationships between new behaviors and the conditions under which they are acquired.

SELF-TEST

1. Three roles of the teacher are _____ , _____ , and _____ .
2. Productive behavior
   a. helps students meet their goals
   b. produces a visible product
   c. produces financial gain
   d. increases the number of students in a class
3. Structured observations use
   a. real behavior in the classroom
   b. observations of physical growth
   c. responses to tests and scales
   d. observations made at standard times of the day
4. Accountability in teaching means
   a. financial bookkeeping for school records
   b. maintaining a head count for students each day
   c. teacher responsibility for student learning
   d. teacher responsibility for student health and safety
5. Prerequisite skills describe
   a. student learning before coming to school
   b. student learning in previous classes
   c. student entering behavior necessary for learning a task

   d. a and b only
   e. all of the above
6. Learning objectives are defined as _____ _____ .
7. Underline the objective behavior descriptions.
   Susan loves math.
   Paula looks at the floor and cries.
   Bryan turns to page 38.
   Donna is unmotivated.
   Marlene understands matrix algebra.
   Alvin turns in his homework every day.
8. The basic teaching model has four parts. These are:
   _____ , _____ ,
   _____ , _____ .
9. Consequent conditions describe
   a. whether or not an event is true
   b. what occurred before a student's behavior
   c. what occurred after a student's behavior
   d. discipline procedures in the classroom
10. Teacher roles are
    a. determined by the school policies
    b. determined by parent and student demands
    c. integrated into a personal style
    d. separate and distinct

SELF-TEST KEY

1. Manager of the learning environment, mediator of human relations, facilitator of individual development
2. a
3. c
4. c
5. c
6. statements of what the student should be able to do at the end of an instructional unit
7. Paula, Bryan, Alvin
8. learning objectives, preassessment, instructional strategy, evaluation
9. c
10. c

PART 2
Mediating Social and Cognitive Development

Bryan is starting first grade today. He comes into the classroom full of enthusiasm, high in activity level, and eager to make new friends. He expects his teacher to like him, his peers to be friendly, and that he will do well in school (Barclay, 1974; Smith & Worell, 1980).

If you are Bryan's teacher, you will want to know all about this small human being and what you can expect of him. What can he do well, what does he need to learn, and what are his interests? As a new student, Bryan is facing the ladder of academic progression and achievement. When he reaches the top and is ready to graduate, consider how he will have changed. What developmental patterns will have carried Bryan from a just-barely-socialized first-grader to a young adult who is ready to face the world on his own? How do students change over time and what factors are responsible for the changes you observe? The study of development involves an examination of progressive changes in behavior over time and of the factors that produce these changes. Your knowledge of these patterns of development will place you in a better position to understand the growing individual, to provide for his or her educational needs, to tolerate changing moods, and to enjoy each student's emerging capabilities.

In your teaching activities, you will find developmental information useful for dealing with individual and group behavior in a wide array of situations. Knowledge of how students grow and change over time will increase your skills in dealing with academic topics as well as in facilitating positive student attitudes toward school. Developmental information will tell you something about student entry behaviors, student expectancies about school, and student interaction patterns. In your management of the academic and interpersonal climate of your class, your knowledge and application of developmental information can help your students mature toward effective cognitive, social, and self-regulation skills. You will have an opportunity to apply the three roles for teaching we described in Chapter 1. Your starting point in learning about these roles begins with a knowledge of developmental patterns.

In the following section, we will describe Bryan at two ages: 6 and 18. You can imagine what he might be like at 12 or 28. We will describe Bryan's behavior in four important areas: physical-motor, cognitive, social, and self-regulation. In later chapters, we shall be comparing Bryan with Jim and Ted as well as with Kathy and Donna. The major focus of Chapter 2 will be Bryan: Chapter 3 will focus on Kathy; Chapter 4 will bring Bryan and Kathy together to consider their cognitive development.

CHAPTER 2

Patterns of Development

LEARNING OBJECTIVES

After reading Chapter 2, answering the self-monitoring questions, completing the learning activity, and reading any further references of your choice, you will be able to:

1. Define and give examples of key terms.

2. Identify individual differences among students according to norms, the normal curve, and the mastery curve.

3. Contrast the development of readiness skills from the viewpoints of stage theory and developmental learning theory.

4. List and describe four sources of information provided by the learning environment.

5. Identify characteristics of physical and motor development that are likely to affect (a) student skill development and (b) student stimulus value.

6. Explain how socioeconomic, ethnic, and cultural factors can influence student behavior and progress in school.

7. Match parent behavior patterns with probable student behavior patterns.

8. Compare how parents, television, and schools teach new behaviors.

9. Conduct a natural observation of a child. Write descriptive statements of observable behaviors. Make inferences and draw conclusions about patterns of behavior.

FOCUS ON DEVELOPMENT

BRYAN AT 6

Physical-motor skills

Bryan has developed many physical-motor skills. He can run a race, throw a ball, climb a tree, and balance himself on a fence. He is very active and enjoys using his body in space. He is not quite so adept at fine motor coordination, however, and has trouble in holding his pencil correctly.

Social skills

Bryan has learned many social skills that will help him integrate himself into the classroom community. He has formed basic attachments to people. Therefore, he is responsive to attention and praise and is usually eager to please. He frequently reaches out toward other children as he forms new alliances. Although you now see him on the playground chasing girls, by third grade he will strenuously avoid them.

Bryan is learning to manage his behavior in terms of some basic prosocial expectancies. He understands and can follow many rules. He is learning to take turns in a game, share his crayons, help other children in distress, and engage in a cooperative project with another child. He understands property regulations, including what is his and and what is yours. Being first is important for Bryan, however, and he often pushes to get to the head of the line.

Cognitive and academic skills

You will observe that Bryan demonstrates a number of cognitive and academic skills that will be useful to him in the primary grades. He can print his name, identify four colors, name simple shapes, and count to ten or more. He follows simple directions and can sit in one place for a reasonable length of time. He is an eager participant in class and often volunteers his answers before you call on him. He is curious and asks many questions. He is able to project himself into the future, but his goals are unrealistic; he tells you he wants to be an astronaut when he grows up.

Bryan also has a good command of language. He can communicate his needs and ideas as well as listen and respond to yours. Language provides him with the ability to plan ahead, to anticipate future events, and therefore to predict the consequences of his own behavior. His language is generally concrete in nature, referring to the familiar and real events in his life. His thoughts may race ahead of his language skills, however, so that he stammers at times and then forgets what he wanted to say.

Self-regulation skills

Finally, Bryan has learned some degree of self-regulation and independence. He demonstrates many self-help skills that enable him to operate on his own without outside assistance. He is capable of dressing and grooming himself, handling small amounts of money, getting around his home and school neighborhoods, and using the telephone. He has learned that the exercise of these skills, as well as the acquisition of new ones, is a source of reward and pleasure because it opens up new potential for experience and stimulation.

Self-regulation skills enable Bryan to manage much of his own behavior without adult intervention. He can cope with small frustrations involving delayed fulfillment of his wants. He tolerates and adjusts to his inability to complete every task successfully on the first try. He has developed some control over his emotions, although he is still prone to sudden bursts of uncontrolled laughter and may become involved in loud, angry disputes. He can carry out small responsibilities and can participate in some decision-making activities. Although he seeks help and guidance at times, he delights in doing things on his own. He feels quite ready for school and is confident of his ability to cope with his small world. This is Bryan at 6.

BRYAN AT 18

Let's skip ahead to Bryan's high school graduation and consider what changes have taken place in him.

Physical-motor development

Bryan has reached his full physical growth, although some of his pals are still growing taller and heavier. His physical sex characteristics are fully developed: his voice is deep, he shaves every day, and he has an abiding interest in the opposite sex. His early development of strength, speed, agility, and coordination, combined with intensive daily practice, has placed him on the school tennis team.

Social development

Bryan's early interest in his peer group has developed into a social network of friends with common interests and activities. Some of these friends may be lifelong companions, and perhaps the redhead he is so often seen with will be one of them. Bryan is active in the social life of his school and was elected student body representative for the senior class. He has an open, friendly manner and a gentle sense of humor that attract others to him. He is coping with the problems of defining his role as a man in contemporary society. He is somewhat undecided about "women's lib" and whether he really believes women are as smart and capable as men.

He has worked out his earlier conformity to the demands of his peer group and is now capable of making his own decisions apart from his friends. By working out his individual philosophy of life, he is setting standards for his behavior which may or may not conform to social expectancies. Having developed a personal moral code about ethical behavior, he frequently leans toward idealism in his political and social opinions.

Cognitive development

Bryan now has language and conceptual systems that allow him to deal with abstractions, complex logic, and advanced problem solving. Except for future additions to his vocabulary, he has become a fully "rational" adult. He enjoys intellectual debates with classmates and is willing to challenge or disagree with his teachers. Adults who tangle with him intellectually may find his arguments tinged with idealism and inexperience. Since Bryan is college bound, he takes his schoolwork seriously and is concerned about keeping up his grades.

Self-regulation

For the most part, Bryan has developed an autonomous manner of functioning in his daily life. He is independent in deciding how to use his time and his money, whom to select as a friend and how to deal with parents and teachers. He wants reasons for rules and regulations and will marshal arguments against those he feels are unfair. Because he is still working out his own system of values, he often appears moody and unpredictable to adults. He has also learned to drive a car, thereby achieving more independence from parents and mobility in his environment.

Finally, Bryan has a set of realistic future goals. Rejecting his earlier desire to become an astronaut, he is now more aware of his capabilities and lifetime options. He has decided to enter college and study engineering, possibly with an aeronautical emphasis. He has spent a great deal of time considering his future—"what I want to do with my life"—and feels optimistic about the opportunities that lie ahead. At the same time, however, he does not feel quite ready to face the world on his own. In spite of occasional disagreements, he maintains a comfortable relationship with his parents and relies on their advice and help. He still has one foot touching the world of childhood while the other foot reaches out to walk alone.

We have described our student's development from the primary grades to the completion of high school and have seen the child mature into an adult (well, almost an adult). Bryan's development will not stop at 18. Researchers now tell us that development proceeds throughout the life span. Significant changes will occur as Bryan meets new situations and copes with the many joys and crises that are to come. Although your job as his teacher is completed, you know that his patterns of living will undergo continuous change and revision.

PRINCIPLES OF DEVELOPMENT

Will you meet another Bryan someday in one of your classes? Of course, none of your students will be exactly like him. He is a unique individual. Although he resembles every student in some manner, none of your students will look, behave, or think just like Bryan. In this chapter, we will introduce some of the major factors that seem to influence similarities and differences among students. We will take a look at alternative ways to describe these differences and similarities in student behavior. Students can be described in terms of norms or typical behaviors, age and stage characteristics, and the contributions of an effective learning environment. Similarities and differences in student behavior are also influenced by broad moderating factors that are defined by physical makeup, family and home environment, and experiences outside your classroom. You will want to become knowledgeable about all the important factors that may influence student behavior in school.

INDIVIDUAL DIFFERENCES

Each of your students will come into your class with a particular background of learned experiences, special capabilities, and expectancies about school. Each new student will react differently to your teaching strategies and your personal style. Every student will be a unique individual, with a particular set of reaction patterns. These variations in any given characteristic that we observe among members of any group are called INDIVIDUAL DIFFERENCES. With so much diversity, how can we describe students in order to deal with the similarities among them? How can I teach, you may ask, when each person reacts in a different manner from every other person?

Developmental norms: Student similarities

Students do behave in ways that are similar. Many student behaviors are predictable for groups. We shall describe these similarities in terms of DEVELOPMENTAL NORMS. You will use NORMS to describe the most frequent or "typical" set of traits or behaviors observed across large groups of individuals. If most students in Bryan's class can count to ten when entering the first grade, then the norm for digit counting in that class is ten digits. As we discuss developmental patterns in later chapters, we shall be referring to norms of behavior that are demonstrated by most students within a particular group. The group may be an age group, a sex group, or a cultural group. The norms for any behaviors or characteristics in these groups indicate some similarity among members of the group.

When you wish to evaluate how Bryan compares with a group, you will need to use appropriate norms. For example, you might want to know how 6-year-old Bryan compares with the norm for his class in reading readiness skills. This kind of information is very helpful to the first-grade teacher who wants to select appropriate reading materials for Bryan. Years later, you might want to know how 18-year-old Bryan

"Many student behaviors are predictable for groups." (Sybil Shelton/Monkmeyer)

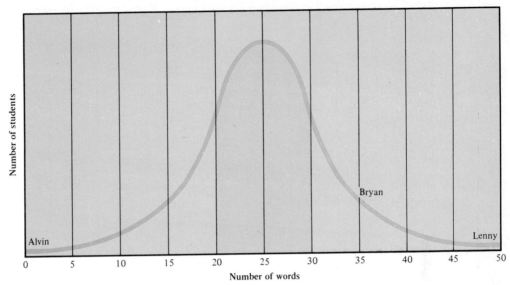

Figure 2-1   Hypothetical distribution of number of words correctly read by first-grade students in Kentucky. The shaded portion represents about 68 percent of all students. Bryan, who read 35 words correctly, reads better than about 84 percent of all first-graders. Lenny reads better than about 99 percent of all first-graders. Alvin does not read at all; he is surpassed by about 95 percent of first-grade students.

compares with all high school graduates on advanced verbal skills. This information might be helpful to a senior class adviser who is helping Bryan to complete his college placement application. For each skill, you will select the norms that are appropriate to that skill for a particular group.

The normal curve: Comparing individuals and groups

For any given behavior, students such as Bryan help develop NORMAL CURVES. Some first-graders (such as Lenny, for example) are very advanced in reading skills. Other first-graders (such as Alvin) have not yet learned to identify their letters. Large groups of student performances can be plotted so that a normal curve is produced. Figure 2-1 demonstrates a hypothetical NORMAL CURVE of distribution for numbers of words read correctly by 6-year-olds in Kentucky. You can see that most of the scores fall within the middle two-thirds of the distribution, from twenty to thirty words read correctly. A smaller number of students at each end of the curve can read either five or forty-five words. Bryan enters first grade with well-developed reading skills; he can read thirty-five words correctly before instruction. Therefore, his word-identification skills are above the norm for first-graders in Kentucky.

Many behavioral and developmental characteristics are distributed among students in a manner similar to the normal curve. Most students cluster in the middle range and some, like Lenny and Alvin, appear at the higher and lower end points. You will rarely compare any one student on

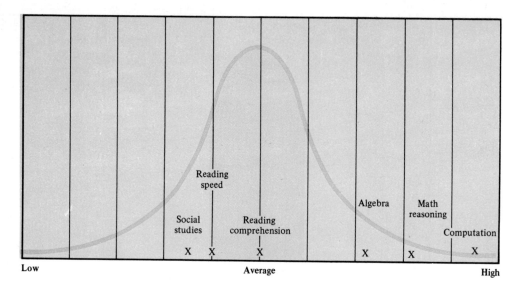

Figure 2-2   Comparison between Bryan's achievement scores and national distribution of scores. The X marks Bryan's scores.

only one behavior. Usually, teachers, parents, and principals look at several different behaviors in describing a student. When Bryan was assessed by his teacher and the guidance counselor at age 18, the results resembled the display in Figure 2-2. As you can see, Bryan is very strong in some skills, average in others, and weak in some areas. When we compare him with other students over a range of skills, we find that Bryan is both average and unique.

PROBE 2-1

The normal curve of distribution describes both _____ and _____ in student characteristics.

Dealing with individual differences

What does this range of individual differences have to do with teaching? There are two major possibilities. Many teachers use the normal curve of distribution to determine their instructional objectives and expectancies for student learning. This means that most students will fall into the center range of achievement and will receive a grade of C. A few will show outstanding achievement and will receive an A. Some students will perform far below their classmates and are likely to fail. You may have been graded this way yourself. Is this a desirable outcome? What might be the impact of this adherence to the normal curve on young children? How did it affect you? A second way to handle individual differences has been proposed by Benjamin Bloom and his colleagues (1968, 1971).

Bloom (1968, 1971, 1976) describes a MASTERY LEARNING approach, in which all learners are expected to meet a set of learning objectives. When teachers assess entering behavior, adjust their objectives accordingly, and develop strategies to encourage each individual student to meet these objectives, then the distribution of skills may be transformed. These teacher behaviors are some of the same activities that we described in the basic teaching model. Figure 2-3 demonstrates the shape of the curve for reading scores in a first-grade class when the teacher has followed a mastery approach to learning. It shows that, at the end of an instructional sequence, most students are expected to meet the learning objectives. Those who do not are given additional instruction and practice and retested until they meet the goals for the unit. In this manner, the teacher can reduce the individual differences among students on specific skills developed from learning objectives. Chapters 9 and 10 cover mastery learning in greater detail and provide you with specific ideas on how to manage it.

PROBE 2-2

Is it desirable to reduce all individual differences? Try making up two lists of behaviors and skills. In one list, include some skills and behaviors that you believe should be fairly similar among all students at a given grade level. In your second list, include some skills and behaviors for which you would like to encourage a wide distribution among these same students. How do these two lists differ?

AGES AND STAGES

Since Bryan obviously changed as he matured, we were able to observe, describe, and classify these changes according to certain norms. At 6 he was highly active and eager to go to school. At 14 or 15 he was frequently moody and argued with his teachers. Can we say that these

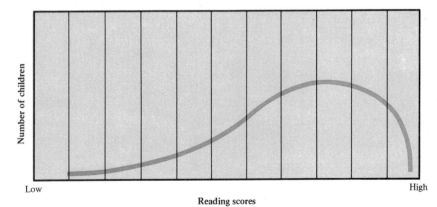

Figure 2-3 Distribution of reading scores for a first-grade class taught for mastery. Most students earn high scores and fewer students earn moderate or low scores.

Number of children

Low   High

Reading scores

changes in Bryan's behavior were due to an increase in age? Or was Bryan just passing through an adolescent stage?

Using age norms

Age and stage norms are frequently used to account for similarities in behavior among students (Gesell & Armatruda, 1947; Gesell, Ames, & Ilg, 1976). Parents and teachers find age norms useful in anticipating what children can accomplish. Knowing that most children don't toilet train before age 2, tie shoes before age 4, or write cursive script before age 8 gives the trainer—be it parent or teacher—some rough guidelines as to what kinds of tasks to expect of the learner. It will be helpful to you in your teaching to be aware of the major behavioral and learning characteristics of the age group to which your students belong. When you move to the level of each individual student, however, there are a number of drawbacks in dealing with Bryan as a typical 6- or 16-year-old.

Pitfalls in using age and stage norms

Several theories of development to be considered in the following chapters are based on a "stage" concept, in which new behavior is thought to depend on DEVELOPMENTAL STAGE as well as age. We believe that there are at least three pitfalls in using norms focused on either age or developmental stage to account for the changes we observe in student behavior.

Some children learn to read early. (Erika Stone)

Individual differences are ignored We have seen that norms for groups do not describe any one student accurately. Although the age norm for learning to read is 6, Lenny taught himself to read when he was 4 but Alvin still can't read at age 8, in the third grade. Each student may have some of the age-typical characteristics, but each also varies on many others. The individual is very rarely "on stage" in all areas of competency. For example, we have see that Bryan, on his senior high achievement tests, fit the norm on some skills but was quite deviant on others. Age and developmental stage norms describe how some students are similar to one another, but they do not explain student differences. If teachers and parents expect all the "normal" behaviors from each student, they are going to set up expectancies that can't possibly be met. Bryan will be assigned an inappropriate text or you may select an ineffective strategy.

Stages are used to explain behavior Frequently, many teachers and parents rely on a stage norm to "explain" student behavior. If Bryan is moody and argumentative at 16, you can say "Oh, it's just a teenage stage he's going through." You might then ignore or dismiss Bryan's objections to classroom procedures or his critical approach to class discussion. It would be more helpful to you to discuss with Bryan some current classroom conditions that may be producing his disagreements rather than to dismiss his behavior as "adolescent rebellion." That way, you may be able to introduce changes in classroom procedures that will accommodate to Bryan's new behaviors. Frequently, student participation in developing objectives and curriculum will encourage positive student contributions to class activities (Solomon & Kendall, 1979).

Stages do not account for learning Descriptions of developmental change in terms of age or stage do not tell us anything about how the student moves from one stage to another. Therefore, the parent or teacher who wishes to change behavior or to move it forward has few guiding principles other than to "wait until the child is ready." From this point of view, a student cannot learn until he or she is "ready." If readiness is dependent upon arriving at a specific age or stage, then you have no alternative but to wait until development or "experience" takes the student forward (Rosenthal & Zimmerman, 1978).

On the other hand, readiness can be regarded as dependent on certain prerequisite skills that the student must acquire before new learning can occur. If new learning is related to particular prior skills, then we can determine what these skills are for any learning activity and how they can be taught (Gagné, 1977; Smith & Worell, 1980). In the following section, we will apply the concept of prerequisite skills to learning and development.

A DEVELOPMENTAL LEARNING POINT OF VIEW

We shall take the position here that development does not proceed by means of stages that are separate and discrete from one another. Indeed, it is continuous, cumulative, and hierarchical. We view development as a *continuous* process of new learning as the student moves from one situation to another. We see development as a *cumulative* process, in that each new learning experience is added to previous ones to form new behaviors. We regard development as *hierarchical,* in that new learning depends upon the skills the student has already mastered. Thus, whether this new skill is learned depends less on age or developmental stage and more on the demonstrated present behaviors that are prerequisite to learning the new skill. In each instance, the development of more advanced or complex behavior depends upon the mastery of more simple behaviors (Baer, 1970; Gagné, 1977). Learning to perform a long-division problem, for example, requires skills in addition and multiplication. Likewise, Bryan cannot read until he has learned to attach sounds to printed symbols.

The development of new behavior is a product of the child's specific social learning experiences and of the social learning opportunities provided by the child's current environment. The same principles of learning will apply to the development of new behavior, whether we are considering, for example, Bryan's reading skills, his tendency to swagger like his father, or his unwillingness to cheat on a classroom test (Bandura & Walters, 1963; Bandura, 1976a). We call this approach to development and learning a *developmental learning* point of view.

Development and teaching

From a developmental learning view, your task as a facilitator of individual differences is to determine what skills are prerequisite for the mastery of any task, to sequence these skills in order, and to apply established principles of learning to the teaching of these skills (Gagné & Briggs, 1979; Gewirtz, 1969; McCandless & Evans, 1973). This approach assumes that, within the limits of the child's physical capabilities to master the required skill, many tasks can be taught at an earlier age and to more diverse students than had been previously thought possible. You can begin to teach new competencies to any child if (1) you initiate the learning sequence at the present skill level of the learner and (2) you use teaching strategies appropriate to the student's present capabilities for responding. Another way of saying this is that the correct time for teaching is a point in the sequence of experience of the student, not a point in time according to age or stage. As a teacher who is interested in promoting behavior change that moves the student toward maturity, you will find a knowledge of learning theory more useful than a description of age norms (Gewirtz, 1969; Rosenthal & Zimmerman, 1978).

═══════ **PROBE 2-3** ═══════

Researchers have recently been able to demonstrate that we can teach reading and typing skills to children as early as age 2. Some preschool programs begin teaching reading at 3 or 4. Do you think it is desirable to begin instruction on academic tasks before the traditional age of 6? Give reasons to support your answer. Turn around and give some arguments against your answer.

Development, maturation, and learning

Recall some of the changes in Bryan's development we described earlier, from the first to the twelfth grades. As Bryan developed over time, his physical structure changed and he learned to make new responses both to his environment and to himself. What, then, is the difference between development and learning? DEVELOPMENT is a lifelong process in which the individual changes over significant periods of the life span. The process of development ends only with death. During these periods of development, the individual may or may not be learning new response patterns. Development includes not only what is learned from internal or external stimulation but also the physical and structural changes that take place as growth proceeds toward maturity. This process of structural change that accompanies age change is called MATURATION. Learning cannot occur until the appropriate physical structures develop (Anastasi, 1958; Hebb, 1966).

LEARNING, on the other hand, involves a stable change in behavior as a person interacts with specific environmental stimuli. At varying periods in his development, Bryan may pay attention to different stimulus conditions and his physical and cognitive capabilities for responding may change. Therefore, environmental or stimulus conditions will have a differing influence on his behavior at various times in his life. The concept of *learning*, then, is narrower than that of *development* and is restricted to the specific changes that occur under specific environmental conditions. Both learning and development are similar, however, in that they involve an interaction between the developing person and his or her learning environment (Singer & Singer, 1969). In the following section, we shall discuss the interaction between the developing child and the learning environment.

THE LEARNING ENVIRONMENT

We have seen that both learning and development involve an interaction between the growing child and the environment. The LEARNING ENVIRONMENT is that part of the real world which directly affects the responses of the child.

**The learning
environment is
social**

Because other people provide the conditions under which Bryan can learn
and develop, Bryan's learning environment is primarily a social one. A
number of psychologists have taken the principles of learning theory and
applied them to the social impact of the behavior of significant others in
the child's environment. The result is called *social learning theory*
(Bandura, 1976a, 1976b; Mischel, 1973, 1976; Rotter, 1954). We shall be
using the concepts of social learning theory throughout the following
chapters to describe and explain developmental processes.

**The social
learning
environment is
developmental**

How is the learning environment both developmental and social? As
youngsters grow, they look different, behave differently, and become
different people to others. As significant people in Bryan's world notice
these physical and behavioral changes in him, they will react differently
to him. They will change their expectancies for his behavior. As a result,
his social-interactive environment will change constantly as others modify
their behavior toward him (Sears, 1957). His parents and teachers will

provide him with more complex toys and books. They will allow him more freedom to explore and to move further from home or classroom. They will place more demands on his behavior as they observe that his capabilities are increasing, and they will refrain from rewarding him for less mature behavior.

The learning environment is dyadic

Bryan is not a passive receiver of the learning environment. According to social learning theory, he reacts to the social and physical stimuli around him with new behavior that, in turn, changes the way in which others react to him. Bryan is a shaper of his environment as well as being shaped by it. His relationships with others are both dyadic and reciprocal; each is influenced by the behavior of the other (Bandura, 1976b; Bell, 1970; Lewis, 1974; Rheingold, 1966). Study 2-1 describes how the behavior of teachers is shaped by the differing ways in which their students react. It demonstrates that teachers use reciprocal behavior with their students and respond to the individual differences they observe in student behavior patterns.

STUDY 2-1: CHILD EFFECTS ON ADULT BEHAVIOR

To what extent are the behaviors of the adult and child dependent upon one another? In an interesting study to examine these interaction effects, two adult women were trained to be either highly nurturant or nonnurturant with groups of young children. The highly nurturant woman was instructed to demonstrate interest, praise, attention, and affection to the children. The nonnurturant woman was instructed to withhold these reactions but not to show hostility or rejection. The researchers found that children reacted differently to these two women in their frequency of dependency and attention-seeking requests. Over four days, the nurturant woman received more than twice as many bids for attention and help from the children than did the nonnurturant one. In turn, these two adults behaved differently to different children, despite their previous training and instructions. Over the four days, the nonnurturant woman became consistently *less* helpful and more negative to dependency bids from boys. In addition, the nurturant woman became significantly *less* nurturant with highly dependent or clowning boys. This study provides strong evidence that the same behavior on the part of the adult may bring out different responses from children. Likewise, certain children received different reactions from the adults, regardless of the adults' previous behavior patterns. Behavior between two people is thus reciprocal and dyadic.

Adapted from: Yarrow, M. R., Waxler, C. Z., & Scott, P. M. Child effects on adult behavior, *Developmental Psychology,* 1971, 5, 300–311.

As students interact reciprocally with their social learning environments, they are receiving information to help them guide their future behavior. On the basis of the information Bryan receives about the world around him and how it will react to him, he plans and adjusts his response patterns. We will describe four major sources of environmental information that are available to youngsters in the course of their development. These sources of information are potentially under the control of social agents, such as parents or yourself. Therefore, you can use these sources constructively in your teaching and intervention procedures. From a social learning point of view, the environment provides the developing child with (1) stimulation, (2) models of behavior, (3) consequences for behavior, and (4) structure. We will discuss each of the four sources of information in turn.

Stimulation The availability of STIMULATION determines what the developing child sees, hears, and touches. The STIMULUS events provided by a child's environment can vary from simple to complex, from few to many, and from seldom to frequent. The amount and quality of early and continued stimulation to which a child is exposed can affect the learning and response capabilities of that child when he or she is presented with new situations (Deutsch, 1964; Hunt, 1972; Lewis, 1976; Zeigler, 1970). In general, an environment rich in available stimulation such as toys, books, colors, sounds, people, places, and language will tend to increase Bryan's later learning capabilities.

Models The environment introduces new patterns for complex skills, language formation, and social roles by means of MODELS. The verbal and physical behavior of other people will serve as primary sources for new learning. As Bryan observes the actions of other people and the consequences that follow these actions, he will later attempt to imitate some of these behaviors in his own manner. The parent or teacher who says, in effect, "Do what I say and not what I do" will soon find out that this is often not possible. If Bryan's father hits him in anger across the face but cautions him to be kind to little brother, he may find Bryan someday hitting his brother just as his father had done to him. Children are able to observe, recall, and later imitate parts of many events to which they are exposed. Whether or not they do so depends upon a number of factors, such as the power and status of the model and whether the model is rewarded or punished.

Consequences The environment provides consequences for behavior that influence whether or not the behavior will be repeated. Some consequences are positively reinforcing. When Bryan receives POSITIVE REINFORCEMENT such as praise or rewards for his new behaviors, he tends to repeat them. He also develops a positive expectancy that new behavior will lead to favorable outcomes for him. On the other hand, some environments provide many negative consequences, so that new responses are less likely to be repeated. If Bryan is provided with frequent negative consequences, such as criticism or punishment, he will develop an expectancy that new and alternative behaviors are undesirable.

Regardless of their positive or negative consequences, all environments provide STANDARDS for competent and acceptable behavior. Standards define the level of competency for behavior to be reinforced. Some parents praise their children for achieving C grades in school; Bryan's parents praise him only when he gets A's and B's. Bryan's parents have higher standards for school achievement than many parents; they withhold reinforcement in the form of approval and praise until Bryan reaches their standards. The standards for competence set by Bryan's parents, teachers, and peers in all areas of his behavior will determine how hard he tries to achieve and how much positive feedback he receives. The standards that others set for him will also determine the standards that he later imposes on himself (Bandura & Kupers, 1964; Mischel & Liebert, 1966). Throughout this book we shall be discussing the ways in which teachers set standards and control learning outcomes for students and how these consequences can be channeled into useful and constructive approaches. Figure 2-4 demonstrates how varying standards for acceptable class participation by three teachers might affect the amount of positive teacher feedback received by students.

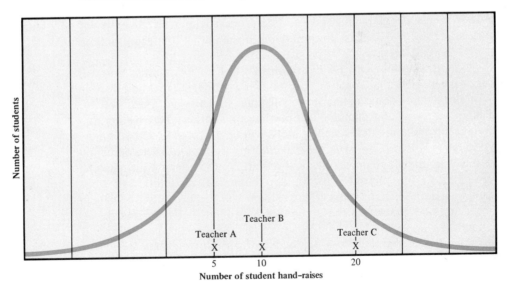

Figure 2-4 Distribution of student participation in class. X marks the number of hand-raises required for teachers A, B, and C to give an S grade for satisfactory student participation. Teacher C has higher standards for satisfactory participation than teachers A and B. Few students in Teacher C's class receive an S for participation.

Structure   Finally, you can see that the learning environment provides the developing child with STRUCTURE. The amount of structure in the learning environment will determine the availability to the child of stimulation, models, and opportunities for reinforcement. Parents provide information about structure by means of instructions and rules which regulate behavior: for example, "Go wash your hands," "Don't hit your brother," "Clean up your room," "Turn off the light." Highly structured environments have many rules and regulations that tell the child what to do and what not to do at all times. A highly structured environment also provides consistent consequences when children comply with these rules. Environments with very little structure have few rules and little, inconsistent, or no reinforcement of these rules. Low-structure environments provide very little information and guidance for younger children who are still trying to learn the social ways of their world. Highly structured environments may unduly restrict sources of information for older students who want to strike out on their own. The amount of structure in the learning environment at all ages will determine how free Bryan can be to try out new behaviors and to learn many alternatives for leading a satisfying life. As you develop your teaching style, you will want to arrive at your own conclusions about a productive balance between too little and too much structure in the learning environment.

How do these development and learning processes affect your behavior with students? We suggest the following possibilities for future action:

GUIDELINES FOR TEACHING

Coordinating the Learning Environment

- *Develop teaching skills for individuals as well as for groups.* You will be aware by now that some of your teaching strategies will be effective with all students some of the time. All your students will need individualized attention and planning at one time or another. This means that both group and individual teaching skills will be useful to you at all times.
- *Acquire skills in observing and evaluating behavior.* Developmental changes in student competencies will require you to adjust your teaching strategies to the physical, social, and cognitive capabilities of your students. In order to be most effective, you will want to acquire skills in observing and evaluating these changes in student behavior and development.
- *Learn to observe your own behavior toward individual students.* The reciprocal nature of human interaction sensitizes both you and the student to the possibilities for bias in how you behave toward individual students. You will want to learn more about how you react to particular student behavior patterns. Do you find yourself becoming less helpful with some students and more critical with others? You will want to learn methods for observing and managing your reactions to particular students.

• *Develop multiple skills in providing stimulation, modeling, reinforcement, and structure.* The power of environmental events to influence behavior provides you with a means of helping all students to make some changes in their learned behavior. Within the limits of the students' physical structure, all behavior can be modified and changed to some extent. As a teacher, you never know what these limits for change will be in any particular student. Therefore, each student has potential for change and you can have a role in shaping some of these changes. You can become knowledgeable in the appropriate use of stimulation, modeling, reinforcement, and structure in the learning environment. You can learn to be judicious in the use of these environmental conditions to encourage each student to reach his or her maximum development of academic, social, and self-regulation skills in school.

MODERATING FACTORS

Each day when your students come to school, their learning environment sets the stage for what they do with their time and how much they learn. The behaviors that emerge in school, however, are influenced by broad factors, both within students themselves and within their social worlds, that moderate their development. Some of the major moderating factors which are most likely to have an impact on the interactions between students, teachers, and the peer group are physical and motor development, socioeconomic and ethnic background, family, and the public media. While learning principles account for many changes in student behavior, these broad moderating factors can expand or limit the possibilities for individual growth and development.

Remember this important point: moderating factors in development do not cause behavior. However, they do provide differential opportunities for learning. Indeed, they may influence Bryan's entering behaviors, learning strategies, and success on each task that he attempts. For example, Bryan's blurting out in his first-grade class may have been related to a number of factors: his mother's permissiveness when he interrupted at home, his "impulsive" cognitive style, his limited experience with peer groups, or his reaction to being the smallest boy in the class. No one of these factors necessarily explains Bryan's behavior. At times, knowledge of possible moderating factors in development may help you to make hypotheses about what might be the most probable antecedents. Knowing more about the determinants of Bryan's behaviors, you may be in a better position to look at them objectively and, when appropriate, encourage more effective behavior patterns. At times, a knowledge of moderating factors leaves you with no immediate strategies. You will have to be patient and tolerant of some behaviors that do not appear easily amenable to change within the time that you have with a given student.

The remainder of this chapter will consider each of our moderating factors and some of the ways in which each can interact with student development. For each factor, we will look at its impact on the developing person and its relevance for how your students perform in school. For each student, these factors may vary in their intensity and influence on behavior. Many other factors might be considered as well; we have chosen those which appear to be particularly useful for your future teaching purposes.

PHYSICAL AND MOTOR DEVELOPMENT

What do you need to know about Bryan's physical development? When might this information become relevant for your interactions with Bryan and his peers? Each student's physical characteristics may affect his or her school progress in two major ways: (1) they may affect the development of skills and (2) they may affect the reactions of others, or the student's STIMULUS VALUE. We shall consider each of these in turn by comparing Bryan's development on each characteristic with that of Ted, who looks very different than Bryan, comes from a different cultural and family background, and is progressing in school in a very different way than Bryan. For each boy, we shall compare how these moderating factors might have contributed to his present behavior in school.

"Speed and agility will help a youngster to achieve competence in all kinds of active games." (P. J. Bailey/Stock, Boston)

PHYSICAL-MOTOR DEVELOPMENT AND
STUDENT BEHAVIOR

First, skill development affects many activities. Each boy's physical structure and rate of growth define and limit what he is capable of performing. Ted and Bryan differ on speed of reaction, eye-motor coordination, physical strength, height, weight, and rate of maturation. Any or all of these factors may affect how skilled each boy becomes at sports, interpersonal play, writing, drawing, and dancing. Strong boys like Bryan can fight back, protect themselves from danger, and become bullies or heroes. Bryan's height can determine success in some activities such as basketball. Speed and agility will help a youngster to achieve competence in all kinds of active games. Do not underestimate the importance of physical strength, build, and prowess for peer acceptance, for boys as well as for girls (Barclay, 1974). Sex differences may influence coordination of large and small muscles, heart rate, muscle-fat ratio, and recovery after physical stress. Regardless of such physical differences, the development of motor skills is equally important for both sexes.

Second, a student's stimulus value affects the reactions of others. Physical development is one factor that determines the stimulus value of students to their teachers and peers. By stimulus value, we mean the ways in which Bryan and Ted's appearance and physical skills affect the responses that others make toward them. These responses can be open approach or avoidance—whether, for example, peers ask them to play, choose them for teams, sit with them at lunch, talk to them at recess, or don't go near them at all. Responses can also take the form of more indirect emotional or verbal reactions that communicate to each boy how others feel about him: facial expression of pleasure and friendliness or disinterest and disgust as well as verbal labels such as *handsome, strong, neat,* or *clumsy, fat, sloppy.* All these reactions result in an evaluation of each boy in terms of his status and acceptance within the peer group. From these evaluative reactions of others, Bryan and Ted will gradually begin to evaluate themselves. As we shall see in Chapter 3, this is part of a process whereby their "self-concepts" are learned.

PHYSICAL GROWTH

For each child, growth is orderly and continuous. Bryan and Ted will follow their own growth rates and will remain fairly stable in their size relationships to other students until adolescence. There are general growth curves at each age level that represent an average for each age and sex. However, within these comparisons, individual variability is great; some children are as much as two years ahead of others in growth. Figure 2-5 displays growth curves for boys and girls from birth to 19 years of age. Comparison between the sexes shows that boys are only slightly ahead of girls in height until puberty, when the adolescent growth spurt occurs.

For students like Ted who are concerned about their short stature, it is important for teachers to know that height after the adolescent growth spurt is more predictive of adult height than is height before adolescence. Poor nutrition can measurably affect both height and weight, however; if it is prolonged and chronic, lifetime effects may occur.

Adolescent growth spurt

Adolescence is a period of marked change in cognitive, social, and personal orientation to life. Its onset is marked by the physical changes that accompany PUBERTY, or maturation of the reproductive system. All students will notice the appearance of pubic hair. Ted and Bryan will observe the growth of testes, while girls will notice breast development. During puberty, there are great changes in height, weight, muscle strength, and vital lung capacity. In general, boys exceed girls in each of these measures, which may give Ted and Bryan an advantage over many though not all girls in athletics. However, Figure 2-6 shows that girls enter puberty earlier than boys and complete their physical growth at an earlier age as well. You can also see from this figure that there is wide variability in the age at which both boys and girls enter puberty. Bryan, who was an early maturer, had already developed sex characteristics at age 11, while Ted had not begun puberty at 15. Teachers of middle-school students note especially the wide variation in physical development and related social behaviors starting at about the fifth and sixth grades. This variability is especially noticeable in girls, since they have an early start.

Early and late maturers

What are the effects of early and late maturing on behavior? There are great differences for both boys and girls on behavioral ratings. Research indicates that boys like Bryan, who entered puberty at about 11, will

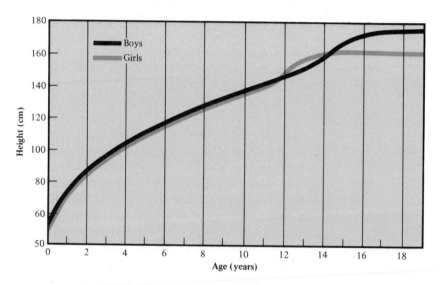

Figure 2-5 Curves for average height attained by boys and girls from birth to 19 years of age. (Source: J. M. Tanner, "Physical Growth," in P. H. Mussen (ed.), *Carmichael's Handbook of Child Psychology.* New York: John Wiley & Sons, 1970, p. 82.)

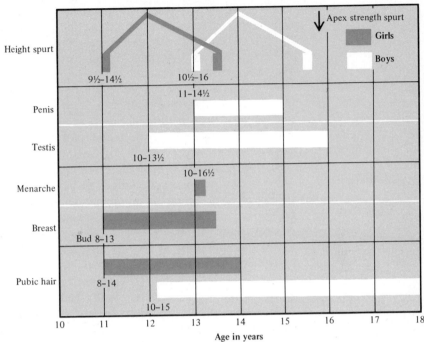

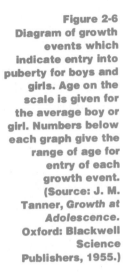

**Figure 2-6
Diagram of growth
events which
indicate entry into
puberty for boys and
girls. Age on the
scale is given for
the average boy or
girl. Numbers below
each graph give the
range of age for
entry of each
growth event.
(Source: J. M.
Tanner, *Growth at
Adolescence*.
Oxford: Blackwell
Science
Publishers, 1955.)**

show an early advantage. Teachers, peers, and Bryan himself rate him as more popular, self-confident, better accepted, more "mature" behaviorally, less attention-getting, and more independent than late-maturing boys like Ted. Ted is the same age as Bryan but did not enter into puberty until he was 15. In contrast to boys like Bryan, boys like Ted are likely to be rated on the same measures as less attractive, more attention-getting, talkative, "immature," less confident, and less popular (Mussen & Jones, 1957, 1958). A follow-up study at age 33 found that late-maturing boys remained more dependent and continued to rely on others for help (Jones, 1957).

For Kathy and Donna, the picture is quite different. To date, few studies have been completed on rates of maturation in girls, but we do know that early maturity is, at the outset, an interpersonal handicap to girls. Kathy, who had visibly matured by age 12, is less likely than the later-maturing Donna to be rated as popular or a leader. However, by 16, Kathy has overcome the negative reactions to her advanced physical development and is rated comparatively high on self-esteem and social prestige (Faust, 1960; Jones & Mussen, 1958; Weatherly, 1964). Apparently, for girls, physical build takes on a different social value, depending on the age of the girl. For boys, advanced physical build is socially valued at all ages.

How can we account for these differences in behavioral ratings that accompany early and late entry into puberty and adolescence? We assume that these behaviors are learned in response to differential expectancies and reinforcement by others for independent and self-assertive behavior. For example, Bryan was tall and muscular at an early age. He was more likely than Ted to be assigned responsibility at home and at school, to be treated as an adult rather than as a child, to gain attention from both boys and girls for his athletic and interpersonal skills. Given the opportunity and encouragement, Bryan tended to adopt and practice these new behaviors. He will continue to use those behaviors because they are positively reinforced and therefore successful. Especially for boys, *instrumental* behaviors are valued in most cultures (assertiveness, independence, decision making, dominance, and leadership) and are likely to be reinforced once they appear (Rosenkrantz, Vogel, Bee, Broverman & Broverman, 1968).

How about Kathy at age 12? Her friends and teachers knew she had reached puberty by her obvious breast development and her early interest in boys. Peers may judge these changes to be age-inappropriate, and they therefore ignored or rejected Kathy at this age. By the time she is 16, these same characteristics become socially valued because they signal an ability to attract the opposite sex. Traditionally, a woman's success in attracting men has been regarded as one of her prime assets. Kathy at 16 acquires social prestige value for her advanced physical development. Since expected behaviors for the two sexes are changing in today's "liberated" culture, we may see a shift in the social stimulus value of early and late maturing for girls.

Body build and physical attractiveness

Bryan is tall and muscular and is regarded as attractive by both his teachers and his peer group. Ted, on the other hand, is short and chubby and is not especially noticeable in his group. How do these characteristics influence Bryan's and Ted's development? Many research studies indicate that body build and physical attractiveness bias the reaction of others and form one basis for evaluations of personality and behavior.

Body build tends to bias personality ratings in favor of boys who are built like Bryan. Several studies have used silhouettes to measure the influence of body build on how people rate behavior. Regardless of whether the raters are teachers with some knowledge of psychology (Walker, 1962) or children in elementary school (Staffieri, 1967), body build affects the stereotypes assigned to boys and men. Strangely enough, girls have been either missing from these studies or have shown no differences in their ratings. These studies show that Bryan, with a muscular body type, would probably have been rated by his teacher as generally more masculine, independent, and successful. Ted, on the other hand—with a short, chubby stature—might be seen by his teachers as being more dependent and lazy.

Similar biases become evident when teachers are asked to rate behaviors of children who have been independently selected as "attractive" or "unattractive." The general thesis of the research in this area suggests that "beautiful is good." Study 2-2 suggests that Bryan, who is physically attractive by our cultural standards, is more likely than Ted to be rated as having higher intelligence, to have parents who are interested in his schooling, and to enjoy good social relationships. He will also be seen as more likely to finish school (Clifford & Walster, 1973).

STUDY 2-2: DOES PHYSICAL ATTRACTIVENESS MAKE A DIFFERENCE?

A set of twelve photographs of actual children previously rated as either "attractive" or "unattractive" was shown to 404 fifth-grade teachers individually. Half the pictures were of fifth-grade boys and half were of fifth-grade girls. The teachers were also given a standard report card which indicated that all the children in the pictures had received above-average grades. Each teacher was sent one report card, with picture attached, by the school principal and was asked to rate the child on the following characteristics:

- Estimated IQ: possible range, *96* to *130*
- Social relationships with peers: *very bad* to *very good*
- Parents' attitudes toward school: *indifference* to *strong interest*
- How far student will progress in school: *grade*

The hypothesis of the researchers was confirmed through statistical tests: on all four questions, teachers rated attractive students significantly more favorably than they did unattractive students. Teachers expected at-tractive students to have *higher* IQs, *better* peer relationships, and parents who were *more* interested in their school progress. They also saw these children as more likely to continue in school. Both male and female teachers produced similar ratings, and there were no rated differences on any of the questions for boys or girls.

This study demonstrates how a student's entering physical characteristics can bias the responses of teachers to their educational and social achievements. The critical question becomes this: How do these teacher expectancies affect the way in which they react to these students? Do these teachers actually provide different opportunities for positive learning? Do these teachers give differential attention or reinforcement to these two groups of students? You cannot change the appearance of your students. You *can* change the manner in which you respond to students. You can also have an impact on the manner in which students respond to each other.

Adapted from: Clifford, M. M., & Walster, E. The effect of physical attractiveness on teacher expectations. *Sociology of Education*, 1973, *46*, 248–258.

MOTOR SKILLS

In first grade, Bryan and Ted gradually gain greater control over their motor behavior. Any day before or after school, you will notice Bryan running more than he walks, jumping over hydrants, balancing on fences, throwing balls and sometimes rocks, hopping through hopscotch squares in the schoolyard, and skipping rope with Kathy. In class he frequently fidgets and moves from chair to desk to pencil sharpener. A survey of over fifty elementary classrooms indicates that "out of seat" behavior averages about 15 to 20 percent of total class time (Worell & Nelson, 1974). Elementary teachers should not expect young children to sit still and be quiet all the time. Ted, on the other hand, walks from the school bus to his classroom, runs only when he is late, and walks around hydrants and fences rather than jumping over them. When a ball comes his way in the schoolyard, he ducks rather than try to catch it. In class he tends to remain in his seat most of the time, counts on his fingers for math problems, and writes a clumsy manuscript with his left hand.

"For the most part, boys' and girls' motor development is very similar." (Bruce Roberts/ Photo Researchers)

Trends in skilled motor performance

Specific motor skills are learned, but they are also related to individual differences in physical structure, activity level, and coordination. Some of the developmental trends in motor behavior that appear from first grade through high school are useful to consider. Let us look at these trends briefly and consider their possible contributions to classroom teaching practices. For the most part, boys' and girls' motor development is very similar except for fine motor coordination in the early grades and skilled performance after puberty. In general, development proceeds in the following manner.

Movement from kinesthetic (motor) cues to visual cues   The use of visual cues for motor performance increases through the early grades and is fairly well developed by age 8. From then on, youngsters become more adept at using visual cues to guide their movements. Note the application of this trend to counting behavior. While Ted is using his fingers in first grade, he will soon learn to count by looking at objects in sequence and later he will transfer these counting skills to a covert process that takes place in his head (Lockhart, 1973).

Coordination of sensory modalities   Many students tend to use only one mode of processing information. Bryan remembers better by looking at his work, while Ted finds listening (auditory stimuli) and touching (tactile stimuli) more helpful. Ted is also having difficulty in reading and writing skills. His teacher might use several SENSORY MODALITIES, or channels for receiving information, in teaching these skills. For example, teachers can combine tactile (touch) and kinesthetic (motor) methods with either look-see or phonetic (auditory) approaches to reading. For many students in elementary school, concrete motor activity associated with the learning of concepts and skills is an aid to understanding and recall.

Movement from large- to fine-muscle coordination   In first grade, Ted still jumps or hops with both feet; Bryan hops on one foot and can balance for long periods of time. While Ted is barely able to cope with lowercase manuscript, Bryan is trying his hand at cursive script. The teaching of cursive script is usually delayed until the third grade, on the assumption that fine motor skills are better developed by then. However, research indicates that most students can become quite adept at this skill by the latter half of second grade (Herrick & Okada, 1963; Otto & Rarick, 1969). In the past, girls have been somewhat ahead in fine motor skills (Maccoby, 1966), so that Kathy is ahead of both Bryan and Ted in her handwriting skills. Since some of this difference may be due to differential motivation and training in girls, these findings may change as motor skill education becomes more equalized for boys and girls in future years.

Movement from clumsy to skilled performance Ted, Kathy, and Bryan will refine their performance of jumping, running, throwing, and writing as they practice these within their daily activities. Ted, who uses his skills less frequently, may need some extra help, instruction, and reinforcement for improving the development of both his fine and gross motor skills. There are many curricular materials available for helping students to refine their motor coordination. With a normal amount of practice, motor skills improve continuously until early adolescence. At that time, boys show a significant spurt ahead of girls in most motor skills. Figure 2-7 shows the advantages that boys have over girls in many physical and motor tasks. While some of this advantage may be due to increased muscle development in boys, the role of cultural and social factors cannot be ignored.

Traditionally, girls have not been encouraged to develop physical skills or rewarded for attaining proficiency in them. While active motor behavior is accepted in elementary school girls, parents tend to discourage "tomboy" behavior as girls move into adolescence. Some girls also feel that skill in sports will be a social disadvantage with their peers. These factors may contribute to the impressive retardation of motor skills in girls, starting at about age 12. Experts are now advising increased emphasis on motor skill training for girls. This is especially important at the elementary school age, when possible differences in physical strength between the sexes are not so apparent (Lockhart, 1973). There is no evidence that motor skills training is any more important for boys than for girls. For all students, skilled performance contributes to self-esteem and to peer approval.

Speed increases While Ted may not increase his skill by performing faster, he can generally perform more efficiently when he learns speed as well as accuracy. Negative feedback to Ted that he is "too slow" may

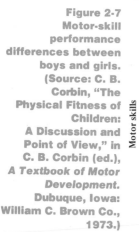

Figure 2-7 Motor-skill performance differences between boys and girls. (Source: C. B. Corbin, "The Physical Fitness of Children: A Discussion and Point of View," in C. B. Corbin (ed.), *A Textbook of Motor Development.* Dubuque, Iowa: William C. Brown Co., 1973.)

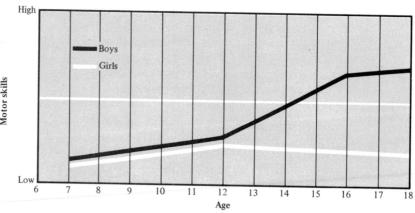

be discouraging, since his skills are initially at a low level of proficiency. However, boys like Ted may benefit from "hurry-up" games, which may stimulate them and help them to increase their efforts. Research suggests that both self-instruction (talking to oneself) and positive feedback (reinforcement for responding faster) can help youngsters increase their efforts at motor skills (Meichenbaum & Goodman, 1969).

Handedness

Ted is one of about 10 percent of school children who use their left hand at one time or another; hand preference becomes stabilized during primary grades (Hildreth, 1948). Considerable research comparing children from different countries on hand preferences suggests that there is a wide variation in use of one or both hands for motor tasks. Cratty (1970) also suggests that hand preference may be learned and culturally determined as children observe what others do and are reinforced for right-handed performance. While research does not support long-term personality damage when teachers and parents attempt to reverse left-handed performance (Cratty, 1970), it also does not suggest that there are any advantages to this practice. Reading difficulty, for example, is not related to handedness (Crinella, Beck, & Robinson, 1971). Rather than discouraging Ted's left-handed tendencies, you can help by adjusting tasks that may be more difficult for him. Show him how to use a pencil or lap tray and how to hold the paper comfortably.

What relevance do these physical and motor factors have to your activities in the classroom? Differences in growth rates, attainment of puberty, physical appearance, and motor skills will all have a continuing impact how children like Ted, Bryan, Kathy, and Donna view themselves and how others react to them. You have three major avenues open to you:

 GUIDELINES
FOR
TEACHING

**Facilitating
Physical and
Motor Development**

• *Refine your observational skills.* You can become a sensitive observer of how you and your students respond to the physical characteristics of others. Are you basing your reactions on stereotypes—for example, what you believe to be true of fat boys, clumsy girls, or students like Bryan who appear to be more adept at all ages? If so, what can you do to change these biased reactions? In Chapters 3 and 8, we will discuss some alternatives for coping with stereotyped responses.

• *Encourage motor skills training.* You can become knowledgeable in methods for training physical and motor skills within the confines of your class. Rather than criticize or ignore clumsy performance, you can take positive steps to encourage more skilled performances. All classrooms can provide opportunities for integrating activity and physical skills games into the academic curriculum. Chapter 4 discusses the use of classroom games for teaching.

• *Provide alternative activities for students who cannot keep up with the others*. In every class, some students will have difficulty in physical-motor participation. Students may be slower, clumsier, or physically handicapped. For each student, you can provide alternative activities, new ways to increase skills, opportunities for practice, consistent encouragement (reinforcement for small efforts), and calm patience (willingness to overlook errors).

SOCIOECONOMIC AND ETHNIC BACKGROUND

Suppose you find yourself teaching in a school which lies at the fringe of a middle-sized city. Your students will come from families with different levels of education and income as well as different racial, ethnic, and religious backgrounds. You may find that these students bring into your classroom organized patterns of behaviors, attitudes, values, and ways of viewing the world that are shaped by the cultural and economic circumstances of their outside lives. Some of these values and patterns of behaving may be compatible with yours and some may seem very strange and different.

You will want to be familiar with the varieties of cultural standards that appear among your students. You will want to be aware of how these standards for behavior differ from your own. You will want to learn about the family and neighborhood circumstances in which these behaviors have developed. You can then be prepared to accommodate some of your teaching strategies to the entering behaviors of students from differing backgrounds. You may also decide to develop differing strategies for dealing with students who enter school with particular language styles, codes of conduct, attitudes toward learning, and prior experiences with educational materials such as books and newspapers.

ADVANTAGED AND DISADVANTAGED ENVIRONMENTS

Each of these observed variations in entering behavior may be related to the SOCIOECONOMIC STATUS (SES) of the student's family. Socioeconomic status can be determined from the parents' employment, education, and income level (Hollingshead & Redlich, 1958). While each family has its individual patterns of living, research suggests that the child's socioeconomic background has a significant impact on probabilities for successful school experiences (Coleman et al., 1966; Havighurst, 1970; Zigler, 1978). As an example, consider how the background factors for Bryan and Jim, described below, might influence the behaviors they bring to your class.

The advantaged environment: Middle-class values

Bryan's family can be described as middle-class. They provide Bryan with a physical environment of open space for play, a room of his own for privacy, and plenty of books, games, and educational toys. The family maintains a comfortable style of living with sufficient food, clothing, medical care, and leisure-time activities. Family goals are future-oriented; Bryan is expected to bank part of his weekly allowance, and his parents are planning college and a professional career for him. They keep a close check on his school progress and offer help with homework; they attend PTA meetings and teacher conferences. They expect Bryan to do well and to persist in whatever he attempts.

Middle-class parents like these generally use positive methods of discipline; they praise their children for good behavior and explain the reasons for their rules. They stress democratic processes at home; they usually listen to their children's opinions and try to include them in family decision making. Thus, Bryan has had a model of family living that emphasizes cooperation, self-control, democratic processes, achievement, material well-being, and educational attainment (Deutsch, 1973; Hess, 1970; Wrightsman, 1977). These middle-class families in ADVANTAGED ENVIRONMENTS also have the education, employment security, and economic means to translate their ideas into the realities of living. Children from middle- or higher-SES environments usually impress teachers positively and receive more teacher support (Barclay, Stilwell, & Barclay, 1972).

Figure 2-8 Disadvantaged defined? Cartoon by Jules Feiffer, 1965. Hall Syndicates, Inc. (Source: M. D. Fantini and G. Weinstein, *The Disadvantaged: Challenge to Education*. New York: Harper & Row, 1968.

Economically disadvantaged environments: The impact of poverty

Jim, on the other hand, is one of the 32 million individuals whose family income is below the poverty line (Havighurst, 1970). Families in DISAD-VANTAGED ENVIRONMENTS typically have low levels of income and education as well as relatively unskilled occupations. You can see in Figure 2-8 that a number of other definitions of "disadvantaged" have been used. You may find that all, some, or none of your students will come from families that meet those descriptions.

By comparison with Bryan, students like Jim are more likely to live in crowded and inadequate housing facilities, to experience family instability, and to be subject to illness and poor nutrition. Their parents are caught up in a cycle of low education, high unemployment, and economic uncertainty. The resulting tensions strain the bonds of marriage and increase the probabilities of family conflict, neglect, and negative child-rearing practices. By comparison with Bryan's parents, Jim's are likely to give more physical and verbal punishment; they are less likely to use reasoning or offer praise in order to control their children. They are also less likely to take a constructive part in their children's schooling.

"Students from disadvantaged environments are more likely to live in crowded and inadequate housing facilities, to experience family instability, and to be subject to illness and poor nutrition." (C. Harbutt/ Magnum)

Jim may obtain less help with homework, and his parents may be less interested in his progress and in his future goals than are Bryan's. Not having done well in school themselves, Jim's parents are unlikely to have the skills to stimulate Jim's achievement (Lynn, 1974; Hess, 1970; Miller & Swanson, 1960; Zigler, 1970).

Read about the study by Bee and coworkers (1969), for a comparison of how some middle- and lower-SES mothers interact with their children (Study 2-3). Studies such as this suggest that disadvantaged students, on entering school, may be "cognitively deprived" as well as culturally different. They may not have had the opportunities at home to learn such skills as those involving language, listening, and problem solving which are essential to competent performance at school.

STUDY 2-3: MOTHERS AND CHILDREN

Helen Bee and her associates studied the interaction and teaching styles of seventy-six mothers with their 4- and 5-year-old children from two SES groups, lower and middle. Interaction was observed by rating the behaviors of mothers in the waiting room before they participated in the experimental phase of the study. Then, each mother-child pair was observed in a teaching situation in which the parent was to help her child construct a house with blocks. In both waiting room and teaching settings, the lower-SES mothers were more controlling, gave more negative feedback, and gave fewer helpful instructions for problem solving. They told their children what to do more specifically in ways that were less likely to transfer to other problem-solving situations. They used less complex speech patterns, asked fewer questions, actually worked on the house more themselves, and less often told their children that their responses were correct (less

positive feedback). In their teaching methods, these mothers were depriving their children of the opportunity to solve problems effectively on their own. In contrast, the middle-SES mothers allowed more freedom for their children to discover ways of solving the problems themselves. These mothers gave more general problem-solving hints and more positive feedback when the child was doing well. They used a more complex and elaborated language structure (as defined by Bernstein's categories). These mothers were providing their children with problem-solving skills that were likely to transfer to new situations. Despite the fact that the task involved building a house with blocks, these children were learning skills that would be helpful to them for the academic tasks encountered in school.

Adapted from: Bee, H. L., et al., Social class differences in maternal teaching strategies and speech patterns. *Developmental Psychology*, 1969, *1*, 726–743.

SOCIOECONOMIC STATUS AND STUDENT BEHAVIOR: SOME GROUP DIFFERENCES

The differences you observe between Bryan and Jim may not apply to any other two students. The effects of SES on behavoir are found for groups only and do not describe any one particular student. You will certainly find more behavioral differences among the members of each group than between one SES group and another. However, research does support group differences on some characteristics that have relevance for school behavior and achievement. We have selected six characteristics which have some probability of influencing the entering behaviors of your students: scores and changes on intelligence tests, use of language, academic retardation, social reinforcement effects, and locus of control.

Intelligence test scores

Measures of intelligence consistently favor middle-class students (Dreger & Miller, 1960, 1968; Jensen, 1969; Tulin, 1968; Whiteman, Brown, & Deutsch, 1967). These differences are consistent across various levels of SES and intelligence, and they hold for both black and white groups of children.

Changes in intelligence test scores

There is a progressive decline in intelligence test scores for children who remain in disadvantaged environments (Gray & Klauss, 1970; Deutsch & Brown, 1964; Weiner, Rider, & Opel, 1963). This finding suggests that students who remain in unstimulating environments are likely to suffer from a "cumulative deficit" in measured intelligence. This fact is important for students and teachers. Scores on intelligence tests are often a major criterion for special class placement; they also bear a strong relationship to school achievement in general.

Use of language

Some differences in use of language appear for the disadvantaged and some minority groups, such as blacks. Bernstein (1961, 1974) found that lower-SES children have more "restrictive" and less "elaborated" language patterns. He contends that these patterns impair abstract thinking and concept-formation skills. Lower-SES children have been found less able to listen to complex speech (Cherry-Peisach, 1965) and less able to give verbal instructions to others to aid problem solving (Krauss & Rotter, 1968). Disadvantaged children have also shown more errors in discrimination of sounds used in speech (Clark & Richard, 1969). Since "following instructions" is an important factor in first-grade reading skill (Cobb, 1970), inadequate listening skills may handicap the lower-SES child in reading performance.

Academic retardation and school dropout

Disadvantaged students have higher rates of academic retardation and they more frequently drop out of school (Passow & Elliot, 1968). Reading retardation reports indicate as many as 33 percent of all disadvantaged children read below grade level (Wittig, 1966). Studies of specific cities show that by the end of sixth grade, a majority of lower-SES students are two years behind the citywide average in reading (Hentoff, 1967; Langer, 1972). Dropout rates from high school are highest for disadvantaged

"Dropout rates are highest for students from disadvantaged environments." (E. Stone/Peter Arnold)

students. Some studies indicate that the high school dropout rate reaches 50 percent; and this group has the lowest rate of college attendance (Passow & Elliott, 1968). If we consider students who are both disadvantaged and members of minority groups, such as blacks and Puerto Ricans, the dropout rate from high school among them ranges as high as 80 percent.

Reinforcer effectiveness

For disadvantaged groups as a whole, immediate reinforcers are more effective than delayed ones. When the daily outcomes in their lives are uncertain, students are more likely to choose what they can get today than to wait for the hopes of tomorrow. This means that year-end grades will be insufficient to motivate many of these students; they will require immediate and more tangible evidences of their success (Mischel, 1976).

Locus of control

Disadvantaged students frequently have an external locus of control for academic achievement. Students with an external locus of control perceive positive and negative outcomes as unrelated to their own behavior. As a result of their life experiences, disadvantaged students come to expect that the important rewards in life are under the control of others (Rotter, 1966). An external locus of control may result in a sense of powerlessness, so that these students might say "It's no use trying, there's nothing I can do to get good grades." Students with an external locus of control are less likely to persist and more likely to blame their failures on others (Battle & Rotter, 1968; Phares, 1975).

Taking all of these intellectual and achievement factors into account, what are the implications for educational policy? For teaching strategies? For educational testing? Large-scale interventions are relevant here: *Head Start, Follow Through,* and *Upward Bound* are but three approaches to compensatory education. They are all aimed at reducing the progressive academic lag of the disadvantaged student. In view of the enormity of the problem, there are no easy solutions. Many research projects are currently under way. These research efforts are comparing and evaluating the effectiveness of differing intervention programs in preventing, remediating, or accomodating to the distinctive learning characteristics of the disadvantaged student (Zigler, 1978). Chapter 4 will discuss some of these intervention efforts in greater depth.

ETHNIC DIVERSITY

Bryan and Jim are white Caucasian Americans whose parents were born in the United States. Compare their environments and experiences with those of Roy and Manuel, whose parents are, respectively, black and Mexican-American. Roy and Manuel both have dark skin, which makes them visibly different from other students. Their families are likely to have a subculture and a langue structure that is at variance with some of the values and ways of speaking that we find in Bryan and Jim. Many of the differences that are found between racial and ethnic groups are due to the same economic strains that Jim's family experiences, since many minority groups in the United States are economically and socially disadvantaged. However, ethnic subcultures often have their own individual patterns that will bring particular entry behaviors to your attention at school. Behavior patterns that you judge to be "incorrect" and deserving of remediation may actually be acceptable and commonly seen in the student's own community. Before you jump in to provide intervention strategies for Roy's peculiar English (I's be ready), or Manuel's refusal to look you in the eye when you talk to him, consider how these behaviors may relate to their life experiences. Many questions are currently being asked about "black English"; do the language patterns of many American black students reflect a *deficit* to be remediated or a *difference* to be accepted and understood? We shall consider this question more fully in Chapter 4. Similarly, you might consider how best to react to students whose nonverbal behavior is quite different from your own. A recent study on Army men, for example, suggests that white men who touched black men on the hair or who impulsively threw their arms around the other's shoulders, were seen as "invading a personal space," which was distasteful to the blacks (Grove, 1976). Read Study 2-4 for an example of how eye contact is used by an Indian child.

STUDY 2-4:
LISTENING AND LOOKING

When I was working with the Navajo Indians, I was fortunate to have friends who were good models for interacting with the Navajos. A small point, but one which I learned was crucial to the entire tone of a transaction with a Navajo, is the way he uses his eyes. Unlike middle-class whites, Navajos avoid the direct, open-faced look in the eyes; more likely, they froze when looked at. Even when shaking hands, they held the other person in the peripheral field of the eyes, letting the message of warmth and pleasure at seeing a friend seep through a long-clasped but delicately-held hand. I ultimately learned that to gaze directly at a Navajo was to display hostility. . . . What must it have been like to have been a small Navajo Indian child in schools—where white teachers, frustrated by behavior they couldn't understand, would unconsciously raise their voices, fix the child with a beady eye and say "What's the matter? Can't you talk? Don't you even know your own name?" Finally, after much embarrassment on everyone's part, some other child would intervene, saying in a barely audible voice "His name is Hosteen Nez Begay." Some teachers were more gentle than others; others were made so anxious by behavior they couldn't fathom that they allowed their own frustration and rage to break through. "Stupid Indians won't even look at you and won't even tell you their own names!"

What does it mean to listen, and what is meant by being a good listener? More than you might think! Most of us take listening for granted, yet the way people show they are listening (that is, paying attention . . .) is as varied as the languages they speak. In fact, it's part of language—not explicit but implicit, not spoken but silent.

Source: Hall, E. T., Listening behavior: Some cultural differences. In R. H. Anderson and H. S. Shane (Eds.), *As the twig is bent—readings in early childhood education,* Boston: Houghton-Mifflin, 1971.

PROBE 2-4

Whether you have just one minority-group student in your class or one large group of them, you will want to become informed about relevant cultural patterns of language, nonverbal behavior, and acceptable social practices. A simple way to do this is to take a walk around the student's neighborhood, visit the stores, observe the people in the streets, and listen to their language. Can you learn anything in this way? We think so.

What can the teacher do about socioeconomic, cultural, and ethnic differences in students?  GUIDELINES FOR TEACHING

Planning for Socioeconomic and Ethnic Differences

• *Obtain information about the socioeconomic and ethnic background of your students.* Visit their neighborhoods and observe the environment: the stores, the open space or lack of it, the opportunities for safe play or productive activities, proximity to transportation and recreational facilities. What is it like to live there? Would you wish to live there?

• *Learn about the different cultures that characterize many of your students.* Obtain information about what is important to their way of life, what the parents want from the school system, and what the parents and students feel is valuable in life.

• *Reflect on your attitudes toward the students in your class who are different.* Observe your behavior for any distinctive ways in which you may be reacting to these students. What kinds of stereotypes do you hold about these racial or ethnic groups? Do you let these stereotypes influence your behavior?

• *Obtain preassessment information about the language and cognitive skills of your class before starting instruction.* Become aware of deficits and differences in learning styles before you start teaching. The more students you have who come from diverse backgrounds and have had divergent experiences, the more you need to determine how each child measures up to the class on a variety of learning-skill prerequisites.

• *Develop a curriculum that is oriented toward the skills, interests, and experiences of these diverse groupings.* Especially important to you as a warm and caring teacher will be specific curriculum and management strategies for children who cannot easily delay reinforcement and who have short attention spans, ineffective listening skills, an external locus of control, and low motivation for academic achievement.

PARENT-CHILD RELATIONSHIPS

Within each student's cultural, social, and ethnic group, each family unit will have individual patterns of family living. These family patterns will determine some of the behaviors Bryan and Jim bring to class. The most widely studied of these patterns is parent behavior. How does the pattern of interaction between Bryan, his mother, and his father invade your academic space? How can your understanding of these patterns of parent-child interaction help you to deal with Bryan and Jim more effectively in class?

THE PARENT IS A TEACHER

Remember one very important fact: the parent is a teacher (Becker, 1971; Cooper & Edge, 1978; Patterson & Gullion, 1976). Some parents teach knowingly and some teach behaviors they wish they could erase, but all parents teach. Like other environmental agents, parents may serve as models whose behavior the child can imitate. Parents are stimulus providers who determine how enriched the developmental life-space will be. Parents are social reinforcers who can deliver rewards and punishments to control behavior. Finally, parents are agents of control who provide structure by means of rules, instructions, and restrictions. Through the ways in which they control, structure, model, reinforce, and punish, parents teach their children not only observable behavior patterns but also many values, attitudes, and beliefs that will pervade your academic space. You will want to know what parents teach, how they teach, and how their training practices affect their children's behavior at school. Consider how teacher and parent roles overlap. As a teacher in school, you are also a surrogate parent, and you will perform many functions similar to those we have described for the parent. What we learn from parent-child relationships may also tell us something about teacher-student relationships.

Relationships are dyadic

Most parents are caring, concerned, and involved in the welfare of their children. Parents will demonstrate this interest in different ways. In your contacts with Jim's and Bryan's parents, remember also that parents may interact differently with each of their children. Earlier, our discussion of dyadic relationships made us aware that children bring their own responses into the world. They serve as stimulus persons for parents. Thus, if Jim's mother seems excessively punitive to you, it may be that Jim has been

"Most parents are caring, concerned, and involved in the welfare of their children." (Ginger Chih/Peter Arnold)

a very active, intense, and irritable child. Perhaps he has given his mother much provocation for a punitive reaction. Several longitudinal studies (Hetherington, 1976; Thomas, Chess & Birch, 1968) have shown that parent behavior is shaped by the child's response; the more irritable and difficult the child, the more the parent reacts with negative and controlling child-rearing practices. What does this dyadic interpretation mean for you as a teacher? It implies that in your conferences with parents, you refrain from criticizing or evaluating their behavior. If parents appear to be passive, unloving, or overcontrolling, they may have reacted to behaviors they observed in their child. Chapter 12 will discuss conferencing skills and provide suggestions on effective interaction with parents.

Some relationships are abusive

Occasionally, your observation of a student indicates abuse: injuries, scars, black-and-blue spots, or obvious indicators of physically punitive practices. When this is your suspicion, it is certainly your ethical and, in some states, legal responsibility to report it to the school nurse or counselor for further investigation. Child abuse is an increasing problem in the United States (Parke & Collmer, 1975; Helfer & Kempe, 1974). At times, students may need help in protecting themselves from an abusive parent. In turn, the abusive parent can benefit from referral to experienced professional consultation. Abusive parents can be helped to understand the motivational and situational sources of their punitive reactions; they can be counseled toward more effective parent-child interactions.

PATTERNS OF PARENT-CHILD INTERACTION

Parent-child interactions can be observed and measured. A series of research studies by Diana Baumrind (1971, 1973, 1975) have been concerned with patterns of parent behavior that lead to INSTRUMENTAL COMPETENCE in their child. Children who are high in instrumental competence are described as having the following characteristics:

Social responsibility: behavior with peers that is friendly, facilitative, and helpful rather than restrictive, hostile, or disruptive

Independence: behavior that is ascendant, purposive, and persistent rather than aimless, submissive, or passive

Achievement-oriented: behavior directed toward intellectual challenge, and persistence at problem solving rather than giving up in the face of difficulty or acting impulsively in problem solving

You will probably want to see your students display many of the behaviors that are included in instrumental competence. These are behaviors that will encourage student achievement in academic learning tasks. Students who are rated high on instrumental competence are liked and accepted by both peers and teachers.

Parent behavior and instrumental competence

Baumrind found three major patterns of parents' behavior that showed signficant relationships to their children's competence; she termed these AUTHORITARIAN, AUTHORITATIVE, and PERMISSIVE. Of the three patterns, the authoritative was most likely to produce instrumental competence in the children.

Authoritative parents These parents establish rules and exert firm control, but they use reasoning and explanation to support expectancies of mature behavior. The parents expect compliance to rules but use warmth and positive reinforcement more than punishment to enforce rules. Authoritative parents also listen to the child's point of view and encourage the child's own strivings for independence. They have high standards for mature behavior and encourage the child to meet these standards gradually, using positive reinforcement such as praise.

Authoritarian parents These parents set arbitrary rules, do not ask for the child's point of view, and do not use reasoning. They also use more punishment and offer less positive feedback to the child. Children of authoritarian parents are more likely to be withdrawn, passive, dependent, and irritable.

Permissive parents Here are the parents who are lax in setting rules, do not expect household chores to be done, are passive in the face of the child's noncompliance, and are very nonrestrictive. Permissive parents are less punitive but also give less positive reinforcement of desirable behavior. Children from permissive families are more likely to be impulsive and aggressive and to show little self-control.

In comparing these three groups of parents, Baumrind points out that the authoritative parent offered a balance between a high level of control, or firm expectations, and a willingness to encourage independence; that is, they gave as much as they demanded. The other two groups of parents either expected more than they gave (authoritarian) or gave more than they expected in return (permissive). Do these patterns of parent behavior tell us anything as teachers?

We see three valuable applications from the research on parent behavior. The implications of these studies should not appear threatening or intimidating to you. You, too, were raised by parents who were at some time either permissive, authoritative, or authoritarian. Probably you have acquired some of their values. In many cases, you may deal with your

 GUIDELINES FOR TEACHING

Responding to Parent Behavior

students in the same way as your parents dealt with you. Therefore, we want to emphasize the following three points:

• *Take your cues from the success of parents who have instrumentally competent children.* Moderately firm control procedures (reasonable rules), warmth (attention and praise for appropriate behavior), reasoning, and listening to the viewpoint of the student are all likely to lead to effective student behavior in the classroom, just as they do at home. In contrast, failure to establish rules and to set limits on disruptive behavior, to adjust rules to the requirements of your students, to give a rationale for these rules and their enforcement, and to provide warmth and positive feedback to students in return for their cooperation with rules—these patterns are likely to encourage hostile, impulsive, and dependent behavior in your students.

• *Provide more structure for students with special problems.* Some students come to school with behaviors that are immature for the students' age. You may find these students to be persistently overactive, disobedient, and dependent (they may ask for help or be unable to initiate activities). These students have probably been exposed to overly authoritarian or permissive parent structures. They will require more attention in terms of clarity or rules, reasons for these rules, and immediate positive consequences for cooperative behavior.

• *Establish regular conference times for parents to discuss students' behavior with you.* Parent behavior is open to modification and change, as is all behavior. Parents are not "stuck" with their behavior and can learn to modify the ways in which they deal with their children cognitively, affectively, and in terms of control techniques. Teachers of students with learning and behavior problems are often in a position to organize and operate parent groups and can help parents to be more effective with their children. Guidance counselors and school psychologists can do the same and may be the more appropriate ones for this job. However, all teachers, at one time or another, are in a favorable position to counsel parents and to be helpful about those student behaviors that are contributing to difficulties in school.

MASS MEDIA: TELEVISION

While all the sights, sounds, and smells of the outside environment will have an impact on Bryan and Jim's behavior, no other stimulus is so prevalent and insistent as television. When Jim was a preschooler, he probably watched television between five and eight hours a week. By the

sixth grade, Bryan watched anywhere from not at all up to five hours a day. Studies have shown these patterns to be common (Stein & Friedrich, 1972; Lyle & Hoffman, 1972). For most students, this is a substantial amount of time; it enables TV to affect them in significant ways. While you may not have much influence on the duration and content of your students' TV time, you should be aware of the significant impact of TV on behavior.

TELEVISION IS A TEACHER

The importance of TV lies in its easy accessibility, its attractiveness to parents for keeping children out of mischief, and its inherent appeal to the student in terms of novelty, excitement, and escape into fantasy. To the extent that television portrays positive models and prosocial behavior, it may be an influence for productive developmental learning (Stein & Friedrich, 1975). However, recent studies on TV violence suggest just the opposite. That is, prime-time TV tends toward excessive violence, interpersonal conflict, and both sex-role and ethnic stereotypes (Murray, 1973).

Does TV violence really influence what children do in other situations? In a well-designed study on young children's aggression, students were matched in groups for equal amounts of initial aggressive behavior during regular school activities. One group was then exposed for four weeks to television films showing aggressive behavior, while the other group observed TV films about cooperative and friendly behavior. A third group viewed films with neutral content. Comparison of the children's behavior afterwards, during free play periods, indicated that those children who showed initially higher levels of aggressive behavior increased their hitting, pushing, and shoving after observing violent TV films. However, all children who watched the prosocial, cooperative films either maintained or increased their friendly and helpful behavior toward their schoolmates (Freidrich & Stein, 1973).

What do these studies tell us about the impact of TV on your students? It seems clear that when children frequently watch TV models of people using violence, resorting to physical aggression, or making abusive remarks, they may be more likely to use these types of behaviors themselves. Moreover, they may use these behaviors in later situations when the aggressive TV models are no longer present. On the other hand, there is also persuasive evidence that prosocial behavior can be facilitated by TV models who demonstrate helping, caring, sharing, and cooperative behavior (Bryan, 1975; Zimmerman, 1978). These results, however, have been demonstrated mainly with younger children in controlled settings such as nursery school. Very little planned prosocial television time for elementary and high school students presently exists. Consequently, you may anticipate that some of the aggressive interpersonal behaviors you observe in your students at school have been modeled and supported by the family TV.

The implications for teachers of the influence of television are multiple. Although you have no direct control over the programs your students watch at home, you can use your classroom time to moderate some of the lessons they are learning through TV.

GUIDELINES
FOR
TEACHING

Moderating the
Influence of
Television

• *Help your students to be informed observers.* When students discuss and evaluate the theme and content of TV sequences, they may be less likely to transfer the aggressive behaviors to their everyday lives. Discussions can center on the feelings of the victims, the outcomes to the aggressor, and the prosocial alternatives that might have been practiced. Students can also role-play, or act out, filmed sequences and practice alternative approaches to conflict solution.
• *Integrate TV time into your teaching strategies.* You can assign programs which you know demonstrate some prosocial and cooperative behavior (you may have to search hard for these) and work the content into your current teaching units. You can also assign selected programs and ask students to describe and evaluate the violence or cultural

stereotypes they portray. Student teaching units can be built around how to modify the content or outcomes of programs to increase their productive social value. High school students can develop and film their own movie scripts which present contrasting ideas and solutions to interpersonal conflicts.

Regardless of what you do in class, you know that your students will probably watch some TV. Why not use this TV time for positive teaching purposes?

LEARNING ACTIVITY: OBSERVING PATTERNS OF BEHAVIOR

OBJECTIVES

When you have read Chapters 1 and 2 and you have completed the learning activity in this chapter, you will be able to:

1. Complete a fifteen-minute observation of a child. Write decriptive statements of observable behaviors. Make inferences and draw conclusions about patterns of responses that you observe.
2. Select descriptions that are not observable behaviors. Revise descriptions so that they are observable.
3. Compare behavior descriptions of two children. List differences in behavior frequency and outcome. Compare and contrast behavior patterns.

You will be using observations in all your teaching procedures to make good instructional decisions. You will want to be able to look at student behavior and record it in many different ways. Why do you need to look at a pattern of behaviors rather than just one behavior? Take a look at Ted and answer this one. If you manage to discourage Ted from hitting Jane in the hallways but he continues to hit her on the playground, to kick her under the lunch table, and to call her names in the library, where are you? Students will use many similar behaviors to achieve the same goal. In order to be an effective mediator of the learning environment, you will need to look at all the behaviors students use to reach their goals.

You will want to look at patterns of behavior for three good purposes:

Patterns of behavior can give you useful information for determining appropriate entry levels or prerequisite skills for learning new tasks.

Patterns of behavior can cue you in to possible learning difficulties.

Patterns of behavior can help you make inferences about possible antecedents or consequences of student behavior. In Ted's case, all the hitting and kicking behaviors were being followed by attention from you, Jane, and Ted's friends. This observation can give you information about what you might do to help Ted and Jane get along together without fighting.

USING BEHAVIOR PATTERNS TO IDENTIFY ENTRY SKILLS

Suppose you are planning a curriculum for developing physical-motor skills. You might observe some very specific motor skills that form a pattern of physical-motor behavior. For Ted, you might observe him on the playground and in his physical education class. Perhaps you would note the following:

Throws the ball overhead at least 20 feet

Throws a ball underhand

Hops on one foot at least five times

Catches a ball with two hands

Catches a ball with one hand

Skips 15 feet in rhythm

From these observations and many more, you will draw a pattern of skills that will help you to make a decision: "Yes, Ted is ready for this new program." You will need to watch Ted on several occasions, across several specific skills, to conclude that he has a total pattern of entry skills that are prerequisites for your learning task.

USING BEHAVIOR PATTERNS TO DETECT LEARNING PROBLEMS

A second way to use behavior patterns cues you in to possible difficulties in learning that require attention. Consider Carla:

Carla frequently has red eyes

Carla squints when she looks at the board.

Carla complains of headaches when she reads.

Carla reads incorrectly from board work, saying *b* for *d*.

Carla stumbles frequently when running on the playground.

Carla calls you by the wrong name from a distance down the hall.

What do all these behaviors mean to you? Any one taken by itself may have little significance. Taken together, you may infer that Carla has a vision problem. You follow through on your hypothesis by contacting her parents for a possible physical examination. Two weeks later, Carla comes to school with a new pair of glasses. Not all of the behavior patterns you observe will be as clear to you as this one. Notice that you may want to observe Carla in several different situations over a period of time before you come to any conclusions.

LOOKING FOR BEHAVIOR PATTERNS

Students like Carla are behaving all of the time. You can't possibly record everything they do. When you are looking for response patterns, you will start with one or two situations and write down what you observe. You might want to write down the situation, the observable behaviors, and possibly the outcome or consequences of the behavior. This procedure will give you short descriptions of what Carla does each time. If you don't write these down immediately, you may find that you quickly forget. Now that you can select observable behaviors, try your hand at the next step: observing patterns of behavior and recording short decriptions. You might want to use a form that looks like this one.

Observation: Carla Smith   OBSERVATION RECORD

Observation #: _____   Time of day observed: _____

Activity: _____

Setting: _____
Behaviors: (List all of the behaviors you observe within a set amount of time—fifteen minutes, for example)

Conclusions and inferences: (List any patterns you can observe that appear to tie these behaviors together. Does Carla appear to have a goal? Are there specific antecedents that trigger or stimulate her actions and words? Are there consistent outcomes?)

TASK 2-1: OBSERVING BEHAVIOR PATTERNS

Select a student or child to observe for fifteen minutes. Use the form presented in the preceding discussion. Describe each observable behavior in short sentences. Can you detect any patterns in this behavior? Can you describe a pattern in one sentence? Hint: if you are not now observing in a classroom, try one of the following:

Follow a child and parent around in a supermarket.

Wait in line behind a parent and child in a supermarket.

Walk behind a parent and child in a shopping center.

Visit a friend who has a child and observe that child at meals, at play, or with the family.

Watch a TV program that centers on a child.

Any of these situations can give you enough material for your observations.

TASK 2-2: OBSERVATIONAL FEEDBACK

Select a student partner in your class and exchange your observation forms. Underline any descriptions that are not observable. Look at the pattern of behavior and decide whether you would come to the same conclusion as your partner. Now, revise any descriptions on your form that are underlined. Check back with each other to obtain agreement on all decriptions. Discuss disagreements and come to a consensus.

TASK 2-3: COMPARING OBSERVATIONS

For any of the situations named above, select another child and complete a second observation. How do these two children compare? Can you detect differences in their (1) frequency of behaviors; (2) types of behaviors; (3) outcomes of behaviors? If you can select students from different grades or age ranges, neighborhoods, ethnic backgrounds, etc., you may find it easier to detect differing patterns. Would you want to make any general statements about these students on the basis of your observations?

 ## SUMMARY

1. A useful way to look at changes in student behavior over time is by means of four systems of development: physical-motor, social, cognitive, and self-regulation. Each of these systems of development can be traced across age levels and has particular patterns of behavior associated with it.

2. INDIVIDUAL DIFFERENCES in development can be considered in terms of their frequency or distribution among many students. Some characteristics are distributed according to a NORMAL CURVE in which most students cluster around the middle or average range. When teachers develop instruction according to learning objectives and prerequisite skills, some student characteristics can be redistributed according to a MASTERY CURVE. The mastery curve reduces individual differences in behavioral skills.

3. Descriptions of development according to age or DEVELOPMENTAL STAGES may be useful for describing general trends in behavioral development. Age and stage descriptions fail to account for individual differences in learning and behavior. Age or stage of development should never be used to explain behavior.

4. DEVELOPMENT is a process which involves changes in the individual over significant periods of the life span. LEARNING is a stable change in specific behaviors at a particular point in time. According to a developmental learning framework, both development and learning involve interaction with the environment. Thus, development is continuous, cumulative, and hierarchical in that new learning depends upon the presence of prerequisite skills.

5. The LEARNING ENVIRONMENT is dyadic and reciprocal. The developing child is shaped by his or her effective environment and in turn, shapes the behavior of others. Thus, the learning environment is a social one which serves four major functions: it provides STIMULATION, BEHAVIORAL MODELS, CONSEQUENCES of behavior, and STRUCTURE.

6. Moderating factors influence the development of behavior by providing for both similarities and differences among students. Each moderating factor we discuss contributes to some of the different entering behaviors you will observe in students.

7. Physical and motor development affect student behavior in two important ways. Differences among students in physical and motor development influence the specific skills that students can demonstrate and affect the STIMULUS VALUE of students, or how others react to them. The section on physical and motor development lists and discusses those developmental characteristics which are most likely to affect skills or the reactions of others.

8. The SOCIOECONOMIC STATUS (SES) of the student's family frequently accounts for differences in student health, economic security, and living conditions. Some of these SES differences typically found among certain groups of students involve factors that have an impact on school entering skills, continued progress in school, and social and academic effectiveness. Ethnic differences among students

account for entering behaviors that may affect the way in which teachers and peers react. Teachers need to be aware of both the ethnic and SES backgrounds of individual students so that their teaching strategies can be adjusted effectively.

9. Patterns of parent behavior fall into three general groups: AUTHOR-ITATIVE, AUTHORITARIAN, and PERMISSIVE. Students with well-developed skills in social responsibility, achievement, and independence tend to come from authoritative families. Teachers need to be aware of these parent-student relationships when interacting with parents.

10. The public media provide both powerful learning inputs of new information and behavioral models. Teachers can use the public media to reinforce positive behavior. They can also attempt to mitigate negative effects through the use of classroom discussion and other activities.

11. Patterns of observed behavior can be useful for teaching in three ways. Student behavior patterns can be used to identify appropriate entry levels for learning new tasks, for detecting possible learning difficulties, and for analyzing problem situations. You will want to become skilled at writing descriptive statements of observable behaviors and in drawing conclusions based upon your inferences about these patterns of behavior.

KEY TERMS

ADVANTAGED ENVIRONMENT: Living arrangements characterized by middle-class levels of income, education, employment, and child-training values.

AUTHORITARIAN PARENT BEHAVIOR: Characteristic of parents who have arbitrary rules, fail to use reasoning, and who use punishment to control behavior.

AUTHORITATIVE PARENT BEHAVIOR: Characteristic of parents who use firm control combined with reasoning and explanation. Authoritative parents use positive reinforcement to support expectancies for mature behavior.

DEVELOPMENT: A lifelong process in which the individual changes over significant periods of the life span.

DEVELOPMENTAL NORMS: Observed similarities in characteristics, traits, or behaviors among members of a particular group.

DEVELOPMENTAL STAGES: Describe similarities in development or behavior according to fixed sequences, such as age or stage level.

DISADVANTAGED ENVIRONMENT: Living arrangements characterized by low levels of income, education, and employment skill.

INDIVIDUAL DIFFERENCES: Observed variations in characteristics, traits, and behaviors among members of any group.

INSTRUMENTAL COMPETENCE: Baumrind's term for behaviors characterized by social responsibility, independence, and achievement orientation.

LEARNING: A stable change in behavior as a person interacts with specific environmental stimulation.

LEARNING ENVIRONMENT: That part of the real world which directly affects the responses of the individual. The learning environment provides four sources of information: stimulation, models, consequences of behavior, and structure.

MASTERY LEARNING: An approach to teaching in which students are expected to achieve the learning objectives at the end of an instructional sequence.

MATURATION: Physical and structural changes that accompany age changes.

MODEL: The verbal or physical behaviors that provide patterns for the developing child to imitate.

NORMAL CURVE: A bell-shaped distribution of characteristics for groups of individuals. The normal distribution can be used to compare any one person with other members of this group on this characteristic.

PERMISSIVE PARENT BEHAVIOR: Characteristic of parents who are lax in setting rules, passive in the face of noncompliant behavior, and nonrestrictive. Permissive parents give both punishment and praise in moderation.

POSITIVE REINFORCEMENT: Consequences of behavior that increase tendencies to repeat the behavior. Positive reinforcement provides information about the probable consequences of behaving in the same manner in the future.

PUBERTY: The period between ages 10 and 16 when observable physical changes accompany maturation of the reproductive system.

SENSORY MODALITIES: Channels for receiving sensory information from the environment. The modalities most frequently used by students are auditory, visual, tactile, and kinesthetic.

SOCIOECONOMIC STATUS: An index of social class which includes similarities in levels of employment, education, and income.

STANDARDS: These define the level of competency required for behavior to be reinforced.

STIMULATION: The variety and quality of stimuli to which the developing child is exposed.

STIMULUS: Any event to which the individual responds.

STIMULUS VALUE: Determines the way in which a person's appearance and skill development affect the responses of others.

STRUCTURE: Instructions and rules which regulate behavior.

REVIEW KEY TERMS

Earlier, we talked about some important ideas which we discussed again in this chapter. We have listed some of them as review key terms.

ANTECEDENTS
BEHAVIOR
CONSEQUENCES
LEARNING OBJECTIVES
PREREQUISITE SKILLS

SELF-TEST

1. Developmental norms describe
   a. differences between normal development and normal behavior
   b. typical behaviors at each age level
   c. the developmental level required for school entry
   d. the principles of normal development
2. Draw a sample mastery curve and a normal curve.
3. *Maturation* refers to
   a. adolescent interest in the opposite sex
   b. structural changes that accompany age changes
   c. changes in skills as children grow older
   d. readiness for entering first grade
4. Four sources of information in the learning environment are:

   _____, _____, _____, and _____ .
5. Student stimulus value
   a. influences status and acceptance within the peer group
   b. depends upon the educational values of the parents
   c. has no relationships to physical development or motor skill
   d. all of the above
6. Which of the following is true of physical growth (height)?
   a. Boys are ahead of girls at all ages.
   b. Girls are ahead of boys until age 8; then they fall behind.
   c. Boys and girls are about equal until puberty, when boys spurt ahead.

   d. Girls are ahead of boys until puberty, when boys spurt ahead.
7. Academic retardation and school dropout rates are higher for
   a. students with slow physical growth curves
   b. students from urban environments
   c. students from disadvantaged environments
   d. students with authoritarian parents
   e. none of the above
8. Parents who are described as authoritative have children who
   a. are submissive and shy in school
   b. are abused and emotionally scarred
   c. are hyperactive and impulsive
   d. are described as instrumentally competent
9. As students develop in school, at least three changes in motor skills can be observed. These are
   a. _____
   b. _____
   c. _____
10. Television programs which portray aggression have been shown to have which of the following effects?
   a. Increase aggressive behavior of the children who watch.
   b. Decrease aggressive behavior of the children who watch.
   c. Increase both cooperative behavior and aggression.
   d. Have no observable effects on children's behavior.

SELF-TEST KEY

1. b
2. (See Figs. 2-3 and 2-4.)
3. b
4. stimulation, models, consequences, structure
5. a
6. c
7. c

8. d
9. speed increases, a shift from motor to visual cues, coordination of sensory modalities, progression from large to fine muscle coordination, shift from clumsy to skilled performance
10. a

CHAPTER 3

Development of Social Skills

LEARNING OBJECTIVES

After reading Chapter 3, answering the self-monitoring questions, completing the learning activity, and reading any further references of your choice, you will be able to:

1. Define and give examples of key terms.

2. Compare the behaviors of students who display high and low skills in affiliation, independence, achievement, prosocial behavior, self-regulation, and self-competency.

3. Compare sex-role stereotyped behaviors with observed sex differences. Account for the comparisons you find.

4. List strategies for reducing sex-role stereotyping in education.

5. Discuss the rationale for encouraging reciprocal peer interaction. Develop three strategies for increasing peer acceptance.

6. List do's and don'ts for moderating aggressive student behavior.

7. Design a plan for increasing a specific example of self-regulation in a classroom setting. List behaviors you wish to encourage and general procedures you will use.

8. Compare the development of self-competency and self-esteem. Justify self-competency as a learning objective.

9. Record frequencies for two different response patterns of social behavior. Compare your frequencies for two or more people.

FOCUS ON SOCIAL DEVELOPMENT

Students move forward in time as whole persons. As a sixth-grader, Kathy seems to be Kathy wherever she goes. But observe her closely as she moves from one situation to another; *is* she always the same Kathy? When you praise her warmly for her perfect math paper, she smiles with pleasure and works even harder on the next one. However, after you correct three errors on her spelling paper, she apologizes, looks ashamed, then sits and stares at her paper. If Ted mimics you by saying: "Oh Kathy, what a nice math paper you have," she takes a swing at him and tells him to "bug off." At recess, however, you observe her laughing and talking warmly with two friends. She icily ignores Ted as he hoots at her from across the yard. Back in the classroom, she gets down to work quickly, maintains her attention to work, participates actively in class discussions, and volunteers to return some books to the library. You know that when she leaves the classroom, she will follow through on her job without being reminded. Therefore, you frequently assign responsible tasks to Kathy. However, when you report her cooperative behavior to her mother at the midsemester conference, her mother says: "That doesn't sound like my messy, forgetful, and irresponsible Kathy at all. Are you sure you're talking about Kathy?"

TRAITS IN SOCIAL SITUATIONS

Kathy, like all growing people, has developed behavior patterns that are somewhat similar for certain situations, certain people, and across time spans. You can also observe that Kathy reacts differently than Donna in each of these situations. The similarity of a person's behavior in different situations has led many theorists to talk about personality TRAITS. You may refer to traits frequently in describing sets or patterns of behaviors that students use to obtain a goal. When adjectives like *helpful* or *friendly* are used to describe Kathy's behavior, does that mean she is always helpful and friendly? Probably not. If Kathy had a trait of friendliness, how can you explain her angry reaction to Ted's teasing? But you do notice that Kathy *is* friendly more often than Donna, and it seems to be a convenient way of telling her mother about how she reacts in school much of the time.

The important fact to remember about behavior traits is that a student does not carry these traits along from situation to situation. Rather, he or she reacts in terms of both typical behavior patterns and the situation at hand (Mischel, 1968, 1976). Figure 3-1 shows how Kathy reacts to criticism from different people. In each situation, she responds in terms of the positive or negative consequences she expects for her behavior. Is Kathy aggressive, apologetic, withdrawing, or remorseful? She is all of these, depending on the situation.

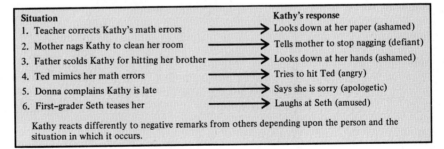

Figure 3-1
Kathy's responses to criticisms from different people.

Situation | Kathy's response
1. Teacher corrects Kathy's math errors ⟶ Looks down at her paper (ashamed)
2. Mother nags Kathy to clean her room ⟶ Tells mother to stop nagging (defiant)
3. Father scolds Kathy for hitting her brother ⟶ Looks down at her hands (ashamed)
4. Ted mimics her math errors ⟶ Tries to hit Ted (angry)
5. Donna complains Kathy is late ⟶ Says she is sorry (apologetic)
6. First-grader Seth teases her ⟶ Laughs at Seth (amused)

Kathy reacts differently to negative remarks from others depending upon the person and the situation in which it occurs.

===== PROBE 3-1 =====

When is a trait not a trait? Explain.

In your interactions with your students, you will want to observe two facts about their social behaviors: (1) how different students respond to the same situations and (2) how each student responds to differing situations. For each student, the more typical responses are called traits. In the following section, we will consider how behavior traits are organized into larger systems of social behaviors.

SOCIAL BEHAVIOR SYSTEMS

In most cultures, children seem to develop very similar kinds of traits or behavior patterns. These behavior patterns become clustered into larger sets of related behaviors. We can follow the development of these clusters over time. A cluster of similar behaviors that develops across a significant period of a child's life is called a SOCIAL BEHAVIOR SYSTEM. As children grow, they learn that what they have done in the past they can do in the present and, with modification, in the future. Some of these behaviors, therefore, remain fairly stable. At 3 years of age, Kathy was already sociable and friendly in her nursery school. In high school, she continues to seek and maintain some close, intimate friendships. But as environments change and individuals grow, new behavior patterns and new goals emerge. Kathy now learns new skills for relating to people of the opposite sex and she becomes more selective in the kinds of individuals she chooses for friends. We find that the term *social behavior system* conveniently describes how a student's behavior remains somewhat similar across time yet is constantly changing.

In high school, students learn new skills for relating to people of the opposite sex. (E. Stone/Peter Arnold)

In this chapter, we shall be talking about those social behavior systems that contribute to your students' entering behaviors, their progress in learning, and their status as cooperative class members. These systems include sex-role behavior, affiliation, independence, achievement, self-regulation, and self-competency. Each of these behavior systems contributes to a broad behavioral goal of *interpersonal competence*. In addition, we will discuss aggression as an example of a social behavior system that frequently interferes with effective interpersonal competence. We next consider the concept of interpersonal competence as a yardstick for the evaluation of effective social skills.

INTERPERSONAL COMPETENCE

As you observe the social behavior of children like Kathy, Donna, Bryan, and Ted, you may be asking yourself, "How are they doing? Are they making progress toward their goals? Am I satisfied that their classroom behavior is constructive and age-appropriate?" When we talk about social behavior, what are appropriate goals? Each student may have his or her own goals, but these are seldom clearly defined. As a teacher, you will want to organize these goals to help you manage learning and to help students plan their lives. We shall use the concept of INTERPERSONAL COMPETENCE to describe a network of social skills that is appropriate at any particular age level. Students who demonstrate interpersonal competence have learned a number of social skills that enable them to meet group goals and their own personal goals as well. They use behaviors that are effective in (1) meeting the social expectancies of others and (2) bringing personal reinforcement and satisfaction.

Three clusters of social behaviors contribute to interpersonal competence. Recall Baumrind's (1971) findings from Chapter 2. She pointed out that children who were rated high on interpersonal competence were also highly rated on (1) *social responsibility* (friendly, cooperative, self-controlled); (2) *independence* (self-assertive, purposeful); and (3) *achievement orientation* (accepting challenge, being persistent). These sets of social skills provide for effective group participation and help students find personal satisfaction. Students such as Kathy will be judged to be competent if others are generally happy with her and she is usually happy with herself.

GOALS FOR SOCIAL BEHAVIOR

The social behavior systems we describe in the remainder of this chapter can contribute to or detract from each student's interpersonal competence. Each social behavior system is composed of a great many teachable behaviors or skills (Cartledge & Milburn, 1978). You can choose to adopt any of these skills as behavioral goals for some or all of your students. You can encourage those students who appear low on certain skills and you can plan to discourage some behaviors that appear to interfere with effective interpersonal functioning. Donna can be helped to develop some peer friendships and Ted can learn to stop shouting insults at students who make mistakes. However, what is desirable and appropriate in your classroom depends upon you, your students, possibly their parents, and many other factors in your school situation. If you do decide to adopt some behavioral goals related to interpersonal competence, we suggest that you do so with forethought and planning. We also suggest that you communicate your intentions to your students and obtain information about their goals as well.

PROBE 3-2

Select a grade level that you would like to teach. List one social skill (teachable social behavior) you would present as a behavioral goal for your students. Justify your choice. If this one gives you some trouble, read the next section.

Whether or not you choose to intervene with any student's social skills remains a personal decision. This decision may involve your values as well as those of your students. Your understanding of the processes by which each set of skills develops will place you in a better position to observe and evaluate each student's progress and to make wise decisions. In your role as a mediator of human relations and a facilitator of individual development, you will wish to create a learning environment which enhances student growth toward mature interpersonal skills.

 **SEX-ROLE DEVELOPMENT**

If all students conformed to their culturally defined sex roles, Kathy would be very "feminine" and Bryan would be very "masculine." Social conceptions of masculinity and femininity include many of the response patterns in our social behavior systems: friendliness, aggression, and achievement. When Kathy's interpersonal competence is judged, these characteristics are frequently evaluated differently than when we are looking at Bryan. Many social behaviors are considered to be more appropriate for one sex than the other. Whenever clusters of behaviors are judged to be more desirable for either boys or girls, we are talking about SEX ROLES (Kelly & Worell, 1977; Worell, 1978, 1980). Since social competence is often judged in terms of sex-role categories of masculinity and femininity, we shall consider first the development of sex-role behaviors. We will look at how sex roles are socially learned and what

It is safe to say that boys and girls are more alike than they are different. (A. Kandell/Photo Researchers)

research has to tell us about actual differences between boys' and girls' social behavior. Finally, we will consider how educational systems contribute to maintaining SEX-ROLE STEREOTYPING.

HOW SEX ROLES ARE LEARNED

While certain physical differences between the sexes are universal, most personality and behavioral differences are not. It is safe to say that boys and girls are more alike than they are different (Maccoby & Jacklyn, 1974). Frequently, teachers, parents, and peers react as though boys and girls were different kinds of people. This universal tendency to respond differently to boys and girls is called SEX-ROLE STEREOTYPING. The people who make up a child's environment mold the attitudes and behavior of children from the moment of birth. "It's a boy" means father can start collecting baseball bats, gloves, and season football tickets. "It's a girl" means that mother can dress her child in pretty clothes. Sex-role stereotyping is relentless. The child will get the message.

Growing up male or female

Let's see how sex-role messages are communicated to children. Bryan will be given active toys such as trucks, cars, and guns. He will be encouraged by these toys to move around in space (Fagot, 1974; Fein et al., 1975). His mother will very early teach him not to cry and not to be a "sissy." Both parents will encourage him to explore his environment, to be independent, and to assert himself to get what he wants. By the time he has reached first grade, he will have established his sex-role learning. He will be able to: (1) tell you the differences between boys and girls and their appropriate activities; (2) say that he prefers to be a boy rather than a girl, and (3) behave according to cultural sex-role standards

(Weitzman, 1979). His teachers are likely to describe his behavior in school as active, assertive, adventurous, curious, and independent (Pottker & Fischel, 1977). For Kathy, however, life proceeds very differently. She is given quiet housekeeping toys to play with such as dolls and tea sets (Seavy et al., 1975). She will be encouraged to "play nicely" and not to shove the little boys around. Her mother will give her more nurturant attention: smiling, touching, and talking (Goldberg & Lewis, 1969; Lewis & Rosenblum, 1974). Her teachers are likely to rate her as conscientious, cooperative, calm, and mannerly. Also, they will reinforce her when she behaves accordingly (Carpenter, 1979; Lee & Kedar-Voiradas, 1976; Lockheed & Ekstrum, 1977; Serbin, 1979). Quite often, however, girls will tend to resist sex-role training. They may continue to prefer "boys' " activities until well past the primary grades. Kathy, for example, frequently says that she would rather be a boy because they have so much more fun (Minuchin et al., 1969)!

Grown up: Masculine or feminine

By the time they graduate from high school, most students are likely to be seen by others as well as by themselves as sex-role stereotyped according to an "instrumental-expressive" dimension. Figure 3-2 shows us that college men and women agree on many behavioral traits that are considered appropriate and desirable for males and females in our society (Bem, 1976). Bryan is expected to use more masculine and instrumental approaches—to be more dominant, competitive, and self-sufficient. Kathy will be seen as more expressive in her behaviors: affectionate, gentle, and tender. Neither intellectual nor social characteristics escape the sex-role stereotyping process. To what extent do these stereotypes reflect the actual behavior of boys and girls in school? Do teachers, school curricula, and textbooks encourage and perpetuate sex-role stereotypes? What are some of the ways in which schools and teachers can modify sex-stereotyped practices? We will try to answer these questions in this chapter.

Figure 3-2 Some sex-stereotyped instrumental and expressive characteristics. (Source: S. L. Bem, "Probing the Promise of Androgyny," in A. G. Kaplan and J. P. Bean (eds.), *Beyond Sex-Role Stereotypes: Readings toward a Psychology of Androgyny*. Boston: Little, Brown, 1976.)

Instrumental (masculine)	Expressive (feminine)
Ambitious	Affectionate
Acts as a leader	Cheerful
Assertive	Compassionate
Competitive	Gentle
Dominant	Loves children
Forceful	Loyal
Independent	Sensitive to needs of others
Makes decisions easily	Sympathetic
Self–reliant	Tender
Willing to take a stand	Warm
Willing to take risks	Yielding
Self–sufficient	Soft spoken

College students rated adjectives as more desirable for males or for females in our society. Some of the characteristics rated by both sexes as more desirable for males (masculine) and for females (feminine) are shown above. These traits, as well as some others, form part of a scale to measure masculinity, femininity, or "androgyny." Since these descriptions are not unique to any one person, they are stereotypes.

SEX DIFFERENCES IN BEHAVIOR

A number of researchers have tried to find out what stable differences do appear between boys and girls. This problem is difficult to answer. First, we know that few really stable sex differences in behavior have been found at birth. Yet some differences do appear at later ages (see Table 3-1). Are these differences learned, or are they a delayed genetic (inherited)

Table 3-1. Some major sex differences in behavior

Behavior or skill	More marked in	Age of onset	Comment
Aggression	Boys	2–3 years	Physical attack or counterattack. Relatively early onset. Found in most cultures. Persists and increases through high school and college.
Verbal facility	Girls	11–12 years	Wide variety of tasks: language, comprehension, spelling, some creativity tasks, vocabulary, reading speed. Continues through college.
Mathematical skills	Boys	12–13 years	Not related to number of math courses taken. May relate to male superiority on visual-spatial skills as well.
Visual-spatial skills	Boys	12–13 years	May relate to math skills.
Reading	Girls	6–10 years	Continues through college. Girls start earlier but boys catch up by age 10.
Anxiety-fearfulness	Girls	14–24 months	No difference in many studies. Where differences *are* found, there is fearfulness in new situations with new stimuli, self-reported fear, teacher-rated fearfulness.
Achievement	Girls	4–5 years and through high school	Lower expectancies for success; greater "fear of success"; withdrawal from competition, especially with males; girls tend to attribute success to luck rather than ability and to attribute failure to lack of ability.
Activity level	Boys	2–6 years	Boys move around more in space at the preschool level.
		age 6 through high school	Some teachers rate boys higher in restless movement. Most studies show no differences.
Referred behavior, learning problems	Boys	6–12 years	Teacher referral for disruptive or hyperactive behavior; early reading and learning disabilities.

Sources: Clarizio & McCoy, 1976; Cook & Stingle, 1974; Deaux, 1976; Hoffman, 1977; Hoyenga & Hoyenga, 1979; Kaplan & Bean, 1976; Lenny, 1977; Maccoby & Jacklyn, 1974.

reaction? Possibly the answer to both parts of the question is "yes." Aggression seems to be observed more frequently in boys. Some writers believe that male hormones contribute to increased aggression in boys. Of course, the fact of being a boy or a girl quickly interacts with the child's social environment to elicit more or less aggressive behavior (Maccoby & Jacklyn, 1974). In one large report of 110 world cultures, girls were more often socialized toward nurturance and obedience, while boys were more often pressured toward achievement and self-reliance (Barry, Bacon & Child, 1957). For our purposes as educators, it is useful to take a look at the learning environments that support or inhibit the full development of important behavior systems. Knowing that most behavior is teachable and can be modified, we can examine the situational conditions that encourage youngsters like Ted and Kathy to hit and others like Bryan and Donna to cooperate.

A second problem in finding stable sex differences comes about when we take a look at developmental ages and stages. Many skills develop at a similar rate in the primary years but begin to diverge during adolescence. For example, starting in early adolescence and continuing on throughout

Table 3-2. Some behaviors in which few or no consistent sex differences appear

Behavior	Comment
Sociability	Boys congregate in larger groups. Girls' groups are smaller and more intimate. Both groups are equal in acceptance of new student in group.
Response to social reinforcement	Both sexes respond with increased effort and persistence.
Conformity	Early studies show higher conformity for girls on spatial tasks only. When task is social or nonspatial, no differences are found.
Dominance	Boys are more assertive with each other in same-sex groups. Males are more assertive early in mixed-sex groups, differences disappear with time spent in group or dyad.
Compliance	Girls comply with adult requests in grades 1 through 6 but are not more compliant with peers. Compliance with peers is equal among boys and girls. Boys' groups are more susceptible to compliance with a "dare" challenge.
Helpfulness	No consistent differences.
Self-esteem	No consistent differences.

Sources: Clarizio & McCoy, 1976; Cook & Stingle, 1974; Deaux, 1976; Hoffman, 1977; Hoyenga & Hoyenga, 1979; Kaplan & Bean, 1976; Lenny, 1977; Maccoby & Jacklyn, 1974.

high school and college, boys excel in mathematics and tasks involving spatial visualization. Take your choice of two possible interpretations. Possibly, mathematical ability may be biologically sex-linked, and this relationship increases when boys reach puberty. Alternatively, we might suppose that math performance becomes increasingly irrelevant to girls. At puberty, girls may become more concerned with marriage, nontechnical careers, or with loss of femininity for appearing to excel at "quantitative" tasks. As you can see, the question of how sex differences develop is really difficult to answer.

In Table 3-1, we have given you a list of the most stable differences between boys and girls. Table 3-2 lists some behaviors in which few or no consistent sex differences appear. There is no evidence that any of the differences listed stem from behaviors that are exclusively either innate or learned. Therefore, it is not clear which behaviors might change with different sex-role training procedures. Certainly, boys know how to put on makeup and girls know how to hit back. The fact that each sex actively refrains from participating in what society regards as "inappropriate" sex-typed behavior may have a great deal to do with the observed differences.

HOW SCHOOLS ENCOURAGE SEX-ROLE STEREOTYPING

Schools, and the people who attend and run them, frequently encourage sex-role stereotyping. It probably happens to some degree in every school, either overtly in textbooks and class assignments or covertly in attitudes and expectancies for behavior. We know that stereotyping appears in various settings: in curriculum materials such as films, in opportunities for enrolling in classes (mechanics, home economics), in teacher reinforcement of passive or active behavior in each sex, in guidance counseling for career planning, in athletic programs and resources, and in the visible distribution of male and female teachers. Each of these factors has an impact on encouraging either "masculine" or "feminine" behaviors to the exclusion of alternative styles of interacting.

Textbooks are frequently stereotyped

Let us take some examples of educational stereotyping. Textbooks have typically shown boys in active, independent, and adventuresome roles and girls engaged in homemaking or various passive and dependent activities. Boys are more often shown in achievement and recognition roles while girls appear in helpmate and subservient roles (Burton, 1974; Child, Potter, & Levine, 1957; Jacklyn & Mischel, 1973; Pottker, 1977). In a recent study of 134 textbooks, women were portrayed in 24 differing occupations while men appeared in 147. Further, female occupations were mainly traditional—teacher, homemaker, nurse, secretary (Sexton, 1976). Missing from school texts have been role models of assertive,

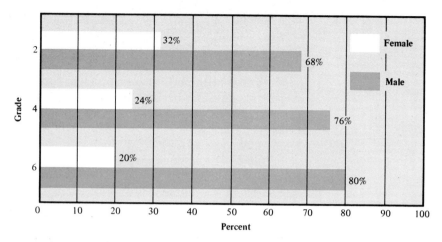

Figure 3-3 Percent of illustrations in children's textbooks for grades 2 through 6 which show males or females. Over 8000 pictures were analyzed; over 5500 of them were of males. (Source: L. J. Weitzman and D. Rizzo, *Biased Textbooks: A Research Perspective—Action Steps You Can Take.* Washington, D.C.: National Foundation for the Improvement of Education, The Resource Center on Sex Roles in Education, 1974.)

achieving women and gentle, tender males. While many textbook companies are attempting to correct this practice, this trend is not yet widespread either in the publishing industry or in school text adoptions. Figure 3-3 shows that males are also more visible in texts; the percentage in representation for males and females increases by grade level, so that by sixth grade there are four pictures of males for every one of females (Weitzman & Rizzo, 1974). The message is clear. Through a biased selection of pictures and stories, textbooks restrict students' exposure to role models with unique or different career aspirations.

=== PROBE 3-3 ===

Think back to your high school. In what ways did sex-role stereotyping appear? Select three different examples to illustrate how it occurred.

Career choices are stereotyped

Sex-role stereotyping in curriculum appears to occur at a relatively early age. Generally, boys select an academic or career choice when they are quite young, and they—more often than girls—elect professional, business, and scientific careers. Girls, on the other hand, delay their vocational decisions until late in high school, and they tend to choose more traditionally "female" occupations (Matteson, 1975). In many schools, counselors "track" boys and girls by both college preparatory courses and vocational selection. Girls are less frequently counseled into nontraditional careers or those that have been typically male-dominated (Pietrofesa & Schlossberg, 1977; Sexton, 1976). Vocational schools have similarly guided boys and girls into separate careers, with females concentrated into fewer and lower-paying occupations (Harway & Astin, 1977). While social and cultural factors are certainly involved here, educational practices in schools are also responsible. School hierarchies provide for female teachers at the lower level and male administrators at the top of the structure. Figure 3-4 shows that while more than two-thirds of all elementary and secondary teachers are women, only 15 percent of principals and less than 1 percent of school superintendents are women (Sexton, 1976).

Teachers support stereotyping

Patricia Sexton (1969) has criticized the schools for "feminizing" boys by reinforcing neat, quiet, and passive behavior rather than allowing them to demonstrate active and exploratory patterns. She uses this view to support her contention that, as a result, boys are slower in reading and are more frequently referred for problem behavior (see Table 3-1). Others have found that teachers seem to be more positive toward girls than toward boys in the elementary grades (Barclay, 1974) and to encourage girls to be more dependent on the teacher (Serbin, O'Leary, Kent, & Tonik, 1973). Thus, in many different ways, sex-role stereotyping does occur in the schools. Let us look at some alternatives for dealing with these problems.

Changing sex-role stereotyping

Schools are beginning to bring their educational and employment practices into line with the provisions of Title IX of the Civil Rights Act (Figure 3-5). When this process is completed, some of the more obvious evidences

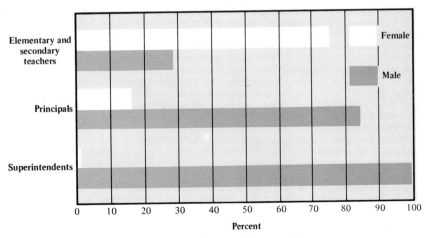

Figure 3-4
Percentages of males and females in public school positions. (Source: P. Sexton, *Women in Education.* Bloomington, Indiana: Phi Delta Kappa Educational Foundation, 1976.)

**Figure 3-5
Title IX—federal
laws help reduce
sex stereotyping in
schools.**

Title IX; education amendments (1972) to the 1964 Civil
Rights Act "No person . . . shall, on the basis of sex, be
excluded from participation in, be denied the benefits of,
or be subjected to discrimination under any education
program or activity receiving Federal financial assistance."

of sex-role stereotyping will disappear. Boys and girls will be taught
physical education together except, probably, for contact sports. Bryan
will no longer be kept out of home economics courses if he chooses to
enroll, and Kathy will be allowed to take shop and industrial arts. Their
school will be required to use the same testing and guidance materials
when counseling boys or girls about educational or vocational opportunities during and after high school. If Kathy wishes to join a girls'
basketball team, she will have the same access to equipment, coaching,
extramural games, and so on as would Bryan on a boys' team. Legal
remedies can provide a background for attention and concern. However,
laws do not automatically change sex bias in attitudes or in many specific
teacher practices that reflect such bias. More needs to be done. Think
about the following suggestions for reducing sex-role stereotyping in your
school.

**As some of the
more obvious
evidences of sex-
role stereotyping
disappear, girls will
have equal access
to equipment,
coaching, and
extramural games.
(P. Travers/Peter
Arnold)**

===== **PROBE 3-4** =====

Paraphrase and give the key words to Title IX. List three areas where Title IX might affect school practices.

If our educational system were to encourage both boys and girls to be active, assertive, independent, and self-confident (instrumental) as well as nurturant, tender, and playful (expressive), what might the result be?

A well-known researcher on sex roles, Sandra Bem (1976), suggests that traditional masculine and feminine sex roles are restrictive. She proposes a more flexible alternative called ANDROGYNY. She suggests that both boys and girls should feel free to adopt the more successful behaviors of both sexes. Androgynous boys and girls should perform more flexibly and adaptively in a variety of situations. They can each be both instrumental and expressive, depending upon the requirements of the situation. When you work to modify sex-role stereotyping in schools and society, you may help your students to move toward increased androgyny.

You can approach the problem of sex-role stereotypes on three levels: awareness, clarification, and action (Sadker & Sadker, 1976). You can also monitor your own behavior to determine where you stand on these issues:

* *Prepare a unit on sex-role awareness.* Lessons on awareness are similar to "consciousness-raising" efforts. Awareness exercises help students to be sensitive to both the overt and subtle indicators of sex-role stereotyping. You might want to try some of the following ideas. Assign TV programs and have students tally male and female roles, activities, and ideas. Discuss whether a man or woman could be a President, nurse, explorer—and why or why not. Ask students to describe how rules for boys and girls seem to diverge ("boys don't cry," "girls don't hit," and so on).
* *Include exercises for clarification of values.* The clarification level helps students (and teachers as well, we suspect) to take a look at their personal values about sex roles and to decide where they stand. One exercise asks the student to complete the unfinished sentence: "When I see a famous football player doing needlepoint, I _____ _____" (NEA, 1974).
* *Develop action plans.* Complete your unit on sex-role stereotyping by implementing a plan of action. The action level gives students the opportunity to take a stand on issues and to use their problem-solving

skills. Here, they can develop nonsexist materials for different grade levels and subject areas. They might even complete a survey of stereotyping practices in their school or community and propose plans to modify these practices.

• *Take a look at your own behavior and attitudes.* What can you do to ensure that your behavior is not biased toward rigid sex roles? Observe your typical behavior toward boys and girls. Do you line up your students by sex? Do you ask the boys to do the heavier chores and the girls to water plants and be class secretary? Do you admonish girls to be ''little ladies'' and boys to ''stand up like a man?'' Do you express more concern about career planning for boys than for girls? Would you look surprised if Kathy said she wanted to be an astronaut? (Frazier & Sadker, 1973). These and many more tough questions can tune you in to your own stereotypes. We hope they set you thinking about where you stand.

• *Use professional resources.* When you are ready to take action on sex-role stereotyping, you will find many useful resources available. Several large-scale projects have developed instructional units and accompanying materials on reducing sex-role stereotyping. These programs will be helpful when you are ready to implement your lessons on awareness, clarification, and action (American Personnel and Guidance Association, 1975, 1976; Campbell, 1978; National Organization for Women, 1976; National Education Association, 1973, 1974).

Sex-role stereotyping has implications for social behavior

By now you may have begun to wonder why we chose to put this section ahead of a discussion of more specific skills such as friendship, achievement, and self-regulation. The reasoning is simple. If you refer to Figure 3-2 and Tables 3-1 and 3-2, you will easily see that actual sex differences in behavior as well as sex-role stereotypes cut across many social behavior systems. We want to emphasize to you that the full development of competencies in all the areas to follow requires that sex-role stereotyping be eliminated from the social and academic curricula of homes, schools, and communities. As you read about some of the sex differences we are going to discuss, consider for yourself how these might have been modeled, taught, and reinforced by the social environment. Consider too how cultural expectancies for sex differences in social behavior might interfere with the fullest development of each individual student.

AFFILIATION: INTERPERSONAL SKILLS

The student who is relatively competent in AFFILIATION SKILLS has learned a number of specific behavior patterns that maintain and increase positive contact with other people. As a result of these social skills, such a student will be (1) responsive to your praise as well as your criticism, (2) more compliant with adults, (3) more conforming to peers, and (4) more skilled at maintaining peer friendships. Let us take a closer look at affiliation skills in school, the conditions under which they develop, and their contribution to positive classroom climates.

DEVELOPMENT OF AFFILIATION

Kathy is described by her teachers as sociable. She is frequently seen in the company of others. She approaches others to talk, to ask for help, or to offer a hand. When she talks to you, she smiles frequently, nods her head in agreement, and goes along amiably with your suggestions. Given a project to complete, she would prefer to work with other students rather than alone. Consequently, Kathy is often chosen as a group member by other students. It is clear that Kathy enjoys the presence of her peers and is comfortable in finding and maintaining friendships. In her interactions with you, her responsiveness to approval and positive feedback makes her a cooperative and constructive class member. Her desire for approval will sensitize her also to your disapproval: Kathy wants to avoid the loss of your positive regard, and constructive criticism of her behavior will motivate her to work harder.

Keep in mind that not all of your students will develop the variety of affiliative skills we see in Kathy. In your future classrooms, you can expect to cope with students who show varying degrees of sociability and group cohesiveness. Paula is always alone and will not talk to peers. Donna stays close to her teachers and is seldom chosen to play games. Ted and Ike are too disruptive to work cooperatively in groups. Alvin smiles sweetly but cannot carry on a conversation. You will want to know how affiliative skills develop and what conditions encourage effective interpersonal behavior. Let us take a brief look at some of the conditions and consequences of the affiliative behavior system.

Attachment to people

When Kathy was a small baby, her parents cared for her physical needs, gave her much attention (rocking, cuddling, smiling and cooing at her), and provided her with lots of interpersonal stimulation. By the time she was a year old, Kathy showed visible ATTACHMENT to her parents; she followed their movements with her eyes, clung to them when picked up, and showed distress when they left her with strangers (Ainsworth, Blehar, Waters, & Wall, 1977; Sroufe & Waters, 1977; Weinraub & Lewis, 1977). The clear demonstration of love and caring by her parents is the strongest antecedent to the development of Kathy's positive approach responses to them and to other people. Many writers contend that a strong attachment to caretakers by the age of 2 or 3 is critical to the emergence of trust and caring for other people throughout the life span (Bowlby, 1951, 1969; Erikson, 1963; Sullivan, 1953).

The clear demonstration of love and caring by parents is the strongest antecedent to the development of positive approach responses to them and to other people. (Erika Stone)

Social learning theorists stress the importance of early attachment for determining the effectiveness of parents and teachers as social reinforcers (Hetherington & Parke, 1975; Sears, Maccoby, & Levin, 1957; Sears, Rau, & Alpert, 1965). Kathy's experiences with her family (including consistent positive and warm interactions) will increase her sensitivity to the feelings of others and her responsiveness to their requests. However, some students have family backgrounds which provide very little warmth, encouragement, or praise. With these students, your verbal praise may not be effective and you may want to use other types of reinforcers for effective instruction and classroom management.

Social and task dependency: Some results of attachment

The obvious helplessness of Kathy as an infant made her physically dependent on others to meet her needs. As a result of their caretaking, she became both *socially dependent* on them for love and attention and *task-dependent* on them for help and assistance. In nursery school, Kathy transferred both her social and task dependency to her teacher; she went to her teacher for comfort when she was hurt or afraid and asked for help with difficult tasks like tying her shoes. In first grade, Kathy will spend less and less time near her teacher and more time with her peers. By the end of the first grade, you will notice that Kathy seeks your attention and approval for her good work; by now, she asks for help only when she really needs it. Most students will use social behavior to please their teachers and task behaviors to obtain help.

Some students like Donna, however, appear to gain comfort from hanging around their teachers and seeking extra attention. Donna asks for help continually and fails to initiate projects until you tell her exactly what to do. She doesn't seem satisfied even when you assure that her work is adequate. With such a student, you may not be able to determine whether her behavior is social or task-dependent: does she want affection and reassurance that you like her, or does she lack the skills to initiate and carry through tasks on her own? Understandably, you are eager to let Donna know you like her. Therefore, you help her whenever she asks and you go over to her desk when she sits and looks perplexed. Your problem here will be to communicate to Donna that you like her as a person but you are not willing to help her do things that she can well do for herself. However, some research studies on adult rejection of children's dependency bids suggest the following: a complete refusal to be helpful to dependency requests will increase continued dependency as much as will your consistent help and assistance (Sears et al., 1957; Hartup, 1958). Perhaps the answer lies in a gradual reduction of support. We will talk about gradually fading your support in later chapters.

PEER-GROUP AFFILIATION

As Kathy became less dependent on you for support and assistance, she increases her attachment to her peer group. Figure 3-6 demonstrates the

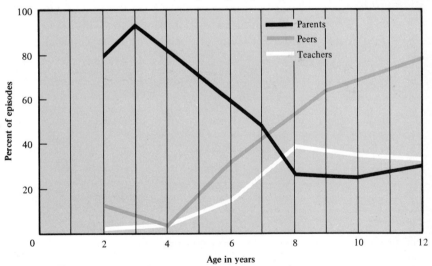

Figure 3-6 Percentage of waking episodes spent with parents, peers, and teachers. Observers followed children around for sixteen hours a day, recording the amount of time, in behavior episodes, spent with varying people and activities. The trend toward increasing time and activity spent with peers increases from age 4 onward. (Adapted from H. F. Wright, *Recording and Analyzing Children's Behavior.* New York: Harper & Row, 1967.)

changes that take place with age in relative frequency of peer, parent, and teacher contacts. You can see that Kathy and Donna will spend more and more time with peers as they progress through school (Wright, 1967). What are the effects of this increased contact with peers?

Peers are teachers

Like teachers and parents, peers exert social control. Peers are effective teachers of new behaviors (McGee, Kauffman, & Nussen, 1977). Kathy's peers influence her behavior in at least three ways: (1) by providing models for appropriate (or deviant) behavior; (2) by their power to reinforce or not reinforce what she does; and (3) by the rules they set for her social behavior (Tyler, 1981). The teaching effects of peer contact will appear in the impressive similarity you will observe in the appearance and behaviors of your students. In second grade, you see lots of Dan'l Boone fur caps; in ninth grade, it's Led Zeppelin T-shirts. This similarity is called CONFORMITY to group norms. The reinforcement effects will be reflected in Kathy's *acceptance* and *status* among her peers. Such evidences of peer support are found when other students ask Kathy over to play after school, to sit near them at lunch, or to be a member of their club. Let's consider each of these peer effects separately.

Peers teach conformity to group norms

CONFORMITY is a kind of modeling behavior practiced in groups. Students will try to match their behaviors to what some or most members of their peer group are doing. Peer norms are like rules: they define for each student what social behaviors will be accepted or rejected by that student's age or social group. It seems clear that a certain amount of

Comformity is a kind of modeling behavior practiced in groups. (Lejune/ Stock, Boston)

conformity to peer standards is desirable and helpful; it teaches new behavior. Through observing and imitating their peers, young people learn many rules and how to get along with one another. Some students, like Elton and Paula, seldom conform or go along with peer norms. These nonconforming students are likely to become, as we shall see, social ioslates or rejected members of the group. Conformity to peer-group standards increases with age through early adolescence and begins to decrease as the older adolescent develops his or her own values and standards for behavior (Costanzo & Shaw, 1966; Landsbaum & Willis, 1971).

PROBE 3-5

Peers exert social control by means of _____, _____, and
_____.

Although Kathy does not conform to her peers in all situations, she is most likely to do so when (1) she is uncertain about what to do and therefore follows those who appear confident (Berenda, 1950); (2) her reference group is small or she is in the minority (Costanzo & Shaw, 1966); (3) her group contains high-status or especially competent peers (Hollander, 1960); or (4) she fears rejection by the group for nonconformity (Schacter, 1951).

Using peer power productively

Peer power can become a headache or a challenge. These peer-group standards may be compatible with your values as a teacher or they may conflict with what you regard as proper and desirable. You can react to the power of peer influence by ignoring it, fighting it, or submitting to it. We believe that your teaching goals can be met most effectively, however, if you use peer-group processes for productive purposes. How effectively you accomplish this depends on your skills in observing, assessing, and integrating your procedures into the structure of the peer group. Considerable research has shown that students themselves do not submit entirely to peer pressures. Rather, they make a compromise between what peers, parents, and teachers require for acceptance and status (Bandura & Kupers, 1964; Stukat, 1958). If you set your standards too high, your students will be far more likely to adopt the lower and more comfortable standards of their peers. Study 3-1 provides an example of how children will follow peer models rather than those of adults when this course of action seems to result in higher reinforcement (Bandura, Grusec, & Menlove, 1967).

STUDY 3-1: PEER STANDARDS OR ADULT STANDARDS?

A bowling game was used by researchers at Stanford University to study children's patterns of self-reinforcement. Scores on the game were controlled by means of preset patterns of lights on a scoreboard. Children observed an adult model "playing" the bowling game. Opportunity for self-reinforcement was provided by a box of tokens which were exchangeable for "value prizes" at the end of the game. The adult adopted *high standards* and rewarded herself with a chip only when her score exceeded a stated high level. Then she would make comments such as "That's a good score, that deserves a chip." When her score fell below this level, she refrained from taking a chip, and she remarked, "That's not a very good score, that doesn't deserve a chip." Subsequently, half the children observed a same-age peer play the game. The peer models took chips for *both* high and low scores, thus rewarding themselves for inferior performance. When given the opportunity to play the game themselves, children who watched both the adult and the peer lowered their standards for self-reinforcement and took chips for lower scores. Children who watched only a high-standard adult were less likely to take a token when their performance fell below the criterion set by the adult. This study shows us that children will follow the example of peers rather than adults when this behavior results in higher reinforcement.

Adapted from: Bandura, A., Grusec, J. E., & Menlove, F. L. Some determinants of self-reinforcement monitoring systems. *Journal of Personality and Social Psychology,* 1967, 5, 449–455.

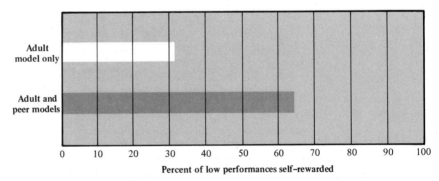

Figure 3-7 Adult and peer models and percent of low performances that are self-rewarded.

Percent of low performances self–rewarded

PEER-GROUP SUPPORT

Peer acceptance and status determine the degree to which each student will obtain reinforcement and support from his or her peer group. Not surprisingly, students who use many affiliative or sociable behaviors with their peers are rated high on popularity or peer status. These students, who are liked by many others, are reinforcing to their peers. As a result, they receive reciprocal social reinforcement.

Measuring peer support

You can determine the level of any student's PEER-GROUP SUPPORT by asking students about their peer contacts (Kane & Lawler, 1978). An appropriate set of questions might look like this: "Whom do you sit next to at lunch? Who is helpful in class? Who is a good leader? Who can draw well?" Questions such as these make up what is called a *sociometric*

Some students are social isolates and appear withdrawn from peers. (Bob Combs/Photo Researcher)

measure of peer support and acceptance. A student who receives many nominations by many students on many questions is judged to rate high in peer support. We shall have more to say about sociometric methods in Chapter 11.

Social skills increase peer support

Students who are rated high in peer acceptance have characteristics other than sociability that cement their attractiveness to others. Peer status will be assigned to students who demonstrate skills or competencies that are highly valued by that peer group. These skills may be in areas of leadership, athletic prowess, or just-plain-funship, to name only a few. Research also suggests that popular students at all ages are more likely to be physically attractive, higher in intelligence, nonaggressive, and helpful to others; they also tend to achieve successfully in school (Barclay, Covert, Scott, & Stilwell, 1978; Hartup, 1970). You can see that some of these characteristics, such as helpfulness, are more open to constructive intervention than others, such as physical appearance.

Students who are low in peer acceptance are rated higher in task dependency, anxiety, negative attention-getting behavior, and aggressiveness and lower on positive social skills. Some students such as Paula are social isolates and appear withdrawn from peers. Paula demonstrates some negative and unskilled behaviors that make friendship patterns difficult to establish and maintain. Whether or not you elect to intervene in the social patterning of the peer groups to help integrate isolated or unskilled students like Paula is a matter of personal choice. However, we do feel that all students should be given the opportunity to develop peer friendships by being helped to integrate themselves into dyadic or small-group activities. Once Paula develops some outgoing social skills and is seen in a more positive light by her peers, the choice will be hers: to integrate socially or to remain independent of others. Since Paula lacks the social skills to approach others and is actively rejected by her peers, her choices are limited; she seems to have no acceptable alternatives to self-isolation and withdrawal.

Positive peer contact and acceptance can be integrated into the normal classroom procedures. Teachers generally have four approaches to use when they decide to integrate students toward more positive interactions. As a prospective teacher, you can:

GUIDELINES FOR TEACHING
Increasing Peer Support

• *Use yourself as a model of positive behavior with students.* When teachers use positive interpersonal behaviors in their classroom teaching styles, their students are more likely to imitate them and to use similar affiliative behaviors themselves (Baird, 1973; Harvey et al., 1968). Teachers who are negative and very critical tend to encourage students to criticize one another.

• *Discriminate between task dependency and social dependency.* Provide temporary assistance to students who need help to get started on a task or to overcome a tough hurdle. Then encourage independent effort and make your approval contingent upon some independent work. Peer support will be higher for students with good self-management skills who do not constantly hang around the teacher.

• *Arrange for students to increase their interactions with peers.* You can do this in a number of ways by integrating the withdrawn or isolated student into peer-group activities and projects. You can group together students with high and low social skills for independent projects. In this manner, high- and low-status students are brought into active contact with one another. You can assign high- and low-status students to adjacent seats. You can also determine what special skills the low-status student may have and provide opportunities for him or her to teach or demonstrate this to the other students. You can make certain that high-status class roles are rotated, so that each student gets a chance to be line leader, recess monitor, record keeper, or teacher of the day. You can also develop rotating small groups that are assigned cooperative projects to complete. Here, you will want to make certain that all group members assume their share of the work and that group goals are not blocked by uncooperative or inactive members. Reciprocal friendliness among peers tends to increase in successful cooperative groups (Johnson & Johnson, 1974).

• *Praise low-status and isolate students in the presence of peers.* If you make certain that Donna's successful performance is rewarded in the presence of her peers, her attractiveness to others will increase (Flanders & Havumaki, 1960; Lott & Lott, 1966).

All students can learn more effective social skills that will enable them to maintain some positive peer contact. Not all students will be a Popular Peg, but no student need remain a Fearful Flora.

=== **PROBE 3-6** ===

Pair off with another person and debate the following issue: "Teachers should (should not) be active in modifying student peer-group interactions that lead to acceptance and status." Be sure you can each develop at least three reasons for your position. Consider possible outcomes in terms of student, peer, teacher, and parent reactions.

INDEPENDENCE AND ACHIEVEMENT SKILLS

The development of independent and achievement-related behaviors begins before students arrive at school. You will observe an increase in both INDEPENDENCE SKILLS and achievement-oriented behavior throughout the elementary and secondary years. While independence and achievement may appear to be separate systems of behavior, they include many skills which overlap and interrelate. Effective achievement in school depends upon many of the skills that indicate an independent approach to problem solving in both academic and interpersonal situations.

INDEPENDENCE AND AUTONOMY

Students gradually decrease their task dependency on others. They learn to cope with their environment in a more independent manner that will progressively free them from external supervision of their behavior. In small steps, Kathy is learning to (1) take initiative in starting on projects, (2) assume responsibility for following through on an assigned activity, (3) complete a task without asking for help, (4) make decisions among alternative choices in the world, and (5) demonstrate self-assertive behavior in obtaining what she wants (Parke, 1969). While these are all separate and teachable skills, they form a cluster of behaviors that will help move Kathy toward a self-directed style of life.

Independence skills are learned

Kathy's independence was probably first noticed by her parents when she said "No, I won't" at the age of 2. Although her parents and later you as her teacher become exasperated at her refusal to comply, let's take a second look. At the age of 2, she asserted her independence by saying "no" to everything. At ages 6 and 16, she is using this capability for self-assertion more constructively. She contributed ideas for the new class play and she made some positive suggestions for a senior class citizen's day. She may also use her independent thinking to disagree with you openly in political science class and to organize a petition to object to the new school rules on off-campus activities.

Kathy's independence is encouraged by a wide range of learning conditions which increase her opportunities for freedom to move around her environment, to control her motor skills, and to use problem-solving effectively. Parents who encourage "early acceleration" of independence expect their children to help with household tasks, to assert themselves with others, to make decisions at home, and to take care of their possessions (Winterbottom, 1958).

As she develops her independence, however, Kathy is still oriented to pleasing her parents and teachers, and sometimes she acts helpless in the face of an apparently small problem. This conflict between a student's emerging independence and the desire to remain dependent and cared for becomes particularly apparent at adolescence (Elder, 1968; Matteson, 1975). Kathy wants and demands more freedom to make her own decisions, but she retains her needs for periodic guidance and support from you and her parents.

You can encourage independence skills at school with careful planning to include students in democratic decision-making procedures, negotiating class rules, choices of activities, and opportunities for taking responsibility without constant supervision.

ACHIEVEMENT SKILLS AND ACADEMIC LEARNING

From the start of first grade, every American child is faced with requirements for competition, competence, and accomplishment in school. Your final evaluation of your students' success at this enormous and continual task can be objective. You can consider the amount and quality of work assigned and completed, class grades, or scores on an achievement test. Each student's personal success at academic tasks is dependent upon a host of factors, many of which are probably not under the control of your teaching strategies. For example, some of the most important developmental factors that have been found to contribute to academic performance are socioeconomic and ethnic background, intellectual or aptitude measures, and parent training practices (Lavin, 1965; Solomon & Kendall, 1979). On the other hand, some of your students will have behaviors that are effectively contributing to academic performance regardless of their scores on an intelligence test (Crandall & Battle, 1970; Kifer, 1975). We shall concentrate here on some of the socially learned behaviors or ACHIEVEMENT SKILLS that contribute to the differences you observe between Kathy, who does well in many academic tasks in school, and Donna, who frequently has problems in completing her schoolwork.

Achievement behaviors contribute to mastery

Students who have effective ACHIEVEMENT SKILLS in school can be described by four broad sets of behaviors which set them apart from their less competent peers. First, you will observe that in many situations, students like Kathy strive to attain mastery of a problem; they attempt to do well in most of the work that is assigned to them. Second, Kathy is competitive with herself; she tries to do better today than she did yesterday and to increase her competence on each task that she attempts to master. Third, Kathy is competitive with others; she watches the performance of her peers and attempts to match or exceed it. She not only compares her achievements with her own previous ones but with those of her peers as well. In both cases, she is matching her performance to a standard of excellence. Finally, Kathy reacts with obvious pleasure and renewed effort when she receives approval or recognition from you, peers, and parents. She wants not only to feel good about her own performance but to gain recognition from others as well (Crandall, Katkovsky, & Preston, 1960; McClelland, Atkinson, Clark, & Howell, 1953; Solomon & Kendall, 1979).

Achieving students: Hard work, persistence, and positive expectancies

In addition to an orientation toward mastery, competition, and recognition, you will also notice that many achieving students like Kathy use a number of other specific behaviors which increase their academic success. They show (1) high persistence, (2) some moderate risk taking, and (3) a POSITIVE EXPECTANCY for doing well.

Task persistence is a strong predictor of academic success (Crandall & McGhee, 1968). Kathy works hard and does not give up easily when the problem appears difficult. As a result of her effort, she frequently completes more work correctly than do other students. In being a moderate risk taker, Kathy is willing to take some chances of failure as long as she expects some chance of success (Atkinson, 1965). If you offer Kathy a choice of problems, she may select one of the moderately difficult ones rather than one that is very easy or very hard. Finally, students who have a positive expectancy to do well on tasks generally do so (Battle, 1965; Crandall, 1967, 1969; Parsons, 1978). Of course, success follows itself to some extent, so that more accomplished students state higher expectancies for achievement. Like "the little engine that could," Kathy gets better and better. "I know I can, I know I can" has a very positive effect on her achievement competency (Masters, Furman, & Barden, 1977).

Students who have a positive expectancy to do well on tasks generally do so. (Doug Wilson/Black Star)

Achievement is situational: To do well or not to do well

It is important to note that Kathy does not show these achievement behaviors all the time at school, nor does she demonstrate them in every situation or for every activity. While she is generally positive and persistent in English and social studies, she frequently slows down in math, looks bewildered, and asks for help on her paper. Furthermore, she has no interest in doing well in home economics or football. Achievement behaviors may characterize some students more than others, but few students try to be good in everything. Some writers have discussed a "need for achievement" or an "achievement motivation" to account for the behaviors we have described above (McClelland et al., 1953; Atkinson, 1958, 1965). We believe that it will be more useful for you to take a look at the specific patterns of behavior that your students use in achievement situations and decide whether or not these behaviors will be helpful for meeting their goals. If you then observe that Donna gives up easily and frequently says "I can't," you can employ some strategies to help her overcome these specific responses that interfere with the completion of her math assignment. You will find this a much easier task than trying to increase her "achievement motivation," and it will be more productive for Donna than giving up on her because she is "unmotivated."

DEVELOPMENT OF ACHIEVEMENT

Parents are important to the development of achievement. Students who come to your classes with well-developed achievement behaviors are likely to have parents who (1) set high standards for accomplishment, (2) stress early acceleration of independence and self-help, (3) give positive reinforcement and praise for accomplishment, (4) show moderate rather than intense warmth and acceptance, (5) allow their children considerable freedom to explore the environment, (6) encourage their children to ask questions and think for themselves, and (7) criticize them for lack of effort and incorrect responses (Crandall, Preston, & Rabson, 1960; Kagan & Moss, 1962; Kelly & Worell, 1976; Rosen & D'Andrade, 1959; Stein & Bailey, 1973).

Some recent research also suggests that children like Kathy and Bryan, who are both moderately high achievers in school, may have somewhat differing early experiences with parents. For Bryan, it seems that high maternal involvement and early acceleration are important. For Kathy, her father plays a more active role and may spend more time with her. For both boys and girls, high educational aspirations on the parents' part will accelerate performance, but this is especially important for girls. Since high achievement is not part of the traditional female sex role, Kathy's parents have had to provide an increased amount of support and encouragement to help her to succeed as well as she does (Hennig, 1974).

The power of early achievement training by parents has a long-term influence. Both Kathy and Bryan are likely to persist in their intellectual and mastery behavior beyond adolescence and into adulthood (Kagan & Moss, 1962). It appears that with repeated experience, attaining one's standards can become rewarding and pleasurable in itself (Masters et al., 1977).

Sex differences in achievement begin in school

Some very interesting differences appear in the achievement behavior of boys and girls. As we shall see, measures of ability or intelligence do not differ for the two sexes. In preschool, teacher ratings of the kinds of behaviors we have discussed above are also quite similar for boys and girls (Maccoby & Jacklyn, 1974). But looking back at Table 3-1, you can see that many specific achievement-related skills begin to appear in the primary grades. By high school and college, more differences emerge. Although Bryan and Kathy have done equally well in school, Bryan is more likely to increase his efforts when competing with other boys, to overestimate his probability of success at many tasks (he boasts more), and to take greater risks in order to win (Maccoby & Jacklyn, 1974). In contrast, Kathy is more likely to withdraw somewhat when competing with her friends, to underestimate her abilities, and to lower her expectancies for success on a new activity (Crandall, 1969; Parsons & Ruble, 1977; Parsons, 1978).

These sex differences in competitiveness and expectancy for achievement, especially on masculine-typed tasks, persist throughout the high school and college years (Deaux, 1976; Lenney, 1977). Matina Horner (1972) proposed that the observed decrease in women's achievement behavior can be attributed to a "fear of success." She suggested that some women withdraw from competitive achievement situations when they feel that their femininity or acceptance by others is at stake. Certainly, this is a useful notion to explain why girls do as well as boys in math until adolescence and then fall behind. It seems clear that some of the behaviors that lead to effective achievement (assertiveness, independence, and competitiveness) are incompatible with a traditional sex-role orientation for girls (passive, compliant, dependent). Indeed, more traditional women who show fear of success do withdraw from direct competition with others (Peplau, 1976). We may continue to see these achievement differences between the sexes until stereotyped sex roles disappear from the academic scene.

You can teach persistence and positive expectancies. All of your students will require effective management strategies to maximize their academic performances, but students like Donna and Ted are prime targets for special attention. Take your cues from parents who have taught achievement behavior successfully.

GUIDELINES FOR TEACHING

Facilitating Achievement Behaviors

• Let your students know you have confidence in their ability to succeed.
• Provide them with activities and learning materials at a level that they are capable of mastering.
• Encourage mastery and accomplishment by being generous with enthusiasm and praise.
• Increase your standards of accomplishment gradually, so that students always have a reasonable goal to anticipate.
• Read Chapter 6 for many more ideas on increasing both achievement behaviors and objective academic accomplishments.

Published reports of programs to increase achievement motivation suggest that you can take positive steps to stimulate students whose levels of effective achievement behavior are low (Alschuler, Tabor, & McIntyre, 1970; McClelland, 1972). You will want to help Donna and Ted to develop more persistence, raise their sights for accomplishment, and work compatibly with their more achieving peers.

=== **PROBE 3-7** ===

Explain how a low expectancy for success can affect future achievement behaviors.

AGGRESSIVE BEHAVIOR

In any free-play situation where students are unsupervised, you will observe many instances of AGGRESSIVE BEHAVIOR. Spontaneous hitting, pushing, punching, or calling of names and insults are all likely to occur in the halls and on the playground during the primary grades; frequently, they occur in high school as well. Whether these aggressive behaviors appear as physical or verbal, they are all behaviors aimed at harm or injury to another person (Bandura, 1973).

SOCIAL AGGRESSION

As students mature, their aggression becomes better controlled, more verbal, and less frequently physical. Most of the developmental changes in the overt use of aggression result from repeated discrimination training provided by both adults and by the victims of the aggressive behavior (Bandura, 1973; Patterson & Cobb, 1971).

Two major changes take place. First, children learn the occasions for aggression; that is, "Don't hit smaller or younger children, don't hit girls, don't hit your parents or teachers, don't hit first." Second, children learn the occasions when aggression is permissible. The concept of *intentionality* becomes important, so that Ted learns it is OK to knock Donna down if he says it was an "accident" and he didn't see her standing there. Bryan learns that aggression is OK when he retaliates but not when he initiates hostilities. That is, Bryan learned that he might fight back if the other boys "picked on him" or called his sister names but that he should not start a fight or hit first. This discrimination tells these boys that aggression is sometimes "manly for self-defense" and desirable and sometimes "cowardly and bullying." Furthermore, failure to use aggressive responses in some situations would elicit the label of "sissy." Bryan's father certainly expects him to fight back (retaliative aggression), and so do his peers.

Finally, many children learn that aggressive reactions are permissible when a person is under emotional stress. For example, if mother is angry, tired, frustrated, or sick, it is OK for her to shout and yell at you. Similarly, children are frequently treated with more leniency when they are tired or hungry and are allowed to display more temper and anger. Such learning conditions teach Ted and Bryan that there are many situations in which aggressive behavior is appropriate and desirable or at least permissible.

Given the choice, we hope that you prefer students to solve their conflicts with cooperative and prosocial tactics. However, when they appear in your classroom, many of your students will not yet have learned to inhibit their aggressive reactions. They just don't know how to solve their conflicts with other people in mutually satisfying ways. In the following sections, we shall discuss some of the major conditions which encourage the expression of aggressive reactions. We shall then suggest alternative approaches to coping with aggression in your classroom and school environment.

LEARNING AGGRESSIVE REACTIONS

As a third-grader, Donna is observed to hit, push, and poke other students many more times than Kathy. Donna probably learned these responses as a means of getting what she wanted. Furthermore, she very likely gets what she wants—the teacher's attention, first place in the lunch line, or Bryan's soccer ball—through aggression more easily than by friendlier methods. An immense amount of research on the antecedents and consequences of aggression tells us that there are two major ways in which aggressive reactions are learned: (1) vicariously, by observation of the performance and consequences of aggression by others, and (2) by

Aggression is learned by observing the performance and consequences of aggression by others. (Erika Stone)

the direct reinforcement of aggressive responses. We may suppose that if children never saw aggressive acts in their environment and were never reinforced for trying out such acts themselves, you would see very little of such behavior in your school and classroom. However, we know that opportunities for the observation and practice of a variety of harmful behaviors are everywhere. How does it come about that some students use these responses much more frequently than others?

Social models for aggression

Models for aggressive solutions to interpersonal conflict are a continual source of information for American children on "how to do it better." As we indicated earlier, television is a constant teacher. In several studies of TV violence, 80 percent of the programs surveyed included at least one incident of violence. Cartoons for young children had the highest frequency, with thirty instances of violence per hour (Gerbner, 1972; Stein & Friedrich, 1975). These studies do not even include the more subtle forms of hostility such as insults, derogatory remarks, and aggressive humor. Furthermore, the "good guys" show as much aggression as the "bad guys," but they are less often punished for it (Stein & Friedrich, 1975). Available research shows clearly that when children observe unpunished aggressive acts, their subsequent aggressive behavior increases. In addition, continued observation of violence reduces the child's emotional empathy or feelings of sympathy for the victim of the violence (Berkowitz, 1973).

Family models: Parents are teachers

Parents themselves provide a second source of observational learning about how to be aggressive. Under the guise of discipline, the use of physical punishment such as hitting, slapping, or using a belt is reported by 93 percent of American parents; 50 percent report using such punishment by the time a child is only a year old, and 52 percent are still using real or threatened physical punishment with high school seniors (Parke & Collmer, 1975). You can see that physical punishment is extremely common in American society. Ted's parents, who use it exclusively or in preference to other methods, have children who are rated in school as unusually high on aggression against their peers (Lefkowitz et al., 1972). Continued physical punishment provides Ted with a model of how to hurt others, especially if they are smaller than he is. The use of physical punishment on into adolescence will also increase Ted's hostility and anger and increases the likelihood that he will use aggression against others (Parke & Collmer, 1975). From TV, movies, books, parents, and peers, Ted and many other children learn a variety of techniques for hurting and injuring others. While Ted is not aggressive in every situation, he may use the behaviors he has observed when he is angry, frustrated in obtaining his goals, or in conflict with others.

Reinforcement of aggression: Three sources of encouragement

The reinforcement of aggressive reactions encourages further aggression. Ted has probably been rewarded in three ways for his aggression. First, his parents may have encouraged it by telling him to stand up for his rights and not let anyone "push him around." (His father wrestles and boxes with him every night after dinner.) Second, Ted usually gets what he wants when he pushes Kathy: he will elbow his way past her in the lunch line to reach for the biggest piece of pie. Finally, he may have been reinforced by Mary's squeal of disgust when he dangled a frog in her face and by your ten-minute lecture to him on proper classroom behavior. When he is quiet, he never gets this much attention! So you see, Ted is reinforced by others in many different ways for his disruptive and harmful tactics. All children observe violence and hostile behavior; those who are consistently reinforced for it are more likely to use it (Bandura, 1973).

Sex differences in aggressive behavior appear very early

Aggressive behavior is one of the few areas in which consistent sex differences are observed from about age 3 onward into adulthood. These persistent trends, combined with similar differences in lower animals, have led many theorists to conclude that males are biologically more aggressive than females. Go out to the playground or into the halls any day at school recess and you are likely to observe these differences yourself. Boys are shouting louder, pushing each other around, wrestling and jostling. Girls may be running and playing actively or just talking to each other. Kathy and Donna do push and pull each other, but less frequently and less vigorously than the boys. When girls observe films about fighting, they even report seeing less violence than do boys (Maccoby & Wilson, 1957). On the other hand, when the incentive or payoff for the use of aggressive responses is high, girls do perform as vigorously as boys (Bandura, 1965). When boys and girls are asked about how anxious or concerned they feel about showing aggression, girls report more discomfort (Sears, 1961). Have girls been socialized to be ladylike and nonaggressive, or are they "by nature" less violent? As a teacher, you can expect the boys in your classes to engage in open fighting and disruptive activity more often. But don't be surprised if you find Donna and Sue slugging it out in the halls one day. Some girls use aggressive behavior as often as some boys.

We don't have any magic formula you can use to transform the behavior of the student who reacts toward others with hurtful or destructive behaviors. However, there are many alternative teaching practices that may work for you. Your success with any technique will depend upon your students' learning background, their expectancies for getting what

GUIDELINES
FOR
TEACHING

**Coping with
Aggressive Behavior**

they want from aggression, and their present skills in using cooperative behavior. What you do need is a wide range of alternatives, so that you do not give up on students who continue to fight and shout insults after you have asked them politely to "behave like responsible people." We offer you eleven do's and don't to try out when dealing with students' aggression.

- *Don't allow unsupervised fighting to continue.* Every available research study supports the finding that violence produces violence. When you tell yourself that "boys will be boys" and turn your back on student fights, you are encouraging another round of the same behavior.
- *Don't accept the student's "justification" for fighting.* Indeed, it may be true that Donna took Kathy's lunch money, put her foot out and tripped her in the hall, or called her mother a name. However, *no* reason can justify a knock-down fight. If Donna continues to support her fighting with statements that her opponents (or victims) "deserved what they got," then she is more likely to fight again next time (Berkowitz, 1973).
- *Don't substitute one form of fighting for another.* Don't encourage students who slug it out on the playground to slug it out with boxing gloves on the gym floor instead. Research evidence is very clear about this point: "letting it all out" by means of competitive contact sports, hitting a pillow or a bobo doll, or telling people how angry you are does

Teachers can encourage and reinforce prosocial alternatives to aggression. (C. Higgins/Photo Researchers)

not reduce further aggression. At times, these pressure reducers seem to make people feel better. Retaliation, or getting even with your opponent, also reduces your anger immediately. However, it also increases the chance that you will retaliate again. Students who are encouraged to substitute one form of aggression for another only complicate their interpersonal problems. They do not learn new ways of solving their conflict.

- *Don't punish aggression with physical aggression.* This means that students who are paddled for fighting learn who has the power. They *don't* learn why they should try not to fight. They also learn to be angry at you and less willing to cooperate in finding a peaceful solution.

Now that you know what not to do, let's consider some constructive approaches to aggressive behavior.

- *Do encourage and reinforce prosocial alternatives to aggressive behavior.* Help students to share, cooperate, take turns, discuss their disagreements, or negotiate solutions that are agreeable to all. Let them know that compromise is not necessarily defeat. Frequently, students do not have any behaviors other than aggression that are acceptable to them. Punishing or reprimanding them without teaching them new ways of behaving will not be an effective strategy.
- *Do help students to look at the other person's point of view.* Help students to understand the reasons for other people's behavior or for your rules. When students feel that you or others have been arbitrary, unreasonable, or unfair, they are more likely to react with hostility and aggression (Malik & McCandless, 1961). When they are helped to understand how others might feel about being victimized or disturbed, they are more likely to attempt to establish some self-control (Hoffman, 1970).
- *Do try to make certain that students' aggression is not reinforced.* One good way to do this is to use "overcorrection" techniques. If Ted snatches Alice's dessert from her tray, he will be expected to stand in line twice and get her two desserts (Foxx & Azrin, 1972). After that, he won't try that tactic for a while. A similar method is to expect "restitution": students who break windows or damage school property can be asked to work to repay the damage.
- *Do try using short, temporary consequences to suppress aggressive behavior as soon as it occurs.* Give a quiet, mild verbal reproof, remove students who fight from the halls or playground, or ask them to sit separately until they calm down. Be sure to read Chapter 5 on punishment before you try it. The point in using mild punishers is to let your students know that disruptive behavior will not be allowed but avoid providing them with an aggressive model.

• *Do, with younger children, deal with fighting first by distracting them into another activity.* Not every fight needs to be moderated, judged, and juried. Frequently, the parties to small disagreements are successfully distracted with a new activity (Brown & Elliot, 1965).

• *Do try to organize your classroom environment so that students are not under extreme stress.* Aggressive responses are more likely to erupt when students are hungry, tired, bored, fearful, frustrated in reaching their goals, disappointed by missing a field trip, or angry at your arbitrary rules. Your sensitive observation of their reactions to your management policies will probably give you some clues.

• *Help your students to discriminate between responsible self-assertiveness and harmful aggressiveness.* Donna can stand up for her personal rights and express herself without hurting or degrading Kathy. Instead of telling Kathy ''Shut up, you don't know what you are talking about,'' Donna might say ''Excuse me, I'd like to finish what I'm saying'' (Lange & Jakubowski, 1976).

You can be helpful to students in rephrasing their requests to you so that they use ASSERTIVE BEHAVIOR rather than resorting to aggression, and you can help them to ask for what they want in prosocial ways. You can also model this responsible, assertive behavior for your students by acting in a responsible, assertive manner yourself rather than timidly or aggressively.

=== **PROBE 3-8** ===

Ted and Kathy are arguing over the new art materials. Kathy has laid them out carefully and says she has an important project to complete. When Ted grabs two of her paint tubes, she pushes him angrily and he falls over a chair to the floor. Other students egg Ted on to ''give it to Kathy.'' You are their teacher and you must develop a plan right away. Use as many of our suggestions as you can to help Kathy, Ted, and the rest of the class to solve this problem constructively. Try role-playing this situation with another person and see how comfortable you feel in using different strategies. Then reverse your roles. Try playing Kathy or Ted and see how it feels when the other person (who is now role-playing the teacher) says different things to you.

Study 3-2 suggests how both a teacher and a student can learn to be responsibly assertive. Students who can use responsible assertive skills successfully with both adults and peers are well on their way to effective self-management and high self-esteem.

STUDY 3-2: PRACTICING AND TEACHING ASSERTIVENESS AND INDEPENDENCE

Though the high school teacher had laid out explicit guidelines for the term paper, the student nonassertively presented himself as a helpless victim: "I don't know where to start. How should I start off the paper? I don't understand about linking paragraphs together. What would be a good topic for the paper? Would you give me some ideas on how to end it?" The student did not even try to help himself. The teacher rescued the student, denied her own needs, and ended up essentially writing the paper for the student. The teacher then became the victim and felt trapped, manipulated, and angry. The next time the teacher saw the student, she aggressively criticized him in class. Predictably, the student became the aggressive persecutor, accusing the teacher of being unclear, never giving help, favoring other students, expecting too much from the student, and so on.

In this case, if either the teacher or student had acted assertively, the entire scene could have been prevented. If the student had assertively asked for help, the teacher would not have felt manipulated and then become abusively aggressive. For example:

Student: I've started my rough draft of the paper and it's going fairly well. I've gotten stuck in one spot though, and would appreciate it if you could help me learn some more interesting ways of starting the lead sentence. I'm also having trouble linking the paragraphs together. Here's what I've done so far. How does it look to you?

If the teacher had assertively set limits when the student played the nonassertive victim, the rescuer-persecutor-victim triangle would have been avoided.

Teacher: I'm willing to give you help on your paper. However, I am uncomfortable giving you all the help you want when at this point you haven't done any work at all on the paper. If you would start a rough draft, I'd be willing to help you learn how you can improve it.

Source: Lange, A. J., & Jakubowski, P. *Responsible assertive behavior.* Champaign, Ill.: Research Press, 1976.

SELF-REGULATION

Wouldn't you be pleased if all your students could pace themselves through a day's activities without constant supervision, reminders, reprimands, and monitoring? Wouldn't you be happy to see students following their independent learning schedules, sharing materials and responsibilities on group projects, taking turns in class discussion and in recess play, keeping their eyes on their own papers when taking tests, and helping fellow students? When students can perform a variety of socially expected behaviors without external supervision, we can say that they have learned SELF-REGULATION or self-management (Bandura, 1977; Thoreson & Mahoney, 1974).

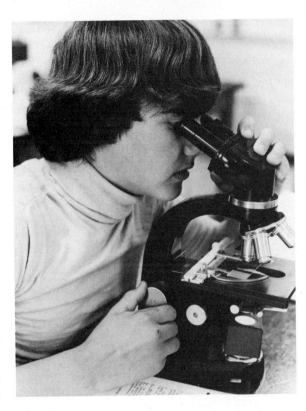

Students who are high on self-regulation skills are well on their way to independent, responsible adulthood. (Suzanne Szasz)

LEARNING SELF-REGULATION

In order to achieve SELF-REGULATION in a great many situations, Kathy has to master two very broad tasks. First, she must learn to inhibit or delay behaviors which are immediately gratifying and frequently attractive to her. Here, self-regulation means that she resists the temptation to take Bryan's lunch money from his desk, to lie to her mother about what she did after school, to cheat on her math test, or to hit Donna in the hall. In each instance, she avoids breaking a number of school and parent rules even though no one is there to check on her behavior.

Second, you notice that Kathy engages in some prosocial behaviors which do not appear to pay off immediately. That is, Kathy (1) helps you straighten up the bookshelves, (2) shares her toys and games, (3) studies and works on assignments, (4) contributes some pennies to the Easter Seal box, and (5) gives up her time to help Donna with math. None of these activities may be immediately rewarding to Kathy and they all require her to give up something she might have preferred to do. Students who are relatively high on self-regulation skills are well on their way to independent, responsible adulthood.

Kathy's early training in self-regulation was provided by her parents. They had the job of teaching her not to use undesirable behavior in many situations as well as to engage in positive, prosocial behavior. What an enormous task! Entire books have been written on this process. Let us see if we can boil it down to just three major procedures which must occur if effective self-regulation is to take place. Since Kathy is relatively high on self-regulation skills by comparison with others her age, her parents probably (1) set clear rules and followed them up with consistent, mostly positive consequences, (2) provided reasons and rationales for their rules, and (3) set a good example of self-regulated behavior by their own actions. Take a brief look at each of these three procedures.

First, it is clear that effective self-regulation starts with consistent external regulation. Kathy's parents probably got together and decided upon many rules for household living, self-care, family relationships, and community behavior. They decided when she had followed or broken these rules. They praised her "good" (rule-following) behavior and probably punished her "bad" (rule-breaking) behavior. They gave her this training in an atmosphere of warmth and positive concern. Kathy learned to avoid displeasing them and tried to do things that would bring expressions of love and approval from her parents. Children who are rated high in self-control skills in school have parents who very early provide clear rules and who enforce these rules consistently and positively (Baumrind, 1973; Burton, Maccoby, & Allinsmith, 1961).

Second, Kathy's parents began to label her behavior to help her discriminate ("You were careful, careless, clean, dirty, selfish, sharing") and to give her feedback on what she did right and wrong (Aronfreed, 1968). They also gave her reasons for their rules and frequently indicated to Kathy how her behavior might affect other people ("It hurts Donna when you hit her"). In this manner, Kathy was learning to label her own good and bad behavior, to give herself reasons for her actions, and to become concerned for the welfare of others (Hoffman, 1970). This type of training helped Kathy to set standards or rules for her own behavior and to reinforce herself for meeting those standards. We shall see in the next section that these are sometimes referred to as "moral standards." In Chapters 5, 6, and 7 we will discuss how these standards are similar to *mediating links* that help Kathy to anticipate the consequences of her behavior. For effective self-regulation to take place, Kathy must be able to anticipate future behavior and thus to regulate it in advance.

Finally, we know that Kathy's parents must provide her with appropriate modeling of the behavior they wish her to adopt. By setting high standards for their own behavior, by using calm reasoning and personal control, by demonstrating responsibility, kindness, and sharing, they provide a model of appropriate self-control.

SELF-REGULATION AND MORAL BEHAVIOR

If Kathy had all of the self-regulation behaviors we have described, she would be a pretty unusual person. Most students (and most people) are probably not honest, helpful, responsible, cooperative, generous, and kindly all of the time in every situation. You can expect to have students in your class who show these behaviors more consistently than do other students (Burton, 1976). However, most studies show that different forms of self-regulated behavior are not very predictable for any one student in differing situations. For example, in a large study of over 1100 children's honesty scores across many situations, Harteshorne and May (1928) found that it was difficult to predict whether the same student would lie or cheat from one task to another. That is, students who cheated on a math problem might not do so on an English test. These researchers concluded that "honest" behavior in these contexts was determined more by the situation than by the individual.

In many more recent studies, self-regulation has been found to be determined not only by whatever self-management skills the student may have but also by the following factors: (1) the probability of being detected or observed ("Is the teacher looking?"); (2) the value of the outcome for the student ("Will this help my test grade?"); (3) the importance of the outcome ("I really want to get a high grade"); (4) the behavior of others in that situation ("I saw Sally cheat also"); as well as many other situational factors (Aronfreed, 1968; Becker, 1964; Burton, 1976).

The situational influences on self-regulated action suggest that none of your students will be totally self-managing individuals. They will be honest, helpful, and responsible in some situations and not in others. Therefore, we must caution you to resist the temptation yourself to label students as "helpful" or "selfish," "honest" or "deceitful." We have stressed before that labels about behavior are never accurate for every situation in which your students will find themselves. Negative labels are often damaging to a student's self-esteem. Labeling a youngster as deceitful because you caught her once in a lie may encourage her to use that behavior again, since she'll figure that you obviously don't trust her anyway. Labeling may become "self-fulfilling" in that students may begin to match their behavior to your labels.

Self-regulation and moral judgment

We pointed out earlier that Kathy's parents gave her rules about "good" and "bad" behavior and some reasons for following these rules. Kohlberg (1964, 1976) has described this reasoning process in terms of MORAL JUDGMENT, or verbal standards of right and wrong. Kohlberg believes that many aspects of self-regulated behavior are influenced by the level of a person's moral judgment. He has developed a six-stage scale for

Table 3-3. Levels and Stages of Moral Judgment

Level	Stage of Reasoning
Preconventional	1. You should obey authority and avoid punishment. Good or bad behavior is judged by its consequences.
	2. You should serve your own needs but recognize that others have needs as well.
Conventional	3. You should follow the golden rule, placing emphasis on interpersonal conformity to gain approval and to be a "nice" person.
	4. You should conform in order to maintain the social system. Social order would break down "if everyone did it."
Postconventional or principled	5. You have an obligation to abide by the law for the welfare and protection of everyone. The guideline is "The greatest good for the greatest number of people." Personal values are relative.
	6. You choose to follow the ethical principles of universal justice, equality, and respect for human beings as individuals.

Adapted from: Kohlberg, L. Moral stages and moralization: The cognitive developmental approach. In T. Lickona (Ed.), *Moral development and behavior,* New York: Holt, 1976.

describing the development of moral judgment (see Table 3-3). Kohlberg's scale assumes that these stages are universal in all societies and that they progress with age. Accordingly, Kohlberg also suggests that teachers should take an active role in increasing the level of their students' moral reasoning. By exposing them to examples of reasoning at higher levels than those at which they are presently functioning, the level of students' moral judgment should increase (Kohlberg & Mayer, 1972; Scharf, 1978). In this manner, Kathy should become more helpful, honest, and self-regulated as she moves to higher stages of moral judgment. In general, research has shown a very modest relationship between Kohlberg's moral stages and actual self-regulation behavior (Kurtines & Grief, 1974; Mischel & Mischel, 1976). Does this mean that Kathy's standards of judgment about right and wrong do not influence her behavior?

Let us suggest that Kohlberg's levels of moral development operate like any other standards or rules for behavior. Moral standards may represent one type of rule or criterion that Kathy will use when judging her own actions or those of others. To the extent that other factors are important to Kathy, she may or may not follow her expressed verbal standards. Saying and doing are thus two different things. As with other learned behaviors, moral judgments are subject to modeling and reinforcement effects (Brody, 1977; Dorr & Fry, 1974; Tracy & Cross, 1973). One of your concerns may be to help students clarify and profitably use their own standards to guide behavior without imposing your personal beliefs on them. It may also be helpful to encourage students to discuss the reasons for following different kinds of self-regulated behavior. By means of group discussion, children may be exposed to many differing kinds of reasoning processes that will guide them in forming more flexible and mature standards for themselves.

SELF-MANAGEMENT SKILLS

As a teacher, you will want to know how you can facilitate the effective development of these many self-regulation skills. Just as with any social behavior, specific competencies in self-management can be taught by means of social learning principles (Bandura, 1977; Mischel & Mischel, 1976; Liebert, Poulos, & Strauss, 1974). Certain of these behaviors that directly affect your classroom management will be of more interest to you than others. You may be more eager to have Kathy refrain from cheating on your math test than to play fair at Monopoly against her brother at home or to avoid cheating in Mr. Dunn's classroom. You can help students to develop self-regulation in specific situations by teaching them self-management skills. Kathy can learn to manage her own behavior in test-taking situations by, among other tactics, keeping her eyes on her own paper.

Self-management and personal values

We have been using the term *self-management* to apply to a specific set of procedures for teaching self-regulation in any particular situation. As with many social behaviors, you will find that deciding upon appropriate self-management skills may involve your values or beliefs about what is right or wrong. At times your values may conflict with your students' values and with those of their parents. In your encouragement of any of these self-management skills, remember that what you judge to be right and good may conflict with what your students believe is right. We shall discuss value conflicts in Chapter 8 and suggest some ways to bring these appropriately into your teaching activities.

===== **PROBE 3-9** =====

Select two student behaviors or classroom situations that might involve a value conflict between you and your students. State your position on each situation. Now try to state the position of the student.

Procedures in teaching self-management

Procedures for self-management involve a set of very teachable skills. These skills can be taught to students by classroom teachers such as you and have been shown to be effective in helping students to maintain their own behavior (McLaughlin, 1976). You can teach young people like Kathy to follow these four steps to self-management:

1. *Observe and describe their own behavior* ("What did I do?") and *record its frequency* ("How often do I do it?").

2. *Set standards or goals for their behavior* ("What should I do? Why should I do it?").

3. *Anticipate the consequences of alternative things they might do* ("What will happen if I do this? What has happened in the past?").

4. *Monitor their progress and evaluate their behavior.* In this step, youngsters like Kathy will administer self-reinforcement when their behavior meets their goals ("Did I meet my standards or fall short of them? Did I like what I did or do I feel badly? Am I ready to take my break?") (Bandura, 1976; Grusec & Kuczynski, 1977; Kanfer, 1972; Mahoney & Thoreson, 1974; Mischel, 1976).

Each of the four self-management skills requires that you be a knowledgeable manager of the learning environment. Your students may not learn these procedures without your competent guidance. You will want to keep in mind some guidelines to ensure the success of your program to teach self-management.

GUIDELINES FOR TEACHING

Facilitating Self-Management Skills

• *Watch out for student value systems that differ from your own.* When you develop self-management programs for specific behaviors, value conflicts can occur. Use these as material for class discussion and role-playing procedures. If fighting is necessary in Ike's neighborhood to "save face," recognize this and deal with it openly.

• *Avoid labeling students with evaluative terms.* Always describe the specific desirable or undesirable behavior and the situation in which it occurred. Don't tell Donna that she is lazy. Rather, suggest to her that she can learn to plan her work periods more efficiently.

• *Look for the situational determinants of your student's behavior.* Try to adjust events that interfere with effective self-management. When, for example, would Donna be more likely to stray from her task and read her comic books instead of her math text?

• *Help students to set personal goals that are within their capabilities for accomplishment.* Can Donna be expected to show the same self-management skills as Kathy?

• *Encourage students to anticipate the consequences of their behavior, both for themselves and for others.* Has Ike considered what will happen after he plays truant for two weeks?

- *Provide specific behavior feedback to students that they can use to evaluate their behavior.* Encourage students to use self-grading and self-evaluation procedures.
- *Be certain that your words match your actions.* Meet the standards you set for yourself. Let your students observe you as a model of self-regulation for any behavior you wish them to achieve. Do you, for instance, yell at Donna and pound on the desk when she turns her back on you?

SELF-COMPETENCY AND SELF-ESTEEM

When students can describe themselves as competent and successful on a skill which is important to them, we can say that they have SELF-COMPETENCY for that skill. Self-competency on any skill involves the student's evaluation of these skills and his or her expectancies for future achievement. Our observations of Kathy have shown her to demonstrate many of the interpersonal skills that are effective in making friends and in relating to others in work and play groups. She also demonstrates many of the specific skills that facilitate achievement, self-regulation, and prosocial activities. You may recall that in some areas Kathy is probably not satisfied with herself and does not expect to succeed. However, the positive self-evaluation of skills outweighs the negative, and we can say that Kathy is relatively high on SELF-ESTEEM. When students describe themselves as competent on many skills that they consider important, we judge them to be high in self-esteem. You may observe that such students appear "self-confident," or you may tell their parents that these students seem to "feel good" about themselves. The diagram in Figure 3-8 shows the relationship between self-esteem and self-competency. As Kathy becomes more skilled at many activities in many situations, her self-esteem increases.

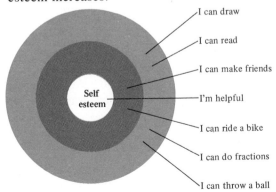

**Figure 3-8
Self-esteem grows
with self-
competency.**

I can draw
I can read
I can make friends
Self esteem
I'm helpful
I can ride a bike
I can do fractions
I can throw a ball

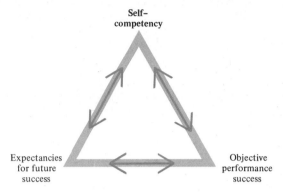

**Figure 3-9
Diagram of the
relationship
between a student's
self-competency,
expectancies for
future success, and
actual performance
success.**

IMPORTANCE OF SELF-COMPETENCY

The importance of self-competency in your students is threefold. First, Kathy's positive self-evaluation promotes a positive approach to school and academic activities (Barclay, 1974). Students like and enjoy school more when they evaluate themselves positively and tell themselves that they are doing well. Second, this positive evaluation spreads or generalizes to skills other than the ones on which Kathy feels specifically competent. This means her expectancies for success on new tasks will increase as she meets with more success. Following successful performances, Kathy's self-evaluation increases. In this manner, we find a relationship between measures of self-esteem and most school subjects (Purkey, 1976). Students who are successful in school tend to evaluate themselves more highly than students who are less successful. You can see that this results in a circular relationship, where self-competency and actual performance success feed into each other. This relationship is shown in Figure 3-9. Indeed, when students are compared across grades on self-competency for school ability, you can see (Figure 3-10) that the successful school achievers (class grades) increase their self-evaluation in this skill domain while the unsuccessful achievers progressively lower theirs (Kifer, 1975).

Finally, a student's positive self-evaluation relates to his or her prosocial behavior in many situations. Since Kathy expects to be generally competent, successful, and accepted by others, she is less likely to resort to problem or deviant tactics. In contrast, students who are referred for problem behavior by teachers and parents are often low in self-competency in many areas. Boys with low self-esteem are described by their mothers as having more disruptive behaviors than are boys with high self-esteem (Coopersmith, 1967). If Donna does not expect to obtain your positive attention by good class work, she may talk, giggle, and disrupt the lesson frequently. Chapters 11 and 12 discuss problem behaviors and how you can handle them in your class setting.

DEVELOPING SELF-COMPETENCY AND SELF-ESTEEM

We are talking here about both special skills and a broad and inclusive self-evaluation that cuts across many skills in numerous contexts. Specific self-competency increases as students develop realistic skills in any of the social, academic, physical-motor, or career areas we have been discussing. As you can see from Figure 3-8, these self-competencies are additive and cumulative. However, since a generalized self-esteem does not depend upon any one skill or situation, it develops slowly. Further, a person's positive or negative self-evaluation is subject to change throughout the life span as new experiences occur and are added to or subtracted from the current set of self-competencies. Two major processes provide a framework for children's reactions to themselves: the responses of significant others to their behavior and a SOCIAL COMPARISON between themselves and their peers.

Developing self-competency: Significant others

First, Kathy's parents and family gave her positive feedback about herself in the form of praise, warmth, and reinforcement for accomplishment. They also placed reasonable demands on her for appropriate behavior and followed through with firm enforcement. In addition, her parents themselves demonstrated high self-esteem (Coopersmith, 1967). Once she arrives at school, she will be exposed to many different teachers, each with individual ways of reinforcing or criticizing her behavior. Each time you tell Kathy, "That's a good answer," or "No, that's not right," you

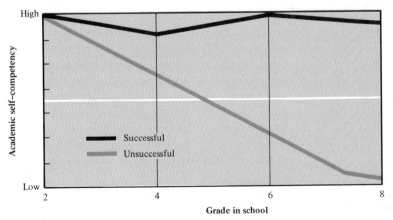

Figure 3-10 Self-competency for ability at academic tasks for students from grades 2 through 8. Students who are successful in school remain high on self-competency. Among students who continue to be unsuccessful in school, academic self-competency declines dramatically. (Adapted from E. Kifer, "Relationship between Academic Achievement and Personality Characteristics: A Quasi-Longitudinal Study, *American Educational Research Journal,* **1975, 12, 191–210.)**

are giving her feedback which tells her something about her work, her behavior, and herself. From either of these statements, she might conclude "I am smart" or "I am dumb." Kathy's peers give her feedback as well in the form of approval or rejection of what she does. As a result of repeated home and school experience with success and failure, Kathy begins to develop her own standards for achievement, sociability, or physical skills. At the same time, she is learning to evaluate her own performances and to reinforce herself with feelings of self-confidence and success for meeting her own standards.

Social comparison and self-evaluation

A second process of SOCIAL COMPARISON influences Kathy's learning of self-evaluation. She began to watch other children and compared her emerging skills and physical attributes with theirs. The resulting combination of high positive regard from others, meeting her personal achievement standards, and a favorable comparison of her skills with those of her peers produced a positive self-competency for Kathy.

Self-esteem changes with school exposure

Individual differences on measures of self-esteem between Kathy and her peers began to appear as early as kindergarten (Purkey, 1976). It is especially interesting that student self-competency for academic tasks is relatively high in the early primary grades but tends to decline by third grade (see Figure 3-10; Kifer, 1975). Both realism (objective accomplishments) and a broadened social comparison (peer accomplishments) may dominate as students move through school. Since many factors contribute to academic achievement besides self-competency, you will find some students with high self-esteem who fail to succeed in school (Brookover, Erickson, & Joiner, 1967). For these students, school may be irrelevant, uninteresting, or unresponsive to their needs. Conversely, you will have some students with high academic achievement who nevertheless evaluate themselves in a negative manner. Too often, these are students with high standards for accomplishment whose performance seldom matches their goals. When students set goals that are far above their accomplishments, they may interpret their objective successes as personal failures. We shall have more to say about this problem in Chapter 6. In either case, you can see that self-esteem is a helpful but not necessary condition for successful school achievement.

PROMOTING SELF-COMPETENCY SKILLS

Of course, you want your students to feel good about themselves. How do you know whether Kathy and Donna are high in self-competency? You can ask them, make your own observations, or ask their peers. Kathy comes up with statements such as "I can," "I like," or "I'm best at," which are all positive statements of ability. Donna, on the other hand, says "I can't," "I don't want to," or "I'm not too good at that." These negative statements reflect her low evaluation of her skill in particular situations. You realize that either girl may have higher self-competency for some skills than for others. This is important. Donna's self-competency for math can be changed if she is given specific successful experience in math. But she is unlikely to improve in general self-evaluation simply by becoming a better math student.

Increasing the level of self-competency

As Donna's teacher, you have decided by means of interview and observation that Donna needs some strengthening of her self-competency skills. Where will you start? Teachers have generally taken two courses of action in dealing with low self-esteem. Some teachers (and experts) suggest that you need to "accept the whole child." This approach assumes that when Donna feels loved and accepted, she will automatically have high self-esteem and self-confidence. We believe that the evidence is generally contrary to this point of view. Of course, as a facilitator of positive growth, you will want to give all your students the notion that you like them as people and you are glad they are in your class. However, your unconditional acceptance of Donna will not alter the fact that her math skills are low, she gives up easily, and she feels that no one likes her. Therefore, you add specific training in skill development to remediate her deficits. Each time you teach and reinforce new skills, Donna will "feel better" about herself and her self-competency will increase. For a student with low self-esteem, it may take many, many trials of experiences with positive feedback and objective success before she changes her level of self-evaluation. Here, your broad goal is to change Donna's statements of "I can't" to an objective statement that says "I can!" However, this outcome is the product of realistic change and the development of new skills (Becker, Engelmann, & Thomas, 1975a). Therefore, we believe that student self-competency will result from your successful application of the teaching approaches suggested throughout this book.

As students become more skilled at many activities, their self-esteem increases. (Peter Vandermark, Stock, Boston)

Let us look at some of the broad approaches you will use in your program to teach self-competency skills. Specific methods for implementing these ideas will come later.

• *Organize your classroom so that all students can succeed.* Since success—not failure—leads to further expectancies for success, it is your job to ensure that success will occur. Your programs for success can emphasize mastery of academic, interpersonal, or physical-motor skills. The opportunities to program for accomplishment and skill development are there in your class: find them and use them.

• *Be alert for opportunities to reinforce and praise successful perform-ances.* Don't assume that students "ought to be" working, paying attention, and trying hard. Develop your skills in providing constructive and positive feedback and use them freely when student performance indicates increased effort, persistence, and success.

• *Help students to make constructive use of failure.* They can use past failures to assess their skills, readjust their goals, and employ alternative methods of attack to solve problems. Continual failure will produce low self-esteem, discouragement, and refusal to try again. However, the constructive use of failure can be instructive to students when it provides realistic feedback on the quality of their responses. We shall consider the constructive use of failure more specifically in Chapter 6.

• *Remember that the same steps that teach effective achievement and self-management will also contribute to the development of self-esteem.* To refresh your recall, these steps are accurate assessment of one's capabilities, setting of realistic goals that match these abilities, persistence at tasks, and self-reinforcement for attaining one's goals. These are all separately teachable skills that students can apply to any learning activity.

In the role of teacher, learning manager, and facilitator of growth, you can do much to contribute to student self-competency. In the long run, however, each student must learn to manage his or her own living environment with self-esteem for present activities and confidence in the future.

**LEARNING ACTIVITY:
COUNTING BEHAVIORS YOU
OBSERVE**

OBJECTIVES

After reading Chapters 1, 2, and 3 and the instructions for this learning activity, you will be able to:

1. Select an observable behavior or pattern of behaviors.
2. Define specific, countable behaviors to observe.
3. Record the frequency of these behaviors on a tally chart.
4. Compare the response frequencies for verbal and physical response patterns.
5. Compare the response frequency for two or more persons.
6. Make a judgment for the situation in which the behavior appears. Would you like to see the behaviors increase, decrease, or remain about the same?

WHY COUNT BEHAVIORS?

Let us say you are interested in how frequently Bryan, Donna, and Jim participate in class. On the basis of your casual observation, you notice that Bryan asks lots of questions and Donna doesn't seem to have anything to say. If you wish to plan a way to increase Donna's class participation, you will need to know more precisely how often she participates, under what conditions, and what happens after she does, if ever, raise her hand. The procedures for determining the answers to these questions are quite similar for a great many student behaviors. For instance, you also notice that each time there is a fight or argument in class or in the halls, Ted seems to be in the middle of it. Before you send Ted to the principal, call his parents, or punish him severely, you ought to determine just how often Ted actually does fight and what seems to be happening at the time. For each of these two *response patterns*—participation and fighting—and for many others as well, you can use similar methods of counting and then recording these behavior counts.

WHAT KINDS OF BEHAVIOR CAN BE COUNTED?

In your own classroom, you will want to determine frequency counts when you observe student behaviors that appear (1) inadequate, (2) inappropriate, or (3) intolerable for that situation. *Inadequate* behaviors are those which are unskilled or appear infrequently (Donna seldom speaks up in class). *Inappropriate* behaviors are those which are disruptive to student or classroom goals and interfere with learning (Bryan's yelling is fine on the playground, but his yelling throughout a class discussion is disruptive). *Intolerable* behaviors are those which you cannot accept anywhere because they interfere with the safety or rights of others (Ted's punching and kicking others is helpful to no one).

HOW TO USE BEHAVIOR COUNTS

You can use your frequency counts to determine one of the following:

1. How does this student's behavior compare with that of others in

your class? (Are Paula and Donna really that quiet in class or do you have a whole roomful of nonparticipants?)

2. Would it be helpful for that student or for your classroom environment to plan a behavior change strategy? Would your class discussion go more smoothly if Bryan raised his hand before blurting out? If a change is indicated, do you and the student involved wish to increase or decrease that behavior? You and each of the students involved might decide that Bryan could raise his hand more and Ted could be fighting less.

3. If you and the students do decide to make some changes, how effective are your procedures? If you decide to look at Bryan and call on him only when his hand is raised, does that really change his blurting out in class? Your behavior counts over time will give you this information. You can evaluate your strategy by means of your behavior counts.

RECORDING YOUR OBSERVATIONS

You have selected a response pattern to observe and you have carefully defined each of the behaviors you will include so that it is observable and countable. You can use the sample tally chart, Figure 3-11, to record your behavior counts, or you can construct one of your own. Some teachers use a golf counter strapped to the wrist to clock off frequencies for one or two particular students. Students can chart their own behavior with cards taped to their desks. Each time Paula speaks up in class, she can give herself a check mark. If you are counting behaviors at the same time each day—math class, for example—you will be in a position to set your information on a graph for ready reading. Chapter 6 will include a learning activity on developing graphs to display your observations.

TASK 3-1

Select a TV program with plenty of action, preferably one which is shown during the time schoolchildren might watch. Set up a tally chart and count the total frequency of aggressive or fighting behaviors. Divide your chart into two sections: "verbal insults or criticism" and "physical aggression" (hitting, punching, kicking, shouting, and so on). How do these two types of aggression compare? What do you think about the amount of fighting or aggression on TV programs that are available to school-age children? What kinds of behaviors are being modeled? Compare the frequencies for two persons on the program.

TASK 3-2

Select a second TV program which centers around a family situation. Set up a behavior chart to count the frequency of warmth or positive feedback

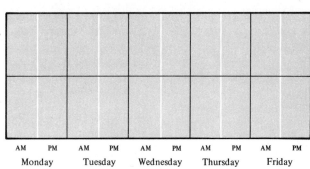

Verbal: praise, agreement, initiates contact, responds to question

Physical: pat, hug, handshake, smile, nods, etc.

| AM | PM | AM | PM | AM | PM | AM | PM | AM | PM |
| Monday | | Tuesday | | Wednesday | | Thursday | | Friday | |

**Figure 3-11
Sample behavior
tally chart.**

behaviors (praise, agreement, smiles, nods, hugs, and so on). Now divide your tally chart into verbal behaviors (telling others positive things) and physical behaviors (showing physical reactions or using ''body language'') as means of communicating warmth. How do the verbal and physical demonstrations compare here? What kinds of behaviors are being modeled here? Compare the frequencies of positive responsiveness between mother and father or between parent and child. What do you observe?

TASK 3-3

If you are in a classroom situation, select a response pattern and chart its frequency for thirty minutes each day at the same time over five observation days. If you are not placed in a classroom, select one of your own behaviors (for example, giving positive feedback to others) or that of a roommate or friend. Tally the frequency of this behavior for five consecutive days. Do the results look like you or your friend? Is this a response pattern you might wish to increase, decrease, or keep the same?

 **SUMMARY**

1. Social behavior can be described in terms of response patterns called TRAITS. A trait describes a student's typical behavior across similar situations. Typical social behaviors may change as situations alter. Traits clustered into larger patterns are called SOCIAL BEHAVIOR SYSTEMS. We can follow social development by describing the progression of each social behavior system across significant time periods of life. We suggest INTERPERSONAL COMPETENCE as a general goal for all students. Interpersonal competence includes broad social skills such as social responsibility, achievement, and independence.

2. SEX ROLES are learned patterns of behavior which generally match societal expectancies for approved ''masculine'' and ''feminine'' behaviors. Sex roles are also stereotypes which do not match most observed sex differences. Sex-role stereotypes include behaviors from different social behavior systems. Teachers and students tend

to stereotype these behaviors into the sex-role categories of "instrumental" for masculinity and "expressive" for femininity.

3. The observed behavior of boys and girls is more similar than it is different. When differences are found between boys and girls, these are mainly in the areas of ACHIEVEMENT SKILLS, AGGRESSIVE BEHAVIOR, and learning problems. These differences first appear at differing ages and are not clearly due to either biological or learning influences.

4. Schools in the past have accepted SEX-ROLE STEREOTYPING through curriculum, personnel, and administrative practices. Teachers and schools can do much to help alter these practices through awareness, clarification, and action programs.

5. AFFILIATION SKILLS are behaviors that include patterns of sociability, dependency, compliance, CONFORMITY, and responsiveness to social reinforcement. The peer group is an important source of affiliation for school-age children. PEER-GROUP SUPPORT takes the form of social reinforcement, acceptance, and status. Peers also provide social control through modeling and demands for CONFORMITY to peer-group norms.

6. Teachers can use peer-group processes productively to achieve teacher and student goals. Teachers can help students with status problems and low peer acceptance to interact positively with other students. Four ways to increase peer interaction are suggested for teachers who decide to take an active part in facilitating positive peer support.

7. INDEPENDENCE and ACHIEVEMENT SKILLS are separate but related systems of behavior. Students with independence skills show competence in taking initiative, assuming responsibility, making decisions, completing tasks, and showing ASSERTIVE BEHAVIOR. These are all teachable skills which contribute to effective achievement behaviors. In turn, ACHIEVEMENT behaviors lead to skill mastery in many activities. Students can be taught many important achievement behaviors such as persistence, trying hard, taking some risks, and striving for mastery. Sex differences in achievement relate mainly to differing expectancies for success among boys and girls. These expectancy differences may reflect cultural sex-role stereotyping. Teachers can encourage achievement behaviors by promoting persistence, mastery, and a POSITIVE EXPECTANCY for success.

8. AGGRESSIVE BEHAVIOR results in harm or injury to another person. Students learn aggressive responses vicariously by observing the aggressive performance of others. Aggressive responses are also learned by direct reinforcement of aggression. Boys have been observed to use more physical aggression than girls. Most students

use aggressive responses to resolve conflicts, to retaliate, or as a reaction to stress. We suggest ten procedures for reducing student aggression in school. Most importantly, we suggest that teachers model and support cooperative and prosocial alternatives to interpersonal conflict.

9. SELF-REGULATION occurs when students can perform a variety of socially expected behaviors without external supervision. Students can learn to use self-management procedures to avoid inappropriate behaviors and to engage in constructive prosocial activities. Self-management skills can be taught by means of a four-step procedure which is useful for modifying any social behavior.

10. SELF-COMPETENCY and SELF-ESTEEM result from realistic skill development in many areas of social, academic, and physical-motor behavior. The term *self-competency* describes a student's positive expectancy on a set of skills. *Self-esteem* is an umbrella term that describes positive self-evaluation resulting from the sum of student self-competencies. Teachers can encourage realistic self-competency by offering their students specific training in many important skills that contribute to objective social, physical, and academic competence. Student self-esteem is judged to be high when the student says "I can do that" about many skills. We suggest four guidelines for helping to increase self-competency and self-esteem.

11. Frequency counts of observable response patterns are useful for student behaviors that are inadequate, inappropriate, or intolerable. Behavior counts can be used in classrooms to compare students with others, to plan strategies for behavior change, and to evaluate the effectiveness of intervention.

 KEY
TERMS

ACHIEVEMENT SKILLS: Behaviors that contribute to attaining mastery on difficult tasks. Students high in achievement skills are likely to be competitive with self and others, to match their performance against standards of excellence, and to seek recognition.

AFFILIATION SKILLS: Behaviors that are effective in maintaining positive interpersonal relationships.

AGGRESSIVE BEHAVIOR: Physical and verbal behaviors intended to hurt or injure another person.

ANDROGYNY: Pattern of sex-role behaviors which includes characteristics of both masculinity (instrumental) and femininity (expressive). The androgynous person should perform more adaptively in a wide range of situations.

ASSERTIVE BEHAVIOR: Behaviors that are effective in obtaining personal goals without hurting or injuring others.

ATTACHMENT: The affectional bond between child and caretakers. Attachment is reflected in proximity-seeking behaviors such as looking, smiling, and following and by signs of distress when separated from primary caretakers.

CONFORMITY: Modeling behavior practiced in groups. When students conform to group norms, they match their behavior to what most of their group is doing.

INDEPENDENCE SKILLS: A set of self-initiated behaviors that result in completing tasks, making decisions, and obtaining important reinforcers without requiring help.

INTERPERSONAL COMPETENCE: A network of social skills that is appropriate at a particular age level. Baumrind included three markers of interpersonal competence: social responsibility, independence, and achievement orientation.

MORAL JUDGMENT: Verbal standards for evaluating right and wrong. Kohlberg has proposed a six-stage scale for describing the development of moral judgment.

PEER-GROUP SUPPORT: The degree of acceptance and status given by peers to individual students. Peer-group support can be measured by means of a sociometric test.

POSITIVE EXPECTANCY: A person's anticipation that the outcomes of his or her behavior will be positively reinforcing, or successful.

SELF-COMPETENCY: Students' evaluation of their skills and their expectancy for future achievement.

SELF-ESTEEM: Self-evaluation resulting from the sum of self-competencies on highly valued activities.

SELF-REGULATION: Performing a variety of socially expected behaviors without external supervision. Self-regulation includes skills in avoiding inappropriate behaviors and engaging in constructive, prosocial activities.

SEX ROLE: Sets of behaviors that, in a given culture, are judged to be more desirable for one sex than the other. Masculine sex roles include instrumental behaviors while feminine sex roles include expressive behaviors.

SEX-ROLE STEREOTYPING: A judgment about an individual's personal characteristics on the basis of gender or cultural sex roles.

SOCIAL BEHAVIOR SYSTEM: A cluster of similar goal-oriented behaviors that develops across a significant time period of an individual's life.

SOCIAL COMPARISON: Evaluating one's skills on the basis of the level of competency of peer reference groups.

TRAIT: A student's typical behavior across similar situations.

REVIEW KEY TERMS

DEVELOPMENT
LEARNING
MASTERY
MODEL
POSITIVE REINFORCEMENT

PROSOCIAL BEHAVIOR
SELF-MANAGEMENT
SOCIAL BEHAVIOR
STANDARDS

SELF TEST

1. The term *friendliness* stands for a trait and
   a. describes typical behaviors in many situations for a group of students
   b. describes how a student behaves all the time
   c. can never be used to describe any one student

d. describes one person's typical behavior in similar situations
2. Which of the following is most accurate?
   a. Boys and girls are more alike than they are different.
   b. Boys and girls are more different than they are alike.
   c. Boys are more aggressive and girls are more friendly.
   d. There are no differences between boys and girls in observed aggressive behavior.
3. Interpersonal competence includes three developmental patterns of behavior:
   a. _____
   b. _____
   c. _____
4. Schools have encouraged sex-role stereotyping by means of:
   a. textbooks which depict boys and girls in rigid roles
   b. curricula which are different for boys and girls
   c. counseling which tracks boys and girls into differing careers
   d. all of the above
5. Title IX of the equal education act states that (in your own words):
   _____
   _____
   _____
6. Three ways to reduce aggressive behaviors in schools are:

a. _____
b. _____
c. _____
7. Peers exert social control by means of:
   a. _____
   b. _____
   c. _____
8. Conformity to peer norms
   a. decreases in adolescence
   b. is higher in girls than in boys
   c. is a sign of emotional instability
   d. depends on many personal and situational factors
9. Students who are rated high on independence demonstrate skills in
   a. taking initiative
   b. completing tasks unaided
   c. self-assertiveness
   d. making decisions
   e. all of the above
10. Sex differences in achievement behavior suggest that:
    a. Boys underestimate their probability for success.
    b. Girls underestimate their probability for success.
    c. Boys and girls do not differ in expectancies for success.
    d. Boys take greater risks but lower their sights after failure.

SELF-TEST KEY
1. d
2. a
3. social responsibility, independence, achievement orientation
4. d
5. See text, Figure 3-5.
6. See text, "Guidelines for Teaching: Modifying Aggressive Behavior"
7. modeling, reinforcement, demands for conformity
8. d
9. e
10. b

CHAPTER 4

Development of Cognitive Skills

CHAPTER OUTLINE

LEARNING OBJECTIVES

After reading Chapter 4, answering the self-monitoring questions, completing the learning activity, and reading any further references of your choice, you will be able to:

1. Define and give examples of key terms.

2. Diagram and give examples of the S-M-R sequence in cognitive development.

3. Explain and compare how Bruner and Piaget account for changes in cognitive behavior at different developmental stages. List instructional applications and limitations of each theory.

4. Explain cognitive development in terms of Gagné's learning hierarchies, intellectual skills, and cognitive strategies. List instructional applications and limitations of Gagné's cumulative learning theory.

5. Describe how language contributes to cognitive development and symbolic mediation. Apply the concepts of modeling, feedback, and rules to account for the development of language structure and communications skills.

6. Distinguish between difference and deficit approaches to nonstandard English and match intervention strategies to each.

7. Explain how attention and self-instruction contribute to intellectual skills.

8. Contrast three views of intelligence. Match each approach with an appropriate use of measurements of intellectual skill in education. List the advantages and disadvantages of using intelligence tests in education to assess entering behaviors.

9. Compare two views of readiness for instruction. Contrast each view with the preassessment of entry behaviors in the basic teaching model. Describe intervention procedures which are suitable to each view. Summarize the results of early intervention for school readiness skills.

10. Develop, practice, and apply a set of systematic visual scanning skills.

FOCUS ON COGNITIVE DEVELOPMENT

As Bryan and Kathy progress through school, they will face a variety of learning activities that challenge their cognitive capabilities. At differing times in your teaching procedures, you may expect students like them to: (1) remember what they read or hear, (2) think about a problem before giving the answer, (3) understand the meaning of what they read, (4) know a variety of facts, (5) perceive the difference between *b* and *d*, (6) solve a problem in mathematics, (7) reason logically in their solutions, and (8) create a theme about their summer vacation. You may sometimes describe your students to others as "bright" or "slow." In doing so, you are making estimates of the general level of their intelligence. What do all these activities have in common? They are alternate ways of describing some of the competencies that appear during the course of a student's cognitive development.

Our discussion of cognitive development will begin by considering what we mean by the term *cognitive*. We shall introduce the concept of MEDIATION to describe cognitive activity. We will also propose that what develops in the course of cognitive change are skills in more effective mediation (Brown & DeLoache, 1978). We will then discuss cognitive development from three differing viewpoints: (1) structural stage theory as represented by Jean Piaget, (2) the stage-sequence approach of Jerome Bruner, and (3) the developmental learning theory of Robert Gagné. These three approaches will be compared and contrasted to determine, first, how each one views cognitive behavior, and second, how each accounts for changes in cognitive skills over time. We will try to draw from each theory what might be useful to you as a future teacher of young people who you hope will think, reason, and be logical in your classes. Following this comparison, we shall present the development of two major mediation skills that are basic to both theories: language formation and cognitive strategies. The development and measurement of intelligence will be considered next. Measures of intellectual functioning are used in many school systems to group students for instruction. Intelligence test scores can also be used to make predictions about the outcomes of instruction. Finally, we will introduce you to some alternatives for encouraging preschool readiness skills by means of early cognitive training programs.

COGNITION AS MEDIATION

The description of students' cognitive development frequently refers to internal or covert processes that we do not ordinarily observe. How do you know that one of your students is thinking or reasoning or considering alternative strategies? You will infer these processes from her observable performances. Therefore, the study of cognitive development must consider first the observable performances of children as they meet increasingly complex sets of environmental situations. We know that in first grade, Kathy can perceive or discriminate the difference between *b* and *d* because she calls out these letters correctly when you present them

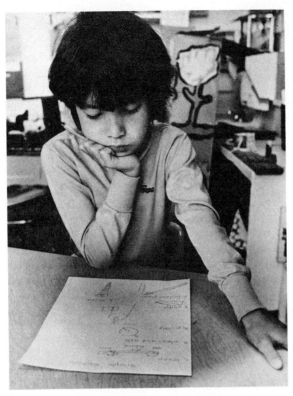

"How do you know that students are thinking or reasoning or considering alternative strategies? You will infer these processes from their observable performances." (Alice Kandell/Photo Researchers)

to her. At a younger age she might have pointed to them in the correct order. By the time she reaches the third grade, she can explain to you that the circle on the *b* goes to the right and one on the *d* goes to the left. At three periods in her cognitive development, Kathy's performance showed in different ways that she was perceiving and thinking. The addition of language and explanation to her responses, however, tells us that she was using different information each time. In many instances, we can't observe what is going on in a child's head but we *can* observe (1) her changing responses to the same stimuli or (2) her similar responses to differing stimuli (she can point out that *h, k,* and *p* are different than *b*). The process underlying these responses is called MEDIATION (Reese & Lipsett, 1970).

WORDS AND PICTURES AS SYMBOLS

MEDIATION refers to the covert verbal and imagery cues that people use to represent objects and events in the environment (Gagné, 1966). These cues are symbols that "stand for" patterns of stimuli to which we can make different responses. For Kathy to discriminate *b* from *d*, mediation includes VERBAL SYMBOLS (what Kathy tells herself) and the IMAGERY she uses to picture the way each letter looks or how it sounds. Figure

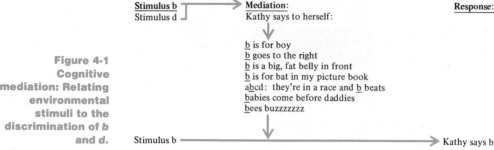

**Figure 4-1
Cognitive
mediation: Relating
environmental
stimuli to the
discrimination of *b*
and *d*.**

4-1 shows the relationship between environmental *stimulus* patterns confronted by the child (S), her inferred thinking or *mediation* response (M), and her overt *response* to these stimuli (R). This s-m-r sequence is a basic unit of Kathy's activity as she matures from toddlerhood to adulthood.

Let's look at some other examples of mediation. When Kathy says "dog" to a four-legged furry creature or to a line-drawing of a dog, she is mediating by means of a verbal symbol—language. The simple word *dog* stands for, or represents, a complex array of shape, color, texture, and possibly sound. Kathy learned before the age of 2 that many stimulus patterns can be represented by short verbal symbols which stand for the object: *mommy, daddy, car, bottle.* In doing so, she learned that one thing stands for another. In addition to verbal symbols, self-produced imagery is another kind of mediation. If you ask her at age 6 how she gets from home to school, she probably flashes a picture or image to herself of the route she walks every morning. This image is also a symbol of the actual pathway that Kathy takes to school. Imagery can probably take the form of pictures, sounds, tactile experiences (rough, smooth), kinesthetic experiences (going down a fast elevator), or even smell (thinking about rotten eggs). We shall see later that these many forms of imagery may be helpful in teaching children who are having difficulty learning symbolic tasks like reading.

════════ **PROBE 4-1** ════════

Think of a pleasant experience you had in the past, such as a day you spent at the beach. Make a list of all the sensory mediators you used to recall the location, the people, and the events. How much did you rely on words, visual images, sounds, smell, movement, touch? Do you use one sense modality more than another? Do you recall more bits of information when you use more or differing mediators?

GAINING FREEDOM FROM STIMULUS CONTROL

Although Kathy at age 2 said "dog" out loud, she gradually learned to "think" the word or to say it to herself (Luria, 1961). This self-produced response then linked together the external environment and Kathy's reaction to it. Mediation procedures gradually freed her from the direct control of immediate external objects and enabled her to consider and deal with the world in the absence of direct contact. Jerome Bruner, a well-known Harvard psychologist, calls this "gaining freedom from stimulus control" (Bruner, 1966). Mediation also allows Kathy to distance herself from the environment and thus to deal more effectively with the past and the future (Sigel & Cocking, 1977). As her mediation skills become more effective and systematic, Kathy will increase her capabilities to anticipate, plan, imagine, recall, create, and evaluate. These multiple skills in planning and evaluation are important for Kathy's developing self-regulation. As we shall see, self-regulation for both social and academic skills may involve the development of some very similar strategies in verbal mediation, or systematic self-talk and self-instruction (Brown & DeLoache, 1978; Worell & Nelson, 1974).

As a prospective teacher of young and developing mediators, don't expect accomplished performance at the start. Research tells us that the relationship between external patterns and mediation skills is somewhat predictable across both age spans and tasks. First, young children and new learners tend to "overinclude" or place too many objects in a symbol class. When Kathy was 18 months old, she said "doggy" to all four-legged creatures, even cats and cows. Probably, when you first looked at the motor of your new car, you said to yourself "Look at all those shiny parts in my motor."

Between the ages of 5 and 7, Kathy increases her use of specific verbal mediation (Kendler & Kendler, 1962; White, 1965). She refines her class inclusion symbols and can even point out Dalmatians and Chihuahuas as she discriminates their critical properties. At some point you, too, may have learned to name the carburetor and the alternator in your new car (especially if they failed to operate properly). Finally, Kathy gradually frees herself further from the absolute properties of dogs and begins to use more inclusive symbols—*dogs, mammals, animals, quadrupeds*—which no longer match the doggy qualities at all. The most advanced types of mediation, we shall see, consist of abstract rather than concrete symbols and are increasingly independent of their specific object referents (Bruner, 1966; Kendler, 1976). How about you and your car? If you learned as fast as Kathy, you were soon talking about the relative advantages, in terms of emission control, of piston as opposed to Wankel-type engines and their implications for environmental pollution. So you see, for growing youngsters and people learning new skills, verbal mediation tends to move from general to specific to differential.

"Students will come to class with individual differences in a variety of specific cognitive skills." (D. Strickler/Monkmeyer)

LEARNING S-M-R SKILLS

Given that children do seem to get smarter as they grow older, what is it that changes and develops over time? In the course of their home and school experiences, Kathy and Bryan will start out on many tasks as novices and end up as experts. As they start to acquire new skills, they may begin with incompetence and end with mastery. We are proposing that all three parts of the S-M-R SEQUENCE will change as students become older, wiser, and more experienced. With increased age, students can react to increasingly more complex and abstract stimuli (S) or patterns of events in the environment. They also learn more sophisticated and efficient mediation (M) skills as they mature, and they can generally show increases in discrimination, recall, problem solving, and logical reasoning—or responses (R). Now we don't believe these changes come about simply because students grow older. Rather, students are learning new skills, putting them together in new ways, and becoming more aware of the complexities of the world in which they live.

COGNITIVE DEVELOPMENT AND
TEACHING

Here is where the study of cognitive development will be of most use to you as a teacher. In your teaching procedures for any grade level, you will have many choices to make in selecting curriculum materials or stimuli (S), providing for effective mediation (M), and encouraging skilled performances or responses (R). The strategies that you select will be more effective in reaching your goals if they match or coordinate with the level of your students' cognitive skills. Students will come to your classes with individual differences in a variety of specific cognitive skills. It will be helpful to you to be able to assess these skills separately for each student or for an entire class and to match your instruction to those students' entering behaviors.

What about students who do not demonstrate the entering skills necessary for the level of instruction you anticipated? Your advance knowledge of the range of teachable cognitive skills will give you some clues. What might be helpful when Kathy can't recall the names of the state capitals or Bryan has difficulty in matching chemistry elements to their symbols? You may suggest techniques of mediation, or COGNITIVE STRATEGIES, that Kathy and Bryan can use to help in organizing and recalling such seemingly unrelated series of facts. The S-M-R sequence of cognitive development will thus be useful to you in two ways: (1) in matching teaching materials and strategies with the students' current cognitive skills and (2) in teaching new skills to facilitate learning. In Chapters 6 and 7, we will suggest ways you can integrate the S-M-R model into your teaching activities.

We have considered the question of what cognition is and how it develops. We now move on to three well-known theories that provide differing views of this same question. Each theory can help you to understand cognitive changes over time. Each has something to say about how development, learning, and instruction can interact.

PIAGET:
A STAGE THEORY

We shall consider Piaget's theory in two ways. First, we will summarize the general way in which he looks at cognitive processes and human development. Second, we will introduce his four stages of cognitive development and the capabilities he describes within each stage. (References for Piaget's theory include Flavell, 1963; Ginsburg & Opper, 1979; Piaget, 1952, 1970, 1971, 1973; Piaget & Inhelder, 1969.)

COGNITIVE STRUCTURE

Piaget views biological maturation as a major force in cognitive development. Taking his cues from the natural living patterns of all organisms,

Piaget sees cognitive activity as a progressive biological adaptation to the environment. This adaptation takes the form of successive qualitative changes in the child's internal COGNITIVE STRUCTURE. All thinking and reasoning come from the cognitive structure which directs and organizes patterns of experience into a whole. Changes in cognitive structure occur (1) as the child matures physically and innate structures emerge and (2) as the child interacts with the external world by means of direct action. Across all stages of cognitive development, adaptation consists of two complementary processes: ASSIMILATION and ACCOMMODATION. As the child meets new experiences, he or she *assimilates* the information into the existing cognitive structure, modifying it to fit with what is already known. Thus, 1-year-old Kathy first saw an orange and called it "ball." When this new information did not fit with previous structures (the orange doesn't bounce, but it tastes good), she modified her cognitive structure to *accommodate* it to the new information.

Equilibrium: Resolving cognitive conflict

Piaget says that once a child has adapted to a set of new information, equilibrium is established. Kathy's cognitive structure reaches EQUILIBRIUM when no conflicts or discrepancies exist between her cognitive structure and the external environment. This is an important point for you as a teacher. According to Piaget, the child will assimilate and accommodate to new information only when he or she confronts a *disequilibrium* or cognitive conflict between what is "known" and what is "perceived." If the new information is not too discrepant or novel, Kathy can assimilate it and thereby "learn" it. If the incoming information is too far above her present cognitive level, Kathy will be unable to adapt. Thus, she cannot profit from experiences which are beyond her cognitive stage.

While Piaget does not discuss learning as we have defined it (see Chapter 2), he accounts for new structures by means of the organization of new schemata. The SCHEMA is an internally represented response-action sequence (Kathy rolls the ball to Jeff and she eats the orange). The cognitive structure consists of organized schemata which enable the child to respond to the outside world. Within this context, your job as a teacher is to provide new materials that are just above the present cognitive level of your students. In this manner, they will be presented with sufficient *disequilibrium* to motivate them to adapt the incoming information to their present cognitive structure.

These processes of adaptation, assimilation, accommodation, and equilibrium operate across all developmental stages and determine the course of growth. Regardless of the content or period of learning, all people have the innate tendency to structure the incoming environment (assimilation) and to modify their schemata accordingly (accommodation).

Action and operations: Promoting cognitive growth

A final topic of importance to Piaget's approach is the role of action in promoting cognitive growth. Kathy assimilates new information by means of acting upon the environment and observing the results. When she bounced the orange, it behaved differently than when she bounced her ball. From the result of her active manipulation of oranges and balls, she began to gain objective knowledge about their characteristics. Later on in her development, she internalized this action into operations. Piaget considers operations, or "internalized action," to be the basic conveyor of intellectual activity. The issue of action in learning has implications for teachers. Does all new learning require the student directly to manipulate the materials to be learned? We shall discuss this question in the following section.

=== PROBE 4-2 ===

Do you think all new learning requires the student to use overt action in relation to some part of the materials to be learned? How would a teacher use action in teaching the concept of "tourist"? How about the concept of "atom"?

STAGES OF COGNITIVE DEVELOPMENT

According to Piaget, there is only one way to go. In Piaget's theory, cognitive growth occurs in discrete stages. These stages occur in a standard order, so that all children go through the same stages in the same sequence. Each stage is thought to represent a *structure of the whole*. This means that within each stage all specific capabilities are determined by the underlying cognitive structure. Accordingly, a child cannot learn operations, such as multiplication, that are beyond the limits of his or her cognitive stage. The importance of structures of the whole is reflected in Piaget's view that new information cannot be taught or "tacked onto" existing knowledge. Rather, the children themselves must reorganize their thinking by means of their own actions or operations which restructure the environment. And in turn, the new information can be assimilated only if their cognitive structure is at the proper stage.

Cognitive development across Piaget's four major stages moves broadly from sensorimotor and external to abstract and internal. Table 4-1 outlines these four major stages, the approximate age ranges during which they are expected to occur, and some of the cognitive functions which dominate the child's thinking at each stage. We shall discuss each very briefly in turn.

The sensorimotor stage

Bryan remained in the sensorimotor stage until about the age of 2 years. During this early developmental period, Bryan learned to separate himself

Table 4-1. Piaget's stages of cognitive development

Stage	Age range in years	Major cognitive functions
Sensorimotor	0 to 2	Causality: own behavior causes events Object constancy: out of sight, but not out of mind Intentionality: "I can make things happen." Internal representation: evidence of imagery Deferred imitation: imitates in the absence of a model Imaginative play: seeks stimulation and novelty
Preoperational	2 to 6	Symbols: uses symbolic language Simple concepts: classes, numbers, relationships Simple relationships: dogs are larger than cats Centration: focus on one dimension at a time Egocentricity: sees the world from own view
Concrete operations	6 or 7 to 11 or 12	Decentration: focus on several dimensions of a problem Reversibility: dimensions are reversible Conservation: of mass, weight, length, volume Seriation: to order objects by size, height, etc. Inferential logic: given premises, consequences are true—if $A = B$ and $B = C$, then $A = C$
Formal operations	11 or 12 to 18	Abstract thinking in the absence of concrete objects Hypothetical reasoning: considers all possible alternatives to solve problems Formal logic: hypothetico-deductive reasoning Idealism: reality vs. possibilities

from his surroundings. He developed simple reflexes (head-turning to sound), and motor responses to interesting events (rattles and balls). He developed some simple notions about how the world operates in relation to his own behavior: that objects have permanence as they move about or disappear from sight, and that his own hand pushing could cause the ball to roll. He also developed simple imitative behavior with and without a model (waving bye-bye) and had some notion of means-end relationships (searching for pennies in a closed fist). These two processes of *deferred imitation* and *object permanence* reflect early indicators of representational or covert thinking. In each case, children mediate their behavior by means of internally represented pictures or images. They achieve a basic skill in symbolic representation that remains with them throughout their problem-solving years.

The preoperational stage

Additional symbolic and representational capabilities emerge in the PREOPERATIONAL STAGE. Bryan developed facility with language as symbols for external events and could thus represent the world in his mind. His symbolic abilities helped him to create imaginative play; he took a stick and said "bang-bang," and he pushed a row of blocks yelling

Figure 4-2
The three-mountain
task. The child
who sits at position
1 is asked to move
the mountains
around to show
how they look to the
person who sits in
position 2.

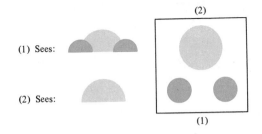

(1) Sees:

(2) Sees:

(2)

(1)

"toot-toot." He could sort objects into simple classifications based on one observed dimension: put the red blocks in a pile. Sorting red and blue squares requires an additional skill. Piaget considers the preoperational child to hold an *egocentric* view of the world and thus to perceive things from his or her own viewpoint. Figure 4-2 shows you a standard three-mountain task Piaget uses to demonstrate that the child, who is in one relationship to the mountains, cannot imagine how they would look to someone seeing them from another perspective. Piaget assumes that this egocentric position also prevents Bryan from feeling "empathy" for Kathy when he hits her, because he cannot understand how she feels.

The stage of
concrete
operations

Many cognitive changes are ushered in during the stage of CONCRETE OPERATIONS. Central among these changes is the move toward *decentration*, which enables Bryan to consider problems from more than one perspective. This shift to a more advanced position in logical thinking is shown by Bryan's responses to relationship questions. Consider Bryan's answers, at age 4 and at age 10, to these questions about Alice:

Age 4: Q: Who is Alice?
A: Alice is my mommy.

Q: Who is John?
A: John is my daddy.

Q: Who is John's mommy?
A: Alice is his mommy.

Age 10: Q: Who is Alice?
A: Alice is my mom. She is also dad's wife.

Q: Who is John?
A: He is my dad. He is also my mother's husband.

Q: Who is John's mother?
A: My father's mother is my grandmother.

You can see that at age 4, Bryan saw Alice on only one dimension: as a mother. At age 10, when decentration has presumably taken place, Bryan describes a mother as both a mother and a wife as well as a grandmother.

Once Bryan can consider more than one dimension at a time, his logical thinking can also include *reversibility*. Bryan can now complete a mental operation (internalized action) and then reverse it covertly. He is now ready to consider that $2 + 2 = 4$ and that $4 - 2 = 2$.

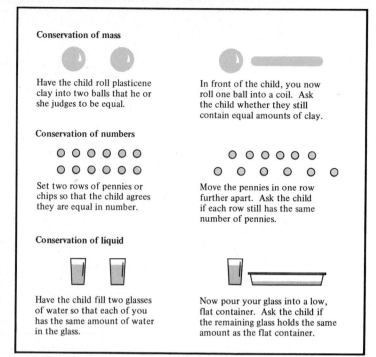

Conservation of mass

Have the child roll plasticene clay into two balls that he or she judges to be equal.

In front of the child, you now roll one ball into a coil. Ask the child whether they still contain equal amounts of clay.

Conservation of numbers

Set two rows of pennies or chips so that the child agrees they are equal in number.

Move the pennies in one row further apart. Ask the child if each row still has the same number of pennies.

Conservation of liquid

Have the child fill two glasses of water so that each of you has the same amount of water in the glass.

Now pour your glass into a low, flat container. Ask the child if the remaining glass holds the same amount as the flat container.

Figure 4-3
Simple tests you can perform to demonstrate conservation of mass, number, liquid.

The most dramatic and widely researched example of decentration is CONSERVATION. Figure 4-3 contains three examples of conservation of liquid, number, and mass. A conservation response to each of these demonstrations would recognize that, while the observed shape or form changes, the amount, length, or identity can remain the same. The evidence for and against conservation as a teachable skill has been one of the most controversial issues surrounding Piagetian theory. We shall consider this issue briefly below.

The stage of formal operations

The highest form of cognitive functioning is thought to emerge during the stage of FORMAL OPERATIONS. Now Bryan's thinking has been freed from concrete and observable evidence to solve more remote problems. He can remove himself from the here and now and consider the alternatives as logical possibilities. He is no longer bound by what presently exists at the moment; instead, he can consider what might be and what ought to be. For example, Bryan is now able to come up with a variety of possibilities if you present him with a problem such as "What if the world's natural oil supply should be depleted in twenty years?" He will be able to test these possibilities by using hypotheses and logical inference. With a new set of skills at hand, Bryan renews his interest in argument and debate. While he increases his ability to take both sides of an issue, his thinking tends toward idealism as he considers the possibilities of a new order in the world.

There are a number of good reasons why you may want to familiarize yourself with Piaget's concepts. Let us first suggest five ways in which Piagetian theory may be useful.

- *Take advantage of Piaget's description of development.* Within the broad framework of Piaget's descriptive stages, you can develop some expectancies or norms for group differences. Children of 6 *do* think differently from youngsters of 16. You can't present the same problems in the same manner to 4-year-olds and 14-year-olds.
- *Consider the match between your students' cognitive stage and the level of complexity of your teaching methods.* Include more action-oriented activities for the early grades, and, throughout the elementary school years, offer concrete things for students to manipulate. Elementary-level students will learn better if they can work directly with learning materials rather than just reading about them. One approach here is to teach a project across different content areas. For example, in studying maps, students are not expected to memorize rivers and mountains. Instead, they begin by drawing maps of their desks, their classroom, and their school. Here, they can become actively involved in measuring, conceptualizing what they cannot directly see, and reducing areas down to scale. In this manner, math skills come into play and students have direct experience with the concept of a map.
- *Provide curriculum variety and freedom of choice in some activities.* If they are allowed a variety of options, students can match their abilities and interests with relevant learning tasks. Some current educators advocate the open classroom, with freely available curriculum materials, as the only solution to the problem of providing variety in task activities. We believe that the opportunity to explore alternatives can be provided within any classroom structure. A discussion of *traditional* as compared with *open* schooling is presented in Chapter 9.
- *Remember that students are frequently enticed by novelty and intrigue.* You can capitalize on Piaget's notions about cognitive conflict by using paradoxes, contradictions, and information discrepancies in your teaching. In Chapter 6, we will discuss the motivational effects of novelty and surprise in encouraging a self-directed learning style. While Piaget recommends these methods for inducing a higher level of cognitive functioning, we see them as primarily motivational in their effectiveness.
- *Consider using the wrong response to diagnose thinking problems.* When children did not give the correct answer, Piaget typically questioned

them to determine the quality of their reasoning. You will want to question Ted further when he tells you that the square root of 144 is 13. You may find out where he is making his errors and how he can avoid them the next time around. Instead of telling Ted that he is wrong, ask him: "What is your evidence? How did you get that answer?" This type of questioning can help Ted to be more reflective and to consider his thinking procedures as he solves problems.

We shall now consider four limitations of Piaget's theory for your needs in teaching.

• *Individualized instruction from Piaget's theory may be unrealistic.* The wide age range at which children reach the Piagetian stages and master the underlying processes makes individualized instruction impractical. If the period of concrete operations ranges from 6 through 12 (and perhaps much earlier and much later), then we don't have many different specific strategies for 8- and 11-year-olds. On the other hand, if we talk about specific cognitive skills that are prerequisite to higher-level skills, then we can examine the presence of these at any age and stage. Thus, we are questioning the educational *utility* of the notion of cognitive stages, not the attention you may give to cognitive skills.

• *Concrete operational skills can be learned by preoperational children.* Recent research suggests that many advanced cognitive skills can be taught to children as early as age 4 (Brainerd, 1975, 1977; Charbonneau et al., 1976; Gelman, 1969; Rosenthal & Zimmerman, 1972, 1978; Zimmerman, 1977a; Zimmerman & Lanaro, 1974). Study 4-1 describes some interesting research on the problems of teaching an advanced skill to younger children. These findings on early instruction are consistent and persistent. They point to the fact that, given the appropriate training conditions (modeling in most instances), even younger children can learn skills that are above their Piagetian cognitive stage levels. Findings such as these place some limitations on the usefulness of stage theory.

Now, we don't propose that you teach conservation of liquids to 3- or 4-year-olds. The desirability of early acceleration will be taken up in a later section of this chapter. What these results tell us is that—given the appropriate materials, methods, and procedures—young children can learn some concepts at a higher Piagetian stage than had previously been thought possible. The reasons why many early studies were not able to produce these results is complex and beyond the scope of this text. It is sufficient to point out that when we do not find evidence of task learning such as in conservation, there may be a variety of factors involved other than a lack of "capacity," such as low motivation; inadequate teaching methods; difficult instructions; ambiguous words (such as *more, less,*

STUDY 4-1: TRAINING CONSERVATION IN YOUNG CHILDREN

Researchers at the University of Arizona have been looking at the possibility of teaching conservation skills to preoperational children. They selected a set of tasks that demonstrated conservation principles in space, number, and weight. A familiar example was the clay ball task, where one of two equal balls of clay is rolled out into a coil and the child is asked to judge if they are still equal (see Figure 4-3). In a series of studies, first-grade children were trained in conservation skills. First, they watched an adult model solve the task by saying "There is just as much here as is there." For some of the children, the model also explained her choice with a rule: "Because they were the same in the first place."

Figure 4-4 shows you the effects of these training conditions on children's correct judgments of equality and on providing a rule for their judgments. Observation of conservation

judgments by a model increased conservation skills on two measures: when children repeated the training task (imitation) and when they gave responses to a new conservation task (generalization). Having a model provide a rule along with her judgments helped children both to conserve and to give a rule as well. However, many children also gave correct judgments and verbalized the rule after having seen a model giving only the correct conservation choices. The authors repeated the procedures and found that even 4- to 5-year-olds could learn from observation of the model. However, when these younger children were asked to give the rule, their restricted language development interfered. They said things like: "That one was a ball." What does this study tell us? That modeling with choice behavior and rules is helpful in teaching even young children to increase their conservation skills.

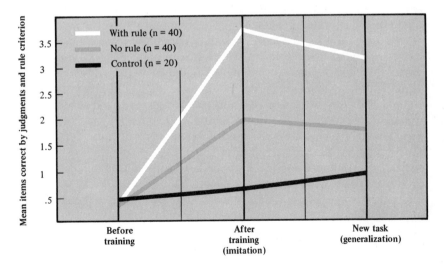

Figure 4-4 Teaching conservation by modeling and instruction. (Source: T. L. Rosenthal and B. J. Zimmerman, "Modeling by Exemplification and Instruction in Training Conservation," *Developmental Psychology*, 1972, 6, 392–401.)

taller, bigger); inattention by the child; and meaninglessness of the activity, to name only a few. As a prospective teacher of students who will show many deficits in many areas, we don't want you to give up on Ted by saying, "Oh, he is not in the right stage yet."

• *Skills are learned in sequence rather than in stages.* As you may recall, Piaget proposes that, at each stage of cognitive development, a single cognitive structure enables all relevant skills to appear. For many skills, we know that this is not found to be true (Brainerd, 1977). The many subskills involved in conservation of length, number, and volume, for example, are acquired slowly and over a period of many years. These skills are probably learned sequentially in terms of difficulty and subskills required, not according to a structure-of-the-whole prediction (Brainerd, 1975). The implications for teaching are clear. You may get more mileage from teaching sequentially in terms of related sets of skills than from teaching to a cognitive-stage classification. You probably can't teach "conservation," but you may be able to teach the prerequisite skills that will lead to conservation responses.

• *Formal operations are not for everyone.* Prospective high school teachers should be aware that your high expectations for formal operational thinking may be unrealized for many if not most of your students. Recent research tells us that most adolescents do not reach this advanced stage until somewhere between ages 15 and 20. Many teenagers and adults do not use formal operational thinking at all (Erickson & Jones, 1978; Keating, 1975; Martorano, 1977; Schwebel, 1975). What does this tell you about advanced methods of teaching hypothetical-deductive thinking and abstract reasoning? We believe that two suggestions will be of use to you. First, most adolescents cannot operate in the abstract alone without considerable concrete manipulation, pictorial images, and direct modeling or demonstrations. While they may like to be hypothetical about marijuana and men on the moon, their interest in Shakespeare may soon lag if it is all taught by way of a high-level hypothesis-testing approach. Second, we ask you not to give up on formal operational thinking merely because you do not find evidence of it in every student. Hypothesis testing and scientific thinking are teachable skills. Look ahead to Chapters 7 and 8 for ideas about how to teach advanced problem-solving skills. Many of your students may never reach the formal operations stage of reasoning unless you give them a head start by showing them how to go about it on their own.

BRUNER: STAGES AND SEQUENCES

Jerome Bruner (1964, 1966, 1971) proposes a different type of stage theory. According to Bruner, a child's thinking progresses through three stages which are determined by the way he or she represents the environment.

THREE STAGES OF DEVELOPMENT

The earliest mode of representation for Bryan was through his own action. He banged two blocks together and acted out the sensation of "twoness." Bruner calls this stage *enactive*. In the second stage, Bryan used *iconic* or visual representation of the two blocks. Now, he no longer needed to manipulate the blocks physically in order to count them. He could recognize them in pictures and visualize them mentally. Iconic representation helped to free Bryan from the physical presence of external stimuli and allowed him greater flexibility in thinking. Finally, Bryan learned to say "two." He could now say "two dogs" and "two books." Representation now moved into the *symbolic* mode as Bryan learned to deal with the world with labels and with increasingly abstract ideas. You can see the similarity of these three stages to Piaget's sensorimotor, operational, and formal stages of thinking.

THE SPIRAL CURRICULUM

In contrast to Piaget, Bruner is not willing to wait until the child moves spontaneously from one stage to another; he feels that children can learn elements of more complex ideas at earlier ages if the content is appro-

"You can encourage cognitive development by sequencing the material to be learned and presenting it at the child's present skill level." (D. Strickler/ Monkmeyer)

priately arranged. Therefore, we can encourage cognitive development by sequencing the material to be learned and presenting it at the child's present skill level. Says Bruner: "Any subject can be taught effectively in some intellectually honest form to any child at any stage of development." Taken seriously, this is a truly radical notion. It tells us that, if we go about it in the right way, we don't need to wait until Bryan is in the concrete operations stage to teach ideas of *bigger* and *smaller*. Bruner proposed that even difficult subjects such as math can be simplified and presented when the child has developed the necessary readiness skills. This approach has been called a SPIRAL CURRICULUM, in which more advanced topics are taught at a level which is appropriate to the student's existing cognitive development. The same topic is revisited in "spiral" fashion at later periods in such a way that the student digs deeper into the subject each time.

Let us look at an example of the spiral curriculum in your school. The history of the American Indians might first be enactively presented to Bryan and Kathy by teaching them to grind corn, do an Indian rain dance, and build a simple teepee. At a later time, stories of Indian life are woven iconically into a visual picture history of different tribal dress, customs, and living arrangements. Finally, students can encounter symbolically the migration of Indian tribes across the continent and the controversies that arose as they were pushed further and further from the lands of their ancestors. For Bryan to develop a full understanding of Indian wars, reservations and the Indian Bureau, he would need to grasp difficult concepts having to do with treaties, concessions, and government.

=== PROBE 4-3 ===

Take one topic in your area of interest or expertise. Suggest how to teach the content and concepts of this area using Bruner's spiral curriculum approach. Include the three modes of representation.

Bruner's theory is an important one for prospective teachers like yourself, who are interested in theories of development as they relate to learning and instruction. Bruner helps bridge the gap between Piaget and learning theorists like B. F. Skinner and Robert Gagné. You will meet Skinner in the next chapter on learning theory. We shall introduce Gagné's developmental learning theory to you here, and then we will follow it up in Chapters 5 and 7 with a detailed analysis of how you can use developmental learning theory in all your teaching activities.

GAGNÉ: DEVELOPMENTAL LEARNING THEORY

Robert Gagné is an educational psychologist whose research centers on the events and conditions necessary for learning the kinds of tasks that children face in school. He has applied his ideas on learning to the way children develop intellectually (many writers, including Gagné, use the terms "intellectual" and "cognitive" interchangeably). As is true with all scientific theories, Gagné's ideas have been modified as new research uncovered new facts and more useful ways of accounting for behavioral change. In the following sections we shall draw upon a series of Gagné's ideas which have developed over a period of time (Gagné, 1968; 1970; 1974; 1977; Gagné & Briggs, 1979). Because of his interest in learning, Gagné's approach to cognitive development is particularly useful for teachers.

DEVELOPMENT AS CUMULATIVE LEARNING

Basic to a developmental learning theory is the idea that cognitive capabilities are learned behaviors. Within the limits of physical growth, the changes that we observe in Bryan's cognitive skills as he moves from first to twelfth grades result from the cumulative effects of learning. His intellectual development is the result of the accumulation of learned skills or capabilities. These skills can be ordered or sequenced from simple to complex. Therefore, Bryan's ability to perform more advanced skills depends upon his mastery of the more basic skills (check back to Chapter 2 if you need to refresh your recall of the concept of mastery).

Bryan appears much smarter at 16 than he did at 6 because he has learned many basic and complex skills in association, discrimination, conceptualizing, and problem solving. Age itself is not a factor except that it denotes more time and opportunity to learn.

Learning complex tasks

Let's look at how Gagné applies his approach to Piaget's well-known task involving the conservation of liquid (see Figure 4-3). According to Gagné, "conservation" is an abstraction or label for a set of specific skills related to "judging equalities and inequalities of volumes of liquids in rectangular containers"—or cylindrical containers if you are using a glass (Gagné, 1968). A possible sequence of these skills is shown in Figure 4-5. You can see that all the hypothesized skills involve concepts and rules, which are advanced intellectual skills. This procedure is called a *task analysis*. In a task analysis, a complex task is broken down into its separate component skills. Gagné does not propose that this is the only possible sequence of skills or that each child actually rehearses each step in turn. He points out, however, that in the natural course of development,

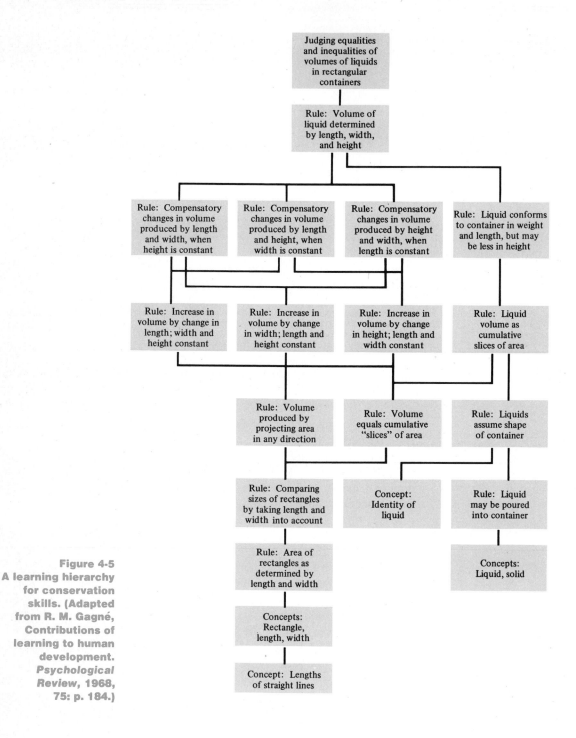

Figure 4-5
A learning hierarchy
for conservation
skills. (Adapted
from R. M. Gagné,
Contributions of
learning to human
development.
*Psychological
Review*, 1968,
75: p. 184.)

older children "pick up" or learn these concepts and rules one by one. In order to teach conservation of liquid to a "nonconserver" on this particular task, you may need to know which of the subordinate or prerequisite skills the child lacks. Many early training programs may fail to "teach" conservation and other concrete-operational skills because certain basic skills are missing. For conservation of liquids, these may include information about lengths, containers, volumes, areas, liquids, and heights, to name just a few.

How would you determine whether Bryan had the necessary subordinate skills to correctly judge the transformation of liquids from one container to another? You would start at the top of the hierarchy with the task itself. If he failed the conservation test, you might move down the hierarchy skill by skill to determine which of the more simple skills were lacking. We can hear you groaning now at the prospect of teaching all these skills from bottom to top. It does look tedious. This is why you may want to match the tasks to be taught with the prerequisite skills the student is capable of using at the start of learning.

LEARNING HIERARCHIES

According to Gagné, the kinds of logical thinking and reasoning that Piaget describes depend upon the prior learning and combinations of many prerequisite cognitive skills. Therefore, the "stage" which Bryan and Kathy appear to have reached at any point in their development depends upon two factors: (1) what skills they can demonstrate at that time and (2) the skills and LEARNING HIERARCHIES they need to perform a given task. A learning hierarchy is an organized set of intellectual or performance skills (Gagné, 1977). This means that as individual skills are learned, they *transfer* or *generalize* to each other and to new skills that are as yet unlearned. In this manner, two outcomes appear: (1) Kathy and Bryan demonstrate more advanced and complex INTELLECTUAL SKILLS with both increased age and training on a task and (2) both children learn more quickly on each new task as they practice COGNITIVE STRATEGIES for approaching problems more efficiently. Let's look at these two learning outcomes—intellectual skills and cognitive strategies.

Intellectual skills

The six major forms of intellectual skills are arranged into a hierarchy from simple to complex. Take a look at Figure 4-6 for the arrangement of these skills, their definitions and a sample of Kevin's behavior for each. You can see that the six types of learning describe Kevin's behavior from thirsty kid to crafty entrepreneur. Each of the higher skills depends upon mastery of the lower ones. In Kevin's case, he already has all of the prerequisite skills to master the sequence right up to the point of problem solving. He is now faced with a set of math calculations and economic decisions. We may have to construct another hierarchy to see

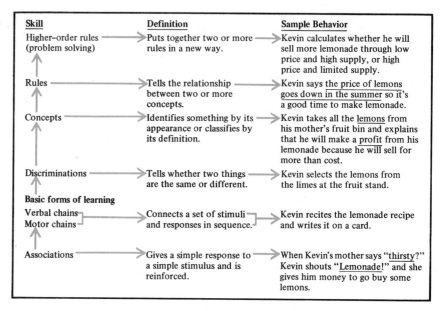

Skill	Definition	Sample Behavior
Higher–order rules (problem solving)	Puts together two or more rules in a new way.	Kevin calculates whether he will sell more lemonade through low price and high supply, or high price and limited supply.
Rules	Tells the relationship between two or more concepts.	Kevin says the price of lemons goes down in the summer so it's a good time to make lemonade.
Concepts	Identifies something by its appearance or classifies by its definition.	Kevin takes all the lemons from his mother's fruit bin and explains that he will make a profit from his lemonade because he will sell for more than cost.
Discriminations	Tells whether two things are the same or different.	Kevin selects the lemons from the limes at the fruit stand.
Basic forms of learning		
Verbal chains Motor chains	Connects a set of stimuli and responses in sequence.	Kevin recites the lemonade recipe and writes it on a card.
Associations	Gives a simple response to a simple stimulus and is reinforced.	When Kevin's mother says "thirsty?" Kevin shouts "Lemonade!" and she gives him money to go buy some lemons.

Figure 4-6
Gagné's intellectual
skill hierarchy.

if he can solve the problem at hand; how to adjust price with supply and demand. At any step in this hierarchy, we could stop the show and teach him the skills he needs to move up to the next level. In order to do this effectively, Gagné contends that we need to know the conditions of learning for that skill.

**Conditions of
learning**

In the natural course of children's growth and development, a variety of conditions may influence the learning of new skills. When those conditions are appropriate for the particular behavior, new learning is more likely to take place. Take our example in Figure 4-6. Had Kevin's mother not given him money for lemonade, Kevin's shout of "Lemonade!" would not have resulted in the sequence of events outlined in the chart and Kevin would not have had these learning experiences. We know from earlier discussions that one important condition for many kinds of learning is reinforcement or feedback to the child following his behavior. Likewise, if no one buys Kevin's lemonade, he may decide to go into another business.

Gagné proposes that we take into account two sets of conditions which influence the developmental learning of skills: (1) *conditions internal* to the learner, such as prerequisite skills and self-initiated learning strategies, and (2) *conditions external* to the learner, such as reinforcement, repetition, and a variety of stimulus arrangements. These conditions may differ for each of the six types of intellectual skills. For parents and teachers who wish to maximize the development of certain skills, knowledge of the conditions required for learning each skill will be helpful. Chapters 7 and 8 will cover these six types of learning more completely. These chapters will also provide you with student and teacher activities which will help to ensure favorable conditions for each type of learning.

Cognitive strategies

While Kevin is learning intellectual skills, he is also using cognitive strategies. These cognitive strategies are mediating skills which Kevin uses to regulate his own learning procedures. Some examples of cognitive strategy approaches include the way in which Kevin: (1) pays ATTENTION, (2) encodes (uses words or images to himself), (3) retrieves (remembers and recalls information), and (4) achieves mastery or solves problems (uses plans and self-instruction). Kevin can use such strategies to help himself learn, remember, and use any information in any situation. By using these strategies, Kevin becomes a more independent learner. Many of these strategies are very similar to our concept of self-regulation skills. They enable the learner to organize and manage learning procedures and outcomes. We believe that they are so important in learning that we shall devote an entire section of this chapter to these cognitive strategies.

GUIDELINES FOR TEACHING

Using the Best of Gagné's Theory

We believe that Gagné's conceptions of cognitive development are particularly useful for teachers. Since the remaining chapters of this book rely heavily on Gagné's ideas and concepts, we shall be expanding more on guidelines for teaching as we proceed. In particular, you will find many specific teaching guidelines in Chapters 7 and 8.

In general, we find many useful ideas in Gagné's theory. He tells us that learning and thinking are teachable skills. He provides us with a sequence of learned skills that you can use for all your teaching activities. His system of cumulative learning directs you to look at the student's prerequisite skills at the start of a learning task. You may recognize these as the entering behavior we described in our earlier model of teaching. Gagné suggests conditions and activities to promote the learning of each intellectual skill. He encourages the development of mediating cognitive strategies that will help all your students to be better and more independent learners. Finally, he emphasizes observable skills that the student can demonstrate when the learning task is mastered.

Since no theory has a corner on the truth, we offer some cautions in applying Gagné's theory to classroom practice.

• *Be careful to temper your enthusiasm with a bit of realism.* There is much to be learned about the "best" conditions of learning for each intellectual skill. We still know relatively little about how cognitive strategies operate and how they can be taught.
• *Remember that any sequence of learning skills you devise may not be the correct one for a particular student.* Research tells us that some students can skip steps in a hierarchy and some may need more steps

than you provide at first (Resnick, 1976). Few learning hierarchies will fit all your students. If you ignore this rule, you may "lose" both types of students. "Fast learners" have developed many prerequisite skills before they arrive in your class. You will bore them with detail if you expect them to climb the ladder in small steps. "Slow learners," on the other hand, have often missed many important skills prerequisite to the activity you are teaching. Too few steps on the ladder may discourage them, so that they fail to progress. You must cut these patterns by measuring each student. We hope your reward will be a good fit.

We have reviewed three theories that will be useful to you in developing teaching strategies. The following section moves into a discussion of two major systems of cognitive mediation: language communications and cognitive strategies. These systems include a range of many specific skills your students can develop to increase their productive learning.

LANGUAGE AND COMMUNICATION

From the time she wakes up each day until she falls asleep at night, Kathy is probably using some form of language. She listens to and understands the conversations of her parents, her teacher, and her friends. They ask her questions, make requests, and tell her about their experiences. Their language communications maintain Kathy's social interactions and her responses frequently result in pleasant outcomes like food, friendship, and fun. In turn, Kathy communicates with others; she reciprocates their verbal messages and reinforces them in turn.

The reciprocal speech communication between Kathy and her social environment has two important results: (1) it is instrumental in helping Kathy to obtain important reinforcers and (2) it is educational: Kathy is learning about the structure and use of language. At the same time, she is developing her cognitive skills and gaining information about the world around her. In addition to communication, Kathy uses private language for self-communication or talking to herself as she plans her day, decides what to wear, solves her math problems, and reads her science book. The development of language and communication skills is an important link in most of Kathy's social and cognitive behavior.

DEVELOPMENT OF LANGUAGE SKILLS

Language is critical for cognitive development because it is an effective mediator. It provides the symbols and rules that help us to think. For Kathy, language mediates the external objective environment, the behav-

"Language communications maintain student interactions with others." (Haun/ Black Star.)

ior of other people, and her own covert self-management strategies. We shall briefly consider the development of three broad language skills: (1) language structure, which includes grammar, vocabulary, and syntax; (2) communicative language, which includes the meaning of words and sentences; and (3) interpersonal communication, which examines what people say when they talk to each other. Each of these areas includes a countless array of specific skills, many of which are not entirely understood at the present time. Finally, we shall include a discussion of dialect differences in the use of the English language.

Controversy on language development

How does Kathy move from an infant who can only babble and coo to a highly articulate adolescent who can generate hundreds of thousands of words, sentences, and dialogues? Two major positions dominate the theorizing on language production: a nativist position and a learning approach. Between these two extremes are many variations and modifications. The nativist approach (Chomsky, 1968; Lenneberg, 1967; McNeill, 1970) views the emergence of speech and language as a biological given for humankind. Investigators who favor this point of view point to evidence such as the limited success of efforts to teach language to lower primates, some universal progressions of language structure across all languages, and the coordination of language skills with motor development. The nativist approach agrees that some exposure is necessary, since French children speak French, not English or Spanish. However, they assert that learning processes have a minimal effect and that biological maturation will account for all final forms of language.

The environmentalist or learning approach (Mowrer, 1960; Skinner, 1957; Staats, 1975; Whitehurst, 1977) stresses the conditions under which language is acquired and the principles of learning which favor its development. Although this position does not ignore the biological structures required for speech, it is more interested in exploring the possibilities for facilitating language skills. In the following, we will indicate some of the developmental regularities that occur as children mature with time. In support of the learning view, we shall also suggest three learning factors that facilitate language development: modeling, feedback, and the acquisition of rules.

Language structure: Sounds, sentences, and syntax

Sounds appear early   No one taught Kathy to coo and babble. Between the ages of 2 and 12 months, she increased these noises regardless of whether or not her verbal advances were returned. According to a prominent learning theorist, O. H. Mowrer (1960), the infant's early vocalizations become attached to the presence of comforting adults. As a result, these noises become "good sounds." When Mom and Dad are not around, Kathy can use these sounds to make herself feel better. Kathy later learned that some sounds produce other pleasing events, such as parents' smiles and reciprocal sounds, as well as cookies and bottles. Therefore she gradually shaped her speech to match the sounds her parents modeled for her (Staats, 1975). Her parents were delighted when she produced a recognizable word, and they repeated it with corrective feedback: Kathy said "ba-ba" and her mother replied "Here's your bottle." In the process, Kathy achieved some important goals for herself that helped to increase her further use of speech.

PROBE 4-4

The theory that language is learned because the child's own speech reproduces the positive sounds of parent speech has run into a knotty problem. How is it that children repeat unpleasant speech sounds, such as calling each other names, or telling you they did something wrong? Do children also imitate a critical model as well as a rewarding one? Recall our discussion of the modeling of aggression and see if it can apply to this problem as well.

Sentences are next By the time she was 2 years old, Kathy was putting two and three words together to form "telegraph" sentences. These short sentences were reduced forms of adult speech which kept the same wording (Bloom, 1975). Let's look at how Kathy retained the important parts of the sentence to tell her mother what she wanted.

Kathy	*Mother*
More milk.	Do you want some more milk?
See kitty.	Do you see the pretty kitty?
Daddy bye-bye-school.	Daddy is going bye-bye to his school.

Both Kathy and her mother were showing forms of modeling. Kathy modeled by reducing her sentence. Her mother modeled Kathy's speech but expanded on it (Brown, 1965). Since Kathy's language included thousands of sentences by the time she was 3, it seems improbable that she learned each sentence separately by means of direct modeling. How did Kathy move from novice to expert in her language skills?

Sentences follow rules Although Kathy's speech was less elaborate than her mother's, she did follow some simple rules of grammar and word order. Psycholinguists, who study speech and language development, have found that children show many similarities in the rules they use to construct sentences and express ideas. Children seem to learn some basic rules of *syntax,* or how words are ordered into sentences. They use these rules to generate many different sentences that they never have heard.

Cognitive social learning theorists believe that these rules are acquired by means of modeling, or observational learning (Whitehurst, 1977; Zimmerman & Rosenthal, 1974). The rule is then transferred to new and unfamiliar situations. Sometimes Kathy used a rule across situations and failed to learn the exceptions: when she said "Daddy goed to school" and put his "shoes on his foots," she was applying some rules that she would have to revise. While observational learning and corrective feedback may not hold all the answers to language development, they will be useful concepts that you can apply to your teaching repertoire.

By the time Kathy and Bryan enter first grade, they will have learned most of the characteristics of their native language. However, their language skills will continue to expand as they approach adolescence. Throughout their school years, they will show improvements in articulation or pronunciation, in syntax and sentence length, in vocabulary, and in correct application of grammatical rules (Palermo & Malfese, 1972). At times, you may still expect students to have difficulty in applying some of the more subtle rules. For example, the rules for using *ask* and *tell* may be confused by many students.

Teacher: Ask Joanne what color this book is.

Child: What color's that book?

Teacher: Tell Joanne what color this ashtray is.

Child: Tan.

Teacher: Ask Joanne what to feed the doll.

Child: The hot dog. (Adapted from Chomsky, 1969)

Be prepared for rule confusions in grammar and word use throughout the elementary and secondary school years.

Semantics: Making sense of words and sentences

We have been talking about language as though Kathy were an architect building a structure. When children use words and sentences, they are using symbols that stand for something else. A symbol conveys meaning by providing information about objects or events. Words become associated with objects and events in the environment and thereby acquire meaning in words, concepts, and sentences.

Word meaning   When people in Bryan's world labeled things for him, word meaning developed. Each time Bryan reached for the cat, his mother said "Kitty." As Bryan played with the cat, he learned many more labels for how a cat looks, acts, feels and sounds: *tail, scratches, soft, meows*. These labels will form an *associative cluster* (Deese, 1966; Worell & Worell, 1966) which define what Kitty meant to Bryan. Now, the meaning of *kitty* became all the associations Bryan could make to the cat. You can test yourself on word meaning in Probe 4-5.

===== **PROBE 4-5** =====

Test yourself on the associative cluster you can form for the following words: Which words have more meaning to you?

supine	highway
lemur	table
frigate	rose

Concept meaning   Discrimination learning precedes concept meaning. At first, Bryan had to tell the difference between cats and dogs on the basis of their similarities and differences. Concepts will become very important for Bryan in mediation learning because they are building blocks to more advanced cognitive skills. *Concrete concepts* involve things Bryan can see and point to—*boat, bottle, book;* these are learned first. Concepts such as *longer, shorter, smaller, equal* are *defined concepts* because they have no specific referents in the environment. Defined concepts are more difficult to learn and are acquired much later. Many problem-solving situations cannot be solved until the child masters certain defined concepts. Concepts are so important for further learning that we will devote a large section of Chapter 7 to concept development.

Sentence meaning More complex learning enters into sentence meaning. A two-word sentence may stand for many objects or events, depending on the associations for each word and the situation in which the child uses them. If 2-year-old Bryan says, "Kitty eat," does he mean "the cat ate his dinner," "the cat wants to eat," or perhaps "the cat ate my dinner"? Many times, and for youngsters of all ages, you may have to *decode* what is being said to you. It will be useful for you to remember that Kathy and Bryan's comprehension or *receptive* language frequently exceeds their production or *expressive* language. That is, they can frequently understand more than they can say. In order to decode their speech and to determine what they mean, you may have to use some probes and clarifying questions.

Individual differences in meaning: Good dogs and bad dogs

Bryan and Ted have very different meanings associated with *dog*. Bryan's parents bought him a dog and taught him to care for it. Bryan learned many positive associations to his dog ("good dog," "nice dog," "pretty dog") as well as activities associated with his dog ("feed the dog," "brush the dog," and so on). Bryan grew to like dogs and had a positive attitude toward them. Dogs mean fun to Bryan. For Ted, dogs mean fear, danger, and suspicion. Ted was told "Dogs are dirty and they bite. Don't touch strange dogs." Ted now avoids dogs and has a negative attitude toward them. You can see that almost any word or concept can become engaged in a positive or negative associative cluster. Your students will have many differing associations to concepts like *democracy, communism, Chicano, Blacks, women's liberation,* and *hippie.* Each of these concepts may have different meanings to Ted and Bryan, depending on their previous associations. Be prepared for individual differences in the meanings that your students assign to words and concepts. Chapter 8 discusses value and attitude conflicts in the classroom and how to deal with them.

COMMUNICATION: TALKING AND LISTENING

Once children acquire some language skills, they talk to each other. All communication involves a speaker and a listener. Speaking and listening skills improve across grade levels and do not approach adult competence until adolescence. Effective communication requires Bryan to construct a clear message so that Kathy receives the message he intended (Worell & Nelson, 1974). Let's consider four skills Bryan will want to use in

order to tell Kathy how to get to the city library (Glucksberg, Krauss, & Higgins, 1975):

1. Bryan must have sufficient language development to tell Kathy about directions, intersections, and stop signs.

2. He has to know enough about what information Kathy will need to get there—street names, number of blocks, left and right turns.

3. He will want to know something about Kathy as a listener. He will explain it differently to her if he knows that she is new in town, younger than he, or has been to the library before (Shatz & Gelman, 1973).

4. Finally, he listens carefully to Kathy's feedback to determine whether she has received his message clearly; that is, whether she can tell him how she will find her way to the library.

Clearly, this task involves social interaction as well as cognition. Effective communication requires skills in a number of competencies (Whitehurst, 1977). Communicative skill is a relatively new topic in development and learning studies, and we know relatively little about how to teach these skills. You should recognize that many of your teaching activities will involve speaker-listener roles. As a concerned teacher yourself, you will play both of these roles alternately. We will consider how you can sharpen your communication skills in Chapters 6 and 11.

NONSTANDARD DIALECTS

Until now, we have been discussing typical patterns of language and communication. However, you will encounter some students, like Manuel and Joe, whose speech patterns appear markedly different from yours. NONSTANDARD DIALECT describes the speech of any student whose verbal patterns do not match the expected speech patterns of the classroom (Shuy, 1973). Consider some of these samples of speech that Joe hears every day in his neighborhood. Compare them with the same ideas expressed in Bryan's standard dialect.

Joe	*Bryan*
I done forget my books.	I forgot my books today.
My mother, she go downtown.	My mother went downtown.
He have a car but he don' go.	He has a car but he didn't go.
Nobody didn't know nothing.	No one knew anything.
Sometime he be busy.	Sometimes he's busy.
I'ma go; I sees you tomorrow.	I'm going. I'll see you tomorrow.

(Adapted from Shuy, 1973).

Does Joe's language seem incorrect to you? This is only one example of a dialect that is different from that in standard classroom use as well as written textbook English. What are the problems for students who arrive at school with differing dialects, pronunciations, or a second language spoken at home? Two major hurdles loom ahead for Joe and Manuel. First, language differences will handicap them in activities which involve speech and reading skills. The failure of large numbers of black students to score at or above the norm on national reading tests has been attributed to their use of nonstandard dialect (Baratz & Shuy, 1969). Second, teacher attitudes may be shaped by the student's failure to use nice, correct, standard English. Faced with Manuel, who says, "Theez beeg feesh, she no can sweem," a teacher may conclude that Manuel is (1) not too smart, (2) retarded in language development, or (3) probably not able to learn much in her class.

Difference or deficit?

Two opposing hypotheses have been used to explain children's use of nonstandard dialect: (1) that it represents a deficiency of proper language development and (2) that it stems from a difference in language structure and usage. The deficiency hypothesis was popularized by Bernstein (1961), who described low-SES speech as "restricted." In contrast to an "elaborated" code of middle-class language, restricted speech uses short, frequently unfinished sentences and few adjectives or adverbs. Thoughts are repeated and sentences are strung out without the use of grammatical sequences. A deficiency hypothesis implies that (1) students who use a restricted code cannot use higher levels of logic and reasoning that require advanced language skills and (2) remediation is required to make up for the deficit (Bereiter & Engelmann, 1966).

In contrast to the deficit approach, some researchers stress that nonstandard dialect follows its own rules and that students can think logically but differently in their own grammar. These researchers point out that, when faced with the standard English of the classroom, such children are confronted by the new rules of grammar, which interfere with their previous (dialect) speech patterns. In this view, Joe and Manuel's speech is not deficient but merely different (Baratz, 1973; Labov, 1970a, 1970b).

Dealing with dialects

What can be done to help Joe and Manuel learn language and reading skills in school? Three proposals are currently in use. First, you can ignore the differences. Manuel and Joe should be expected to use standard English in both speech and reading and to keep up with the other students. Baratz contends that the results of this procedure are students who are significantly retarded in reading skills (Baratz, 1973). Recent research suggests that most young black children understand standard English but do not choose to use it on a learning task (Gay & Tweney, 1976). Thus, it is still possible that the knowledge of two separate dialects interferes with learning to read standard English for these children.

Second, you can develop specific training programs to remediate children's language deficits (Harbor & Beatty, 1978). This approach is frequently integrated with COMPENSATORY EDUCATION, or programs designed to serve children with deficits in academic readiness. Head Start is a well-known example of compensatory education. We will consider some alternative early training programs in the last section of this chapter. Finally, some experts suggest BILINGUAL EDUCATION, or adaptation of reading materials to fit the different language patterns of the dialect-speaking student. This means that some early reading materials are printed in the child's own dialect, so that the printed words match his or her speech (Leaverton, 1973). Once Manuel grasps the process of transforming speech sounds to written symbols, he can be weaned to standard English texts. Then standard English is, in effect, taught as though it were a second language.

=== **PROBE 4-6** ===

Put yourself in the place of a bilingual first-grader. You enter a school in which only Russian is spoken and printed in your text. A new program offers you temporary instruction in English until you learn how to read, after which you will switch to Russian. Which do you think you would prefer? Under which system do you think you would learn best?

Unfortunately, the research literature is too premature to tell us which alternative is the better one. A number of language training programs aimed at deficit speech have shown moderate to considerable success in modifying both speech and reading skills. Whether the strategies based on the difference theory will be equally effective remains to be seen. We must point out, however, that many factors other than nonstandard dialect enter into reading skill. Any approach based on a single strategy will probably be too limited.

Specific instruction in language arts is beyond our scope. We can draw some general guidelines for you which should be useful for all of your students.

GUIDELINES FOR TEACHING

Mediating Language Patterns

* *Take your cue from parents who use elaborated speech patterns.* Model for your students the standard English you want them to use. When Joe says "It be lunchtime?" you can reply, "Yes, Joe it is lunchtime. You have been working very hard and you must be very hungry." Here you are not only reflecting Joe's idea back to him in standard English but also expanding his ideas into a new sentence. This way, you can help Joe preserve his self-esteem by accepting his communication while providing him with a model of standard English in reply.
* *Avoid using the dialect of your students.* You may believe that you are showing them that you care enough about them to speak at their level. However, you are also providing them with a model that will interfere with your attempts to teach standard English (Johnson, 1970).
* *Accept the language and speech patterns of each student.* The speech you hear is Joe's native language. Then, diagnose his language differences so that you can help him to modify these patterns gradually. You can diagnose his differences by listening to him speak spontaneously or by asking him questions that will elicit the patterns in which you are interested.
* *Treat yourself to some ethnic reading.* If you are teaching in a school with many students who use nonstandard dialect, learn about their culture and the ways in which they communicate. You may get some cues about how to proceed with your teaching.
* *Consider adopting a structured language training program.* Many language programs are available for students who appear to be having trouble with listening, speaking, and reading skills. As an alternative consider referring specific students for further help if their speech patterns seem very different from those of the rest of your class. Early assessment and remediation may save a student from a lifetime of inadequate language and reading skills (Harbor & Beatty, 1978).

COGNITIVE STRATEGIES

Cognitive strategies describe plans and procedures that students use to maximize performance. These procedures help youngsters like Kevin to gather information (attend), organize (encode), retrieve (recall), and use information to solve problems (develop and follow a plan of action). You can expect three positive outcomes from the development of effective cognitive strategies: (1) efficient learning, (2) effective problem solving, and (3) independent action. First, Kevin can become more efficient in his learning skills. He will take less time to solve problems and will make fewer errors. A simple ratio of time in relation to errors will give you an index of efficiency. Second, Kevin will solve more problems correctly if he follows a plan of action. He will be able to focus his attention, develop a plan in advance, test his alternatives, and evaluate his solutions. These are all useful strategies for self-directed problem solving. Finally, when Kevin develops his own self-monitored strategies for learning and problem solving, he can become more independent of you. He can now proceed on his own in many new activities. For these three reasons, you will want to encourage a variety of cognitive strategies in attending, encoding, retrieving, and problem solving. Let's take a look at some specific skills in attention and mediation that facilitate learning.

ATTENTION SKILLS

Every day in Kevin's classroom, hundreds of stimuli bombard his senses: books, people, voices, lights, wall decorations, blackboard material,

"Students can solve more problems correctly if they follow a plan." (Sybil Shelton/Peter Arnold)

instructional equipment and much movement about the room. As his teacher, you raise your voice above the din: "Kevin, you're not paying ATTENTION." What does Kevin have to do to inform himself and you that he is "paying attention"? Kevin can perform one or all of four activities: (1) he can orient himself to the task by turning around and looking at you or at the blackboard; (2) he can scan the problems on the blackboard by looking from one to the other; (3) he can select and focus on the problem you wish him to solve; and finally, (4) he can ignore the distraction of Kathy and Bryan who are giggling behind him. When Kevin can orient himself to a problem, scan its contents, focus on the relevant aspects, and screen out the irrelevant ones, we can probably conclude that he is "paying attention" (Bandura, 1977; Hagen & Kail, 1973; Reese & Lipsett, 1970).

Attention: Building block for further learning

Once Kevin has mastered these skills and is focusing on the task at hand, he increases his attention span. He learns to maintain these attending behaviors over longer periods of time and across larger amounts of information. Teaching units can increase in length and study periods become longer as Kevin learns to control his attentional behavior. Attention skills will help Kevin to follow directions: "turn to page 26." Ted frequently ends up on page 28 or just sits there looking at his book because he seldom focuses on your directions. Attention skills are critical to all further cognitive procedures in encoding, retrieval, and problem solving (Hagen & Kail, 1973). Kevin can't implement any further self-control strategies in his cognitive behavior until he gains control over his attention. Let's take a look at how these attention skills affect some of Kevin's related behaviors.

Many of the mediation strategies that Kevin uses appear to be spontaneous. That is, he picks up ways of learning without systematic, formal instruction. Kevin learns these procedures through observing other people, trying things on his own, and informal instruction from his parents and peers. As his language skills increase, Kevin learns to deal with problems more symbolically. He begins to pay attention to verbal or semantic cues to find lost ideas (to recall) and to keep important ideas in focus. Even young children can extract the "gist" of a story read to them and ignore the irrelevant details (Brown & DeLoache, 1978). As children progress through school, their verbal and mediational skills help them to pay more attention to central themes. They will increasingly ignore materials that are unnecessary to the task at hand. Again, attention skills are critical here. Of course, other mediation skills are now coming into play, as Kevin and Bryan learn strategies in how to organize, rehearse, and give themselves verbal cues to facilitate recall.

For many of your students, getting all these behaviors together at the same time in order to "pay attention" is a tough task. Most of your students will need some help in focusing and concentrating. Certain of your students, such as those with learning problems, may need more help than others. How can you assist Kevin in his struggle to pay attention to math instead of to Kathy?

Teacher activities to increase attention will depend on the subject matter and the developmental level of your students. We shall brief you on some general strategies for focusing attention. More will be said regarding attention in Chapter 6.

- *Depend upon some classroom management procedures to set the stage for attending behaviors.* Classroom management here will include your own interpersonal attending skills (look at Kevin when he talks to you) as well as your monitoring of learning activities, pacing of lessons, and reinforcement for good attending behavior.
- *Develop cognitive techniques that emphasize management of classroom cues and materials.* Choose instructional approaches that encourage your students to *stop, look,* and *listen* (Figure 4-7). Materials that are salient will stand out and demand attention from your students. You clap

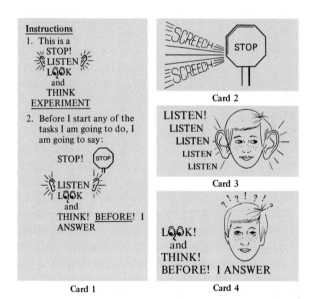

Figure 4-7 Training cards for attention and planning skills. Nine-year-old boys were trained to give themselves instructions to stop, look, listen, and think before completing a task. A picture of each step accompanies the self-instruction. (Source: Palkes, Stewart, and Kahana, 1968; as cited in D. Meichenbaum, *Cognitive-Behavior Modification: An Integrative Approach.* New York: Plenum Press, 1977, pp. 37, 38.)

your hands and say "OK, everyone listen." You use three colors of chalk to demonstrate the phases of caterpillar life. Materials that are relevant and meaningful are also likely to hold interest and command attention. You relate fractions to cutting equal pieces of pizza. You help Kevin to assign meaning to new materials by relating them to what he already knows. Finally, novelty and surprise in your teaching procedures will stimulate students to wonder what's coming next.

• *Use verbal cues prior to a learning task to help direct and focus selective attention.* Verbal cues can be directions about what to look for, instructions about how to organize a task, hints about what cues to focus on, or strategies for how to go about remembering. When you give a broad summary of what a learning task is about, we call this an *advanced organizer*. In Chapter 9, we shall see that advanced organizers help students remember things. When you give learning objectives for a unit, you are telling students what information is central to mastery of the activity. All of your advanced verbal cues will provide active models for Kevin and Bryan on how to go about organizing their own learning. Once you have told them about how to look ahead and plan, they can begin to tell the same kinds of things to themselves.

• *Help students to develop self-managing strategies.* We believe that in the long run, students can learn self-management skills for establishing and maintaining selective attention. Once you have their attention on a learning task, you want them to stay with it, to resist distraction and irrelevant stimuli, and to recall the material they are learning. Beginning with first grade and on into senior high school, Kathy can use many mediation methods to maintain her attention. One example is *covert rehearsal*, or repeating something over and over to herself. A second example is SELF-INSTRUCTION, in which Kathy tells herself how to go about managing a learning task. Chapter 7 will discuss rehearsal strategies. In the following section, we will focus on self-instruction and how Kathy may be encouraged to tell herself how to learn and solve problems.

MEDIATION SKILLS: SELF-INSTRUCTION

In this section we want to introduce you to a fascinating set of research studies being conducted at the University of Waterloo, Canada, by Donald Meichenbaum and his associates. These researchers asked the general question we are talking about right now: "How shall we get children to plan, to think before they act, to stop, look, and listen?" (Meichenbaum, 1977, p. 24). The answer seems simple enough: for any task, teach these children to talk to themselves about what to do and how to go about it. How successful is this approach?

Meichenbaum decided to test out these ideas on some of the toughest prospects around, impulsive and hyperactive children. Children who fail to use covert language or self-talk to control their overt verbal and motor behaviors are sometimes labeled as hyperactive or impulsive. These children act before they think. Consequently, they make many errors in problem solution. These are also the children who later give teachers many headaches because their inadequate skills in self-regulation lead to disruptive classroom behavior and peer conflicts. We shall assume that techniques that can teach self-management to ''impulsive'' children ought to be pretty powerful for all teaching situations.

Teaching children to talk to themselves

The challenge of teaching children to talk to themselves was approached with a cognitive social learning format which resembles our four-part teaching model. The goals or objectives were provided at the outset as skill development in self-instructional strategies. The remaining three parts of the procedures in teaching children self-talk or self-instruction provide an example of the teaching model in practice.

Identifying problem learners The first step in this research program was to identify students who are ''cognitively impulsive.'' Figure 4-8 shows a sample array of pictures from the Matching Familiar Figures Test (Kagan, 1966). The child is asked to select the picture that matches the standard at the top. Impulsive children tend to respond very quickly and make many errors on this task. When observed in other situations, these same children (1) had difficulty in maintaining verbal control of their motor responses (Meichenbaum & Goodman, 1969), (2) did not appear to use planful behavior in solving tasks (Ault, 1973; Goodman, 1973), (3) showed immature and irrelevant speech patterns during free play (Meichenbaum, 1971), and (4) made more reading and reasoning

**Figure 4-8
The Matching Familiar Figures Test—sample pictures for measuring impulsivity in children. (Source: J. Kagan, "Reflection-Impulsivity: The Generality and Dynamics of Conceptual Tempo,"** *Journal of Abnormal Psychology,* **1966, 71, 17–24.)**

errors (Kagan, 1965; Kagan, Pearson, & Welsch, 1966). These were clearly students with many learning problems.

Meichenbaum then asked: "Could we teach these children to talk to themselves differently? And would this new strategy of self-talk be helpful to them in guiding and controlling other behaviors?" This second question is a critical one for cognitive mediation. It asks whether we can teach some basic self-regulation skills on one activity that will carry over to subsequent activities. The answer is an important one for teachers. As a prospective teacher who will meet many students with "impulsive" behavior patterns, you will be interested to know what Meichenbaum and his associates found.

Training new skills Children were trained on a variety of activities that require motor control: tracing a maze, copying patterns, coloring within lines, and verbal sequencing—that is, following directions or ordering parts of a story. The training went like this:

1. An adult model performed the task while repeating the instructions out loud (cognitive modeling).

2. The child performed the same task under the direction of the model's instructions (overt external guidance).

3. The child performed the task while repeating the instructions aloud (overt self-guidance).

4. The child whispered instructions while performing the task (faded, overt self-guidance).

5. The child performed the task while guiding performance by means of private speech (covert self-instruction). (Adapted from Meichenbaum, 1977, p. 32.)

Let's look at an example of how this program was carried out in practice. For a simple maze task, the model provided the following cognitive patterns:

Okay, what is it I have to do? You want me to copy the picture with the different lines. I have to go slowly and carefully. Okay, draw the line down, down, good; then to the right, that's it; now down some more and to the left. Good, I'm doing fine so far. Remember, go slowly. Now, back up again. No, I was supposed to go down. That's okay. Just erase your line carefully . . . Good. Even if I make an error I can go slowly and carefully. Finished. I did it! (Meichenbaum & Goodman, 1971, p. 117)

You can see in this example that the model was demonstrating some important skills: (1) defining the problem ("what do I have to do?"), (2) guiding his responses and focusing attention ("draw the line down, down"), (3) self-reinforcement ("Good, I'm doing fine"), and (4) self-correction ("That's okay. Just erase . . ."). These are very similar to the self-management skills we have been discussing.

Evaluating outcomes   How successful was this program? In one follow-up study (Meichenbaum & Goodman, 1971), impulsive children showed improved performance on the maze and Matching Familiar Figures Test, as well as some improved scores on an intelligence test. Moreover, this improvement was evident one month later in a new situation. These same procedures have since been applied to a number of differing student populations, and the outcomes have generally been successful. The training pictures in Figures 4-7 and 4-9 are examples of visual supports through imagery to help these children mediate their verbal and motor control. Pictures of the behaviors the models wish to teach are used as intermediary steps between direct demonstration and the child's own self-management. Other researchers have applied these methods to academic behavior and find improvement even in math and reading skills (Henderson, 1980; Robertson & Keeley, 1974).

While these research studies are quite recent and still in the experimental stage, they tell us one important fact. Mediation by means of self-imposed verbal or imagery cues is an essential component of learning. When you give your students opportunities to observe and practice these mediation skills, you may well be rewarded with improved academic skills and increased self-management. Your students will be the real winners. They will be learning skills that can last a lifetime.

What is my problem?   How can I do it?   Am I using my plan?   How did I do?

Figure 4-9   Training pictures to cue self-verbalization in problem solving. (Source: M. Bash and B. Camp, "Think Aloud Program: Group Manual," in D. Meichenbaum, *Cognitive-Behavior Modification: An Integrative Approach.* New York: Plenum Press, 1977.)

You can try some of these modeling and coaching methods with any of  your students who seem to need an extra boost. You don't need to wait until you have diagnosed Ted as impulsive or Donna as hyperactive to use some strategies in cognitive self-management. We do not know right now how many differing activities and situations will respond to self-instruction methods. But you will want to consider some suggestions in carrying out any program of self-instruction:

• *Combine self-instructional methods with external reinforcement at first.* For many students who have never learned to use covert self-reinforcement (''I did a good job''), some outside support is useful at first (Robertson & Keeley, 1974). Then, when students are managing on a more self-regulated level, you can remove the external reinforcement and allow the self-evaluation skills to take over.

• *Teach self-instruction before the student begins a task.* This procedure can prevent later errors and careless responding. If you depend upon students to remember later what they did wrong, they may not be able to apply self-correction instructions the next time around.

• *Do use visual imagery to assist in mediation.* Take your cue from Figures 4-7 and 4-9. Devise some pictures that will help students remind themselves of the next step.

• *Be sure to have the students rehearse the procedures aloud before saying them covertly.* You might try having two students direct each other in how to go about planning and completing a task carefully. By observing how Joe responds to his instructions to assemble a dry cell, Ted may gain some insight into his own errors in verbal planning. A cautionary note here relates to older students, who may be too embarrassed to repeat instructions aloud. If you run up against this problem with Ted, be flexible and allow him to complete the program in his own way (Meichenbaum, 1977).

• *Use the student to help you assess mediation problems.* Ask Kevin how he goes about solving a problem and how he thinks he could improve. Follow through on some of his suggestions by modeling them first while he observes you. Then have him evaluate the success of his strategy. This may help him to diagnose his own problems, and to generate new solutions. He may also discover in the process that you can offer some good suggestions. In this way, Kevin becomes a more independent partner in improving his own learning skills.

Addenda on cognitive strategies: Learning to learn

We have been discussing only two of many possible strategies to promote self-regulated learning. In subsequent chapters we shall return to attentional and self-instruction procedures. Your students will find that these skills are useful for mastery of any cognitive and social behaviors they wish to improve. Once your students become more proficient in the techniques of learning, they will find that *learning to learn* is fun. Each new activity becomes easier as they master some of the fundamental skills they need to become efficient and effective learners.

INTELLECTUAL SKILLS

One outcome of cognitive development is the emergence of intellectual skills. As Bryan progressed from first grade through high school graduation, his cognitive and academic skills became increasingly adept and complex. The concept of INTELLIGENCE is frequently used to describe the sum of students' cognitive capabilities at any point in their development. Intelligence tests represent one approach to measuring current outcomes of cognitive development in students. In the following sections we will consider (1) differing views on the nature of intelligence, (2) some widely used tests of intellectual functioning, and (3) some precautions about the use of intelligence tests in schools.

INTELLIGENCE: TRAIT OR SKILL?

No single definition of intelligence is accepted by all educators and psychologists. Two broad views have been proposed: (1) that intelligence is a general learning and ability trait which is reflected in all aspects of behavior and (2) that intelligence involves the combined application of many specific skills.

Intelligence as a trait

Some theorists see intelligence as a general ability trait. Thus, a person who shows ability in one situation on one intellectual task should show ability on many tasks. Alfred Binet, who developed the first successful test of intelligence, defined intelligence as the ability to carry out abstract thinking in the solution of problems. Another well-known test developer is David Wechsler. He defines intelligence as "the aggregate or global capacity of the individual to act purposefully, to think rationally, and to deal effectively with his environment" (1958, p. 7). This view of intelligence has had a profound impact on the way in which we have dealt with students in schools. The tests to measure intelligence devised by these two men have been the most influential in educational decision making in the United States.

Intelligence as many traits or skills

In contrast with a single-trait view of intelligence, several educational psychologists propose the idea that intelligence reflects the composite of specific, measurable skills. Accordingly, Bryan might be a whiz at math

Table 4-2. Thurstone's Primary Mental Abilities

Ability	Description
Verbal comprehension	Understanding the meaning of words: vocabulary
Word fluency	Using words rapidly: speed of association
Number	Working with numbers: computational skills
Space	Visualizing space-form relationships
Memory	Recalling verbal stimuli
Perceptual speed	Discriminating visual stimuli quickly
Reasoning	Forming rules about ideas or numbers

Adapted from Thurstone & Thurstone, 1963.

but a real plodder in English. Even within a specific area such as math, Kathy might have good computational skills but come to a full stop when you ask her to solve a problem in arithmetic reasoning. Thurstone (1938) proposed seven "primary abilities" which together make up what he called "intelligent behavior" (Table 4-2). Thurstone developed the Test of Primary Mental Abilities (PMA), which is still in popular use today. While the idea of specific skills is appealing and certainly reasonable, the factors on Thurstone's test tend to be related to each other. People who score high on one skill seem to score high on many skills. Earlier, Spearman (1927) had proposed a general intelligence factor (g) as well as some specific factors (s). Thus, Bryan might score higher than Ted on a test of general intelligence, but Ted might have higher scores on numerical and musical abilities. Guilford (1967) went even a step further and proposed that intelligence consists of 120 separate skills and abilities. It seems clear that we could generate skills almost infinitely.

The findings at the present time suggest that (1) the intellectual skills measured by tests tend to be related to each other and (2) individuals do show particular talents in special areas. A long-term study of exceptionally competent children (Terman & Oden, 1925, 1954) showed that while they were well above the crowd on general tested intelligence, there were also individual areas of special skills. However, we can have little insight into the nature of intelligence until we understand how it is measured.

Intelligence as skill attainment

The cognitive social learning view of intelligence takes observed performance as a starting point. Scores on intelligence tests can be seen as performance samples which tend to be consistent across a number of situations (Anastasi, 1978; Mischel, 1976). However, these performances are learned skills which depend upon many subordinate skills. Bryan can not learn to read until he can discriminate the letters. Similarly, he can not deal with higher-level abstract problem solving until he learns labels and simple concepts. We speak of performance samples because we believe it will be most useful for you to observe and measure the skills

"Students cannot learn to read until they can discriminate the letters." (O'Neil/ Stock, Boston)

that Bryan can demonstrate at the present time. Intelligence tests will tell you about a particular sample of the possible cognitive behaviors that Bryan might be able to demonstrate. From the sample that you observe on any particular test, you are going to make inferences and predictions about his future performance in similar situations. At the same time, you will be gathering many other sets of information about Bryan. You will also be using many other samples of his entering cognitive behaviors on achievement tests, classroom academic work, and group discussions. Each of these performance samples will give you some information about Bryan's prerequisite skill attainment. Intelligence tests will be useful only if they can tell you something more than the sum of your other accumulated information. Whether an individual's test scores reflect his or her "true" intelligence is less important than whether the test scores you receive can be helpful to you in planning the student's academic experiences.

MEASURES OF INTELLECTUAL SKILLS

Aside from our theoretical notions about what intelligence "really is," how do we go about measuring intellectual skills? How can we use information about intellectual skills in our educational decision making? Frequently, intellectual skills are measured by intelligence tests. In this way, the definition of intelligence is an operational one: "Intelligence is what intelligence tests measure." Let's see how these tests fit into our conceptions of intelligent behavior.

Purposes of intelligence testing

In many school systems, measures of intellectual functioning may be used as one source of information for any of the following purposes:

1. To predict how well students will do on school-related tasks
2. To explain why, in fact, they did or did not do as well as expected
3. To select students for special instruction who may not be benefiting from regular class instruction

Let us look at how these procedures might have applied to Bryan. Suppose you had been Bryan's first-grade teacher and you wondered how well he would perform in your class by comparison with the others in his group. Your school might administer some intelligence tests to determine children's intellectual ability. These tests result in a ratio between Bryan's performance on the test and that of most people of his age. This ratio is called an *intelligence quotient*, or IQ. If Bryan's IQ score is below a certain level and he seems to have trouble learning in class, you might tell the principal that Bryan does not belong in your class. You might express this judgment in several ways: "He is a slow learner," "He is retarded," "He can't learn to read," "He's not ready for school yet," "He needs special help," "He's not very bright."

Since, in fact, Bryan's IQ score is relatively high, you probably would say, "He's really bright. I expect him to learn to read by the end of the first grade; he can probably do simple arithmetic, and I know he will be a cooperative class member." By the end of first grade, Bryan has met all your expectations and is well on his way into the second-level reader. Now, if Bryan fails to perform equally well in the next few grades, his third-grade teacher might look at his high IQ score and decide that he should be doing better. This teacher might report that Bryan is just lazy, or unmotivated, an underachiever, or perhaps that he has some emotional problem. It might be decided that some special help is in order.

Tests of intelligence are typically used for these three purposes: to predict future performance, to explain good or poor performance, and to select students for special instructional methods. None of these decisions should ever be made without additional information such as may be provided by achievement tests and an evaluation of social and adaptive skills. What does the intelligence test score add to this student evaluation and how should the IQ be used? As a teacher concerned with individual progress, should you make use of IQ scores? And if so, in what manner? Before we consider these important questions, let us take a look at how intelligence is measured.

The Stanford-Binet Test: First and still running

The first widely used intelligence test was devised in 1905 by Binet and Simon in France. They were commissioned to determine which children in the Paris school system were incapable of benefiting from regular instruction. Binet interviewed teachers to find out what skills successful students actually did demonstrate. The test he constructed was so successful for its purposes that it was later revised by Louis Terman at Stanford University and is now called the Stanford-Binet (Terman, 1916). Terman standardized the test several times by developing age norms (see Chapter 2) on large groups of children and writing a careful manual to administer the test. On this test the IQ is expressed as a single score which compares a given student's performance with that of other students in the same age group on whom the test was standardized. As we shall see, the nature of the standardization group becomes extremely important when we consider IQ testing with minority-group students.

IQ: Computing a score

Terman devised a clever way of computing the IQ, which was given as the ratio of a child's mental age (MA) to his or her chronological age (CA). Thus, $IQ = MA/CA \times 100$ (multipled by 100 to eliminate decimals). Mental age was determined by comparing the number of test items a child answered with the age norms. Thus, if Bryan answered as many questions as the average 8-year-old, his mental age (MA) would have been 8. However, this will result in a different IQ depending on Bryan's chronological age (CA). At the age of exactly 8, Bryan would have had an IQ of $^8/_8 \times 100 = 100$. The average IQ at any age is thus 100. However, if Bryan had produced the same test at age 10, then his IQ would have turned out to be 80 ($^8/_{10} \times 100 = 80$). Similarly, if a 6-year-old achieved an MA of 8, then his IQ would have worked out as $^8/_6 \times 100 = 133$. While this method of computing IQ is no longer in use, it shows you the reasoning that underlies the resulting average of 100 for tested IQ. Table 4-3 shows how selected IQ scores compare with others.

Table 4-3. Percentage of children who score at differing IQ ranges on the Stanford-Binet

IQ range	Description	Percent in group
Above 139	Very superior	1
120–139	Superior	11
110–119	High average	18
90–109	Average	46
80–89	Low average	15
70–79	Borderline	6
Below 70	Retarded	3

Source: Terman & Merrill, 1937.

The fact that a single IQ score is assigned to each child is important. It tells us that the user of this test will tend to accept a global or trait view of intelligence. It tells us that decisions about this student may be made on the basis of this one score. Keep this in mind as we consider some alternatives.

Individual and group tests: Many ways to go

While the Stanford-Binet is still in use in some school systems, it has been replaced by many other tests of intelligence and ability. The second most widely used test of intelligence is the revised Wechsler Intelligence Scale for Children, or WISC-R (Wechsler, 1974). Like the Binet, the WISC-R must be given individually to each child and requires several hours to administer and score. To give you the flavor of the types of test items included, we have displayed samples (not the real test items) of each subtest of the WISC-R in Figure 4-10. You can see that three scores were obtained: a verbal IQ, based on items which require use of language; a performance IQ, which requires motor responses (but assumes the child can understand and use language); and a total IQ computed on the basis of both verbal and performance factors. In your experience as a teacher, you will encounter many more tests of intelligence and ability. In contrast to the individually administered Stanford-Binet and the WISC-R, most of

Scale and subtests **Verbal**	Sample test questions
Information	How many legs does a dog have?
Comprehension	What's the thing to do if you got lost in a big city?
Arithmetic	If you had a basket of 10 apples and you lost 4 of them on the way home, how many apples would you have left?
Similarities	How are a blanket and an overcoat alike?
Digit span	Repeat these numbers after me: 5 7 4 2 6 etc.
Vocabulary	What is: pajamas skyscraper hollow etc.
Performance Digit symbol	
Picture completion	What is missing? 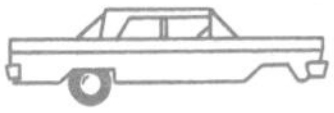
Block design	 Use these blocks to make a design like this one 
Picture arrangement	Put these pictures together so they make a good story 
Object assembly	Put these puzzle pieces together to make a picture 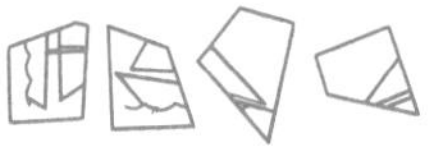

Figure 4-10
Sample items of the type used on the WISC.

these will be group tests which your entire class can take at one time. Chapter 10 will compare the advantages of group and individual tests for obtaining useful measures of performance.

USING MEASURES OF INTELLECTUAL SKILLS WISELY

Earlier we suggested that intelligence test scores have been used in schools for three purposes: prediction, explanation, and grouping for instruction. In your teaching career, you may never use an IQ score for any of these purposes. Many school systems have replaced intelligence testing with other measures of performance skill. Other school systems reserve IQ scores for use by specialists, such as counselors and school psychologists. However, you may encounter IQ scores on a student's record. You may also see IQ scores if you are part of an educational team responsible for planning individualized instructional programs. You will want to be familiar with (1) the purposes for which the IQ score is used and (2) the limitations of these IQ scores for school personnel.

Using IQ scores to predict

IQ testing has survived for three-quarters of a century because it accomplished one important purpose. The Stanford-Binet or WISC IQ has been the best single predictor of students' school and occupational performance after the age of 5 (Kennedy, 1969; Kennedy, Van De Riet, & White, 1963). The IQ score has been used to determine how well students will respond to schooling and how they will probably fare in the world. IQ scores have been used to select those who are likely to perform at outstanding levels as well as those who will probably fall further and further behind. For example, some correlations between Stanford-Binet scores and a standard achievement test were found to be as follows:

> Reading achievement .69
> Arithmetic achievement .64
> Language achievement .70
> (Source: Kennedy, Van De Riet, & White, 1963, p. 106)

Remember that the highest possible correlation between two tests is 1.00.

The strong relationship between IQ and academic achievement has encouraged the continued use of intelligence tests for prediction. Therefore, IQ scores are sometimes added to the many other considerations involved in deciding how well a given child will progress under differing educational arrangements. Alvin, for example, whose IQ score is consistently below 90 percent of all other students his age, may benefit from a special classroom for part of his school day and some long-range vocational planning (see Chapter 12). Counselors and teachers may also use IQ tests to supplement the information they provide students to help them make their own educational and vocational decisions. Students may want to be knowledgeable about their probability of success in college, training school, or a job placement. Based on test norms for people already in college or a profession, Bryan and Kathy can then judge their own chances of success. IQ scores will not guarantee the effectiveness of these educational decisions, but they may help reduce some of the guesswork involved in making long-range plans. Chapters 10 and 12 discuss alternative kinds of information that can be helpful in making educational and career decisions.

How can we account for this predictive power of IQ tests? It should not be a surprising outcome. Recall that these tests were originally constructed to select youngsters who would do well in school. Individual test items were dropped if they did not discriminate between students who were successful at school tasks and those who were not. Accordingly, IQ tests typically measure the same kinds of skills that help students to succeed in school: good vocabulary, a command of standard English, familiarity with cultural information, effective attention skills, and the kinds of cognitive strategies we discussed earlier in the chapter. These are all learned skills which are moderately predictive of future school learning. The student who can display these skills on an IQ test is likely to display them over a period of time during the school year.

Cautions in using IQ scores to predict: Consider many other factors

Despite our positive recommendation above, we have many reservations about using IQ scores for prediction. The list below covers only the most important of these. Each problem has been supported by research and has taken up columns of discussion itself.

The conditions of testing The score that Ted achieves may be influenced by the testing situation. Since the IQ score is a performance sample, it will depend upon any of the following factors: the skill of the examiner who administers the test, Ted's interest and motivation at the time of testing, and Ted's familiarity with the type of test items presented. For Joe, who is black, the presence of a black examiner may encourage a better performance than a white examiner. If it is a group test, Joe may also be distracted by the other students, misunderstand the instructions, or sit and daydream. If you are giving a group test, you will want to be certain that you follow standard instructions and procedures carefully. You cannot guarantee a valid IQ score, but you can increase the chances of obtaining one.

Time of testing The results of IQ tests that are given before children reach age 2 have no relationship to later school-age IQ or school achievement. When Bryan was about 5, his IQ score had a moderately good relationship with the scores he achieved at later times in his life. However, a test administered to 5-year-old Bryan will tell you less about his chances for college success than a test given at age 16. The relationship between IQ scores and other measures of the individual's behavior decreases over long time spans.

=== PROBE 4-7 ===

Some school systems now discard all test scores that are more than two years old. Do you believe this is a wise practice?

Individual differences The growth pattern of IQ scores varies from one student to another. For many students, the IQ score is relatively stable over time. A stable IQ score tells you that Bryan remains about the same IQ level in comparison with his peer group at different ages. However, longitudinal studies which periodically retested children from age 3 through 18 and even into adulthood show dramatic changes in IQ scores (Bayley, 1970). Sometimes these changes are upward or downward swings at particular periods of the student's development. Some students show a progressive increase or decrease over time, so that by the age of 18 they are significantly higher or lower in tested IQ than they were at age 6 (Sontag, Baker, & Nelson, 1958). In one study which retested eighty children from ages $2\frac{1}{2}$ to 17, one out of three children showed a progressive increase of 30 points in IQ and one of every seven children increased 40 points (McCall, Applebaum, & Hogarty, 1973). How can we account for these changes in IQ over time?

Additional factors in IQ change A number of factors have been found to predict increases or decreases in tested IQ. For Bryan, a continued increase in IQ may be related to any of these conditions: his high motivation, competitiveness, and independence as well as a stable, middle-class home with well-educated parents who tend to accelerate, encourage, and give firm discipline. On the other hand, Ted's decrease in IQ across the years may be related to one or more of these conditions: a lower-SES family background, low competitive and achievement goals, a father who was often away from home, a large family, little parental involvement in his school progress, and overly strict or lax discipline (McCall, Applebaum, & Hogarty, 1973; Rees & Palmer, 1970). Finally, we have evidence that early training programs can improve IQ scores as much as 20 points for some children. We shall discuss the evidence for the modifiability of tested IQ in the next section.

Economic and cultural background   Taken together, the foregoing research studies tell us that the IQ score is not always the best estimate of how well any individual child will achieve in school. There is considerable evidence from several large-scale studies that children from culturally deprived or isolated environments tend to score below the national average on IQ tests. Certain minority groups also score below average (Kennedy, Van De Riet, & White, 1963). These group differences have been used to support three divergent positions about the nature of intelligence and the appropriate use of IQ scores.

First, some people believe that the major portion of intelligence is inherited. Furthermore, the majority of certain economic and racial groups are thought to be innately less intelligent than the majority of Caucasian Americans (Jensen, 1969, 1973). If you subscribe to the hereditary position, you might believe that the IQ reflects a student's true functioning level. You might not recommend compensatory education programs and you might group students for different instructional methods based on IQ scores. The view that intelligence is largely inherited has raised some stormy controversies in recent years. A full discussion of both sides of this controversy is beyond our scope. You may wish to refer to writings by Kamin (1974) or Loehlin, Lindzey, and Spuhler (1975) for an in-depth treatment of innate factors in IQ.

A second view proposes that IQ tests are biased against minority cultures in their use of language and vocabulary. Accordingly, it is thought that many students like Ted are not deficient; they are just different (Labov, 1970b). If you agree with the cultural difference hypothesis, you

"There is considerable evidence that children from culturally deprived or isolated environments tend to score below the national average on IQ tests." (C. Harbutt/Magnum)

might throw intelligence tests out entirely, or you might look for an alternative way of measuring intelligence. Several "culture-free" tests have been devised which attempt to avoid questions and materials that are unfamiliar to particular groups of children (Cattell, 1949; Davis & Eels, 1953; Mercer, 1977). While the goals of culture-free testing seem humane and fair, no test yet has been able to erase social class differences in measured IQ. Middle-class children still do better than others. Moreover, culture-free tests do not predict future school performance as well as standard IQ tests.

The third approach to intelligence testing takes the position that IQ tests measure a sample of the present functioning of any student as well as his or her learning history. One reason for the wide variation in IQ scores is that some learning histories have been impoverished, different, or inappropriate to the goals of the middle-class American classroom. If you view the IQ score as a reflection of the student's present intellectual functioning, you may take a deficit and remediation approach to group differences in IQ.

You will never know how much any particular student's present IQ and classroom functioning is fixed by heredity and how much you can stimulate toward change (Bronfenbrenner, 1972). You may conclude that cultural differences are legitimate but not functional for academic achievement. That is, Ted and Joe may have their own lingo, but this will not help them to succeed in school or in the world at large. You may accept such differences but decide to adopt a deficit model to remediate language and conceptual patterns. You would also refer to the results of several recent programs for intensive preschool intervention. You might be impressed by evidence of some startling increases in IQ scores and cognitive skills brought about by several programs (Bereiter & Engelmann, 1966; Blank & Solomon, 1968; Heber et al., 1972; Karnes et al., 1968; Klaus & Gray, 1968). You will probably not have the time and resources to duplicate these intensive programs for change. However, you might want to investigate the many possibilities within your classroom for stimulating and encouraging cognitive growth in all of your students. You would therefore treat the IQ as a rough measure of selected entering skills and proceed with a further assessment of prerequisite skills to meet your learning objectives.

IQ and school achievement Many factors other than IQ affect school achievement. Among the most forceful of these factors are the quality of the home environment, previous stimulation toward language and intellectual skills, parental support of the student throughout school, and good or poor teaching practices. Wolff (1966) found that an index of intellectual environment at home, such as language models and corrective feedback, was almost as predictive of school achievement as the IQ score.

What can we conclude from all this information about measures of intellectual skills? Knowing the IQ can give you some broad leads, but it is clear that IQ is by no means the only predictor of school success. You should be encouraged to learn that you will have an important impact on Bryan, Kathy, and Alvin's progress in school. After all, that's what you will be there for, isn't it?

Using IQ scores to explain school achievement

Since so many factors other than tested intelligence enter into school performance, don't blame it all on the IQ! When you say that Ted gets low grades in class because he has a below-average IQ, you may be quite off target. There may be many other reasons for Ted's achievement problems. Be careful to look at the total learning situation. On any particular learning skill, Ted's IQ will reveal less than would a careful task analysis of where he is and what he needs to learn. The IQ score is related to achievement; it does not explain achievement.

Using IQ scores to group students for instruction

Large differences in tested IQ between Bryan and Ted have some implications for instruction. In comparison to Bryan, Ted is likely to have fewer entering skills for the planned instruction, he may take longer to learn the material, he may need extra help along the way, and he may require a different curriculum and special teaching methods. For all of these reasons, teachers frequently prefer to teach *homogeneous* groups. In a homogeneous teaching group, most of the students are at about the same level on some factor: age, IQ, or entering skills. When you teach a *heterogeneous* group with a wide range of IQs or entering skills, you tend to teach to the middle group. When this happens, some students fall behind and some become bored. You may wish to consider some kinds of grouping arrangements so that students with similar entering skills are learning together. The IQ score is only one way to accomplish this purpose. In most schools, students in the primary grades are grouped according to reading skills. These entering reading skills may or may not coincide with IQ. Students who are grouped only for reading are then *mainstreamed* into regular classes for other school activities. Chapters 9 and 12 will discuss some alternative ways to group students so that you can teach and they can learn. We believe that some kinds of homogeneous groupings are helpful. For selecting groups with extreme learning problems, such as the severely handicapped, IQ scores can be one useful tool in a battery of procedures.

By now, you should know enough about IQ scores to be able to support the following conclusions:

GUIDELINES FOR TEACHING

Cautions in Using IQ Scores

• *Never use the IQ score alone to make decisions about special classes, instructional groups, institutional placement, or college planning.* To do so is to misuse the IQ score and possibly to abuse the student. Any instructional decision which selects students for special treatment should be based on many other factors in the student's adjustment, interests, and specific academic skills. The IQ score is better used as an adjunct to decision making rather than as the only factor.

• *Keep your instructional decisions based on IQ scores tentative, and review them frequently.* Having placed Ted in a lower reading group or a special classroom, you need to evaluate your decision frequently. Perhaps Ted needs extra help for only a few months or one semester. Possibly he will do even less well in this new situation. If Ted does not show measurable progress in comparison to his previous class placement, a change should be made as soon as it is practical to do so. Too often, children are placed in homogeneous groups and then remain in that track for the remainder of their school careers. In Chapter 12, we will further discuss the flexible placement of students with special learning requirements.

• *Develop measures of intellectual skills that are specific to your learning objectives.* Rather than trying to teach on the basis of some broad traits such as intelligence, concentrate on prerequisite skills. Decide what you want to teach and what skills are necessary for success on your objectives. Remediation of deficit skills will bring you far greater return on your efforts than assignment of intelligence test scores.

Recap on intelligence tests

The worst use you can make of an IQ score is to label the student with a number and then react to that number instead of the student. We have seen that Ted's IQ score is only a sample of all of his possible performances. IQ scores tend to be fairly stable over time, but for many students they may change impressively in either direction. A better use you can make of the IQ score is to regard it as a moderate predictor of student achievement. This means that IQ scores are one source of information to use in grouping students, planning instructional arrangements, and advising students on their relative chances of success in college. However, the best use you can make of IQ is to supplement it with lots of additional information. We believe that all your instructional purposes can be better met by assessing entering skills that are specific to the material you wish to teach. Ted's IQ may tell you something about his general READINESS to participate in class activities. However, careful diagnostic assessment of his readiness skills for the specific curriculum you planned for his class will be far more useful than his IQ in making further decisions about Ted.

READINESS FOR INSTRUCTION

When Ted was in kindergarten, his father said to his teacher "He's so young and unsettled; do you think he is ready for first grade?" What did Ted's father wish to know? He probably wondered (1) whether Ted would be able to master first-grade reading and math and (2) whether Ted could sit still long enough to pay attention and follow directions. Most concepts of school READINESS include two kinds of entering behaviors: the cognitive skills required for academic work and the prosocial behavioral skills children need to adapt to the requirements of a structured classroom situation. In this section, we shall discuss some differing concepts of readiness for school and several programs which have been designed to increase preschool cognitive and behavioral readiness skills.

TWO VIEWS OF READINESS

In answer to Ted's father, his teacher might have taken one of two major approaches. Many teachers advise delayed school entrance: "I don't think he is ready for first grade yet. Perhaps we ought to hold him back another year." Other teachers believe that waiting around for cognitive development to occur spontaneously is inefficient and unnecessary: "Ted needs to develop some important skills for first grade. I believe he will benefit from some extra attention and instruction."

Maturation viewpoint: Wait a year

In advising Ted's parents to wait another year for school entrance, his teacher was influenced by a maturational point of view on readiness. She judged him to be low on important behavioral and cognitive skills that are prerequisites to first-grade success. She noticed that Ted found it difficult to "settle down" to schoolwork and frequently failed to follow instructions given to the class. In addition, he had not mastered the alphabet and could not count to 10. His teacher reasoned that he was a little young for first grade and might do better if he stayed out another year until he "matured."

If Ted's teacher had subscribed to a stage-theory approach, she might also have concluded that he was still preoperational in his thinking and therefore not ready for first-grade learning activities. A maturation or stage-developmental position on readiness for school learning generally tells us to wait until the child is "ready." Some educators are opposed to attempts to accelerate the skills that do not appear spontaneously during development (Almy, 1966). In their view, since readiness has roots in both biological and cognitive structures, it is futile and perhaps undesirable to push Ted ahead of his natural course of development.

Social learning viewpoint: Why wait?

If Ted's teacher had a cognitive social learning view of readiness skills, she might have taken another approach. Earlier in the kindergarten year, she might have (1) given Ted a diagnostic test to determine specific learning deficits (Smith, 1969; Smith & Worell, 1980), (2) programmed small lessons for Ted to help him remediate some of his diagnosed learning problems, and (3) called a conference with his parents to plan some activities they could carry out at home. From a learning point of view, readiness consists of Ted's existing entry skills in relationship to what his teacher expects him to learn (Gagné & Briggs, 1979). Rather than wait for him to develop these skills, his teacher will teach these skills directly or provide some opportunities for them to develop. In this approach, the emphasis is on what the environment can provide as well as on what the student brings to the learning environment.

The action toward skill development moves from labeling the child as immature to environmental programming for skill development. Of course, you will recognize that readiness now resembles our old friend "entering behavior." We believe that it will be most useful for teachers to approach readiness for school, for a subject, or for an activity in terms of student entering behaviors that are prerequisite to further learning. What does Ted need to be able to do in order to begin instruction in your class? How can you help him with these entering skills?

ACCELERATING READINESS SKILLS

Your first question about increasing readiness skills is this: Does additional schooling make a difference? Starting in the 1930s, many studies were completed on the effects of nursery schools on tested IQ and academic competence. Generally, nursery school experience increases the social competence of young children but does not affect readiness skills. More recently, interest has shifted to disadvantaged and minority-group children who have shown depressed IQ scores, lower school achievement, and a higher school dropout rate. Can remedial programs be helpful in preventing any of these cognitive deficits? If so, at what age should we start intervention and how should we go about it?

Head Start and early intervention

In reply to the public pressure for increased school readiness skills among disadvantaged children, government agencies poured a tremendous amount of money and effort into the development of *Head Start*. The Head Start effort began with summer programs prior to entrance into first grade. These programs were diverse and used many differing educational theories and methods. Evaluations of these early programs were disappointing. More recently, experimental programs to enrich the social and cognitive environment of disadvantaged children begin at an earlier age and include full day-care programming. When all programs were evaluated for effectiveness in raising IQ levels and increasing school readiness skills, they have been moderately successful for short-range goals (Zigler, 1978). At the end of one to three years of intensive preschool experience, the students in several programs have shown impressive gains in both IQ and school readiness skills (Karnes et al., 1968; Klaus & Gray, 1968, 1970; Miller & Dyer, 1975; Weikert, 1972). Study 4-2 outlines the Klaus and Gray research in more detail. However, when these same children were returned to regular school programs, most of the early gains faded away by the end of the second grade. In an attempt to counteract these

"Children in well-designed remedial programs, such as Head Start and Follow-Through, continue to make gains in academic competence." (I. Hamberger/Black Star)

STUDY 4-2: IMPROVING COGNITIVE PERFORMANCE

One of the earlier intervention studies with long-range follow-up information was started by Rupert Klaus and Susan Gray in 1963. These researchers selected 3-year-old black children from poverty-line parents who had less than eighth-grade education and low-skill occupations. These are the children who are typically doomed to academic retardation, failure, and dropout. Two experimental groups were given several ten-week summers of intensive remedial training. The programs were organized around two broad areas of preschool functioning to replicate the environments of more middle-class children: motivation for academic achievement and cognitive competence. Motivational goals included achievement motivation (to compete, to try harder, to improve prior performance), persistence (to continue in an activity until a goal was at-

tained), delay of reinforcement (to select delayed rewards over immediate ones), and identification with achieving role models (to expose children to teachers who used achieving behaviors). The cognitive goals included perception (to discriminate visual and auditory similarities and differences), concept formation (to apply the same label to different objects and events), and language development (to use and comprehend elaborated spoken language).

An interesting addition to this summer-only training program with the children was a weekly home visitor who maintained some family contact throughout the first year. The visiting teacher worked with the parents (usually the mother) during summer school to encourage and reinforce the types of training experiences to which the children were exposed at school.

A battery of tests in achievement, reading readiness, intelligence, and cognitive skills was given at intervals before and after training as well as three years after the project was terminated. The results of these tests were compared with results obtained from local and distant nontreated control children who lived either in the same town or 65 miles away. At the end of two years, the combined Stanford-Binet IQ of the training groups was significantly higher than that of the controls (92.2 versus 81.8). On two school readiness tests, the trained children outperformed the control children on 10 of 11 subtests. The initial impact of this training program was clearly impressive.

However, when all intervention was withdrawn and the researchers returned one, two, and three years later for further testing, many of the differences between the training and control groups had gradually declined. For example, by fourth grade, IQ comparisons lost ground (85.6 versus 80.3) for both groups. Reading achievement was still superior at this point for both experimental groups and the local control. While the early dramatic gains tended to fade out somewhat, some residual benefits remained. The authors concluded their final follow-up with "cautious optimism," pointing out that a limited program "cannot carry the entire burden of offsetting progressive retardation." Indeed, they calculated that the training staff's contact with these children over the first six years of their lives consisted of only about 2 percent of the children's waking hours. Total contact with the mothers averaged 110 hours, or only 0.3 percent of the child's waking hours. In view of this limited degree of direct interaction, the effected changes are impressive indeed.

Adapted from:

Klaus, R. A., & Gray, S. W. The early training project for disadvantaged children: A report after five years. *Monographs of the Society for Research in Child Development,* 1968, *33* (4), whole no. 120.

Klaus, R. A., & Gray, S. W. The early training project: A seventh-year report. *Child Development,* 1977, *41,* 909–924.

"fadeout" effects, Follow-Through classrooms were established to carry the programs through the primary grades. A recent review of the Follow-Through classrooms (Stallings, 1975) suggests that students in well-designed remedial programs continue to make gains in academic competence.

Effectiveness of early intervention: Modest gains

Two striking outcomes of the many early intervention programs are becoming clear. Both the age at which children enter them and the character of the program may be determining factors. Most researchers agree that programs reaching the very young child have a better chance of succeeding. Two recent programs which intervened with intense cognitive and social interaction before the age of 1 year found preschool IQ differences as high as 30 points in comparison to children in a nontested control group (Heber et al., 1972; Robinson & Robinson, 1971). Of course, you cannot hope (nor do you wish, we suspect) to start teaching your students while they are in the cradle. However, these studies do suggest that cognitive functioning is flexible at early ages. The characteristics of the training program is a second important factor in determining cognitive outcomes. Table 4-4 shows some of the major training charac-

Table 4-4. Classroom structure and interaction in seven different Follow-Through programs

Variable	Far West	Univ. of Arizona	Bank Street	Univ. of Oregon	Univ. of Kansas	High/ Scope	EDC
398, all adult praise to children		X		X	X		
412, adult feedback to child response to adult academic commands, requests, direct questions				X	X		
420, adults attentive to a small group	X			X		X	
421, adults attentive to individual children	X	X	X		X	X	
423, positive behavior, adults to children	X	X	X				
435, total academic verbal interactions							
438, adult communication or attention focus, one child	X		X		X	X	X
440, adult communication or attention focus, small group				X		X	
444, adult movement	X						
450, all child open-ended questions							X
451, adult academic commands, requests, and direct questions to children				X	X		
452, adult open-ended questions to children	X	X	X			X	X
453, adult response to child's question with a question						X	X
454, child's extended response to questions		X	X				X
456, all child task-related comments	X	X				X	
457, all adult positive corrective feedback	X			X	X		
460, all child positive affect	X	X					X
469, all adult reinforcement with tokens					X		
509, child self-instruction, academic				X*			
510, child self-instruction, objects			X			X	X
513, child task persistence			X		X	X	
514, two children working together, using concrete objects						X	
515, small group working together, using concrete objects			X			X	
516, social interaction among children	X		X				X
574, child movement	X						X
599, child self-instruction, nonacademic	X	X				X	
Total N critical variables	28† 27*	21	27	16* 17†	17	29	20† 22*

* Third grade only.
† First grade only.
Source: Stallings, 1975.

teristics of the seven Follow-Through programs referred to above. You can see that there are large differences in the amount of structure, adult directiveness, reinforcement, and the child-adult interaction among the programs. We shall discuss these factors of classroom structure and interaction in later chapters.

The net outcome of early intervention programs tells us that many cognitive readiness skills are teachable. It is still too soon to decide which of the many ongoing programs will be the most successful in helping students with inadequate school readiness skills to maintain satisfactory progress as they proceed up the academic ladder. Each of the programs in Table 4-4 has somewhat differing goals. Therefore, our evaluation of their success and failures may depend upon how these outcomes match particular teaching objectives. However, in your first-, fifth-, or tenth-grade classroom, you will still be faced with students like Ted, Donna, and Kathy who may have inadequate entering skills for some parts of your instruction. In Chapters 10 and 11, we shall discuss some alternative approaches to the assessment of entering skills. We will emphasize a variety of techniques in observation, interviewing, and the use of standardized tests to help you evaluate the cognitive and behavioral readiness of your students for the curriculum you plan to teach.

LEARNING ACTIVITY: IMPROVING SCANNING STRATEGIES

In the years ahead, you will be in a position to help many students increase their skills in efficient learning. In Chapter 4, we discussed some ideas on teaching students to use mediation strategies. We suggest that you may be more effective in teaching these skills to your students if you are familiar with the strategies that you use in solving problems. In the following exercise, you will examine your typical strategies in a visual scanning task and apply these to a new series of problems.

LEARNING OBJECTIVES

1. Complete visual scanning of problem A and write down the procedures you used to solve it. Use a stopwatch to time yourself from start to finish.

2. Compare your procedures in visual scanning with the self-test questions and determine whether your scanning procedures were *systematic*. Did you follow a plan, look for a rule, attend to distinctive features, ask yourself questions, develop hypotheses?

3. Read the example of a planning strategy for scanning and compare it with yours. Determine the differences between your plan and the sample plan we provide.

4. Try the new plan on problem B. Does this help or hinder your progress?

5. Now revise your plan to include anything new you learned about your scanning strategies that helped you to select the correct solution quickly. Write the plan out step by step. Follow this new plan with problem C. Time yourself and compare how efficiently you reached your solution. *Caution:* Sometimes a new strategy takes longer than your old method because it is a new pattern of behavior or it interferes with your established pattern of problem solving.

TASK 4-1

Complete the following problem as quickly as you can in the manner that you would usually proceed.

A.

Figure 4-11   Visual scanning tasks A, B, and C. (Adapted from B. Egeland, Training impulsive children in the use of more efficient scanning techniques. *Child Development*, 1974, 45, 165–171.)

TASK 4-2

Self-test questions:

1. Did you follow a plan? If so, write it down step by step.
2. Did you look for a rule? If so, write it (them) down.
3. Did you look for distinctive features?
4. Did you ask yourself questions?
5. Did you develop hypotheses about what aspects of the pictures were important?

TASK 4-3

Now try the following scanning strategy (Egeland, 1974).

1. Look at the standard and all the alternatives.
2. Break the alternatives down into component parts.

B.

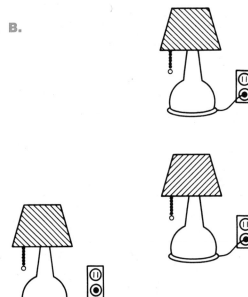
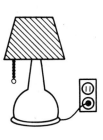
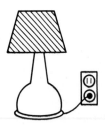

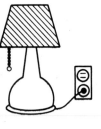

C.

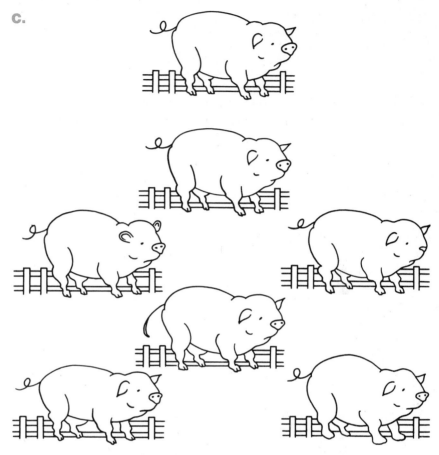

3. Select one component part and compare it across all alternatives. Look for similarities and differences across alternatives on the particular part being studied.

4. Check the standard to determine the correct form of the component part.

5. Successively eliminate alternatives that deviate from the standard on the particular component being studied. Continue to eliminate alternatives based on an analysis of component parts until only the correct alternative remains.

TASK 4-4

If you used the plan in Task 4-3, you have developed effective scanning skills for this type of task. Now, find a youngster between ages 7 and 11 and try the sample problems out. Watch how the youngster proceeds. Ask him or her how to go about solving the problems. If no plan is evident, try to teach the plan in Task 4-3. You might use direct instruction by explanation, or you might wish to try out Meichenbaum and Goodman's self-instructional modeling procedures.

SUMMARY

1. Cognitive development involves progressive changes in MEDIATION skills. Mediation procedures use VERBAL and IMAGERY SYMBOLS to represent the external environment. Mediation skills will help students to recall the past, plan for the future, and develop increased self-regulation.

2. Piaget's theory of cognitive development describes four stages of cognitive growth: SENSORIMOTOR, PREOPERATIONAL, CONCRETE OPERATIONS, and FORMAL OPERATIONS. Within each of these stages, COGNITIVE STRUCTURES change by means of ASSIMILATION and ACCOMMODATION as the child adapts to the environment. One of the most widely researched processes is *conservation*. Evidence to date suggests that the skills required for conservation may be sequenced and taught at an earlier age than Piaget has suggested. The usefulness of Piaget's theory was outlined and drawbacks were proposed.

3. Bruner's approach to cognitive development introduces three modes of cognitive representation: *enactive, iconic,* and *symbolic*. Bruner's concept of the SPIRAL CURRICULUM can be seen as a link between stage theory, which sees learning as discontinuous, and learning theory, which emphasizes that all learning is continuous.

4. Gagné's approach to cognitive development tells us that learning and thinking are teachable skills. Gagné proposes a sequence of six intellectual skills: association, chains, discriminations, concepts, rules, and problem solving. These skills are learned under differing conditions. Additionally, each of these skills involves the application of COGNITIVE STRATEGIES such as ATTENTION, encoding, retrieval, and mastery. Gagné's theory, like those of Piaget and Bruner, is particularly useful for teachers and students.

5. Language is a symbolic mediation skill that develops gradually from early infancy on through the high school years. Language is important for communication, for thinking and problem solving, and for understanding written symbols in reading. Although some theorists believe that language structures are innate, learning a language probably involves modeling, feedback, and learning rules for grammar and syntax. Meaning is acquired through multiple associations which form associative clusters. For students to communicate effectively, they must develop skills in sending clear messages that are adapted to the needs of the listener.

6. Students who come to school with NONSTANDARD DIALECTS may be seen as using either a different or a deficient language system. Nonstandard dialects interfere with effective communication and reading skills and contribute to significant retardation on standardized reading tests. Intervention with students who use nonstandard

dialects includes COMPENSATORY EDUCATION to remediate deficits or BILINGUAL EDUCATION to recognize two concurrent language systems. We suggest that teachers provide a model of elaborated standard English, avoid using the student's dialect, and maintain respect for the communication pattern of each student.

7. COGNITIVE STRATEGIES help students to learn and solve problems more efficiently and independently. ATTENTION SKILLS require the student to orient, scan, focus, and ignore irrelevant stimuli. Teachers can improve student attention through classroom management as well as by cognitive techiques that emphasize salience, relevance, and meaning. Self-instruction skills can be taught through modeling and rehearsal procedures. It was suggested that all students will benefit from some coaching in self-instructional strategies.

8. INTELLIGENCE has been viewed as either a general trait or a combination of specific traits or skills. It can also be seen as a performance sample that is moderately predictive of student progress in school and in many vocations. The two most widely used individual intelligence tests are the Stanford-Binet and the Wechsler Intelligence Scale for Children. The IQ score is useful for prediction and grouping only when a number of the limitations of intelligence tests are taken into consideration. These limitations are especially relevant to minority groups, who may be unfairly classified on the basis of standardized IQ tests.

9. READINESS for instruction includes both cognitive skills required for academic achievement and behavioral skills necessary for adapting to structured classroom situations. Readiness can be equated to the entering behaviors of students in relation to what teachers expect them to learn. Intervention to increase readiness for instruction is more effective if it is started early and followed through consistently in later grades. Head Start and Follow-Through programs use many different methods, each of which can produce different outcomes for student readiness.

10. The cognitive strategy of visual scanning requires skills in systematic planning. These skills include following a plan, looking for rules, attending to distinctive features, asking self-questions, and developing hypotheses about important aspects of the task.

 KEY TERMS

ACCOMMODATION: Piaget's term to describe reorganization of the cognitive structure to adapt to the assimilation of new stimuli.

ASSIMILATION: Piaget's term to describe modification of a new stimulus to fit the present cognitive structure.

ATTENTION: A cognitive strategy that includes four skills: orienting to a problem, scanning problem content, focusing on relevant aspects, and ignoring irrelevant stimuli.

BILINGUAL EDUCATION: Adaptation of learning materials to fit the different language patterns of the student with a nonstandard dialect. Standard English is then taught as though it were a second language.

COGNITIVE STRATEGIES: Gagné's term to describe mediating skills which students use to regulate their learning behavior.

COGNITIVE STRUCTURE: Piaget's term to describe the stage-determined organization of the mind.

COMPENSATORY EDUCATION: Preschool and early elementary academic programs designed to remediate deficient readiness skills. Head Start programs are one example of compensatory education designed for lower-SES groups.

CONCRETE OPERATIONS: Piaget's term to describe the period between ages 7 and 11 when the child's thinking moves toward decentration. In the concrete operations stage, the child can consider experience from more than one perspective.

CONSERVATION: Piaget's term for a child's knowledge that the quantity, length, or identity of substances remains the same even though the observed shape or form may change.

EQUILIBRIUM: Piaget's term to decribe a state of the cognitive structure in which no conflict exists between internal organization and the external environment. *Disequilibrium* describes a conflict between cognitive structure and discrepant information which leads to reorganization and movement to a new stage.

FORMAL OPERATIONS: The final stage of cognitive development in Piaget's theory. During adolescence, formal operational thinking becomes increasingly abstract and logical.

INTELLIGENCE: The sum of cognitive capabilities at any point in a person's development. Intelligence tests provide a measure of current intellectual functioning called the IQ.

INTELLECTUAL SKILLS: Gagné's term to describe the hierarchy of skills that enter into all learning situations. The six intellectual skills range from simple associations to problem solving.

IMAGERY: Covert, nonverbal cues that are symbols of external events.

LEARNING HIERARCHY: Gagné's term to describe an organized set of intellectual or performance skills that students need to learn a particular task or concept.

MEDIATION: The use of covert verbal and imagery cues to represent objects and events in the environment.

NONSTANDARD DIALECT: Culturally different verbal patterns that do not match the expected speech patterns of the classroom.

PREOPERATIONAL STAGE: Piaget's term to describe the period between ages 2 and 7 when children can represent their experiences by means of symbols.

READINESS: The cognitive and prosocial skills that will help students adapt to academic learning environments.

SELF-INSTRUCTION: Using covert language or self-talk to control overt motor and verbal behavior.

SCHEMA: Piaget's term to describe an internally represented response-action sequence.

S-M-R SEQUENCE: A unit of mediation consisting of a stimulus, a mediator, and a response.

SPIRAL CURRICULUM: Bruner's system of instruction in which more advanced topics are taught at a level which is appropriate to the student's cognitive development. Later, the same topic is presented at more advanced levels as the student's cognitive development matures.

VERBAL SYMBOLS: Brief language cues that are symbols of external events.

REVIEW TERMS

AGE NORMS
DEVELOPMENTAL STAGES
INDIVIDUAL DIFFERENCES
NORMAL CURVE
SOCIOECONOMIC STATUS

SELF-TEST

1. *Mediation* refers to
   a. covert processes we can't observe
   b. visual and verbal imagery
   c. changing responses to the same stimuli
   d. all of the above
2. The most advanced type of mediation consists of
   a. adult thinking processes
   b. attention skills
   c. abstract symbols
   d. concrete symbols
3. Piaget sees development as a change in
   a. cognitive structure
   b. mediation
   c. intellectual skills
   d. intelligence
4. When a 2-year-old child says "ball" when she sees an orange, Piaget calls this
   a. adaptation
   b. equilibrium
   c. generalization
   d. assimilation
5. The spiral curriculum was proposed by
   a. Bruner
   b. Piaget
   c. Gagné
   d. Worell and Stilwell
6. Gagné proposes that cognitive development is
   a. determined by conditions internal to the learner
   b. completed by the eighth grade
   c. cumulative and sequenced
   d. sequenced by stages
7. Four cognitive strategies outlined by Gagné are:
   a. _____
   b. _____
   c. _____
   d. _____
8. Four skills in effective interpersonal communication are:
   a. _____
   b. _____
   c. _____
   d. _____
9. Teaching techniques that encourage students to stop, look, and listen are ways to increase
   a. listening skills
   b. cognitive skills
   c. intelligence
   d. attention
10. Four steps in teaching children to talk to themselves are:
   a. _____
   b. _____
   c. _____
   d. _____

SELF-TEST KEY

1. d
2. c
3. a
4. d
5. a
6. c
7. Refer to page 173.
8. Refer to page 180.
9. d
10. Refer to page 189–190.

PART 3
Facilitating Learning Experiences

What do you need to know about learning to become a good teacher? How can knowing about motivation help you manage human relations and facilitate individual differences among your students? For many of you these questions will become very real. Each individual pupil is sure to present unique challenges to you. On a typical day in a typical classroom, it would not be unusual to observe the following incidents—all occurring at once:

Sid jabs Joe with a pencil, Joe yells.

Janice raises her hand for the fifth time; she is now more insistent.

Julie glances at her friend Melody and starts laughing.

Sam and Bruce walk to a discussion area and begin planning their project report.

How you conduct yourself in the classroom will be largely related to how well you understand learning theory and its application. You will want to understand how to apply learning theory in the classroom. You will recognize that learning experiences occur everywhere. These experiences can be simple and exciting. Learning occurs in the classroom, on the playground, during a part-time job, in front of the TV, in the kitchen with a parent, and in many other places. We want you to be able to apply your knowledge of learning and behavior to yourself, your friends, and your students.

In Part 3 we will discuss learning, behavior, and motivation. Our definition of learning will suggest ways of observing students and teachers and will help select a direction for changing behavior. A manager of the

learning environment can choose from among five directions for change. You may want your students to (1)
acquire a new behavior, (2) increase the frequency of a
behavior, (3) maintain the present level of performance,
(4) decrease the frequency of a particular behavior, or
(5) eliminate a behavior. You will try to motivate your
students to make some decisions about the frequency and
variety of their behaviors. In order to facilitate a change
in student behavior, you will need to know about several
important theories of learning. Once you have these
theories organized in a learning skills hierarchy, you can
apply them with precision and skill. Yes, we do believe
our three teacher roles can be combined scientifically and
artfully.

CHAPTER 5

Principles of Learning

CHAPTER OUTLINE

LEARNING OBJECTIVES

After reading Chapter 5, answering the self-monitoring questions, completing the learning activity, and reading any further references of your choice, you will be able to:

1. Define and give examples of key terms.
2. Analyze a descriptive label into its behavioral elements.
3. Apply the ABC model to a real-life situation.
4. Explain the models for classical, operant, and cognitive social learning.
5. Explain differences among the four intermittent schedules of reinforcement.
6. Select events in which the rules for reinforcement have been followed.
7. Explain potential difficulties in using only reinforcement procedures in your classroom.
8. Select examples of verbal and motor chains.
9. Summarize the arguments pro and con on aversive control strategies.
10. Analyze behavioral events in cognitive social learning.
11. Compare self-management with the four components of the basic teaching model.
12. Compare the use of natural and managed reinforcers.

FOCUS ON LEARNING AND BEHAVIOR

As a classroom teacher, a manager, and a facilitator, you will be looking at learning in this way: Learning is a process in which the person (student, parent, another teacher, or yourself) interacts with the effective environment to produce a stable change in behavior. This definition has four very crucial parts which we will look at closely.

LOOKING AT LEARNING

You can't have learning without each of these parts: a person, interaction, environment, and behavior change. Let's look at them.

Learning involves a person

When you were very young, you picked up cues (the "fridge" closing, mother's footsteps, the jostled crib) that told you food was coming. As you grew up, the environment gave you new cues (teacher smiling, assigning A+ on a term paper) that told you school is fun. Still later you learned to recognize cues from friends (laughing, touching) that said you were a valued person. Your learning is a continuous process which will go beyond your formal education.

Learning involves an environment

The person is surrounded by a learning environment. As we pointed out in Chapter 2, an environment is not stable. It is changing from moment to moment. It is not constant for any person. Environment is different in more ways than we can easily specify. Each child, each small discussion group, each classroom, each school, each family, and each community has its own very different, distinctive, and important environment. As a teacher, you will want to be sensitive to the many different environments in which you and your students find yourselves. Recognizing these individual differences and relating them to the various classroom environments will facilitate behavior change.

Learning involves interaction

The people who make up your environment interact to promote learning. As you learned in Chapters 2, 3, and 4, we develop through a process of interaction with our family and friends. Possibly, your father and mother are learning how to live without you. Their lives were constantly bombarded with slammed doors, requests for advanced allowances, or your demand for food. Now your parents may be fumbling about trying to talk with each other. You are not there to fill those moments of silence. Through these new interactions they will adjust to the family environment without you.

Learning involves behavior change

The fourth part of our definition of the learning process contains two ideas. First, behavior change requires us to look at behavior on several different occasions. If the behavior is repeated at time 1, time 2, and time 3, we would probably say the behavior change is stable. Of course, we would want the environmental conditions at time 1, time 2, and time 3 to be as similar as possible in order to test whether the behavior has been learned. Second, behavior change may be visible and *overt* or it may be invisible and *covert*. Sid, a student in driver training, may say, "I watched the safety film and I read the manual"; but we won't know until he becomes involved in actual highway conditions whether he can handle an emergency situation. Some behavior change may not be seen! How can that happen? We know that covert behavior change occurs when we observe the evidence in overt behaviors.

At this point we have discussed our definition of learning as a process. We have identified four necessary prerequisites to learning: a person, interaction, environment, and behavior change. The challenge for you is to develop ways to answer the following question in your own classroom: What is the most *appropriate* learning strategy for this *particular* individual with that *distinctive* educational goal in these *different* environments?

"We know that covert behavior change occurs when we observe the evidence in overt behaviors." (M. Reinhart/Photo Researchers)

For example, you will ask, "Which learning strategy, film simulation, or behind-the-wheel experience will improve Sid's stop-and-go driving in a downtown area?"

LOOKING AT BEHAVIOR

In your daily classroom activities, you will want to assess and balance learning strategies, student characteristics, educational goals, and the uniqueness of your classroom environment. The results of your assessment and analysis can be your plan for facilitating a particular student's or group's program of behavior change. You will want to develop this program of changing behaviors in cooperation with Sid, Janice, and Sam, their classmates, and their parents. This kind of cooperation will challenge your abilities to manage, mediate, or facilitate a change for a classroom or a student in a sensitive manner.

Notice that you will need to consider behaviors as well as behavior. A person does not perform a single behavior. People demonstrate sequences of behaviors, often at the same time; for example, drinking water, smiling at you, and deftly throwing a paper cup into the wastebasket. Let us look at some ideas about behavior and behaviors.

Characteristics of behavior

Behavior has a number of interesting characteristics. Understanding these characteristics is a prerequisite to management, mediation, and facilitation in the classroom. You will want to master the meanings and applications of the key words and underlined sentences in learning to be an effective teacher.

Behavior is a simple, measurable, and observable event which appears to be under the control of either antecedents or consequences. It is simple because it can be described in words which each of us—you, the student, a parent, your principal, and an observer—can understand. It is measurable because it has a distinctive beginning, duration, and ending. Behavior is observable because it is simple and measurable and because an objective observer—you, a child, a parent, or your principal—can record the behavioral event, usually a series of behaviors linked together in a chain. A number of observations of nearly the same behavioral event can help you focus on the frequency or on the variety of behaviors. This focus on simple, measurable, and observable behavioral events can help you manage a classroom or facilitate individual mastery of skills.

Behavior is learned   Through a process involving people interacting with their environments, a stable change in behavior which we call learning occurs. The process of learning continues far beyond the end of formal schooling.

Behavior is predictable   For years, psychologists have been studying learning. Each study has tried to develop a better understanding of "What happens if . . .?" Sometimes psychologists find that apparently nothing happens! Other times they discover a new answer to "if-then" questions. In an early example, Brackbill (1958) asked the question, "If an adult smiles and tickles a smiling 3-month-old child, then, will the child's smiling increase?" The simple answer was "Yes, smiling will be increased." Brackbill also found that an adult who smiles once in a while helps a child keep on smiling more than an adult who smiles all the time. Studies on "if-then" questions about behavior help the psychologist get more information to put together into laws of learning, guidelines for classroom management, or rules for self-management (Scandura, 1977). These laws, guidelines, or rules are really statements about what typically occurs in a given situation. Events that typically occur are predictable.

Psychologists have patiently described how people learn by observing specifiable and measurable behaviors, usually in laboratory-like conditions. Educational psychologists and social learning theorists, in particular, have tried to translate laboratory learning results into meaningful ways to manage learning and human relationships and to facilitate human development. In your teaching, you will find that psychologists and teachers have been working on the same thing. Our first sentence in this paragraph could be easily rewritten as "Teachers have patiently described how their students learn through observations and specifiable and measurable behaviors, usually in the classroom." Indeed, we want you to be able to rewrite this sentence in two or three years to read, "I can patiently describe . . ."!

Behavior can be overt or covert We can see behavior or we can feel and think behavior. You can see behavior in the environment. OVERT BEHAVIOR which is seen easily lends itself to theory building, prediction, and managing. The problem is that many behaviors are COVERT. Only the person who is doing the behavior can really observe COVERT BEHAVIORS such as tightening of muscles, drying of the mouth, or feelings of fear or love. While Sid or Joe appear to be studying busily, they may actually be thinking about ice cream, girls, and Saturday night. This is an example of covert behavior. In the long run, the covert "stomach pain" of the high school junior just before her Practice Scholastic Aptitude Test (PSAT), can be a recordable behavioral event. A very important challenge for you is to become sensitive to evidence of covert behaviors as well as those that are overt.

=== **PROBE 5-1** ===

Think of a recent important event in your life. List five overt behaviors and five covert behaviors related to the event. Did the two sets of behaviors say "the same thing"?

An exciting experience for you or your students is to become aware of your covert behaviors. Sometimes the covert behaviors do not match the overt behavior. For example, Sid might really be feeling quite sad yet say "I am very happy." For another example, you might think that the symphony was a horrible experience because the strings were flat, but when your date gently asked for your opinion, you say "Oh, I enjoyed the Beethoven immensely!" When covert thoughts and feelings do not match overt behavior, stress or discomfort can result. The challenge for you or the student is to match up the overt and covert behaviors. Kazdin (1974) has suggested PROBE 5-2.

=== **PROBE 5-2** ===

Suppose you pick a course which is a little bit of a "pain." Such an undertaking usually enters one's thoughts from time to time. We want you to count how often you think negatively about this particular course. Also, record how often you raise your hand in the class. Probably you don't raise your hand very often. Try something different and repeat "I like this class. I like it a lot." Force yourself to say it over before your class. Remember to say it to yourself. By doing this, you are practicing a covert behavior. Do you raise your hand more often or do you look at your students more frequently?

Behavior may be learned but not performed   In driver education class, for example, the defensive driving strategy for slipping on ice may be learned during the semester, but it may never be performed during the class. As a teacher, you will want to get your lesson plan across to the students, use all the appropriate film strips and pictures, test the students, and reteach parts of the lesson. The entire process can fall very flat if some of the learned material is not performed. You will meet students who say, ''I know the material, but you didn't ask the right questions.'' Has this ever happened to you? The tricky part of measuring learning is to set up the kind of situation in which the learned behavior can be performed and observed (Chapter 10). Given a situation in which the behavior can be performed, you will be able to assess learning.

Behavior may be appropriate or inappropriate   A great number of variables enter into the decision on appropriateness. You will have to consider the past frequency of the particular behavior as well as the existing situation before deciding whether or not the behavior is appropriate. For example, some children are very shy in class. They seldom speak up. When a quiet child does speak up, it may be the wrong time. When Marilyn finally asks a question, it might be such a singular event that you will want to give her a hug. Often the timing of the behavior tries your patience. Patiently encourage the Marilyns in your classroom and help them learn the appropriate times for the question.

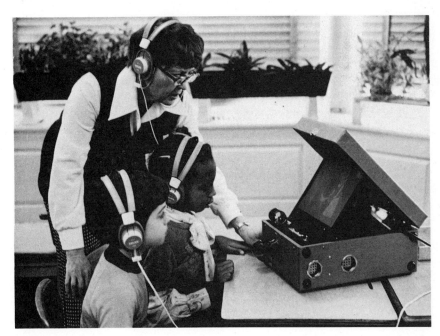

"You will want to get your lesson plan across to the students, use all the appropriate film strips and pictures, test the students, and reteach parts of the lesson." (Sybil Shelton/Peter Arnold)

Behavior may be unlearned   Earlier we said behavior is learned in a predictable manner. Now we are going to say that behavior may also be unlearned or performed less frequently. As a teacher, you will frequently want to reduce the frequency of a particular classroom behavior (for example, the passing of notes between Joe and George). Some learned behaviors simply do not help students study, interact with their classmates, or ask creative questions. You will want to help students unlearn some of their behaviors.

CAREFUL USE OF LABELS

Earlier, we talked about using labels to describe people and their behaviors. In Chapter 1, we said that people use labels to code their descriptions of behavior. For example, a "great gal" or a "cool guy" brings to your mind a host of very positive feelings and a cluster of behaviors which make up the labels. We are concerned about your use of labels to describe your students during your coffee-drinking sessions in the teachers' lounge. For example, you might hear someone say "The kid's an absolute pain!" Such a remark is probably just as harmful as "You know his sister was terribly stupid also." The repeated use of these labels can create problems for you as the classroom teacher and for the student as well (Reynolds & Birch, 1977). When students and teachers tend to use the same label, they seem to expect certain things. For example, the "country boy" who is enrolled in the city school is expected to know all about farming conditions in New England. A number of other things such as knowledge about cows and tractors seem to be uniquely ascribed to the "country boy." Indeed, the people who use a particular label seem to develop a set of expectations for the person to whom the label is applied.

A label is made
up of behaviors

Let's take a look at the first intense pair of eyes that meet you after that momentous occasion when your supervisor-teacher says, "OK, now you're on your own!" Sid is not really bad, but he does hum frequently. In addition, Sid has thrown one or two paper planes. Also, a pile of books fell on a girl's foot as she walked past Sid. Last, the thumbtack on the teacher's chair may well have been placed there by Sid. Probably you would think of this fairly normal boy as a little "wild" in the classroom. What does this label mean? Table 5-1 shows several behaviors related to the label "wild".

Table 5-1 shows four specific behaviors which are numbered b_1, b_2, b_3, and b_4. Several other behaviors can be specified and numbered b_x. You can see in Table 5-1 that a number of behaviors seem to be related to the label *wild*. In making up our list of behaviors, we have used present participles to show action. Sid's "wildness" is made up of a large number of different action behaviors. In Table 5-1, we can look at the several

Table 5-1. Several behaviors related to "wild-ness"

Label	Behaviors
Wild	b_1 Humming frequently
	b_2 Throwing paper planes
	b_3 Hitting girl
	b_4 Placing thumbtacks
	b_x Swinging on fire door

behaviors (b_1 to b_x) and say "a child who does all those things is really wild." In this case, we are using the behaviors to define the label. From our experience, we have observed that many teachers and counselors use behaviors to define the label when they talk about a student like Sid. Be careful when you talk about your students' behaviors. There are many problems in using labels.

A label predicts behaviors

Let us take a slightly different look at Figure 5-1. Some people use the label to explain the behaviors. Probably, in your own experience, you can remember a classmate with a reputation for being wild. In that case, the student's reputation probably preceded him or her into the room. The labeled wildness was probably used to predict or to explain the student's observable, specific behavior. Indeed, probably you expected this student to live up to a "wild" reputation! Often, the label predicted the behavior.

Logical circularity in a label

Do you see the problems? On the one hand, the behaviors (b_1 to b_x) are used to define the label *wild*. This way of thinking about people can get us into trouble. On the other hand, the label *wild* is used to explain or to predict the same behaviors (b_1 to b_x). We believe that either one of these ways of using labels is misleading. Everyone of us—experienced teachers,

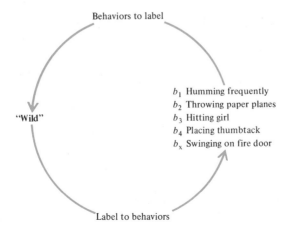

Figure 5-1 Does the label or the behavior come first?

psychologists, social workers, teenagers, parents, and even you—frequently uses labels in both of these ways.

The problem with labeling is that it creates a circle from the observed behaviors to the label and from the label to the specific, measurable, and observable behaviors (Figure 5-1). Using the behaviors to define the label or the label to explain the behaviors is a logical circularity. It doesn't help us answer the important questions about the management of classroom learning or the facilitation of learning experiences. You as a teacher will simply chase yourself and your behavioral definition if you use a logical circularity.

Breaking the logical circularity

As a classroom teacher, you will not be able to afford to indulge in logical circularities. Thirty unique children and your professional colleagues in the school need your special skills as a manager of learning, mediator of human relations, and facilitator of development. Please do not waste your time, so that your students will not lose your unique contribution to them. Consider a more useful alternative for focusing on learning.

AN ANTECEDENT-BEHAVIOR-CONSEQUENCE MODEL

In this new model, we want you to consider each of Sid's behaviors (b_1 to b_x) as a separate event. You should be able to answer three questions about the behavioral event: (1) What did he do? (2) What happened after the event? and (3) What happened before the behavior? For example, we have developed some answers for these three questions related to Sid's "throwing paper planes." These events probably occurred in this way: (1) it was a few minutes before lunch and Sid was probably tired and hungry, (2) Sid threw the plane, and (3) you gave a very standard lecture which brought snickers from Sid's classmates. In this example, we have tried to answer our three questions about the behavioral event, its

Table 5-2. Listing behavioral events

Antecedent	Behavior	Consequence
a_1 Reading silently	b_1 Humming	c_1 Laughing classmates
a_2 Getting tired	b_2 Throwing planes	c_2 Lecture by you
a_3 Walking near Sid	b_3 Hitting girl	c_3 Attending to Sid
a_4 Thinking of spring	b_4 Placing tack on teacher's chair	c_4 Laughing, explaining to principal, gaining new status
a_x Leaving school	b_x Swinging on door	c_x Meeting with principal

antecedents, and the consequences. In Table 5-2, we have tried to relate behavioral events to their antecedents and consequences.

USING BEHAVIOR AS AN EVENT

In this new model for focusing on learning, each specific, observable, measurable behavior now has other antecedent and consequent events tied to it. The humming (b_1) has a special payoff—classmates laughed (c_1). The tack on your chair (b_4) got a rise out of everybody! Probably the more important consequences were new status for Sid, a meeting with the principal and counselor, and a serious talk with Mom or Dad (c_4). Thus, in this new model for focusing on learning, we have considered each behavior as part of a separate sequence of events. The label (*wild*) which we used to discuss Sid in Figure 5-1 has disappeared in Table 5-2. We have broken the logical circularity, so that now we consider each behavior as a separate event with unique cues and payoffs. In Table 5-2, we have given you a cue to the next section of this chapter: What do the *a* and *c* stand for?

USING ANTECEDENT AND CONSEQUENT EVENTS

The *a* and *c* refer to events which surround a particular behavior. Earlier we called these events "cues" and "payoffs." In looking at Table 5-2, we can think of each line as a sequence of events. For example, we have antecedent events, behavioral events, and consequent events. Each of these three events has a special title. "Walking near Sid" can be called

"The classroom environment helps contribute to both the list of antecedents and the table of consequences." (Lejeune/Stock, Boston)

an antecedent event or the DISCRIMINATIVE STIMULUS event (S_D). The sight of the girl sets the stage for Sid to participate in a sequence of events. We can also say that the girl walking near Sid either (1) structures his role, (2) obtains his attention, or (3) provides the occasion for his subsequent response (hitting). In each of these examples, the discriminative stimulus controls the sequence of Sid's and his classmates' behaviors. On the other end of the sequence, "attending to Sid" can be called a consequent event or the reinforcing event (S_R). The glare of the female classmate provides a large payoff for Sid! In this sequence of events, Sid's *behavior* (b_1 to b_r) seems to be facilitated by the *antecedents* (S_D) or reinforced by the events listed in the *consequences* (S_R). In this way, we have the ABCs of a particular behavior (Table 5-2).

The classroom environment helps contribute to both the list of antecedents and the table of consequences. When you begin to list antecedents and consequences, you can think of them as single events or as clusters of events. Also, antecedents and consequences may be overt or covert. Overt consequences are usually administered by teachers, peers, or parents. In contrast, covert antecedents are usually things that people say to themselves. One may, for example, say "take it easy" or "be careful, practice each move" before becoming involved in a particular behavioral event. Similarly, when the consequences are covert, people administer the reinforcers by saying to themselves "I did well," "That was a nice thing to say," or "Keep it up, you are about finished!" Thus, the environment surrounding the behaving students and the students themselves can be the sources for both antecedents and consequences.

===== PROBE 5-3 =====

Think of a recent specific, important event in your life such as meeting "the person," getting fired, or getting a new job. Create a table and fill in the ABCs of the event.

Now we expand our ABC MODEL for focusing on learning. By going through a behavioral analysis such as the one we have just completed on "wild" Sid, you can get a pretty good idea of how a behavior or cluster of behaviors is being maintained. You will find it useful to apply the ABC approach to the facilitation of learning in a variety of classrooms. Frequently, a parent or another teacher may ask for help with the management, mediation, or facilitation of student behaviors. The questions usually have the same emphasis: "I need help with Bruce!" How will you focus on Bruce? It is a long way from that insistent cry for help to the well-thought-out, appropriate learning strategy for the unique individual with a distinctive goal in this particular environment. We believe that your use of the ABC model to focus on learning will set you well on your way to reaching an answer.

APPLYING THE ABC MODEL TO
BEHAVIOR CHANGE

Once we agree that behavior is learned and that it can be unlearned, the roles for a teacher become very different. You are expected to know that each student's behaviors and learning can be managed. Some behaviors which you want to manage can easily be changed by modifying the antecedent: assign different textbooks, change the daily schedule, or reorder the classroom seating assignments. Some other behaviors can be managed by changing the consequences: allow the student to use free time with a friend, offer the student a choice in the next learning activity, simply praise the student on a paper, or provide creative games. Still, some other behaviors, such as incomplete assignments and speech mannerisms, will seem impossibly difficult to influence and very resistant to change. The ABC model can help you analyze a particular student such as "wild" Sid in a manner that will suggest alternative plans.

Consider the alternatives

In classroom and playground situations, the ABC model will guide you in one of five directions. Your analysis might help you decide (1) to maintain the specified behavior at its present rate, (2) to increase its frequency, (3) to decrease its rate, or (4) to eliminate it entirely. Should none of these four alternatives be acceptable to you and Sid, you might help him (5) acquire a new behavior. Sometimes your ABC analysis and your plans based on the analysis will result in referral to a specialist such as a reading teacher, school psychologist, school social worker, or special educator.

Analyze the ABCs

The basic ABC model can be applied on the playground, in the home, and in your own interpersonal relationships. On the playground, the ABC analysis might help you pinpoint the sequence of events leading Sid to bully the same two or three others day after day. Indeed, you might try to create your own diagram of the several ABC sequences involved in a playground scuffle. In the home, the antecedents to the quiet and careful closing of a door can be a very gentle discriminative stimulus—the word "quietly" (Krumboltz, 1966). In your own interpersonal relationships, you might apply the ABC model to get your roommate to clean the kitchen sink. The model can be useful in a variety of settings.

Changing student behavior

Let's take an example and apply the ABC model to "wild" Sid. As his teacher, you do not want him to continue throwing paper planes in class. You would be glad to see him reduce or eliminate this particular behavior completely. Further, since Sid is a fairly responsible middle-schooler, he is willing to agree to the goal of reducing his plane throwing during class time.

	Antecedent	Behavior	Consequence
Sequence 1	Nearly lunchtime	Throwing of plane	Lecture by you
Sequence 2	Negotiation of learning contract	Work for fifteen minutes	Read favorite book for five minutes

Figure 5-2
Sid's ABC analysis of two sequences.

At this point, you can set up a special ABC table for Sid (Goodwin & Coates, 1976). This unique ABC table has at least two sequences, as shown in Figure 5-2. Each of these sequences represents three time frames (antecedent, behavior, and consequences) in Sid's learning management. The first sequence represents the initial situation. The second sequence shows what occurred after you and Sid talked about his behavior and negotiated a new goal. This negotiation was backed up by a "contract" involving you, Sid, possibly the principal, and Sid's parents. The contract becomes an S_D (or discriminative stimulus event) for Sid because it specifies what he has to do to receive a reinforcing event. It is therefore a cue for his appropriate behavior. In situations of this kind, the ABC model can become dynamic and meaningful to you.

LEARNING THEORIES TO GUIDE YOU

In this part of the chapter we will talk about learning theories and how they are helpful for teachers. In Chapter 1, we talked about theories and how they can be helpful in your teaching activities. In order to be useful for you, a theory must be *simple, testable,* and *heuristic.* Very few theories meet these criteria. The person who first rolled a heavy object by using a wheel apparently had developed a simple, testable, and heuristic theory of motion. First, a simple theory has very few parts. When a theory can be stated briefly and simply, it usually means that the theory builder has stated the ideas in the most basic way. Second, testable theories so state their ideas that the constructs and concepts are measurable. When the constructs and concepts can be stated in operational (measurable) terms, it usually means that the theory can be tested. (Also, the theory conforms rather closely to the real world when it is simple and testable.) Third, heuristic theories suggest many more questions than they answer. When more questions can be generated, it usually means that the theory can help people discover more new ideas based on the theory. In this book we shall limit our discussions to the simple, testable, and heuristic theories of learning.

In the 1980s, you as a classroom teacher will be able to use a number of learning theories. We will emphasize three useful ones: classical, operant, and cognitive social learning. Simple, testable, and heuristic criteria can be successfully applied to these theories. Indeed, these theories have so much in common that once you understand classical conditioning, it is a small step to operant learning and a slightly larger step to cognitive social learning. We show this in Table 5-3.

As you can see, each theory has the basic elements of stimulus (S) and response (R). Each successive theory adds to this basic theme. In classical learning, the S and the R are closely related, almost automatically. Operant conditioning recognizes the linkage between the stimulus (S), the response (R), and reinforcement (the little r). The important addition is reinforcement. Last, cognitive social learning added a model's behavior and self-control variables to mediate cognitively the person's behavior before responding. These theories will help you focus on behavior, discover antecedents and consequences, and develop programs for behavior change. By using combinations of these theories, you will develop an appreciation for the way in which distinctive behaviors are learned and maintained and what can be done to change them with the particular individual.

PRINCIPLES OF CLASSICAL LEARNING

One basic variety of learning is called CLASSICAL or respondent LEARNING. The model for CLASSICAL LEARNING was presented in Table 5-3. In this model we say that the simplest kind of learning occurs when an antecedent stimulates a response. We can describe classical learning in several ways—for example, "an antecedent elicits a behavioral response" or "an unconditioned stimulus controls an unconditioned response" (Figure 5-3). Whatever way we talk about classical learning theory we are still describing the SR format presented in Table 5-3.

Ivan Petrovich Pavlov, a Russian physiologist, was studying the digestive process of dogs. He had hooked up some tubes which allowed him to measure the saliva secreted by his dog in response to food placed in the dog's mouth. Said another way, Pavlov was looking at the relationship between the antecedent (food placed in the dog's mouth) and the salivation response. You can imagine Pavlov's surprise when he discovered that the dog salivated as soon as he saw his food dish.

Table 5-3. Three formats of learning

Name	Format	Prominent researcher
Classical learning	SR	I. P. Pavlov
Operant learning	$S–R_r$	B. F. Skinner
Cognitive social learning	S–M–R	A. Bandura

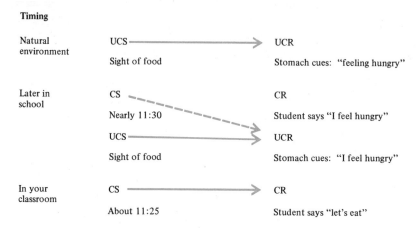

Figure 5-3
Classical
conditioning around
lunchtime.

The classical learning theory studied by Pavlov has been applied to the behavior of students in the classroom, on the playground, and at home. Let us look at classical conditioning in a diagram (Figure 5-3). In the simplest setting, we say that a natural UNCONDITIONED STIMULUS (UCS) controls or elicits a particular UNCONDITIONED RESPONSE (UCR). In the learning environment, the simple model gets two new terms: CONDITIONED STIMULUS (CS) and CONDITIONED RESPONSE (CR). The distinction between *unconditioned* and *conditioned* is that one is natural and the other is learned. Figure 5-3 shows the difference.

A closer look at Figure 5-3 shows that in the "Natural environment" line there is an unconditioned stimulus, the sight of food, that controls the stomach's "feeling hungry." Of course, there are many stimuli controlling a similar number of unconditioned responses (for example, bright lights in the eyes influence pupil size and sudden loud noises increase heart rate).

In the "Later in school" line, the situation is becoming more involved. We have added a conditioned stimulus ("nearly 11:30") which occurs a few minutes before the student sees food. The timing is important in classical conditioning because a new or neutral stimulus, which occurs just before the unconditioned stimulus, takes over the influence of the older unconditioned stimulus. The effect in classical learning is that the new conditioned stimulus (nearly lunchtime) controls the old unconditioned response (hunger pains) and probably some other unanticipated behaviors. In Figure 5-3, the dashed line shows that the conditioned stimulus (lunchtime) is beginning to control the unconditioned response (stomach), and a new cue conditioned response ("I feel hungry") is developing. As you can see, classical conditioning will appear daily in your classroom management.

Finally take a look at the "In your classroom" section of Figure 5-3. We find that the more natural examples of classical conditioning have been replaced by some behaviors which function under the classical conditioning format. In this classroom, Sid, Janice, and the gang begin to get a little restless around 11:25 a.m. Over time in your school, they have learned that they will actually eat shortly after 11:30. Further, the feeling of hunger and the sight of food have been controlled by the thought of food and the time of day! Presto! In this kind of model, we can show you how classical conditioning seems to work in your classroom.

PROBE 5-4

Examples of classical learning can be found in the natural environment. Select a CR such as a fear response and diagram its probable development to include UCRs, UCSs, and CSs. Look at Figure 5-3 for a model. You may have to repeat that sequence several times in order to reach the selected CR.

Now we want to make a point about classical conditioning. As a classroom teacher who is strongly committed to children's learning, you will probably use classical learning procedures to help your students develop positive attitudes toward school. At the earliest stages—reading, doing art work, and studying arithmetic—the teacher will probably be fairly neutral. We want these parts of the school environment to become conditioned stimuli so that the children will develop some positive feelings toward school. School and learning can be fun for children. The teacher can be "fun," "pretty," or even "great"! And when teachers provide interesting books, exciting topics, and lots of praise and positive attention for good work, these activities become enjoyable as well. Depending on how you use classical conditioning procedures, the children will develop their unique attitudes about school. You will have the great responsibility of developing such positive attitudes in your students.

PRINCIPLES OF OPERANT LEARNING

Classical learning is not the only way people learn. Another very basic way of learning is called OPERANT LEARNING or instrumental conditioning. It is operant because the person is operating on the environment to effect a consequence. Thus, in Table 5-2, instead of looking at the antecedents or stimulus events which control a behavior, we are looking at the consequences or rewarding events which appear to control a behavior. In classical learning, we look at the S in our format and in operant learning we will expand our focus to include S, R, and (r) in the format. Mostly we will focus on the consequence of a particular behavior. In the classroom, you will smile at Sid, you will draw a happy face on his paper, or you will say something nice about his behavior. On the playground, reinforcing events or consequences also occur, such as kicking a long ball, skipping rope with a friend, or holding hands with someone special. The point is, behavior that is reinforced has a tendency to increase in frequency, strength, or probability of occurrence.

Positive reinforcement

B. F. Skinner, an American psychologist, developed a number of useful ideas about operant learning. He learned that a thirsty or hungry pigeon will peck in the cage until it happens to hit a button which releases a drop of water or a pellet of food. Skinner watched the pigeon wander around the cage, pecking, until again the button was hit and water appeared. The average thirsty or hungry pigeon soon gets the hang of life in the "Skinner box." The pigeon hits the button at an increasingly stable rate and receives food or water until it is satiated or filled up.

Let's look at operant learning in a classroom. Before they enter school, boys and girls appear to like to hear their names. In many homes, the name is especially important and appears to be a highly valued word to the child. Once in school, these young students engage in a wide variety of activities which result in their name being called by peers and/or you. Sometimes the message following the name is warm, pleasant, enjoyable, and positively reinforcing. Primary-level students quickly learn which particular classroom behaviors have positive consequences. In Table 5-4, we have Joe once again. Very simply, Joe learns fairly quickly that smiling at you results in hearing his name, probably couched in a warm or pleasant sentence. Similarly, he discovers that running in the halls results in a brief, but aversive (unpleasant) meeting with the hall monitor or principal. You will probably discover during your first year of teaching that young boys like Joe will quickly learn the most effective behavior for obtaining your undivided attention. They will usually repeat that behavior again as long as they are rewarded for it.

In the last two paragraphs, we have presented you with a very important idea proposed by Skinner. Earlier, we said that reinforced behavior has a tendency to increase in frequency, strength, or probability of occurrence. In the classroom situation, Joe smiled and/or helped Mark and obtained some positive reinforcement from his environment. Indeed, future behavior is usually determined by past consequences.

Table 5-4. Some positive and negative consequences for Joe

| Behavior | Probable consequences | |
	Positive	Negative
Hitting Beth		Sitting in the corner
Smiling at you	Hearing his name	
Helping Mark	Mark sharing	
Running in halls		Principal becoming "angry"

	Present	**Remove**
Positive stimuli	Positive reinforcement	Extinction, "time out"
Negative stimuli	Punishment	Negative reinforcement

**Figure 5-4
Possible conditions
for positive and
negative stimuli.**

Reinforcement may be positive or negative. A positive reinforcer increases the behavior that produces it. Let's take a look at Figure 5-4. So far we have talked only about positive reinforcement. Later in this chapter we will discuss what happens when a negative stimulus is presented, when a positive stimulus is removed, and when a negative stimulus is removed. As a classroom teacher, you will want to learn how to manage positive and negative stimuli in the classroom and on the playground.

**Schedules of
reinforcement**

Skinner and his students did not stop watching pigeons with his discovery that reinforced behavior will probably recur. At first, every time the pigeon pecked at the button, it received some grain or water. Skinner was curious. What happens to the pecking behavior when the pigeon is not rewarded every time it pecks? This simple question helped to open up more ideas about reinforcement. Skinner and his coworkers made a lot of discoveries which have been translated into useful ideas for individual, group, teacher, and student behavior.

Skinner was able to look at many different patterns of behavior which occur when a person is reinforced. Originally, he studied the effects of a CONTINUOUS REINFORCEMENT schedule (CRF). Under a CRF schedule, Julie, for example, upon raising her hand, is rewarded every time with attention from the teacher. Fortunately for you as a teacher, a continuous reinforcement schedule is seldom necessary. Later, Skinner considered the effects an intermittent reinforcement schedule might have on a student. For example, people may be reinforced after a fixed number of behaviors are performed or after a fixed amount of time has passed. Skinner also tried varying the time interval and the number of behaviors needed to earn a reward. In addition to CRF, Skinner and his associates observed four basic intermittent patterns: FIXED INTERVAL (FI), FIXED RATIO (FR), VARIABLE INTERVAL (VI), and VARIABLE RATIO (VR). The task of identifying five schedules of reinforcement and applying them to the classroom, playground, and home settings was not enough for Skinner. He also studied the characteristic performances of people in a combined VARIABLE INTERVAL–VARIABLE RATIO (VI–VR) or mixed schedule. Each of these schedules appears to result in its own unique pattern of behavior. Let's look at each schedule in turn.

"Under a continuous reinforcement schedule, students are rewarded with attention from the teacher every time they raise their hands." (Robert Smith/Black Star)

Continuous reinforcement   Some children start their day demanding immediate and continuous parental attention. Very few parents are able to respond with their own CRF schedule. First thing in the morning, the typical 2- to 4-year-old pays a great deal of attention to the parent. Then, amost abruptly, the child leaves the parent for Captain Kangaroo. We would say the child was *satiated* by the parental reinforcement. Indeed, CRF schedules are rarely used because the person quickly becomes satiated and stops performing the desired behavior.

Fixed interval reinforcement   First graders can be given their allowance every Friday, no matter what they are doing at the precise moment of reinforcement. This FIXED INTERVAL (FI) reinforcement schedule is not CONTINGENT upon any particular behavior except possibly "being good" all week. Similarly, as a classroom teacher, you will probably be reinforced once or twice a month by the school board treasurer, no matter what you are doing at the precise moment of reinforcement. These two situations are examples of FI schedules of reinforcement. The occurrence of the reinforcer is contingent upon the passage of time rather than upon a specific response.

Fixed ratio reinforcement   In English class, Sam can be assigned fifteen pages to read and report on. As soon as Sam turns in his report, he will earn a set number of points, say five. In this case, he is being rewarded on a FIXED RATIO (FR) reinforcement schedule. Certain jobs such as telephone solicitation and farm work appear to be paid by the number of units of work completed. This is another example of the FR reinforcement schedule. In such a schedule, the occurrence of reinforcement is contingent upon the performance of a planned number of acceptable responses.

Variable interval reinforcement   In your social studies class, Melody does not talk frequently. Recently, you have made a point of calling on Melody once during each class session—either near the beginning of the class, about halfway through, or near the end of class. It is very important in this schedule to call on Melody at least once during every class. Surprisingly, Melody pays closer attention in every social studies class. Since she is a good student, you can call on her frequently (Good, 1970; Rowe, 1974). On the average, you call on her two seconds after she raises her hand. Both of these average length of times she is called on during social studies classes can be used to describe the VARIABLE INTERVAL (VI) reinforcement schedule. These reinforcement schedules, which are designed to change behavior, take an extra amount of care so that students like Melody are rewarded (being called on) at the planned average interval.

Variable ratio reinforcement   Joe may be reinforced upon completing a variable number of math problems. For example, he might have to answer six problems correctly one day for an A; on another day, he might have to give fourteen correct solutions for the same grade. Under the control of this VARIABLE RATIO (VR) reinforcement schedule, Joe works quickly and accurately to earn his A. As a classroom teacher, you will find that planning the ratio is crucial to maximize on Joe's interest in completing the math problems. You have probably thought about going to Las Vegas, but please remember that there the slot machines will reward you on a VR schedule that has been carefully planned to benefit the management!

Each of the four intermittent reinforcement schedules that Skinner has described is presented in Figure 5-5. In the FI pattern, we see a brief pause after the reinforcement and before the person resumes work. Probably, on payday, you daydream that you could easily spend twice the amount on your check before you resume working. The behavior pattern from the FR schedule shows a long flat period of no production after each reward. The person working under an FR schedule typically performs at a zero rate or at a very low rate immediately following the reinforcement. The total number of behaviors completed under the VR schedule suggests

Figure 5-5
Patterns of four
intermittent
reinforcement
schedules.

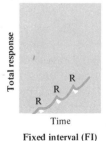

Fixed interval (FI)

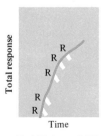

Fixed ratio (FR)

Variable interval (VI)

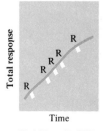

Variable ratio (VR)

that the person does not know when the reinforcement is to be provided and therefore works in "bursts" of activity. You might have a charming little troublemaker in your class who gets a large number of "jollies" out of being disruptive. For a while, this child works quietly and then, with no warning, puts on a show for the sake of the class's (and your) attention (reinforcement). Last, under the VI schedule, the student really does not know when a reinforcer will be made available. Sometimes, several payoffs occur rapidly and other times the student has to work for a long time before there is any reward. (It is something like writing a book!)

PROBE 5-5

Consider your own life and list two examples each of FI, FR, VI, and VR reinforcement schedules provided by your experiences. Which of these behaviors would be easy for you to change? Which behaviors would be difficult for you to change? Why?

Now that you are quite familiar with these five schedules of reinforcement, we want to point out that the real, natural world in which we all live follows a variety of reinforcement schedules. For many of our behaviors, we function under a combination of variable interval–variable ratio (VI–VR), or a mixed schedule. Indeed, many of us work very hard to order our lives in such a way that we will be able to predict and plan our courses of action. Still, numerous other people—many of whom will be the parents of your students, your teaching colleagues, and sometimes even yourself—appear quite often to behave as if they were operating under a VI–VR schedule. For the record, the behaviors controlled by the VI–VR schedule are the most difficult to reduce or to eliminate.

In sum, six operant conditioning schedules can be identified for your consideration and possible use in the classroom. Each of these reinforcement schedules produces a unique set of management challenges.

Organizing schedules of reinforcement: A management challenge

As a classroom teacher, you will observe and try to analyze behaviors which have been learned with different schedules. Each schedule seems to suggest a different set of challenges for the classroom teacher. We can think of this challenge under the general heading of behaviors which are persistent, or "resistant to change." The six schedules can be ranked in terms of their resistance to change. At one end of the continuum we can put the CRF schedule. Here, the person is accustomed to reinforcement after every occurrence of the particular behavior. Should the reinforcement not be forthcoming, the behavior will probably not occur. At the other end we have the combination VI–VR or mixed schedule, in which the person really does not know how often the behaviors will be reinforced. In VI–VR, the performance of a behavior does not appear to be influenced by the omission of a reinforcer. As you can imagine, behaviors controlled by a continuous reinforcement schedule should be pretty easy to change, while those operating under a mixed schedule are extremely resistant to change.

Applying fixed reinforcement schedules Arranged between these two endpoints of our continuum are the four intermittent schedules of reinforcement (FI, FR, VI, and VR). As you might expect from our discussion following Figure 5-5, each schedule produces behavior patterns with unique characteristics. In general, the fixed schedules produce behavior patterns which are less resistant to change than behaviors reinforced under the variable schedules. Let's look at some examples. Suppose Joe grew accustomed to earning an A grade for the completion of ten problems. In this case, he was working under a fixed ratio of 10 (or FR_{10}); that is, his A grade (reinforcer) was provided upon the correct completion of ten problems. Suppose that Joe suddenly fell upon "hard times"—such as word problems or solid geometry—and obtained low grades for a week or more. He might then become very discouraged and lose all interest in math, or at least in word problems or in solid geometry. As a classroom teacher, you will have to be aware of the possible consequences when students who have been reinforced under the FR schedule find themselves getting no reinforcement. The same kind of decline in performance can occur when a child is reinforced on an FI schedule. In both situations, the behaviors maintained by a fixed schedule are not especially resistant to change.

Applying VR schedules The variable schedules provide a different picture and one which is more challenging to you. Let's look at some examples of the variable schedules in the classroom. Suppose you decide to give an assignment in chemistry, such as balancing equations, and then walk among your busy students. You would be applying a VI schedule as you stopped once in a while and complimented Melody for her work. On some days you might stop at Melody's desk two or three times, and other days you might stop only once during the study period. After a few weeks of using this VI schedule, you might observe that it had the desirable effect of keeping her "on the job" throughout the study period.

In another class, you might decide to reduce the number of times you reinforced Bruce for volunteering during a discussion. Let us suppose that when you started to work with Bruce, you reinforced him every time he raised his hand (CRF). Once this particular behavior begins to occur fairly frequently, you decide to reinforce Bruce on an average of every third time he volunteers. We would call this a VI_3, meaning a schedule that provided reinforcement every three behaviors on the average. Of course, you remember that if reinforcement is suddenly withheld after CRF, there may be an abrupt drop in or elimination of the performed behavior. In order to avoid losing Bruce's volunteering, you might say something like, "I'll call on you next time, Bruce. Let Joe have a chance." Such a message lets Bruce hear his name but lets him become accustomed to being called on less frequently. In these examples of intermittent reinforcement schedules, the behaviors of Melody and Bruce appeared to persist and to be resistant to change, so that Melody continued to do chemistry equations and Bruce volunteered in class. In short, we are saying that as a classroom teacher who is extremely sensitive to the needs of children and to the various reinforcement schedules, you will be able to choose and plan effective patterns of classroom reinforcement.

GUIDELINES FOR TEACHING
Using Reinforcement Schedules

In order to help you manage schedules of reinforcement for yourself or in your classroom, we suggest four guidelines for reinforcement. These rules will not provide you with all the answers, but they will help you to use the ABCs of behavior change more effectively.

• *Select and use reinforcers that you are fairly certain will be effective with each child.* This guideline is probably the most difficult for people to implement. On the one hand, we want to treat each child as an individual. On the other hand, does this really mean thirty individual children with their own individual reinforcers? The best solution lies somewhere between the extremes of using the same reinforcing activity for everyone in the class and creating a REINFORCEMENT MENU so that everyone will be satisfied. The list of potential classroom, playground, or home reinforcers for a reinforcement menu is endless. Probably you can think of several other reinforcers. We believe these five areas cover the most useful ones:

1. Peer group approval (for example, being a member of a club or being chosen first or second on a team)
2. Independence (for example, reading alone or putting a puzzle together with no help)
3. Competition (for example, being first in line or receiving an A grade in the class)
4. Approval from teacher or parent
5. Conventional rewards (such as ice cream, candy, or stars)

In every classroom, some or all of these kinds of reinforcers are provided. The list of the natural classroom reinforcers might include working on math puzzles, free time to visit the library or to be alone, drawing a picture or writing a creative story, and playing a flash-card game with a friend. Try to find out what each student particularly likes to do. (You will learn more about these preferred reinforcers in Chapter 11). You and your students can make up a reinforcement menu. By agreeing to two or three choices in each area, you will probably have enough alternative reinforcers in your classroom to answer this important question: How can we select a maximally effective reinforcer or reinforcing event to promote a rapid change in this particular behavior for that unique person? We believe that by using the ABC model for focusing on behavior and simply by asking the student, you will be well on your way to stating an answer to the question.

• *Use the reinforcer only after the child has demonstrated the response which you wish to encourage.* This guideline is hard to follow, especially for "grandmothers" who reward before, during, and after the desired behavior! We want your reinforcement of the child to be contingent upon

"You can use immediate reinforcement more easily when you walk about the classroom than when you 'teach' from one position in the room." (Doug Wilson/Black Star)

the performance of the desired behavior. This guideline calls for patience on your part for two reasons: (1) when you are working with the whole class, you will want to set your expectations or goals so that every student can reach them, and (2) when you are working with an individual child, you will want to reward each behavioral response as it comes closer to the goal behavior. Both these challenges to your patience mean that you will have to be sensitive to small changes in behavior and to the unique behavioral goals of your students.

• *Use immediate reinforcers whenever possible.* As a teacher you will have a choice: to sit at your desk and manage the class from there or to walk about your room and manage the class with your "body language" and your voice. Should you elect to sit, you may find this reinforcement guideline very difficult to follow. Bobby might finish his work early and then start talking to Millicent. Your immediate reinforcement as a sitting teacher might come too late. However, by moving about your classroom, you can follow the first two guidelines and make a positive comment about his accomplishments while Bobby is working. You can use immediate reinforcement more easily when you walk about the classroom than when you "teach" from one position in the room.

• *Use small steps on your way to the goal behavior.* It is unfair to ask a child or a classroom to reach a behavioral goal immediately. A more reasonable request would be that the student(s) reach the goal in a series of small steps. In this series, each step represents a closer approximation of the behavioral goal. Indeed, you must be very patient in shaping the child's successive small steps or approximations into the final goal behavior. SHAPING a behavior by SUCCESSIVE APPROXIMATIONS is an art. Shaping requires sensitivity, timing, and alertness. In applying this guideline, you will gradually be shaping a new word, phrase, or more complex behavior. You might be asked to help a young person learn to say the *R* in grass, and you would use shaping procedures. As a middle-school teacher, you will probably use shaping to increase study time for some easily distracted child. In any case, the guidelines are probably fundamental to your successful shaping of a student's self-management behavior.

PROBE 5-6

Think back to the best teacher you had in high school and cite examples of how he or she followed our four guidelines for reinforcement.

The guidelines for reinforcement which we have just covered are most useful for a teacher who is trying to increase a particular behavior. In the course of following these four guidelines, you will make use of many different reinforcement schedules. You might begin by using a CRF schedule. Once the student demonstrates the desired behavior at a stable or dependable rate, you will probably change the reinforcement schedule, perhaps to one of the intermittent schedules. In all likelihood, the student will maintain the behavior change under the mixed reinforcement schedule. In the long run, students will be able to find their own covert reinforcers. Let's put this material on operant learning into a perspective by reading, in Study 5-1, about a project involving a group of men who did not have the kind of teacher which you will be.

STUDY 5-1: STREETCORNER RESEARCH: REINFORCEMENT "AU NATUREL"!

Robert Schwitzgebel and David Kolb undertook a nearly impossible task: they tried to use operant learning procedures with real juvenile delinquents in a storefront building. They worked with twenty tough kids. *How* tough were they? These were their average characteristics: age, 17.8; age of first arrest, 13.5; number of arrests, 8.2; length of incarceration, 15.1 months. A very tough group!

The study was unique because the researchers found their clients and collected their data in a natural setting, the delinquents' own neighborhood. Earlier studies (prior to 1964), usually with college freshmen in carefully controlled laboratory environments, looked at the reinforcement of small, specific behaviors such as self-referent statements and plural nouns. Schwitzgebel and Kolb carried out their pioneering study under very different conditions.

The two authors and their staff used a storefront building located at the intersection of two busy streets in a tough part of town. To find their delinquents, they searched pool halls, drugstore hangouts, and street corners. The initial contact, usually at a local eating establishment, centered on whether the young man was willing to talk to a tape recorder for an hour and earn a dollar. This employment approach for getting people involved in a study may be creative, but such an approach is not unusual among Harvard researchers.

The uniqueness of a storefront laboratory, tape recorders, and the prospect of earning a dollar merely for talking won the boys over for the study in reinforcement. At the end of his first interview, each young man was given an unexpected bonus of a dollar. Each was encouraged to bring friends along to the first few sessions until he felt comfortable talking to a tape recorder and a staff member.

The rules of reinforcement were used throughout this study. The authors and their staff started each person on the CRF schedule, which was later modified to a VR schedule. Finally, once the man was showing up promptly and fully involved in the program, a VI–VR schedule was used. Let's see how the rules were used and how the schedules were modified by the staff.

Shaping procedures were used to develop promptness. As soon as the man arrived for his second interview, he was welcomed and given coke and food. In following sessions he was provided with modest, simple reinforcers—such as a pair of white socks (this was early 1960s), cigarettes, or food—in a VR schedule. Once attendance became dependable (about the fifteenth meeting), a VI–VR schedule was started. This new schedule was complex and full of surprises (for example, a bonus quarter for arriving *only* an hour late, followed by nothing for arriving on time at the next session; or a bonus quarter for exploring a dream or making an important affective, self-referent statement; and so on). Under the VI–VR schedule, each delinquent received reinforcers, but he was never sure when or why they would come. Promptness was established by the twenty-second meeting.

The VI–VR reinforcement schedule produces a high frequency of behaviors which are resistant to change in the absence of reinforcement. By using this mixed schedule, the staff of the street-corner laboratory was able to maximize performance in a variety of areas. Thus, throughout the tape-recorded interview sessions, the staff member listened attentively. The staff encouraged the young men to explore their own feelings as much as possible. Sometimes the staff member provided bonuses for interviews in which the subject talked feelingly about his plans. However, once the young man's anxiety appeared to be aroused, the usual staff procedure of listening attentively would be dropped, so that the man would be able to regain control of himself.

The typical participant's life began to change after about two months of working in this program: he looked for a part-time job, signed up for a correspondence course, and—

along with such positive moves—committed fewer crimes. These young men generally seemed to stay on with the program for up to ten months. They returned for tape-talking sessions on an as-needed basis, once they found full-time work.

A three-year follow-up of the twenty project men showed that they had fewer arrests and shorter sentences than twenty other men who had been carefully selected for comparison purposes. The behavior changes among the participants in the program showed that the intensity of delinquency (frequency or kind of crime) could be reduced but that the full repertoire of delinquent behaviors was not eliminated entirely.

In this pioneering operant learning program conducted in the natural community setting of juvenile delinquents, the staff of the storefront laboratory adhered to three guidelines: (1) each person was treated as a unique individual, so that reinforcers were empirically and operationally defined for each participant; (2) each person was free to leave the program at any time, so that freedom of choice was a condition of participation in the program; and (3) each was encouraged to explore his feelings, to plan ahead, and to engage in "self-direction" activities. These guidelines reflect the values of the program director, Robert Schwitzgebel, a truly committed teacher.

Adapted from: Schwitzgebel, R., & Kolb, D. A. Inducing behavior change in adolescent delinquents. *Behavior Research and Therapy,* 1964, *1*, 297–304.

APPLYING OPERANT LEARNING: MANAGEMENT OF REINFORCERS

As a classroom teacher, a facilitator, and a manager, you will have many opportunities to use reinforcement procedures. You will also face many problems and frustrations. Still, when you get it all together, you will have mastered an exciting combination of skill and art. First, you will be aware of the ABCs of student behavior. Second, you will know about and be skilled in many management and facilitative techniques. And third, your timing and judgment in using reinforcement techniques will appear as a work of art. In the following section, we will talk about how you can apply the principles of operant learning.

Satiation of reinforcers

Suppose a group of eighth-graders negotiates a contract with you. When they complete their math assignment (with at least 90 percent of the problems correct), they may play Parcheesi in the quiet area for 10 minutes. As far as you are concerned, the youngsters are doing well in math and are earning reinforcement time in an activity of their choice. After a week of this daily game, the noise level seems high to both you and the rest of the class. At this point, Bryan tells you "We have played Parcheesi for ten days and we are getting tired of it!" This is simply another way of saying "We are becoming satiated with this reinforcer."

The skill involved in reinforcement is to prevent SATIATION. Probably a good way of preventing satiation is to offer two preferred reinforcing activities upon completion of the learning activity. You can ask, "Do you want to play Parcheesi, or do you want to play three-dimensional tic-tac-toe?" In addition, you might try using different forms of verbal praise. You can say, "You are doing well on your project," "I am proud of you," or "Wonderful! Well done, Sid." A skilled manager tries to have alternatives.

The art of preventing satiation involves good timing in changing the reinforcers. A teacher using reinforcement procedures will have to be sensitive to the verbal, bodily, and facial cues that suggest that a particular reinforcer is no longer effective. If Bob and Millicent are bickering over where the marker landed or Sid begins to daydream during spelling class, these may be signs that their reinforcers have lost their effect; these youngsters have been satiated.

Shaping behaviors

Suppose one group of sixth-graders turned in uniquely different papers. Lazy letters—such as *i*'s and *e*'s that look alike and *b*'s that might be uncrossed *t*'s—seem to sprinkle their papers. After about three weeks of trying to interpret this writing style (and usually doing a poor job), you decide that now is the time for a change. You try to encourage this change by asking the entire class to make their *e*'s, *i*'s, *b*'s, and *t*'s more distinct. No change. You try asking each "lazy" writer to change his or her ways. Still no change. Then you try finding one good letter on each student's paper, circling it, and writing, "Leo, this is a good *e*!" On another paper, you write, "Leo, this *t* is neat!" Each note you write indicates to Leo that his letters are coming closer to their proper shape (Kulhavy, 1977).

In reading about changing behaviors such as Leo's handwriting or a child who says "muthfer," you will encounter SUCCESSIVE APPROXIMA-TIONS and SHAPING. In successive approximations you reinforce behaviors

Start | *measure* | *easel*
Cue letter | *measure* | *easel*
Shape | *measure* open the loop | *easel* touch the line!
Shape | *measure* good l | *easel* great!!
Shape | *measure* | *easel*

which are closer and closer approximations of the goal behavior. For example, Leo's l's and e's look very much alike and cause confusion to anyone reading his projects. Figure 5-6 shows how *measure* and *easel* can be shaped over several attempts. As a classroom teacher, you will be able to cue, shape, and reinforce students whose handwriting needs some differentiation. In Leo's case, the e's become different from the l's in a series of approximations. Or the child who says "Muthfer" slowly learns to say "Muther" and then "Mother." What is happening is that the specific behavior is becoming similar in shape or form to the goal behavior. We call this process SHAPING.

As you can appreciate, shaping a behavior requires a combination of skill and art. Skill is necessary to select the best reinforcers and to create the best learning conditions. Since shaping can take such a long time, it is probably a good idea to use reinforcers that will not satiate quickly or to use a variety of reinforcers. Another skill in shaping is to simplify the problem so that the student can easily focus on the behavior and the reward. As a classroom teacher managing a learning experience, you are an artist who sensitively molds the weak or poorly defined behavior into a masterpiece. It calls for patience on your part to reward the student's work with just the right amount of enthusiasm and with the best timing.

Extinguishing behaviors

Suppose 9-year-old Sid figured out the best way to annoy you. Once he perfects this special skill, the entire class will watch with glee while he works his special magic. Support for this deviant skill will come from two directions: his classmates and you. Every actor in this drama can get trapped into a role: the class titters and you fume. Every actor plays out a part and receives his or her own kind of reinforcer: in this case, status for Sid, entertainment for the class, and the temporary stopping of the deviant behavior for you. What do you do to stop the drama?

This drama can have a different ending if you use EXTINCTION, a gradual procedure for reducing behavior. When you use extinction, you withhold the reinforcer that was maintaining the behavior. Since social reinforcement from you and the class seems to be maintaining Sid's behavior, why do you not simply stop fuming? That is, when Sid begins to act up, you might call on Millicent, ignoring Sid's behavior. Praise Milly for her class participation! Later, try to catch Sid doing his assignment (catch 'em and praise 'em).

Extinction is not this simple. It requires that the major sources of

"Social reinforcement from the teacher and the class seems to be maintaining the behavior." (Diane Koos Gentry/Black Star)

reinforcement—the titter of the classmates and your fuming—have to be withheld. Such cooperation of the entire class in the extinction of deviant behavior requires a special approach. Probably, you could discuss the situation on the day that Sid is absent and obtain agreement with the class not to laugh; or you could praise the class for not attending to the disruptive behavior; or you could praise Sid before he starts his act. In any case, you will want to make certain that the particular disruptive behavior is consistently extinguished. Any deviation from a consistent plan of withholding reinforcement can produce an intermittent (very low but variable ratio) reinforcement schedule. As you know by now, a VR pattern will encourage Sid to continue his antics indefinitely.

Extinction has its problems. As soon as you start a program of extinction, there is typically a burst in the specified behavior and it appears to increase in frequency. You will have to ride through this tough period. Probably, you will make a mistake in your initial identification of reinforcers and therefore continue a VI–VR schedule. Ask yourself, "Do I want to change Sid's behavior, or do I just want to lash out at him because he upsets my class?" A sensitive teacher—supported by caring parents, an interested principal, and perhaps also guidance counselors, and possibly the students themselves—will help identify through observation and self-report the reinforcers maintaining the disruptive behavior. Last, eliminating a disruptive behavior through extinction is a very gradual process and will try the patience of many people involved with the student.

Skill and art are called for continuously in your classroom management of learning and social development. You might analyze some situations according to the ABC model and decide simply to ignore the disruptive behavior. In other situations, you might ignore the student's behavior and call on a classmate whose behavior can serve as a model for effective classroom behaviors. Art in this extinction program means that you have to be skillful in enlisting the support of your students, in calling on a classmate to demonstrate an alternative behavior, or in asking Sid to perform a behavior that is incompatible with his disruptive activities.

Delayed reinforcement

Suppose you encounter a young girl, Janice, who simply cannot wait; in class, she insists on getting her question answered "right now." On the playground, she must be first and she is often unwilling to take turns. This young lady is becoming so demanding that she appears to be losing friends and is trying your patience. We might say that she needs immediate reinforcement and she needs to learn how to accept DELAYED REINFORCEMENT.

Teaching a child to accept delayed reinforcement can be one of your biggest challenges. For eight to ten years, Janice has "had it her way." Statements such as "Wait your turn" and "Be patient, Janice" have probably served to reinforce her demanding behaviors and to maintain her insistence upon immediate answers to her questions or demands. If you are successful, she will learn about sharing and delayed gratification. Your planned behavior change, skillfully and artfully managed, can begin with an individual tutorial relationship. Later it can be modified. At first, you can be immediately available to Janice. You can provide immediate reinforcement by checking her math problems upon request. Later, you might nod briefly at her but be "busy" for the moment. These moments of delay can be lengthened until she has mastered delayed reinforcement. Once Janice can work with delayed reinforcement (like a trip to the zoo or a six-week grade), you can go ahead with your daily management of learning and human relations.

As a classroom teacher, you will have to make sensitive decisions about whether to reinforce immediately or to delay reinforcement. Generally, you will reinforce immediately for new skills, for difficult or complex tasks, and with young or unmotivated students. As the learning responses are performed more competently, you can stretch the interval between reinforcers and thereby delay reinforcement. Once more, skill and art integrate with reinforcement procedures to bring about behavior change.

Generalized reinforcers

Suppose Sam, one of your eleventh-grade students, seems to be reluctant to try anything but science. Sam seems to be a very different person in science (volunteering, showing classmates procedures, and leading study teams) than he is in English (silent, muttering answers, apparently absent-minded). This young man has developed a style of looking at school so that only very specific times and places are reinforcing to him. Indeed, when Sam is praised for his work in science, he responds attentively. However, when Sam is praised in English class, he usually mutters unintelligibly. In this situation, you have a problem of success in science as a specific reinforcement. You want to generalize this success into other areas of study. You will want to facilitate students' generalized reinforcers across a variety of situations.

As a classroom teacher, you will be concerned about students like Sam, who seem to find only limited reinforcement in school. Sam finds joy only in science class. You will want to facilitate the use of positive GENERALIZED REINFORCERS from his science class to other classes and the playground. Probably building a positive relationship with Sam is the first step. A warm smile or wink can do wonders for a boy who feels that he has been left out of a project in English or activities on the playground. You can develop this dyadic relationship so that it will be very positive and your comments about Sam's work in science will generalize into a positive attitude toward school. Usually things like grades, praise, and attention are reinforcers which generalize across a variety of situations in school and on the playground. In trying to build these generalized reinforcers, you are pairing your positive comments about Sam's work in science with his work in English. Gradually, you can comment positively about his appearance (shirt, shoes, and so on) and ask him to describe a scientific process in your English class (you are aware that science demonstrations are easy for him, so the next step would be to use the demonstration skill in a new environment). As Sam has more and more positive successes in English, you can plan class activities with other teachers so that he can enjoy positive experiences in math and social studies. The potential of generalized reinforcers is great once that force is activated. Your skillful planning of facilitative activities can help even the most reluctant students to broaden their enjoyment of school through the use of generalized reinforcers.

Differential reinforcement

Suppose you are dealing with Barbara, a young lady who is talkative, loud, spontaneous, and full of surprises both in the hall and in your classroom. In the hall you have sometimes smiled, winked, or started a conversation with Barbara. A relationship exists between the two of you. Still, you have a problem: in the hall, Barbara's lively sociability is appropriate, but in your classroom she tends to disrupt lessons. We can say that Barbara has not learned to discriminate between the stimuli inside and outside your classroom.

As a classroom teacher, you will closely follow the guidelines for reinforcement and for extinction in differentially reinforcing Barbara's talking. Essentially, you want Barbara to learn both the stimulus cues for talking (S_D's) and the stimulus cues for nonreinforced behavior (S_Δ's) in your classroom. On the one hand, should Barbara establish eye contact, pay attention and volunteer, you must promptly and massively reinforce her. On the other hand, should Barbara begin to chatter or stray from her assignment, you can walk away, call on someone else, or ignore her and not reinforce these particular disruptive behaviors. In this way you are using DIFFERENTIAL REINFORCEMENT for Barbara's talking.

As you can judge from reading this section, it can be difficult to use reinforcement effectively. Over time, you will develop the skills to become an effective manager of learning and human relations. Reinforcement learning can facilitate your accomplishment of these teaching roles. We hope that, in the long run, you will be able to integrate reinforcement learning ideas into your own style ''automatically'' so that your teaching becomes a work of art.

APPLYING OPERANT LEARNING: STIMULUS MANAGEMENT

Very shortly, you will have to consider the ABCs of learning and performance. As we have discussed earlier, the antecedents and consequences of learning have a profound effect upon the rate of learning. How well you can identify and relate the antecedents and consequences of learning will be an important part of how effective you will be as a teacher. The management of learning and human relationships will make you very sensitive to the ABCs of learning and the interplay between people. In the remainder of this section, we will talk about some ways to organize events for learning. Thus, part of your managerial role will be to organize the environment by using stimulus discrimination, stimulus generalization, verbal chaining, prompting, and fading. These procedures will help you carry out the three roles of a classroom teacher.

=== PROBE 5-7 ===

Compare the ''stage setting for learning'' in your elementary school and your high school to that of schools today. Consider three major aspects—physical, academic, and social—in the comparison. Give examples for each aspect of each level in your education.

Stimulus discrimination

Suppose your third-period literature class is impossibly noisy. It is not disruptive, but very quickly each day the discussions become aggressive, personal, and very uncomfortable for some students. In your teacher training, you prepared to manage your discussions by quiet, intense, and polite means. In this situation, you have a problem, since the students do not seem to be able to carry on a calm discussion of John Updike. From your brief experience as a teacher of advanced literature, Updike has never generated this kind of enthusiasm. What's going on? By applying the ABC model, you will quickly discover that in the period just before your class, most of the students have a sociology class with Mr. Ham, the football coach. In his class, confrontation, aggression, and sharp comments seem to be valued and reinforced. In fact, Mr. Ham seems to encourage confrontation and aggression most of the time. We would say that students in your class have failed to discriminate between Coach Ham's classroom stimuli and your own. STIMULUS DISCRIMINATION occurs when the student responds differently to environmental stimuli that appear to be very similar.

In stimulus discrimination training we try to help students find two kinds of distinctive cues in a particular classroom setting or dyadic relationship. These discriminative stimuli (S_D) or cues set the occasion for positive reinforcement. "Set the occasion" is a technical way of saying "arrange the environmental stimuli that typically precede a specific response." So far, your literature class has not recognized the environmental elements that make your class uniquely different from Coach Ham's sociology "happening." The class as a group has not discriminated the environmental stimuli which will result in your positive reinforcement. Thus, your immediate task will be to communicate those cues, antecedents, or discriminative stimuli (S_D's), that signal reinforceable behaviors. The students in your literature class will have to learn, probably by observation, which hand gesture means "Tell me more," which glance means "Everything is OK," and which body posture means 'You're on your way to trouble, Mister!''

As a classroom teacher committed to facilitating individual student development, you will use stimulus discrimination training skillfully and artfully. When the discrimination is too difficult and the stimuli are too similar, the student may become frustrated and make mistakes. We want you to use stimulus discrimination to help you avoid creating an uncomfortable classroom atmosphere. Remember, teacher, "Keep the S_D difference clear!"

Stimulus generalization

Suppose that the career education program in your school is so open that girls are permitted to enroll in your basic car maintenance class. To many students, teachers, administrators, and parents, it will seem that Millicent's election of "Basic Car Care" is inappropriate, atypical, and risky. However, as a wise, calm teacher, you argue that women's changing roles and opportunities make Millicent's decision to enroll in your class wise and farsighted.

In the course of teaching your students how to choose the proper automotive tools, you will have many opportunities to use stimulus generalization activities. As you might expect, stimulus discrimination and STIMULUS GENERALIZATION are fundamental to classroom learning. On the one hand, you will use stimulus discrimination procedures to differentiate the variety of car wrenches (such as socket, crescent, torque, Allen-head, and single-head wrenches). In this discrimination training, you will try to help Millicent recognize the appropriate mechanical cues for selecting the proper wrench for the job. At the same time, you will use stimulus generalization techniques to point out the common elements in all these tools. For example, they all are hand-held, they are used for twisting or holding, and they are usually made of tempered steel. When a tool has these common general characteristics, it belongs to the *wrench* category. As a career educator, you will have the opportunity to teach many concepts such as *triangle, curvature, seal, weld,* and a host of others. Indeed, you will frequently use discrimination and generalization together in classroom and playground learning situations.

As a classroom teacher in any kind of class, you will sometimes present the discrimination problem first; at other times, you will start the learning activity with a generalization exercise. In most cases, you will discover that effective mastery of ideas or concepts occurs when the two procedures are skillfully and artfully merged into a well-planned learning activity.

Verbal chaining

Suppose Janice has her own way of saying the alphabet. Her "h, i, k, j" and "s, t, w, x" are two unique parts of a twenty-six-letter verbal chain. In CHAINING, two or more behaviors are linked together. Each response becomes the stimulus for the next response. For example, saying "a"

"In chaining, two or more behaviors are linked together. Each response becomes the stimulus for the next response." (D. Strickler/ Monkmeyer)

cues saying "b." You had noticed that several classmates laughed when Janice said her alphabet. At PTA Open House, you talked with Janice's parents. The mother was concerned. The father said, "You are responsible for teaching the alphabet!"

As a reasonable classroom teacher interested in pleasing parents and teaching students, you have a double-barrel problem. Probably, getting the child to go home with a standard twenty-six-letter alphabet would do wonders for your next PTA Open House. We would say that Janice has an incorrectly learned verbal chain. At some point in school or on the playground, she got the idea that her version of the alphabet was the correct version.

In building a verbal chain such as the alphabet with a student like Janice, you will want to make sure that seven guidelines are followed:

GUIDELINES FOR TEACHING

Building Verbal Chains

- *Tell the student what the entire chain sounds like*. In this way she will learn the objectives. You will have her say the entire alphabet. You will discover which letters are missing from the chain.
- *Make sure she has the skills she needs to complete the alphabet*. She might, very simply, not be able to say one of the letters.
- *Encourage her to pay attention*. In this guideline you will practice your shaping skills so Janice pays more attention to you.
- *Make sure that the student works on the missing parts of the alphabet*. It is unreasonable to ask her to say all twenty-six letters over and over. Let her focus on her skill deficits. Probably the "s, t, u, v, w" sequence can be done first. It is near the end of the complete verbal chain so Jan can feel the full sense of relief by singing "Z"! It is important that you try to listen to the verbal chains so you can say whether each is correct or not.
- *Reinforce her immediately whenever the correct part of the verbal chain is recited*. Later, you can go through these same guidelines for creating a new "h, i, j, k" verbal chain.
- *Prepare her for generalization so that she will be able to say the alphabet at home*. You will want her to perform the alphabet with her parents or in a new setting.
- *Give her the opportunity to retain her new skill through practice in your classroom*.

Motor chaining

The guidelines for successful verbal chaining can also be applied to motor (body movement) chaining. As an effective classroom manager, you will frequently be asked to put several motor behaviors into a chain. For example, post-recess hubbub can be reduced through effective motor chaining. In your classroom, two behaviors—sitting fairly quietly and paying attention—will probably be rewarded by you ("Thank you, Joe, for quickly getting ready for math"). Additionally, those boys and girls who perform three behaviors—(1) sit down in their seats, (2) sit quietly, and (3) pay attention—will also be rewarded. The motor chain can be longer. For example, those students who (1) play hard during recess, (2) return promptly to their seats at the end of recess, (3) sit down quietly, and (4) pay attention to you will indeed be rewarded by you. In other words, you can take a behavior that is usually performed (like attending to you in class) and usually is rewarded ("Good question, Jan") and add a series of preceding behaviors to form a complex motor-behavioral chain. In the long run, you will be able to help students develop their own chains of motor behavior for their schoolwork and their work at home, as we will discuss in Chapter 7.

Backward chaining

One last note will be useful in chaining. BACKWARD CHAINING from the final behavior toward the first behavior in the chain appears to have a great deal of merit. The conditions for learning and the seven guidelines for chaining can be performed in backward chaining over and over again. In backward chaining the Gettysburg Address or a class play, for example, the students learn the last line first and the first line last. It may be hard on the principal who drops in to observe your class or a play rehearsal, but backward chaining is an effective instructional technique.

===== **PROBE 5-8** =====

Compare forward and backward chaining in your next memory assignment, such as the dates for a history examination or the bones of your hand for physiology. Does backward chaining take fewer trials than your normal techniques for learning the complete verbal chain?

Prompting and fading

Suppose one slightly younger boy in your class usually cannot finish his long-division problems. He can copy the problem and write the first digit of the long-division answer but no more.

As a creative person interested in helping each child develop his or her fullest potential, you recognize that this young man could benefit from tutoring in long division. In your unique school, a "cross-age" teaching program has been developed so you can obtain the assistance of an older student to help this young man learn long division (McGee, Kauffman, & Nussen, 1977). As you casually listen to and observe this dyad, you notice that the older student (Bill) has been giving the younger boy (Joe) some cues on what to do next in long division. These cues about the correct response are also called PROMPTS. In Table 5-5, we have given

Table 5-5. Prompting math skills: Fading gradually

Prompting and fading are two important techniques for use in learning complex behavior chains such as manual long division. Since you believe students should learn the four math functions manually first, before using a calculator, let us listen to the dialogue between Bill (the tutor) and Joe (your student):

Bill:	There you go! Four into nine goes two times. Right on!	In this early session, Bill is obliged to provide frequent prompts in a very close supervisory role. Each prompt is an S_D for the immediately subsequent behavior. In a sense, Joe depends on Bill's prompts for completing the long-division problem.
Joe:	(Winces, but also smiles. This session has not been the most exciting so far. The third problem has just been started.)	
Bill:	Now subtract eight from nine . . . And you have . . .?	
Joe:	One (looks at Bill)?	
Bill:	Put the one below the eight . . . there. . . . Next?	
Joe:	(No movement except a glance at Bill)	
Bill:	Bring down the seven. Write it next to the one. Four into . . .	Over time, the prompts can be made shorter and less frequently.
Joe:	Seventeen.	When fading is under way, the prompts serve two functions: antecedents or S_D's for the links in a behavioral chain that are sometimes weak and consequences or rewards for completing a particular step in the chain.
Bill:	Right. . . . Seventeen goes . . . [Later. Probably one or two twenty-minute sessions have passed.]	
Bill:	Umhum . . . good. The six goes . . .	
Joe:	Here (writes) next to the four.	
Bill:	Seven into forty . . .	
Joe:	Six goes five . . . no, six times!	
Bill:	(Smiles) OK. Put the six . . .	The older tutor has a chance to sharpen his skills and to practice positive reinforcing statements at appropriate times.
Joe:	Here. Multiply six times seven. Forty-two. Subtract . . .	
Bill:	Yeah (softly) forty-two from forty-six . . .	
Joe:	(Quickly) equals four. The remainder is four!	
Bill:	Hey, Joe, you've got it. I think you've really got it!	

From what we know about cross-age tutoring in which a slightly older, more knowledgeable student helps a younger student with a specific learning need, both students seem to improve their knowledge or competency in the given area. Cross-age tutoring such as that between Bill and Joe has the desirable effect of helping both students (Paolitto, 1976).

you parts of the training session involving Bill and young Joe. Indeed, a close reading of this transcript may remind you of your own learning experiences as a seventh-grader. The classroom is one of the few settings in which prompts are acceptable and used frequently.

Later, your tutorial student reports that he and Bill can do an entire math assignment with no difficulty. At this point, many other teachers would believe that Joe had mastered long division and his tutorials could be terminated. Usually, when prompts are abruptly removed, the verbal or motor chain cannot be continued. Rather than abruptly stopping the tutorial, you ask Bill to give fewer and fewer prompts during the long-division solution. The use of fewer prompts is called FADING and allows Joe to gain control over his new skill. Usually, as you will discover, prompting and fading go hand in hand. You start with prompting and gradually fade the support or cues as the child gains mastery of the particular skill.

CAREFUL USE OF AVERSIVE CONTROLS

Sometime soon, you will confront a student or your entire class in a troublesome situation. You might finally act on your urge to nag a girl who is slow getting in line or a boy whose handwriting is absolutely unintelligible. In another situation, you might really want to say, "Sister, you have a dilemma: keep it up and you are on the third team for two games" (or "Stop that particular behavior and you are free until I decide to restrict you")! Or, in a still more tense situation, you might consider raising your voice to say, "Stop it! Do that again, Buster, and pow!" In each one of these situations, you have begun to use strategies involving aversive control.

Aversive control

Aversive control is really an umbrella term for several teacher strategies that have common characteristics. When you elect to use aversive control techniques, the consequence may be that a behavior is increased *or* decreased in frequency or intensity (Walters & Grusec, 1977). Indeed, when you plan on using aversive control techniques, you should be very sure about the ABCs of the situation. You can consider both classical and operant learning models in this ABC analysis. Your view of the situation might suggest whether you use (1) negative reinforcement, (2) punishment by withdrawing reinforcers, or (3) punishment by presenting aversive stimuli to bring about the desired behavior change.

Let's take a look at each of these three ways of changing behavior. The temptation is to label the behavior "problem," "undesirable," or "inappropriate." A label of this type means that we (you and us) have a special understanding of desirable and appropriate behaviors. In making this judgment about another person's behavior, remember to consider carefully the situation, the effect, the intensity, the frequency, and the variety of behavior that seems to need changing. Please be careful about making judgments on the appropriateness of behavior and about arriving at decisions to use aversive control procedures.

Negative reinforcement   Suppose Leonard, a student in one of your classes, feels particularly uncomfortable about your regular Friday afternoon spelling test. He squirms, looks out the window, and tries to sleep. Indeed, Leonard tells you that the spelling test "ruins" school for him. The number of correct words on his spelling tests drops so far that you have a conference with him and later with his parents.

As a classroom teacher, you will have several options for managing this particular, common learning activity. An unfortunate approach would be for you to say something like this: "Leonard, you look pale; you must be sick; you better go to the nurse." Miraculous recovery occurs! You have given Leonard a way to avoid the dreaded, aversive spelling test. Indeed, were you to create this monstrous, negative reinforcement situation, Leonard would, in all probability, get sick every Friday! A powerful alternative approach, based on your ABC analysis, might be to let Leonard's pride work for him: place him in a remedial spelling group. Leonard might well consider this assignment an aversive event. Therefore, he might—through his own hard work and less squirming, daydreaming, and resting—learn his lessons well enough to return to his regular spelling group. Should Leonard follow your management plan, work on his spelling, and remove the aversive stimuli, he would strengthen or increase his spelling behaviors. In this manner, the aversive stimuli which, when removed, increase or strengthen a preceding behavior are called NEGATIVE REINFORCERS. Negative reinforcement increases or maintains a behavior by the removal of an unpleasant or undesirable object or activity.

The effects of negative reinforcers are very important for you as a future manager of learning experiences: students who have been trained almost exclusively with negative reinforcement learn only those precise behaviors which result in the avoidance of aversive stimuli. When they enter a multiple-choice, positively reinforcing environment such as high school or college, they appear to flounder because they do not know how to take risks and to explore. In our view, these are not desirable consequences.

If you decide to use negative reinforcement in your classroom, you will have to do the following: (1) select the best aversive stimuli, (2) time the presentation of these stimuli, and (3) provide a way for students to engage in the desired, appropriate behavior. Without this last element— a way to engage in appropriate alternative behavior—your use of a negative reinforcer can backfire. School for Leonard can become terribly aversive. Thus, you will find yourself delicately balanced between two choices: classically conditioning Leonard to dislike school, particularly the remedial spelling group, and operantly conditioning him, by using negative reinforcement, to achieve spelling mastery. This aversive control procedure must be carefully planned or it may backfire. Without your careful supervision, Leonard may decide to give up his efforts to learn spelling and resign himself to a permanent place in the remedial group.

PROBE 5-9

Have you ever been placed in a negative reinforcement situation? What were the aversive stimuli? How did you find the "best" behavior to remove the stimuli? What was it? Did you do it more often?

Punishment by withdrawing a reinforcer Sometimes class can get a little rough, especially for a beginning teacher. Suppose your student Edgar tells you what to do with his paper. In previous encounters with Edgar, you have turned the other cheek. The class has smirked. Later, while walking around between classes, you hear, "Edgar really put it to that new hot-shot from the university!" Well, Edgar and his friends do not know that you have set aside a special chair to be placed in the hall by your door. Next time Edgar gets a paper back, reads the grade, and recycles his direct suggestions, you—without comment—take his hand and lead him to the special chair. Ten minutes later by the wall clock in the back of the room, you invite a somewhat puzzled Edgar back into the class. Later, you meet with him and explain the guidelines for classroom behavior when talking with you.

In an aversive control procedure of this kind where you withdraw the reinforcers, you are not using strongly aversive consequences (Nelson & Gast, 1978). Indeed, you remain restrained, polite, and very calm. In Edgar's case, the consistent removal of positive reinforcement will probably reduce his particular troublesome behavior. A frequently used strategy in withdrawal of reinforcers is known as TIME OUT from social support. In this procedure, the child is removed from a reinforcing situation. The strategy will work as long as Edgar gets social support in the classroom and *not* while sitting in the hall. You should be aware that too much time out can encourage Edgar to be creative while sitting in the chair; indeed, chair-sitting might, therefore, become desirable. You don't want that to happen!

In addition to withdrawing social support through time out, you can withdraw a variety of other desirable reinforcers as an aversive consequence. Your goal is to decrease or eliminate a troublesome behavior. You will be wise to consider withdrawing reinforcers that are naturally tied to the inappropriate behaviors. Joe, for example, might be moved to another seat for a time and lose his opportunity to be with Alice. A temporary loss of abused privileges is often an effective use of aversive control.

Punishment by presenting an aversive stimulus   Suppose Buford has developed special skill in tripping people who are running on the playground. So far, several knees have been scraped and two parents have called. Buford's unique behavior, while reinforcing to him, is causing physical harm to his classmates and making him a threat. Your response to Buford will be stronger than mere negative reinforcement or the withdrawal of a reinforcer. Indeed, you want, as quickly as possible, to present an aversive consequence that will reduce or stop Buford's destructive antics.

PUNISHMENT by presenting an aversive stimulus is a kind of aversive control that might work with Buford. Punishment is a procedure in which the presentation of an aversive stimulus immediately after a particular behavior reduces the rate with which the behavior occurs (Walters & Grusec, 1977). The choice of this management technique—punishment by presenting an aversive stimulus—usually means that other strategies have not reduced or eliminated this particular behavior. In Buford's case, the presentation of an aversive stimulus might bring about a reduction in his tripping.

As a classroom teacher in the manager role, you will have five important guidelines to follow if you elect to punish a child like Buford:

GUIDELINES FOR TEACHING

Using Punishment Carefully

- *Develop a simple set of rules.* You will want to involve your students as much as possible in this decision making.
- *Specify clearly consequences for following or breaking the rules.* You will want to encourage students to follow rules. Send home "good news" reports whenever possible.
- *Make sure that the consequences are applied immediately and consistently.* Buford will "get the message" as long as you are quick and consistent. Any delay can result in Buford asking, "Why me?" You will want to be able to specify which rule was broken.
- *Make sure that the consequences are more powerful than the reinforcers maintaining the undesired behavior.* In order to master this guideline, you will want to use the ABC model to plan your strategies.
- *Provide an alternative and rewardable behavior.* By suggesting another response, you can help Buford avoid punishment. You can whisper the rule and prompt a rewardable behavior (O'Leary et al., 1970).

Aversive control is a very controversial area of classroom management (MacMillan, Forness, & Trumbull, 1973). The debate has gone beyond "old school" and "new ways." Psychologists and educators have spent much time looking at the good and bad sides of aversive control. As a teacher, you should be aware of the arguments.

Let's use aversive control   As a classroom teacher, you will probably run into many people who advocate the use of aversive control techniques. By their definition, they mean simply punishment or the use of aversive consequences. Their arguments will be based on personal experience and common sense. The advocates of punishment, especially physical, will be very direct in letting you know how they feel. Punishment stops the behavior immediately, it is instructive to other students, and it helps the student learn right from wrong. At least their position is clear. Finding a way to work with these people will be a challenging experience for you.

At this time we want you to think about the five guidelines for using punishment by presenting an aversive stimulus. We want to make the point that this particular kind of aversive control will work as long as the guidelines are closely followed. Please try to match these guidelines with our three teacher roles. We believe that the realities involved in playing these roles will prohibit you from inescapably, immediately, and consistently administering aversive stimuli as a punishment to students. Indeed, the difficulty of meeting the guidelines for effective use of punishment provokes an image of helplessness and of frustration for you. When a teacher uses punishment in a haphazard way and fails to provide an alternative behavior, we believe that teacher has probably lost control of both self and classroom. We hope that no reader of this book will fall into the trap of resorting to physical punishment to solve every problem or of imposing punitive tasks (such as writing out "I will not talk in class" 550 times) as a routine method of classroom control.

Let's prohibit aversive control   Five major arguments seem to suggest that aversive control procedures, in particular physical punishment, can have several very negative effects on Leonard and on the rest of his class. The arguments seem to be as follows:

• In some aversive-control procedures, Leonard receives a destructive message. The message is "You are no good." This soon becomes "I am no good" and "I can't do it." The "it" generalizes to all sorts of classroom and playground activities, so that soon we have a real "problem kid."

• When you are physically aggressive toward Leonard, you are sending a mixed message. As a result, he may think, "Here is my high-status teacher, whom I am supposed to imitate, paddling me for something I

Punishment–Does It Help or Hurt?

"Physical aggression can make students angry, and it gives them a model for aggressive behavior." (*Science World*, vol. 22, no. 4, March 1, 1971)

really didn't do. Is it OK to hit people?" In other words, the teacher-model appears to the student to be condoning a "punishable" behavior! We know from Chapter 3 that this experience will encourage the student to hit others. Physical aggression can make students angry, and it gives them a model for aggressive behavior.

• Leonard will escape from the situation by withdrawing (for example, by looking out the window).

• External control by the teacher promotes lying, cheating, and other evasive behaviors to avoid punishment. The classroom should be a place where young men and women learn how to control themselves rather than how to submit to control by others (Rosenbaum & Drabman, 1979).

• The fear of a teacher can generalize to become fear of a classroom. Certainly the worst possible atmosphere for learning is one that generates fear; a nation of sheep can be taught through fear, but that approach does not facilitate individual differences, positive human relations, and creativity.

PROBE 5-10

Look around you. Can you identify three uses of aversive control procedures in your community or school? How well are they working? Why? Discuss your observations with your classmates.

We do not want to appear to be too harsh on aversive control. You will have opportunities to consider using one or more of these aversive procedures. At very select times, particularly when there is risk of physical harm to another child or yourself, the prompt administration of punishment by presenting aversive stimuli is appropriate. In your teaching, we hope that you will consider the ABCs of the situation. After analyzing the situation, you will probably find that aversive control (negative reinforcement or punishment by withdrawing reinforcers) will enable you to deal with the problems you encounter on the playground or in the classroom.

COGNITIVE SOCIAL LEARNING THEORY

COGNITIVE SOCIAL LEARNING theory is a third way for you to look at classroom behavior. In this theory, the emphasis is on the social setting, on how a person observes and thinks about the environment. Cognitive social learning theory is important because it will give you choices for management, mediation, and facilitation in the classroom. By now, you might suspect that we believe the strict application of a single theory is nonproductive in a classroom. For example, limiting each student to trial and error learning for using a lathe, driving a car, or baking a cake can be dangerous, foolish, and costly. Instead, we want you to take advantage of this fairly new theory which combines the strength and power of classical and operant learning with a flexibility that adapts to a variety of social settings (Bandura, 1969, 1971, 1977; Mischel, 1968; Rotter, 1954).

PRINCIPLES OF COGNITIVE SOCIAL LEARNING

Cognitive social learning has three main components: stimulation from the environment, reinforcement, and mediation of the self. Each of these three components interacts with the others so that they are interdependent but not independent. We have presented a simple version of cognitive social learning in Table 5-3. The straight line model is expanded in Figure 5-7 to show the full range of potential interactions among the three components. In this diagram, each component has a two-way influence upon the others. For example, should the environmental stimuli change (from football game to church), the fact of change is mediated by the self and a new pattern of responses is chosen. In turn, these new responses have an influence upon how well the person is reinforced in the social setting. Mediation or cognition plays an equal role with the stimulus environment, and the degree to which a person is shaped by that environment will influence how well he or she will finally manage the personal environment.

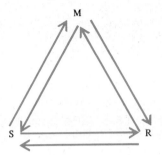

Figure 5-7
Interactions among
three components
of cognitive social
learning theory.

Cognitive social learning theory suggests that one can learn through two major processes: MODELING or observational learning and SELF-MANAGEMENT. As a classroom teacher, you will want to use three types of models for teaching complex patterns of behavior: (1) physical or behavioral demonstrations (as with a lathe); (2) pictures such as film strips or TV; and (3) verbal instructions (as with a recipe for angel-food cake). Models are discussed in Chapter 2. As you and your students gain more confidence in each other (as your behaviors become more predictable), you will try to develop self-control, self-regulation, or self-management skills among your students. We believe that a primary goal of education is to prepare people not to be dependent upon their environment but to be as independent as possible. Cognitive social learning theory suggests many ways to reach that goal. Let's explore the highly interrelated components of this theory, involving both stimulation and reinforcement from the environment and the self.

OBSERVATIONAL LEARNING

We learn from our environment by watching what other people do and say. The influence of the social environment in cueing and reinforcing a person has been extensively studied. For example, Study 5-2 describes how Albert Bandura and his students at Stanford University tried to understand the ways in which people acquire a range of simple and complex behaviors. Observational learning can be a powerful influence on children's learning to hit a Bobo doll (Study 5-2) or accepting a new moral judgment (Bandura & McDonald, 1965) or on client behaviors in therapy (Bandura, 1976). Bandura has worked on the idea that when an observer watches a model performing a pattern of behavior, there is a fairly good chance that the observer will try to imitate the model (Bandura, 1977). The observer learns by watching the model and by practicing the new behavior. Usually, an observer who sees behavior succeed for others is more likely to behave in a similar manner. The observer has been reinforced *vicariously* when he or she watches the model being reinforced. In a similar manner, an observer who views a sequence or pattern of behavior being punished is less likely to behave in the same way. Indeed, modeling and imitation are learning activities that occur continuously at home and in the classroom.

STUDY 5-2:
LEARNING FROM MODELS

Albert Bandura and his colleagues at Stanford University have carefully studied the modeling process. Their work on modeling, or learning by observation, has opened up vast new areas for educational psychologists. Now we are raising questions and experimentally determining how, by modeling, students affect their peers and teachers and how teachers affect their students. The results of these studies on modeling have made us more sensitive to the impact we have on each other.

In one of the earliest modeling studies, Bandura and two of his graduate students studied aggression. The topic is important because aggression in its many different forms (spanking, yelling, teasing, and sometimes grading too strictly) abounds at home, on the playgrounds, and in the classroom. Bandura, Ross, and Ross wanted to determine the extent to which aggressive behaviors can be transmitted to young children through observation of aggressive adult models.

Three groups were used in this study. One group of children watched a model hit and throw a plastic Bobo doll. Another group of children watched the adult model quietly play with the Bobo doll. A third group did not watch a model. Bandura arranged the models so that half the children observed models of the same sex as themselves and the rest viewed opposite-sex models.

After the experimental program, the children were given a Bobo doll. The children who had not seen the doll with a model did not pay much attention to it. The children who had watched the model play quietly with Bobo also played quietly with the doll. Finally, the violent model elicited violence among the observers. The children became very aggressive; they hit, kicked, and pummeled Bobo as they had seen the adult model do, and they imitated some of the model's specific verbal behaviors.

Subsequent studies of modeling suggest that when a child is punished physically, the effect is often just the reverse of what was intended: the child imitates the punishing (aggressive) adult in dealing with a friend, a sibling, or a pet.

Adapted from: Bandura, A., Ross, D., & Ross, S. A. Transmission of aggression through imitation of aggressive models. *Journal of Abnormal and Social Psychology,* 1961, *63,* 575–582.

As a manager of learning, you will have four guidelines for learning by observation:

GUIDELINES FOR TEACHING

Using Observational Learning

• *Be sure the students have mastered the prerequisite skills.* Two important prerequisite skills for observational learning include (1) the student is able to pay attention and (2) the student is able to imitate. Not everyone has these two skills. In some families, imitation is a valued activity: "Watch me, son. Good!" However, confusion reigns in other families. Therefore the children find it difficult to pay attention to anything for very long. Rewards for imitating each other or their parents are absent from the family (Chapters 2 and 3). Children raised in such families will frequently become your students. Remember that an observer needs certain skills before vicarious learning can occur (Bandura, 1977).

• *Make certain that the model has some unique characteristics.* The more important of these are status, prestige, similarity to observer's sex or ethnic group, age, and competence. In some classrooms, the most likely model is the teacher, who has size, age, and prestige in his or her favor. In other classrooms, the more likely model is a good athlete or a knowledgeable student. The model should be fairly similar to the observer in sex, race, and interests. The similarity between model and observer appears to promote an affinity or bond which increases the tendency to imitate. Indeed, you might have to point out some of the model's characteristics to the observing children. In addition to having unique characteristics similar to those of the observer, the model should also perform behaviors which the observer can imitate. If students simply can't master each part of the complex behavior chain, then you will have to train them to perform these behaviors by operant learning.

• *Make sure that the model is reinforced for the particular behaviors.* Later, when the student imitates the model's performance, the student is said to have experienced vicarious reinforcement.

• *Reinforce students for selecting and imitating appropriate models.* As a classroom teacher, you might want to add your own ample amount of direct reinforcement to support your student's new behavior. Thus, attention to the model, similarity between model and observer, and reinforcement of both the model and observer behavior are the four guidelines for you to use modeling in your classroom.

PROBE 5-11

Modeling has probably influenced your life in many ways. Identify one instance in which you modeled another person's behavior and specify how the four guidelines for effective modeling were met.

Applying observational learning

Suppose Aaron has been in your room for several weeks. You have assigned A grades to his homework. Aaron has smiled when you have returned his paper, yet he has not participated in your class discussions. Also, you have observed that Aaron and Martin eat together during lunch. In contrast to Aaron, Martin frequently volunteers during class discussions. In the long run, it is probably important for Aaron to learn how to participate in class. As a teacher, you will often call upon your knowledge of individual differences and human relations to use modeling in promoting classroom learning. In your plan for increasing Aaron's classroom participation, Martin will play the role of the model. The plan must

"Modeling and imitation are learning activities that occur continuously at home and in the classroom." (Griffiths/Magnum)

consider the conditions which are necessary for successful modeling in your classroom. Let's look. First, Aaron pays attention to Martin and they both appreciate good grades. Second, Martin and Aaron are good friends and they appear to have common interests. Last—and you are not too sure about this—Aaron does have most of the behavioral skills necessary to speak up in class. Selecting a math problem as the starting point, you may ask Martin, the model, to count to six on the base of two. Martin does this easily and receives your warm praise. Then, you immediately ask Aaron to do the same thing so that he has a simple verbal statement to imitate. In all probability, Aaron will be able to imitate a part of or all of Martin's answer. You then reinforce him quickly, being careful not to be too gushy and thus spoil a good beginning.

SELF-MANAGEMENT

As time goes by during the school year, your students will become more and more aware of the ABC model for learning. Don't keep the model a secret. After all, you will be using the ABC model over and over again as you follow and imitate the symbolic models we offer you here. A few students will begin to use your terms. Indeed, you may feel that something (a behavior change) is happening to you, too! This will mean that the time is ripe to teach certain students how self-management or self-control procedures can be helpful to them. In preceding chapters we discussed the development of self-management skills. Now, we will expand on those ideas. Let's look at the second major procedure for cognitive social learning.

Suppose bubbly, slightly plump Oscar asks to speak with you after social studies class. Usually, Oscar makes one of these visits about halfway through the marking period. The topic is usually the term project, so you are ready with your best problem-solving suggestions. This visit is different, since Oscar confesses: "I'm fat. There's no way around it. The girls don't like me because I'm not lean and mean." The floodgates open and the Kleenex box suddenly has a new, unanticipated user.

As a teacher who is performing the three teaching roles, you are aware of the upcoming ninth-grade prom and some of the not-so-pleasant dynamics related to dates and to wallflowers. In Oscar's case, he wants to redistribute his weight and go with Millicent to the prom. This clearly stated objective did not fall easily from Oscar's lips; it took some shaping, prompting, and fading! Of course, it will take a carefully worded conversation to help Oscar build his own self-management plan. In developing a self-control or self-management plan, recall from Chapter 3 that there are four basic steps: (1) observe your own to-be-changed behavior in several settings; (2) set standards and goals for the behavior to be changed; (3) consider and assign consequences for behavior-change strategies; and (4) monitor the plan and progress toward the goal (Kahn, 1976; Mahoney & Thoresen, 1974; McLaughlin, 1976).

Mastering self-management skills

If Oscar is going to manage his own behavior, you will want to help him follow these four SELF-MANAGEMENT skills:
- Oscar will have to specify the behavior that he wants to change. From your casual observations of Oscar, eating between class periods seems to be a logical starting point.
- Oscar will want to observe how often and what he eats. A week is a good length of time for self-observation. In this step, you want to learn more about the antecedents and consequences of his eating. Also, self-observation has a very special consequence: probably Oscar will begin to change his behavior in the desirable direction. He will eat less frequently or he will eat less. At the end of the first week, you and Oscar

will discover that he eats almost all the time—between periods, between meals, during commercials—but not at breakfast. Once more you have a carefully worded conversation with Oscar. In this second step, Oscar and you discover that Oscar's eating occurs when other people are around. It would therefore seem that some social-environmental influences are maintaining Oscar's eating.

• You and Oscar will want to consider a variety of plans. Three alternative plans quickly come to mind: removing noncontingent social rewards for eating, such as talking with friends between class; practicing self-denial by eliminating snacks; and regulating the amount and kind of food. Oscar will be the primary person to choose the strategy for change.

• A plan with no monitor is like a ship without a compass. So you will ask Oscar to weigh himself every other day, to give you a record of his eating, and to smile at Millie once a day. Oscar can practice covert self-reinforcement by saying, "Good boy. Another snack passed up means I'm closer to pleasing Millie." Or "Steady. Walk on by the coke machine. Good work." Further, you might add to the contract the *contingency* that as soon as Oscar loses 6 pounds, he may ask Millie to the prom. Throughout this self-management program, Oscar will evaluate his performance and maintain his new physique. Who knows what new and pleasing things will happen to a nearly lean and mean Oscar?

Cognitive social learning theory, particularly self-managment procedures, serves a crucial role as you play the three roles of the classroom teacher. It is an integrated theory which is simple, testable, and heuristic. The concepts of modeling and self-management suggest a wide range of alternative strategies for management, mediation, and facilitation. We believe that as a classroom teacher, you will help students to become scientists about their own behaviors, to integrate their past learning experiences artfully with their present social stimulations and rewards, and to manage themselves more effectively in the future.

LEARNING ACTIVITY: SELECTING YOUR OWN REINFORCERS

What's it going to take to keep you on the job? Where will you find your sources of reinforcement? Who will be willing to provide the kinds of reinforcement that you will want? These questions are not lightly asked, and you will want to answer them. After all, as you read this learning activity, several groups of teachers may be loudly protesting their inadequate support. These men and women are concerned about . . . (you can fill in the blank). Actually, teacher strikes and boycotts have received a great deal of mixed publicity, depending upon the views of the teachers, the reporters, and the voters. Often, no one really understands why teachers are dissatisfied. Indeed, we can say that the concepts and/ or principles related to the employment confrontation have not been adequately defined: the issues are unclear. Relationships among concepts have not been stated, and communications over some basic issues have broken down.

TWO KINDS OF REINFORCERS: NATURAL AND MANAGED

Why does anyone become involved in teaching? One way of looking at this question is to consider the potential and real sources of reinforcement. On one hand, you might obtain *natural* reinforcers from students, other teachers, principals, and the community. Friendship and social support might be readily available to you from these people. On the other hand, you might find that selected, *managed* reinforcers are available from the same four sources. For example, students who have unique educational needs might be assigned to you as a management strategy. You may request slow learners, for example, because you are certain that you are especially competent with them. Or perhaps you might work on an instructional team in order to maximize your special and unique skills. Again, you might find that your community or your industrial employer can strongly support your work by keeping the class size small. In any case, natural and managed reinforcers will become extremely important to you. Some students will gradually acquire self-management skills, others will become successful in problem solving, and still others will master the alphabet. All these students can become sources of reinforcement for you. Think about your natural and managed reinforcers. As a future teacher, you will want to explore your many opportunities for reinforcement.

Your applied learning task

You will complete the task of selecting reinforcers for teachers in three separate steps:

1. Select two of these three groups—teachers, principals, and/or community members—and identify each group's list of "best" reinforcers. You may use any of the three assessment techniques: observation, interview, and paper-and-pencil inventory. It may be easier for you to use a pencil-and-paper survey than an observation or an interview assessment. For teachers, your task will be to find out which reinforcers they would want to receive as a consequence of their work. For principals (possibly an alternative would be an industrial employer), you can find out which reinforcers they would be willing to provide. This set of questions is important for your professional development. Be careful, because some respondents might feel uncomfortable about completing your questionnaire.

2.   Prepare a table for your data. We have drawn up a sample for you:

Reinforcers by name	Rank assigned by teachers	Rank of principal's or taxpayer's "willingness to provide"
Dental plan	1	3
Another day off	3	2
More filmstrips, etc.	2	1

We suggest that you collect data on two or three teachers and on two or three community members. Compare the rankings: do they match?

We have some suggestions for the paper-and-pencil survey. You might ask teachers questions about reinforcers that are available within the classroom or the school (and possibly visible to the principal). For example, you can ask, "When you finish working with a student, do you like her to smile at you (to say, 'Thank you,' to perform a second problem correctly, etc.)?" You can anticipate that some teachers would want the child to smile and others would be content to see the student perform another problem correctly. That difference is something that you are trying to determine. On the other hand, you might ask teachers questions about the managed reinforcers available to them from their employers. "When you submit a request for new equipment, do you like to receive a written or oral explanation about the lack of funds?" "Would you prefer to meet with your principal about the request?" "Would you hope to obtain community sponsors for the materials?" These are some of the possible questions you might ask regarding the managed reinforcer approach to this learning activity. As you can see, the entire issue of reinforcers available to teachers can become extremely complex.

3.   Explain the difference between ranks for the two lists, using the developmental materials from Chapters 1 through 5 and your own experience. The encounters which you can have during this learning activity will probably be as reinforcing as the two sets of ranks. Should you have any interesting or unique results, please share them with us. We will be delighted to hear from you.

 **SUMMARY**

1.   Learning is a process in which the *individual interacts* with the effective *environment* to produce a stable *behavior change*. The italicized terms are crucial parts of this definition. Each term can be varied so learning may apply to an older or younger person. It can apply to a career education program or a retirement planning course. All people can learn to develop and master the skills necessary to cope with new environments.

2. Behavior is *simple, measurable,* and *observable*. This definition allows us to further specify whether the behavior can be seen by others (OVERT BEHAVIOR), or whether it is observable only by the individual involved (COVERT BEHAVIOR). All behavior is learned, and these same behaviors can be unlearned. The environment, antecedents, and consequences influence the learning and unlearning of behaviors.

3. A common practice is to label people, and this is usually destructive. When used in this manner, labels describe people and/or explain their behavior. But in actuality a label cannot either describe or explain behavior, and its use in this manner is a logical circularity. Usually, a label can be analyzed into a list of specific behaviors which can be further specified as a series of events.

4. The ABC MODEL for learning considers each behavior in terms of the related antecedents and consequences. Each sequence of events can be listed by its antecedents (A), behaviors (B), and consequences (C). You will analyze a behavioral event by the ABC model, consider educational goals and objectives with the students, and decide whether to increase, decrease, eliminate, or maintain the present behavior or to acquire a new behavior. The application of the ABC model will become fully integrated with your life-style as you develop your competencies as a teacher.

5. The three learning theories discussed in this chapter—CLASSICAL, OPERANT, and COGNITIVE SOCIAL LEARNING—are closely related. Classical learning has the simplest functional parts and deals primarily with antecedent control of behavior. Operant learning expands the model to include the stimulus events—such as cueing and reinforcing—which increase and strengthen behavior. The third theory, cognitive social learning, suggests that the person mediates the stimulus and reward messages from the environment. Cognitive social learning theory describes how people acquire new behaviors by observing models, choosing alternative strategies, and managing their own behavior. The functional components of the theory are interactive, interrelated, and interdependent.

6. In operant learning, we know that a reinforcer appears to increase the frequency of a behavior. The schedules of reinforcement tell us what happens when the person is not reinforced continuously. Four distinct intermittent schedules have been identified and studied. They are called the FIXED INTERVAL, FIXED RATIO, VARIABLE INTERVAL, and VARIABLE RATIO reinforcement schedules. As a group, they are called *intermittent* schedules of reinforcement. The behaviors that are controlled by the variable ratio and variable

interval schedules are more resistant to change than the behaviors controlled by the more predictable schedules.

7. There are four rules for using reinforcement—select effective reinforcers, apply contingent rewards, reward promptly, and use small steps toward the goal. These suggest that you must be observant, patient, and sensitive in applying operant learning. Behavior change does not occur overnight, so care must be taken to avoid confusion and frustration for both the student and yourself.

8. Most of the behaviors which students perform are not isolated events. Rather, they are parts of long, complex behavioral chains. Such diverse activities as tieing shoelaces, repairing a flat tire, or singing "America the Beautiful" are examples of motor or verbal chains. CHAINING can be practiced until it occurs with no errors; some people might want to explore learning a verbal chain backwards.

9. Aversive control is an umbrella term which includes NEGATIVE REINFORCEMENT and two kinds of PUNISHMENT: withdrawal of positive reinforcement and presentation of aversive stimuli. Negative reinforcement is the procedure in which the removal of an aversive stimulus increases or strengthens a preceding behavior. Aversive control procedures can be extremely effective. However, there is disagreement about whether certain kinds of aversive control should be used in the schools. We believe that physical punishment is not appropriate in academic settings. Other forms of aversive control are preferable and are more effective in prompting behavior change.

10. Learning by observation is probably the most powerful and most common kind of learning in a social setting. COGNITIVE SOCIAL LEARNING theory considers how the individual thinks about or mediates the environmental stimuli and rewards. In contrast with other learning theories which deal with external stimulus events or reinforcement schedules, cognitive social learning theory considers the process by which a person mediates the meaning of the stimulus and reinforcing events.

11. The end product of cognitive social learning theory is SELF-MANAGEMENT for the student. In the long run, self-direction, self-control, and self-management are the primary aims of education. Cognitive social learning theory suggests how you can help students develop and carry out their own self-mangement programs.

12. Natural and managed reinforcers are available in the educational environment. The former reinforcers occur as parts of the day-to-day events in school and in the community. The latter reinforcers are carefully planned and used to produce the greatest possible effect upon students, teachers, or parents.

KEY
TERMS

ABC MODEL: A model designed to help teachers analyze the antecedents and consequences influencing a particular behavior. The analysis helps prepare a plan for action.

BACKWARD CHAINING: A procedure whereby the last response is learned first, and then the entire chain is learned backward to the first stimulus in the chain.

CHAINING: A procedure involving two or more behaviors that are linked so that each response becomes the stimulus for the next response. Verbal chains include the Gettysburg Address and motor chains include riding a bike.

CLASSICAL LEARNING: Learning that occurs when an antecedent event stimulates a response or behavioral event.

COGNITIVE SOCIAL LEARNING: Learning that occurs when an observer mediates antecedent and consequent information from models, self, and the environment before responding.

CONDITIONED STIMULUS: A learned antecedent event which controls or elicits a conditioned response.

CONDITIONED RESPONSE: A learned response which is controlled by a conditioned stimulus.

CONTINGENT or CONTINGENCY: Conditions under which reinforcement will be given.

CONTINUOUS REINFORCEMENT: The CRF schedule describes the reinforcement of a specific response after every occurrence.

COVERT BEHAVIOR: Behavior that can be measured and observed only by the person who is performing the behavior (for example, feeling happy).

DELAYED REINFORCEMENT: A procedure in which the person is rewarded some time after the performance of the response.

DIFFERENTIAL REINFORCEMENT: The selective reinforcement and nonreinforcement of specified responses.

DISCRIMINATIVE STIMULUS: The stimulus that sets the stage or cues the person to perform a sequence of events.

EXTINCTION: A procedure to reduce behavior by withholding the reinforcer that was maintaining that behavior.

FADING: A procedure in which prompts are used less and less frequently in order to maintain the performance.

FIXED INTERVAL REINFORCEMENT: A reinforcement schedule that provides reinforcers contingent upon the passage of a time interval.

FIXED RATIO REINFORCEMENT: A reinforcement schedule that provides reinforcers contingent upon the performance of a planned number of specific responses.

GENERALIZED REINFORCERS: Reinforcers that have an influence upon a specific behavior in a variety of situations.

MODELING: The procedure of selecting, from the patterns of observed physical and verbal behavior, specific patterns of behavior to imitate.

NEGATIVE REINFORCEMENT: The use of aversive stimuli which, when removed, increase or strengthen a preceding response.

OPERANT LEARNING: Learning that occurs when a reinforcing event influences the performance of a specified response.

OVERT BEHAVIOR: Behavior that can be observed, measured, and specified.

PROMPTS: Cues used to elicit or to maintain a response.

PUNISHMENT: A procedure in which the presentation of an aversive stimulus immediately following a particular behavior reduces the rate at which the behavior occurs.

REINFORCEMENT MENU: A list of potential reinforcers from which one or more may be selected as a reward.

S_D: The symbol used to represent discriminative stimuli or antecedents in the ABC model.

SATIATION: The condition that exists when a reinforcer no longer has an effect upon a specific response.

SELF-MANAGEMENT: A four-part sequence in which the person observes himself or herself, specifies a goal, chooses a strategy, and monitors progress toward that goal.

SHAPING: The procedure of reinforcing successive approximations to the behavioral goal.

STIMULUS GENERALIZATION: The spread of effects in which a response occurs in situations that are similar to an initial learning situation.

SUCCESSIVE APPROXIMATION: The procedure of developing a goal response by reinforcing responses which more and more resemble the behavioral goal.

TIME OUT: A procedure that involves removing the person from the reinforcing environment contingent upon the performance of a particular behavior.

UNCONDITIONED RESPONSE: A naturally occurring response which is controlled by an unconditioned stimulus.

UNCONDITIONED STIMULUS: A natural antecedent event which controls or elicits an unconditioned response.

VARIABLE INTERVAL REINFORCEMENT: A reinforcement schedule that provides reinforcers contingent upon the passage of a variable time interval. The time interval has a specified range and a specific average.

VARIABLE RATIO REINFORCEMENT: A reinforcement schedule that provides reinforcers contingent upon the performance of a variable number of specific responses. The number of responses prior to reinforcement varies around a specific average.

SELF-TEST

1. Learning has four crucial parts. They are:
   a. _____
   b. _____
   c. _____
   d. _____

2. Feelings, attitudes, and thoughts about a person are examples of _____ which can:

   a. not be observed by others
   b. be specific
   c. be measured
   d. be all of the above

3. A model for analyzing and for planning change in an educational setting has three parts which are:

a. cost, supply, and excess
b. cost, antecedents, and behavior
c. payoff, environment, and behavior
d. behavior, antecedents, and consequences

4. In planning a behavior change program with a student or with another adult, you will want to decide from among five different directions for the behavior, depending on the student and your own goals.
   a. _____
   b. _____
   c. _____
   d. _____
   e. _____

5. Match the appropriate theories, people, and ideas:

Theory	People	Ideas
operant learning	Pavlov	stimulus
classical learning	Bandura	models
cognitive social	Skinner	reinforce-
learning		ment

6. In classical learning the natural environment has _____ stimulus and _____. Later as learning occurs the _____ gains control over _____.

7. A reinforcement menu can be prepared by the student and teacher working together. In all probability, the menu will include items from one or more of the following reinforcers:
   a. _____
   b. _____
   c. _____
   d. _____
   e. _____

8. Many long sequences of behaviors such as speeches, bike riding, and going to work are simply responses which serve as cues for subsequent behavior. They are called:
   _____ or _____
   _____.

9. In cognitive social learning, three components seem to interact to produce behavior change. The three components are:
   a. _____
   b. _____
   c. _____

10. Several kinds of models occur in our day-to-day environment. As a rule, models who are similar to the observer and who are _____ are more influential than similar but _____ models.

SELF-TEST KEY

1. person
   interaction
   environment
   behavior change
2. covert behaviors
   and d
3. d
4. increase
   decrease
   acquisition
   extinction
   maintenance
5. classical learning Pavlov   stimulus
   operant learning   Skinner reinforcement
   cognitive social   Bandura models
   learning

6. unconditioned
   unconditioned response
   conditioned stimulus
   the conditioned response
7. conventional
   adult approval
   competition
   independence
   peer-group approval
8. verbal or motor chains
9. environmental stimulation
   reinforcement
   mediation
10. reinforced
    unreinforced

CHAPTER 6

Positive Motivation for Learning

LEARNING OBJECTIVES

After reading Chapter 6, answering the self-monitoring questions, completing the learning activity, and reading any further references of your choice, you will be able to:

1. Define and give examples of key terms.

2. Compare self-motivation and environmental motivation according to the ABC model.

3. List and describe cognitive factors in motivation.

4. Summarize the arguments for and against the use of external rewards in classrooms.

5. Explain the effects of success, failure, and feedback on future performance.

6. List ten changes in classroom procedure that will improve student motivation for learning.

7. Select examples of classroom reward structures that will increase or decrease positive motivation for learning.

8. Describe three situations that produce anxiety reactions in school and match intervention strategies to each.

9. Select examples of effective and ineffective teacher feedback responses. Revise examples of teacher feedback to increase positive motivation and self-motivation.

 **FOCUS ON MOTIVATION**

Today is parent-teacher conference day. You are meeting with the parents of your seventh-grade class to report on student progress. Bryan's and Ted's parents show up for individual conferences with you. Consider the following brief reports you make to each set of parents:

Ted just doesn't seem to be settling down in my class. He has trouble getting started with his math assignments and he gives up when he has some difficulty. He doesn't really seem to be interested in math and I have a hard time getting him involved in working the problems. He just doesn't seem to have much motivation.

On the other hand, to Bryan's parents you might say:

Bryan is really a self-motivated student and he seems to be very interested in math. He always gets started with his work promptly and he works

**Figure 6-1
Positive motivation
leads to mastery.**

*hard at his projects. He usually completes his class assignments on time,
too. When he's having some trouble with a problem, he just works hard
until he has solved it.*

In each situation, you have been talking about MOTIVATION, describing
three aspects of each boy's activity in class: (1) initiation of activities
(showing interest, paying attention, choosing to engage in some task);
(2) amount of effort (trying hard, spending time, going to the library for
more references, using allowance money to buy materials for a class
project); and (3) degree of persistence on task (concentrates on completing
tasks, does not give up easily, overcomes small obstacles). Students who
initiate or get started on a particular task and who work hard and
persistently can be described as highly motivated in that situation (Figure
6-1).

The contribution of these motivating behaviors to academic success
is apparent to the facilitating teacher. Figure 6-1 suggests that motivation
leads to mastery. Bryan's efforts and persistence in math will pay off in
increased knowledge and problem-solving skills. He will probably enjoy
his math assignments more than Ted, since he shows increasing competence and participation. In turn, you will probably enjoy students when
they reward your teaching efforts with involvement and accomplishment.
You will also be concerned about students who appear unmotivated to
put forth their best efforts on many tasks and in many situations. For any
student, you will recognize that not all sources of motivated school
behavior come packaged inside the individual. What can you do as a
teacher to improve and increase the productive motivation of each of
your students?

SOURCES OF MOTIVATION

In this discussion, we shall be looking at motivation from two perspectives:
(1) SELF-MOTIVATION, which is internal to the student, and (2) ENVIRON-
MENTAL MOTIVATION, which is provided by others. Self-motivation is
cognitive because students provide their own antecedents and consequences. Each student will have a unique pattern of self-motivation. In
any situation, the self-motivated student sets realistic goals, takes concrete
steps to meet these goals, and evaluates personal progress accordingly.
When students meet these goals, they feel pride in accomplishment; when
their achievement falls short of the goals, they take corrective action.

"The self-motivated student sets realistic goals, takes concrete steps to meet these goals, and evaluates personal progress accordingly." (Suzanne Szasz)

You will observe that self-motivated students take responsibility for their learning and can work independently.

Environmental motivation is provided by the situation, the tasks on which the student is working, and the objective consequences of his or her efforts. Social learning theory proposes that all useful motivation is an interaction between factors contributed by the student and factors provided by the effective environment. As a teacher, you will have more control over the external determinants of your students' motivation. However, your skillful management of classroom ABCs can exert a positive effect on internal or self-controlled motivation as well. Your long-range goal may be to have all your students setting their own goals and reinforcing themselves for accomplishment without external or artificial inducements. Indeed, we believe this to be a worthy goal for all education. Your immediate task, however, will be to arrange a favorable environment so that self-maintaining academic behavior is most likely to take place.

In this chapter, we shall discuss differing concepts of self-motivation and environmental motivation and how you can apply these concepts to your classroom management procedures. Within every school situation, there are multiple opportunities for stimulating and increasing productive student motivation. We shall also take up some deterrents to positive motivation. We will offer some suggestions on how to deal with academic anxieties and fear of failure; your management and facilitation skills become useful here. In applying the many alternatives for encouraging productive motivation in your classroom, you can offer opportunities for effective learning to all your students.

SELF-MOTIVATION

There are at least as many theories of motivation as there are theories of how learning takes place. We can divide these theories into two broad groups: (1) Trait theories, which emphasize needs within the individual, and (2) cognitive theories, which focus on the student's mediating skills. In the following sections, we will discuss differing approaches to both traits and cognitive mediation as motivators for learning.

TRAITS AND NEEDS IN MOTIVATION

The final source of motivation has often been placed within the individual. In some theories, each person is held responsible for his or her own effort, persistence, and accomplishment. Since the motivation is assumed to be within the individual, it is similar to a trait which is functional across many situations. Among such internal theories are those which emphasize *needs* within each person that motivate her or him to act. Let's consider the classroom utility of theories that propose (1) internal needs to motivate effortful behavior and (2) the trait of competence as the basis of motivation.

Internal needs as motivators

Internal needs have been used to explain why people pursue some activities and avoid others (Maslow, 1943; Murray, 1938). These needs are seen as forces or tensions within individuals that drive them toward particular goals. When you infer a need as a motivator of Ted's behavior, you imply that he annoys Donna because he "needs attention" or that he hangs around you frequently because he "needs love." In either case, you assign the cause of Ted's behavior to an internal need, ignoring the outcomes of his actions—such as Donna's squealing or your concerned attention. The list of personality needs is endless: we observe that students seem to have needs for achievement, affiliation, self-esteem, self-actualization, exploration, stimulation, activity, safety, and social approval. For example, how do you conclude that Ted needs social approval? You observe that he frequently says "Look at me," and he asks you to look at his work. From your earlier reading on reinforcement, you can see that these are situational consequences or reinforcers that have as much explanatory power for Ted's behavior as an internal need.

As a manager of the classroom environment and a sensitive observer of all of your students, you will note the particular antecedents and reinforcers that appear to elicit and maintain certain high-rate or frequent behaviors. Careful observation of student-situation interactions may be more useful to you in organizing a motivating learning environment than taking guesses about the internal needs of each student.

You are probably shaking your head by now. In every classroom you have observed, some students do ask for more help, more attention, and more support. Doesn't that mean that they need what they are asking for? Let's apply some principles of reinforcement here and consider the student's learning history. We know that each student has a unique background of reinforcement experiences. These experiences have included different reinforcers, different reinforcement agents, and certainly a variety of reinforcement schedules. Remember that students with a history of intermittent reinforcement on any task will tend to persist longer at that activity in new situations. Ted has probably received attention intermittently from parents, relatives, and siblings for displaying his work and asking for help. Probably he learned that if he kept "bugging" his mother, she would say "Ummm, very nice." Now, he has learned to keep asking for adult attention until you give it to him. The resulting attention-getting behavior looks like a "need for attention" to you. The problem in translating your observations of Ted's behavior into internal needs is that you may give him lots of attention inappropriately when he could be working independently. Your solution, therefore, is to observe the reinforcers that appear to motivate Ted and to provide these contingently for constructive effort and achievement.

Competence motivation

In recent years, it has been common to attribute all achievement behavior to an underlying need for competence (White, 1959). According to this view, all your students have an innate need or desire to explore the environment and to deal with it effectively. Robert White called this COMPETENCE MOTIVATION. He proposed that the motivation for mastery over the environment is the basis for all cognitive and motor behavior such as exploration, play, curiosity, activity, language, and learning. Accordingly, external outcomes of behavior become secondary in importance. Satisfaction is achieved by arousal and the maintenance of activity that leads to competence. Once the student gains competence in an activity, he or she performs this activity for its own sake rather than to reduce internal needs or to gain external incentives. Therefore, the desire to learn is seen as intrinsic to all students. White believes that INTRINSIC MOTIVATION occurs when students are working for no apparent external rewards.

The view of competence as intrinsic motivation for learning is understandably attractive to teachers. White's position suggests that Kathy can learn math just for the enjoyment of being able to complete her long-division problems. A competence motive also suggests that Kathy will be equally motivated by any challenging task. As Kathy's teacher, you can best arouse this competence motive by arranging stimulus conditions that will facilitate Kathy's involvement in math activities. The conditions favorable to mastery here include a sufficient amount of novelty in Kathy's math to arouse curiosity but also enough familiarity that Kathy can relate to the problem and solve it. You may recognize here a similarity to Piaget's conception of the conditions favorable to equilibrium: moderate newness to provide a challenge to the student. Both White and Piaget would suggest that Kathy's math problem be presented in terms of a familiar setting (such as cutting up pizza pie). At the same time, you should introduce an interesting twist that will challenge Kathy's competence motive (such as how to adjust the portions for big and little eaters).

PROBE 6-1

Think back to all the subjects you studied in high school. Can you recall one class in which you had very little interest? How hard did you apply yourself in that class? List three things the teacher might have done to increase your active participation and effort. Would these strategies also have increased your interest in the topics?

Can you apply White's idea of universal competence motivation to all your teaching activities? Will you be able to "turn on" all your students to work enthusiastically and persistently in every academic subject by arranging a continual succession of novel and stimulating topics and problems? Certainly, White offers you the challenge of finding materials and strategies that will appeal to a wide range of individual student interests and skills. Of course, we want to develop in every student an underlying sense of personal competence. The development of individual competence across a wide variety of academic and personal skills has been a major theme of this book. However, the conditions of learning proposed in earlier chapters suggest that a number of factors other than innate competence motivation and stimulus novelty will combine to arouse and sustain student effort. In the following sections we will look at some of the ABC conditions that contribute to effectively motivated learning: cognitive student *behaviors* (B), and environmental conditions related both to tasks, or *antecedents* (A), and incentive factors, or *consequences* (C).

"We want to develop in every student an underlying sense of personal competence." (Doug Wilson/Black Star)

COGNITIVE MEDIATION IN MOTIVATION

It should come as no surprise to you that cognitive mediation in motivation is directly tied to self-competency skills. Here we shall expand our earlier description of self-competency to cover situations which require positive motivation for a specific activity. Table 6-1 shows six self-competency skills that will contribute to Kathy's motivation in math: *self-evaluation, task preferences, expectancies for success, achievement standards, locus of control,* and *self-reinforcement.* All six of these concepts have been introduced in earlier chapters. You may recall that all self-competency involves the first three factors:

1. Self-evaluation of math skills.
2. Preference for math over other activities.
3. Expectancies for success on these problems.

When Kathy can score positively on each of these factors, she will probably agree to get started on page 31 of her math workbook.

What additional self-motivating factors are required to keep Kathy working to complete her math assignment? In achievement situations, three more conditions will contribute to Kathy's positive motivation:

4. The setting of standards or goals for math achievement ("I want to get them all correct") and striving to meet those self-imposed standards.

5. The application of an internal locus of control for math achievement ("If I get my math problems correct, it's because I'm smart and I tried hard"). Therefore the student works harder to meet the goals.

6. Self-reinforcement contingent on meeting goals; students can congratulate themselves with good feelings when they succeed.

Each of these six factors provides a separate but interdependent source of internal cognitive motivation for Kathy's efforts in your math class. Let's look briefly at these six factors and consider how each one contributes to Kathy's positive effort.

Self-evaluation   Self-evaluation involves Kathy's personal assessment of her general skills in math. If she believes strongly that she can tackle long division, she is more likely to pay close attention to your instructions and to try working

Table 6-1. Kathy's self-competency and motivation for math

Source of self-competency motivation	Kathy's covert behavior, or what she tells herself	Kathy's overt behavior in math class
1. Self-evaluation for math (specifically: long division)	"I am good at long division."	Attends to instructions; starts working the problem.
2. Task preference	"I like math and I want to be good at it."	Keeps working the problems; does all her homework.
3. Expectancies for success	"I'm pretty sure I can do this set of problems if I think about them and try hard enough."	Keeps working the problems. Even though she is unable to solve one, starts the next one.
4. Goal-setting standards	"I really want to get them all right. I've got to keep going till I get them all finished."	Keeps working the problems; goes back to complete unfinished ones.
5. Locus of control	"If I get a good grade in math, I know it will be because I am smart and I worked hard."	Keeps working the problems; seeks more information from book and teacher; tries alternative solutions.
6. Self-reinforcement for meeting goals	"Wow! I finished my work ahead of time. I feel so good because I got them all right."	Tells her teacher she is ready for some harder problems next time.

"The instructional challenge is to design learning environments where all students can expect to succeed." (Dennis Brack/Black Star)

the problems. It is important to remember that actual skill is less important for motivational effort and choice of activities than the student's perceived skill. Students with low achievement as well as competent students can develop confidence in their ability to master certain kinds of tasks that match their present capabilities.

Self-evaluation for math relates to two major factors: (1) the student's learning history of success in math and (2) a social comparison with the observed math accomplishments of peers. This dual standard for self-evaluation has implications for group cooperation and competition strategies. If Kathy's math skills are high and she has been personally successful on her assignment, competition with peers will tend to increase her self-evaluation. However, for Ted, who has been having difficulty with long division, open comparison with his peer group can only embarrass and discourage him. As a result of negative comparisons with others, Ted's self-evaluation for math may decrease. You can relate these issues to alternative grading systems and their impact on student motivation. For all students, success in the skill area is essential for future positive self-evaluation. Therefore, the instructional challenge is to design learning environments where all students can expect to succeed.

Task preference

Task preferences will help determine how willing Kathy is to start working and how hard she will persist in the face of difficulties (Crandall, 1969; Gold & Berger, 1978; Stein & Bailey, 1973). Three factors contribute to Kathy's personal preferences for classroom activities: (1) previous experiences (either real or vicarious); (2) the anticipated usefulness of the tasks to her; and (3) the degree to which the tasks are interesting or challenging.

First, activities in which Kathy has experienced some positive interactions or success will take on increased preference value for her. Kathy may prefer math because her mother is a computer analyst, or she may dislike math because she feels the boys won't like her if she is a math whiz (Condry & Dyer, 1976; Janda, O'Grady, & Capps, 1978). Second, Kathy will prefer activities that are useful and relevant to her present and future life. It is clear that all school tasks are not immediately useful to students. Your challenge will be to place learning tasks into meaningful contexts so that all students, whatever their background, can value them and generate some enthusiasm for learning (Banks, McQuater, & Hubbard, 1978).

Finally, tasks themselves will have differential interest or challenge for Kathy and Ted. Long lines of math computation are probably dull for everyone. Repetitive drill is hardly exciting enough to raise Ted's eyebrows in anticipation. You may find that certain tasks are inherently low in interest for some students. At these times, you will welcome external sources of motivation to keep initial activity and persistence high (Ross, 1976). The place of environmental incentives in learning is discussed below.

Expectancy for success

On any particular set of problems, expectancy for success is critical to all effort and persistence. Regardless of Kathy's general self-evaluation, she may have low expectancies for successful performance at particular tasks. For example, in art class, she tells you she can't draw and her figures come out "funny." Students who do not expect to do well on an activity tend to avoid the activity. Some students try half-heartedly and give up easily (Crandall, 1969; Parsons, 1978; Weiner et al., 1971). As a result, Kathy is less likely to perform well when she has a low expectancy of success than when she has confidence that she can succeed or meet her goals (Battle, 1965; Feather, 1966). Therefore Kathy works harder at her math problems than she does at her art assignments. She also completes her math problems every time and tends to get most of them correct. In art class, she looks out the window or talks to Ted. At the end of her hour, she produces a messy, half-drawn figure which she crumbles and throws away. How can we account for these differences in Kathy's expectancies for math and art?

Generally, students expect to do well (1) following positive information or feedback, (2) on tasks they perceive as not too difficult, and (3) in areas in which they have done well in the past. You can see that these requirements for a positive achievement expectancy suggest that teachers (1) give clear feedback, (2) match task difficulty to student skills, and (3) help students to anticipate some degree of success regardless of past failures.

Certainly you will not always meet the challenge of encouraging a positive expectancy for success in all of a student's activities. In those tasks where objective success is unclear or ambiguous, such as music or art, students will be able to impose their own standards for success. Interestingly enough, girls have lower expectancies for achievement than do boys where the external criteria for competence are unclear. When the standards for skilled performance are vague, many students need more encouragement to use their own internal standards of judgment (Lenney, 1977). Remember that a student's expectancy for success can be helped by your careful management of learning.

PROBE 6-2

Providing clear feedback is important for establishing positive expectancies. How does the feedback procedure differ for subjects where there are objectively "correct" answers and for those where the criteria for excellence are more subjective? List three different things you might say to a student who (1) asks you how you like her picture in art class and (2) disagrees with you in a topical discussion.

Standards for achievement

Goal-setting standards for achievement will determine Kathy's demands upon herself. When her goals are moderately high, she may work hard to meet them and will reward herself with good feelings and satisfaction in accomplishment (Locke, Cartledge, & Koeppel, 1968). Two problems are common when students set their own goals: (1) goals are set so low that no effort is involved in meeting these goals or (2) goals are set so high that they are impossible to achieve; the student becomes discouraged and gives up. You will want to watch out for student goals that are far out of line with your students' apparent skills. Let's consider what happens in each of these situations.

When standards and goals are too low, motivation is also low and Kathy will get no satisfaction from completing her work. You may observe in art class that she "doesn't seem to care about her work"; she produces sloppy or incomplete papers, and she also spends a good deal of her work time in distracting off-task activities. Students who appear to work consistently below their capabilities are frequently referred to as *under-achievers*. Sometimes, however, students set very high standards for themselves. They want to produce a perfect paper, always to be right when answering in class, and always to be the best student in the class. Frequently, these self-imposed demands are unrealistic and unreachable. In art class, Kathy may be comparing herself to Jim, who has had an artistic flair since first grade. Since none of Kathy's efforts match Jim's drawings, she concludes that she is "no good" and gives up. When students consistently strive for exceedingly high goals or standards, they are seen as *overachievers*. Under- and overachievement are both related to the level of goal setting and the student's present level of skill.

The teaching challenge here fits into your roles as both manager and facilitator of learning. You will want to work individually with students who appear to set their goals too high or too low. In each case, it will be helpful to have students state their goals in advance and to discuss reasonable goals with you. The skills involved in realistic goal setting are not always learned before students show up in your class.

Goal-setting skills are teachable. Study 6-1 shows you how one high school teacher helped students to set realistic goals for typing skills. You can help Kathy to match her goals with her present capabilities for meeting these goals. In art class, it will be important to help Kathy to compete against herself, rather than comparing her performance with Jim's. Alternatively, she can decide to practice her skills, take a Saturday art class, or check out some books on drawing from the library. You will observe that some students can maintain high goals and satisfy their achievement standards by increasing effort and personal development. Whether Kathy decides to lower her standards for good art work or to increase her skills, she will be wise to make her goals specific and attainable. Being a "good artist" is less attainable than being able to draw a landscape scene in perspective. In addition to helping students set realistic goals, you will want to make certain that the goals are clear and specific. A specific goal helps each student state what behaviors must yet be learned to attain the standards the student has set.

Locus of control for achievement

Locus of control describes Kathy's general expectation about the relationship between her effort and skill and her objective success and achievement. You may recall from Chapter 2 that students with an internal locus of control tend to attribute (explain) their success or failure to their own skill and efforts or lack of them. Students with an external locus of control tend to attribute or explain their success and failure as due to the outside environment: good or tough luck, a hard or easy test, a fair or an

STUDY 6-1. TEACHING GOAL-SETTING SKILLS

Many students in a large suburban high school are not college bound. Those who end up in business education courses are frequently unmotivated and low-achieving. One typing teacher decided to increase motivation by placing more responsibility on the students. She instructed them in determining goals in relation to their skill and the difficulty of the typing assignments. The dramatic success of her project is presented in Figure 6-2. Students in the class which developed goal-setting skills increased their interest and effort during the school year. Look at the effects of this increased motivation on typing speed. In comparison with a control class that received no special goal training, students' typing speeds increased significantly over the school year. How did this teacher accomplish such impressive results? First, she had students assess their capabilities in relation to the difficulty of the assignment. Typing materials were ana-

lyzed for specific sources of difficulty. Students examined how their personal skills matched each typing problem. They considered alternative tactics for overcoming each typing deficit. Second, the teacher changed the goal-setting and grading structure. Each student kept a graph of daily progress. On the basis of these graphs, students set short- and long-term typing goals. Students then decided when they would take the tests. They also selected the level of the tests on the basis of their skills and chosen goals. These procedures shifted the locus of control from the teacher to the students. When students took greater personal responsibility for goal setting, they learned how to take moderate risks and to meet their goals.

Adapted from: Alschuler, A. S., Tabor, D., & McIntyre, J. *Teaching achievement motivation: Theory and practice in psychological education.* Middletown, Conn.: Educational Ventures, 1970.

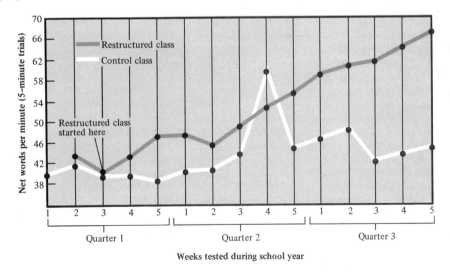

Figure 6-2
Number of words typed by students trained (restructured) or untrained (control) in goal-setting skills. (*Source:* Alschuler, Tabor, & McIntyre, 1970).

unfair teacher. A striking demonstration of the relationship between belief in personal control over academic rewards and academic achievement was shown in the now famous Coleman report on school achievement (Coleman et al., 1966). Coleman and his associates, who based their findings on a large-scale study of schools throughout the United States, concluded that

A pupil attitude factor, which appears to have a stronger relationship to achievement than do all the "school" factors together, is the extent to which an individual feels that he [sic] has some control over his own destiny. . . . The responses . . . show that minority pupils, except for Orientals, have far less conviction than whites that they can affect their own environment and future. (p. 23)

Many other studies have found similar relationships. Where students demonstrate a belief or conviction that they are responsible for their grades and achievements, they indeed earn higher grades. These students also spend more time on their schoolwork and other intellectual activities (Buck & Austin, 1970; Crandall & McGhee, 1968; Lessing, 1969; Messer, 1972). How can we account for higher achievement in students who maintain a belief in their own control over reinforcers? When specific skills are examined separately, students with an internal locus of control show up with more cognitive behaviors that lead to mastery. Specifically, internal control has been found to predict many of the student behaviors that lead to mastery: attentiveness to instructions, information seeking, using relevant situational cues, and developing rules and strategies for retention (Phares, 1976). It seems that these skills contribute directly to the higher academic achievement of students with an internal locus of control. This is a motivational factor because an internal orientation is related to greater effort and persistence at problem solution in many situations.

Since an internal locus of control appears to contribute to positive motivation in school, what can you do to encourage students to attribute their achievements to skill and effort? Remember that Kathy's beliefs about the outcomes of her behavior have been built up over the years. These beliefs are still developing by the time she reaches your third-grade class. We know that third-grade students are generally more external than they will be in high school (Penk, 1969). An internalized approach to one's performance develops slowly over time. However, we believe that, in any situation, students have a choice. You can help them to decide on internal rather than external attibutions.

Several massive programs designed to increase student awareness of how they can control the outcomes of their lives have demonstrated a positive effect on achievement (Alschuler et al., 1970; deCharms, 1971;

Kolb, 1965). While each of these programs may be too detailed to implement in your classes, several themes run through them. Each program emphasized (1) self-evaluation, or assessment of skills in relation to particular tasks; (2) teacher-student contractual planning for tasks, responsibilities, and grades; (3) positive expectancies for accomplishment and success; and (4) realistic feedback for task completion. Each program also placed personal responsibility on the student for his or her own accomplishment. Don't these ideas sound similar to the self-competency motivation we have been discussing?

We should caution you that internal beliefs may be difficult to change without consistent and intense programs such as these. However, you can be helpful to students like Kathy and Ted if you encourage an internal orientation through wise management of the learning environment in your class. Take some of the suggestions in this chapter's Learning Activity for giving constructive feedback to increase self-motivation. Each small effort on your part can add a measure of self-motivation to Kathy's and Ted's efforts.

Self-reinforcement   Self-reinforcement for meeting goals is the final outcome of Kathy's self-competence in math. Once Kathy sets realistic goals and organizes her mastery skills to achieve effectively, she persists until she attains her goals. Her self-reinforcement through feelings of competency or feelings of failure are the major motivational factors responsible for her hard work and persistence in math. Having achieved her goals, Kathy will now set new goals and will again reward herself for meeting her self-imposed standards. You can see how self-reinforcement becomes a continuing process.

=== **PROBE 6-3** ===

Describe how the relationship between standards for achievement and the students' actual achievement can determine the level of self-reinforcement. What happens to self-reinforcement when goals are set (1) too high or (2) too low in terms of the student's actual achievement?

You must be wondering by now how we can get Kathy to this ideal state of self-determined goals, persistent effort, and self-reinforcement for achievement! Is it really possible? It should be perfectly clear to you by now that self-reinforcement depends in part upon objective success and mastery. Students who routinely reward themselves with good feelings of accomplishment must have objective FEEDBACK for their efforts. Therefore, the development of effective self-reward skills depends in part

"The development of effective self-reward skills depends in part on a consistent, contingent, and informative environment." (Paul Conklin/Monkmeyer)

on a consistent, contingent, and informative environment. Here is where your job as Kathy's teacher becomes critical and extremely important. Teacher management of the learning environment, especially with regard to the consequences of learning, is essential for the development of student self-reinforcement skills. Students will transfer external evaluations of their performance to their self-evaluation. Consistent corrective feedback and approval by others for good performance will teach Kathy to provide these outcomes for herself in the future (Bandura, 1974).

Take your cues from two topics we discussed earlier: self-management and self-competency. These are related groups of skills that effectively contribute to student motivation. Students who can effectively manage their own learning sequences will have mastered many of the fundamentals of self-determined motivation. In teaching for self-motivation, you will want to focus more closely on the goal-setting and self-reinforcement skills of each student. It is therefore important that (1) both you and the student make these specific skills clear and explicit and (2) you help students to bring the steps for self-management increasingly under their own control. Consider the following suggestions:

• *Provide opportunities for objective self-observation.* Many times the particular behaviors that would help students remain on task and working hard are unclear or undefined for the student. What does it mean to tell Ted that he must "pay attention" or "try harder"? In a carefully controlled study with an eighth grader named Liza, study behavior was

GUIDELINES FOR TEACHING

Encouraging Self-Motivation

defined in the following four ways: facing the teacher, writing class notes, looking at students who were answering teacher questions, and answering questions when called upon (Broden, Hall, & Mitts, 1971). Liza was given a card and instructed on how to mark a plus or minus sign each time she felt she was or was not "studying." Figure 6-3 shows you the form of Liza's self-recording card. At the outset of the project, Liza was "studying" only 30 percent of the time. Figure 6-4 shows you the results of Liza's self-recording strategies. Notice that external reinforcement (teacher praise) was added to support Liza's efforts. Finally, both self-recording and teacher praise were removed and Liza was able to maintain her own study skills. What an exciting change for both Liza and her teacher! Please note, however, that if you plan to set up external contingencies—such as awarding points and privileges based on self-recording—you may encourage students to cheat (Turkewitz, O'Leary, & Ironsmith, 1975). Therefore, self-recording skills should be accompanied at first by teacher monitoring to ensure accuracy (Drabman, Spitalnik, & O'Leary, 1973).

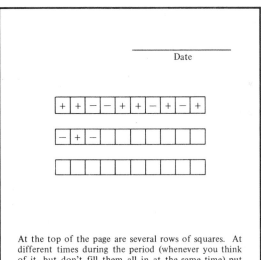

**Figure 6-3
Sample of a self-
recording sheet.
(*Source:* Broden, M.,
Half, R. V., & Mitts,
B. The Effects of
Self-Recording on
the Classroom
Behavior of Two
Eighth-Grade
Students. *Journal of
Applied Behavior
Analysis,* 1971, 4,
191–199.)**

Date

At the top of the page are several rows of squares. At different times during the period (whenever you think of it, but don't fill them all in at the same time) put down a "+" if you were studying, a "−" if you weren't. If for example, you were ready to mark a square you would ask yourself if, for the last few minutes you had been studying and then you would put down a "+" if you had been or a "−" if you hadn't been studying.

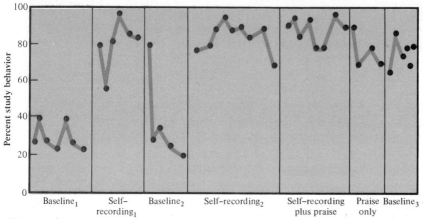

Figure 6-4
Study behavior during baseline and self-recording with and without teacher praise for study. Baseline sections show study behavior with no intervention added. (*Source:* Broden, M., Hall, R. V., & Mitts, B. The Effects of Self-Recording on the Classroom Behavior of Two Eighth-Grade Students. *Journal of Applied Behavior Analysis,* 1971, *4,* 191–199.)

• *Adjust difficulty level of activities to ensure positive self-evaluation and expectancies for success.* You may be satiated by now, since we keep insisting on an appropriate level of difficulty as a prerequisite for effective motivation and learning. The mechanics of matching difficulty on all tasks to student entering skills is one of the greatest challenges in teaching (Glaser, 1977). Your success at this task will determine many outcomes in student motivation and learning.

• *Provide multiple opportunities for students to engage in activities that have high personal value and interest.* You can accomplish this objective in two general ways. First, you will want to assess student interest and previous experiences and orient your assignments toward individual student choice. In order to achieve this goal, your teaching assignments should allow flexibility and student input. Second, you will want to salt and pepper your teaching strategies with imaginative curriculum materials that spark interest and involvement. We shall discuss the use of classroom games as an environmental motivator for this purpose in the next section.

• *Develop student-teacher contracts in order to teach realistic goal-setting skills.* Frequently, students are uninformed about how much work they can complete within a specified amount of time. A CONTINGENCY CONTRACT specifies what each of two persons will do to achieve a mutually desirable outcome. Contingency contracts can be used to teach students to set realistic goals and then work hard to meet them. A student-managed contract states: ''When I have completed X, I can then let myself do Y.'' As a manager of learning, your teaching job will be to help students (1) evaluate their skills in relation to the task at hand and (2) set reachable goals. If Kathy correctly completes ten math problems, she can start doing her homework, go to the library, or help Ted with his math. Chapter 11 will discuss how to develop a fair self-management contract.

• *Maximize opportunities for students to provide self-reinforcement for effort and persistence.* Even elementary-age children can be taught to monitor and reinforce their behavior. You can help students to increase their self-reinforcement skills. You can encourage self-evaluation and self-congratulation by asking the right questions. When Kathy completes her ten math problems, ask her how she did on her math. You can set the stage for Kathy to tell herself that she met her goals. Then, at a later time, Kathy can tell herself again how well she did (Pressley, 1979).

ENVIRONMENTAL MOTIVATION

Most of Kathy's and Bryan's behavior in school is determined by what they expect will happen. We have seen that many situational cues and events can serve as signals to let them know what to expect. On the basis of her expectancy for interest, challenge, peer acceptance, teacher approval, or perhaps free time at recess, Kathy usually applies herself to her math studies and works hard at learning each new method.

Let us make this point clear. Each of the environmental motivators to be considered here has an impact only in terms of how it interacts with the student's personally determined cognitive motivation. The interesting stimuli you provide, your enthusiastic voice, corrective feedback, or the incentives you add for effort and accomplishment may affect each student differently.

How can you teach thirty students when each of them is operating under an individualized motivational system? Fortunately, we know through research and experience that many situations and consequences are effective with most students in most settings. This means that most students are concerned with mastering new skills, getting good grades, obtaining teacher or peer approval, and discovering interesting new things about the world. For any individual student, however, a good grade may mean an A or a C; teacher approval may mean "Uh-huh" or "Hey, that's really great"; peer status may be gained through leadership or disruption; and interesting topics may be Shakespeare or tropical fish. Finally, many students are not touched by any of the traditional motivational devices used by most school systems and most teachers. You will soon discover who these are in your classes: Donna sits and stares out the window; Jim clowns during math class; and Edward often fails to show up at all.

Remember at all times that our three-part definition of motivation lies in the observed behavior of the student: initiation, effort, and persistence. Only Kathy can decide when and how to direct her attention to the task at hand. Only she can decide how hard to work on a given project. Your job will be to provide the conditions under which each student can most effectively mobilize his or her behavior toward reaching self-determined goals. This means that your most effective motivational approach will be to obtain your students' cooperation with positive incentives rather than pushing them from behind with a stick. Regardless of how you choose to operate in your class, the students ultimately make the choice: to be cooperative and work hard or to alienate themselves from learning and involvement. Your teaching and group management procedures will help determine whether students choose to stand still, to balk and pull back, or to go forward with enthusiasm and commitment.

ANTECEDENTS: POSITIVE EXPECTANCIES FOR LEARNING

You can play an important part in determining the positive expectancies that students develop about the activities and procedures in your classroom and in your school. Some of these positive expectancies can set the stage for motivating learning. You will want to use these positive expectancies as conditions that are likely to motivate Kathy to attend, to listen carefully, and to apply herself with sustained interest.

You will have some control over three major sources of stimulation that can help increase positive motivation in math for students like Kathy: (1) task management in the form of task difficulty and novelty; (2) models, standards, and goals for accomplishment in math; and (3) instructions for action which increase positive expectancies for achievement. As we discuss each of these ideas, refer to Table 6-2 for examples for how Kathy's positive motivation interacts with her math activities.

Task management: Setting the stage for attention

Task management includes all the curricular stimulus arrangements that contribute to student attention and sustained involvement. In task management, you will want to focus on both task difficulty and novelty factors that contribute to student motivation.

Task difficulty   The difficulty of the problems facing Kathy in math may determine whether or not she begins to work and how long she continues to struggle along. We saw in a previous section that the level of task difficulty will interact with the skills and learning history of the student. For students like Kathy, who have well-developed entering skills and a history of success in math, self-directed learning will probably occur. Moderately difficult tasks will be most likely to challenge her interest and result in satisfying performance. For Ted and Jim, who constantly struggle with math, lower levels of difficulty may be necessary.

Table 6-2. Situational factors in Kathy's positive motivation for math

Source of motivation	Kathy's covert behavior, or what she tells herself	Kathy's overt behavior in math class
I. *Antecedents: Situational expectancies*		
1. Task management: Difficulty, stimulus change, novelty	"This is interesting: I want to do it some more."	Attention to task: spends more time with task.
2. Models, standards, and goals: Models— displaying motivated behavior	"I want to be like Bryan; he is so good at math."	Uses attention and work behaviors she observes in Bryan.
Standards and goals set by others	"Bryan is doing square roots now; I should be able to do square roots too. My teacher says I am ready to calculate square roots now."	Reads the text section on square roots.
3. Instructions for action	"My teacher says that doing square roots is useful and he keeps telling me I'll really like it when I get into it."	Tries some of the practice problems in her workbook.
II. *Consequences: Situational incentives*		
1. Mastery information: Corrective feedback	"Good. I got more problems correct today than I did yesterday and I know where my mistakes were. I can do even better next time."	Works hard to correct errors, revises strategies.
Progress charts		Shows progress on math skills chart.
2. Positive outcomes: Rewards or privileges contingent on correct or complete work:		
Social approval and attention	"My teacher says I am doing well for a beginner at square roots. I want to show Bryan I can be good at math."	Completes homework problems on square roots. Smiles with pleasure when Bryan says "not bad."
Current incentives: Tokens, reinforcers, and privileges	"Oh boy, I get 10 minutes free time at the end of the hour if I finish my math paper."	Works hard and quickly and completes her math problems.
Delayed incentives: Grades, honors, promotion, graduation	"I really want an A in this course and I hope I get an A on this test."	Works as hard as she believes she needs to in order to get an A on test or course. Is likely to be distracted in particular situations.

They may need help to decide whether they want to master these skills. Why take long division at all if you won't ever use it? Remember too, that long, tedious tasks may be seen as more difficult by some students. Very difficult tasks will lower the level of motivated behavior. For all students, you will want to adjust the individual difficulty level of tasks so that moderate effort can take place. In this way, you will increase the chance that students like Ted, as well as those like Kathy, can attribute success to their own skills.

Task novelty   During work and study periods, novel or unexpected events will be useful to arouse student interest and attention. A variety of curriculum, activity, and schedule arrangements can be used to produce occasional novelty, variability, and unexpected outcomes. Repeated tasks and activities that Bryan has mastered—or that occur every day in the same format and without much variation—tend to make him increasingly bored and disinterested with math. Under prolonged periods of low or inadequate stimulation, people tend to become uncomfortable, restless, and irritable. Under such unstimulating conditions, students will provide stimulation for themselves (Zubek, 1969). If Bryan has to endure the same dull math drills every day, he may begin to kick his chair, poke at Kathy, doodle on his workbook, or ask to go to the bathroom. However,

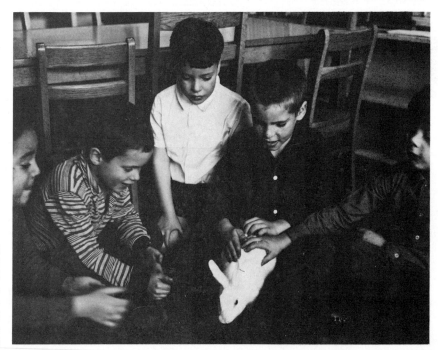

"During work and study periods, novel or unexpected events will be useful to arouse student interest and attention." (Suzanne Szasz)

when unexpected, unusual, or incongruous events occur, students ask more questions, persist longer at a task, and may work hard to master the problem (Berlyne, 1965; Day & Berlyne, 1971).

Why, indeed, do we become bored with excessive sameness while we are excited by novelty and challenge? Many theorists have grappled with this problem and a number of differing explanations have been offered: a need for competence (White, 1959); physiological arousal and homeostasis (Day & Berlyne, 1971); or reduction in uncertainty (Gibson, 1969). We believe that no single or simple explanation is sufficient to cover all stimuli, situations, and students. However, the observed motivational effects of moderate novelty and uncertainty challenge you to use this resource creatively in your teaching activities.

Educational games   Consider the use of educational games to stimulate interest and involvement. For educational purposes, a game is a simulated real-life situation. Players set goals, make decisions, compete, negotiate, and use strategy. It is all safe and no one gets hurt. In well-constructed games, no one loses and everyone wins, although some may win more than others. The magnetic appeal of games is that they allow the student to learn within a context of fun and make-believe. Well-constructed games can transform dull math drill into dramatic activity or simplify complex economic questions by translating them into concrete and manageable formats.

Games for learning are intrinsically motivating; they contain novelty and uncertainty, they require active participation, and they provide players with a sense of efficacy and personal control. Games can be played repeatedly with differing strategies and unexpected outcomes. Ted is the loser today, but he may be the winner tomorrow. Games are also educational when they require the use of relevant information, problem solving, decision making, interpersonal cooperation, judgment and planning, and when they transfer to real-life situations. You can develop your own games for particular purposes. You can also use any of the games currently on the market. Commercially developed games now appear in many topics, including math, social studies, international affairs and government, economics, group behavior, reading readiness, and civil rights, to name a few (Gordon, 1970). Figure 6-5 describes a life-style game designed to help students make decisions about the advantages and disadvantages of further education.

Models, standards, goals: Looking ahead toward achievement

In planning ways to stimulate your students' interest in achievement, you might consider using such potent sources of motivation as models, standards, and goals.

**Figure 6-5
AIM: A life-style
game which you can
construct to
demonstrate
alternative
educational and
employment
decisions. At each
turn, players must
choose to move up
the scale of more
education or across
into the present job
market. (Source:
Gordon, A. K.,
Games for Growth.
Palo Alto, Calif.: SRA,
1970.)**

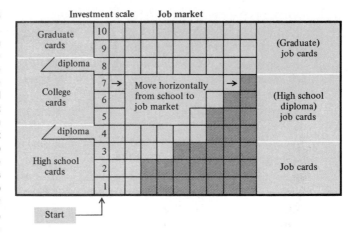

Models Parents, peers, teachers, and community figures can be used as models to influence your students' levels of entering motivation. You can bring community models into your classroom by means of examples, actual visits by guests, or trips into the community to observe people at work. By openly praising their behavior, you can use peer models who demonstrate effective attention and work habits. Watch out that this technique does not backfire on you; avoid selecting a specific student all the time. For minority students or those of low economic status, successful models from their own ethnic or community group often serve to raise expectancies for future achievement.

Teacher goals as standards Teachers frequently set standards and goals in the form of learning objectives. As we have seen in earlier chapters, clear objectives provide achievement standards toward which students can strive. Instructional goals help Kathy to focus her learning activities and to experience a sense of accomplishment when she meets these goals. Many teachers are understandably concerned about possible conflicts between teacher-centered and student-centered goals. Can you continue to hold Ted's interest when your instructional goals are very different from what Ted wants to learn? It seems clear that there is continual compromise and adjustment between teacher and student goals. When students are given the opportunity to follow only their personally set goals, enthusiasm runs high at the outset but soon disappears (Bernstein, 1968; Rafferty, 1970). Clear structure and positive directions can motivate students to strive toward teacher-set goals. Careful programming to integrate these goals with student interests and skills will increase your score in positive motivation. Teacher-set goals which ignore and exclude student goals are likely to elicit low motivation in the form of listlessness, little effort, and absenteeism. In Chapter 9, you will learn more about how to develop student-teacher goals.

Group norms as standards A potent source of motivation in every classroom can be found in peer-group norms and goals. Remember that peer groups have considerable control over goal-setting standards, norms for work output and cooperation, and acceptance and approval for adjusting to group goals (Bany & Johnson, 1975). The nature of the classroom groups will determine whether their influence on individual motivation is positive or negative. Groups that are competitive, hostile, and in conflict will inhibit rather than motivate productive achievement. On the other hand, groups that are *cohesive* and supportive can motivate individual students to adjust to their norms and to work hard toward goals set by the group (Bany & Johnson, 1975). You will find it extremely useful to develop effective working groups in your classroom within which each student can feel acceptance, support, and direction. Characteristics of cohesive groups will be covered in Chapter 11.

Instructions for action: Promoting positive expectancies

You have now carefully arranged the learning environment. You have provided interesting and challenging tasks, appropriate models, and reasonable standards and goals. What else can you do to promote positive expectancies so that Kathy and Jim will try to read a new text or begin to solve a tough problem? For many students, your motivating skills have been successful and they attack a new subject with enthusiasm and vigor. Others like Ted and Edward, however, just sit looking down at their hands. You know that you will have to go one step further with these boys. For many students with low initial interest, additional motivators

"Positive motivation is frequently no farther away than an exciting new activity, a revised learning objective, or an encouraging word." (J. Karales/ Peter Arnold)

may be helpful to get them started on course. These may be students with a history of past failures and a low expectancy for future success. If you believe that math is an interesting subject, tell them so with enthusiasm. If you think Ted can master square roots by working these examples, tell him so! While students may not believe everything you say, your positive support of their ability to master a skill can encourage them to try. Positive expectancies for involvement and achievement can be encouraged for many students who are, as yet, unable to encourage themselves.

The three sources of environmental motivation discussed above will suggest endless management and facilitation strategies for you. Positive motivation is frequently no farther away than an exciting new activity, a revised learning objective, or an encouraging word. Now let's look at the additional advantages of using two situationally motivating consequences: mastery information and positive outcomes.

CONSEQUENCES: INCENTIVES FOR EFFORT

You certainly know by now that all your students will be affected by the results of their actions. We have seen that self-delivered consequences are the most desirable because they are effective in maintaining effort over time. However, we know that most students do not come to school with highly developed self-competency in all areas. Isn't it fortunate that you have so many opportunities within the natural learning environment to provide INCENTIVES for effort and persistence? Incentives are like reinforcers; they are used to increase desirable behaviors. We call them incentives here because the student is usually informed in advance that particular outcomes will be available, depending upon performance. The rationale for using incentives is simple. Social learning theory assumes that whether or not your students choose to engage themselves in the learning process and to perform what they have learned is strongly influenced by the anticipated outcomes of such action (Bandura, 1976a).

Incentives provide information and positive outcomes

Motivational incentives can be used for two major purposes: (1) to provide mastery information about competence and skill development and (2) to produce positive outcomes for task effort and involvement. Table 6-2 shows how each of these incentive conditions will interact with Kathy's self-competency and her observable task behavior in your math class.

Are extra incentives necessary for all students? This critical issue is frequently raised about the use of external incentives in classrooms. Let us consider this important question. In general, you will find yourself spending more time, planning, and effort in developing incentives for students like Ted in math class than for others like Kathy. Ted's math skills are low in comparison to those of his classmates and he is convinced that he can't do square roots. He tells you that he dislikes math and that it will be of no use to him in life. Incentives for students like Ted will be directed at two levels. First, incentives can provide mastery information so that students know when they are meeting their goals. Ted can reward himself with competency feelings for good work. Second, incentives will help to develop and maintain Ted's attention, on-task effort, and goal orientation. For students like Kathy, incentives can be milder and less frequent. Kathy is already interested and motivated toward math as a goal activity. She primarily likes to know when she is on the right track. Of course, she will also enjoy receiving your approval for a well-done homework paper because she still wishes to please you.

For both Ted and Kathy, then, some kinds of incentives are useful on some occasions. For students with low achievement and low interest in a specified topic, incentives should be stronger and more frequent. Students who are happily engaged in some involving activity may require only periodic encouragement to maintain their high productivity. No student should be expected to perform continuously with little hope for a constructive comment or recognition for good performance.

Feedback provides mastery information

You can use performance FEEDBACK for three major benefits: (1) to provide information about correct or incorrect responses, (2) to offer remediation for improving the quality of performance, and (3) to add motivational incentives for future good performance.

Feedback includes a variety of procedures designed to tell your students whether their responses were right or wrong. You can vary your feedback in length, positiveness, and complexity. Feedback can be either a simple "yes" or "no," reinforcing or critical comments ("That's very good" or "This is not the right formula"), or even complex remedial information. At the remedial end, your feedback may resemble instruction by reviewing steps or procedures for mastery (Kulhavy, 1977). Feedback following Ted's correct solution of math problems reinforces his responses and tells him that his learning strategies have been successful in meeting his goals. When you give feedback about incorrect responses, you are not only telling Ted that his answers are wrong but also that you want him to put another one in its place. You will be far more successful in helping Ted to correct his errors if you give him information or guidance to select the correct response rather than just telling him his answer is wrong (Travers et al., 1964). Following this type of CORRECTIVE FEED-BACK, Ted can rehearse the correct answer and be better prepared next time. This helpful feedback can be informative about both correct and incorrect responses. You can see in Figure 6-6 that feedback adds to our picture of positive motivation. Having achieved mastery, the feedback to positive motivation encourages the student to further effort.

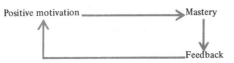

**Figure 6-6
Feedback adds to
positive motivation.**

Positive motivation ──────────▶ Mastery

Feedback

How much feedback is enough? For any one student, you may have to judge how much information is necessary to motivate him or her to revise study or problem-solving strategies. It may look impressive to have a range of comments available to you for student feedback. Surprisingly, extended comments are not always more effective than a simple "right" or "wrong" with a correction for errors (Kulhavy, 1977). From a motivational view, however, additional comments ("Keep it up; I like the way you approached this; take another look at Chapter 5") may tell your students that you are interested in their work and willing to support their efforts. For Ted, who is low in both skill and interest in math, these comments may be encouraging. In all your feedback procedures, be sure to observe the effects of what you do on subsequent responding. Did your sarcastic comments about Ted's spelling discourage him for the rest of the week? Or did your hints for sentence structure show up in Kathy's revised English paper? For all students, the following guidelines for using feedback should be tried first. Individual adjustments can follow.

• *Make certain that student entry skills match the task.* Feedback on very difficult problems is confusing. Rather than helping students, this kind of feedback discourages them from active rehearsal of the correct answers (Kulhavy & Parsons, 1972). Feedback is useful only if the student can use it profitably to revise and correct errors.

• *Provide feedback frequently.* Some moderate delay in feedback allows students to forget incorrect responses (Sassenrath, 1975). Excessive delay, however, decreases motivation and feedback loses its effectiveness. This means handing back tests quickly, grading papers conscientiously as they are handed in, and making use of programmed materials when possible. It also suggests making use of student-controlled feedback by means of correction templates and self-grading keys.

• *Let the student control feedback when possible.* Objective tests and fill-in workbooks can be self-graded for immediate reinforcement or correction. Here, you want to be careful to have students marking their responses before the answers are available. Otherwise, the "lazy" or low-motivated student will take the easy path and look ahead. When students are given the opportunity to peek ahead at correct answers, many of them do so (Anderson, Kulhavy, & Andre, 1972) and thereby learn little.

GUIDELINES
FOR
TEACHING

**Providing
Constructive
Feedback**

● *Make your comments specific and suggest corrections.* Students cannot correct mistakes unless they are informed concretely of their errors and, in most cases, are directed toward correct responses. One of your friends might have given feedback on Ted's English paper as follows: "This paragraph confuses me and is illogical." However, you might read the same paragraph and say, "This paragraph confuses me; rewrite and include (1) an introductory sentence, (2) a central section which clearly explains your thesis, and (3) a closing sentence which summarizes your main idea. I really like your interesting ideas here."

You can see that your friend's comments would make Ted's rewrite job fairly difficult; Ted may become frustrated, angry, and unwilling to try revising the paragraph. Would this mean he is lazy? You know better. Your constructive feedback offers information, remediation, and motivation to try again.

● *Avoid sarcasm and personal criticism.* Your purpose here is to motivate students toward positive effort and task involvement. Without constructive alternatives, negative or critical remarks will only lower interest and increase the student's avoidance of further effort.

● *Have students revise their incorrect responses.* Motivation to mastery increases each time you provide opportunities for students to exert effort and persistence, which you can reinforce with praise or a revised grade. A set of incorrect problems staring Ted in the face will very likely discourage him from trying again. When your feedback comments are specific and positive, however, students can hand in the corrected task with a sense of achievement.

● *Have students chart their progress toward individual learning goals.* Progress toward each student's learning goals can be displayed on goal cards, learning ladders, or checklists. Samples of methods to provide visual evidence of progress are shown in the Learning Activity for this chapter. Progress charts should be individually prepared and filled out as each student completes a skill. Goal charts which are publicly displayed in class will increase competition. The advantages and disadvantages of competition as a motivator will be discussed below.

● *Provide verbal feedback to increase self-motivation.* Your verbal feedback about student performance can emphasize either external or self-motivating outcomes. When you tell Ted that his good solutions to the math problems ought to gain him a high grade on a quiz, you are emphasizing an external outcome. Rather, think about telling him how proud he must be to have completed these problems on his own. You can be instrumental in helping Ted to look to himself for sources of good feelings by pointing out situations in which he can practice self-reinforcement. The Learning Activity will give you some practice in providing feedback to encourage self-motivation.

All students require periodic encouragement and direct reinforcement for effort. Not all subjects are immediately fascinating. Not all answers are correct. Many necessary drill sessions can be tiresome and boring. Frequently, it's more fun for Bryan to talk to Mary than to work on math problems. Distractions to persistent work are always present in classrooms and efforts can lag in spite of effective teacher management of interesting learning materials and dynamic teaching strategies. Your use of a variety of positive reinforcers to stimulate interest and effort do not reflect your failure as a teacher. On the contrary, your wise management of current and delayed reinforcers (See Table 6-2) can make the difference between student apathy and student enthusiasm.

Any of the reinforcers for learning discussed in Chapter 5 are appropriate for increasing the effortful and persistent behaviors that we have defined as motivational. In using these reinforcers, you will want to consider both the guidelines for applying reinforcers and the cautions we suggest for applying these guidelines. We have stressed previously that external reinforcers can easily be misused and abused. However, do not allow this possibility to blind you to the rich sources of school motivation: teacher and peer approval; access to free-time privileges or interesting activities; and grades, awards, and honors. None of these positive outcomes is a substitute for self-motivation and the pride and pleasure that come with competent achievement. Keep in mind, however, that some external supports are necessary for all students some of the time and for some students most of the time.

The skill and art of teaching includes making careful discriminations about when to reinforce and deciding on what types of reinforcers to use for each student. The most critical skills involve learning when to phase out heavy use of these reinforcers once students are working competently on their own. The following guidelines will help you to apply the principles of reinforcement to incentive management in natural classroom settings. The cautions for using incentives that follow our guidelines tell you that a good thing can frequently go wrong.

STUDY 6-2: TEACHER ATTENTION PAYS OFF

Tom, a 13-year-old boy, seldom attended to his math lessons. His arithmetic was usually full of errors and incomplete. Tom's teacher decided to present him each day with a set of twenty arithmetic problems, giving him twenty minutes in which to complete them. During the *baseline* phase, she corrected all problems at the end of twenty minutes and put the number correct at the top of the paper. In the *experimental* phase, a fixed ratio reinforcement schedule was begun (refer to Chapter 5 for refresher on reinforcement schedules). At first, for every two problems completed, Tom's teacher praised with remarks such as "Good work," "Excellent job," "Great, you got fourteen right today," or "Since you did so well today, it won't be necessary to check your work so often." The number of problems

Tom was required to complete before his teacher praised him was gradually increasing, so that Tom was finally finishing sixteen problems without special attention (over a total of eight days). Then, to check on the effectiveness of continued teacher attention, a *reversal* procedure was introduced for three days, during which Tom was asked to complete his twenty problems with no further teacher attention. Finally, the fixed ratio praise treatment was again provided. Figure 6-7 shows the changes in Tom's rate of arithmetic completion during these baseline, experimental, and reversal phases of the study. You can see that the treatment had a stable and increasing effect on Tom's arithmetic progress. Interestingly, Tom's rate of attending behavior also increased. The second part of Figure 6-7 shows you that his observed attending changed from a baseline rate of 51 percent to an average of 97 percent during treatment phases. What a rich reward for so little teacher effort!

Adapted from: Kirby, F. D., & Shields, F. Modification of arithmetic response rate and attending behavior in a seventh-grade student. *Journal of Applied Behavior Analysis,* 1972, *5*, 79–84.

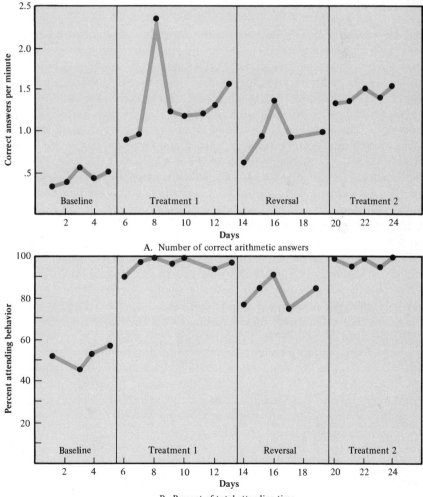

A. Number of correct arithmetic answers

B. Percent of total attending time

Figure 6-7
Correct arithmetic and attending behavior with and without teacher praise.

• *Start with incentives that are natural to the classroom and school environment.* Whenever possible, you will want your consequences for effort to match the probable outcomes in other classes and in other situations. This means liberal use of teacher and peer approval, access to educational activities, free time, library time, and recess. When you program natural reinforcing consequences, you maximize the possibility that Ted's increased attendance in your class will carry over to his other classes as well. If special privileges and rewards are available only in your class and nowhere else, the good effects you obtain in math may not show up in Ted's English or physical education classes (McLaughlin, 1976). Study 6-2 is an example of increased arithmetic output and classroom attending in a seventh-grade student when teacher praise was present or missing.

• *Start with incentives that are immediate.* For students who appear disinterested in the task at hand, far-off goals such as year-end grades and honors will have little current effectiveness. You should always try low-strength natural consequences first, such as attention, smiles, and approving comments. If your social reinforcement value is sufficient, these immediate responses can gradually be stretched to an intermittent schedule. Your comments of "Good thinking" and "You really worked hard on that one" can be given at less frequent intervals and with longer delays from the actual completion of the work.

• *Consider the use of token systems.* Praise and privileges are sometimes ineffective in reaching the more "unmotivated" students like Joe. You might consider using TOKEN REINFORCERS to facilitate task mastery. In a token system, you can give Joe frequent points, checkmarks, or tokens for desired performance. Later, Joe can trade in these tokens for important rewards and privileges, called *backup reinforcers*. Token programs are helpful in temporarily motivating students who do not respond to natural classroom contingencies. Well-managed token systems have been extremely effective in bringing about rapid and dramatic changes in both academic and social behaviors (Kazdin, 1977; Kazdin & Bootzin, 1972; O'Leary & Drabman, 1972).

Once Joe is working under his own steam, the backup reinforcers for the tokens can be reduced from tangible rewards to stars, points, or privileges. Finally, you will fade out the tokens altogether as natural reinforcers take over to maintain Joe's newly established behaviors. An exception to this fading rule exists for students with more severe behavior or learning disorders, who frequently operate best within a structured token system (O'Leary & O'Leary, 1977). However, the use of tokens as a systematic procedure is not natural to the average school classroom and should be reserved for situations in which naturally programmed incentives such as praise and privileges have not been effective. Chapter 11 will give you some tips on how to develop and manage a token system in your classroom.

• *Make some incentives available to all students.* A common problem with classroom incentive systems is that they are typically competitive. You can adjust the classroom REWARD STRUCTURE so that all students have access to some important reinforcers. Classroom reward structures define the conditions or standards students must satisfy in order to receive important reinforcers, such as grades (Michaels, 1977; Slavin, 1977). Reward structures based on grades or access to privileges are of two standard types: COMPETITIVE and CONTINGENT. Competitive grades, given either to individuals or to groups, reinforce some students and deprive others. Not everyone wins the spelling bee and not everyone receives an A. However, individual competition is the single best motivator for about one-third of the students who are high achievers (Michaels, 1977). In contrast, group competition in which groups or teams work together increases group cooperation and positive attitudes toward both task and group members (Johnson & Johnson, 1974).

How do you reinforce students like Ted and Joe who always lose the games or fail to achieve high grades? Contingent rewards based on mastery to criterion will be a possible solution here. You can develop grading, progress charts, or point systems based on either individual or group contingencies. Incentives for Ted on an individual contingency system might consist of points that he earns on a progress chart for math

"Group competition in which groups or teams work together increases group cooperation and positive attitudes toward both task and group members." (F. Bodin/Stock Boston)

skills. Ted competes against himself and gains pride in accomplishment and progress over his previous performance. Points can be traded in like tokens for privileges such as free time.

Alternatively, you can develop GROUP CONTINGENCIES in which the performance of individuals, small groups, or of the entire class earns grades, points, or privileges for the classroom. Both individual and group contingency incentive systems are extremely effective in motivating prosocial as well as academic behaviors (Hamblin, Hathaway, & Wodarski, 1971; Hayes, 1976; Johnson & Johnson, 1974; O'Leary & Drabman, 1971). Chapter 11 will provide some ideas on how to set up a group contingency system in your classroom. Study 6-3 gives an example of a group contingency system in which the entire class was awarded points and backup reinforcers for the academic progress of selected students.

STUDY 6-3: GROUP INCENTIVES CAN IMPROVE ACADEMIC PERFORMANCE

Group contingencies are used to reinforce all members of a group for the social or academic behaviors of only some members. Sometimes this is done by averaging the total group performance and making reinforcement contingent on some specified criterion, such as 50 percent on a test. At other times, the whole group may receive a privilege when one particularly troublesome student improves to a preset goal. In these cases, students tend to encourage and help one another and to tutor the peers with deficits, so that all may benefit from the outcome.

Researchers in an inner-city school in St. Louis compared several different systems of group and individual contingencies for accelerating performance in the spelling, math, and reading of fourth-grade students. Group I was reinforced on the basis of high performance in the group; the top three scores in the group determined the number of points all group members would receive. Group II received points on the basis of low performance; the bottom three scores on the weekly test had to reach a minimum level before all group mem-

bers could receive points. A third group received points on the basis of the average performance of the entire group. Finally, two comparison groups were included, in which students received points for either individual scores or for attendance in class. All groups could trade their points at a later time for tangible rewards. Figure 6-8 shows the outcomes for the five contingency conditions on gain scores in classroom tests. The overall improvement was highest for either low or high group contingency conditions and lowest when students received points just for coming to class. When the system was compared for the three most gifted and three slowest students, look what happened! Parts *B* and *C* of Figure 6-8 show that the gifted students performed best under the high contingency condition, while the three slowest students were shining lights under the low performance condition. These results suggest that while a group contingency appears to be more effective than individually awarded points, it affects student performance in differing ways. In a follow-up study, it was found that the major effect of the low performance condition was to stimulate increased peer tutoring of the slower students.

Adapted from: Hamblin, R. I., Hathaway, C., & Wodarski, J. Group contingencies, peer tutoring and accelerating academic achievement. In E. W. Ramp & B. L. Hopkins (Eds.), *A new direction for education: behavior analysis, 1971.* Lawrence: University of Kansas, Department of Human Development, 1971, pp. 41–53.

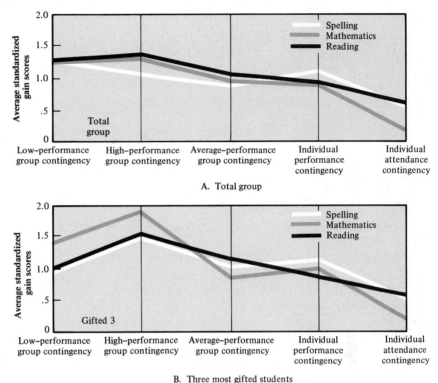

A. Total group

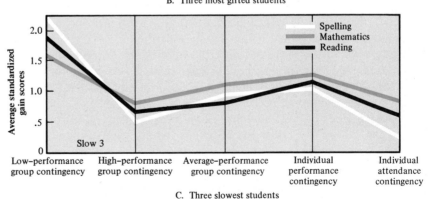

B. Three most gifted students

C. Three slowest students

Figure 6-8 Average gain scores in spelling, mathematics, and reading for five types of group and individual contingencies. (A) Results for the total group. (B) Results for the three most gifted students in the group. (C) Results for the three slowest students in the group.

* *Combine teacher contingencies with increasing opportunities for self-management.* Concentrate your efforts at motivating students toward greater productivity and social responsibility. Once you have organized some effective incentives into your teaching strategies, arrange to move toward student control of the outcomes. Consider especially that freedom and self-determination can be used as incentive outcomes for encouraging productive academic behaviors (Premack, 1965).

You can construct a variety of student-teacher contracts that will give students increasing degrees of freedom (or free time) in exchange for voluntary assumption of task responsibility. Read Study 6-4 for an interesting approach toward programming responsible freedom into math instruction. Given the opportunity for full freedom to choose academic tasks, these students accomplished little work and displayed disruptive and rude behaviors. Once their freedom was made contingent on increasing amounts of competence in math, students applied themselves with enthusiasm. Many students completed the equivalent of three years of math work in one term. Further, their subjective evaluation of the school increased; they reported liking school better, doing more homework, and learning more math. Most importantly, they chose to work hard for free time rather than have no requirements placed on their efforts (Salzburg, 1972).

* *Be creative in developing special incentives for special students.* Most students will work for free time, teacher praise, or access to privileges such as hall monitor or ditto-machine operator. However, you will frequently come across one or more students like Ted or Jim who find none of these events reinforcing. When nothing you try with the entire class seems to get such students going, move off in new directions. Develop some creative solutions. Sometimes events that other youngsters dislike can be used as incentives for a resistant and difficult student: going to see the counselor, spending ten minutes chatting with the principal, or having access to special help from you after school. Keep in mind that every student will work for something.

* *Fade artificial incentives to natural ones when self-motivation takes over.* Heavy doses of praise, points, and privileges are useful in gettting productive behavior started. Only the uninformed or desperate teacher resorts to these extreme procedures for maintaining desirable behaviors over long periods of time in regular classrooms. When Ted learns to read easily, he will be less interested in tokens than in an exciting adventure story. No one gives Ted points for watching TV! However, we caution you, please, to remember that all students (and all people) require some positive feedback from their social environment. When Ted no longer receives points for numbers of pages read, he will still be pleased to know that you are happy with his new reading skills. While it is unwise to continue excessive external rewards, it is also unrealistic to assume

that students will continue to perform for no social approval and no rewards at all. You certainly don't want your students to operate in a meaningless vacuum where the reactions of others are no longer important. So when you phase out the tokens, keep smiling!

STUDY 6-4: FREEDOM AND RESPONSIBILITY IN AN ELEMENTARY SCHOOL

Freedom cannot exist long in a school unless it is accompanied by responsible behavior. This study attempted to develop and maintain responsible behavior in two groups of elementary school students. When students were allowed to do as little or as much as they wished, they did less than one half of a page each day. When the freedom to leave class was made contingent on finishing one page of math their rate of work (problems/minute) almost doubled. A procedure in which children recorded their own progress in math on special charts generated much interest but little change in their rates of math progress. A third procedure in which students were required to pass a quiz each week in order to leave class early almost doubled the rate of work. Students in the older group were subsequently permitted

to elect a condition in which they did not have to attend class at all if they passed two quizzes per week. Sixty percent of the older students elected to try this procedure. Their rate of work once again doubled. Those students were progressing at four times the normative rate of their public school-age peers. With the onset of the last two conditions students began to take initiative for their own academic progress. They began to come to class early to get a fast start. Students also began to voluntarily take some work home. They were beginning to demonstrate behavior that the teachers would call *responsible*.

Source: Salzburg, C. I. Freedom and responsibility in an elementary school. In G. Semb (Ed.), *Behavior analysis and education*. Lawrence: University of Kansas, Department of Human Development. 1972, p. 62.

Cautions in using motivational incentives

As a teacher in control of thirty lives for a good portion of the day, you hold a great deal of power. Your inappropriate use of rewards and privileges may create injustice, hostility, boredom, and apathy. How can a good thing turn so sour? Watch for three major pitfalls:

• *Don't make important reinforcers contingent on meaningless activity.* Will you expect and demand that students perform repetitious and dull activities in return for valued events such as recess? Does Bryan have to complete forty additional problems before he can go to physical education? Do you use important reinforcers for your own purposes rather than for student benefit? If the answer to any of these questions is "yes," you are

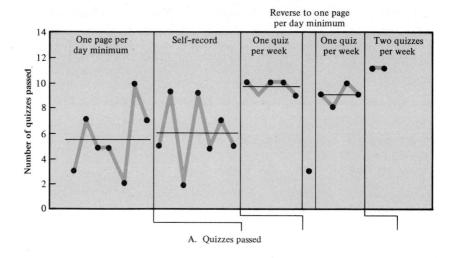

A. Quizzes passed

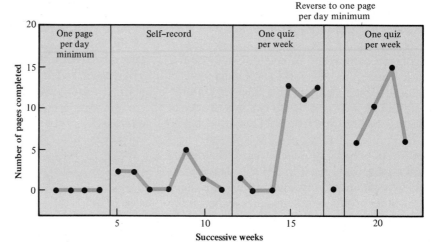

Figure 6-9
Number of quizzes passed (a) and amount of homework completed voluntarily (b) when leaving school early was an incentive for passing quizzes.

B. Total number of pages of homework completed (N = 10)

exploiting and manipulating students. Be sensitive to this issue. The result may be resistance and uncooperative behavior. Let's clear up a confusing point about manipulating students. We believe that teachers who use positive contingencies are usually contributing to productive motivation. The use of promised rewards or inducements to good behavior becomes manipulative only when the use of these valued outcomes is for *your* benefit: to keep students quiet, docile and obedient, or involved with meaningless busywork (Bandura, 1977; Winett & Winkler, 1972). Please don't confuse motivation with manipulation; they are by no means the same.

• *Don't make important reinforcers impossible for some students to attain.* If you require the correct completion of forty problems from all students before they go out to recess, some of them may frequently miss their recess. When Ted and Donna don't have the skills to achieve your preset goals, no amount of incentive will get them to meet these goals. Instead of inducing positive motivation, you will produce discouragement and a low level of effort. Rather, you will want to set achievement criteria that are based upon a joint decision between you and the student. Here, the three R's for teachers might run like this: be reasonable, responsible, and relevant. Be all three R's and your students will respect you.

• *Don't add unnecessary reward to activities that are intrinsically interesting.* When students are busily engaged in an interesting activity, your additional rewards may communicate the wrong message. Rather than telling them they are doing a good job, unnecessary rewards may induce feelings of being pressured, dominated, or controlled. Under some conditions, children lose interest when excessive rewards are dispensed for activities which initially held their attention (Lepper, Green, & Nisbitt, 1973; Lepper & Green, 1975; Notz, 1975). Remember that extra motivational incentives are useful only to stimulate and maintain behaviors that might otherwise not occur. Once students are actively involved in projects that are challenging and enjoyable, additional incentives are not required and may produce some undesirable side effects.

===== PROBE 6-4 =====

Suppose you are assigned to be the new teacher for a low-achieving, disruptive fourth-grade class. You decide to establish a token system whereby students earn points for both academic work and appropriate classroom behaviors. Your principal challenges your approach and wants to know why you are bribing your students to learn. Develop a rationale for your approach, listing at least three reasons why you believe that some extra incentives may be necessary. Then, suggest three possible problems you might expect to encounter in your system.

ANXIETY REACTIONS IN SCHOOL

Good management of motivation pays off. You now have Ted working hard on his math project, and his mother reports he is finally completing his homework. But you are still concerned about Millicent and Joe. Millicent becomes speechless every time you call on her for an answer in class. You know that she can give the correct reply, but she just reddens and looks down at her hands, twisting her fingers together. The last time there was a class test, she told you her stomach hurt and she didn't think

"Fear and apprehension about schoolwork are not uncommon throughout the school years." (M. Reinhart/Photo Researchers)

she could go on. You encouraged her to complete the test, confident that she knew the material. She handed in a blank answer sheet. Millicent is probably experiencing ANXIETY about her school work, and you wonder whether her *fear of failure* is interfering with her performance.

Fear and apprehension about schoolwork are not uncommon through-out the school years (Hill, 1978; Sarason et al., 1960). Many students are particularly anxious about being evaluated and may doubt their ability to succeed. Since some students with a high IQ are also found to be anxious (Sarason et al., 1964), factors other than ability may be involved. Frequently it is not real failure but the anticipation of failure that starts them off (Phillips, Martin, & Meyers, 1972). How can you cope with fears and anxiety about schoolwork in your students? Do you want to remove all sources of tension and anxiety from your classroom?

ANXIETY AND SCHOOL BEHAVIOR

Think of anxiety as a learned fear of an aversive or unpleasant situation. While fear and anxiety are sometimes differentiated, we will use these two terms interchangeably.

Effects of anxiety in school

How do Millicent's anxieties about school affect her behaviors? Three aspects of student anxiety reactions may be of concern to you as a teacher: (1) excessive worrying, (2) physical distress, and (3) poor performance. First, Millicent is aware of her anxious feelings and consciously worries about tests, schoolwork, class discussions, and how she compares with other students. Second, Millicent frequently experiences signs of physical distress; when called on in class, her heart beats faster and her throat feels tight. Before a test, her stomach hurts and sometimes she feels nauseated. Third, Millicent performs poorly in situations where she feels she is being evaluated. Her problem-solving skills seem to disappear under stress and she can't recall material she has studied (Maher, 1966).

Anxiety in school: Harmful or helpful?

We can measure Millicent's anxiety about her schoolwork in an objective way with the Children's Test Anxiety Scale (CTAS) (Sarason et al., 1960). Some of the items on the CTAS are displayed in Table 6-3, divided according to the four factors measured by this test (Feld & Lewis, 1969). These four factors tell you that some students worry specifically about test situations, while others worry about teacher and peer evaluations in class. Still others are plagued by physical signs of discomfort. Millicent scores relatively high on all four factors of the CTAS, while Joe scores relatively low. You might want to take the test yourself. Do any of the items apply to you?

Anxiety can be harmful   How do these anxiety-provoking conditions affect Joe and Millicent in school? In many classroom situations, Millicent will perform less well than Joe. She is especially likely to perform poorly when (1) she feels she is being evaluated, as on an examination, (2) the material to be learned is complex or difficult, (3) she is being timed and under pressure, and (4) she is in a situation that lacks structure and has no clear set of rules (Gifford & Marston, 1966; Grimes & Allinsmith, 1961; Sarason et al., 1960; Spielberger, 1966).

These four anxiety-provoking conditions will provide some suggestions for helping students like Millicent to relax their apprehensiveness and to be more efficient in stressful situations. If Millicent is not helped with her fears of inadequacy and failure, her anxieties about schoolwork will increase throughout her school years. She is likely to experience increasing difficulty with her work and her fear of tests and evaluation will intensify (Gaudry & Spielberger, 1971; Gibby & Gibby, 1967; Sarason et al., 1964). In its more severe form, anxiety about school can result in *school phobia*, where the student remains home and refuses to come to school. Students

Table 6-3. Four Factors from the Children's Test Anxiety Scale

Test anxiety	Remote school concern	Poor self-evaluation	Somatic signs of anxiety
25* When the teacher says that she is going to give the class a test, do you become afraid that you will do poor work?	8* When you are in bed at night, do you sometimes worry about how you are going to do in class the next day?	10* When the teacher is teaching you about reading, do you feel that other children in the class understand her better than you?	24* When you are taking a test, does the hand you write with shake a little?
20* Do you worry a lot before you take a test?	32* Do you sometimes dream at night about school?	7* When the teacher is teaching you about arithmetic, do you feel that other children in the class understand her better than you?	9* When the teacher asks you to write on the blackboard in front of the class, does the hand you write with sometimes shake a little?
19* Are you afraid of tests in school?	31* When you are at home, do you think about your schoolwork?		
29* While you are taking a test, do you usually think you are doing poor work?	18* Do you sometimes dream at night that the teacher is angry because you do not know your work?	14* Do you sometimes dream at night that other boys and girls in your class can do things you cannot do?	16* When the teacher says that she is going to find out how much you have learned, do you get a funny feeling in your stomach?
23 Do you sometimes dream at night that you did poor work on a test you had in school that day?	23 Do you sometimes dream at night that you did poor work on a test you had in school that day?	4* When the teacher says that she is going to call upon some boys and girls to answer arithmetic problems out loud, do you hope that she will call on someone else and not on you?	28 When the teacher says that she is going to give the class a test, do you get a nervous or funny feeling?
28 When the teacher says that she is going to give the class a test, do you get a nervous or funny feeling?	22* After you have taken a test do you worry about how well you did on the test?	15 When you are home and you are thinking about your reading group for the next day, do you worry that you will do poor work?	6* When the teacher says that she is going to find out much you have learned, does your heart begin to beat faster?

Table 6-3. Four Factors from the Children's Test Anxiety Scale (continued)

Test anxiety	Remote school concern	Poor self-evaluation	Somatic signs of anxiety
21 Do you worry a lot while you are taking a test?	30 While you are on your way to school, do you sometimes worry that the teacher may give the class a test?	12 When you are at home and you are thinking about your arithmetic work for the next day, do you become afraid that you will get the answers wrong when the teacher calls on you?	17* If you did very poorly when the teacher called on you, would you probably feel like crying even though you would try not to cry?
15 When you are home and you are thinking about your reading group for the next day, do you worry that you will do poor work?			
12 When you are at home and you are thinking about your arithmetic work for the next day, do you become afraid that you will get the answers wrong when the teacher calls on you?			21 Do you worry a lot while you are taking a test?
30 While you are on your way to school, do you sometimes worry that the teacher may give the class a test?			
M = 2.253 SD = 2.427 Range = 0–10	M = 3.241 SD = 1.715 Range = 0–7	M = 1.717 SD = 1.515 Range = 0–6	M = 2.633 SD = 1.933 Range = 0–7

Note: For the Sarason TASC (30 items), Mean (M) = 10.173, Standard Deviation (SD) = 5.889, Range = 0–30.
* Item appears on only one index.

who become phobic about school may become physically ill or cry and scream if required to remain in class. Students with debilitating fears about school are estimated to number as many as one in every hundred (Leton, 1962). You will want to obtain professional or counseling advice to help such students overcome their fears and to be quickly integrated back into the classroom.

Anxiety can be helpful On the other hand, anxiety can facilitate behavior in three ways. First, Millicent may do especially well when there is one single answer to a problem and she has studied it well. High anxiety seems to facilitate responses to simple, as compared to complex, problems (Spence, 1958). This fact will give you some clues about how best to help students like Millicent in math and reading. Second, some concern and tension would be helpful in motivating a student like Joe to work hard and to apply himself when there are no external demands on his behavior. At times, some anxiety and concern about his schoolwork may be motivating to Joe, who sometimes acts as though he couldn't care less. You will notice that Joe's low effort is reflected in incomplete assignments, school absence, and careless errors. Frequently, a student's unwillingness to express any anxiety or concern about how he or she is doing in school may reflect a defensive attitude—a desire to avoid facing and admitting one's own failures. Finally, recent work on experimental stress tells us that exposure to mild amounts of pressure and stress during the formative years increases our abilities to "cope with" or handle later stress situations. Students who are sheltered from all pressures may never learn to work under pressure when it becomes necessary to put forth increased effort and concentration.

In summary, we can conclude that the relationship between anxiety and school behavior is complex. High anxiety about schoolwork usually, but not always, interferes with effective functioning during the elementary and secondary school years. Very low anxiety about school progress takes the pressure off the student but may result in little effort toward reaching mastery goals. In either case, the nature of the task and the situation in which the student must perform complicate the simple anxiety-performance relationship.

SCHOOL CONTRIBUTIONS TO ANXIETY

Do the academic realities of school attendance and requirements for accomplishment affect student anxiety? Clearly, many students experience real failure, lower grades than their standards demand, and negative reactions from peers or teachers. For some students, school is so unpleasant that they withdraw entirely. Indeed, the majority of school dropouts are of average intelligence but two years retarded in reading and arithmetic by the seventh grade! Moreover, the typical dropout has failed one or more years in school (Cervantes, 1965). In these cases of continuing failure, the student becomes completely discouraged and just gives up. Interestingly enough, however, the phobic or hyperanxious child is usually an average student who is not failing at all (Coolidge, Brodie, & Feeney, 1964). Regardless of the "real" causes of school-based anxiety, you can alert yourself to the existence of student fears and you can be helpful in dealing with excess anxiety reactions. Here, all three teacher roles will be appropriate to prevent student failure, to mediate the school environment for students in academic trouble, and to facilitate the efforts of students who wish to swim with the tide.

Suggestions for helping students to cope with anxiety in school include general guidelines for creating a pleasant and nonthreatening classroom environment as well as more specific interventions for reducing intense anxiety reactions. As a warm, facilitative classroom manager, you will probably try to prevent student anxiety by applying the following guidelines:

GUIDELINES FOR TEACHING

Dealing with Anxiety

- *Avoid the use of critical and sarcastic remarks.* While students are positively motivated by corrective feedback and knowledge of errors, personal criticism is demoralizing and a source of anxiety. Keep your comments specific to the work at hand rather than directing your negative remarks to the student as a person.
- *Provide structure for students who appear uncertain and anxious.* Your structure can include rules, instructions, and guidelines for action. Ambiguity and uncertainty increase anxiety in students who are afraid of doing the wrong thing. Programmed learning materials are especially good for the anxious student because learning programs give clear directions; require single, small-step responses; and provide immediate feedback.
- *Reduce the pressure of strong competition among individual students.* Since these students are afraid of failure, personal mastery goals and small, progressive steps will ensure goal attainment. Be sure to give lots of support and reinforcement for progress toward mastery of goals. Public performances that heighten individual differences tend to increase threat, so approach these situations carefully. If you want Millicent to respond in class, select subject matter that she has studied or that you know is familiar to her.
- *Remove pressure from your test and evaluation procedures.* There are a number of ways to build evaluation procedures into your teaching strategies without excessive pressures on students. Avoid strictly timed tests, where speed is the most important factor. Keep high-tension remarks during tests to a minimum ("Anyone caught cheating on this exam will automatically fail"). Provide frequent evaluation by testing small amounts of progress rather than large chunks of work where a great deal of memorization is required. Do not make large portions of the class grade dependent upon one major test. Give students an opportunity to drop the grade from one or two tests along the way. Give students the choice of making up lost points on tests by means of a retest which earns either full or part credit. See that tests are helpful rather than punitive and critical by giving positive corrective feedback. All these suggestions are intended to preserve the teaching and learning value of classroom evaluation while reducing the stressful aspects.
- *Encourage overlearning of skills and information.* Since high anxiety frequently facilitates simple, well-rehearsed responses, take advantage of

this fact. Help Millicent to practice, drill, study, and rehearse her work so that she can repeat correct answers while under low stress. Then, these answers are more likely to be available to her in tension-arousing situations.

=== PROBE 6-5 ===

Think back to your reaction to examinations or to speaking up in class. Do you feel tense or uncomfortable in these situations? Have you ever felt acutely frightened so that you could not think or speak effectively? What might your instructor have done that would have been helpful? List three teacher strategies that might have been helpful to you in these situations.

LEARNING ACTIVITY: PROVIDING USEFUL FEEDBACK

Feedback will be one of your most useful tools in encouraging positive motivation. Let's review the concept of feedback. Giving feedback to Bryan means providing information about his present or past behaviors which he can use to monitor future behavior. This information may tell Bryan that he is on the right track or it may signal a required change in his responses next time around. In addition, effective feedback can contribute to Bryan's self-motivation. Earlier, we discussed the functions of feedback and suggested some rules for increasing its effective impact. Now, we want you to practice feedback responses in the context of probable student responses.

OBJECTIVES

1. Provide graphic feedback. Given a set of response data, develop a graph (line, bar, cumulative) which displays the frequency of an observable student activity. Label the graph correctly and indicate the goal.

2. Select examples of effective and ineffective verbal feedback. Given a set of teacher responses to student answers, select verbal feedback responses which will benefit student motivation and those which will lower student motivation to respond.

3. Revise verbal feedback responses to increase positive motivation. Given a set of ineffective teacher feedback responses, revise them to increase positive motivation.

4. Select examples of verbal feedback to strengthen self-motivation. Given examples of teacher feedback responses, select those which are likely to strengthen the student's self-motivation.

5. Provide verbal feedback responses that are likely to increase self-motivation. Given a set of student responses, write short feedback responses that will increase self-motivation. Be ready to explain how each of your responses contributes to self-motivation.

PROVIDING GRAPHIC FEEDBACK

Three kinds of graphs will be useful in giving students visual feedback and in monitoring their progress: line graphs, bar graphs, and cumulative graphs. You should be able to construct each type of graph quickly to help students like Ted and Millicent chart their progress.

Line graphs

The simplest graphs to construct are called line graphs. You mark a point for the student's progress each day or following each study unit. Then, you draw lines to connect one graph point to the next. For Ted's completed homework assignments, the results would look something like this:

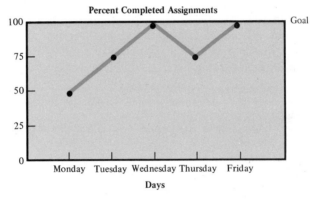

Bar graphs

Younger students find bar graphs somewhat easier to read because they present a dramatic appearance. A bar graph fills in a designated space below the point of progress. A felt-tipped pen is a handy way to fill in bars on a graph. Ted's correctly completed math problems each day might look like this:

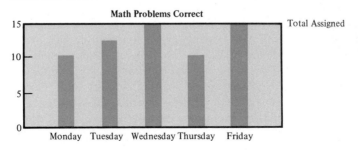

Cumulative graphs

The most difficult for students to decipher, a cumulative graph includes all previous performances with each new entry. However, the display on a cumulative graph can be highly motivating to the student who sees total accomplishment increasing daily. A cumulative graph on the new words Bryan has learned in French class is shown below:

Number of Words Learned in French

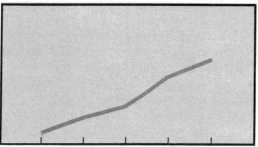

Monday   Tuesday Wednesday Thursday   Friday

TASK 6-1

Construct a graph to display the number of pages Millicent has completed in her workbook. The data are shown below. Try all three types of graphs on the data provided. Which one would be most effective in keeping Millicent working hard to complete workbook pages?

Number of pages completed in workbook

Goal: To complete the 15-page unit by the end of the week.

Monday	2
Tuesday	1
Wednesday	3
Thursday	3
Friday	5

What can this graph tell Millicent about how to schedule her time and effort for next week's unit? Do you think the graph had any effect on Millicent's motivation to complete the workbook?

Selecting and revising examples of effective and ineffective feedback

Student responses in class tend to be either (1) question-asking, (2) question-answering, or (3) contributing information to a discussion. Your feedback to student responses can exert considerable influence on whether students continue these behaviors, try harder next time, or just give up in discouragement. The tone of your voice can communicate interest and involvement or apathy and disgust with the answers you receive. The specific content of your responses can tell students that they are trying hard and you appreciate their contributions or that they are dumb indeed and had better think before they speak next time. Your responses can encourage students to attribute their correct answers to good thinking, hard work, or just a lucky break. Developing the skill and art of effective feedback is indeed a challenge.

TASK 6-2

For each of the following student responses, decide whether the teacher's feedback was helpful (+) or not helpful (−) for encouraging positive motivation. Where you judged that the teacher's response was not helpful (−), rewrite the teacher's response to make the feedback positively motivating according to our discussion in Chapter 6. For the responses that you judge to be helpful motivationally (+), be prepared to explain your reasons in class. Remember that your feedback can be positively motivating regardless of whether the student's answers are correct or incorrect.

Student	Teacher	Your evaluation (+ or −)
1. Ted: "I don't understand why the spacemen jump so high when they walk on the moon."	"You should know that, Ted; it was right there in your textbook."	Revise? _____ _____ _____ _____
2. Joy: "Columbus was born in 1451 in Italy."	"That's right, Joy; I can tell you have been keeping up with the class reading."	Revise? _____ _____ _____ _____
3. Ann: "I didn't bring my book today. Can I look on with Millicent?"	"Well, I suppose, but you two always get into trouble. Now, I don't want you fooling around today."	Revise? _____ _____ _____ _____

Student	Teacher	Your evaluation (+ or −)
4. Jay: "Twelve times four is forty-eight."	"Stan, how much is twelve times five?"	Revise? _____ _____ _____ _____
5. Tom: "I think that there's less gravity on the moon because it's a smaller mass, or something like that."	"Good thinking, Tom. Now let's see if we can state a general rule from that."	Revise? _____ _____ _____ _____
6. (Donna looks down at her feet when asked a question.)	"Donna, I'll ask you again, what is Costa Rica's major export? Well, Donna, you certainly don't have this unit under your belt, do you? Did you do your homework?"	Revise? _____ _____ _____ _____ _____ _____
7. (Joe smiles but says nothing.)	"Let's look at that in another way, Joe. Did they always build their homes with thatched roofs? Joe, was there an-	Revise? _____ _____ _____ _____ _____

Student	Teacher	Your evaluation (+ or −)
	other type of hut used there sometimes?"	
Joe: "Could they use palm leaves?"	"That's a good guess, Joe; they probably did. Class, does anyone want to add another idea?"	_____ _____ _____ _____ _____
8. Sue: "I think they layered their roof materials to give insulation against he heat."	"That's a good point, Sue. How can we find out if they layered their roofing?"	Revise? _____ _____ _____ _____ _____
9. Ted: "Seven times five is thirty-two."	"Ted, you're wrong again. Sally: seven times five?	Revise? _____ _____ _____
10. Sid: "The cause of the French Revolution was economic unrest and political tyranny."	Sid, you're talking so much back there, I surely thought you knew everything. That's a pat answer—or a safe guess. What do you think, Dan?"	_____ _____ Revise? _____ _____ _____ _____

	Student	Teacher	Your evaluation (+ or −)
11.	Bill: "Sixteen . . . no, it's eighteen."	"Well, which one is it? We can't wait all day. And don't count on your fingers, Bill. Come on!"	Revise? _____ _____ _____ _____
12.	Alice: "Some insects commit suicide—look at the bees who die after they sting you!"	"You're doing some creative thinking, Alice; keep it up. What other insects sacrifice themselves for the good of the group?"	Revise? _____ _____ _____ _____ _____ _____

Selecting and revising examples of verbal feedback to strengthen self-motivation

Now that you have been able to select and revise feedback statements that provide positive motivation for learning, you are ready to go one step further. You will want to develop skills in providing feedback that is either externally motivating or self-motivating. Feedback that provides situational incentives suggests to students that others are pleased or displeased with their progress or that desired awards will be obtained for good achievement. Feedback statements that encourage self-motivation suggest to students that they have been working hard, that they must be pleased with themselves, or that the work in which they are involved is very interesting.

TASK 6-3

For each of the following student responses, decide whether the teacher's feedback is likely to encourage self-motivation or reliance on external sources of motivation. If the feedback response was self-motivating, your answer to "Revise?" will be "no." If the teacher's response is externally motivating, revise the teacher response to encourage self-motivation. Be prepared to explain your changes in class.

Student response	Teacher feedback	Your evaluation
1. Ted: "Seven times five is thirty-five."	"Nice work, Ted; you've been working hard on that one, haven't you?"	Revise? _____ _____ _____ _____
2. Tom: "I think there's less gravity on the moon because it has a smaller mass."	"Good, Tom; I bet you'll do well on the test Thursday."	Revise? _____ _____ _____ _____
3. Ted: "I don't understand why the spacemen jump so high on the moon."	"That's really an interesting problem, Ted. Find me the section in the text where it is discussed and let's see if we can figure it out."	Revise? _____ _____ _____ _____ _____ _____
4. Jay: "Twelve times five is sixty!"	"Terrific, Jay. You should be proud of yourself for not making a single error today."	Revise? _____ _____ _____ _____
5. Alice: "And the lemmings all swim into the sea."	"I really don't see how that relates to what we're discussing. Pay more attention, Alice!"	Revise? _____ _____ _____

Student response	Teacher feedback	Your evaluation
6. Sue: "I just don't under- stand how to do this prob- lem—it doesn't make any sense."	"Well, if you don't get it pretty soon you're going to miss some recess time."	Revise? _____ _____ _____ _____
7. Mike: "I'm fin- ished!"	"Nice work, Mike. You certainly showed yourself you can do it if you try hard."	Revise? _____ _____ _____ _____
8. Joe: "I'm fin- ished!"	"Wow—I bet you'll get a good grade in this class, Joe."	Revise? _____ _____ _____

SUMMARY

1. You can observe that students who are positively motivated on any activity will (a) show interest, pay attention, become involved (initiation); (b) work hard and spend time at the activity (effort); and (c) continue working until the task is completed (persistence). The sources of MOTIVATION may be internal and self produced, or external and situationally produced. You will have many opportunities to contribute to positive student motivation in both your teaching strategies and classroom management procedures.

2. SELF-MOTIVATION can be viewed as either a result of needs and drives within the individual or as cognitively mediated interaction with particular situations. Theories of motivation which emphasize internal needs propose specific needs which motivate individuals across all situations. Of particular interest is White's concept of COMPETENCE MOTIVATION, which proposes an innate desire for mastery over the environment. According to White, motivation for learning is INTRINSIC to activities which lead to feelings of compe- tence and mastery. Teachers can provide favorable conditions for

competency motivation by arranging for moderate novelty and incongruence.

3. Cognitive factors in motivation include six self-competency skills. These skills are related to the particular activity in which the student is engaged and include self-evaluation of skills for the task, value of the task to the students, expectancies for success on the task, standards for task achievement, locus of control for the task, and self-reinforcement for mastery or meeting of goals. Some students are highly motivated on most activities, while others seem to show little enthusiasm or effort at anything. Most students are selective and become more involved with certain preferred subjects or topics. *Underachievers* and *overachievers* may be those students who set standards for themselves that are either too low or too high for their capabilities. Teachers can be helpful in providing conditions under which useful self-motivation is most likely to flourish.

4. Sources of ENVIRONMENTAL MOTIVATION are essential for all students some of the time and for some students all of the time. You can approach motivating strategies from either antecedent or consequent factors. The way that you set the scene and arrange the conditions of learning will help establish positive expectancies for learning activities. Antecedent conditions include task management, goals for accomplishment, and instructions. Of particular interest here is the use of educational games to stimulate interest and involvement. Games have intrinsic interest for many students and they teach many useful skills in planning, negotiating, and problem solution. While any of your plans may backfire for individual students, the behavior of the student is your cue to success. When any of your plans result in apathy, low achievement, or hostility, then you know it's time for a change.

5. INCENTIVES can motivate in two ways. They provide information to the student about competence and progress and they provide positive outcomes for achievement. FEEDBACK informs the student about success, failure, and level of competence. CORRECTIVE FEED-BACK can encourage increased effort, revision of errors, or rethinking of the problem. We suggest that your feedback should be frequent, constructive, and specific. Allow students to participate in the feedback procedure by means of self-monitoring, self-grading, and individual goal charts. You can contribute to self-motivation by giving feedback that attributes students' success to their own skill and effort.

6. Positive outcomes other than feedback will be in the form of peer and teacher approval, rewards, and privileges contingent on correct or complete work; TOKEN REINFORCERS (points); and delayed

incentives such as grades and honors. We suggest that you follow careful rules for using outcome incentives to avoid some of the problems that can result from an excess of external rewards. We prefer incentives that are natural to the school environment, contingently available to every child, tailored to individual students, and combined with opportunities for self-management. When you do strenghten the reinforcers by using immediate rewards, tokens, and points, these should be gradually stretched to interval schedules and faded to natural classroom events.

7.   REWARD STRUCTURES determine the availability of reinforcement outcomes. COMPETITIVE REWARD STRUCTURES reinforce a few and deprive many. CONTINGENT REWARD STRUCTURES are based on student mastery and make reinforcers available to all students. Watch out for pitfalls in incentive motivation; avoid reinforcing repetitive or meaningless activity and don't add rewards to activities that have intrinsic interest. Once more, the behavior of the student will tell you when and how much to use external outcome incentives. Let this behavior be your guide.

8.   ANXIETY and *fear of failure* are deterrents to positive motivation. Both real and anticipated failure can interfere with efficient learning. When anxiety rises too high, it produces worrying, physical distress, and low performance. Anxiety and fear of failure tend to increase if they are not dealt with early; they may lead to massive failure, *school phobia*, and eventual dropout. For students who are showing signs of persistent anxiety, we suggest that you avoid excess criticism, provide added structure, reduce competition, remove pressure from evaluation situations, and encourage overlearning.

9.   In providing useful feedback to students, you can use graphic or verbal methods. Graphic feedback includes line graphs, bar graphs, and cumulative graphs. Verbal feedbacks should always promote positive student motivation. Verbal feedback can be designed to increase either external motivation or self-motivation in students.

KEY
TERMS

ANXIETY: A learned fear of an aversive or unpleasant situation.

COMPETENCE MOTIVATION: A trait approach to motivated behavior in which satisfaction is achieved by arousal and maintenance of activity that leads to mastery over the environment. Once competence is achieved, the student performs the activity on the basis of INTRINSIC MOTIVATION.

CONTINGENCY CONTRACT: An explicit agreement between two or more persons that specifies what each will do to achieve a mutually desirable outcome. Contracts may be written or verbal.

ENVIRONMENTAL MOTIVATION: Motivated behavior in which the antecedents and consequences are provided by the situation, the task, or the objective consequences of the behaviors.

FEEDBACK: Procedures to inform students about success, failure, or level of competence. In CORRECTIVE FEEDBACK, additional information provides guidance in selecting another response.

GROUP CONTINGENCY: A classroom incentive system in which the performance of individuals, small groups, or of the entire class earns grades, points, or privileges for the classroom.

INCENTIVES: Reinforcers that are made available contingent upon appropriate student performance. Reinforcers become incentives when students are informed about them in advance of performance.

INTRINSIC MOTIVATION: Motivated behavior in which students are observed to work hard with no apparent external rewards.

MOTIVATION: A broad term describing three aspects of activity: initiation, effort, and persistence.

REWARD STRUCTURE: The conditions or standards students must satisfy in order to receive important reinforcers. Reward structures can be competitive or contingent. COMPETITIVE reward structures reinforce some students and deprive others. CONTINGENT reward structures reinforce all students who meet their goals.

SELF-MOTIVATION: Motivated behavior in which the student provides the antecedents and consequences. Self-motivation is cognitively mediated and internal to the student.

TOKEN REINFORCERS: Points, check marks, or tokens that are given contingently for desirable classroom behavior. The value of tokens lies in the important rewards and privileges, called backup reinforcers, for which they can be exchanged.

REVIEW TERMS

CONTINGENT
POSITIVE EXPECTANCY
POSITIVE REINFORCEMENT
STANDARDS

SELF-TEST

1. We can define motivation as
   a. initiation of activities
   b. amount of effort
   c. degree of persistence
   d. b and c
   e. all of the above
2. The idea that all persons have the innate desire to explore the environment and to deal with it effectively has been called
   a. secondary reinforcement
   b. drive reduction

   c. competence motivation
   d. self-motivation
   e. attribution
3. Students work harder and longer on a task when they have
   a. a high expectancy for success
   b. a high IQ
   c. a high value for the task
   d. high peer status
   e. a and c
   f. all of the above

4. External incentives are useful when
   a. the task is difficult
   b. the task is dull and repetitive
   c. the student has low entering skills
   d. the student does not expect to do well
   e. all of the above
5. Effective self-reinforcement is most likely to occur when
   a. goals are set just above present achievement
   b. goals are set very high above present achievement
   c. goals are set below present achievement
   d. goals are set just at present achievement
6. Students who use effective achievement behaviors tend to attribute their success to
   a. an easy test
   b. their own skill as well as their effort
   c. just plain good luck
   d. superior IQ
   e. your good teaching techniques
7. Teachers can add interest and attention to classroom activities in three ways, by
   a. _____

b. _____
c. _____
8. Feedback can be used for three purposes:
   a. _____
   b. _____
   c. _____
9. Incentives that are natural to the classroom include
   a. token reinforcers
   b. grades
   c. teacher approval
   d. free time
   e. all of the above
   f. b, c, and d
10. In competitive reward structures,
    a. all students can earn high grades
    b. some students are reinforced and some are deprived
    c. all students are motivated to succeed
    d. all students are penalized by fear of competition
    e. students are rewarded for individual accomplishment

SELF-TEST KEY

1. e
2. c
3. e
4. e
5. a
6. b
7. Adjusting task difficulty, providing novelty, using games.
8. Evaluating information (correct or incorrect), remediation, motivation (self or external).
9. f
10. b

CHAPTER 7
Teaching a Cognitive Skills Hierarchy

CHAPTER OUTLINE

LEARNING OBJECTIVES

After reading Chapter 7, answering the self-monitoring questions, completing the learning activity, and reading any further references of your choice, you will be able to:

1. Define and give examples of key terms.

2. Analyze a short verbal chain, three related multiple discriminations, and two concepts.

3. Apply the basic teaching model to the learning of a principle or a rule.

4. Diagram and explain the parts of a verbal chain.

5. Explain and give examples of rules for verbal chains, rules for discrimination learning, and rules related to forgetting, concept learning, and principle learning.

6. Compare three alternative approaches for managing learning concepts.

7. Diagram a principle in terms of concrete and defined concepts, discriminations, and selected verbal associations.

How can you use principles of learning in your own classroom teaching? How can you apply a cognitive skill hierarchy in your classroom? At any time, you will have students like these who need your help: Barbara wants to learn the alphabet; Edward needs help in remembering state capitals; Laura tries to balance chemistry equations; Elizabeth keeps forgetting the geological ages; and Ned wants you to explain the meaning of kinship terms.

How you perform in the classroom will be related to how well you can analyze a learning situation, choose an appropriate strategy, and effectively carry out the plan. The ABC model presented in Chapter 5 is our fundamental model for the analysis of a learning situation. The results of the ABC analysis can specify in precise, easily understood language the information which you, the student, the principal, or a parent will consider in selecting an appropriate goal and learning strategy.

The choice of learning strategies will be influenced by answers to two questions: (1) What is it that you (and your student) want the student to be able to master? and (2) What does the student have to be able to do to reach mastery? The first question helps you specify the learning objectives (Edward wants to be able to match the fifty state capitals with their respective states). The second question helps you list the prerequisite skills for mastery (pronounce the fifty states, spell and recognize the fifty state capitals, relate the name of the capital to the name of the state,

"What does the student have to be able to do to reach mastery?" (Suzanne Szasz)

check on whether Columbus goes with Georgia or with Ohio, change the response if necessary, and a host of other specific skills). The answers to these two questions provide the starting points for analyzing Edward's or any other student's learning skills.

HIERARCHY OF LEARNING SKILLS

Robert M. Gagné, a well-known educational psychologist, has had an impressive impact upon the planning of learning activities for the classroom. He has created a learning skills hierarchy which orders activities from the most simple to the most complex (see Chapter 4). In Gagné's hierarchy, mastery of a more simple skill is prerequisite to the performance of more complex activities. This idea of organizing skills into a hierarchy will affect the way you approach Elizabeth's forgetting or Ned's need to master kinship terminology. We believe that students can master many complex activities as long as the learning activities have been carefully constructed in advance.

Two words, *simplify instruction*, seem to be the best way to describe Gagné's hierarchy. For years, psychologists studied learning—verbal associations, nonsense syllables, insight, problem solving, discovery, operant conditioning, creativity, retention, proactive inhibition, and many more. These various psychologists seemed to claim that they were making "the" important contribution. Gagné benefited from their sound and fury. He must have used many 3 by 5 cards in ordering theories, activities, procedures, and the like. In the long run, Gagné selected eight skill levels of learning which he ordered into a hierarchy (Gagné, 1965). The impact of the hierarchy was immediate. Educators recognized it as a model for organizing learning.

As Gagné looked more closely at learning in schools, he simplified his hierarchy into six skill levels on each of five learning outcomes (Gagné, 1977). These five learning outcomes are intellectual skills, cognitive strategies, verbal information, motor skills, and attitudes. Throughout this book, we will talk about these learning outcomes. In the new hierarchy, Gagné started with response chains. He reasoned that the new hierarchy applies more to intellectual and academic tasks than to all kinds of elementary social and motor skills. Indeed, students have usually mastered classical and operant learning skills prior to entering school. In the new hierarchy, the six levels are response chains, discriminations, concrete concepts, defined concepts, rules, and problem solving (Table 7-1). As a classroom teacher, you will be asked time and time again to facilitate student mastery of these learning skills. Let's take a look at the first level of the hierarchy, response chains. Later in this chapter, we will discuss discriminations, two kinds of concepts, and how to retain the learned skills.

TEACHING VERBAL ASSOCIATION SKILLS

The simplest element of an idea—a concept, a rule, or a principle—appears to be a two-word verbal chain. It is upon these simple chains that more and more words are linked until phrases, sentences, paragraphs, and ideas are enunciated. (One might say "from small verbal chains do large principles grow"—sorry, acorns!) You will find students who have mastered long, complex verbal chains. Many of your colleagues will call these young men and women "bright" and "intelligent" as long as the verbal chains are flattering and grammatically accurate. Of course, you will find children who have not yet mastered simple verbal associations such as *boy-girl; cat-dog; red-stop;* and *tall-short*. Probably, some of these colleagues will say these children are "dumb," "ignorant," and "inarticulate"! Indeed, many school systems try to avoid labeling children as "bright" or "dull" by using a preschool assessment program. As we said in Chapter 4, intellectual skills such as those involved in verbal learning are tested in this program. Those boys and girls who do not appear "ready" or who have not mastered response chains are usually asked by the school system to remain at home for another year or are provided with special readiness training. We prefer the second strategy.

Table 7-1. A learning skill hierarchy

Robert Gagné has ordered classroom learning into a hierarchy of six skill levels, from simple to complex (Gagné, 1977). The simplest kind of learning serves as a prerequisite for the next higher learning process. Gagné's organization fits closely with the ABC model for learning by helping you prescribe the next learning task. The six levels of the hierarchy are briefly described as follows:

Response chains: These are motor and verbal chains that consist of a sequences of behavioral responses acquired as units. In a chain, the stimulus serves to cue the response (such as *green-go; boy-girl;* and *black-white*). Students generally master these very simple chains before they start school.

Discriminations: Our operating definition of discrimination is a sequence of behaviors in which a student tells whether two or more stimuli are the same or different. Motor or verbal chains are prerequisites to the extended chain of a discrimination. Usually, physical discrimination (such as comparing different colors or hearing different tones) is learned by late first grade. At times, a student will have to learn new discriminations, as among tissues in a physiology class or among sounds in a machine repair class.

Concrete concepts: Students have learned a concrete concept when they can identify an object as having a particular characteristic in common with other objects. Concrete concepts may have attributes (round, flat) or position (above, below, left, right) properties which can be checked with a pencil, grasped, or pointed at by the student. Discrimination, the prerequisite skill, requires a student to identify or to discriminate a particular object from others. Concrete concepts may vary in property or position (for example, GM and BMW cars), but they belong to the same concept—*car.*

Defined concepts: Students learn a defined concept when they can demonstrate the meaning of an object. Because they involve verbal definitions, defined concepts depend upon verbal associations or links and upon discriminations. The prerequisite levels of learning must be mastered before a person can assign a meaning to an event (*party, emergency*), a relationship (*uncle* as "my father's brother"), or objects. A defined concept requires more skill than simply rattling off a long verbal chain without meaning!

Rules or principles: A rule or principle has been learned when a student can consistently apply a relationship among two or more concepts. For example, a student can learn *evaporate, water,* and *heat* as three separate concepts. The relationship among these three concepts can be stated as "heated water evaporates." Other principles or rules can be found in grammar, math, and sports, and every other field. Rules and principles emphasize the way the student "puts together" concepts.

Problem solving or higher-order rules: Students engage in problem solving when they put together two or more rules with very little help or learning guidance. For example, one of your uniquely gifted students may be able to open your car door with a coat hanger (once you have locked your key inside). Problem solving is the highest level of the hierarchy and requires the student to master many prerequisite skills. As a classroom teacher, you will strive to promote problem solving among your students. Indeed, you might suggest models for problem solving which your students might adopt or adapt. A true instance of problem solving occurs when the student creates a new set of relationships among the rules and principles.

   As you can see, the hierarchy is more complex with each level. However, in this complexity there are a number of very important ideas for you as a manager of learning or as a facilitator of individual development.

Adapted from: Gagné, R. M., *Conditions of learning,* New York: Holt, 1977.

HIERARCHY OF VERBAL ASSOCIATIONS

Let's talk about verbal chains before we discuss how they can be learned at school. The smallest example of a verbal chain is a simple stimulus-mediation-response (S-M-R) unit such as *green-go* or *sit-down*. The basic chain has three parts: (1) stimulus, (2) mediating link, and (3) response or behavior. From Chapter 5, you are familiar with the ideas of stimulus and response. The new term, MEDIATING LINK, is similar in meaning to the kind of mediation that goes on in cognitive social learning (Chapter 4). It is thinking about (picturing an image or repeating to yourself a verbal chain) the relationship between the stimulus and response. Thus, covert behavior, or coding, is a shortcut for picturing the mediating link. Mediation (for example, visualizing a green light) is used to link the stimulus object or word *green* to the response word *go*. Each of these three parts must be learned separately before the student can learn a verbal response chain.

In the broad hierarchy described by Gagné, there are two levels within verbal associations. Figure 7-1 shows the relationship between verbal chains and verbal associations. The difference between each level in Figure 7-1 is the addition of a specific mediating link to help make a verbal association. Let's look at each level in this hierarchy for verbal associations.

At the simplest level of verbal chain, the wiggly line between the stimulus and the response headings is our way of saying that mediation is occurring. In this simple chain, the stimulus and response are joined by a spontaneous mediating link. "Good dog" or other pairs of words seem to occur "naturally" in the home and before children start school. Indeed, even three-word verbal chains are very common in conversation. Students will often say, "You're OK" or "You said it" when they are still preschoolers. Thus, phrases which students typically use in conversation are examples of longer verbal chains.

The apparently simple act of "naming" or labeling an object is the second level of this verbal association hierarchy. In Figure 7-1, you can see a three-part S-M-R sequence which is very similar to the three parts of the basic verbal chain. In the "naming" verbal chain you see a stimulus link, a mediation link, and a response link.

In Figure 7-1 we have presented a special case of the "naming" verbal association, the translation example. As a classroom teacher, you might decide to plan an instructional program for helping students to learn selected Spanish words. In the *casa-house* translation, we see how *casa* can become *house* and vice versa with the use of a mediating link.

ACTIVITIES TO FACILITATE VERBAL ASSOCIATIONS

You can see that simple verbal chains are an important beginning for learning complex thinking skills. In the learning of verbal chains, certain

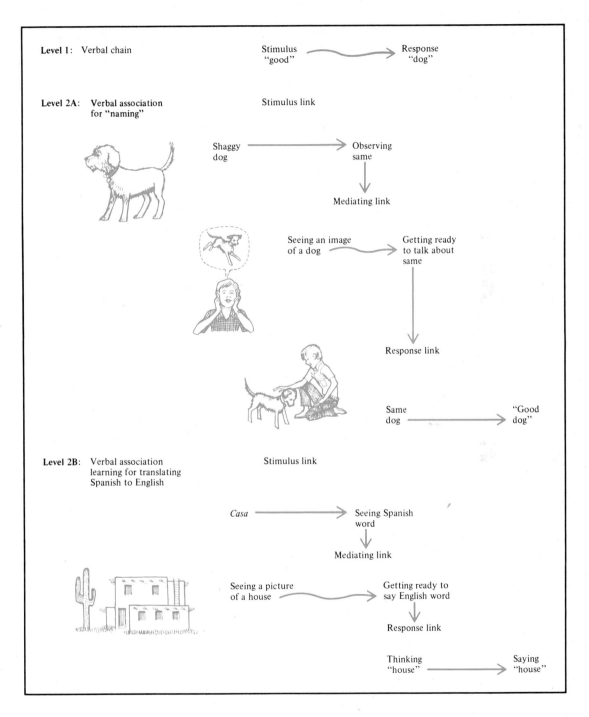

Level 1: Verbal chain

Level 2A: Verbal association for "naming"

Level 2B: Verbal association learning for translating Spanish to English

Figure 7-1
Two levels of verbal response skills.

student and teacher activities must occur to facilitate mastery. Suppose Elizabeth, a ninth-grader, comes to you a week before midterms. Elizabeth, tearfully, simply cannot remember the order of the geological periods for her environmental studies course. It does not matter that you are teaching literature this semester; here is a young person with an educational crisis. A few minutes of sensitive questioning reveals that Elizabeth cannot come up with any way to remember the seven geological periods. Elizabeth's fears turn to mild panic when you calmly ask, "Does Campell's onion soup develop mysterious pains in Peter?" Too polite to ask, Elizabeth probably wonders whether you have gone bonkers! You quickly tell her that the first letters of the words in that question are cues or a MNEMONIC DEVICE for the first letters of the seven geological ages. Indeed, you point out, the words in your question sound like these seven names—Cambrian, Ordovician, Silurian, Devonian, Mississippian, Pennsylvanian, and Permian. Let's discuss the student and teacher activities which must occur in verbal learning and see how learning the Campbell's soup jingle can help Elizabeth learn her terms.

Student activities in verbal associations

The student is an active participant in verbal association learning. In order to learn these important skills, the student must (1) be able to distinguish stimulus and response and (2) have learned the mediating link.

Distinguishing stimulus and response   The student must discriminate the stimulus part of a verbal chain and must pronounce the response. This means that Elizabeth will be able to distinguish both the stimulus and the response from all other possible S_D's in the environment.

Learning the mediating link   The student must previously have learned the mediating link or the third part of the chain. The mediating link for most people is a self-produced code that is either verbal or pictorial (Mahoney, 1974; Trabasso, 1963). Thus, in Elizabeth's learning of the geological periods, she must be able to recognize *Campbell's,* be able to say *Cambrian,* and be able to mediate (picture, verbalize, or code) *Campbell's* and *Cambrian* in order to perform one verbal association.

As a classroom teacher, you will frequently try to find out whether students like Elizabeth can perform each part of the verbal chain. We hope that most of your students will have learned how to perform basic verbal associations at home or in your school's readiness program.

=== **PROBE 7-1** ===

Think of a series of terms that you want to learn. Analyze them as if they were a verbal chain. Specify the stimulus, mediating links, and response.

The cognitive social learning theory approach emphasizes interactions in the classroom. These interactions in verbal learning may be between students and classmates, student and teacher, or teacher and the entire class (Becker, Engelmann, & Thomas, 1975b). You will want to provide for a high level of interaction between student and environment in facilitating mastery of verbal learning. Frequently, students like Elizabeth will ask for help in learning verbal associations. Usually, students will try to use verbal associations to learn stable or factual material such as traffic laws, lines in a play, a second language, or chemistry symbols. As a classroom teacher helping students like Elizabeth, you will find the following guidelines useful in teaching verbal associations:

• *Help the student assign meaning to the verbal chain.* A great source of frustration in learning verbal chains is their apparent lack of meaning. On the one hand, this lack occurs because the children's experiences have not yet caught up with their need to learn the verbal chain. A 2-year-old would probably have difficulty with "Please, may I have the milk?" followed by "Thank you," because his experiential base had not

"Students will try to use verbal associations to learn stable or factual materials such as traffic laws." (Christy Park/ Monkmeyer)

yet been established. However, a 4-year-old would be able to learn those two complex chains fairly rapidly because she had had the necessary experiential base to make the chains meaningful. On the other hand, lack of meaning inhibits the learning of verbal chains such as a second language or chemistry symbols. Familiar experiences from the student's life seem to be a good starting point for relating the student's experiences to new learning materials. As a classroom teacher, you might suggest to the students that they (1) use visual images to help build mediating links, (2) incorporate the new words into a story, or (3) find mnemonic devices to serve as external cues. The Campbell's soup jingle is one attempt to use these three suggestions.

• *Present each verbal unit* (*chain*) *in the proper order.* You will try to present the stimulus before you present the response. Sometimes, however, when you are teaching several separate verbal chains, the student will remember (mediate) a new link between the two responses! You will have to plan whether you want the pattern in Figure 7-2 or not. In this learning skill, Elizabeth probably would want to learn more complex verbal chains than *Campbell's-Cambrian!* In other verbal learning situations, such as naming chemistry symbols, you might try mixing up the stimulus words so that the responses do not develop into long, complex verbal chains.

• *Use external cues to guide the correct performance of each verbal chain* (Melton & Martin, 1972). While Elizabeth uses the Campbell's soup jingle for her external cues, you might use "Every good boy does fine" for the five lines of the treble clef in music. You will probably learn many other mnemonic devices in preparing yourself for teaching in a particular area.

• *Have the student respond overtly to the stimulus event.* While we believe that covert performance is helpful for learning new behaviors in many situations, we recommend that you encourage overt responses in verbal learning. The student is active in this way. The student who hears, sees, and/or feels the motor response, is stimulated by these overt responses. The student's full involvement helps him or her to associate a large number of secondary stimuli (Becker, Engelmann, & Thomas, 1975b). Elizabeth will have to say or to write each verbal chain. In either case—saying or writing—you and Elizabeth will be able to monitor her progress and to get an idea of how she is doing.

			Stimulus	Link	Response
Figure 7-2 **Sometimes responses in verbal chain units become verbal chains themselves.**	Each unit	(1)	Campbell's	→	Cambrian
		(2)	Onion	→	Ordovician
	Becomes one unit	(1 and 2)	Cambrian	→	Ordovician

● *Provide students with immediate feedback on their performance* (Skinner, 1968; Kulhavy, 1977). The fundamental law of operant learning applies to verbal association learning. A behavior, in this case the correct verbal response, will occur more frequently if it is reinforced. The required information or KNOWLEDGE OF THE CORRECT RESPONSE (KCR) may come either from external feedback or from self-produced feedback. This information about correct and/or incorrect responses will serve as a reinforcer for the verbal response. For example, a classmate working with Elizabeth in a dyad can provide reinforcement either by giving the correct response or by providing social reinforcement. For example, "Keep it up; you almost have it!" In the self-produced feedback example, Elizabeth might be given flash cards with which to reinforce herself. As a classroom teacher involved in helping selected students such as Elizabeth develop their verbal chain skills, you will work with your students both as a manager of stimulus materials and as a facilitator of verbal chain learning (Barringer & Gholson, 1979).

● *Instruct the student to review recently learned verbal chains frequently.* Missed verbal chains must be restated correctly. Two things usually happen: either students forget certain verbal associations or they have a more difficult time learning certain associations. When a student has a long list of verbal chains (such as the Preamble to the Constitution), you can be pretty certain that mastery will occur in this pattern (Figure 7-3).

The first third will be learned quickly, the last third will be learned somewhat slowly (about the same number of errors), and the middle third will be filled with frustration, errors, and additional time (Underwood & Schultz, 1960). Probably the beginnings and ends of sequences are rehearsed more frequently (Atkinson & Shiffrin, 1971). As a classroom teacher helping Elizabeth or any other students learn verbal chains, you might suggest that they budget more time for the middle third of the second-language word list or the Preamble. You want to make sure that these reviews occur after small amounts of material have been learned. Later, as the lists of words or the paragraphs are learned and retained, overt and closely monitored reviews can be scheduled less frequently.

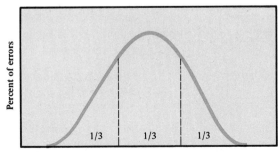

Figure 7-3
Error rates for a
long verbal
passage.

Portion of entire verbal learning series

• *Make certain that the student distributes verbal association learning over time*. One of the themes that we have emphasized frequently is preparing students to be self-managing. In acquiring verbal chains or in using verbal association learning skills, the student has an excellent opportunity to practice three self-management techniques.

First, verbal learning occurs more rapidly (with less errors) when the actual learning sessions are distributed over time. Many students will try to mass their practice the night before the exam or rehearsal. Too many things seem to *interfere* with the learning of verbal chains under the massed-practice condition. As a classroom teacher, you can suggest that students budget their time so they learn a few lines or new words each time they practice.

Second, verbal learning is retained longer (not forgotten) when the student overlearns the materials. OVERLEARNING is repeating the material after mastery has occurred. The mediating links in the longer chains apparently are embellished and reinforced as the students overlearn a Shakespearean soliloquy. As a second-language or chemistry teacher, you might suggest that students frequently reorder the stimulus words or symbols so the responses themselves do not link into a verbal chain.

Third, verbal learning takes place quickly (with fewer tries) when the student adds a new verbal chain (such as another phrase from the Preamble) as he or she continues to practice the previously learned chains. This self-management technique for learning verbal chains is called the progressive- or whole-part method. By using this method, the student can master several small parts of the entire, long verbal chain. In this way, the student can avoid the frustrations of trying to learn too much (more than seven plus or minus two verbal links) at one time (Miller, 1956). Essentially, these self-management techniques can be practiced by a student such as Elizabeth to distribute verbal association learning over time.

PROBE 7-2

Consider two learning assignments. Keep track of how long it takes you to learn the first assignment. Now apply the guidelines for learning verbal chains. How much time did it take you to learn the second assignment? What happened?

Learning verbal associations or response chains is the first skill level of the hierarchy. Mastery of this skill is a prerequisite for learning the next level, multiple discriminations. Later in this chapter, we will discuss how a student can recall verbal chains and discriminations. Recalling these important skills and transferring them to new situations appears to be helpful for learning the two kinds of concepts.

TEACHING DISCRIMINATION LEARNING SKILLS

Once a student can perform a variety of verbal chains—name numerous objects and engage in simple conversation—he or she is ready for the next skill level in the hierarchy. Learning how to make multiple discriminations can be fun for the student and a source of enjoyment for you. Through the expanded use of language, the young student gains control over more of his or her environment. The mediation linkage which is so important in cognitive social learning begins to involve more of the student's environment. At the same time, you will have many opportunities to promote brief periods of self-management. For example, a student who has mastered many verbal associations can process covert reinforcement and can master self-management for specific learning outcomes. In this way you will have more opportunities to be less "smothering" and to use more indirect facilitation.

HIERARCHY OF DISCRIMINATION LEARNING

Learning the discrimination skill requires the student to make appropriate responses to environmental stimuli that differ in one or more ways. If Barbara is to master this skill, she must learn (1) the differences between two or more stimuli and (2) the unique response chains associated with these differences. For example, the letters *P*, *R*, and *B* are very similar and distinctly different. Barbara would have to learn how the three letters are different and how to respond to those differences.

Discrimination is a two-step process in which differences or similarities are recognized and this recognition cues a response chain. The discriminations may involve matching letters or colors in the elementary grade levels, discriminating among different textures in art class, or comparing two minerals in petrology lab. As you can see, no single discrimination is performed, so we call this learned skill the making of *multiple discriminations*. It is a basic learning skill but one which must be relearned or refined in many new learning environments.

ACTIVITIES TO FACILITATE DISCRIMINATION LEARNING

In learning the discrimination skill, responsibility rests upon both the student and you. Suppose Barbara, a slow second-grade student, comes to you during recess. Earlier you had worked with a group on word recognition. Barbara was a part of the group, but she was one of the two "nonparticipants." Now, between sobs, she explains that she does not know her alphabet. However, a few days ago you listened to Barbara sing the entire alphabet with nary a mistake! A few minutes of gentle probing reveal that Barbara cannot recognize the differences among the sets of many similar letters. Barbara's skill deficit is not uncommon among many slower second-grade students. She cannot recognize the differences among such letter sets as *B*, *R*, and *P*; *O* and *Q*; and *d*, *b*, *p*, and *q*. Barbara's skill deficit is similar to that of a person who has a "tin ear" and sings different notes by raising or lowering the volume of his or her voice (the authors know which one of them it is). Both Barbara and the singer have a discrimination skill deficit. Let's look at how you might help Barbara discriminate among selected letters.

Student activities in discrimination learning

The activities for learning the discrimination skill are similar to the activities used in mastering verbal association skills. However, on this level of the learning hierarchy, the student is using previously learned verbal associations as the learning units. In order to learn the discrimination skill, Barbara must be able to learn verbal chains and individual letters.

Learning verbal chains Barbara must learn the stimulus verbal chains and the response verbal chains before she can perform the discrimination. In many discrimination learning situations in the classroom, the student has mastered either the stimulus verbal link or the response verbal chain. Essentially, the student has a three-part process to complete in performing a discrimination. The parts are (1) stimulus, (2) coding or mediating link, and (3) response. Barbara has apparently mastered the verbal response chain for letters of the alphabet. She must now learn both the stimulus and coding or mediating links.

Learning individual letters You will want the student to learn the individual printed letters—basic verbal associations of names—in isolation. The particular uniqueness of *P*'s and *Q*'s, and *R*'s will have to be learned and overlearned. Indeed, Barbara will probably bring to the learning experience a host of previous but incorrect verbal associations. The letter *P*, for example, might have been named *R*, or lowercase letters such as *b*'s and *d*'s might have been misidentified. This means that Barbara will have to practice, probably with flash cards, looking at a *B* stimulus, mediating, and saying "B."

As a classroom teacher engaged in helping a student master one learning skill such as discriminations, you will find that your student must master some prerequisite skills before working on the learning skill assigned at present. Let's take a look at your management responsibilities in discrimination learning.

"The student must learn the individual printed letters—basic verbal associations of names—in isolation." (Larry Smith/Black Star)

In your effort to facilitate discrimination learning, you will provide for a high level of interaction between student and environment. Frequently, students such as Barbara and Laura will ask for help in learning multiple discriminations. Students will try to use multiple discrimination skills for learning "correct" responses to verbal or physical stimuli. The correct discriminations follow some set of rules such as the rules for balancing valences in chemistry. These rules have a correct response. As a classroom teacher helping Barbara or her older cousins who have more complex performance needs, you will find the following guidelines helpful in teaching multiple discriminations:

GUIDELINES
FOR
TEACHING

**Discrimination
Learning**

• *Make certain that the student can discriminate among the stimulus words or objects.* Both the stimulus objects and behavioral responses in multiple discriminations can become merged for the student. For example, many young students will look at crocodiles and alligators and give them the same name, "crocodile." Similarity among the stimuli or among the responses can produce behaviors which appear to be "dumb" or "incorrect." For another example, you might present the twenty-six stimulus letters to Barbara and give her prompts such as those in Table 7-2. Since Barbara can already say each letter in the verbal chain, your task is somewhat less complex than it would be if you were helping a student acquire a second language. Your discrimination learning goal is to teach Barbara twenty-six stimuli, mediation links, and responses so that she will be able to recognize each letter of the alphabet.

Table 7-2. Selected letters and possible prompts

Present letter	Suggested prompt
O	This letter is round, just like a Cheerio. It is called "O."
Q	This letter is round like a Cheerio. See the little tail. The tail makes it a Q.
D	This letter has a straight side. It looks like an O, but the straight side makes it a different letter. See the big bulge. The letter is D.
P	The letter is tall. At the top of the straight line there is a circle. The circle points to the right. The letter is P.
R	This letter is tall and it has a bulge like the P. It has a leg dangling from the bulge. The leg is not straight. The letter is R.
B	The letter is tall. It has a straight side. Two bulges point to the right. The letter is B.

As a classroom teacher responsible for learning management, you will have to check frequently to make sure that each stimulus and each resonse is learned and mastered. Barbara will have to master each stimulus letter, each mediating link, and each response. This requirement means that you will frequently fall back to the prerequisite skills of verbal associations to help students master multiple discriminations.

• *Give the student immediate reinforcement for each correct performance.* This guideline appears crucial in the learning of this skill because the absence of reinforcement contributes to extinction and extinction contributes to FORGETTING. Please remember that correct responses should be promptly reinforced (socially by a peer or by a teacher using a flash card). The apparent solution for you and your students is to practice differential reinforcement in discrimination learning. That is, reinforce the correct performance and do not reinforce the incorrect performance. In this way, your students can overlearn the discriminations and prevent extinction and forgetting.

• *Have the student practice frequently the mastered multiple verbal discrimination.* Barbara, for example, must overlearn the discriminations among P, B, and R. You will be able to watch a young child start to enunciate R when the stimulus letter is P. In this case the previously learned verbal chain for *R* may interfere with the verbal chain for *P*. The amount of repetition that is required for a student to master the discrimination seems to increase with the number of chains to be discriminated.

You will want to have frequent practice sessions to prevent interference and to keep mastery at a high level. How often these sessions occur will be a result of your sensitivity, art, and skill in classroom management.

You will have some choices. On the one hand, in working with young children (like Barbara) who are learning very simple and very basic discriminations, you will have to manage learning carefully. The close supervision will help Barbara follow the guidelines. On the other hand, you will have two options with older students: (1) You may use your Rolodex cards and set up the *anticipation method* for learning second-language words. In this method, three cards are used in a set. The first card says *casa-house;* the second, *casa,* and the third, *casa-house*. The students can see, first, the complete verbal chain. Then they can see the stimulus alone. They can delay the presentation of the complete chain until they try to remember *house*. In a sense, the students are learning how to delay reinforcement until they consider possible response words. (2) You may try to offer the student ways to assign meaning to the discriminations. For example, you can assign meaning by communicating in the second language for a portion of the class period or by applying role playing in a social work class. These applied learning situations can reduce the effects of interference and can increase the stability of the recently learned multiple discriminations. Your responsibility will be to provide for frequent reinforcement of the correct discriminations (KCRs) and information about the proper response in the case of incorrect discriminations. Indeed, the addition of meaning in the various discriminations is a prerequisite for learning the skills related to concepts.

=== **PROBE 7-3** ===

Consider your best high school or elementary teacher and cite examples of how he or she followed our three rules for discrimination learning. Why is this self-monitoring question somewhat difficult for you to answer? Are you learning some new skills that your teachers had not really considered?

Let us now confirm your hypothesis about multiple discrimination learning. The guidelines that we provided earlier for verbal associations are very similar to the guidelines for multiple discrimination learning. Actually, you will think of multiple discrimination learning simply as sets of verbal associations. If you can help your students to master the learning of such associations, you can also help them to achieve multiple discrimination learning. And your students' mastery of multiple discrimination learning is prerequisite to the learning of concepts.

TEACHING CONCEPT LEARNING SKILLS

Putting together verbal chains and multiple discriminations can be an exciting challenge for you and your students. The puzzle of learning skills will begin to fit together. Be patient. Review the prerequisite skills and make sure you have mastered them.

Usually, we teach students by using concepts. Unfortunately, we rarely take the time to analyze a concept and make sure our students have mastered the prerequisite skills or the subordinate concepts.

FOCUS ON CONCEPT LEARNING

CONCEPT LEARNING is a skill for naming a pattern of discriminations based on a set of attributes. Concept learning occurs after a number of prerequisite skills in the learning hierarchy have been mastered. The set of attributes for a concept may describe an object or an idea. Of course, objects or ideas which do not share the set of attributes are not included in the concept. Thus, a student who is learning a concept may go through

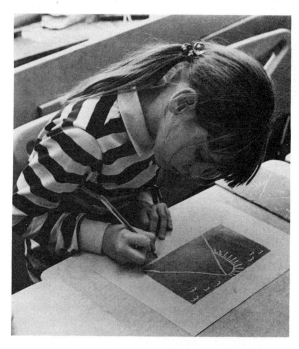

"To learn the concept of straight line, you want students to make the correct selection between a straight line and a curved line." (Bernstein/Peter Arnold)

a series of correct and incorrect performances on the way to learning the concept.

Suppose Barbara were going to learn the concept *straight*. It is possible to determine whether she knows this concept by asking her to point out a straight line or to define the concept as the shortest distance between two points. On the most basic level, you want Barbara to make the correct selection between a straight line and a curved line. Once this skill is mastered, you can check on whether she has mastered the concept *straight* by presenting her with pictures of straight lines—short, fat straight lines and straight chairs as well as some curved or wavy lines and bean-bag chairs. You want Barbara to point to the straight lines, chairs, and so on on a consistent basis. Essentially, you want Barbara to master a series of S_D's to promote her discrimination of attributes that define the concept.

Concepts needed in communications

Too often when a word is used differently by two speakers, they are unaware of their conflicting definitions; they do not take the time to make sure that each is using the word in the same way. Without a set of common shared attributes or characteristics, a word might be incorrectly passed off as a concept. The concepts that depend on verbal descriptions frequently fail to have a common set of attributes for all the users (for example, the concept *fair wage* as used by management is sometimes very different from that used by teachers at the bargaining table). Once a concept is specified, both the speaker and the listener can agree on its common attributes. After that, the full benefit of clearly defined concepts is seen, since they help to facilitate communications. Patience and precision are probably needed by all of us.

Most of our communications to you in this book use basic concepts to describe more complex ideas. Communications in school use higher learning skills almost exclusively (such as concepts in the learning hierarchy to promote, manage, mediate, and facilitate learning of all varieties). At times, you will be assumed to have learned what is meant by the concepts, *we, teach,* and *students*. At other times the assumption is made that certain prerequisite learning skills or selected subordinate concepts must be mastered before higher skill-level learning can occur. In introducing new concepts to you, we try to define them in words that, we hope, you have already mastered. Of course, both sets of assumptions frequently are not supported. Indeed, this lack of mastery promotes confusion and an aversion to textbooks and frequently to school as well!

Characteristics of concepts

Concepts which are clearly defined are fundamental to communication, are often complex, and usually facilitate students' educational progress.

Concepts are fundamental   When we use concepts in communication and in education, we are dealing with the building blocks of ideas. These blocks—verbal chains and discriminations—are ordered in an interdependent manner. The ordering of a concept includes those things or ideas which share a common, specifiable set of attributes. As you can see, your learning about the prerequisite skills for concept mastery is very important because we are now talking about ways you can put together signal learning, stimulus-response learning, chaining, and discriminations into learning the relevant attributes of a concept.

Concepts are complex   The mastery of concepts (even learning about concepts) is based upon your students' mastery of the prerequisite learning skills. Sometimes the prerequisite for learning a large concept involves putting together a number of subordinate concepts. For example, *white leather ball* is really five subordinate concepts (*small, hard, white, leather,* and *ball*). When put together, these subordinate concepts describe a baseball. A host of subordinate concepts may be put together to describe a very complex concept like *justice*. Concepts vary in complexity.

Concepts can be facilitative   Plainly, concepts are on the other side of the bridge from cues and verbal chains. They allow teachers, students, parents, and all of us greater freedom to communicate with each other about special ideas, problems, and solutions. Indeed, correctly used concepts allow us to abbreviate our verbal interactions and to avoid "knowing" every separate item as a verbal chain. Thus, they are the steppingstones to the higher levels in the learning skills hierarchy (see Table 7-1).

Attributes define concepts

Throughout this discussion of concepts we have talked about attributes. As you might expect, attributes have several other names such as *dimensions, aspects,* and *characteristics*. An attribute may be either relevant or irrelevant. A RELEVANT ATTRIBUTE helps define positive instances of the concept. In such an instance, all the relevant attributes are present. An IRRELEVANT ATTRIBUTE may be either an irrelevant dimension or a noncritical aspect of the concept. Irrelevant attributes complicate learning. You will want to keep them to a minimum in concept learning. In a negative instance of the concept, some but not all of the attributes are present. A familiar example of a negative instance is the description of an elephant by the seven blind men.

Let's look at learning the concept *red*. Two attributes, one relevant and one irrelevant, are used in Figure 7-4. The student must learn the correct response in this learning situation. At Time 1, Barbara is presented with two circles—red (I) and pink (II). She is asked to pick one circle and she chooses (*) the red one. You would say "correct." At Time 2, the

	I		II		Teacher's response
Time 1	* (red)	S_D	(pink)	S_Δ	"Correct."
Time 2	(red)	S_D	* (pink)	S_Δ	"No. Let's try another."
Time 3	[pink]	S_Δ	* [red]	S_D	"Fine."
Time 4	[red]	S_D	* [pink]	S_Δ	"No."
Time 5	(red)	S_D	* (pink)	S_Δ	"No."
Time 6	(pink)	S_Δ	* (red)	S_D	*"Great!"*

**Figure 7-4
Learning the
concept *red*.**

student is given two more circles and happens to select the pink one. The choice is not correct. At Time 3, with rectangles (an irrelevant attribute), the procedure is repeated and Barbara receives feedback that the red rectangle was the correct response. The red ellipse was also correct. You then ask Barbara, "What thing usually seems to be right?" Barbara answers, "When I choose red," which is correct. She appears to have mastered this particular concept. The student learned that the relevant attribute was the color and the irrelevant attributes were the shape. Of course, classroom learning rarely occurs in this neat, two-attribute manner. Usually, a host of competing stimuli, one or two competing responses, and a fight in the back of the room interfere with concept learning in the classroom.

CONCRETE AND DEFINED CONCEPTS

Earlier we said that concepts are complex. Some people have defined and described as many as five kinds of concepts (Bergan & Dunn, 1976). We believe that too many definitions can clutter a future teacher's view of concepts. We will consider only two kinds of concepts: concrete and defined (Gagné, 1977). A CONCRETE CONCEPT is learned when Edward can identify (label, point to, or select) an object. You can think of many concrete concepts which your students have probably learned before they entered school. We are talking about such concepts as *chair, horse,* and *car,* examples of which can be identified by pointing and labeling. On the other hand, a DEFINED CONCEPT is learned when Edward can use verbal behaviors to identify it. He can identify an object (an idea such as *freedom*) by its definition. Examples of defined concepts would include *long, longer, family, brother,* and *uncle*. These defined concepts are more difficult to demonstrate and usually require the students to describe several subordinate concepts. For example, *brother* might involve such subordinate concepts as *father, same-generation, sibling,* and *male*. Defined concepts can be very complex!

STUDENT ACTIVITIES IN CONCEPT LEARNING

In the hubbub of even the best-managed classroom, you will find that concept learning does not occur without extensive planning and careful attention to detail. In the classroom, concept learning usually requires the student to master a concept which has numerous real-life attributes. In the real world, concepts are usually the product of several critical attributes which increase the concept's specificity. For example, New England democracy with its town meeting participation is very different from big-city democracy. Your list of critical attributes for democracy is probably fairly long, but for both New England and big-city government the list of common attributes helps to restrict and define the concept *democracy*.

Suppose Edward is wrestling with democracy as a concept. As a classroom teacher committed to helping students like Edward, you might try the historical approach and start with Greece, but Edward might confront you with the Spartans' practice of throwing away sickly babies. You might try Roman law and the use of senators to develop laws, but Edward might ask you about full representation. If you had the patience and the school board gave you the time, Edward might eventually discover the meaning of *democracy,* but we believe that learning by induction is frequently too time consuming. You will want to use learning by induction for certain kinds of students and for selected topics. Let us distinguish between two types of learning: inductive learning, or learning by discovery, is going from examples to a general rule; deductive learning, on the other hand, is learning the rule first and then mastering specific examples of it. We believe it will be easier for you and Edward if you simply tell him what we mean when we speak of democracy.

The learning of concepts, either concrete or defined, depends on the student's mastery of prerequisite skills and of *subordinate* concepts. For concrete concepts, the student must have mastered stimuli, mediating links, and responses. By now, these are old friends to you. They are important. Students like Edward must be able to perform them before you can test for concept mastery. For defined concepts, the prerequisite skills include mastery of subordinate concepts. For example, the defined concept *straight line* involves the subordinate concepts *shortest, distance, between two,* and *points.* As a classroom teacher, you will want to be precise and careful in teaching a concept. You will want to take advantage of your students' prior experiences with concrete, subordinate, and defined concepts. If you take your time and assess your students' present skills, then you can manage the learning environment to help students show their mastery of the concept.

TEACHER MANAGEMENT OF CONCEPT LEARNING

Throughout your own learning experiences, you will probably be flooded with different ways to teach concepts. For some students, strategy A would be helpful. For other students, strategy C will be useful but difficult. For still other students, you will find that AB at first, then followed by a modified C works very well. You will have an advantage over many of your colleagues: you will have the ABC model for focusing on learning!

The ways to manage learning for concept mastery fall into three groups: stimulus-response, mediation, and cognitive social learning. Let's take a look at each of these management strategies.

Stimulus-response concept learning

The stimulus-response (S-R) idea for concept learning considers concept learning as a special case of discrimination learning (Becker, Engelmann, & Thomas, 1975b). In this management strategy, the student is asked to discriminate between sets of positive and negative instances of the concept. For example, "Sesame Street" characters frequently ask viewers to choose the "one that does not belong" from three pictures of birds and one of a truck. In this situation (Figure 7-5), the picture stimulus produces a response for which the child can be reinforced. Big Bird or Gordon then repeats the S-R concept learning task. In S-R concept learning, there are essentially four steps: stimulus, response, reinforcement, and repetition. Concept mastery occurs when the student's choice behavior is consistent.

Figure 7-5 Which one is different?

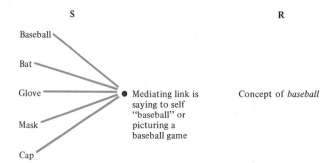

S   R

Baseball

Bat

Glove ———————● Mediating link is   Concept of *baseball*
                    saying to self
                    "baseball" or
Mask   picturing a
                    baseball game

Cap

**Figure 7-6
Mediation model for
concept learning.**

**Mediation
concept learning**

The mediation approach to concept learning suggests that students learn concepts as a result of S-R links and some mediation. The model for concept mediation looks like Figure 7-6. In the mediation model, the several stimuli produce a mediating verbal or pictorial link (baseball) which stimulates the overt response or the concept *baseball*. As you can recognize, Figure 7-6 is a more general model of the verbal chain except that several stimuli unite to develop the mediating link. In turn, the mediating link stimulates the student to say "baseball."

**Cognitive social
learning concepts**

To manage concept learning, we like to use both the stimulus-response and the mediation approaches. As a teacher, you will have opportunities to observe change, to monitor progress, and to manage both the environmental antecedents (prerequisite skills, physical stimuli, experience) and the consequences (rewards, new questions, and so on). In cognitive social learning theory, no one way is seen as the "best" way for learning. Indeed, you will want to adjust your learning management to promote discovery for some students, rule learning by other students, and receptive learning by still other students—depending on the materials to be learned. It is a challenge! Our experience has been that students who have learned concepts with the social learning model have become "turned on" to learning. Environmental and self-reinforcers are frequently available, and many of our students have become self-managers.

Whether you choose the S-R, mediation, or cognitive social learning model for teaching concepts, you will want to follow some guidelines for managing concept learning. You will want to plan and carefully carry out activities which will help students master concepts.

GUIDELINES
FOR
TEACHING

Concept Learning

● *Analyze the concept for instruction.* As a classroom teacher, you will want to ask many questions about the concept. The answers to the following ten questions can help you analyze the concept and put together a sequence of instructional events:

What is the concept to be taught?

What are some relevant and some irrelevant attributes of the concept?

What are some examples and nonexamples for use in learning activities and in assessment?

How does the concept relate to other concepts?

What principles (see Table 7-1) include this concept?

Which real-life situations can I use as sample problems?

What concrete activities can I assign to let students use the concept directly?

What vocabulary is appropriate to the concept and to my students?

What is the skill level of my students?

How will I give feedback?

The answers to these ten questions can be overwhelming, but remember that they can be organized into the basic teaching model which we discussed in Chapter 1.

● *Emphasize relevant attributes.* In the learning environment which we are advocating, students and teachers work together. We want to put an end to the practices which result in "tricky" tests. The idea of emphasizing relevant attributes is a step in that direction. You will want to use several different techniques:

Accentuate the critical attributes so students really observe them. For example, you can help students learn the concept *square* by presenting pairs of squares and triangles. It would be difficult for students to master the concept *circle* if you gave them pairs of circles and ellipses. Later, you can gradually remove the prompt or the emphasis (Trabasso, 1963).

Use a small number of attributes for the concept. Too few attributes appear to limit some students' skills in generalizing the concept, which is not good for the student. Too many attributes also have a mind-boggling effect on students.

Keep the attributes related. When too few attributes are used to define the concept, they will probably be so unrelated that the student will fail to master the concept (remember the seven blind men who were describing the elephant).

Hold the irrelevant attributes constant or try to remove them from the learning situation. If you are unable to remove or fade the irrelevant attributes, vary their position or their intensity so a student masters the concept based on the critical attributes rather than on some irrelevant ones such as order or position.

- *Use familiar examples.* In the analysis guideline, we emphasized your wanting to select the most appropriate examples. You do not want students to stumble over your very novel examples and fail to master the concept. We know of a teacher who brought his full naval terminology into a discussion only to discover that the class was still trying to get the "true meaning" of *bulkhead* and *deck*.
- *Group your examples.* Our fourth guideline is an effort to simplify the learning of the concept. In order to promote generalization of the concept, we suggest that you group the examples so they seem to "hang together." This grouping will allow the students to generalize across irrelevant attributes as well as to learn most of the positive instances of the concept.

BASIC MODEL FOR CONCEPT LEARNING

Let's see how these guidelines can be easily organized into a familiar model. In Chapter 1 we talked about the basic teaching model. We have tried to use the model in our chapters; therefore you should be fairly familiar with it by now. The basic model has four parts: objectives, assessment, instruction, and evaluation. We will briefly discuss each of these parts below.

Present the objectives

Time and time again, we find that students learn more easily after they are given a set of clearly stated objectives. Unless you want students to spend their energies trying to figure you out, you will want to provide them with specific objectives about the concept. You might try to create interest in the concept by using real-life experiences, pictures, or an audiotaped dramatization of the concept.

Assess students' entering behaviors

Earlier we talked about concept analysis. The ideas from this analysis will help you create the "better" assessment questions, demonstrations, and test items. You will want to assess students by using words which are familiar to them. Should you use "tricky" items, you might find out how your students respond to tricky items and not how much they know about the concepts.

Select instructional technique

How you finally decide to present the concept will be a matter of your students' individual differences and your own preferences. The following basic ideas on concept learning will be useful to you:

1. The simplest way to help students learn the concept is to give them the full definition.

2. You may give the concept by modeling it verbally or symbolically.

3. You can speed up learning by giving the student pairs of examples and nonexamples rather than one of each (Bourne, Ekstrand, & Dominowski, 1971).

4. You can use the right number of examples to prevent undergeneralization (too few examples), overgeneralization (too many examples), and misconceptions (emphasis on irrelevant attributes).

5. You can guide the discovery of the concept as long as you have planned the orderly use of learning activities for selected students.

6. You can arrange for appropriate use of the concept through planned, positive *vertical* or *horizontal transfer.*

You will want to use each of these ideas, individually adapted to you and your students' individual learning styles. We cannot say that each one will work for all people, but we are fairly certain that adaptations can help most students reach mastery in concept learning.

Evaluate instruction

Concept learning is very similar to other kinds of learning; student behavior changes with feedback for both correct and incorrect responses. The idea of feedback after an incorrect response is very important, because feedback can help correct an incorrect response pattern. In a sense, feedback can be used to shape the concept. There are three points to remember about evaluating concept learning: (1) beware of the verbal chain, since many students will behave as if they had mastered the concept when they have really learned only a verbal chain; (2) pointing is a satisfactory way to demonstrate the concrete concept (*nickel, cat,* and so on); and (3) letting the student show examples is a good way to evaluate a defined concept. Try to use this evaluation information in

"The idea of feedback after an incorrect response is very important, because feedback can help correct an incorrect response pattern." (Bruce Roberts/Photo Researchers)

planning your next instructional event. We will talk more about this model in Chapter 10.

As a classroom teacher, you will find that helping students to master concept learning skills will facilitate their future learning of other concepts and of higher levels in the learning skill hierarchy. Of course, when you manage concept learning, you will recall the discussions of development in Chapter 4. You will recall that not every student can learn the same things at the same rate and at the same age. Piaget, Bruner, and Gagné have made this point over and over again. We agree: you will want to match your concept learning experiences to the students' entering behaviors.

TEACHING PRINCIPLE LEARNING SKILLS

A major breakthrough in helping students master a broad variety of learning activities occurs when a student masters concept learning. Another breakthrough occurs when students relate concepts to each other. In our own discussions of defined concepts, you might have sensed that the next learning skill level in the hierarchy is relating one concept to another. Students who can relate concepts can usually state PRINCIPLES, or rules. In turn, these can be useful for predicting and explaining related events such as antecedents and consequences in the ABC model.

FOCUS ON PRINCIPLE LEARNING

The definition of *principle* will be important for you. A principle states the relationship between two or more concepts. In our learning skill hierarchy, a principle is based upon concepts which must be mastered by the student. Principle learning occurs after a student has mastered the several concepts which are integrated into a principle. You have probably learned many principles such as "Stop at railroad crossings," or "Respect others' property" which usually are stated as rules. Principles as rules seem to govern predictable interactions among objects, people, or events.

The most fundamental principles demonstrate the relationship between two concepts. "Birds fly," "Water boils," and "gravity pulls" are examples of two-concept principles. These fundamental principles have a close relationship in form to our old friend the verbal chain. In these examples the concrete concept *bird* is related to the defined concept *fly*. Indeed, the relationship is a form of a mediated link. You can use games in which you suggest that "+ means add" and "– means take away." In these two examples, the concept equated with the symbol is related by the "meaning" concept to add or to take away. We say that you are teaching an equivalency rule or principle when you try to teach arithmetic symbols to students. As a classroom teacher, you will spend more time with more complex principles which require student mastery of a host of subordinate defined and concrete concepts. Let us see how principle learning can begin in the classroom.

ACTIVITIES TO PROMOTE PRINCIPLE LEARNING

In the classroom, principle learning is a shared experience which involves interaction between student and "teacher." By now, you may be getting the idea that a teacher can be another classmate, an older student-tutor, a parent, or yourself. As the manager of learning in the classroom, it will be your responsibility to select the "better" teacher for a particular learning activity.

Student activities in principle learning

In principle learning, the student has certain responsibilities. In the first place, Barbara must master all the concepts which appear to be related to the rule or principle which is being taught. This idea has been emphasized in our discussions of the learning hierarchy. Barbara may have been exposed to most of the concepts, but she has not yet mastered each one. If Barbara does not "understand" the concept of *respect*, how can she respect Edward's property? She will have difficulty in learning the principle if some of the subordinate or prerequisite concepts have been incompletely learned. Barbara, for example, learned that showing respect means to say, "Sir," so she grabs Edward's book and says, "Give me that, Sir!" You can see how partially learned concepts can undermine the appropriate application of the principle. By now you will have discovered that mastery is important throughout the hierarchy. When the student has not learned the prerequisite skills, you have a challenge as a classroom manager. To meet this challenge, you will simply recycle the student through the concept until he or she actually masters it. In this case, a class lesson on "respect" and behavioral examples of it would be helpful. In the second place, Barbara must be prepared to go beyond simply reciting the principle. Remember verbal chains? Barbara might give a perfect rendition of the rule, but it is still a verbal chain. She will have to plan on demonstrating how the rule works.

=== **PROBE 7-5** ===

Principle learning requires preparation by both the student and you. Observe principle learning with the ABC model. Were the subordinate concepts restated as prompts? Did the teacher encourage the student through feedback? Lots of practice and planning are necessary for effective principle learning, so don't be too critical.

Both these student responsibilities allow the principle learning to be a shared experience. A class activity of showing "respect" to others for one day might be fun for you and your class. You might define respect or have students provide definitions, give examples, discuss and criticize these examples, role-play for practice, reverse roles so classmates can practice "respect" in a new way, and give points (rewards) each time a student demonstrates a "respect" response. In other words, the question "What does someone do to communicate respect to another classmate?" can be the theme for a day.

Principle learning is the final prerequisite to problem solving and creativity. Therefore, helping students to master principle learning is the final stage in preparing students to encounter unique experiences in school, on the playground, and at home. The skills in problem solving become, themselves, a style of approaching life and its continued challenges. You will want to make sure that your students are ready for those challenges.

As manager of learning experiences in the classroom, you will have several responsibilities to promote principle learning:

GUIDELINES FOR TEACHING

Principle Learning

- *Analyze the principle for all its subordinate concepts.* Earlier, we mentioned task analysis, and you will want to follow this procedure for principle learning. Based upon your analysis of the principle's prerequisite concepts, you will want to make sure that your students have mastered these crucial concepts.
- *State the objectives for today's learning task.* Clearly stated objectives for principle learning can be most helpful for your students and you. For example, you might say, "Today we are going to learn that heating a liquid will cause it to become a gas. For example, at home when your parents heat water for tea, steam usually appears." This objective statement is simply loaded with good things for the student: (1) it gives the student a statement of the principle; (2) it gives the student a goal for self-reinforcement; and (3) it serves as a model. This objective statement is important for another reason; (4) it includes a familiar example of the rule. Students seem to master a rule or principle more easily when an example is presented with the rule (Markle & Tiemann, 1974). As you can see, selecting and stating objectives with examples of principle learning require planning, sensitivity, and an artistic flair!
- *Use questions to prompt the previously learned concepts.* Prompting and fading are two skills which are used in a variety of learning environments (Chapter 5). For example, you might say, "You will remember the difference between gases and liquids. What do we mean by *liquid*? What do we mean by *gas*?" This will prompt important

concepts in this principle learning situation. Thus, principle learning is a closely guided experience.

• *Make sure that the principle has been mastered.* Please don't be fooled because the student can recite the rule. Probe Laura's mastery of the rule in several different ways: (1) give positive examples that show variations in irrelevant characteristics; (2) give negative examples that differ from the positive only in one attribute; (3) ask questions that require Laura to put concepts together in various examples of the principle, such as "Under increased heat conditions _____ expands to become _____. As long as the heat remains constant a _____ can change its state by _____ pressure and by holding _____ constant"; and (4) ask Laura to restate the principle in more or in less technical terms.

• *Reassess the student's mastery of the principle after some time has passed.* The delay is important because principle learning means that the student has integrated many previously learned skills and is ready for the next adventure—problem solving and creativity.

• *Keep the student informed about progress toward mastery of a given principle.* By itself, the feedback can reward and encourage a student to learn more and faster. Frequent feedback also means that you are being highly interactive with your students.

"Clearly stated objectives for principle learning can be most helpful for your students and you." (M. Heron/ Monkmeyer)

TEACHING RETENTION SKILLS

The kinds of skills described in this learning hierarchy do not always proceed smoothly from one level to the next. Problems occur. A skill may not be recalled. When a skill is not recalled, the teacher often says the skill is forgotten. Other mastered skills are limited to a single subject (for example, one may be an excellent singer but a stutterer in conversation). These three problems—ensuring recall, preventing forgetting, and facilitating transfer—inhibit a student's development of many learning skills. As a classroom teacher, you are committed to making sure that skills and information are recalled fairly consistently; therefore the dual challenges of preventing forgetting and promoting transfer will be crucial to your successful classroom management.

MODEL FOR RETENTION

Making sure that students retain the information and skills they have learned can be extremely frustrating to you and probably to the students. Sometimes your planned discrimination learning activities will fail to produce recall of a previously learned response. The student looks blankly at you, "I have forgotten the answer." Well, forgetting the answer is simply the other side of "Sorry, but I don't recall the answer." As a classroom teacher, you will try to help students retain and recall information, experiences, or a chain of verbal or motor behaviors so they can apply that information in new settings.

=== **PROBE 7-6** ===

Think of your most recent "I forgot" experience. Complete an ABC analysis of the event. Was this analysis a complete experience for you or do you want more information?

Let us take a look at a cognitive social learning theory model for retention. Each part of the model uses some fairly specific skills which students like Elizabeth or Ned can master. These sets of skills are (1) attending and organizing, (2) mediating and coding, (3) retaining infor-

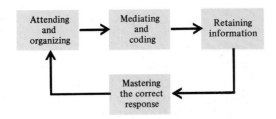

Figure 7-7 How retention works.

mation, and (4) mastering the correct response. The four-part model looks like that shown in Figure 7-7. Let's discuss each part of the model.

Attending and organizing: Paying attention

Throughout Chapters 5, 6, and 7, we have emphasized setting the stage for learning and using planned, ordered learning experiences (Gagné & White, 1978). Usually the stage setting has involved making sure the ABCs are working so the student is paying attention. Sometimes the antecedents or the consequences have to be modified, but in the long run you will want the student to pay attention (Gagné, 1977; Hewett, 1968). You will use ADVANCED ORGANIZERS, which give an overview of what the student will be presented in the learning activity (Ausubel, 1969; 1978). Advanced organizers can be short statements, brief paragraphs, or sets of objectives. Some of your professors might give you their lecture outlines as an advanced organizer. You have heard a class start with "Today we will continue our discussion of emerging nations. Five common characteristics can be listed for most nations. They are . . . ." Probably you will give the students a list of the instructional objectives (Mager, 1962). You will also try to assign meaning to the materials by tying the present learning activity to some previous and future experiences (Melton, 1978). We have tried to give you an advanced organizer by presenting objectives for each chapter. In all these activities, you want students to pay attention, use mediation skills, and acquire the information in the activity. Please refer back to Chapter 4 for guidelines in facilitating attention skills. In other words, you want to facilitate learning.

Mediating and coding: Providing links

The second part of this model for retention is mediation. Early in this chapter, we said that mediating is thinking, picturing, or repeating to yourself a verbal chain. We also said that coding is an abbreviated form of mediation. This part of our model serves as the link between the attending and organizing of new information and the student's retention of the verbal or motor skills (Gagné & White, 1978). As a classroom teacher, you will want to prompt mediating and coding behaviors. Later, you will fade these prompts as your students become more responsible for retaining learned skills.

Retaining information: Long- and short-term recall

In the third part of this model, you will want to find out how much of this learning the students have retained. You will examine your students' ability to recognize or recall information and skills. Recognition is a unique set of skills which a student finds useful, particularly in multiple-choice testing. In a social setting, the student might quickly recognize you as a former teacher but not recall how good you were! Recall will be very important for class discussions, for examinations, and long-term retention of learned materials.

Short-term recall   On the one hand, SHORT-TERM RECALL will be important when you ask two or three students a question about the contributors to American democracy. You will want all the students in the group to retain the question and to respond within the discussion. Not everyone can recall questions over a short period, so you will probably see a blank expression once in a while.

Suppose you watch three or four students in a small group discussion. If you ask a question, their hands will shoot up. What do they do to recall an answer? One student will probably fidget and poke her hand in the air. Another student will be silently saying the answer to himself. Another student will write the answer on a slip of paper and keep her left hand raised. What you are observing are two ways in which people can maintain short-term recall: (1) they practice or rehearse the answer overtly or (2) they code the answer covertly. In recall, rehearsing is simply repeating the answer (preferably quietly to oneself). In the same way, coding involves verbal or pictorial self-cues which are similar to the mediating links in verbal chaining. In this experience, you can observe how students recall information over a short period of time.

Long-term recall   In contrast, LONG-TERM RECALL will be important when students are required to perform a skill several days, weeks, or months after it has been learned. Again, you will want students to recall the information fairly consistently. As a classroom teacher, you will want to facilitate students' performance in long-term recall situations. Probably the most important facilitator of long-term recall is organization (Tulving & Donaldson, 1972). We believe that organizing new ideas by relating them to familiar ones will facilitate their later recall. For this reason, the advanced organizers, instructional objectives, and entire hierarchy of sequenced learning experiences become extremely important. Without these organized and sequenced cues to learning, long-term recall will be difficult for most students. Thus, you will want to help students organize the new materials or information. You might suggest cues or *mnemonic devices* to help cluster and simplify information. [After all, George Miller (1956) says that most people can handle seven plus or minus two ideas fairly consistently, so you will want to help students keep learning tasks as simple as possible!]

Mastering the response

Throughout your efforts to help students develop their long-term recall, you will discover that the "best" organization must continually be revised and reorganized. Instead of encouraging students to "pile their information in neat stacks," you will want them to develop their own evolving organizations so that each student can learn and recall in his or her own way. How well Barbara and Laura retain their information will have an influence upon how they attend and organize any new information. Thus, students and teachers seem to do a better job of attending and mediating new information after they have performed several correct recognitions or recalls. In this sense, we are emphasizing the importance of mastering the correct responses as a kind of reinforcement for the student (see Figure 7-7).

FAILURE TO RECALL

Earlier we said that when a student "forgot" the answer, he or she might say, "I don't recall the answer." For years, students have been trying to recall the three reasons for forgetting. The first reason is that we get older, and we always forget the two other reasons. This typical teacher story probably began shortly before Socrates met his first student. Teachers have remembered the story for centuries because we have practiced the story, assigned positive value to it, altered it slightly to fit each new situation, and generally promoted its retention and facilitated its transfer.

From your early childhood, you have been learning new skills. Some of these new behaviors (such as a funny joke) you remembered only long enough to tell your best friend. She gave you a new joke and you promptly "forgot" the first joke. Some other new behaviors (such as Spanish words) you practiced and practiced. For the Spanish quiz and for Spanish Club, you performed pretty well. Still other childhood behaviors (riding

"You never seem to forget some childhood behaviors." (Sybil Shelton/Peter Arnold)

a bicycle, for example) you seem never to forget. Today, riding a bike without holding the handlebars can be a bit risky for you. Still, bike riding is as much fun as it was when you were 10. Throughout your own development and your students' education, you have been influenced by learning and by forgetting.

Forgetting is common

Forgetting occurs when a previously learned behavior is not produced. In its simplest form, when the behavior is not performed on request, we say that the behavior has been forgotten. As a classroom teacher, you may observe a boy like Edward writing "Lincoln, Nebraska" in his notebook. You announce that, later in the day, you will ask the class to name the capitals of the Midwestern states. This is a part of your daily review and rehearsal activity to promote recall. During the review session, Edward fumbles with the capital of Nebraska and mumbles, "I forgot." Since social studies comes at the end of a hard morning, you lose some cool and suggest, strongly, "Edward, the capital is Lincoln. Don't you *ever* forget that, Edward!" He cannot perform on request, so he calls this experience "forgetting." Edward, in this situation, is embarrassed and quietly burns.

Later, in the teacher's lounge, Edward's name comes up. You are just about ready to join in and blame him for not remembering *Lincoln, Nebraska* when you remember a study described by Worell and Stilwell. In this study, the teachers usually blamed the student for not learning (Baldwin, Johnson, & Wiley, 1970). You bite your tongue and remember. Both you and Edward can become extremely frustrated over reaching mastery, especially after you have followed the learning hierarchy! This frustration can stimulate many destructive consequences. For example, (1) school may become an aversive experience for Edward; (2) he may develop a negative attitude toward school; and (3) you will doubt your own judgment about the teaching profession. Keep cool—some people forget more often than others. In the section on forgetting, we want to talk about how to facilitate recall.

Why do we forget?

The "why" question on forgetting is difficult to answer. Numerous theories have been offered and many have been discarded. We prefer to organize three approaches about forgetting into our ABC model. We shall focus on three theories which emphasize the mastery of learned behavior, the consequences that followed such mastery, and the effects of interfering responses.

We are most comfortable with these three approaches about forgetting. First, forgetting may occur because the behavior was not learned to a very high level of competency. In that event, how can a teacher expect the verbal chain *Lincoln, Nebraska* to be performed on request? Really, we ask a student to perform two activities. Initially we want the student to learn the cue or stimulus word, *Nebraska,* and then to associate it with *Lincoln.* This sequence is called backward chaining (Chapter 5). Later we want the student to mediate this backward chain (*Nebraska*, then *Lincoln*) so it is produced as *Lincoln, Nebraska.* As you may imagine, this two-step hierarchy can be pretty difficult to master.

Second, the reinforcement for learning and recalling was not available. For example, Edward rehearsed his verbal association, but he rarely reinforced his own correct response. In his self-study periods, the mediating link weakened when he performed the verbal associations correctly (Mahoney & Thoresen, 1974). Thus, in the absence of strong reinforcement, the behavior itself became weakened. If you think this idea about forgetting sounds like extinction, you are correct. We believe that a behavior is no longer performed because it is not reinforced, which is what happens in extinction.

In a third theory of forgetting, we are concerned about *competing responses.* The stimulus in the *Lincoln* verbal chain has several different competing responses such as *logs, Steffans,* and *Continental.* These competing responses can interfere with Edward's mastery of the correct verbal chain. A special case of competing responses occurs in "motivated" forgetting. That is, a student may "forget" something he or she does not enjoy ("Oh, I 'forgot' to brush my teeth this morning!"). A second type of motivated forgetting results when students are feeling anxious, tired, or apprehensive. In this case, you may ask Barbara to explain the base 5 and Barbara may say to herself, "Oh oh. I don't know this, she'll think I'm dumb. I should have studied more. . . ." Barbara's self-statements will interfere with recall and can be viewed as competing responses.

Indeed, our three approaches to forgetting sound very much like the ABCs of learning. The resemblance is planned. You will see that this approach, like our ABC model, (1) has to do with the behavior; (2) discusses the consequences; and (3) focuses on the antecedents. Thus, we have brought the ABC model for focusing on learning into our discussion of forgetting.

Interference promotes forgetting

Earlier, in Chapter 5, we spent a great deal of time defining behavior and discussing how reinforcement seems to keep the behavior going (maintain or increase its frequency or strength). The new idea for you is competing responses. This idea has been studied for some time and is usually called the *theory of interference.* Interference is really a happening: when a person tries to learn similar S-R chains and gets confused, we say that interference has occurred. So many people have studied interference for so long that we now have a theory of interference (Underwood, 1957). We will spend some time on interference and then demonstrate the similarity of interference and competing responses.

The studies on interference usually appear to be very simple. In most of these studies, the researchers have used college freshmen in psychology as subjects (the American answer to the white rat). They, however, are not a very typical group. Usually the students have been asked to memorize fifteen to twenty nonsense syllables. Normally, the three-letter nonsense syllables have had very little meaning. However, some of the combinations now have meaning (for example, SDS, NOW, and NFL) and cannot be used. To perform such a study, the students are divided into two groups, control and experimental. The studies have looked either at the RETROACTIVE INTERFERENCE or at the PROACTIVE INTERFERENCE situations. These two kinds of studies are presented in Table 7-3.

In retroactive interference, the students are asked to master list A, headed "Important dates of birth." Here the stimulus is, for example, "1858," and the response is "Booker T. Washington born." Once these students reach mastery, the experimental group is asked to master list B, headed "Dates of important laws." After a little while (at Time 3), both groups are asked to perform list A. As you would expect, the experimental group has a harder time (takes more time to reach mastery) to remember list A than does the control group. It will be little wonder if the students in your classroom face a challenge in trying to recall all the stuff you will direct at them!

In PROACTIVE INTERFERENCE the situation is a bit different. The experimental group is given a prior learning experience involving the French verbs in list C. At Time 4, these students must learn to master this list. At Time 5, both groups are asked to learn a new list, D, made up of Spanish verbs. Of course, the experimental group had a hard time reaching mastery. Many of the Spanish verbs sound strangely like the French verbs these students had already learned. This is like trying to get young children with culturally different dialects to use standard English. They will have a very hard time overcoming the proactive interference from their early childhood.

Table 7-3. Associations to be learned under two kinds of interference

	Retroactive interference			Proactive interference		
Experimental group	A	B	A	C	D	D
Control group	A		A		D	D
Time	1	2	3	4	5	6

=== PROBE 7-7 ===

Select a recent situation in which you have tried to learn something and show how proactive or retroactive interference influenced your failure to remember some important information.

Both kinds of interference apply to the daily activities of a classroom teacher in managing learning. For teachers helping students learning new words or trying to master multiple discriminations (such as important dates), interference will promote forgetting. When you are helping students master specific motor skills—such as painting with watercolors or shooting free throws—you can expect interference to slow your progress. However, there is hope! For instruction related to continuous activities (such as playing kickball or riding a bicycle) or to large clusters of verbal chains (such as an idea), interference seems to be less of an inhibitor to learning. In these related or continuous activities, it seems that no single missing link or weakened response can inhibit performance on request. Planned learning management activities can help a student through situations involving interference or competing responses.

Student Activities in promoting recall

You will want to reach the point where your students can do the following:

1. Respond to cue words from your questions (for example, "Name three Confederate generals who graduated from the U.S. Military Academy). The cue words are *generals*, *graduated*, and *U.S.M.A.*, which would result in an appropriate answer.

2. Make verbal associations (for example, "Spring forward and fall back"). This association can be useful in deciding whether you set your alarm clock forward or back upon the shift from standard to daylight savings time.

3. Recall either the complete verbal chain for a multiple-choice test item or the mediating link for a discussion item (for example, "What are three causes of increased food costs?"). Asking students to respond to this question assumes that they have done a pretty good job of retaining some fairly complex information.

4. Relearn the stimulus cues and the complete verbal chain.

This four-part goal is reasonable and reachable as long as you plan your learning management activities wisely and carefully.

ACTIVITIES TO PROMOTE RECALL

One of the most exasperating experiences for students and teachers is the plaintive admission, ''I forgot.'' As a classroom teacher committed to facilitating individual development, you will want to minimize experiences of this kind. In Study 7-1 we present some ideas on how to promote recall.

STUDY 7-1: HELPING STUDENTS RECALL A STORY

Ann Brown and her associates at the University of Illinois have been studying how people recall long passages such as a story. She has been studying strategies which can be taught students to help them recall important and not-so-important ideas in a story.

Brown, Smiley, and Lawton (1978) studied how fifth-, seventh- and eighth-, and eleventh- and twelfth- graders selected cues for recalling a story. Two unfamiliar Japanese folk tales were used in the study. Each story had been divided into idea units. Brown had also rated each idea unit into one of four levels of importance.

These educational psychologists wanted to find out (1) what kinds of idea units promoted recall and (2) whether experience with the story changed the recall strategy.

They used the same procedure with each age group. For example, the fifth-graders listened to a tape recording of one story while they read the story. At the end of the story, the students were asked to read each idea unit which had been typed on an index card. Half the students were asked to select the twelve most *important* idea units. The other half selected the twelve idea units which were *needed to recall* the story. The results are important for classroom teachers.

Brown and her colleagues found that important ideas are very different from ideas which are helpful for recall. Younger students seem to select very important ideas for recall. Older students, especially those who had heard the story once before, selected somewhat less important ideas to help them recall the story. The less important ideas cued the recall of the more important ideas. As a classroom teacher, you will want to recommend that your students not spend more time studying the same ideas. Instead, you will want to encourage them to restudy the intermediate-level idea units as aids for recall.

Adapted from: Brown, A. L., Smiley, S. S., & Lawton, S. Q. C. The Effects of Experience on the Selection of Suitable Retrieval Cues for Studying Texts. *Child Development,* 1978, *49,* 829–835.

Frequently, students faced with simple learning tasks will ask you for help in maintaining a learned behavior. Usually the problem is that a student like Ned can easily recall parts of the information but not the full sequence. As a classroom teacher helping students to maintain learned behaviors, you will find the following guidelines helpful.

GUIDELINES
FOR
TEACHING

Preventing Forgetting

• *Sequence learning experiences so that students can master them in a hierarchy.* When you plan a learning sequence from its simplest idea, the basic or simple ideas are usually performed over and over again. This overlearning plus the self-reinforcement from mastering each level probably will facilitate a student's recall of the information. Students frequently tell us that the mastered skills are self-rehearsed without any stimulation from us.

• *Try to make the materials easy to recall.* We suggest four techniques to facilitate meaningfulness:

Show the relationship among ideas by using advanced organizers (Ausubel, 1963). Students seem to master ideas more easily and to recall faster when the structure of the information is explained to them in advance.

Show how the new information is dissimilar to the older information. This emphasis on the dissimilarity is another way to make the stimulus cues, the mediating link, and the response as distinctive as possible.

Use declarative, active sentences. George Miller discovered that people usually restate complex sentences as simple, direct, active and declarative sentences (1962).

Require understanding. Too frequently, we will assume that the class understands our beautiful presentation, only to discover later that their nodding heads meant sleepiness, not understanding. One way to promote understanding is to ask questions—either within the learning materials (for example, Stilwell & Thoresen, 1972; Worell & Nelson, 1974) or within the normal class interactions. Indeed, the questions can be used to promote curiosity and focus attention as well as to find out how much Ned can recall. As a classroom teacher, you will want to use many of these techniques to help make their learning materials more meaningful for your students.

• *Present the materials in familiar terms.* The crucial words in this guideline are *familiar terms.* You will want to know your students' experiential history—what they have done, what they like, and where they are going. Once you can talk with your students in their terms, you are on your way. You can think about working with clusters of students who share common experiences, interests, or goals. When you work with small groups, you can phrase your remarks in terms that are familiar to your students.

• *Distribute the practice.* The best way to establish long-term recall is through frequent, short practices over a long period of time. These short sessions allow the student to rehearse information or skills between the sessions. Cramming all the practice sessions into the night before the performance usually leads to forgetting.

• *Expand the summary or review.* On the summary or review, you will set the stage for overlearning and for interrelating verbal chains. You want the information or skill to be recalled even though one or two mediating links have not been learned to mastery.

● *Make sure that students plan the review.* In the long run, we want the students to plan, manage, and evaluate their own learning experiences. Of course, these skills are learned, so you must gradually promote and facilitate them. An objective of this guideline is to get the student *involved* in learning; an involved student is interacting with the information and becoming committed to it.

● *Test immediately after the material is mastered.* An easy way to maintain a high level of recall is to test right after the material is learned. Programmed instruction works this way. You can produce four- or five-item quizzes for students at the end of each learning unit. If you test immediately, you must be fair and give prompt feedback of the results.

● *Keep the original learning and recall environments as similar as possible.* Usually, classrooms are fairly consistent over time. For example, students learning math with Muzak will subsequently be examined with the sound of music. Yet sometimes unthinking teachers do the opposite: they present the new materials in a group simulation exercise and examine individual students by assigning an essay. You may have learned about Freud and Brentano during spring, perhaps while psych class was held on the lawn in the cool shade of big trees. Later, in a stuffy classroom on a hot June day, you may have cursed them as you were trying to finish the final exam. It is often difficult to behave the same way in very different environments.

"Keep the original learning and recall environments as similar as possible." (Ginger Chih/Peter Arnold)

If you can learn how to help students recall information and skills, you can prepare them to transfer these skills to new situations.

⫿⫿ TEACHING
FOR TRANSFER

Once you have helped a student like Oscar learn a very important skill— asking Millie to the ninth-grade prom—you will want him to perform the skill in a new setting. Please don't assume that Oscar will "know" how to ask a question like "Millie, will you go to the prom with me?" in a new, different social environment.

APPLYING SKILLS IN NEW ENVIRONMENTS

In this section you will discover that each new skill requires practice and application to new environments. The use of a recently learned skill in a new context is called TRANSFER, a learned activity. We value the spreading of recently learned skills to new educational and social settings. You will want your students to spread the word from your arithmetic class, where "making change" has been the activity, to their homes and to the grocery store. However, transfer of new skills cannot be left to some incidental happening. Rough spots in mastery will sometimes delay transfer. As a classroom teacher committed to mediating human relations and to facilitating individual development, you will want to plan and manage learning activities to promote transfer.

SIX KINDS OF TRANSFER

Transfer refers to the facilitating or inhibiting effects that a given learning activity can have on subsequent learning or performance. Sometimes you will want to facilitate transfer from the present to a future learning activity, as in applying "making change" to buying ice-cream cones. Other times you will want to inhibit transfer from the present to a future social activity, as in applying "debating skills" to a first-date situation with a warm, sensitive, and vibrant person. Usually, you will want to promote the student's discrimination of the "better" kind of transfer.

Transfer comes in many different sizes and shapes. Transfer may be positive or negative, vertical or horizontal, planned or incidental. Let us take a look at these six types of transfer in Table 7-4.

You will want to encourage transfer as often as possible in the course of your daily classroom management. In the long run, teaching becomes easier when your students master transfer. You will then have more time to work with students who need close supervision.

Table 7-4. Six basic types of transfer

Kinds of transfer	Description of transfer
Positive	Student applies old information or skills in a new setting (for example, ''making change'').
Negative	Student inhibits old skill in the new setting (''You may play on this side, but do not cross the street'').
Vertical	Student uses older skills to master newer, more complex skills in the sense of learning skills in a hierarchy (as when verbal chains precede multiple discrimination learning).
Horizontal	Student masters a skill in the classroom and subsequently applies it to a real-life setting (for example, simulated driver training and real-life freeway driving).
Incidental	Students ''put things together,'' often in mysterious ways. This usually occurs when we have helped students overlearn an idea or a skill and they try it out on their own. Really, you *want* students to make incidental transfers.
Planned	Students frequently benefit from your verbal modeling of several ways in which the information skills may be used. For example, we give a cue to the effect that ''The ideas in Chapters 5 and 11 apply classroom management skills.''

Why does transfer occur?   The "why" question on transfer is somewhat difficult to answer. At the turn of the century, several ideas were suggested; some have fallen by the wayside and others have been modernized. We prefer to focus on the following three ideas to explain transfer.

"Similarity breeds transfer"   The originally learned material is similar to the new learning (transfer) situation. For example, Ned can read about driving a car, but the original learning environment (sitting in a chair with a book) is very dissimilar to the real highway situation. Therefore, you will want a high degree of similarity between the driver simulator and the real car in an urban traffic jam. In other words, "Similarity breeds transfer."

Mastery promotes transfer   The information and skills presented in the original learning situation are mastered as a learning hierarchy. It appears that when students master materials, they overlearn verbal and motor chains. The students develop a profound and desirable self-competency about their mastered skills. For example, Ned, a teenager who was an assortment of arms and legs at the beginning of driver training class, learned new skills in the driver simulator and became a very safe highway driver. Hierarchical learning experiences help students respond to the new environment's cues so that old verbal and motor chains are triggered in the new environment.

Feedback strengthens responses   Feedback from success in the new environment shapes students' behaviors and strengthens them in the new environment. For example, Ned will become more proficient, sensitive, and aware of his own skills, his car's responsiveness, and the irresponsible "yo-yo's" driving on our streets as he drives more miles in city and highway conditions. Reinforcement and information about the correct response tend to influence Ned's behavior as a driver.

As you can see, we view transfer as a special instance of the ABC model. The antecedents are carefully planned and developed to cue proper motor and verbal chains. Each behavior is mastered. Similarly, consequences can be planned and managed by you. Our ideas about transfer apply to skills within a hierarchy and to complex problem-solving skills (see Table 7-1) in new employment or social situations. We are saying that, in a very real sense, the transfer activities will usually occur as long as you carefully plan the antecedents and consequences and you make sure that the student has mastered the prerequisite behaviors.

ACTIVITIES TO PROMOTE TRANSFER

As a classroom teacher, you will want students to leave you with the skills to meet new challenges in school and in the community. For example, when Barbara finishes learning the alphabet, you will want her to master word recognition. Once she can demonstrate that she has learned the letters, the new challenge will be to put those twenty-six letters, with their many different sounds, into words. You will want to help Barbara and other students to transfer previously learned skills to new environments.

In applying the ideas from this section on transfer, you will have a chance to practice transfer on yourself. Indeed, you will want to mediate some of our basic ideas for your own style of working with students.

• *Make sure that all the component behaviors are mastered in the first place.* Nothing can be more foolish than trying to transfer an unlearned skill. The best-laid planned, positive, horizontal transfer is a waste of everyone's time if the required behaviors have not been previously learned.

• *Specify what is to be transferred.* As a classroom teacher, you will want to specify your goals and objectives for transfer. In order to facilitate the management of learning activities, you might try to list each specific learning activity that falls within a bigger task or problem. This listing and showing of the relationships between ideas and activities is called *task analysis.* We will work on task analysis in Chapter 9.

As you specify what and when you want students to learn selected skills, you will discover a baffling variety of ways to promote transfer. On the one hand, you will find students who benefit from simply listening to you talk (lecture). The *lecture* approach usually is fast and well organized. It is probably a better way for those students who prefer to go from the complex to the simple to learn. On the other hand, you will encounter students whose transfer skills are more consistent when they learn on their own. Letting students *discover* relationships and ideas on their own is time consuming, calls on you to arrange the events of instruction, and probably is better for students who want to go from the simple to the complex. The point is, no one way is "best" for promoting transfer. You will want to select approaches which respect your students' individual differences.

• *Present the materials in the best order for the student.* Three points of view will help you on this guideline: (1) order the learning skills in a hierarchy; (2) order the learning activities from simple to complex; or (3) order the activities from complex to simple. This guideline means that you will want to assess your students carefully to determine their individual styles of learning.

- *Encourage students to plan their own frequent practice sessions.* When students plan anything, they are experiencing an opportunity to practice for the future. For that reason alone, this guideline is valuable. You want your students to become involved in learning and to select a distributed rather than a massed learning pattern.
- *Practice what is to be transferred.* One of the surest ways to promote transfer is to practice the skills in both simulated and real-life environments. As a classroom teacher, you will frequently consider new curricular packages. Some of these materials are awkward or complex. We recommend that you practice the complete demonstration in the real-life world of your classroom as well as in the safety of your living room the night before the demonstration! Your easy movements across the living-room rug might actually be limited by a desk and a fishbowl in your classroom. Indeed, you will want your students to complete their practice spelling tests or the Practice Scholastic Aptitude Test (PSAT) in an environment that will resemble "the real thing."
- *Promote the total mastery of the materials.* You will frequently relate the present learning activity to a larger context. A mediated transfer is one that occurs through the students' use of mediating links. In view of the importance of mediated transfer, you will want your students to observe you and other models, to create their own mediating links among these ideas, and to self-manage their independent transfer of information and skills. Once students like Barbara benefit from planned, positive transfer, they are well on their way to meeting the challenges of new ideas and situations.
- *Follow up on your goals and objectives.* How often have you seen a professor wave yellowed notes and say "This is important" or "Usually I examine students on this matter." Be fair and consistent so students can respect your emphasis on an idea. Then you can examine them on the idea and you will give them feedback on how well they have performed.

Learning how to promote recall and facilitate transfer are crucial skills for a classroom teacher. These classroom management skills are especially important for you as you continue up the learning hierarchy (see Table 7-1). Earlier, in Chapter 5, as well as in the present chapter, we discussed the basic theories and ideas which relate to classroom learning. As a classroom teacher, you will want to plan pauses so that students will be able to rehearse, recall, and practice some positive, horizontal transfer. Be patient with yourself and with your students. We are about ready to cross an important bridge in the learning skills hierarchy.

LEARNING ACTIVITY:
WORKING WITH A PRINCIPLE

Each teaching day you will hear the innocent question, "Wha'd'ya mean by that?" As soon as you hear that question, you have a cue: you are ahead of your students! You are using terms that are too complex for your students. The learning hierarchy can help you. In each level of instruction, you will want to make sure that the prerequisite terms or skills are mastered. A student's innocent question (like "What do you mean by that?") signals that you have not laid the groundwork. You will want to make sure that each student has mastered the prerequisite learning skills before you go on to the next learning level.

In this learning activity, you will try to diagram a principle which you will teach. You will actually try to make a task analysis of a principle. We suggest that you select a familiar principle. Please use the hierarchy provided in Table 7-1 (principles, defined concepts, concrete concepts, and so on). In Figure 7-8 we have provided a sample hierarchy for you to complete.

Please remember that each higher level in the hierarchy involves at least two prerequisite skills. For example, two concrete concepts contribute to "Defined concept 2."

In your own diagram you will give a principle at the top of the task analysis. Then you will specify two defined concepts, and so on. The lowest level of this hierarchy will have sixteen verbal chains!

You will find this learning activity a challenge. As a teacher, you will find it a very common experience, however. Try to limit yourself to three pages. Obtain feedback from your teacher and a peer.

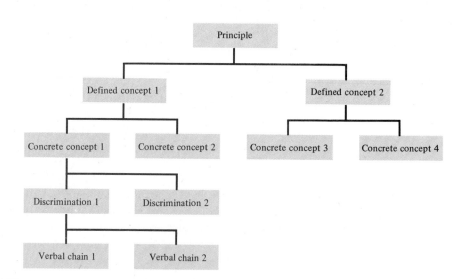

Figure 7-8
Analysis of a
principle.

SUMMARY

1. The learning skill hierarchy developed by Robert M. Gagné emphasizes an orderly approach to the mastery of learning skills. Each level, beginning with response chains, is a prerequisite for the next higher level. The six levels in the hierarchy are response chains, discrimination, CONCRETE CONCEPTS, DEFINED CONCEPTS, PRINCIPLES or rules, and problem solving.

2. Each verbal response chain is made up of three parts: stimulus, MEDIATING LINK, and response. The mediating link may be verbal or pictorial. In longer chains, the response link serves as the stimulus link for the next three-part chain.

3. To promote the mastery of verbal response chains, you will want to do the following: make sure that students respond overtly, provide immediate feedback, allow for frequent reviews of chains, facilitate a distributed practice schedule, and help students assign meaning to the verbal chains. These guidelines will help you promote student learning of verbal response chains.

4. Each discrimination is made up of verbal response chains. The student correctly identifies each cue and completes the response chain in a discrimination learning situation. Students typically learn how to make many discriminations in the classroom.

5. Concepts are the bridge to intellectual manipulations. They are fundamental and often complex, frequently facilitating communications. CONCRETE CONCEPTS can be pointed at (such as *horse, car,* and so on). DEFINED CONCEPTS must be identified verbally (such as *uncle, democracy,* and *love*). The attributes of the concept act as S_D's and help to define its limits.

6. Concepts may be learned by applying the stimulus-response approach, a mediational approach, or the preferred cognitive social learning approach. The latter suggests more flexibility to facilitate individual student's mastery of concepts.

7. Principles or rules state the relationship between two or more concepts. Mastery of the prerequisite concepts is essential to the learning of principles or rules. You will want to make sure that students have mastered the appropriate principles before they try to reorder principles in some problem-solving or creative manner.

8. Retention requires the management of learning into three activities: attention to and organization of the new information; mediating and coding the information with pictorial or verbal links; and retaining and recalling the learned information or skills upon your request or in response to particular environmental conditions.

9. FORGETTING is the bane of all our learning experiences. A student is expected to perform short-term and long-term recall upon request. All too frequently, the student responds, "I forgot." Events in the classroom and in the student's normal course of life interfere with recall. Interference may be either PROACTIVE or RETROACTIVE.

10. Promoting retention can be a major planning goal for managing learning. Usually you will want to highlight the uniqueness of the material, focus on the meaningfulness of the information, expand the review and summary, encourage the student to get involved in planning the rehearsal or review sessions, and test immediately after the students are presented with the learning materials. Be fair and try to keep the examination environment similar (physically and socially) to the original learning environment.

11. Planning for TRANSFER will be a frequent part of your class preparation. Of course, you will have many options: positive or negative, planned or incidental, and horizontal or vertical transfer. Initially, you will want to emphasize planning; but as students become more able to manage their own learning experiences, you will promote incidental transfer.

12. To plan your learning activities, you will want to diagram your principles, concepts, and so on. The diagram based upon a learning skills hierarchy can help you plan prerequisite learning activities, such as the discriminations required to master a concrete concept or the defined concepts used in a principle.

 KEY TERMS

ADVANCED ORGANIZERS: Statements that give an overview of what the student will be offered in the learning activity.

CONCEPT LEARNING: A skill for naming a pattern of discriminations based on a set of attributes.

CONCRETE CONCEPTS: Concepts that are learned when a person can identify, point to, or select an object.

DEFINED CONCEPTS: Concepts that are learned when a person uses verbal behaviors to identify an object (*freedom* is such a concept).

FORGETTING: The process that has occurred when a previously learned response is not produced on request.

IRRELEVANT ATTRIBUTES: Characteristics that define noncritical aspects of a concept. Irrelevant attributes complicate learning.

KNOWLEDGE OF THE CORRECT RESPONSE: Feedback to the student about the correct response. KCR may be external or internal.

LONG-TERM RECALL: A skill in which the individual can organize stimuli, mediating links, and responses for a long period of time—for example, until exam time.

MEDIATING LINKS: Covert behaviors which relate a stimulus to a response. These links can be picures or verbal chains.

MNEMONIC DEVICES: Simple phrases which cue more complete verbal or motor chains.

OVERLEARNING: A procedure to practice a particular skill many times after mastery has been achieved (as in bike riding).

PRINCIPLES: Rules that state the relationship among two or more concepts.

PROACTIVE INTERFERENCE: Response competition that occurs when a skill learned earlier interferes with a student's performance of an activity learned later.

RELEVANT ATTRIBUTES: Characteristics that help define positive instances of the concept.

RETROACTIVE INTERFERENCE: Response competition that occurs when a later learned skill interferes with the performance of an activity learned earlier.

SHORT-TERM RECALL: A skill that requires the individual to keep the stimulus, mediating link, and response available for a short time, as in a class discussion.

TRANSFER: Using a recently learned skill in a new context.

┌┌ SELF-
└└ TEST

1. In a typical learning hierarchy you will find these patterns:
   a. response chains, concrete concepts, and rules
   b. defined concepts, discriminations, and problem solving
   c. response chains, defined concepts, and problem solving
   d. defined concepts, rules, and problem solving

2. In a basic verbal chain, at least three parts can be identified. These parts are _____, _____, and _____.

3. Verbal chains may be mediated by _____ or by _____ links.

4. The error rate for long verbal chains is usually higher in the
   a. first half
   b. first third
   c. second third
   d. second half

5. Knowledge of the correct response can promote learning and prevent forgetting when the information about the response is
   a. only negative
   b. negative and positive
   c. only positive
   d. equally divided among neutral and positive

6. Concepts seem to be made up of
   a. verbal chains and rules
   b. discriminations and verbal chains
   c. fundamental notions
   d. shared, common elements

7. Teachers managing concept learning can try one of these combinations:
   a. classical, operant, and social learning
   b. S-R, verbal chaining, and mediation
   c. motivation, reinforcement, and time out
   d. S-R, mediation, and cognitive social learning

8. A four-part model for analyzing retention comprises the following skill areas:
   a. _____
   b. _____
   c. _____
   d. _____

9. Interference seems to promote forgetting. You will want to be aware that the proactive interference model looks like this:

experimental	———	———	———
control	———	———	———
	Time 1	Time 2	Time 3

10. Transfer comes in several different varieties. Specify six kinds of transfer:

    _____
    _____
    _____
    _____
    _____
    _____

SELF-TEST KEY

1. d   mediating and coding
2. stimulus   retaining information
    mediating link   mastering the correct response
    response   9. C D D
3. pictorial   D D
    verbal   10. positive
4. c   vertical
5. b   incidental
6. b   negative
7. d   horizontal
8. attending and organizing   planned

CHAPTER 8
Applying Problem-Solving Strategies

LEARNING OBJECTIVES

After reading Chapter 8, answering the self-monitoring questions, and reading any further references of your choice, you will be able to:

1.   Define and give examples of key terms.
2.   Analyze a classroom academic problem using problem-solving procedures.
3.   Explain an affective skill using problem-solving procedures.
4.   Compare creativity, values clarification, and life-career activities for similarities in problem-solving procedures.
5.   Prepare a story on which your creativity may be judged.

What do you need to know about PROBLEM SOLVING to become an effective manager of classroom learning? In what ways can you facilitate students' creativity? All too soon you will be thinking about these questions, and the answers can be very complex. You might, for example, be faced with requests for help: Warren wants to solve a Chinese puzzle box; Emily is trying to create a new Junior Achievement product; and Samantha needs to develop some job-seeking skills.

Students will ask for help in the classroom. Later, on the playground, one of Sam's friends may talk about getting along with her parents. How well you perform in each of these situations will be important for your students and for you.

You will want to help your students become self-directing or self-regulating people. We value the ability to size up a situation and calmly work through its ABCs toward a goal. Each goal behavior—affective skill, valuing, creative act, or solved problem—can be analyzed. Each analysis can reveal subordinate principles and concepts. Completing the analysis and mastering the prerequisite skills can help you and your students reach their goals.

The learning theories and skills hierarchy described in Chapters 5 and 7 are fundamental to the skills discussed in this chapter. Classroom and social situations indicate expected performances, and those performance signals must be detected, processed, and solved. Indeed, rule mastery is only a part of problem solving. The oldest ensign in the Navy once said, "If you know the rules, then you can master the system." (He must have been a particularly sophisticated ensign to use such modern terms!) The ensign was right. Today we say, "If you have mastered the rules, then you can reorder them to solve the problem." You will want your students to master problem-solving skills.

Problem solving can be a great challenge for you. In our experience, we have seen teachers who believe that problem solving occurs when a verbal or motor chain is reproduced. You will want your students to go beyond simply overlearning a verbal chain, defining a concept, or stating a rule. Indeed, the problem solving which we value is a skill that you and your students can easily master. Later in this chapter, we will discuss special kinds of problem-solving skills such as creativity, values clarification, selected affective-social skills, and life-career education.

TEACHING PROBLEM-SOLVING SKILLS

Each level of the learning skill hierarchy brings more and more excitement to the classroom. With each newly mastered skill, the student gains a sense of new freedom, new control, and new direction. For example, as the child masters words and discrimination, parents can become more responsive. Later, as the young student learns mastery over social concepts such as sharing and taking turns, your work will become different. Still later, the more experienced child can follow your rules, the class rules, or the rules of physics. As he guides his behavior with rules, Warren appears to be more and more responsible. For many students and for many teachers, excitement—bright eyes, laughter, and grins—heralds the beginning of problem solving and new freedom. A dyad or a classroom can almost buzz with this anticipation of new ways to learn.

"For many students and for many teachers, excitement—bright eyes, laughter, and grins—herald the beginning of problem solving and new freedom." (Burt Glinn/Magnum)

FOCUS ON PROBLEM SOLVING

Problem solving can be defined as the relating of two or more principles or rules to reach a goal. Once a problem has been solved, the problem solver gains additional control over the environment. For example, little brothers feel a great sense of power when they can turn room lights on and off. Let us suppose that your little brother began to work on this power during his afternoon "nap." He moved a chair to reach the light. During this afternoon quiet time, he mastered several skills involved in light switching (moving the chair, reaching to touch the switch, coordinating fingers to touch the switch, and pushing the switch up or pulling it down). He has applied the problem-solving procedure to relate each rule in turning the light on and off. Later, to your surprise, this little boy displayed these several environmental management skills (1) while watching television, (2) after bedtime, and (3) when you asked for help in turning on the light. Of course, you do not always need this kind of help. The child will have to learn which environmental cues signal the better responses. Later your little brother's growing problem-solving skills will generalize to climbing trees, scaling fences at Halloween, and observing you and a friend on a date! Little brothers and sisters, teachers, and parents can master the discriminations as well as related problem-solving skills.

PROBE 8-1

Problem solving starts when children are very young. It is not very complicated—two or three ideas just suddenly click. Describe one of your earliest problem-solving experiences. Write at least an entire page about it. Try to describe the motor chains involved in this early learning activity.

Problem-solving patterns

The question of how people solve problems is not a new one. Many theories of problem solving have been proposed, discussed, and dismissed or revised. John Dewey (1910), in a powerful little book called *How We Think,* described some ideas which have stayed with us. He suggested that problem solvers probably go through the following stages on their way to a solution.

1. *Perplexity.* Presentation of a problem, which is accompanied by a feeling of perplexity. The individual observes, feels, and is discomforted by the information.

2. *Problem definition.* Definition and clarification of the problem. Clarification is an important procedure which helps one to suspend judgment. This stage takes time.

3. *Hypothesis suggestion.* Suggestion of a hypothesis—a period of adventure and speculation. It is a safe time. Judgments are not rendered. A good problem solver does not act in this stage.

4. *Relate and elaborate rules.* Elaboration and relating of rules that help assign values and consequences to alternative hypotheses.

5. *Test hypotheses.* Verification or testing of the hypothesis through "experimentation."

John Dewey's seventy-year-old ideas about problem solving have remained with us, and we shall refer to them frequently throughout the remainder of this chapter. Can you create a mnemonic device to help you retain these five stages?

Cognitive social learning theory suggests that problem-solving skills are learned in a hierarchical manner. A young child, Warren, begins to learn about problem solving by manipulating objects. In the same way, your little brother engaged in problem solving by moving his chair to reach the light switch. Developmental changes described earlier—in Chapters 2, 3, and 4—occur as children grow older. As Warren becomes more experienced, he masters problem solving by manipulating names or concepts instead of physical objects. In the course of this development and hierarchical mastery, prompts and models play an important role. Young people learn problem-solving skills through prompts from their "teachers" and from observing rewarded models. Adults frequently expand a child's or a student's labels (your professors do it all the time). In the cognitive social learning view of problem solving, we see the environment (peers, teachers, or parents) modeling, verifying, and rewarding effective problem-solving skills (Rosenthal & Zimmerman, 1978).

Problem solving can be learned anywhere

Many children learn about problem solving while playing in a sandbox or at naptime. Problem solving occurs frequently throughout the day. Sometimes the problem solving is nonacademic, as when the child finds a shortcut to the store or a way to fix a radio.

Many students with goals and problems similar to Warren's, Emily's, and Sam's will seek your assistance. You will find that helping students to solve problems can be a lot of fun. Indeed, both you and the students become very different people as you master more and more problem-solving skills. We are going to suggest a problem-solving checklist consisting of nine steps. We believe that problem-solving procedures persist after a solution has been identified. Problem solving includes making sure that the solution is a good one. The plan of action is monitored in our problem-solving procedure. Of course, how you will use the problem-solving checklist or change it depends on your students, their goals, and your style of classroom management (see Table 8-1):

Table 8-1. Problem-solving procedure

Activity	Explanation
1. Assess your own strengths and weaknesses with regard to information and skill.	1. When a problem solver begins to work, much information is needed. Data can be collected from test results, observations, and interviews. The assessment should result in an awareness, appreciation, and documentation of the individual's or the problem's strengths or weaknesses. For example, Warren wants to make an Edison light bulb. He will have to assess his resources: physical, financial, and his own skills. He can read the encyclopedia, try to master soldering equipment, and assess his manual dexterity and patience. Without the necessary resources, information, and skills, Warren might decide to (a) learn the skills, (b) acquire the materials, (c) gather the information, or (d) choose a new problem.
2. Consider the broadly stated goals and refine them into manageable objectives.	2. A problem solver must spend time clarifying the goals and specifying the subordinate objectives. The ABC model and task analysis can be used to specify subordinate goals. Basically, the model and the analysis can be used to build a treelike hierarchy of the goal, its subordinate activities, and the antecedent-consequence relationship among these activities. For example, Warren can translate "need a source of energy" into "gather two 6-watt batteries, four short wires, two thin screws." Presto—the stuff for a lightbulb!
3. Match information.	3. Many a career decision has been based upon one or two test results and some vague idea about what women and men should do. For many people, problem solving seemed to follow this sequence, "Well, I know what I can do and I know what I can't do, so I'll get on with it!" Unfortunately, some problem solvers stumble onto an early solution. A quick answer can be a very reinforcing event. The student stops solving and now *you* have the problem! You will want to model, in your classroom, a more complete problem-solving procedure, such as the one we are presenting.
4. Generate and list alternative actions.	4. In this activity of the problem-solving procedure, Warren takes an active role. We like activities. In this and the following

Table 8-1. Problem-solving procedure (Continued)

Activity	Explanation
	activities, the problem solver can demonstrate self-directed or self-regulated behaviors. By generating and listing many alternative actions, he or she can "break a lock" on a single solution and probe what is out there. Excitement can be a valuable reinforcer for students like Emily or Warren when they see that a problem can be solved in many ways.
5. Assign consequences to the alternative actions.	5. Once the long list of alternatives has been generated, many different clusters of information can be used in this activity. Emily can ask questions about her skills, her willingness to master deficient skills, about costs, materials (tools, paints, fabrics), schedules, and a host of other things. The assignment activity helps her discover the importance or value of each bit of information or each skill involved in solving the problem. The answers can be put together to assign a weight to each alternative action.
6. Rank the alternative actions.	6. The weighted alternative actions can be reordered. Earlier, they were simply listed (probably the first or second item on the list was a favorite). Now Emily has a lot more information. The reordering can be perplexing, and this can be a very stabilizing experience. The previously considered information—needed skills, required information, and clarified values—puts a price on each alternative action. (Emily never anticipated that a Junior Achievement project could be so carefully considered.) The reordered list can be put together in a fairly stable way. Emily can probably identify the first and second alternative actions: (*a*) etching monograms on paperweights; (*b*) preparing a calendar with regional scenes.
7. Plan the primary action.	7. All this and still no action! Wait. A plan of action for a problem solver basically answers the question: Who will do what while the goal-directed activity occurs? For example, Samantha might ask you to observe her job-interview skills in a role-play situation. In this example, Sam has involved a cast of

Table 8-1. Problem-solving procedure (Continued)

Activity	Explanation
	thousands in her problem solving. This approach is fine. Later, Sam can manage her own job-finding behaviors. As you may have suspected, we see *problem solving* and *self-regulation* as interchangeable terms.
8. Monitor primary action plan and revise if necessary.	8. Once Emily or Sam starts to act on a primary plan of action, two other activities must also occur: (*a*) continuous monitoring of performance as it approaches a goal and (*b*) prompt revising of the plan should performance fall behind schedule or below some planned criterion. Emily's Junior Achievement partners will be greatly interested in her product development efforts. They will participate in many of these problem-solving activities, including monitoring of the purposeful performance.
9. Integrate problem-solving skill for each individual.	9. Each new problem creates and signals a new sequence of activities. The events which we described are merely a checklist of activities. Each problem solver in each new situation will find new or uniquely different combinations of principles or rules to reorder into a manageable, purposeful plan of action.

All too frequently, the excited young problem solver encounters a new environment in school. The rules and expectations do not support the kinds of spontaneous problem solving that is encouraged among pre-schoolers. Indeed, that style of problem solving is generally extinguished in the elementary grades. Many classroom teachers obtain reinforcement from a quiet, predictable student environment. We want to change that trend. We urge you to try a carefully planned, guided approach to problem solving. Indeed, we are strongly committed to helping you promote problem solving in your classroom.

THREE CRITERIA FOR PROBLEM SOLVING

Our cognitive social learning model is deceptively simple. We say that problem solving requires the person to take two mastered rules and combine them to accomplish a given purpose. By now, you know that complex learning skills are not that simple. Let's do a little refining: *new, correct,* and *common* can help define problem solving. First, the solution must be new to the person. The repeated solution of an old arithmetic problem or a Chinese puzzle is not really an example of problem solving. However, should you or one of your students figure out, for the first time, how to connect nine dots (three rows of three dots each) using only four straight lines, you have solved a problem. That four-line solution meets the criterion of newness. Second, the solution must be correct or workable. Children, students, and some adults "solve a problem" by bashing the parts together. That's not problem solving. The solution (such as connecting nine dots with four lines) commonly exists in only one correct form. (Try it!) Third, the criterion of commonness is an especially important distinction. Thus, in the model of cognitive social learning theory, problem solving requires a person to take two mastered rules and put them together correctly in a way that is new to this person.

Later we will talk about creativity. You will see that creativity is simply a special kind of problem solving. We believe that correctness and commonality play an important part in distinguishing between problem solving and creativity. Creative problem solving produces both correct and incorrect answers as well as less than common products. For the present, let's focus on problem-solving activities.

ACTIVITIES FOR MASTERING PROBLEM SOLVING

Classroom learning of problem-solving skills can involve shared learning experiences. Your students can contribute to your planned learning activities by being models, sources of reinforcement, and "teachers." In the long run, you will want students to master independent problem solving and become self-regulated persons. Let's see how students can share in problem-solving mastery.

Student activities in problem solving Solutions to problems don't just appear without prior experiences. Warren, working on his puzzles, or Emily, trying to create a new product, will have had some prior experiences that prepared them for their tasks. These previous experiences provide the "stuff" of problem solving. To solve a problem a student must be able to (1) search for previous rules and principles and (2) perform prerequisite behaviors.

Search for previous rules and principles Young people learn new rules or principles each day. In Chapter 7, we described how they attend to, code, and retrieve these rules. Many people use these procedures to organize their experiences. In the search activity, the student probably uses many different strategies to find usable rules. Emily might look for common elements of a concept such as a straight line or a common word form. She might restate her problem in the form of a specific objective or in her own terms. Emily might try to relate principles by a series of mediating links. Whatever Emily does use as a search strategy, she will review her mastered principles for the most appropriate ones.

Perform prerequisite behaviors This activity is an old friend. Indeed, for each learning skill level, you want the student to perform each of the prerequisite skills. In the event that a skill cannot be performed, both you and the student can turn to the ABC model, of which you are pastmasters by now. Use it. Bring the student up to competency. Once the student has again mastered the prerequisite behaviors, both of you are ready to get on with learning.

Once in a while students like Samantha will ask for help in learning how to develop some skills for finding a job. On the one hand, you might say, "Sorry, Sam. That's the counselor's business!" For you, the thought of analyzing "finding a job," of encouraging Sam to assess herself with the ABC model, and of structuring the best set of prompts to recall information and skills might be too much. Finding a job is a fairly complex problem-solving skill. After all, Sam has been using the ABC model to analyze problems for several years, so she should be able to do it herself. However, as a classroom teacher who is committed to facilitating individual development, you see Sam's goal as an opportunity to teach problem-solving skills. Samantha may be able to learn how to find a job either by listening to you lecture on a procedure or through your guidance in seeking out the better principles for her particular goal. In helping Sam or her friends, you will want to be aware of these guidelines:

• *Make sure that you have mastered the problem-solving skills yourself.* Throughout your teaching career, children, students, colleagues, and parents are going to watch you solve problems. As a French teacher, you might go to dinner with some friends who ask you to pronounce "go toit," "cho-pho-use," and "mac-hin-ery." You can imagine the hilarity when you mispronounce *go to it, chop house,* and *machinery.* You will always be on a spot, so please be a master problem solver!

You will want to be a unique person who can help students solve problems such as those involved in finding a job. This calls for a special kind of flexibility and planning. You will need to tap Sam's or any other student's previous interests, experiences, and knowledge. The "right" question, its timing, and its delivery must be artfully mixed with your planned curricular and social interaction in the classroom. These questions, their intentions, their effect, and your management of the social environment take us back to Chapter 5. Earlier, we talked about the art and skill of reinforcement. *Art* and *skill* are the creative bywords for you as a manager and a model of problem-solving skills.

• *Clarify the problem-solving goals.* Problem solving, like other learning skills, occurs faster when there are clear goals and objectives. You will want to state the goals in terms of a skill or information deficit. For example, Sam wants to find a job. This kind of goal statement is almost clear. A little probing might reveal the desired working hours, the type of working conditions, and the pay. One of your youngsters wants a 9-to-5 job, good pay, little physical exertion, and an apartment. Given this kind of a "hidden agenda" in a simple goal statement, you will want

"Interaction with peers as well as with teachers can be used to facilitate problem-solving mastery." (Sybil Shelton/Peter Arnold)

to clarify the goals. Three steps seem to be helpful in goal clarification: (1) state the goal as a deficit (for example, "I want to earn more money"); (2) encourage the students like Sam and Warren to apply the ABC model with the original goal stated as the "B"; and (3) restate the goal in the student's own words.

• *Analyze the subordinate goal skills.* A job for Sam is an overall goal. You will want to help her identify the subordinate goals. A good way to get started is to work back from the overall goal. In a sense you are building an activity tree, with "finding a job" as the topmost branch. (The activity tree might look like your product for the learning activity in Chapter 7.) Each subordinate goal can be analyzed by the ABC model so that, finally, you will be able to list competencies, consequences, deficit skills, strategies for change or mastery, and the antecedents. As you can see, the task analysis can be time-consuming. You will remember from Chapter 4 that it must be carefully planned so you and your students can focus on the goal.

• *Encourage the student(s) to propose hypotheses.* Facilitating mastery of the problem-solving skills requires much patience. In many learning situations, the answer is provided to the learner. Often, simply listening and learning produces mastery of a very narrow range of solutions. Warren, for example, has probably been through a period of receptive rule learning (Ausubel, 1978). For many classrooms, receptive principle learning is simply "easier." You will want to guide the learner into a more interactive learning style (Glaser, 1977). Interaction with peers as well as with teachers can be used to facilitate problem-solving mastery. In Sam's case, you might encourage her by using one of the following strategies:

1. Restructure her problem. For example, simply by juggling some of the related ideas involved in the project of finding a job, you and Sam can hit upon alternative hypotheses.

2. Consider each suggestion carefully. Students frequently try to "test" whether you really mean "let's try to solve the problem, Sam. Let's try to help you find a job." They will propose the most outlandish alternatives and watch your eyes, mouth muscles, and knuckles. Once they get the idea that you really intend to help them, you are on your way!

3. Repeat each idea by reflecting it back to the student. Even the most doubting student will want to hear your version of his or her idea, hypothesis, or alternative strategy. Thus the student, a small group, or the entire class will become involved in the job-finding problem-solving discussion.

4. Use role playing to stimulate new hypotheses. Sam and her friends will imitate your presentation of your hypothesis almost down to your mannerisms.

5. Be prepared to "incubate" the idea. When you incubate an idea, you leave it alone for a while to see what hatches. Problem solving takes energy. Alternative goals and learning strategies can really get mixed up. Please don't be afraid to suspend problem solving for a while. By "putting the idea on a back burner," you are encouraging the students to work on alternative strategies at their own pace.

• *Help the student(s) solve the problem symbolically.* A great temptation for students and teachers is to act precipitously. Suspend your judgment. Too often, when you have reached a quick solution, something is left out. In this guideline you will want students to state the solution in their own words; they might, for example, describe their solution orally. Often by simply saying each step in the procedure, the student will uncover "bugs." Emily or Sam could write up the solution. Warren could get materials and demonstrate his solution. Either kind of verbal or symbolic presentation has the same purpose, which is to solve the problem symbolically. By using verbal or written prompts and gradually fading them, you can encourage students to practice the solution before they actually settle on it.

We see three benefits from this patient approach toward a solution:

1. Try out alternatives. Primary and secondary strategies or alternatives are tried out. Each new trial probably is closer and closer to the real world, so that a kind of "successive approximation" occurs.

2. Obtain feedback. The problem solver obtains two kinds of feedback. In the first kind, Emily discovers whether her idea will work. That "go or no-go" information is very important to a problem solver. Second, Samantha can receive critical support from her classmates

and you. She might ask whether she should wear a special suit or how she can best state her interests. Social support from others can be rewarding.

3. Plan for generalization. A strategy that has been carefully selected, tried out, and evaluated by the problem solver (one of the students or you) stands a much better chance of being generalized to a new situation such as another job application.

● *Be open, calm, and systematic.* Throughout these activities we have talked about things which are primarily for the student. This sixth guideline is for both you and the student. You will want to model openness, calmness, and order as much as possible. Each one of these behaviors is itself a masterable skill. The ABC model can be applied successfully, should you want to master these clusters of skills.

1. Keep yourself open to different possibilities. If you close down (so much that you are not open) after one or two alternatives, you may ignore good possibilities. Many people are not aware that they typically consider only the boxlike shape of the nine dots (in the puzzle described earlier) or that the C-clamp can be used to make

"Remember, 'Incubation can work.' " (C. Wolinsky/Stock, Boston)

a longer pole out of two shorter ones (Maier, 1930). Observe yourself. How many different alternative solutions do you typically generate? Should you come up with one or two on the average, you might try to come up with one or two more.

2. Observe how much guidance you give students in their own problem solving. Here we have an art-skill kind of situation. On the one hand, too much guidance (too many prompts, too much information, too many models) can overmanage the learning of problem-solving skills. A very narrow range of solutions can result. Probably the solution resulting from your overguidance would appear to be the same as yours. On the other hand, too little guidance (too little information, too few prompts, and no models) can throw the students into a trial-and-error learning situation. A balance between too much and too little guidance in problem solving is most helpful.

   You will want to find out how much guidance helps a particular student perform better. For example, you can record one of your classroom discussions. Later, you can count how many prompts you gave. How often did you restate the student's suggested strategy? How much time (a half second? three seconds?) do you allow a student for stating an alternative strategy? The answers to these questions can serve as the beginning of your own development of problem-solving skills.

3. Allow sufficient time for yourself and your students. Be systematic. Try to budget enough time for a long classroom or dyadic discussion of the problem and its solution. Remember, "Incubation can work." You might continue the discussion a day or so later. Of course, you can prompt your students to "Please keep the problem in mind. Try to come up with some other solutions. We'll talk about it Friday."

PROBE 8-2

Think of a problem you have had in the last three months. For example, you might have needed help with a chemistry problem, wanted to talk to a friend, or tried to find a job. List and briefly describe your activities. Use the procedure given in Table 8-1 to evaluate your own problem solving. Discuss your analysis in a small group during class time.

Problem solving is the highest skill level in the learning hierarchy. Mastery of this skill sets the stage for a variety of self-directed and self-regulated activities—creativity, clarification of values, affective-social skills, and life-career planning. You might say that our problem-solving procedure is large, cumbersome, and unreasonable. You might be right.

Many problem solvers go through these procedures without making long lists of this and that: first graders divide an allowance, ninth graders select an umpty-umpth boy friend, and bookstore managers or the President perform all the problem-solving activities we have discussed in various levels of detail.

In our experience, the more successful problem solvers seem to benefit from each previous use of the problem-solving procedure. In a sense, the "margin of error" becomes a little narrower on each new use of the procedure. In a larger sense, you will want your students to have many problem-solving experiences so they will gain mastery and become self-regulated people. You might even want them to become creative!

 **TEACHING CREATIVITY**

At some point in the problem solver's regulated life, a dilemma will occur: two or three nearly equal solutions will be developed. If you can help to resolve such a dilemma, you will be facilitating problem solving and creativity.

FOCUS ON CREATIVITY

Creativity and problem solving share the same kinds of criteria. A very important but small difference separates the two. In our opening example, we said the time will come when problem solving produces two nearly equal solutions. Each solution will meet the individual's problem-solving criterion of newness. Each solution can be located on a continuum of commonality (from frequent or very common to unique, singular, rare, or uncommon). We are saying now that creative solutions are fairly uncommon solutions. Further, each solution may be placed along another continuum from correct to not-so-correct (from a tumble clothes dryer to a Rube Goldberg conveyor-belt dryer). Indeed, many creative solutions have often been dismissed because they were not useful at that particular time. Timing of the creative product is extremely important. Creativity, like problem solving, produces a product (Cole, 1969) which can become "old" and can later be used to facilitate new, creative activities.

The creative products themselves have a "life cycle" from newness, uncommonness, and unique purposefulness to oldness, conventionality, and sometimes usefulness. For example, Emily may prepare a truly creative Junior Achievement product. Over time, its newness may change to become common and useful. Indeed, creative products may become fundamental and common elements of principles, concepts, and chains. Look at B. F. Skinner's creative reordering of available information (Skinner, 1953). He built a theory. Later, the theory became a very fundamental element of classroom management, mediation, and facilitation. Skinner's creative theory survives today because it is useful to many people in many situations. The uncreative theories tend to disappear.

===== **PROBE 8-3** =====

Think about one of your creative moments as a very young child or as a student in the primary grades. What did you do? What was the product? Share this experience with a classmate or your teacher.

DIVERGENT VIEWS OF CREATIVITY

In a very real sense, CREATIVITY has been its own victim. Students and teachers have applied versions of creative problem solving, and as a result more definitions and examples of creative skills have appeared. Sometimes this new information is not well ordered. Creativity's divergency has contributed to its present conflicting status.

Usually creativity is discussed in close relationship to problem solving. In view of its singular, usually common, and correct solutions, problem solving is often called *convergent thinking*. After working through problem-solving procedures such as those shown in Table 8-1, the individual converges upon the solution relentlessly. In contrast, creativity with its many, usually uncommon, and sometimes not-so-correct solutions is often called *divergent thinking*. It is this divergency that has produced the problems connected with creativity.

Traditional views of creativity

Many psychologists have tried to account for the causes, characteristics, and consequences of creativity—with widely divergent results. These efforts include Joy Paul Guilford's monumental structure of the intellect (Guilford, 1967; Guilford & Hoepfner, 1971). In a series of studies, Guilford and his associates have developed 120 subtests to assess the elements of the intellect and creativity. That's a lot for a future teacher to recall and use. Paul Torrance has spent a tremendous amount of energy learning about creativity from students' and teachers' points of view. Torrance (1970) looks at the creative product as one which has novelty and value. These characteristics seem to be similar to the ones we discussed earlier. Arthur W. Staats (1971) takes us a step further, holding that creativity occurs when novel environmental stimuli call up novel responses. For example, children who are learning the meanings of selected words often put them together in novel ways. (Each family has its traditional stories about what father said at the wrong time and so on.) As you can see, we can follow a fairly extensive set of definitions and descriptions of creativity. Let's take a look at one set of definitions and descriptions.

A skill approach to creativity

Our approach to creativity is built upon the foundation laid so far in this book. Whatever you want to call creativity, you can help students learn how to manage it. We prefer to talk about creative problem solving.

STUDY 8-1: TEACHING CREATIVE PROBLEM-SOLVING SKILLS

Glover and Gary (1976) worked with eight fourth- and fifth-graders. The procedures were simple. (You can use the same procedures with eleventh-graders in literature or with adults in continuing education.)

First, they defined the four components of creativity. The definition had to be observable, measurable, and specific (remember Chapter 5). Raters were used to judge student performances. Glover and Gary used these four operational definitions: fluency, the number of different uses of a word; flexibility, the number of different verb forms used; elaboration, the number of words per response; and originality, the student's *new* uses of a verb. These definitions are elaborated upon in the original article, which you might want to read.

Glover and Gary wanted a "normal" classroom activity. They decided to play the unusual uses game developed by Torrance (1966), which was played for ten minutes each day during the baseline and the four conditions of the study (Figure 8-1).

The rules were slightly different in each condition. For the *baseline*, the students were simply asked to list as many different uses of a noun (like *box, brick, book*) as they could in ten minutes. The raters applied the four operational definitions to the lists, computing baseline scores in each area for each child. On

the sixth day, the definitions of fluency, elaboration, and so on were explained to the students. On that same day, the students were divided into two teams. They were told that each day the team with the most points would get ten additional minutes of recess, some extra cookies, and another carton of milk. Both teams could win if their scores were close. On the sixth day and every day thereafter, Glover or Gary wrote on the blackboard the creative component words—for example, *fluency, flexibility,* and so on. They circled the one in operation for the week and announced, for example, "one point for each different verb" (fluency). Thus, after the baseline period, the study had four stages (fluency, flexibility, elaboration, and originality). In each stage on each day, the students wrote rapidly for the next ten minutes.

In Figure 8-1, we see some of the different patterns that were obtained. Check marks indicate elaboration responses on each day. The line is the plot of the flexibility responses over the duration of the study. The results show that during the period when the points were awarded for different verb forms (flexibility), more verbs were used by the students. Glover and Gary also found that elaboration behaviors really increased when they were reinforced. Fluency and originality stayed

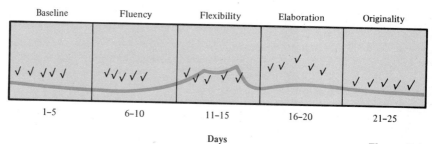

Days

Figure 8-1

Selected patterns of creative problem-solving behaviors. (Adapted from Glover, J., & Gary, A. L. Procedures to increase some aspects of creativity. *Journal of Applied Behavior Analysis,* 1976, 9, 79–84.)

roughly the same throughout the study. Indeed, the five-week program meaningfully raised the students' scores on Torrance's Thinking Creatively With Words test.

Glover and Gary demonstrated that a carefully planned, closely observed, and well-recorded set of systematic classroom strategies can be used to increase behaviors related to creativity and to scores on a test of creativity. As a classroom teacher, you will want to consider these strategies to facilitate selected creative problem-solving skills.

Under the right conditions, any youngster can become creative. We want to discuss these conditions. According to our approach, based on the cognitive social learning theory, creativity occurs when a unique combination of environmental stimuli and planned learning activities produce a new, novel, and useful product. We are using both the ABC model and the learning skills hierarchy to look at the conditions for creative behaviors. With our approach, we believe you can manage the environment, organize the learning activities, and set a proper stage for creative behaviors; you will then be in a good position to facilitate creativity.

First, managing the environment means that you will want to understand the antecedents and consequences influencing the potentially creative person. In Chapter 5, we talked about the ABC analysis. You will want to use this approach as you and your students plan strategies for learning. Paul Torrance (1970) has suggested that creativity has four components—fluency, flexibility, originality, and elaboration. In Study 8-1, we give you an idea of each of these components. You might use the ABC model to help a student like Emily plan how to go about becoming a creative problem solver.

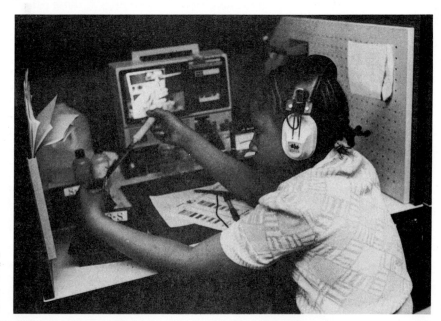

"Creativity is a special kind of problem solving." (Rhoda Sidney/ Monkmeyer)

Second, planned learning activities which lead to creative behaviors have been discussed in Chapters 5 and 7 as well as the present chapter. Indeed, we gave you a problem-solving procedure in Table 8-1. Emily will do well to master the skills that are prerequisite to problem solving before using ideas from Table 8-1 as a checklist. "Hey, wait a minute," you may be thinking, "this sounds too simple." If that's your reaction, you're pretty close to being on the right track. We believe that creativity is a special kind of problem solving.

Third, it is really difficult to set the stage for learning how to be creative. We don't know how to do it. We are fairly sure that creative problem solving occurs under two very unique conditions: (1) when the problem solver—Emily, for instance—has "flooded" a problem with her ideas (indeed, these many ideas can be viewed as many discriminative stimuli) and (2) when unique stimuli are related in a unique manner, as when a mistake occurs. (How often has a mistake led to an important discovery?)

At this point, you should be feeling confident about using the ABC model and about the learning skills hierarchy. Now the challenge is to begin to put them together so that your students will be able to assemble ideas into novel and useful products.

PROBE 8-4

How can you become a creative teacher? What techiques can you use to become fluent, flexible, original, and elaborative? Do you want to? Discuss your answers with your adviser or with a friend.

ACTIVITIES TO FACILITATE CREATIVE PROBLEM SOLVING

You and your students will be highly interactive in creative problem solving. This theme of sharing responsibility is by now a familiar one. Each student will have some responsibilities, and you will use some facilitative prompts as your students become more self-directing and creative.

Student activities in creative problem solving

In creative problem solving, the individual seems to face an overwhelming task: work. Creativity takes perspiration (sorry, Tom Edison). Suppose Emily wants to create a new Junior Achievement product. First, she must become immersed in the field. In this case "the field" can be an idea for an artist or an author, a mud pie for a child, or a stew for father's turn at cooking dinner. You may laugh, but creativity does not belong to an exalted few. You and your students can learn how to be creative problem solvers. Emily must observe all the elements, facts, and rules that are relevant to her field. Second, the result of this observation can be a systematic reporting or organizing of the relationships among these facts, elements, or rules. The student can be asking "How can all these

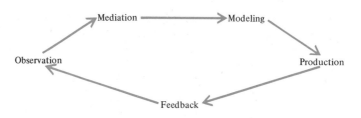

Figure 8-2
Creative problem-
solving activities.

things be put together so they make some sense?'' and ''Does each idea fit? If not, why not?'' This systematic questioning is just like the ABC analysis of learning. This step requires mediation skills.

Later, Emily or any other creative problem solver can observe high-status, valued, competent, or reinforced models perform problem-solving skills in the relevant field. For example, Emily can read *Forbes* magazine for stories about successful business people. It is these three activities—detailed observation, mediation, and modeling—that can produce creative results. In Figure 8-2, we give you a diagram of creative problem-solving activities.

In this figure, detailed observation is emphasized. These crucial observations can help the creative problem solver pinpoint relationships among facts, elements, and rules. Through these observations and the related activities of imitation and mastery, Emily can become immersed in her creative challenge.

Emily can put together her product with some support from you. Production of a Junior Achievement item, for example, tells us that she is not merely performing a modeled behavior but is also putting together skills and observations that were previously separate. This new behavior is an example of mediation (see Chapters 4 and 5). This product might be creative (new, unique, and purposeful). It might not be creative. In Figure 8-2, both kinds of information about the product are returned to Emily so she can change her observations. Students experience these creative problem-solving activities repeatedly until the creative product is produced or until the need for the product disappears.

The approach to creativity based on the cognitive social learning theory emphasizes classroom interaction. This planned interaction may be between you and a student in a dyad, between two students in a group, or between you and a class. You will want to provide for a high level of classroom interaction in facilitating creative problem solving. As a classroom teacher helping students like Emily, you will find the following guidelines helpful:

GUIDELINES
FOR
TEACHING

**Creative Problem
Solving**

Prepare yourself for creative problem solving. You may be asking ''Why do I have to prepare myself for creative problem solving?'' We have found that preparing ourselves for creative problem solving is a giant step toward student mastery of this important skill. You will want to become involved in facilitating creative problem solving in the following ways:

1. Practice prompting questions and statements, reflecting students' ideas, restating their questions, and encouraging their experimentation or risk taking. You will want to communicate your respect for your students' questions, ideas, and statements. We believe that if you practice these activities before you get involved in a creative problem-solving session, it will benefit you as well as your students (Meichenbaum, 1977).

2. Master a balance between providing too many prompts and supportive statements and too few restatements and supporting activities. This is a delicate balance. It is a matter of art and skill.

3. Avoid making judgments that appear to be "premature." Many

"Early in the schooling experience, the bubbly, uncontrolled enthusiasm for creative efforts is dampened." (E. Herwig/Stock, Boston)

experienced and not-so-experienced teachers give students like
Emily "the word." Be patient; you might lose Emily that way.
Maintain eye contact while you are "thinking." Smile and delay
your response.

* *Make sure that the students have mastered problem-solving skills and
procedures.* This guideline has a double message: (1) Be ready to retrain
your students in missing prerequisite skills and (2) Make sure your
students work their way through a procedure similar to that shown in
Table 8-1. This guideline is fundamental to a student's creative problem
solving.
* *Encourage students to go beyond the facts.* A child's enthusiasm for
creative effort is often uncontrolled. A youngster might create stories
about an invisible character or might paint Daddy's picture so he is a
rainbow of colors. However, at some time early in the schooling
experience, the bubbly, uncontrolled enthusiasm for creative efforts is
dampened. We are not urging you to promote chaos in the name of
creativity. Instead, you will want to spend your energies in setting the
stage for creative problem solving.

Many of your students, their parents, and your professional colleagues
will want to "stick to the facts," insisting, for example, that zebras must
be black and white. This is fine for skills which are prerequisite to
problem solving. However, you will want your students to ask "if, then"
questions. (For example, "If we remove . . . or if we add parts, then
what will happen?") Such questions can encourage students to go beyond
the facts. The "if, then" statements call for the use of the hypothesis-
testing idea that we talked about in the problem-solving section of this
chapter. In the classroom, you can encourage students to go beyond the
facts by assigning different colors, shapes, or sounds to objects. What
new verbal chains develop from pink elephants or purple cows? New
discriminations, concepts, rules, and problem solving can result from
simply changing a unique relationship in the problem-solving learning
hierarchy. You will want students to "use their imagination"—to reach
out for new ideas in the classroom, on the playground, and at home.

* *Promote a supportive classroom environment.* One of your most
difficult challenges will be to get your students to take chances. For years
children and students have been urged to "do the right thing." They may
or may not have done so. Then, they have either been ignored for doing
the right thing or punished for not doing it. In either case, they have
probably "played it pretty close to the vest." You will want to encourage
students to be willing to suggest alternatives:

1. Try to create ambiguities. The suggestion that you might not know
   the answer is a fine start. Young people tend to abhor that vacuum.

2. Encourage students to elaborate. "What do you mean?" seems to be an especially facilitating question that brings out an idea in detail. Once more, we encourage you to look more closely at the Glover and Gary study (Study 8-1) for ideas on promoting creativity.

3. Use provocative questions. Specially designed questions can be used to reduce students' rigidity. You will have to generate your own special questions. For you, each week will bring a new set of provocative questions. Issues on prisoners' rights, the rights of women and children, and the environment seem to change weekly. Try to keep ahead of the changes.

4. Put inconsistent ideas into new relationships. In the last few years, some very powerful people have spent time in prison. Many of these people come out of prisons urging prison reforms. The experiences these people have had seem to have produced an openness to alternatives. In the classroom, the situation need not be so severe: place the brown-eyed students first in each class activity for one day. This simple classroom strategy can let selected students experience new relationships. But be careful; in this simple exercise, some students can get hurt. You will want to be sensitive to the new needs of your students in this experience.

• *Help the student produce a product.* Throughout this creative problem-solving procedure, we have been purposeful. A product must be derived from all this effort. The product of creative problem solving might be usable at some later date. For example, many creative products are too advanced for their time. You might recall that, in the 1960's, computer-supported multimedia instructional systems were only gleams in educators' eyes. By the mid-1970s, we dropped back and moved two steps to the side for our assault on the eighties. We are looking ahead. Indeed, the creative product may not be the ultimate solution; it may be merely a plateau on the way to some greater goal.

• *Give students opportunities to maintain their problem-solving skills.* Creative problem solving—like operatic singing, the decathlon events, or a foreign language—has to be practiced. Keep your students in shape for creative problem solving. Keep them primed. Instead of scheduling problem solving between Shakespeare and modern drama, you will want to try to help students maintain their skills in the following ways:

1. Provide "free time" on a once-a-day basis for divergent production of stories or of art work.

2. Set up a special creative problem-solving program for selected students. For example, Chris enjoys watching sports events. He can earn TV-watching points by writing stories. Of course, each

word must be correctly spelled. You can add bonus points for new themes or for using adjectives and adverbs appropriately. (Do these ideas sound like Torrance's flexibility and elaboration?)

3. Integrate selected curricular packages into your regular schedule. Creative problem-solving skills can be maintained by such packages as *Productive Thinking Program* (Crutchfield, 1969) or *Man: A Course of Study* (MACOS) (Bruner, 1966). Both these programs require a good deal of preparation before you use them. You will probably have an opportunity to work with these curricular packages before you meet your future classes.

PROBE 8-5

A teacher of creative children has a special challenge—a challenge not unlike that faced by a teacher of slow learners. Think about teaching activities for facilitating creative problem solving. Do you now have those necessary skills and ways of working with people? If you do not, how are you going to gain or acquire those skills? Try to build your own self-regulation plan. Share it with your teacher or with a helpful classmate.

Recap on creative problem solving

Let's try to bring some ideas together. Earlier in this chapter we said that problem solving is convergent: a relentless pursuit of the solution. You have had friends who have been "untouchable" as chemistry students or as mechanical problem solvers. These friends can give you an idea of what we mean by *convergent*. Later, we suggested that creative problem solving is divergent. The creative problem solver searches for several solutions, works on them, and finally solves the problem with the better solution. For example, you may recall one or two of your friends in English or in drama who have been creative problem solvers.

In many problem-solving situations, a problem is presented to the person. In other situations, the creative problem solver seeks out a problem. To find a problem, the person must make sense out of inconsistencies. Once this is done, it is possible to develop creative solutions and subsequently converge upon the better one. In a sense, each creative problem solver has a self-regulated cognitive strategy—attending to environmental cues, coding data, retrieving experiences and information, and using a problem-solving procedure—for approaching each new situation. How creative problem solvers approach math, English, or a new friend can be viewed as unique or nontraditional. All of us—peers, teachers, principals, and parents—must be sensitive, supportive, and adaptable to one another when we are using these creative problem-solving skills.

TEACHING
AFFECTIVE SKILLS

AFFECTIVE EDUCATION is a relatively new area in the classroom. For years, education has rolled forward relentlessly; grandparents, parents, and probably some of your friends were trained by "*the* curriculum." In those days, fathers could help their children with base-ten math and mothers were able to prompt the diagramming of sentences. Parents were comfortable; they understood what was going on in the classroom. In the last twenty years, however, people have tried to change the curriculum— new math, new science, new reading, new career education, and new "et cetera" have been offered to education. How little did they know! Students could have warned the curriculum changers "Never wake a sleeping curriculum" (sorry dragon). The tranquillity of the past was disturbed; controversy and criticism followed the curricular changes.

FOCUS ON AFFECTIVE SKILLS

Many of these curricular changes really did not involve the "whole student." What had happened is that the math student, the reading student, or the career-planning student was encouraged to master skill after skill. Many people wanted to keep the "emotional well-being" of the whole student out of education and out of the classroom. Opposition to affective education prevailed until data on drug use, early pregnancies, higher divorce rates, and adolescent suicides demanded that young people be prepared to cope with these dimensions of life.

A new area for the classroom

The response to the children's and student's problems has been creative. Since 1970, numerous programs and curriculum packages have been offered to classroom teachers. The program names suggest how creative educational psychologists have been: "confluent education," "humanistic education," "psychological education," and "affective education" have been the most common. To give you a taste of the response, Miller (1976), in an excellent discussion, summarizes seventeen major and ten near-major affective education models for you to use in your classroom. In addition, curricular activities such as Developing Understanding of Self and Others (DUSO) (Dinkmeyer, 1970), values clarification (Simon, Howe, & Kirschenbaum, 1972), Classroom Climate Inventory (Barclay, 1978), Toward Affective Development (DuPont, et al., 1974), and selected affective activities (Thayer & Beeler, 1977) have been developed or organized. More than two hundred affective education strategies are described by these educational psychologists. Let's try to explore affective education.

Affective education: Another umbrella term

In affective education, we are concerned about teaching students problem-solving skills to mediate their daily interactions at work, at play, and within the family. This broad commitment in affective education makes our definition extremely comprehensive. Affective education includes mastery of such skills as self-competency, self-regulation, communications, values, awareness of alternative roles, interpersonal relations, attitudes, and motivation. In earlier chapters we talked about the development and learning of many of these skills. Various programs integrate one or more of these broad skills to produce a composite package.

In affective education you may use curricular packages for the year or minicourses for only a few weeks; specific situational strategies are also available. Affective education programs are designed to coordinate the mastery of many skills and competencies so that students can learn how to meet situational demands. A properly managed and carefully evaluated affective education program may be integrated with your other classroom activities.

From the umbrella of affective education we have selected two areas for emphasis: VALUES CLARIFICATION and the mastery of affective-social skills. Of course, we could have chosen many other areas, but these two seem to be related closely to problem solving and creative problem solving.

VALUES CLARIFICATION

Students, teachers, principals, and parents have VALUES or attitudes toward objects, people, procedures, and so on. For example, Warren might assign a very high value to football, and he goes to all the games. Emily says loudly "Football is a waste of time" and argues with Warren. You need to clarify values in your classroom right now. We say that a value is a combination of emotions, actions, and cognitions which produce a tendency to act in some situations (for example, an effort to get football players' autographs). Sometimes these combinations of influences join forces, making the day-to-day management of a classroom something of a challenge. You cannot continue to teach while Warren and Emily are arguing. You will become involved in many situations which start with a values clarification sequence.

Focus on values

A value can be defined in terms of three components. First, there is the affective component, which deals with the emotions or feelings that accompany an idea. For example, Warren may have positive or negative feelings toward members of different football teams. Second, there is the behavior component, which involves overt and covert actions. For example, Warren may drive to the football game two hours early so he can obtain autographs from his favorite players. Third is the cognitive component, which is mediation among situations, objects, or people. Warren would have had to do some planning (mediation) so he could recognize the players in their warm-up clothes. These three components can be called the ABCs of values. When we talk about values, these ABCs can be translated into the ACEs of values (Table 8-2). In Table 8-

Table 8-2. ABCs become ACE of values

ABC mnemonic	Example	ACE mnemonic
*A*ffective	Like the Bengals	*E*motion
*B*ehavior	Recall Essex Johnson's number	*A*ction
*C*ognitive	Relate no. 19 to other backfield players	*C*ognitive

2, we show the three components of a value as a variation of the ABC model. We also provide examples of each component. The third column is an alternative mnemonic for recalling the components of a value. We suggest ACE (action, cognition, and emotion) as a way to recall the three defined components of an attitude.

Value development

Cognitive social learning theory suggests that values are developed in the same way as problem-solving procedures are mastered. Values in this theory can be seen as a learned hierarchy of concepts, rules, and so on. For example, Warren has some friends like Emily who tease him about his positive feelings toward football players. These classmates have probably learned the concepts "Big males are athletes," "Big athletes are football players," and "Football players are slow of wit." Emily might have brought together these several interesting (and loaded) concepts into the value rule "Big males become dumb football players." Many people have these attitudes about football. The same kinds of concept learning and rule making apply to the development of values related to math, Mexican-Americans, and machines. Indeed, we see value development as a special case of problem-solving learning.

The skills and competencies which make up a value are probably mastered by classical, operant, and/or observational learning. Values probably begin with some unplanned classical conditioning in the home. As a child, Warren, for example, might have "read a book" while sitting in the relative safety of Daddy's lap. The resulting early positive relationship between Warren and reading can be maintained by teachers, peers, and parents once Warren reaches school age. The high value assigned to reading and school can be further developed in a more planned manner: letter grades, smiling faces, and touching. In short, an interactive teacher can shape and maintain a positive attitude. Probably the most effective way to develop values is through the use of models. A classmate or a parent's friend may say something positive or negative about physics, and this can have a delayed but long-term effect on Sam's performance.

You can probably generate other examples of how these three basic kinds of learning can contribute to value development and learning.

Steps in the development of affective skills

We believe that values clarification can be very helpful to you in preparing for the mastery of affective-social skills. Values clarification precedes the application of the ABC model to the mastery of affective skills. You will want to clarify values and then try to help your students act upon their discoveries. At least three important activities must occur.

Prepare for affective education   This preprogram training can vary in intensity. Suppose Kathy values her skills in chemistry and devalues her skills in athletics. This means Kathy finds some activities rewarding or enjoyable and that she tends to find some other activities or people to be undesirable or unacceptable. The pattern of differences may be difficult to untangle. Too often, counselors and teachers do not take the time to look at a student's values. The student is not asked to clarify which skills are prized or valued. Instead, a global decision is made for the student. We encourage you to help Kathy apply a special problem-solving procedure called VALUES CLARIFICATION.

Essentially you will want to make sure that the students are ready for the program and you are ready to manage it. You will probably want to spend several weekends in values-clarification workshops before you try this technique with your students. On the one hand, an intense group encounter in the name of affective-skill education can so terrify students that you will be unable to help them. We do not want this to happen. On the other hand, the same intense group encounter might be too much for you! If a student's telling you "I don't like the way you treated Robert" tends to offend or anger you, call for help yourself.

Apply the ABCs to affective-social skills   Once the values are clarified, you will want to use the ABC model to focus on those competency areas specified during values clarification. The ABC analysis provides you, as the classroom mediator, with some information on your students' behaviors, antecedents, and consequences. It may also suggest your own strengths and weaknesses in value development. You may find yourself threatened by a student who expresses values very different from your own. Warren challenges some of your most cherished values. What are you going to do? Of course, you will be a self-regulated person who will be sensitive to personal limitations.

Choose appropriate models   You will want to consider goals, strategies, individual needs, and the environment in selecting an appropriate affective-social educational model. We asked this same kind of question in Chapter 5, when we considered setting the stage for learning. Your answer to the question will require much work: values must be clarified, goals have to be stated, individual differences have to be considered, the parental-principal support system has to be activated, and the alternative models have to be studied, practiced, and mastered. Purposely, we are making this planning detailed because our experience has warned us to avoid quick decisions.

Values clarification: Beginning to resolve conflict

The biggest step for you and your students is the first step in affective education. We have said that affective education is a broad umbrella term. Under the umbrella, we have identified seven skill areas. Each of these skill areas—self-regulation, group interaction, and so on—can be further defined into a cluster of behaviors, objectives, and related learning activities. A perplexing problem is presented by questions such as these: Which skill area is important to you? To your students? The decision is complex and possibly confusing. We have observed some teachers who have been unwilling to get started. "After all," they argued, "it's a lot easier to follow the teacher's manual." A leap forward for their students was too risky. Our response has been to involve these teachers in activities which help them define issues.

Louis Raths and his associates (1966) proposed a procedure for identifying important or valued issues and actions. This procedure closely resembles the problem solving of Dewey. Since values clarification is so similar to problem solving and creativity, we say that values clarification is simply a special case of problem solving. One of Rath's associates, Sidney Simon, is the acknowledged leader in the values clarification "movement." He suggests that the procedure is based on the idea that people do not clearly know their values and goals. This deficit or lack of knowledge appears to prevent many people from behaving purposively. Let's see how values clarification works.

Values clarification: Seven activities

The seven values clarification activities cluster into three stages: (1) prizing or valuing one's beliefs and behaviors; (2) choosing one's beliefs and behaviors, and (3) acting on one's beliefs. Let's look more closely at each stage.

Prizing In the prizing stage, the clarifier of values engages in two activities: (1) "prizing," which means respecting a behavior or its uniqueness, and (2) "affirming a value," which means that you are willing to let your attitude toward an object, behavior, or consequence be generally known. For example, you might ask a group of students to answer the value survey or value inventory items in Table 8-3 (Worell, 1976). You will want to have conflicting items in your survey. Usually, conflicting values are found when people discuss religion, money, and love. Indeed, you can build your own inventory to help a group identify the objects, behaviors, or consequences that they value.

As soon as the class completes the inventory, rearrange the students into very small groups made up of not more than five and not less than three students. In these small groups, the students can be encouraged to discuss their responses and to affirm their values publicly. In all probability, John Dewey would be very happy with this prizing of values, in the course of which some people will develop a feeling or sense of perplexity. The problem-solving procedure begins with this kind of discomfort.

Choosing In the choosing stage, the student or the values clarifier performs three activities: (1) "choosing from alternatives," which means considering an almost limitless list of alternatives; (2) "choosing freely," which means there is an equal opportunity to choose and that realistic constraints such as wealth, physical prowess, and knowledge do not limit choosing; and (3) "choosing after considering consequences," which means the values clarifier reduces the limitless variety of values by assigning some cost, valence, or variety to each one. We want to emphasize that this activity in clarifying values is very similar to the fifth activity (assigning consequences) in the problem-solving procedure (Table 8-1).

Table 8-3. Sample value-survey items

Parental values	Yes	No
Parents should expect children to work for their allowance.	____	____
Sex education should be taught in the schools.	____	____
A good mother stays at home and takes care of her family first.	____	____
Parents who abuse their children belong in jail.	____	____

OR

Desirable child characteristics		Very	Some-what	Not at all
Kind (gentle, considerate)	boys	____	____	____
	girls	____	____	____
Self-controlled (self-disciplined, restrained)	boys	____	____	____
	girls	____	____	____
Ambitious (hard-working, aspiring)	boys	____	____	____
	girls	____	____	____
Loving (affectionate, tender)	boys	____	____	____
	girls	____	____	____

Acting In the acting stage, Kathy, Warren, or Emily carries out two activiies: (1) "acting upon choices," which means actually doing the things they like to do and (2) "being consistent," which means bringing the "should's" and "want's" and what they do into closer harmony. One of our students, James Garland, used a novel approach for helping students clarify their values. In his eighth-grade classroom, Jim showed how our values can bias the way we perceive and react to ideas:

In his eighth-grade unit on American Heritage through literature, Jim tried to orient his students to five major American minorities. Orientation was not enough: the students wanted to learn about the minorities life-styles, traditions, prejudices, and contributions. [As a values clarifier yourself, you can recognize the potential for conflict in this classroom!]

This class was made up mostly of lower socioeconomic level boys and girls. Their parents were unskilled or unemployed as a rule. About two-fifths of the class was black. A few students were Asian-American and one was a native American. About ten percent of the class was middle class (college educated parents).

In the prizing stage Jim wrote "American" on the board and asked for a definition. Everyone knew the answer! At first the class responded with simplistic definitions. However, this did not last long. The students started to affirm particular values. They clarified their beliefs as appropriate first stage activities.

Jim did not let the classes drag in subsequent sessions. In the choosing stage of values clarification, Jim said, "One day I started the class by asking in my normal intonation, 'What's a niggard?' The class got so quiet that I was a little afraid. The facial expressions were those of bewilderment: had they heard Mr. Garland say 'nigger'? After a few more moments of complete silence, one timid voice said, 'black.' I simply remarked that 'niggards came in black, white, yellow, red, and brown!' More silence."

"Why did you ask that question?" asked one boy. I directed him to look up niggard in the dictionary and to read aloud to the class. "A niggard is a stingy person," he read in a monotone. The students looked at each other; they appeared to be perplexed!"

I asked again, "What color is a niggard?" This time a happy chorus responded very noisily! The class was excited and talked more about taboo words such as Honkie, Crackers, and Jungle Bunny.

In closing his report, James Garland said, "The class appeared to appreciate the unit so much that I'm going to use it next year. I just hope that I will have the same enthusiasm."

When you reread Jim Garland's narrative, you will begin to see how you can create your own values-clarification procedure. Jim applied basic problem-solving procedures. His students were involved. Jim mediated many student-to-student interactions. The self-reports from the students indicated that they had made some changes on their own. Both Jim and his students took many risks in the classroom. The unit and its value-loaded ideas could have exploded into citywide headlines. The students could have become physically aggressive toward each other. Instead, careful and gradual changes in verbal interactions seemed to occur in the classroom and on the playground.

PROBE 8-6

Values clarification can help you and your students. Think about the problem-solving checklist (Table 8-1). Choose a value and build your own values-clarification checklist. Share one copy with your friends and another copy with us.

Recap on values clarification

Values, *valuing*, and *values clarification* are extremely important management, mediation, and facilitation terms. You will be want to apply something like *guided discovery*, but we will call it guided value development. It is a middle ground between imposing values and seeking values. In this approach, children and students are encouraged to explore and to try out new activities after they have assigned a consequence to the choice. The consequence may be to self or others. The parents might say, "Sure you may go to the movies, but how will you earn money for your bike?" You might say in the classroom, "OK, let's try it; what do you think'll happen? What about this? Which do you want?" This middle ground is the most difficult. A balance must be maintained.

PROBE 8-7

Value-free teaching is impossible. Think of two teachers you have had—one whose values were most clearly observable and one whose values were least visible. Contrast these two teachers on three dimensions (your choice). Was either able to make his or her teaching value-free? Support your answer.

As a classroom teacher, you will be a model. We have said that over and over. You will set examples for your students and your colleagues. Your actions may or may not match your words. Some new teachers are fairly certain that they give an equal opportunity to all students. However, when they apply the ABCs to themselves, they discover that they tend to call on the students in the front-center part of the classroom; they reward (with smiles or high grades) the students who agree with them; and they give more time to the more attractive students. Your students, colleagues, principal, and your students' parents will figure you out. Be advised that value-free managing, mediating, and facilitating in the classroom or on the playground is impossible. Try to work at clarifying your own values, both as you get ready to teach and while you are teaching.

ACTIVITIES TO FACILITATE AFFECTIVE SKILLS

Your students will get very close to you during affective-skill development. You will observe very emotional interactions. Some students might even cry. Occasionally teachers respond so intensely that they cry also! For many of you, some of the affective education activities will involve uncomfortable and threatening experiences. It will be "too much." For some of you, the way you look at the classroom and at individuals during affective education will help you develop an effective mediation and

"Your own self-regulation in affective education can serve as a model for your students and your colleagues." (Hanson Carroll/Black Star)

facilitation style. Affective education activities and techniques will grow on you. When you share a fear with a student like Warren, you may reveal something that is very private. Be cautious, be careful, and be confident. Your own self-regulation in affective education can serve as a model for your students and your colleagues.

Student activities in affective skills

In affective education, the student has an important responsibility. Frequently you will want the students like Emily to explore their own values and alternative actions independently. It is hard work. You will want to give them a supportive environment. In affective education, students do two main things: (1) they identify values and (2) they plan reachable goals. Both these activities include smaller tasks. Each activity is mainly the student's responsibility.

Complete the steps for values clarification It is unusual for a third-grader or a high school junior to have a clear-cut idea or goal definition. Affective skills are hard to pinpoint. Too often, students, parents, teachers, and schools want a "correct" answer. In values clarification, all the participants (Emily, her parents, and you) will want to accept or tolerate "possible" answers. That's going to be hard for everybody, including Emily.

Perform accurate self-observation   Students like Sam will master the ABC analysis. In their earlier experiences, you will help them answer your questions "What happened then?" and "What came before?" Over time, the students will be able to observe and record more detailed and complex behaviors. They will master the counting of "eye contacts" and how often they "feel afraid of math." You will help these students to become more accurate self-observers.

Set reachable subgoals   Many students want to reach their goals *now*. They are impatient, they want the whole thing, and yet they don't reach the goal. When Sam task-analyzes job-seeking skills, such as selecting the clothes to wear, she can identify both her hierarchy of objectives and her realistic subgoals. For example, Sam might think the tank top and jeans are easy to wear, but her father says, "Wear a dress or a pantsuit!" You can point out that subgoals include working with Sam's parents. You will want to help Sam schedule these subgoals so that each one can be mastered.

Reward self for attaining goals   In the long run, you want your students to be self-regulating. Students at every level can master self-rewarding skills. You might have to work on the idea with some students. You will want to use successive approximations to help them master self-rewarding skills. Gradually fade your prompts. (Sound familiar?) It works! Sam, for example, might reward herself with "I really looked nice for that interview when I wore that dress."

The performance of these three planning skills—observation, goal setting, and reinforcement—is the student's responsibility. You, in turn, will have the responsibility of providing the environment in which the student can master these skills.

Our approach to valuing and affective education uses a three-level model for organizing strategies. The three levels are modeling, curricular change, and environmental management (Barclay, 1978). As a classroom teacher you might try to use models to bring about the desired changes. Should modeling not work, you might try curricular packages and then environmental management. Indeed, it is possible to cross-reference these three levels to the seven affective-social skill areas (self-competency, self-regulation, and so on). Thus, you can build your own problem-solving package for choosing affective education strategies. Let's look at each of the three levels as guidelines.

GUIDELINES FOR TEACHING

Affective Skills

• *Model affective skills.* Earlier in the discussion of the learning skill hierarchy, we said that children learn many basic skills at home or in readiness classes. Your task will be to improve upon those skills, probably by modeling.

1. Select peers or slightly older students to serve as models for your students. These young people must be selected on numerous criteria such as competency, status, prestige, and ethnic-group membership (Bandura, 1977). As a classroom teacher, you will probably want to select models who are more competent than your observer-students. This aura of competency appears to enhance the model's influence upon observers.

    People will be your greatest resource in teaching affective skills. Use them. Students' peer models can be offered to help observers grasp behaviors and complex ideas quickly. Your students will be watching you intently. Be consistent in your professed values and in your behavior. Young students are often quickest to sense who is a "true" person. Older students and adults seem to mediate inconsistent messages more easily than do the youngsters.

PROBE 8-8

In your own education, you may have wanted to change some of your learning activities, such as attitudes or affective skills. If you had been able to observe this learning situation from the outside, as an uninvolved observer, how would you have described your activities as a student? How would you have described the activities of the teacher? If you were the teacher, would you use modeling, curricular packages, or environmental management? To make things a little easier for you, write about a fairly recent learning experience (in the last two years or so). Share your answer with a friend.

---

2. Demonstrate self-regulation skills. Remember that Bandura and Kupers (1964) reported that models can be used to transmit patterns of self-reinforcement (Chapter 3). For example, students who observed a high-standard model rewarded themselves when they exceeded a criterion. On the other hand, children who observed a low-standard model tended to give themselves minimal rewards. The same kinds of results were obtained by Marston (1965), who studied adult observers.

    Once a person has mastered a set of skills, we would like to think they will maintain them. Many skills simply weaken unless they are practiced. As a classroom teacher, you will want to provide opportunities so students can maintain their self-regulation skills. Indeed, we emphasize self-regulation because we value it as a long-term educational goal for most students and teachers.

● *Use established curricular packages or strategies.* In the late seventies and early eighties, the teaching of affective skills appears to be a frequent theme of books, journals, articles, and curricular packages. You might try some activities from *Dimensions of Personality* (Fischer, 1972), *Toward Affective Development* (DuPont, et al., 1974) and *The Valuing Approach to Career Education* (Smith, 1972). Each one of these activities and curricular packages should be reviewed carefully before you decide to use it. You will want to get answers to such questions as the following:

1. What are your students' and your own objectives for affective education?

2. What are the published objectives of the activity or curriculum?

3. Does the set of materials provide experiences which help a student or you meet those objectives?

4. How does your task analysis fit with the publisher's analysis of the curricular package?

5. Can your school provide the necessary curricular supports—such as space or money—for your classroom?

6. Do you need preprogram in-service training before you can "safely" use the curricular activity?

7. How are you going to get that training?

8. In what ways can the program be evaluated? (Remember we emphasize psychometric measurements, observation, and interviews as the best sources of information.)

9. Can the affective curricular package be integrated within the weekly class activities and the school's overall curriculum?

Probably you can create some other questions. The point is, however, that you will want to get as much information as you can before you commit yourself to an affective curricular package.

● *Reorder the environmental structure.* You might try to change the environmental structure in any or all of the following ways:

1. Identify the students who learn best by listening and then lecture to them.

2. Use some other students as cross-age tutors for selected academic areas.

3. Encourage other students to learn by means of independent study.

4. Mediate small groups to encourage peer-supported learning.

5. Assign new roles to selected students on a rotational basis or in role-play situations.

6.   Encourage each student to sit with a friend for each different subject
      area.

•   *Integrate affective activities into the regular classroom schedule.* No
real comment on this guideline is needed. The skills are important for
everyone from early childhood to old age. We can find no convincing
argument for separating valuing and affective education from the classroom's regular activities (Stilwell, 1977). Indeed, a complete integration
of affective activities can have a powerful impact upon a school, its
teachers, and the students. A well-planned program, sensitively carried
out, can mediate differences among students and facilitate their learning
of a wide range of lifelong skills.

**Recap on
teaching affective
skills**

As a classroom teacher, you will want to consider a great variety of ways
to help students meet the goals of education in values and affective
development. In your daily classroom activities, you will often want
students to consider factual, conceptual, and value levels of learning. For
example, ample evidence suggests that the "Pentagon papers" were
indeed reproduced. On a conceptual level, you could ask your students
to discuss a citizen's responsibility in this situation. On a value level, you
might ask, "What is so valued that you would risk losing your citizenship?" Remember, we told you that values are often difficult to discuss.
In your weekly classroom activities, we encourage you to raise affective
or psychological education to the same status as the three R's. You might
schedule affective activities for three times a week, thirty minutes per
session. This kind of schedule seems to work very well for an affective
education program (Stilwell & Barclay, 1978). By scheduling affective
education regularly, you will let your students and their parents know
that you mean to help your students gain these important skills.

TEACHING
LIFE-CAREER SKILLS

For the rest of this century, LIFE-CAREER EDUCATION will involve a
number of subgoals. We see life-career education as a procedure that
involves the whole person in a carefully planned, lifelong experience of
work, leisure; and family. Our world has changed so dramatically in this
century that work cannot be all-consuming. Indeed, the educated person,
such as your students and you, will learn how to balance family, work,
and leisure. When your parents were in school the theme probably was
"take courses to prepare you for work." Times have changed. Course
work is now available to help people be positive, effective family and
community members and to master leisure activities.

LIFELONG PROBLEM SOLVING

Life-career education enjoys a special relationship with "the four R's"— readin', 'ritin', 'rithmetic, and relationship. First, Sam or Warren needs basic academic skills in order to master career-related activities. Second, the individual needs affective-social skills in order to deal with the many new situations that arise in and after school. Third, the amount of information about the world of work that students have seems to influence their affective and academic skills (Barclay et al., 1972). Thus, we cannot prepare Emily or Sam for what is going to happen by emphasizing only the three R's or life-career education. We believe that a carefully planned, well-implemented, and thoroughly evaluated program of academic, affective, and life-career education belongs in every school. In this way, the important relationships among the four R's and life-career education can be maintained for the benefit of your students.

Life-career and affective skills

Life-career education can be as important as the development of skills in academic and affective education. It is developmental from awareness through exploration and implementation. Each cluster of life-career activities—such as welding skills, working with a supervisor, or finding a job—can be task-analyzed. Mastery can be orderly and can be managed as a part of regular classroom activities. We have this commitment to life-career education because it is similar in a number of ways to affective education and problem-solving procedures. Let's take a look at these similarities.

"Life-career education can be as important as the development of skills in academic and affective education." (C. Wolinsky/Stock, Boston)

Similar history   The sleeping dragon in every curriculum was shaken in the sixties and seventies. Parents, teachers, and educators began to act out their dissatisfaction with education. Changes occurred in many different places, and reams of yellowed notes were thrown out. The changes will continue to occur in the eighties. In life-career education, the push came from Sidney P. Marland, Jr., the U.S. Commissioner of Education (1971). People got on the bandwagon. The ideas of Ginzberg (1952), Holland (1966), and Super (1957) were translated into career-education programs and materials. Some materials were developed vigorously, with objectives and learning skill hierarchies. Unfortunately, too few programs were fully integrated within the regular curriculum (Project PLAN stands out as an exception). Many different kinds of materials were produced either in order to get on the bandwagon or to help students master a few of the many life-career education skills. Much has yet to be done in life-career education to integrate it with academic and affective education.

Similar problem-solving procedures   In our view, career education can be viewed as a special case of problem solving. The procedures used in career education (modeling, work simulation, direct observation, task analysis, and psychometric measuring) are similar to those used in affective education and in mastering basic problem solving. In career education, the procedure can be applied to teaching children in the primary grades different kinds of work—what the salesperson, firefighter, or police officer actually does. Similarly, an older person can use the same skills to gather information about patient-care facilities for a stricken spouse. These career-education skills are useful throughout a person's life (Mitchell, Jones, & Krumboltz, 1979).

Similar importance   We argue that career education should be equal to academic and affective education in importance. A person cannot effectively cope with "the real world" without information, learning skills, and some creative problem solving. This same person—Samantha, Emily, or you—will need skills to communicate, adapt, and adjust to people and situations. A person's experiences in career education can provide a foundation on which are built work, leisure, affective, and academic skills.

Similar classroom management   The classroom management activities for career education will require you to do many familiar things: observe, help set goals, task-analyze, use the ABCs, practice communications skills, and follow the problem-solving procedures. In a series of studies, John Krumboltz and his students at Stanford University developed film and videotape models and problem-solving activities designed to aid in career problem solving (Krumboltz & Baker, 1973). Indeed, we believe that a balanced curriculum integrates affective skills and life-career skill development with the traditional curriculum (Stilwell, 1977).

Similar evaluation   Throughout this book, we have told you that three kinds of assessment data—psychometric, observation, and interview—are better than only one kind. In career education, you will be able to use published interest or achievement tests, develop your own observational records, and conduct your own structured interviews. The data from these three sources can be more meaningful than data from only one source (Thoresen, 1977). Let us take a look at some questions that you could use after completing a career education unit in your class. The questions are similar to those that you might ask a tenth-grader (Table 8-4).

You can give an inventory of fifteen or so questions based on the problem-solving procedure. For example, two questions can be asked about Activity 1 (see Table 8-1), such as our questions 1, 2, and 3. Then you can ask two questions about each of the other eight problem-solving activities in career education. From all the students' answers, you can get a pretty good idea about how powerful your career-education program or activity has been (Stilwell & Thoresen, 1972; Krumboltz & Baker, 1973). Once more we are going to advise dividing classroom time between academic, affective, and life-career education. While we are committed to placing the three areas of education on the same level, we (you and us) recognize that not all school boards will agree with us. You will have an interesting challenge should you try to help educational decision makers clarify their values and change their attitudes toward contemporary and future education.

Table 8-4. Structured interview for gathering career education information

Have you done any of the following during the last three weeks?
Please circle the correct answer.

1. Have you talked with any persons now working at the types of occupations you are now thinking about?	Yes	No
2. Have you written for information on the occupations or on the schools where you could get training?	Yes	No
3. Have you bought, borrowed, or checked out of the library any reading materials that might help you to plan your training?	Yes	No
4. Have you made any definite plans to visit any of the schools where you could get training?	Yes	No

Structured interviews can be helpful sources of information for self-regulation and for monitoring the behavior of others. Please generate nine questions for career education. We have given you a start in Table 8-1. Prepare one question for each activity involved in career problem solving.

Each person in the classroom as well as the principal and parents can become involved in planned programs for change. These programs for behavior change are probably the most complex challenges you will face. However, they are not so great that you will not be able to work your way through the ABC analysis, task analysis, and problem-solving procedures. As you can see, the change sequences integrate the materials presented so far in this book. If you need help in problem solving, do your own task analysis, master the prerequisite skills, select the appropriate change strategies, implement, evaluate, and revise. Be your own self-regulated person!

LEARNING ACTIVITY: CREATIVE PROBLEM SOLVING FOR YOU

In the very near future you will be concerned about how creative your students really are. Many students are diamonds in the rough. Their creative skills must be discovered and polished by you, your colleagues, and the students themselves. Many people simply don't want to take a risk and try to be creative. Therefore, a proper environment must be prepared to support creative problem solving. You will be an important manager of the students' learning environment.

Before you venture out into the classroom, you might try to find out how creative you can be now. Paul Torrance has developed a number of tests and activities that can help you do this. For example, you might look at a brick and try to list as many different uses as you can in, say, five minutes. Now, bricks are fairly common and probably not very stimulating, but some people can list ten to fifteen different uses for a brick! We aren't going to ask you to produce the unusual uses for a brick or to complete an incomplete picture.

Instead, we are going to ask you to read these three lists of words, choose one word from each column to produce a story title, and write a two- to five-page story.

A	B	C
secret	farm	birth
love	peace	joy
river	death	funny
hope	challenge	order
city	plain	goals
warmth	help	home
life	passage	valley

You may expand the title, but you must use one word from each of the three columns (for example, "Life Finds Daily Challenges in Every Birth").

Prepare your story so that you or a classmate can judge its creativity. You should remember that Torrance uses four components in his definition of creativity (fluency, flexibility, originality, and elaboration). You might reread the definitions used by Glover and Gary (1976). However, you or a friend might also consider using the following words as guidelines for judging the story's creativity and your creative problem-solving skills:

humor

flavor (introduces the senses)

vividness (intensity or excitement)

unique setting (that is, an unconventional site)

unusual terms or names

You might create some additional key words *prior* to this undertaking. Throughout this learning activity, we are using the basic four components of Torrance's definition of creativity. You might want to read more about creativity, so we suggest the *Journal of Creative Behavior* and the many books written by Paul Torrance.

SUMMARY

1. PROBLEM SOLVING is an easily mastered skill which can help students become self-regulated. Problem-solving skills can be applied in a variety of settings and may include scientific, literary, and artistic creativity; values clarification; and selected affective-social skills.

2. Problem solving as described by John Dewey involves five steps: (*a*) feeling of perplexity, (*b*) clarification of the problem, (*c*) hypothesizing, (*d*) assigning values to the alternatives, and (*e*) experimen-

tation. Over time, these five steps have been restated into nine activities which apply to many settings.

3. CREATIVITY is a special kind of problem solving. In creativity, the solution seems to be new, uncommon, and possibly not correct or even useless. Indeed, creative solutions seem to have a life cycle which ends in oldness, conventionality, and usefulness.

4. Paul Torrance has made many major contributions to problem solving or convergent thinking and to creativity or divergent thinking. Torrance emphasizes four components of creativity: fluency, flexibility, originality, and elaboration. It is possible to increase creative problem-solving skills by helping students master the four components of creativity.

5. AFFECTIVE EDUCATION goes by many different names, including "humanistic education," "confluent education," and "psychological education." Numerous minicourses and year-long programs are available to teachers, counselors, and parents.

6. VALUES CLARIFICATION activities are selected as a special kind of affective education. In values clarification, seven activities cluster into three stages: *prizing* or valuing one's beliefs, *choosing* one's behaviors, and *acting* on one's beliefs. Usually, attempts to clarify values are intended to resolve some ambiguous or conflicting information about a VALUE.

7. The clarification of values involves a warning: value-free managing, mediating, and facilitating in the classroom or on the playground is impossible.

8. Affective-social skills include a broad variety of self-competency, group interaction, and self-management skills. You will be able either to model affective skills, to use established curricular packages, or to reorder the environmental structure to help students master these affective-social skills.

9. Lifelong problem solving is a real educational goal for every student. Many programs now emphasize LIFE-CAREER EDUCATION in the sense of both preparation for a career or work and anticipation of life's frequent challenges. Life-career education programs apply problem-solving procedures to help students become self-regulated persons.

 KEY TERMS

AFFECTIVE EDUCATION: Education aimed toward mastery of daily problem-solving skills such as self-competency, self-regulation, interpersonal relations, communication, values, and awareness of roles, attitudes, and motivation.

CREATIVITY: A procedure that allows a unique combination of environmental stimuli and planned learning activities to produce a new, novel, and useful product.

LIFE-CAREER EDUCATION: Education designed to involve the whole person in a carefully planned lifelong experience of work, leisure, and family.

PROBLEM SOLVING: A procedure that involves the relating of two or more principles to accomplish a purpose. The product is typically new, correct, and common.

VALUE: A set of emotions, actions, and cognitions that produce a tendency to act in a particular way in some situations.

VALUES CLARIFICATION: A procedure that includes three stages for mediating conflicting values: prizing, choosing, and acting on one's beliefs.

SELF-TEST

1. Problem solving is _____
_____

2. Reinforcement, modeling, and classical conditioning can be used to develop or change attitudes. Usually _____ is more effective than _____ or _____. (Write in the correct answers using the words or phrases listed below).
   a. cognitive learning
   b. modeling
   c. classical conditioning
   d. reinforcement

3. Four of the seven competencies usually found in affective education are (circle the letter which represents the correct answer):
   a. fluency, flexibility, elaboration, and speed
   b. perplexity, problem, production, and product
   c. motivation, self-regulation, self-competency, and communications skills
   d. emotions, actions, cognitions, and behaviors

4. John Dewey discussed stages of problem solving. They were:
   a. eleven in number
   b. branching from complex to simple
   c. written less than forty years ago
   d. five related activities

5. Problem solving and creativity are discussed in the following ways:
   a. both have correct answers
   b. creativity has a correct answer
   c. problem solving is convergent

d. both have products
e. (two answers are correct)

6. Four useful characteristics of creative activities are the following:
   a. resourceful, diligent, committed, and dedicated
   b. flexible, elaborate, fluent, and original
   c. sequential, step-by-step, rewarded, and feedback
   d. calm, self-assured, self-regulated, and self-monitoring

7. The ABC model can be used to produce learning skills hierarchies in:
   a. problem solving but not career education
   b. values clarification but not creativity
   c. affective education but not valuing
   d. creative problem solving but not affective education
   e. creative problem solving and affective education

8. Values clarification employs three activity clusters:
   a. searching, comparing, and choosing
   b. analysis, synthesis, and valuing
   c. acting, prizing, and choosing
   d. perplexity, problem, and production

9. You will consider a hierarchy for planning effective strategies which looks more like
   a. values clarification, goal clarification, and self-clarification
   b. model skills, curricular packages, and reorder environment

c. directing, modeling, and managing
d. convergent guidance, divergent guidance, and problem solving

10. Effective skill training and life-career education have a common set of skills which are called _____ skills.

SELF-TEST KEY

1. See Table 8-1
2. modeling, cognitive learning, reinforcement
3. c
4. d
5. c

6. b
7. e
8. c
9. b
10. problem-solving

PART 4
Managing Teacher and Student Behavior

How can you use a teaching model in your classroom? How can you facilitate each student's individual development? In what ways can you integrate instructional methods and instructional innovations to manage learning outcomes? In just a short while, you will be trying out your answers to these questions. You will have students needing your unique kind of help: Ellen wants to solve each challenge as quickly as possible (*now*); Robert tries to analyze his "mastery" of paragraph writing; and Alice gets tired of learning from filmstrips.

There is a common theme in the questions of each of these students: How am I doing as a self-regulated person? As a classroom teacher, you will want to manage learning experiences so that students have many opportunities for self-regulation.

Student mastery of self-regulation skills can appear in many different areas. Some students can become fully functioning problem solvers in academic, affective, and career areas. Ellen's friend Samantha appears to be well on her way toward developing her own job-seeking skills. Of course, Samantha acquired these skills from a carefully managed and frequently facilitated series of classroom and real-world learning experiences. Given the same sequence of models and experiencs, you will help Ellen become more patient in her problem solving. Some other students develop self-regulated behaviors for academic, affective, or career skill areas. Still other students appear to have large gaps in their mastery of basic problem-solving skills. Your challenge is to help them master those unlearned skills. As a classroom teacher, you will often be the manager, facilitator, and mediator for students whose skills represent a wide range of mastery.

In Part 4, we will discuss the management of teacher and student behaviors. Our definition of *management* will suggest ways to plan, coordinate, evaluate, and change an educational enterprise. You will try to manage the learning environment to benefit each student, each parent, and yourself. In order to facilitate a change in students or in your own behavior, you will need to know about several different learning strategies. Once you have organized learning outcomes, evaluation techniques, and strategies, you can apply them to meet the needs of all students.

CHAPTER 9
Managing Learning Outcomes

LEARNING OBJECTIVES

After reading Chapter 9, answering the self-monitoring questions, completing the learning activity, and reading any further references of your choice, you will be able to:

1. Define and give examples of key terms.
2. List and describe four management styles.
3. List and describe five parts of the basic management model.
4. Explain the benefits of the basic management model for your students and for you.
5. Summarize benefits and weaknesses of individualized, group, and lecture instruction.
6. Explain the benefits and costs of a mastery learning approach for your students and for you.
7. Discuss the roles of students, teachers, and administrators in several instructional systems.
8. Create six learning objectives for your subject area.

FOCUS ON MANAGEMENT

On your way to managing a productive learning activity, you will try to integrate student needs, curricular materials, and learning outcomes with your roles as a facilitator and a mediator. Administrators, parents, colleagues, and students will try to influence your approach to management. How you respond to these various influences will be important for your own approach to management.

We believe that MANAGEMENT is a set of learned skills. From our experience in helping new and not-so-new teachers manage their classrooms, we have found that problem solving is essential to the four kinds of activities found in management. These four kinds of activities are planning, organizing, coordinating, and directing each productive educational enterprise. You will use all these skills in any approach to management you select. As you gain experience, you will adopt one style of management from the many approaches that are available.

STYLES OF MANAGEMENT

As a teacher you will encounter several different kinds of management approaches. We cannot say which approach will be the most comfortable for you. For the moment, we want you to be aware that at least four managerial styles can be identified. In the future, you will want to work out your own typical style for working with the various influences around you. Read our brief descriptions of the four management styles: (1) administrator-imposed style, (2) teacher-directed style, (3) student-demand style, and (4) teacher-student negotiated style. Let's look at each of these.

Administrator-imposed style

A management style can be imposed upon you by the school board or by the principal. Here, the principal collects your lesson plans every Monday morning. Tuesday afternoon, some of the lesson plans are returned—with comments. These feedback statements can range from "Excellent choice of articles" to "You have not thought about this choice, Ms. B." We have found that, in schools that use admiministrator-imposed management, the supervisor makes frequent visits to selected classrooms, usually without warning. In addition, inflexible rules abound, such as a rule that spelling tests must be given on Friday afternoons. Above all, *silence* is the byword for the building. As you may have gathered, we believe that too much imposed management can be unfortunate.

Teacher-directed style

A classroom management approach can be directed upon the students by the teacher. Usually, teachers have clearly defined values. Indeed, one of the authors was exposed for one year to a woman who flatly said, "My values direct me to instill a strong sense of commitment to excellence in grammar." That was one experience we have not yet forgotten! Other teachers direct students "to play sports for the fun of the activity, not for winning." As you can appreciate, teachers with clearly defined values can translate them into approaches for managing learning outcomes.

Student-demanded style

A management approach can evolve from student preferences. Often we have found teachers, particularly substitutes, whose classroom management style has been dictated by the students. For example, Robert might approach you and say, "Our last teacher was a pain. You won't be one also, will you?" How you answer depends, of course, on how big Robert is and how confident and self-managed *you* are.

Teacher-student negotiated style

A fourth approach to management is one which is negotiated between your students and you. In our travels, we have found some teachers and students who can negotiate. Negotiations are difficult; both parties have to give and take. They have to practice interaction and sharing. Indeed, in negotiations, teachers and students are obliged to learn about each other. Suppose Alice, one of your students, comes to you for help in finding some different ways to learn social studies. She is tired of changing the record and moving the filmstrip. In the few minutes she is interacting with you, you will have a chance to learn about her and she will be able to learn about you. The payoffs from this negotiated approach to management can be great.

"Negotiations are difficult; both parties have to give and take." (P. Vandermark/Stock, Boston)

As you may have figured out, we like the negotiation approach better. There are at least five reasons why we prefer this middle-ground approach to management: (1) students can learn how to be problem solvers; (2) teachers can master problem-solving skills; (3) teacher-student interactions can produce mastery of new skills in such a way that each new solution creates new problem-solving opportunities; (4) teachers, students, and parents can join in a "problem-solving community" in which each is learning from the others; and (5) you can become less of a resource person and more of a facilitator or mediator. In the long run, you will have the opportunity to work with each of these managerial styles. Our hope is that you will be able to apply problem-solving skills and to select an appropriate style for each situation.

A MODEL FOR MANAGING LEARNING

The day is coming when your supervisor will say, "They're all yours!" Don't panic now and please don't panic then. Recall (from Chapter 1)

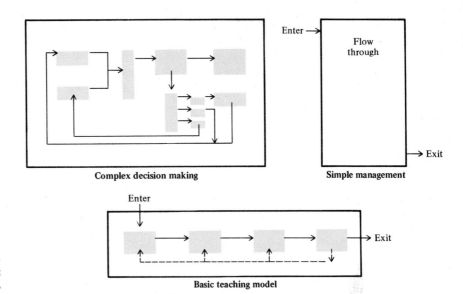

Figure 9-1
Alternative
management
models.

Robert Glaser's basic model for managing learning outcomes. In the early sixties, Professor Glaser, an educational psychologist at the University of Pittsburgh, proposed a simple four-part model (1962). We prefer this model, which has revolutionized education, to some alternatives (see Figure 9-1). By applying the model, a new or experienced teacher, an educational psychologist, or a student can pinpoint where they are in working toward mastery. You will recall from Chapter 1 that the four parts of the model were (1) developing learning objectives, (2) assessing entry skills, (3) developing instructional procedures, and (4) evaluating learning outcomes. We will now highlight a fifth part to the model— providing feedback. We believe that feedback holds the other four parts of the model together. Let's see what this basic management model can mean to you in your teaching activities.

DEVELOPING LEARNING OBJECTIVES

The purpose of this part of the model is to establish what will be mastered during a given learning unit, during a cluster of units, or over a longer period of time. Objectives are designed to communicate to students what they should be able to do to demonstrate mastery of the materials. Learning objectives can be developed on three levels—general, subordinate, and learning. Each level is important and crucial to your work as a classroom teacher.

General
objectives

GENERAL OBJECTIVES represent the most abstract and vague level. Broadly stated educational goals such as "Promote democracy in our schools" or "Prepare the student for successful citizenship" seem to characterize this level. Do not underestimate the importance of general objectives. They are important because (1) the state school board, famous educators, psychologists, and politicians have helped to state them and (2) these objectives often represent the only contact the public will have with what is happening in the classroom. As far as you are concerned, these general objectives are the first step in preparing learning objectives for the classroom.

Subordinate objectives

SUBORDINATE OBJECTIVES appear on the next level. Here, the general objectives are broken down into more specific goals. Subordinate objectives are adaptable to the region, district, or building. It is the subordinate objective which becomes more precise. For our general objective "Prepare the student for succcessful citizenship," for example, a subordinate objective might be "Acquire knowledge about state laws and employment." As you might suspect, broad and general objectives suggest a host of possibilities. These subordinate objectives have a general purpose of communicating to the students what is expected of them (Popham, 1978a). In your day and in our day, our teachers used "lesson plans" which prescribed what was expected of teachers but not of students. The movement toward objectives appears also to have been a movement toward the student. When you are developing learning objectives, you will begin by stating both the general and subordinate objectives (Gronlund, 1978).

Learning objectives

LEARNING OBJECTIVES appear at the third level. Learning objectives specify precisely the learning conditions, the action process, and the criteria for a learning event. For example, you might use "Given a sample city organization (condition), you will match responsibilities with departments (action) eight out of ten times (criterion)." This might be a learning or performance objective in helping students learn about city government. These three-part objectives can be written for each detailed activity in a learning hierarchy. They are narrowly stated and refer to only a small range of behaviors. Since they are so narrow they can be generated by the hundreds. Indeed, you too will have a chance to prepare objectives in the learning activity at the end of this chapter. We shall soon take a look at what happens when too many objectives are generated for an academic topic.

ASSESSING ENTRY SKILLS

The purpose of this second part of the basic learning management model is to decide whether the student has mastered the prerequisite skill or information. In your assessment of prerequisite learning skills, you will want to use psychometrics, observations, and interviews to gather information (for example, see Stilwell & Santoro, 1976; Mannebach &

Stilwell, 1978). We are emphasizing your use of different assessment strategies. When only interviews or only observations and test results are used, crucial information can be missed. For example, Robert's difficulties in paragraph writing might really be traced to an unmastered prerequisite skill. As his teacher, you will want to test, observe, and interview Robert; possibly he has not yet mastered certain discrimination skills. Try to identify antecedents and consequences which appear to be maintaining Robert's dilemma.

SELECTING INSTRUCTIONAL STRATEGIES

The purpose of this part is to generate instructional activities to help students reach their learning goals. As a classroom teacher, you will often be asked to adopt, adapt, or create better learning materials for students. Each challenge will be different. In some situations, you can adopt another set of available instructional materials. Such an approach might be useful to a student like Alice, as an alternative to filmstrips. On the other hand, Robert's desire to analyze his paragraph writing might be facilitated by a specially prepared learning activity on task analysis to help meet his needs. Sometimes you will find that instructional procedures simply do not exist. You must create your own. For example Ellen, who is always rushing to a quick solution, might pose your greatest challenge of the week. You will be asked to select the best reading materials, the best peer model, the best schedule, the best this and that. Indeed, when you create a learning procedure for any of your students, you need both skill and art. As you can see, management of the learning process involves skills in planning, organizing, coordinating, and directing the learning environment (Davies, 1973).

EVALUATING LEARNING OUTCOMES

The purpose of this part of the basic management model is to provide two kinds of information: (1) whether students are making progress toward mastering an educational goal and (2) whether they have reached mastery of the goal. The evaluation information can be helpful to the school, the student, the parents, and to you. Such frequent evaluation can be time-consuming, but we believe it is helpful to an effective classroom manager. In our discussion of entry skills we emphasized the need for three kinds of information—psychometric (paper-and-pencil test results), observational, and interview. You will want to evaluate learning outcomes with these three kinds of information. In this chapter we will discuss how you can teach for mastery learning. Later in Chaper 10 we will give you some ideas on how to evaluate mastery.

STUDY 9-1: USING FEEDBACK TO HELP STUDENTS MASTER CURSIVE WRITING

Four educational psychologists (Trap, Milner-Davis, Joseph, & Cooper, 1978) studied how to use feedback to facilitate student mastery of cursive writing. The study was undertaken to evaluate several strategies for helping students make a transition from printing to cursive writing.

Twelve first-graders were involved in this study. None of these boys and girls had previously demonstrated skill in cursive writing. Each student was worked with for three to five 15-minute sessions per week. The students reached mastery in four and a half to six weeks.

Jennifer Trap and her colleagues wanted to increase the correctness of cursive writing strokes. They carefully defined specific skill areas such as containment (i.e., staying between the lines) and closed circles (i.e., no letter *a* could look like the letter *u*). Seven skills were defined for trained raters.

Three raters were trained to rate students' performance during five probes, a baseline period, and three interventions. Interrater agreement was computed by dividing agreements by the sum of agreements and disagreements (Chapter 10). In each stage of this study, the raters seemed to maintain a high level of agreement.

The raters used these standardized procedures to compare the individual programs by the four educational psychologists. An analysis of tape recordings from each session failed to show any significant differences in the verbal interactions of these psychologists.

The study began with a baseline. Students were asked to copy lowercase letters. The baseline was continued for five sessions or until the percentage of correct strokes appeared to be stabilized. The baseline percentages ranged between 11 or 12 to about 37 percent correct.

In a probe session the psychologist asked the student to copy uppercase cursive letters. No modeling or encouragement was offered by the psychologists during each of the five probe sessions.

The first intervention used verbal and visual feedback and praise. Trap and her colleagues modeled selected letters (*a, f, h, i, o, q, t, w, x,* and *z*). After the student copied the letters a special overlay was placed on each letter. The student was able to see how the letters matched the model on the overlay. Specific verbal feedback was also provided. The first intervention continued either until the student had improved by 10 percent or until ten sessions had been completed. A probe followed each intervention.

The second intervention added rewriting the missed letters. Thus, in this intervention the student copied letters, saw the overlay comparison, reviewed precise feedback, and then rewrote the missed letters. Again, the student remained in this intervention stage either for ten sessions or until the mean percentage of correct strokes had increased by 10 percent. Another similar probe followed this intervention.

In the third intervention the psychologists offered the student a potential reinforcement. A Handwriting Certificate of Achievement was promised as soon as the student improved by another 10 percent and maintained that skill level for three sessions. Once the student reached the criteria, an award ceremony was held in class.

The results suggest some helpful ideas for classroom teachers. The percentage of correctness for these twelve students averaged as follows: 24 percent, baseline; 38 percent, verbal and visual feedback; 60 percent, verbal and visual feedback plus rewriting; and 72 percent, certificate. The students' level of correctness on the ten trained letters improved faster than did their level of correctness on the rest of the alphabet. The probes were also used to measure generalization from the training program. The students improved on the probe letters, but, again, not as fast as they did on the ten letters selected for the program.

In this study Trap and her colleagues used a *multiple-baseline design* to monitor carefully each student's progress through the cursive writing learning strategy. She also collected data on untrained letters to observe any generalizations from the programmatic strategy to the untrained letters. It is this careful approach to program development and evaluation that you will want to try with the programs which will be available to you.

Adapted from: Trap, J. J., Milner-Davis, P., Joseph, S., & Cooper, J. O. The effects of feedback and consequences on traditional cursive letter formation. *Journal of Applied Behavior Analysis,* 1978, *11,* 381–393.

PROVIDING FEEDBACK

This part of the basic management model is often shown as a dotted line which leads back to the other four parts of the model (Figure 9-1). We believe that feedback and/or motivational incentives truly make the management model work. By using feedback, knowledge of correct response or motivational incentives, you can become a more effective manager of learning outcomes. A good example of feedback in the classroom is found in Study 9-1. In contrast with the practices in this study, many teachers fail to use constructive feedback. They seem to prefer to spend time haranguing their students about their failures. On the other hand, you will show your students where they were or were not

"Wisely used, feedback can be exciting." (Charles Gatewood)

successful. Wisely used, feedback can be exciting. You can promote an aura of enthusiasm. Alice, Ellen, and Robert and their friends can be encouraged to increase their own levels of competency. They can become turned on to excellence. The constructive use of feedback is discussed in Chapters 5, 6, and 10.

PROBE 9-1

In your high school learning experiences, how was your performance assessed? Did your teachers use only one form of evaluation or did they use several? Did you receive constructive feedback? Would you want more information for your students? Be prepared to discuss your responses in class.

BENEFITS FROM THE FIVE-PART MODEL

At present, you have already mastered many of the skills that are needed to carry out this five-part model. We laid the groundwork for the model as early as Chapter 1. We talked about the ABCs of learning in Chapter 5. Later in this chapter, we will present some ideas about task analysis and learning objectives. Also in this chapter, we will talk about mastery. This model offers many learning benefits to you and your students.

Student benefits from the model

The application of this basic model in the classroom can bring some benefits to your students. First, the model provides students with a kind of advanced organizer. In the model, we see a certain degree of stability. Over and over again, the students experience learning objectives, entry assessment, instructional procedures, evaluation, and feedback. This stability can bring some order and organization into the classroom, particularly for students like Ellen who lack self-regulation skills (Soloman & Kendall, 1979). In the basic management model, each set of events can cue in the next event and provide incentives to those students who want them. Second, the model fits well with our cognitive social learning approach, which emphasizes mastery of selected skills. We want the learning activities to be related. We also want the student to be immersed but not lost in the problem. Thus, the model provides many of the important cues for students who are mastering learning outcomes.

Teacher and student benefits from the model

At first, the basic model can serve as a simple structure or scaffold upon which you may hang ideas and activities. As a classroom teacher committed to helping students like Ellen or Alice, you will find that the model offers the following benefits:

Table 9-1. Integrating the basic teaching-management model with problem-solving activities

Parts of the model	Problem-solving activities
Specify objectives	Consider goals and refine them into objectives
Assess entering skills	Assess student strengths and weaknesses; match this information with goals and objectives
Select instructional strategies	Generate and list alternative actions; assign consequences to same; rank same and plan primary action
Perform evaluation	Monitor primary action plan and revise (if necessary)
Provide feedback	Integrate problem-solving skills for each individual

It integrates activities In Table 8-1, we presented a checklist for problem solving. You will use these nine activities in working with a whole class, a small group, or a single student. These nine activities fit into the basic teaching-management model in several different ways. In the broadest way, the relationship can be shown in Table 9-1.

In a more detailed sense, we can look at the interaction between specifying objectives and assessing entering behaviors. Suppose Ellen knows what she wants and tells you what she can do. You will be able to apply the nine activities of problem solving (Chapter 8) to clarify objectives and entry behaviors. In the long run, you will want to master the problem-solving skills so you can then master the basic management model. Indeed, the model and the problem-solving skills will have lifelong value for you and your students.

It applies to teachers and students At any point in your sequence of instruction, you and your students will be able to see where you are in the model. Jointly you can prod yourselves in specifying the objectives, assessing entry behaviors, or whatever. You can ask yourself, "What do I want my students to learn?" as well as "What do my students want to learn?" The model provides you with a structure. As long as you and a student can agree on where you two are in the model, you will be able to promote behavior change. Remember the ABCs of learning? If you two can agree where you are in the basic management model, then you can quickly use the ABCs.

It meets student needs In Chapters 2 through 4, we emphasized an important point: students are different. Students are unique combinations of entry skills, learning histories, and learning styles. Because each student is so different, you will want to consider a wide range of instructional alternatives. In our many visits to classrooms, we have watched teachers ''consider'' alternatives and then repeat the same old thing. In contrast, we feel confident that you will apply the problem-solving activities and actually implement several appropriate strategies to help your students.

It evaluates instruction The basic management model provides a simple structure for evaluating learning. We mean that you, your students, and possibly a parent group can develop some checklists for seeing where individuals, groups, or classes really are in terms of reaching their agreed-to goals. Later in this chapter, we will talk about some very comprehensive programs which involve nearly everybody in evaluation.

It provides continuous feedback As you become more familiar with the model, feedback will become more important to you. Feedback is a lubricant to classroom management in two ways. First, feedback helps to relate each activity and person—things within the environment—to each other. Second, feedback promotes the coordinated development of each person's skills. As we saw in Chapters 6 and 7, feedback within the teaching-management model promotes planned changes, since the effects of these changes ''come back'' to the rest of the activities and people in the classroom.

DEVELOPING LEARNING OBJECTIVES

In the last twenty years, performance, instructional, or learning objectives have made a crucial contribution to our educational enterprise. Getting started on developing learning objectives was the hardest step. A map was needed to organize and give direction for preparing these objectives.

DOMAINS OF LEARNING OBJECTIVES

Efforts began in the mid-fifties at the University of Chicago. Benjamin Bloom and his associates began to order learning activities by means of a *taxonomy*. The first work was completed for the *cognitive domain* (Bloom et al., 1956). Later the *affective domain* was ordered into a taxonomy (Krathwohl, Bloom, & Masia, 1964). Ten years ago, the *psychomotor domain* was arranged into a hierarchy by Kibler, Barker, and Mills (1970). Soon *life-career activities* will be ordered into a taxonomy. Table 9-2 shows how three taxonomies appear to be ordered.

A taxonomy suggests learning activities, test items, and a sequence for mastery. The work of such people as Robert Gagné seemed to fill the gaps and smooth out the rough spots in the early taxonomies. We believe

Table 9-2. Taxonomies for skill mastery

Level	Cognitive domain classification (key word)	Affective domain	Psychomotor domain
1.0	knowledge (e.g., remember or define)	receive (e.g., share or accept)	gross body movements (e.g., throw a ball)
2.0	comprehension (e.g., receive communication or interpret)	respond (e.g., discuss or applaud)	finely coordinated movements (e.g., typing)
3.0	application (e.g., use abstractions or relate)	value (e.g., support or deny)	nonverbals (e.g., show interest)
4.0	analysis (e.g., break down communications)	organize (e.g., theorize or formulate)	speech (e.g., recite a poem in German)
5.0	synthesis (e.g., define a new structure or originate)	characterize by a value (e.g., valued by peers)	
6.0	evaluation (e.g., make quantitative judgments)		

that the preparation of taxonomies and generation of learning hierarchies for many different domains will continue for some time.

STRATEGIES FOR DEVELOPING OBJECTIVES

Learning objectives, sometimes called performance objectives, can reach your classroom by one of three ways: adoption, adaptation, and creation. Each way presents a different set of activities. Let's explore those differences. Later, we will emphasize the creation of objectives.

Adopting objectives

Most school systems simply adopt a set of objectives. The school board, through the efforts of administrators and teachers, may adopt a curriculum or a textbook that is available commercially. Often, book publishers offer a ''package'' of text, instructor's manual, and tests. This approach has both positive and negative outcomes. It may be helpful to have much of the thinking and planning done for the district as a whole. However, sometimes districts try a product without fully understanding the package. When the objectives of the package and the school board do not agree, a controversy results. Please be careful when you ''push'' a program for adoption.

Adapting objectives

Sometimes school boards will authorize the use of human and financial resources to adapt a set of objectives for local use. Usually objectives are adapted when the prevailing values of the community, the training of the teachers, and the skills of the students are matched. We can always think of situations when the match is ''bad.'' For example, when teachers are not well trained or students have not mastered the prerequisite skills, a "family planning" course can run into trouble; that is, the community may hold that it is the parents' responsibility to provide this information. Unfortunately, objectives cannot be adapted without adequate planning and training.

You may consider—along with your school board and principal—major sources of educational objectives: libraries of objectives and taxonomies. The two most massive objective libraries are the one developed by Popham (1970) and that produced for Project PLAN (Flanagan, Mager, & Shanner, 1971). The emphasis of these objectives is on academic skills. Career education objectives seem to be gathering in number, particularly through work at Ohio State University (Campbell et al., 1973). Libraries of objectives for affective education are rare.

As a classroom teacher, you will be involved in adapting programs and materials to your district or to your students. You can use the taxonomy sources as a checklist for making sure that many of the important learning activities are included in the adapted program. Indeed, as a classroom teacher involved in adapting programs to meet your students' needs, you might go so far as to create some new objectives.

Creating objectives

Less often, school districts or individual teachers will create their own objectives. After looking at statewide objectives, after reading federal documents on trends, or after a new company comes to town, the school board might encourage you to create a new set of objectives. If you are beginning to worry, please relax. This task is not undertaken by one person using a box of no. 2 pencils! Creating objectives takes time and

"You will be involved in adapting programs and materials to your children." (Owen Franken/Stock, Boston)

patience, art and skill. Creating learning objectives involves applying the problem-solving model, the ABCs, and the basic teaching-management model very carefully. We understand that school districts, textbook selection committees, and you will not often have the time and the support to choose our option of "creating" objectives. At the same time, we believe that the process of preparing learning objectives can help administrators, teachers, parents, and students clarify goals, alternatives for instruction, and ways of evaluating learning.

Creating objectives can follow a script

Sometimes you and your principal will agree that a new set of objectives has to be written. As an aspiring new teacher, you will be "volunteered" for this effort. Find friends fast! Build a working committee for your building. Often, there will not be enough people in the building who want to work on this project. Find friends in nearby buildings. Other schools in your district or community may contain lots of willing minds. The local mental health facility or a local industry may be other sources of willing objective builders. Get these people together in an objective-creating committee (Mannebach & Stilwell, 1978). The purpose of this committee will be to develop a set of objectives for a curricular area.

Objective building follows steps outlined by Robert Mager (1962; 1968). This activity seems to start by speaking about goals and objectives in the most general terms. From this beginning, a concept and a model can be created. This concept becomes the structure on which ideas can be built. Be careful about this concept, because it might be valued by some "important person" (such as the president of the school board). You will often find that unclear and fuzzy statements are offered as objectives.

Four questions for developing objectives

You should ask at least four questions about each objective. Suppose the educational goal (also called an "objective" by the school board) said "The school will 'develop and foster an appreciation of music.' " You can try to clarify this statement by asking questions such as these:

"What do you mean by *appreciate, music, develop,* and *foster*?"

"What does Alice do when she 'appreciates' the 1812 Overture?" That's a tough question, but you are a veteran of Chapter 5, where we show you how to break a logical circularity.

"What are the entering behaviors related to this task? What do we have to teach Alice before she can appreciate the 1812 Overture?" You can see that these questions are related to the basic teaching-management model.

"How do you know when Alice finally appreciates the 1812 Overture? How does the person demonstrate mastery of the particular set of skills that make up the concept?"

These four questions can help you answer a most crucial question for a manager of learning outcomes: "What do you want the students to learn?" Many of your colleagues will become frustrated with you. "You know exactly what I mean!" can be their standard answer. Be patient.

As you begin to clarify a broad, general goal such as "Develop and foster appreciation of music," you will find answers to what students might do to appreciate music. These "do" words are really action words, such as *select, describe, list,* and *match.* You can rewrite the general goals into subordinate objectives. For example, you might write "List the five parts of the 1812 Overture" as a subordinate objective. Your goal is to list the many learning activities that make up the subordinate objective. This list can be used to describe the activities and skills which students must complete in order to master an objective. Essentially, you will want to list all the skills that are needed to reach an objective.

TASK ANALYSIS

By now you have discovered we do not like to leave things unorganized. We like to organize concepts, procedures, and activities into hierarchies. TASK ANALYSIS helps us to order learning activities into a hierarchy. You will want to ask: What subskills and subconcepts must the student perform in order to master this objective? The answer will help you order the many learning activities into a hierarchy. As a classroom teacher you might help a student like Robert task-analyze his paragraph writing. Such a task analysis will help Robert identify the many intermediate behaviors between his entry skills and mastery of his own objective. In this way, task analysis can help a student meet a unique or individual need. As a classroom manager, facilitator, and/or mediator, you will find that task analysis is a kind of bond; it holds program goals and student behaviors together.

Preparing a task analysis

Building a learning hierarchy for a task can be challenging. The simplest hierarchy is a straight line from entry behavior to objective. In this simple hierarchy, mastery of a single prerequisite activity signals the performance of the next activity. (Remember the simple kinds of learning in Chapter 5?) The simple hierarchies are very rare since student behaviors are not usually simple discriminations. Instead of looking for a simple hierarchy, you will want to draw a picture. Possibly you will prepare the following diagram to show the relationships among several learning activities (see Figure 9-2).

Of course, much more detail in a learning hierarchy is possible. In facilitating Robert's mastery of paragraph writing, you and Robert might prepare a task analysis similar to this one. You will show the relationship between the task analysis and Robert's mastery level. Please remember that each student and each task analysis combine to produce a different and unique learning hierarchy.

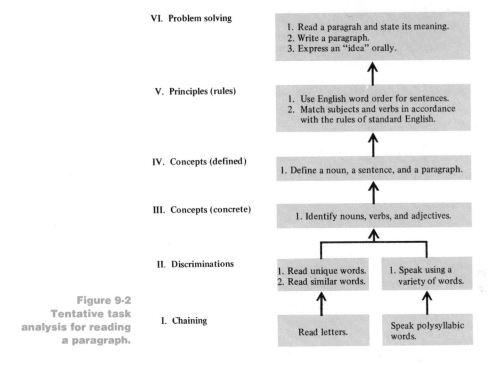

VI. Problem solving

1. Read a paragrah and state its meaning.
2. Write a paragraph.
3. Express an "idea" orally.

V. Principles (rules)

1. Use English word order for sentences.
2. Match subjects and verbs in accordance with the rules of standard English.

IV. Concepts (defined)

1. Define a noun, a sentence, and a paragraph.

III. Concepts (concrete)

1. Identify nouns, verbs, and adjectives.

II. Discriminations

1. Read unique words.
2. Read similar words.

1. Speak using a variety of words.

I. Chaining

Read letters.

Speak polysyllabic words.

**Figure 9-2
Tentative task
analysis for reading
a paragraph.**

You will not learn task analysis overnight. Your first attempts will be full of "bugs." Try out these early versions on small groups, your friends, or a few students. Then take the bugs out and try your task analysis again. On each try, ask yourself this question: What learning activities must students perform in order to reach their objectives? This can help you clarify your task analysis. Please try to ask this question before you start to develop any learning objectives.

PREPARING A LEARNING OBJECTIVE

Once your task analysis is complete, you are ready to write your learning objectives. Robert Mager (1962) suggests that each objective should contain (1) a description of the learning conditions, (2) a statement on the terminal performance, and (3) the level of criterion. Let's take a look at each part.

Conditions of learning

In this first part of the learning objective, a statement of the *conditions of learning* tells the reader which materials will be made available for this learning activity. For example, a condition-of-learning statement might be: "Given a list or map or the following tools, you will . . . ." In this part of the objective, the student is provided with the basic materials for mastering the objective.

Terminal performance

Terminal performance refers to the specific actions which the student will perform. In the terminal performance part, you will specify in detail the action verbs which you want the student to perform. For example, a terminal performance might be "To identify/select/recognize/construct/solve a problem." These action verbs can be ordered in a hierarchical manner (see Chapters 5, 7, and 8) or in a taxonomy.

Criterion level

Criterion level specifies the accuracy required for mastering the objective. This might come as a surprise, but mastery can be set at different levels. This level can be established through negotiation between you and your students. For some performances, like Alice's competition in a spelling bee, you would like 100 percent accuracy. However, for other performances, such as free-throw shooting, you will be very happy with Robert as a 75 percent shooter. The criterion level may vary depending upon the value assigned to the task and a reasonable expectation for Alice's or Robert's performance.

Once these many objectives have been written, they can be synthesized again into learning hierarchies, curricula, and programs of study. We have presented sample learning objectives in Table 9-3. In these two examples, you can find the condition of learning (". . . a set of learning experiences on social power in the classroom"), the terminal performance (". . . identify . . . clarify . . . apply . . ."), and the criterion level (". . . five . . . five . . . one . . ."). Try to identify the three parts of a learning objective in the second sample in Table 9-3.

You can create a complete curricular package for use by other teachers in your school system. Should you and your committee want to help your colleagues in the district, go on and try to prepare (1) sets of examination items for each objective and (2) sets of performance activities for each objective. The development of a complete curricular package will take time. However, by trying to build your learning objectives and the related materials, you will become an effective manager, mediator, and facilitator of learning.

BENEFITS AND LIMITATIONS OF LEARNING OBJECTIVES

Learning objectives can provide many benefits for students and for teachers. Let's look at several potential benefits for students. Later we will look at benefits for teachers.

Table 9-3. Two sample learning objectives

1. Given a set of learning experiences on social power in the classroom, the student will be able to identify five examples of teacher power, to classify five examples of teacher-student communications, and to apply one social-power skill in the classroom.
2. Given a learning unit on chemical equations, the student will be able to balance four out of five equations.

Student benefits from learning objectives

The advocates of learning objectives suggest two benefits for students. First, objectives can help students clarify learning goals. In this clarification function, the objectives facilitate teacher-student communications. Suppose Robert came to you with his paragraph problem. You might respond with "Go read Melville for paragraph structure." This kind of an answer confuses learning. Robert could wander under this kind of educational leadership. The clearly stated response can be "Let's practice identifying topic, content, and closing sentences in paragraphs." This approach is far more facilitative. You can see that objectives provide a focus for learning. Second, objectives can help students find reachable learning goals. For Alice and Ellen, well-stated objectives provide a structure for self-observation and offer a realistic (our fifth "R") set of subordinate objectives for reaching mastery. As you might guess, we are pretty strong in our commitment to learning objectives!

Teacher benefits from learning objectives

Remember that the primary focus of learning objectives is the student. However, learning objectives can also benefit you in two ways. First, objectives arranged in a learning hierarchy can help organize learning activities by (1) telling students what they have to master; (2) suggesting to teachers what they could do to manage, mediate, or facilitate student mastery; and (3) providing a common ground for sharing information about a student's program with parents or another teacher. Our choice of words in the last sentence was purposeful: *telling, suggesting,* and *sharing* do signal the most likely uses of objectives. As a classroom teacher, you will probably want to temper the telling. We have suggested that goals and objectives are actually "reachable learning goals" which have been agreed to by students, you, and possibly the parents as well.

Second, learning objectives can help you select ways to assess a students' entry-level skills. For example our first learning objective (Table 9-3) can require a paper-and-pencil test for classification and identification and observation for evaluating the student's performance. As a classroom teacher, you will want to find out how close a student is to mastery. Once you locate the student's skill on a particular learning hierarchy, you can then facilitate learning. It sounds easy, but the art comes hard *after* you have mastered the many skills related to building objectives.

=== **PROBE 9-2** ===

Think about your teaching area. Try to relate learning objectives to the learning area. Are sample sets of objectives already published? Will you have to adopt or create objectives?

Limitations of learning objectives

Objectives come in all sizes and shapes. You will hear them called *instructional objectives, educational outcomes, expressive objectives,* and probably by ten other names as well before too long. We like *learning objectives* because *learning* suggests a variety of in-school and lifelong activities. We are still concerned about the proper use of objectives.

Acceptance of instructional objectives has not been universal. At first, objectives in education were viewed with excitement and humor (Mager, 1962). As time went on, people began to recognize the potential of objectives. The enthusiasm for objectives was quickly countered by people who offered objections. We will describe some of the objections and suggest a middle ground for using learning objectives. Let's look at three sample arguments that have been raised in opposition to using objectives.

Objectives produce mechanical learning   "Objectives are mechanical and dehumanizing. Analysis of J. S. Bach is impossible. You want us to tear apart a beautiful work of art? It can't be done! You want to quantify something as beautiful as a waltz? We are teaching creative arts and not something mechanical."

Objectives hinder learning   "Students perform no better with objectives than without them." Educational psychologists have tried to find an answer to this argument. Sometimes objectives don't help students reach mastery and some objectives do facilitate mastery (Duell, 1974). The argument, like the other arguments against objectives, does not have a simple answer.

Objectives have a narrow range   "Objectives don't cover everything that's going to be learned." At first, the impression might have been created that objectives indeed do cover the waterfront, but this is probably not practical. Objectives are limited in what they can cover. A different way to look at objectives might be to expand their meaning. At first, objectives described what should be learned. Eisner (1969) wants objectives to be expanded to include something about what students could be learning in a given activity. He talks about expressive objectives. For example, you might suggest "Let's build an ancient city." This expansive objective can become an invitation to create unanticipated outcomes. When you expand objectives, unanticipated outcomes often occur. Students get "turned on" as they work toward mastery. We like this idea for explaining the meaning of objectives.

Middle ground: Reasonable and responsible use of objectives

How can we reconcile these differing positions on objectives? Over time, the two groups have mellowed. The arguments are less loud. Some professors who, ten years ago, would not have tried to write an objective are preparing a few for their affective education programs. Some other educators are trying to reduce the total number of objectives for any single program. They are developing broader objectives that include larger units of information or skills. We believe that early enthusiasm and vigor contributed to much misunderstanding. Indeed, you can select, modify, and create learning objectives that meet your educational needs. For example, you might have to write very specific objectives for students who have low skill levels. If Alvin can't dress himself, you might need separate objectives for socks, shoes, pants, and so on. On the other hand, Lenny is ready to manage objectives on Shakespeare's sonnets. You will want to establish objectives that fit with the basic model you adopt. If you use a model similar to the basic teaching model, your objectives will relate to your educational goals and to the assessed entry behaviors of your students. If your objectives are carefully planned, it will be easier for you to use them reasonably and responsibly in managing learning outcomes.

ASSESSING ENTERING SKILLS

Setting up objectives is only the beginning. Your challenge will be that students won't come to you with the same levels of skill development. Alice and Ellen have mastered paragraph construction, but Robert has not. He knows he has a skill deficit. Robert is rather unusual because he can tell you what he wants to master and what he has not yet mastered.

RECOGNIZE INDIVIDUAL DIFFERENCES

Most students and adults do not know their own skill deficits. Those few people who *do* know are often afraid to tell you. Instead of waiting for a classroom full of eager Roberts, you will have to assess students' skills before they begin to master learning materials. You will discover that students are performing at different levels of mastery. For example, Robert might be weak in paragraph construction but strong in reading comprehension. Indeed, you might discover that Sidney and Millicent are on the same mastery level in English. However, Sid is far ahead in math and Millicent is superior in social studies. In your classroom, you will want to recognize these individual mastery levels. Later, you will arrange your instructional strategies so students at roughly the same mastery levels can learn together.

CONSIDER VARIETY OF INFORMATION

Assessment of a student's entry skills will require information from a variety of sources. In some schools, you will be able to ask the guidance counselor or the school psychologist for help. These professionals usually have time for the more complicated cases. In many schools, you will find that counselors and psychologists are too busy or simply unavailable. Instead, you will be doing your own assessment. You will want to use observations and interviews as well as testing. Smith (1969) has organized several assessment strategies which you may use as a classroom teacher. For example, you might use informal measures of perceptual-motor skills such as having students walk on the 2-inch side of a two by four or by having students imitate your body movements. For another example, you might, in reading, use the *Cloze procedure*. Here, Alice would be required to supply the missing word in a sentence. After the students fill in the blank you can assess their spelling or ability to follow general rules (such as "*I* before *e* except after *c*"). You will want to gather your own set of assessment procedures.

GUIDELINES FOR TEACHING

Assessing Entering Skills

Please be very cautious with your assessment. You might want to ask a teaching colleague for guidance. Parents can also be very helpful in program preassessment. Remember that your best source of information is the student. Robert clearly stated his skills and his goal. You will want to learn how to ask the "right" questions to get at the prelearning activity assessment. You will find that art and skill can again be carefully combined to give you maximum information. Let's look at the guidelines:

• *Consider prerequisite learning experiences.* When the learning manager (you) begins to assess a student's performance, much information is needed. Try to start the student at the right level in the learning hierarchy. In the past, many teachers and parents did not spend time on observing whether students like Robert had mastered spelling, sentence structure, paragraph outlining, and the other skills involved in paragraph writing. Indeed, many preassessments simply did not occur. As a result, students like Robert were "plunked" in the wrong place in the learning skill hierarchy.

• *Consider the learning style.* Students seem to have different styles of learning different kinds of materials. Barclay (1978) suggests that some students learn better in a structured environment, others learn better in an independent study program, while still others seem to work well in small groups with classmates. Finally, there are students who seem to learn more effectively in the tutor role. For example, Alice might learn her social studies by using a filmstrip, but she prefers the small group for learning science.

• *Consider family/social support.* As you begin to get a feel for the information about your students, you might try to assess their support from parents and classmates. Kifer (1975) reports that parental support really made a difference to high- and low-performing students. Barclay (1978) says that children cannot really learn in the classroom without the teacher's approval and classmates' support.

• *Use psychometric, observational, and interview data.* Sound familiar? Never put all your judgments in one basket. Spread out your collection of information so you can measure the same skill in several different ways (Buss & Ploman, 1975; Mischel, 1977).

• *Integrate the assessment information.* Once more you are applying problem-solving techniques when it comes to putting these many different bits of information together. You can apply the formula for entry behaviors: performance objective minus the entering behavior level equals need. This formula can be used to help locate the student on your learning hierarchy. Indeed, you can use the total package to help you select an instructional strategy.

SELECTING INSTRUCTIONAL STRATEGIES

In your classroom, you will frequently be asked for help. Often, students will be able to give you a clear statement of their problem. You will ask yourself a familiar, crucial four-part question: What *strategy* can *we* use to help this unique *student* reach the particular learning *objective*? The key words have been italicized for emphasis.

FOCUS ON INSTRUCTIONAL STRATEGIES

Instructional strategy is a planned sequence of activities directed toward a goal. For Alice, Robert, or Ellen, we don't have a single answer to our familiar, crucial four-part question. We believe that each question can be answered by a list of several "better" strategies rather than by a single "best" answer. You will want to apply problem-solving activities with your students. In this give-and-take exchange, both you and your students can become more confident. During your teacher training program, you will learn about many different ways to organize strategies. In Table 9-4 we suggest five ways in which you might want to organize strategies.

Your great undertaking—managing learning outcomes—can be bound together by the basic teaching model. Really, you are using the model to organize available information. For example, the learning objectives can be found. They have been either imposed by the school board or the book publisher, negotiated by a curriculum team or by you and a student, or created by you, Ellen, and Robert. For another example, the entry-skill information is available, usually in a paper-and-pencil test. We recommend gathering observations and interview data also. You find the information and organize it. Earlier, we said that task descriptions and task analysis produce a hierarchy on which you can place each student or cluster of students. The hierarchy placement suggests a learning strategy for reaching mastery. You will have to make some pretty wise educational decisions.

Table 9-4. Alternative ways to order instructional strategies

Instructional strategies	Activities
Communication channels	In your classroom, you will try to choose a communication strategy to help meet student needs. You might try to lecture or to set up teacher-student dialogues. In other situations, you will ask selected students to lecture (give an oral report). In still other situations, you will try to communicate with a small group or with one student. Each of these communication strategies seems to be appropriate for different situations (Davies, 1973; Worell & Nelson, 1974).
Curricular strategies	Sometimes, changing the educational materials can produce novelty and interest (Berlyne, 1960). You might try to give your students a variety of textbooks, programmed texts, slide-tape presentations, language masters, and packages such as *Man: A Course of Study.* How you help students keep active in learning will depend also on how you mix field trips, projects, library work, visitors and minidramas (Brophy & Good, 1974).
Group arrangements	You will discover that some students seem to learn more and faster in certain kinds of group arrangements. You might use one small group to help selected students learn math. In this small group, you might set up pairs of tutors and students to work together. In another small group, the educational purpose might be very different, so the composition of the group would be different. If you are lucky, you might be able to set aside a part of your room for study carrels. Some of your students might find it difficult to read chemistry because of many distractions. Any noise from a classmate can add to those distractions. In a carrel, the visual and auditory distractions can be reduced.
Motivation management	In Chapter 5, we talked about reinforcement. It is possible to arrange a classroom so that student performance is rewarded on a planned basis. Premack (1959) discovered that activities can be used to reinforce task-oriented work. Recall from Chapter 6 that in the

Table 9-4. Alternative ways to order instructional strategies (Continued)

Instructional strategies	Activities
	classroom, Premack's ideas are called contingency management. We discussed the idea that when a student completes a ''contracted learning activity'' (for example, eight math problems), he or she may enjoy a reinforcing activity (for example, playing Monopoly for five minutes). The ''Premack principle'' has grown to become a ''token economy'' that ''pays'' people for performances and allows them to ''buy'' snacks, free time, and TV (Sulzer-Azaroff & Mayer, 1977).
Management styles	We cannot predict how you will manage learning outcomes. We are fairly certain that your decision will be based upon many different things, such as (1) financial support, which relates to the social status of the student(s) and to the expansiveness of the curricular programs; (2) student learning styles, which might be a preference for independence, leadership, structure or dependence, and group learning (Barclay, 1978); (3) your style of instruction, which might be highly controlled, free-form, or integrated cognitive social learning theory; and/or (4) group sizes, which we will talk about later in this chapter.

Group size: Three ways to go

Frequently in this book, we have urged you to keep it simple. We like simply to count the number of children working with a ''teacher.'' On the first level we have INDIVIDUALIZED INSTRUCTION. One child at a time works with a teacher. You will find this approach rewarding but time-consuming. Remember, not every student learns best this way. On the next level we have SMALL-GROUP INSTRUCTION. For us, a small group is two to nine students. You may have more than one small group at any one time, but keep the groups small. In this way students cannot ''hide,'' as many students seem to do in a class of fifteen to twenty. On the third level, we have LECTURE INSTRUCTION. Up to forty students can be involved in this third level. You will find that you develop certain patterns in these larger groups. For example, you stand in a certain part of the classroom or you call on only a few students. In classes larger than forty, our fourth level, students can ''disappear'' from the group. The quieter people never stand out and it is unlikely that you will be able to interact with the quiet ones in these larger classes. Each level has its own strengths and weaknesses. Let us look first at individualized instruction.

INDIVIDUALIZED INSTRUCTION

As a classroom teacher, you will frequently have single students who need your help; each of these will have unique needs. You have a number of choices for your instructional response. You will plan and manage selected learning activities to meet these unique needs. This highly focused planning and management of curriculum and strategy to help a student master a unique goal is *individualized instruction*. We can order individualized instruction into four types. Let's take a look at each of these.

Packaged individualized curriculum

In the packaged, individualized curriculum, the school determines the objectives and the instructional strategies. Here we are talking about programmed instruction, language laboratories, multimedia programs, and complete curricula such as Individually Prescribed Instruction (IPI). B. F. Skinner (1953) developed the earliest kind of individualized instruction, calling his materials programmed instruction (PI). In applying operant conditioning to the mastering of subject matter, Skinner used a brief presentation of content in frames (Table 9-5). In each presentation, a cue signaled the correct response. These cues usually required an active response (as to fill in a blank). Once the response had been made, the student looked at the next frame. In well-constructed programmed

"You will frequently have single students who need your help." (Miriam Reinhart/Photo Researchers)

Table 9-5. Samples of linear and branching programmed instruction

Programmed instruction can be an effective way for some students to master certain kinds of information. In the following passages, you will learn about frames, cues, and reinforcers. Please place a blank paper over the right-hand side of this figure. You may write your answers in the blanks or you may simply ''think'' them.

The purpose of this short program is to help you become aware of linear programmed instruction. In its earliest forms, _____ instruction was developed by B. F. Skinner.	programmed
Skinner believes that people will learn more and faster when they are reinforced. Thus, _____ developed a teaching technique which would speed up learning.	Skinner
This technique involved the use of frames. Each frame included a cue word, a behavior opportunity, and a _____ .	reinforcement
The cue word usually was one that had been used in the previous _____ . The student read the cue word, retained the idea, and	frame
_____ , usually by filling in a blank.	behaved
As time went on, people began to question the three-part structure of the frame. Skinner had argued for _____ behavior. Others began to ask whether the person could learn as much with a covert response.	overt

This kind of program became known as a linear (or linelike) program. The student reads through frame after frame as you have just done. Later an alternative to linear programming was developed by Crowder (1963), whose branching program looked something like this:

	Congratulations! You have just completed a short linear program. Now we will start you on a branching program.
As you will remember Skinner wanted each frame to contain three parts _____ , _____ , and _____ .	The three parts of a frame are cue, behavior, and reinforcement. If you completed this frame correctly, go on to the next frame. If you did not, you might need some more help with Skinner's ideas about programmed instruction. If you want, read Skinner (1954). If you are not that brave, work on the linear program.

The branching program took the student through a series of activities. As long as the student responded correctly, the student went forward. Whenever the student missed a response, the branching program sent him or her through a series of frames or learning experiences which were designed to help promote mastery of the missed response.

instruction booklets, the student reads the correct answer before going on to the next frame. In this way, knowledge of the correct response reinforces the student. Thus, with each frame, the student is reinforced, cued, and asked to perform. Very simple! The students learn frame after frame. Shortly after its introduction, *linear* programmed instruction was seen as the answer.

Educators really got involved in programmed instruction. Crowder (1963) developed branching programmed instruction, in which you could be sent through a series of corrective frames. Textbooks were developed in this model, such as the *Sullivan Reading Program* and Robert Mager's little books that used Skinner's basic ideas about programmed instruction. Today, even dental educators are using programmed instruction combined with slides and audiotapes for many mastery learning tasks.

Not everyone climbed on the bandwagon of programmed instruction. People began to raise questions about Skinner's guidelines for programmed instruction. The following are some sample discoveries:

Learning is faster   Learning does appear to be faster with programmed instruction than with traditional materials (Jamison, Suppes, & Wells, 1974).

No need for continuous reinforcement   The need for continuous reinforcement, sequential frames, and overt responses has not been upheld in several studies (for example, Brown, 1970; Krumboltz, 1964).

"Teacherproof" is an inaccurate label   It is inaccurate to call programmed materials "teacherproof." Indeed, these materials are used in an interactive environment with teachers and classmates. Other stimuli and reinforcers support a student's learning with programmed materials.

PI is better for drill   Programmed instruction is probably better for memory tasks or for drilling a lesson.

These materials represent only one kind of individualized instruction. You will want to use your programmed materials very carefully. We want to emphasize this idea: Programmed instruction is better for some students, some subjects, and some schools; it is not better for everyone.

Flexible individualized program

In the flexible individualized program, the school determines the objectives but the student decides how to reach them. Here we are talking about the project approach to learning. In addition to teacher-made "six-week term projects" which pepper contemporary education, you will be able to purchase complete projects such as *Man: A Course of Study*. In either case, these projects have academic and expressive objectives. These expressive objectives include such expansive goals as "independence" and "creativity." After using these programs, you should be able to demonstrate that many of your students have mastered creative and independence skills.

Personal individual program

In the personal individual program, the school very loosely establishes the methods for learning and the student selects the objectives. This type of individualized instruction is characteristic of unique learning environments such as the Pacifica School in California and the Outward Bound program. In these learning environments, the students need extremely knowledgeable facilitators and mediators. Learning activities and programs *appear* to develop spontaneously. They do, but the planning and careful mixing of questions, models, silence, and patience lead to the spontaneity. These programs are so untraditional that they are often misunderstood by parents and the community. Given the opportunity to work in one of these very special environments, you will want to apply the problem-solving activities to yourself. A very special set of skills, a large amount of self-regulation, and creative behaviors in several different areas appear to be prerequisites for the staff.

Independent study

In an independent study program, the student sets the objectives and determines the means by which they are to be reached. Only some very unique students appear to be suited for this kind of individualized instruction. You will want to encourage some students to develp the self-management skills to learn in this way. However, please realize that most of your students will be more like Robert or Edward. It would be very unfair to ask such students to master materials in this fourth type of individualized instruction unless you were willing to help them master the prerequisite skills.

Individualized instruction does benefit some students

Selecting and planning the use of the better types of individualized instruction takes time. Once you and your students have decided to go ahead, some very nice benefits occur. For example, Alice, who wanted to find an alternative means of approaching her studies, might really become excited about learning. At least four benefits of individualized instruction can be listed.

Work at own rate   The student has an opportunity to master materials at his or her own rate. Students must learn to be self-regulating before they can do this.

Interaction important   The student has a high rate of interaction with the effective learning environment. You will remember that student-to-environment interaction facilitates learning (Chapter 5).

Immersed in materials   The student is immersed in the materials. You will recall that getting really involved in the materials was a prerequisite for problem solving. The same idea applies to individualized instruction.

Practice self-regulation   The basic four-part model for self-regulation (Chapter 5) can be practiced in individualized instruction. In the future, we hope you will use each type of individualized instruction with selected students.

Individualized
instruction does
ask more of the
teacher

You now have a fairly clear idea of individualized instruction. It can be expensive. It is costly in terms of planning and selection time for any one student. You will want to balance this cost with school goals and student gain. In any case, extensive management is needed to integrate individualized instruction within the overall matrix of classroom management.

We are cautious about using too much individualized instruction. In our visits to classrooms, we have found students immersed in individualized instruction—the entire class, all at the same time. We have found students wandering about with no stated goals while they were supposedly working on their library project. We have found teachers urging students to finish all at the same time "so we can go out and play." Some principals pride themselves on their "individualized instructional programs." As a careful problem solver, you will avoid jumping before you've considered the range of instructional options. If you do decide on individualized instruction, consider a peer tutor, a high school student volunteer, or an educational psychology student. These helpers will help you assure

"If you do decide on individualized instruction, consider a peer tutor, a high school student volunteer, or an educational psychology student." (Nancy Hayes/Monkmeyer)

that your learning environment is effective. Plan ahead and use individualized instruction wisely.

SMALL-GROUP INSTRUCTION

As a classroom manager of learning outcomes, you often encounter small clusters of students who have roughly the same learning goals. Each student is still very unique. However, such a cluster of students—for example Samantha, Ellen, and Millicent—have the same learning goal: mastery of completing application forms. You will plan and mediate selected activities in small-group instruction to help these girls meet their unique and also common learning goals. This special planning of learning activities and facilitation of instruction to meet the common needs of several students is small-group instruction.

Activities of a small group

Two to nine people can be members of a small group. In such a small group, frequent and often intense interaction is common. There is "no place to hide." You will want to facilitate small-group instruction so that classical, operant, and cognitive social learning theory can be used to promote learning. For quiet (shy) Alice you can promote the group as an "island of safety." She can try out new skills, gain self-competency, and develop new attitudes. For outgoing (bombastic) Robert, you can use operant learning to shape up his new ideas. For teenagers, peers are very powerful reinforcers. For impatient Ellen, all the group (including students and you) can become models in a close, intense learning experience. Patience can be learned through modeling (Bandura, 1977). Thus, in these small groups you have a great potential for mediating selected skill development and for managing classroom activities (see Study 9-2).

STUDY 9-2: FACILITATING ACADEMIC MASTERY BY PEER TUTORING

Mastery of introductory educational psychology can be a challenge for some students. Coyne (1978) tried to develop a small-group strategy for mastering the course principles.

Coyne worked with twenty-one students over a five-week period. Each day the class met for ninety minutes and studied a learning unit. The course materials were divided into nine units, each with objectives and an examination. Every other day the students were given an examination. A cumulative exami-

nation was given at the end of the five-week course. The experience was intensive for the participating students!

The study was divided into three parts: baseline I, intervention, and baseline II. In the first baseline, three lectures were given. Each lecture was followed by an examination. The students' performance on these three examinations was ranked high, medium, and low. Based upon these rankings, the students were assigned to peer-tutorial pairs or to an independent study group. The students in the pairs were further assigned to high-low, middle-middle, and high-middle combinations. Five other students worked as members of the independent group.

In the intervention which extended over learning units four, five, and six, the members of each dyad were encouraged to work together. If both students met a 90 percent mastery criterion, each student received five bonus points. Also, if both students met this criterion on all three of the intervention units, each received ten more points. Additionally, these pairs did not have to attend the course review. Thus, each member of the pairs gained from tutoring the other. The five independently functioning students worked on these same three learning units. Points were awarded on the same schedule.

In the second baseline, the lecture-exam pattern from the first baseline was reestablished. All students completed the last third of the course in three lecture-examination units.

The results are important for introductory educational psychology students and for future classroom managers. During the intervention, the academic performance on three examinations for every student who had been paired with a high performer (i.e., high-medium and high-low combinations) improved over their baseline scores. In contrast, the five independently working students did not improve their scores during the same three units. An analysis of the structured interview or questionnaire revealed that more than half the students preferred the peer-tutoring learning strategy.

Coyne has a tentative conclusion from his study. He suggests that pairing students with other tutor/models who are academically stronger and also rewarding the dyads for their combined performance facilitates the lower student's mastery of the required materials. You might try peer-tutoring to facilitate student academic mastery in your own classrooms.

Adapted from: Coyne, P. D. The effects of peer tutoring with group contingencies on the academic performance of college students. *Journal of Applied Behavior Analysis,* 1978, *11,* 305–307.

Alternatives for small-group instruction

Many different kinds of small-group instruction can be used in your classroom. Let's take a look at three alternatives which are fairly common.

Team project   At some point you probably worked on six-week projects. We did. In our classroom visits these projects are still acceptable learning activities. In many situations, the team project was something like this: the teacher listed the topics (such as "The Rise of Mercantilism" and "The Influence of Rivers on European Commerce"). In addition, the teacher provided a detailed checklist for the six-week project report. As long as each student contributed in a planned and anticipated manner, the team project was OK. We've also seen team projects in which the team members, the topic, and the report format were chosen by the students. Between complete teacher control and complete student-managed learning lies a reasonable midpoint for structuring team projects.

You might want to use team projects for their side effects. Suppose, in English class, you tried to assign a good student, an average student, a talker, and a quiet one—plus someone who was none of the above—to each project group. Then you would require each group to work together on specific projects. In our classes, we have watched the quiet ones become more active, the talkers slow down, the good writers become better speakers and so on. In these structured groups, the overt emphasis can be on the development of academic skill. At the same time, unanticipated affective-social changes can occur. You might find that these groups also build up trust, friendship, and peer support (Slavin, 1977). Team approaches do have an important place in the classroom.

We offer another caveat about the team approach. Many students seem to react by becoming very convergent in their work. "The team" seems to control each member's classroom performance. For some students, this kind of external control is very helpful. For many students, however, other kinds of small-group instruction are more appropriate.

Discovery learning   Another useful small-group instructional strategy is discovery learning. We have talked about discovery in Chapter 7. Discovery learning is supposed to promote independent thinking. It looks easy in the classroom. However, discovery learning is a very demanding example of applied, guided problem solving. The advocates of discovery learning—such as Jerome Bruner (1961)—suggest that it facilitates transfer and promotes self-motivation.

As a classroom teacher, you will want to use discovery learning at appropriate times. Both your students and you can suggest limitations in its use. We believe that special kinds of students are more suited for discovery learning than most young people. Since discovery learning is, in our terms, guided problem solving, you already have one cue: It is better for students who have had some successful problem-solving experiences. Successful experiences occur when a student masters some skills. Here is a second clue: Students who are "turned on" to learning seem to benefit more from discovery than students who have low motivation.

In the same way, a special kind of teacher is needed for discovery learning. This teacher is one who has the time and energy to plan each clue, each question, and each piece of curricular material. In addition, this teacher has the patience to let the students learn on their own. If you choose to do this, you must communicate in nonverbal ways. Don't jump in; move your body or tilt your head. With patience and care, you will be able to master many of the prerequisite skills for guiding discovery learning in your classroom.

Discovery learning is not for everyone (McLachlan & Hunt, 1973). By now you know that no one form of learning is good for every student.

"No one form of learning is good for every student." (Peter Vandermark/Stock, Boston)

Still, we want you to question each new strategy that you read about or that you practice. Use our four-part question about which students, which strategy, what outcome, and by whom. Discovery learning is appropriate for certain self-regulated students who can generate their own questions and inferences about learning tasks.

Group discussions A third kind of small-group instruction is all too common. You have had many small-group discussions in high school and college. How many of these discussions can you remember? We've asked this question many times. Our students seem to answer "Those discussions from which we have had a product, such as a decision or a plan for action." They are saying that they took something useful away from these discussions.

Timing is
important

Small-group discussions offer students some wonderful opportunities. Of course, each participant will have to be ready for the discussion. Robert just might not be ready. Remember that he must have mastered the prerequisite skills. Once he has done so, Robert and his classmates can have some fun. In group discussions, students (and you) have the opportunity to become immersed in the topic. They can set the objectives for the discussion. The opportunities in a group are almost limitless. In addition, discussions enable the participants to practice self-expression, adapt to others' points of view, receive constructive criticism, establish common grounds for ideas, and reach conclusions. The students in a well-planned group discussion will "get involved." They will interact with each other. They will have eye contact. They will relate to one another in many ways. The focus, in other words, is upon the students in the group.

You will discover that small-group discussions are better in certain kinds of situations, involving selected students with specific skills and goals. Let's take a look at several guidelines for conducting a small-group discussion:

GUIDELINES
FOR
TEACHING

Group Discussions

• *Clarify different ideas.* Small-group discussions can be used to clarify ideas in areas where there is no agreement. The group-discussion learning activity can be a way to exchange ideas and to build some agreement.
• *Facilitate critical thinking.* You will want group discussions at the right times. Not every student is ready for group discussion at precisely your time! Preassess your students on the discussion topic. For example, Ellen may not be able to listen to a classmate talk about a controversial topic without becoming very angry herself. You will want to be a mediator in some heated discussions. Or Alice might have a hard time expressing herself on a controversial matter. You will want to be ready to facilitate Alice's timid statements.
• *Avoid reanalyzing topics.* You will want to avoid reanalyzing topics, such as a rule or a procedure on which agreement has been reached. Over time, you will gain experience and feedback that will help you to use group discussions more and more effectively.
• *Guide the discussion.* Try to guide the discussion so that each student will have something to remember. You can learn how to mediate a small group. The skills can be mastered. You will want to learn how to surrender some control to the students. You might, for instance, move to the perimeter of the group, restate ideas, prompt, fade, and reinforce the speakers or their ideas. You will have many chances to practice these group discussion skills. Over time, you will master question asking (not speechmaking), encouraging (shaping) participation by some students, offering alternatives, avoiding premature judgments (counting to eight before responding), looking at the speaker, and being silent appropriately. Practice your values-clarification skills (Chapter 8). You will find it very hard work to help a discussion go from a beginning to an end, but it will be worthwhile.

Each choice in managing learning outcomes requires you to look at the possible benefits to your students and yourself. Individualized instruction can benefit your students greatly. It can also take up a great deal of your time. Certainly, individualized instruction will interact with the curriculum and the effective learning environment. Some changes in this equation are found in small-group instruction. For example, more students are involved in small-group instruction, more different learning models (simulation, role play, etc.) are available, and more different media can come into play. In small-group instruction, more students can probably be involved in more different learning activities than they can be in individualized instruction. Group instruction can be less expensive than one-on-one. You will want to weigh the time and management costs versus "missing" a student. How you are going to work with challenging students will be up to you. It's a choice of style. Our book is full of useful ideas. You will be sensitive to students who begin to "miss"; catch them before they fall.

LECTURE INSTRUCTION

As a classroom teacher, you will often speak to the entire class. In such situations, you have made the judgment either that everyone is ready for the information or that everyone needs the information. For example, at the beginning of a learning unit and before the students begin to master the materials in their own unique ways, you might speak to a large number of students. Similarly, you can remember your first fire drill. The teacher might have told you everything there was to be known about the drill, but some of the friends still went the wrong way! You will organize your materials and present them so as to provide some arousal value. The LECTURE INSTRUCTION is one way of providing students with well-organized, important, and easily forgotten information.

Our definition of lecture instruction is a cue to you. Well-organized materials are always hard to find. You will have to spend hours working on your lectures, even to groups of fifteen students. Your words must have some pizzazz. You must keep the students' attention. You must also be aware that the students will forget your pearls of knowledge and wisdom fairly quickly. The students are supposed to be fairly quiet during a lecture. However, many—such as Ellen and Robert—prefer interaction in their learning. They want activity. Whenever you lecture, Ellen and

Robert begin to chat together. A few students can master materials covertly or passively. But there are others who will feel their individuality is not being recognized in the course of a lecture. All the students are not happy during a lecture learning activity. While all these different things are happening among your listeners, you are in control. You've got the chalk! You can see that lectures can be appropriate for selected students and certain learning outcomes, but not for everyone.

Two kinds of lectures

Lectures can involve either small or large groups. Each group size has some unique characteristics. We want to take a look at these characteristics.

Small-group lecture For most of you, a small-group lecture will be a common way to manage your class. You will try to talk to thirty or forty young people at one time. In this learning experience, you will discover that some students can interact with you. A few will ask questions. One or two will smile at your jokes. You might even get a student to answer another student's question. In this small-group lecture involving the entire class, you will lose some students. They will stay in the room but drop out of class. One of the authors remembers a sixth-grader who could not answer the teacher's question but *could* tell the engine make of a passing truck during the last five minutes of the lecture. He was an amazing person! Usually, some careful planning must be done before a small-group lecture is tried. Plan ahead.

Large-group lecture   Some of you will be employed in high schools that use the large-group lecture for certain instructional purposes. In a large-group lecture, you will have several challenges:

• You have an "eye line." Students who are not in the first few rows or along your eye line will probably lose out on the points of your lecture.
• Listening is a prerequisite skill. Students who do not have "lecture listening" skills need prerequisite training (for example, how to take lecture notes). It is really hard to go from a small-group discussion to a long, large-group lecture. Sometimes students find it difficult to handle all of those words.
• Anticipate words, phrases, and ideas. Students who can anticipate the words, phrases, and ideas in a lecture can be covertly rewarded when they do so correctly. You will discover that reinforced students will attend your class. Other unreinforced students will be late for class or perhaps not show up at all. In lecturing, you will want to plan your materials so that the students can anticipate your outline. If you are planning to tell a joke, you might change your tone, move your body, smile, or signal to your students in some other way that they may temporarily stop taking notes.
• Retroactive inhibition hinders lectures. Retroactive inhibition (remember Chapter 7) begins to occur after about fifteen minutes. After about that the students can anticipate your outline. If you are planning to tell more difficult. You might put the outline on the board, summarize after about fifteen minutes, and encourage students to fill out a lecture summary sheet. You can see that you will want to be very cautious about long, large-group lectures.

Student activities in lecture instruction   Students will have some unique and demanding opportunities in lecture learning activities. Lectures offer students opportunities to apply their problem-solving skills. In small-group lectures, a student like Ellen can practice overt and interactive learning skills. Selected active students might find an opportunity for participation in the small-group lecture. Take time out from your notes. Shape up their participation. In the large-group lecture, some of your students will have to practice covert learning and reinforcement. Our self-regulation model will be helpful to many students in a large-group lecture. Both lecture conditions require mastery of the skills that prepare the student for a lecture.

As a manager of classroom learning, you will find several challenges in the lecture approach to facilitating learning. On the one hand, lectures certainly simplify educational administration; in this way many students can be handled at any one time. On the other hand, lecturing is another masterable skill. You can learn how to outline a logical and coherent presentation. You have many choices for an outline. For example, (1) *comparisons and combinations* can be exciting for political parties or issues in the Civil War; (2) *sequential relationships* can bind together ideas in history and chemistry, such as the importance of blood plasma's discovery; (3) *part-whole relationships* can guide ideas about social systems and about mathematics; and (4) *transitional notions* can be used to bridge historical eras and to integrate knowledge. If you really want to use lecture instruction to manage learning in your classroom, you will want to consider these five guidelines:

GUIDELINES
FOR
TEACHING

Lecture Instruction

• *Establish relationship with your audience.* You will want to let your audience know that you are aware of them and concerned for them. You might sit and talk with a few students before starting your presentation, or you might find a special face in the middle of the room and share a point with that particular person.

• *Gain your students' attention.* As you are aware, a student may be peering intently at you and still be "miles away." You will want to encourage the behaviors that go with the label *attention*. In addition, you will want your students to "lock onto" your lecture. Some teachers raise and lower their voices to keep the group's attention. Other teachers use humor, excellent graphics (slides, pictures), and/or costumes to gain and maintain many students' attention. You will want to mix art and skill in this special activity.

• *Make material in the lecture relevant.* Old-fashioned laws of supply and demand and/or modern international trade can be awfully dry. Ellen, for example, may drop out as long as your presentation remains "dry and irrelevant," but she might become more interested if you were to talk about her Japanese radio or her Italian shoes. You will want to find examples from your students' day-to-day experiences for your lectures. Should you want to underline the relevance, emphasize your main points. (Kick the podium!)

• *Use advanced organizers.* You probably expected to find this guideline somewhere in this list. The use of advanced organizers in a lecture provides a scaffolding for the rest of your presentation. Remember that a carefully worded statement of your purpose can really key students in to your ideas *provided that* they are able to receive or understand your cues.

"It takes more enthusiasm to prepare a complete lecture than the ordinary person can supply." (Frank Siteman/Stock, Boston)

• *Convey enthusiasm.* On many topics, it takes more enthusiasm to prepare a complete lecture than the ordinary person can supply. You have run into teachers who have been dull. For some of these teachers and for some of the topics, a different instructional strategy might have been more effective. You have probably had a professor who was a poor lecturer but a great one-on-one helper. In the one-on-one situation (tutoring), you have the chance to interact and to stimulate the student, so that the topic does not seem so dull after all. In your lectures, you will want to change your discriminative stimuli (Chapter 7) by using graphics, coordinating body movements with points in your presentations, and changing the intensity or volume of your voice. Enthusiasm is produced by a cluster of skills which you will be able to master.

Recap on lecture instruction   If you decide to use lecture instruction, please remember these three points:

1. It's really a lot harder than it looks. A large amount of planning is needed before you will be ready to go before your students.

2. Retroactive inhibition tends to erase complex and/or brand new information. You will try to avoid presenting new or complex information for the first time in a lecture. Take time to lay the groundwork. Help your students become aware of the new terms. Give a preview of coming attractions in minilectures followed by small-group instruction.

3. Passive learning seems to be less effective for certain kinds of information and skills than active learning. All the data on active and passive learning are not yet in, even after fifty years of research.

Some studies seem to say that lecturing helps some students and hinders others. The gainers and losers seem to balance each other. In short, the facts on lecturing are not entirely clear (McLeish, 1968). As a classroom teacher on any grade level, you will try to find more precise information about your students, their objectives, and your skills before you decide to lecture. We urge you to apply the problem-solving sequence (Table 8-1) to choosing the better instructional strategies for students in your class.

We hope you are beginning to see that it takes a lot of work to choose the better instructional strategies. We believe that you can cluster most of these strategies into one of three groups: individualized, small-group, and lecture instruction. In a way, these clusters begin to reveal a structure for managing learning outcomes. As you learn more in this teacher training program and in your professional in-service development, you will find that specific strategies can be easily placed in one of these three clusters. In the eighties, nineties, and the next century, more and more precision in goals, objectives, strategies, and management styles will be available to you and your colleagues.

MASTERY LEARNING

You have many choices among instructional strategies. We have discussed some of these, as well as their costs and benefits. No matter which you choose, you will want to plan for your students' mastery of the learning objectives. In the following section, we will discuss mastery learning and how you can use it with all your students.

Basic beliefs about mastery learning

Mastery learning involves four basic beliefs about education (Block, 1971). We shall state and discuss each briefly.

Students have an aptitude for learning This basic value or belief guides the teacher using mastery learning; it is crucial for success. An *aptitude* in mastery learning is the time needed by a student to master a given learning activity. For example, Sally does have the *aptitude* to learn how to drive in traffic; she needs enough time to master the required skills. In a class where all the students finally demonstrate an aptitude for learning, the ''grading curve'' is not normal, such as that in Figure 2-1. Indeed, as students master specific objectives on their way to completing the learning unit, their performance may look like the curve in Figure 2-3.

Differential instructional styles   In mastery learning, the instructional materials and strategies are taken from the objectives and the task analysis. These materials and strategies are frequently revised (Dick & Carey, 1978). You will want to have many different approaches so that students like Sally can work with better learning strategies. This belief also implies that no one instructional strategy is best for all students. You will work very closely with each student. Frequent tests can be used to facilitate Sally's adjustments in learning style. This will help her to reach mastery—meeting the learning objectives—and encourage Sally to stick to her tasks.

Objectives and learning tasks are clearly stated   In mastery learning, students and teachers work in a ''no tricks'' environment. Objectives and the related learning tasks are clearly stated for parents, teachers, and students. A sense of cooperation among students and teachers is facilitated by this kind of environment. Sharing and clarification are encouraged when people are acting on this mastery learning belief.

Stick-to-itiveness   In mastery learning, the fourth crucial belief is that students and teachers will persevere. They will not give up. The objectives and task analysis set up many chances for success. Each mastered performance objective can add to the student's list of competencies. In mastery learning, the environment seems to get students involved, encouraging them to try one more objective.

Student and teacher activities in mastery learning

These four beliefs suggest a demanding kind of learning environment. The student seems to feel pressure to perform. This kind of pressure comes from success—each newly mastered objective is another step toward self-regulation. In mastery, students will demand a supporting, facilitative learning environment. Let's look more closely at mastery learning.

Student activities in mastery learning   Mastery learning is work for students. The emphasis upon individual performance means that there is no place to hide. If she wanted to, Sally could fade into the background of the regular classroom. However, in mastery learning, each student's performance is frequently assessed and reviewed. Supportive feedback from teachers—either adults or peer tutors—is usually available. Indeed, the entire learning activity, from entering behavior to objectives, is laid out for the student. Time will be available; performance schedules can be contracted; and the objectives and learning tasks can be so clearly stated that Sally can monitor her own progress toward mastery. *Formative* tests along the way tell her how she is doing. The feedback of performance results can encourage Sally to do even more. In our experience, students get excited about mastering skills.

Teacher activities in mastery learning   Program planning is primary in a mastery learning environment. Students and parents will not see the preprogram detail, the creation of anticipated remedial and/or supplemental learning activities, or the mounds of records. In mastery learning, you will work with both the slow and fast students at their own pace. This kind of instruction is very different from that in traditional classrooms, where all of the students are given the materials at the same time. This means that you may work with very small groups rather than the entire class. In addition, support for you will be important. Your principal must be involved in mastery learning. Your colleagues will have to understand that mastery can produce some very excited, self-regulated students who want to learn on their own schedule. Try to get them involved in your planning. You might discover one or two parents who can help as program monitors, tutors, or record keepers. In mastery learning, your work will require a careful balance among management, mediation, and facilitation. It will be hard work, but worthwhile.

Mastery costs and benefits

As you might expect, not everyone shares our enthusiasm for mastery learning. Some of the arguments over mastery learning and its related "competency-based instruction" sound convincing. Let's consider some of them.

Selected students   "Mastery learning may not be for everyone." We agree. Not every child, teacher, or community is ready for mastery learning. It takes a lot of planning and preprogram preparation to get people ready for such an educational change (Stilwell, 1976).

Costly undertaking   "The time and effort put into objective writing is wasteful." The argument here is one you have heard earlier, in Chapter 8, and in this chapter: It certainly seems impossible to write objectives for an appreciation activity. We agree that writing objectives is time-consuming and frustrating. However, it it not impossible.

Extensive record keeping   "Mastery learning requires so much record keeping that little time is left for teaching." This argument makes us a bit impatient. Education should help students to grow, not to guarantee the comfort of teachers and administrators. It is clear that when you use mastery learning, you will keep records on objectives mastered, materials to be revised, and projected learning activities. Record keeping can be annoying and demanding. These records will be important, for example, in the case of a student who is advanced in math and slow in English. We are trying to help children learn, and that idea is paramount.

Narrow emphasis   "Mastery learning reinforces people for learning only the performance objectives." This outcome is certainly possible as long as you teach narrowly defined objectives. You can broaden your objectives to include problem solving, creativity, and divergent thinking.

We have seen elementary-age students, counselors, and even dentists become truly creative problem solvers. Thus we find some of the arguments meaningful, particularly those about administration and cost. However, the challenge for us and for you is to make the learning environment powerful and effective. We believe that mastery learning, carefully carried out, can be a giant step in that direction!

INSTRUCTIONAL INNOVATIONS

In the early 1960s, educational innovations became "the name of the game." Social changes brought about by Supreme Court desegregation decisions in 1954 were putting stress on many school districts. Taxes were getting too high, especially taxes for education. Indeed, the quality of American life was in doubt. After all, the Soviets launched the first space flight: would they beat us to the moon too? There were many demands for improved instruction.

NEW DIRECTIONS IN TEACHING

For most of the 1960s, we had innovations in four areas: (1) in teaching, such as computer-assisted instruction and team teaching; (2) in testing, such as criterion reference and performance tests; (3) in curriculum, such as *Man: A Course of Study* (MACOS) and *Developing Understanding of Self and Others* (DUSO); and (4) in multimedia instruction, such as coordinated slides, tapes, or filmstrips. Indeed, in the 1960s, an innovation here and an innovation there began to sound an educational echo as familar as the refrain of "Ol' Mac Donald's Farm." There were so many new approaches to managing instruction that they rarely coordinated with much of anything else. A few innovative efforts have survived into the seventies and eighties. Probably a hundred others will appear during the eighties and nineties. Let's look at six instructional innovations (Table 9-6).

Table 9-6. Current educational innovations

Innovation	Brief description
Educational games and simulations	In an effort to make learning more fun, a broad variety of educational games were identified, adapted, and created. Take a walk through any large toy department and read the labels: When the game publishers talk about games for all ages, they are not fooling. In addition to being fun ways to learn, many of these games offer "safe" simulations of real future experiences. Games and simulations have objectives; the activities are related to the objectives, and rewards are given for reaching goals. Students can really get involved and excited, and will frequently be rewarded by these games which are like learning activities (Coleman et al., 1973). You will want to consider educational gaming in your management of learning outcomes (Chapter 6).
Team teaching	The idea that one person could or even should know everything there is to know about chemistry, English, or any learning-skill area is slowly falling by the wayside. In some innovative educational environments, individual teachers are beginning to team up to manage learning. You can visit elementary schools where one teacher will have his or her own class plus that of a teammate for English and history. This lets the teammate prepare the demonstrations for science and math during the English and history periods. On the secondary level, knowledge is changing so rapidly that some teachers can become experts in only one or two areas. Indeed, some teaching teams assign lecturing and small-group instruction to different team members, depending on their individual strengths and weaknesses.

Table 9-6. Current educational innovations (Continued)

Innovation	Brief description
Modular instruction	An old idea, units of instruction, has been considerably dressed up. You might be old enough to remember something like "Now we are going to start the unit on Greece" or "The diagramming unit will take us the entire marking period." Those old units now have some real class. A typical unit can have (1) learning objectives; (2) texts, films, and activities to help students reach mastery; (3) alternative versions for (a) helping students get ready for the unit and/or (b) providing additional experiences for enrichment; and (4) evaluation items for both knowledge and performance. In the last twenty years, learning modules have matured so they can be purchased as complete educational packages. You will want to examine simple instructional modules before you decide to adopt, adapt, or create your own.
Educational TV	If you are as old as we are, you have missed many exciting learning experiences such as *Sesame Street, Infinity Factory, Inside/Out,* and *Firing Line.* Educational TV is not a new idea; it's over thirty! However, in its new form, thanks to federal monies and grants from foundations, it is competing for viewers with commercial TV. During the day in many states, you can get a full dose of reading, writing, arithmetic, affective skill development, and reality. The programs can be creative, and they appear to help people master many needed skills (Liebert, Neale, & Davidson, 1973). Not stopping with young children, ETV can help you plant a garden, keep trim, pass the GED, and generally experience a liberating education in your own home.

Table 9-6. Current educational innovations (*Continued*)

Innovation	Brief description
Computer-assisted instruction	Ever since Sidney Pressey in 1928 and B. F. Skinner in 1954 talked about using machines to program instruction, educators have been trying to find the best way to apply these ideas. Along came the computer in the fifties and sixties. Post-Sputnik money made the computer available to educators. The computer was viewed by many as the great educational manager: After all, it had a good memory and could do lots of things at the same time! At first the computer was used to modernize Pressey and Skinner's teaching machine ideas. The computers were programmed to "talk" with the student, to provide encouragement, to update each student's academic history, and/or to improve the student's performance on a particular drill-like activity. Indeed, enthusiasm became so strong that computers were drilling tens of thousands of students at one time. Then, in the late sixties, the money began to run out. People found out that computer-assisted instruction was least effective for teaching language, better for tutoring, and most appropriate for drilling (Jamison, Suppes, & Wells, 1974). Later, computer-assisted instruction changed, so the computer was used to support and manage instruction. School districts began to use computers for record keeping and planning on a districtwide basis. In a few programs, such as Project PLAN, the computer was used for record keeping, test scoring, and suggesting classroom management strategies for selected students (Flanagan, 1970; Weisgerber, 1971).
Satellite-supported instruction	The space-age wizards at NASA

Table 9-6. Current educational innovations (*Continued*)

Innovation	Brief description
	have joined with educators to prepare programs for dissemination via satellite. At the University of Kentucky, nearly a dozen in-service programs have been developed for career educators, early childhood paraprofessionals, and classroom managers, to name a few. These programs have been set up so that seminars can be conducted using the satellite for the video and telecommunications for the audio. These seminars are so arranged that more than a thousand students are attending at sites in the thirteen Appalachian states. Alaska is developing such a satellite-supported educational program to help meet the needs of students in remote sites across that large state. The potential exists for large and complex educational programs to be transmitted to thousands of students via the NASA satellites (Bramble, Hensley, & Goldstein, 1977).

COMPREHENSIVE INSTRUCTIONAL SYSTEMS

What seemed to be needed was a more comprehensive approach to the management of learning. Let's look at the following situation to see how an integrated system of instruction might help you.

Can you remember a time when the phone rang, you twisted your ankle on a misplaced shoe, and the cat wanted out all at the same time? You might have limped to the phone, called to the cat, and then discovered that the caller had hung up. Usually, these overload situations seem to occur on the day your supervising teacher is planning to visit. Screaming is an appropriate response to such an overload. After that, you might open the door for the cat, put away the shoe, and sit down to collect yourself. You might ask, "What happened? How can I do a better job? Could I have gotten the cat out earlier, put away my clothes, and answered the phone in time?" Perhaps you'll conclude: "Aha! A system will help . . . I gotta have a system." The same kind of crisis seemed to occur among educators in the 1960s. People began to get together to try to build comprehensive instructional systems.

As a result, several comprehensive instructional systems were developed, implemented, and evaluated. These comprehensive systems took advantage of the work which had been done on the basic teaching model, learning hierarchies, and innovations in instructional strategies. Indeed, these new comprehensive systems have brought about many changes in American education. Let's take a look at three major efforts.

Individually prescribed instruction (IPI)

IPI was started in the early 1960s under the leadership of Robert Glaser at the University of Pittsburgh. In its earliest forms, IPI was an application of programmed instruction for the K-6 curriculum (Weisgerber, 1971). Over time, the learning materials have been expanded to include reading, math, science, handwriting, and spelling. In short, the basic teaching model that Glaser initiated grew into something really big. Research for Better Schools (RBS) in Philadelphia is presently responsible for program implementation and continuous evaluation of IPI.

Program goals The educational goals of IPI are consistent with the program title. Students are to (1) work at their own rate; (2) develop mastery of the specified academic areas and of problem-solving skills; (3) practice self-initiated instruction; and (4) perform self-evaluations. In a way, IPI students have mastery of self-regulation as their program-directed educational goal (Glaser, 1977). Indeed, these goals are fairly similar to education's most general goals and to cognitive social learning theory's highest levels of performance.

IPI management Let's take a look at how IPI tries to help students reach the program's educational goals. Remember that IPI is an example of a comprehensive instructional system. We will talk about four broad areas: learning materials, student roles, teacher responsibilities, and program administration. Each area is both independent and interdependent with the others.

• Learning materials. In IPI, the learning objectives are ordered into subject-area hierarchies. These several hierarchies are further clustered into learning units. Students work through each unit on their way to the top of the particular hierarchy (math, spelling, and so on). More recently, a *Humanizing Learning Program* was added to the basic IPI set of curricula. This program is designed to help educate students for living.

(Sounds suspiciously similar to affective education!) A third learning program was added for the IPI administrators. The *Administrating for Change Program* is designed to help administrators and teachers "get up to speed" in IPI. By our order of presentation, you can get an idea of how a pioneering program can really grow.

• Student roles. In IPI, the subject-area hierarchies are arranged in such a way that students may work in different levels at the same time. For example, Robert might be able to forge ahead in math while going a bit more slowly in the writing or spelling learning units. As you can see, this kind of multilevel learning is fine as long as Robert stays in IPI. Should he transfer to a traditional learning environment, Robert's fifth-grade-level math and third-grade-level writing might present an administrative problem. In IPI, the student's work is frequently monitored. From the time the student starts in IPI, she or he meets a cycle which looks like this: placement test, unit pretest, prescription development, peer/teacher tutoring, group instruction, or project materials (Scanlon & Brown, 1971). As you can well imagine, the "teacher" and each student have many opportunities for interaction.

• Teacher responsibilities. The IPI teacher has a new role. Rather than serving as a traditional dispenser of information, the IPI teacher becomes a learning manager. In this role, the IPI teacher prepares prescription sheets for each child, directs the work of the paraprofessionals, and mediates individual students' learning needs. The IPI paraprofessional plays a crucial role. This person does extensive grading, keeps records, and tutors. As an IPI classroom manager, you will want to have extremely well-trained paraprofessionals to support your students.

• Program administration. IPI administrators are both program managers and instructional leaders. In these two roles, they communicate with parents, provide ongoing research information to RBS in Philadelphia, and maintain staff development. The work of IPI administrators is especially difficult: In the IPI part of their day, they must be flexible enough to handle students who are learning at different rates and levels; in the rest of their day (about half the time), they must be able to manage a traditional learning environment. This kind of dual life is only for brave and committed administrators; they *do* exist, you know!

IPI is the oldest of the three comprehensive instructional systems presented in this chapter. It is an ongoing educational undertaking. Most certainly, IPI calls for a lot of clerical support. Every program you will consider has pluses and minuses. IPI is no different: Some students seem to be able to learn some materials faster in IPI than other students in a more traditional educational environment. In any case, IPI continues to grow; at present, it is in 276 schools in 38 states.

Two other comprehensive instructional systems were developed during the 1960s. These systems—Project PLAN (Program for Learning in Accordance with Needs) and IGE (Individually Guided Education)—tried to benefit from each other's experiences and to improve upon each other. The programs are very similar in many respects and unique in other ways. Let's look at each of these two systems.

Project PLAN John Flanagan and his associates at American Institutes for Research discovered, in their massive survey of 440,000 high school students, that American education was not meeting student needs (Flanagan et al., 1964). Therefore, Flanagan organized Project PLAN for grades 1 through 12.

In this computer-supported instructional system, Flanagan and his associates prepared over 6000 learning objectives which were arranged into two-week learning activities called Teaching Learning Units (TLUs). Language arts, social studies, math, science, and guidance are covered by these objectives. In PLAN, students are encouraged to use available assessment data, parental expectations, teacher recommendations, and their own judgment to plan medium and long-range educational goals. The computer, now an option, can function in PLAN to grade tests, keep records, and help the learning facilitator to plan each week (Flanagan, 1971).

"Language arts, social studies, math, science, and guidance are covered by these objectives." (Westinghouse Learning Corporation)

IGE   For nearly twenty years, educational psychologists at the Wisconsin Research and Development Center for Cognitive Learning have been developing, evaluating, and improving IGE. Under the leadership of Herbert J. Klausmeier, the Center has applied its research skills to (1) preparing materials for math, reading, science, and social studies; (2) training teachers to work with individualized instructional materials; and (3) helping administrators reorganize their school systems for IGE (Klausmeier, Rossmiller, & Saily, 1977).

In this research-based instructional system, each component is continuously studied, evaluated, and revised. For example, the principals in each school supply the Wisconsin Research and Development Center with massive amounts of data on teacher teams, effectiveness of planned instructional strategies, curricular materials, teacher-in-service training, and parent-community relationships. The Center provides extensive support for the reorganization of teacher and administrator roles to provide the greatest possible support for IGE students.

Similarities and differences among instructional systems

You will find similarities and differences in each of these three comprehensive instructional systems. The similarities seem to include an emphasis upon the four-part basic teaching model and special training for teachers and administrators. The differences seem to reflect the varying approaches of the program's originators. In IPI, there is a simple, straightforward approach to individualized instruction and linear programming; in PLAN, a deficit remediation approach helps students reach mastery through a complex variety of TLUs, programs of study, and an optional computer-support feature; and in IGE, a continuous developmental approach invites participation and feedback from an increasingly large number of school districts.

MINISYSTEMS

So far we have talked about the comprehensive systems. Let's now take a few minutes to describe several specialty programs. It will be a lot easier for you to use one of these miniprograms than to convince *everyone* they should use IGE, PLAN, or IPI! For example, you might want a model for classroom management for your entire junior class (the Keller Plan). Or one of your colleagues might need some help in working with affective skills (DUSO or TAD). Should you be really lucky, you might convince your math or reading supervisor to let you use DISTAR. Let's look at these few specialty programs (Table 9-7).

Each of these three sytems is unique. It is almost as if each program has its own set of values. At the same time, these three programs share

Table 9-7. Sample minisystems

Program	Description
1. Developing Understanding of Self and Others (DUSO)	Donald Dinkmeyer and his associates have developed several different packages for young children, their older sibs, and for parents. These programs have an extensive offering in affective learning activities. You can learn how to use these materials with the help of comprehensive teacher guides (Dinkmeyer, 1970, 1973; Dinkmeyer & McKay, 1976).
2. Direct Instructional System for Teaching Arithmetic and Reading (DISTAR)	In DISTAR, the materials are so prepared that students and teachers really work hard, physically and mentally. The program is set up so the students can earn large amounts of teacher praise for specific activities. This means that daily programming and monitoring of each student's performance is necessary. Indeed, a computer-supported planning service is offered (for example, Engelmann & Bruner, 1974; Becker & Engelmann, 1976).
3. Keller Plan	In the mid sixties, college-level teaching was jolted by an old idea. Skinner had talked about it, but Fred Keller did it—set up a plan for individualized instruction on the college level. The plan has many characteristics that are old friends: learning objectives, multimedia lectures, individually paced learning, and orientation toward mastery. Should a student want help, peers who have mastered the materials are available as tutors. Indeed, the plan can work with less actual instructor hours. Of course, the Keller Plan is appropriate for those people who can work without direct supervision

Table 9-6. Current educational innovations continued

Innovation	Brief description
	of a classroom teacher (Keller, 1968; Kulih, Kulih, & Carmichael, 1974).
4. Toward Affective Development (TAD)	In 191 lessons, more than enough for a school year, you can use TADs to stimulate psychological and affective development. You may want to integrate these lessons into your classroom management style. Should you do so, you will find a variety of materials for 8- to 12-year-olds (Dupont, Gardner, & Brody, 1974).

in common a basic teaching model, learning objectives, programmed instruction concepts, mastery learning, and a commitment to educational research. You might feel that the comprehensive educational undertaking is overwhelming. After all, 6000 objectives can't all be right! It's too much. Yet, the excitement of a whole educational program can affect everyone—students, teachers, administrators, parents, and community. That's what education is all about—everyone making a unique contribution.

Still, for everything we've said about these programs, a better comprehensive instructional system and better ways to manage learning outcomes are on your drawing board. Your new program will represent an integration of the experiences being gained in IPI, PLAN, IGE, and the miniprograms. Please share your ideas with us.

LEARNING ACTIVITY: PREPARING LEARNING OBJECTIVES

In the very near future you will be asked to prepare instructional materials for role playing, later for student teaching, and still later for the *real* thing! We want you to begin to gain some experience in preparing learning objectives.

Please use your own teaching area such as Spanish, physical education, or preschool care. Take the learning hierarchy described in this book and prepare a sample learning objective for each level. Thus you will prepare a three-part performance objective for each of the response chains, discriminations, concrete concepts, defined concepts, and principles as well as for problem solving.

SUMMARY

1. As a classroom teacher, you will want to become a manager of learning activities. In this role, you will plan, organize, coordinate, and direct as you facilitate and mediate students' mastery.

2. The basic teaching model provides a structure upon which you may hang your many MANAGEMENT decisions. In this model, you will be involved in specifying objectives, preassessing student behaviors, selecting instructional processes, evaluating student performance, and providing feedback. This basic model is held together by such relationships as TASK ANALYSIS and feedback.

3. Learning objectives have come into their own in education. It is almost impossible to find a curriculum without a set of objectives. You might have to restate GENERAL OBJECTIVES, breaking them down into SUBORDINATE OBJECTIVES and then into LEARNING OBJECTIVES. The last of these are most easily stated in students' terms. Indeed, they are written for the benefit of students.

4. The preparation of learning objectives follows a fairly standard script—from global statements, subordinate objectives, and learning objectives to the specification of tasks. This specification of learning tasks is called *task description*. Once the many activities have been described, they can be ordered by task analysis. This activity helps arrange learning activities in terms of the prerequisite skills.

5. Learning objectives have three major parts: (1) conditions of learning, which describe the ''givens'' in a learning activity; (2) terminal performance, which specifies the actions to be mastered in the learning activity; and (3) level of criterion, which talks about the number of responses or their percentage of accuracy.

6. Choosing a better instructional strategy involves your finding answers to a four-part question about strategy, student, need, and whom. A better strategy is a more realistic search than for the ''best'' answer. Too many competing influences make the ''best'' answer too elusive for us.

7. INDIVIDUALIZED INSTRUCTION can be broken down into four categories: (*a*) school-selected objectives and school-selected instructional strategy—for example, programmed texts; (*b*) school-selected objectives and student-chosen strategies for mastery—for example, six-week term projects; (*c*) school-selected instructional guidance and student-selected learning objectives—for example, the Pacifica School; and (*d*) no school participation in either choice of objectives or method—for example, the students may select objectives and decide how to reach them, as in self-regulated learning.

8. SMALL-GROUP INSTRUCTION for two to nine students can involve less interaction than individualized instruction (such as tutoring) but

far more peer-to-peer and student-to-teacher interaction than lecture instruction. You might consider team projects, discovery learning, or group discussions. In any case, you will have to manage (plan, organize, coordinate, and direct) student learning. Small-group instruction calls for a careful balance of art and skill.

9. LECTURE INSTRUCTION, while common in classrooms, is another example of "different strokes for different folks"—it's not for everyone! Should you lecture, please (*a*) establish a relationship with the audience, (*b*) gain your students' attention, (*c*) make the material relevant, (*d*) use advanced organizers, and (*e*) convey enthusiasm.

10. Three major comprehensive instructional systems were discussed: Individually Prescribed Instruction (IPI), A Program for Learning in Accordance with Needs (PLAN), and Individually Guided Education (IGE). Each program offers unique learning experiences. At the same time, the progams share common elements such as a basic teaching model, learning objectives, programmed instructional concepts, mastery learning, and a commitment to educational research. The three programs were discussed in terms of their learning materials, student roles, teacher responsibilities, and program administration.

11. Although the list can be far longer, the authors suggested several innovations that appear to be here to stay: educational games and simulations, team teaching, modular instruction, educational TV, computer-assisted instruction, and satellite-supported instruction. In addition to being this brave, the authors offered descriptions of four specialty programs or instructional systems: DUSO, DISTAR, the Keller Plan, and TAD.

SELF-TEST

1. Management has been defined as performing four activities:
   a. _____
   b. _____
   c. _____
   d. _____
2. Instructional objectives can be generated by carefully following an analysis such as the following:
   a. task description
   b. educational goals, subordinate objectives, and learning objectives

   c. terminal objectives, learning conditions, and criterion
   d. thorough review of the learning task
3. Glaser's basic teaching model is fundamental to managing learning outcomes. The model has four points:
   a. appraisal, goals, use, and satisfaction
   b. feedback, preassessment, objectives, goals
   c. objectives, preassessment, instruction, and evaluation
   d. planning, organizing, coordinating, directing
4. Task analysis involves _____ skills,

while task description is mainly _____ skills.
a. choosing, trying
b. ordering, listing
c. taking apart, describing
d. using, sorting

5. The assessment of skills involves
a. watching the child
b. talking to the child and observing him or her at play
c. using paper-and-pencil tests, observation, and interview
d. visiting the child in another class and talking to the parents

6. The selection of management strategies can
a. be painstaking and complicated
b. mean choosing among individual, group, and lecture approaches
c. be precisely done in cognitive social learning
d. none of the above

7. Programmed instruction developed by B. F. Skinner and modified by N. A. Crowder
a. permits linear and branching experiences
b. encourages small steps, cues, and reinforcement
c. promotes self-paced learning

d. all of the above

8. Comprehensive instructional systems have many ideas in common, such as objectives and feedback. Choose the correct pair of ideas:
a. PLAN and team leader
b. Klausmeier and Glaser
c. IPI and RBS
d. IGE and TLU

9. You will want to plan learning strategies that will consider
a. what _____
b. by _____
c. for _____
d. with _____

10. Well-prepared learning objectives have three parts:
a. _____
b. _____
c. _____

11. Mastery learning uses the following assumptions:
a. sequenced learning and monitoring
b. unlimited time and sequenced learning
c. objectives and skewed distribution
d. aptitudes control learning time

SELF-TEST KEY

1. a. planning
   b. organizing
   c. coordinating
   d. directing
2. b
3. c
4. b
5. c
6. b
7. d
8. c
9. a. strategy
   b. whom
   c. this individual
   d. that specific goal
10. a. condition of learning
    b. terminal performance
    c. criterion level
11. b

 KEY TERMS

GENERAL OBJECTIVES: Broadly stated ultimate educational goals.

INDIVIDUALIZED INSTRUCTION: A program of study that is individually prepared; for example, an independent project, a tutorial, etc.

LEARNING OBJECTIVES: Statements that precisely specify the learning conditions, the action process, and the criteria for a learning event.

LECTURE INSTRUCTION: The oral presentation of well-organized, important, but easily forgotten information.

MANAGEMENT: A learning skill that includes four subordinate skills: planning, organizing, coordinating, and directing.

SMALL-GROUP INSTRUCTION: Planned and mediated selected activities that help two to nine people meet their unique learning goals.

SUBORDINATE OBJECTIVES: More precise statements developed from general learning objectives. These subordinate objectives are adaptable to local areas such as school districts or individual buildings.

TASK ANALYSIS: A procedure for ordering a hierarchy of subskills that the student must master to reach an objective.

REVIEW TERMS

ADVANCED ORGANIZERS

FEEDBACK

CHAPTER 10

Evaluating Learning Outcomes

CHAPTER OUTLINE

LEARNING OBJECTIVES

After reading Chapter 10, answering the self-monitoring questions, and reading any further references of your choice, you will be able to:

1. Define and give examples of key terms
2. List and describe the procedures in producing teacher-made and standardized tests
3. Compare norm-referenced and criterion-referenced testing
4. Compare pictorial and statistical methods for displaying results
5. Analyze alternative grading practices for your own learning environment
6. Analyze an evaluation situation for a learning activity or a program
7. Observe, record, and graph an individual's performance

In what ways can you find out whether a single student or a group of students is making any progress? How can you match your educational goals, instructional activities, and evaluation? What does a test score mean? In a very short time, you will be trying to find solutions to these questions. Students will be needing your help—Dody wants to master Spanish before her trip to Colombia; Natalie gets discouraged about her "failing" grades; and Sally is trying to improve her driving skills.

In looking for ways to help your students, you will be facing a grand challenge. You will want to be a creative problem solver. In order to begin, you will want to be a reliable observer, keep good records, monitor what is happening, create learning situations, ask questions, give tests, assign grades, and—finally—evaluate learning outcomes. We believe that this order of activities is the one strongly suggested by cognitive social learning theory. Indeed, observing carefully, considering more than one or two variables, and judging the product are important aspects of evaluation. Evaluation is an integrating activity which can be helpful to you and your students in planning and managing learning.

SAMPLING BEHAVIOR BY TESTING

Testing is done in order to sample behavior for a specific purpose. Usually one of three different purposes is considered before a test is used: diagnosis, the sampling of performance, or the monitoring of progress. The first very common purpose of testing is diagnosis. For example, before a student such as Dody starts a program to study conversational Spanish, a test can be given to diagnose how much of the language she already knows. A second common purpose of testing is to sample final performance. For example, final or summative examinations are generally designed to measure how much the student knows in a given area. A SUMMATIVE EVALUATION gathers information on what a student can do at the end of the course. A third and comparatively new purpose of testing is the monitoring of progress. For example, you might want to find out how well Dody is doing with subordinate Spanish-speaking skills. The practice of getting information about a student's progress during the program of study is called FORMATIVE EVALUATION. As a classroom teacher, you will want to consider both the timing (preprogram, in-program, and end-of-program testing) and the purpose (diagnostic, for-mative, summative) in planning how you will sample your students' behavior.

COSTS AND BENEFITS OF TESTING

You will want to consider the benefits and potential aversive consequences of testing. The arguments about testing seem to focus on three areas: (1) benefits to students, (2) benefits to you, and (3) potential aversive consequences (costs). Let's take a brief look at each of these points of view.

Potential benefits to students

In each discussion, we want to emphasize the word *potential*. Throughout this text, we have said that individuals are very different. Some students "freeze" at the very mention of tests. Others seem to do very well on certain kinds of tests but not on other kinds. The authors have reviewed many application folders of students with poor grades and fabulous scores on the Graduate Record Exam. We are not really sure about the benefits—or harm, for that matter—from testing. Still, we will propose that tests can provide three benefits: they can increase motivation, promote un-derstanding, and provide information and reinforcement.

Tests can increase motivation Probably, this means that students will want to do well to avoid some aversive consequence, such as loss of an allowance or fellowship. Indeed, many students seem to want to dem-onstrate knowledge and skill development.

Tests can promote understanding You have a pretty good idea of what this means. Dody will probably work very hard and spend long hours in the language lab in order to master each Spanish quiz, test, and summative examination.

Tests can provide information and reinforcement In Chapter 5, we talked about the use of positive and negative feedback. As long as you emphasize the corrective feedback dimension of testing, we agree that test results can provide reinforcement (Page, 1958) and information for skill development. In order to help you get started on using feedback in testing, we recommend that you try to write a note on each test. This means that you will read each form or essay and generate some positive and/or negative comment for your students. The effort will take time, but it can bring great motivational benefits.

Potential benefits to teachers

Testing can help you manage your classroom in four ways: (1) diagnosis and prescription, (2) measuring mastery, (3) discrimination among students, and (4) program planning. Let's take a look at each of these four areas.

Diagnosis and prescription   Some of you will work in school districts that have an extensive preschool screening program. Others will work in school systems that use their own versions of comprehensive instructional systems (Chapter 9). Still others will become involved in programs for special children (Chapter 12). You will want to use selected tests to help you identify students with special needs and to determine their strengths and deficits.

Measuring mastery   Midprogram and end-of-program assessment can provide you and your students with a variety of important information. For example, Sally can use a mastery test to demonstrate that she has improved her parking skills. You will want to practice using formative and summative examinations in your own work.

Discrimination among students   The idea of using tests to discriminate among students is quite controversial. In some school districts, readiness tests are given to kindergartners to determine in which group a given child should be placed. This idea has given rise to horror stories about children (Albert Einstein, for example) who were placed in the wrong slot but who turned out exceptionally well. Later, in high school, the testing of academic performance is used to "track" students for college prep, general, or other programs of study. Some of you can remember hearing parents talk about the AFQT, which was used to place them in a particular kind of military training program. The use of tests for placement is very common.

Program planning   You will want to use paper-and-pencil tests to facilitate individual educational plans and to manage classroom learning experiences. As you will discover later in this chapter, you will want to consider other kinds of information too, but more about that later.

Potential aversive consequences

The subject of testing can become a very loaded one! How it becomes loaded depends very much on how you use the test results. Let's take a look at some of the arguments against the use of tests (potential costs).

"You will want to use paper-and-pencil tests to facilitate individual educational plans and to manage classroom learning experiences." (Doug Wilson/Black Star)

The teacher-student relationship is disrupted It has been argued that testing can disrupt the teacher-student relationship. You may remember a teacher whose tests were simply torture, or you might have learned to fear testing in a classical conditioning situation (Figure 10-1). Remember our discussion of classical learning in Chapter 5 while you study Figure 10-1. If you were given a choice, you might not have selected that teacher.

=== PROBE 10-1 ===

When you were taking your first test, you probably had some feelings about what was happening. Try to recall those feelings and list them. Did any of those covert behaviors have behavioral antecedents or consequences? Share your one-page narrative with a classmate.

Failing is destructive Some people have pointed out that failure is such a final thing—like the end of the world. Remember Millicent and her test anxiety? She did not perform at her mastered level (Chapter 6). Failing grades, the argument goes, seem to destroy the student emotionally and physically.

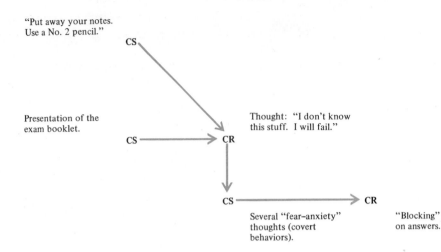

"Put away your notes.
Use a No. 2 pencil."

CS

Presentation of the
exam booklet.

CS   CR

Thought: "I don't know
this stuff. I will fail."

CS   CR

Several "fear–anxiety"
thoughts (covert
behaviors).

"Blocking"
on answers.

**Figure 10-1
A picture of test
anxiety.**

Testing is subjective Then there are those who talk about the "subjective shifts" in grading. One of the authors is certain that his horrible handwriting has influenced one or two teachers. Huck and Bounds (1972) studied the grading practices of teachers. They found that teachers who themselves had poor handwriting were not biased against students with poor handwriting. However, they found that teachers whose handwriting was good had little patience with students whose handwriting was illegible. This word from the wise can be compounded by what else we know about subjective shifts. For nearly seventy years we have known that teachers have a hard time grading essay examinations. Starch and Elliot (1912) gave two essay examinations to about two hundred professors of English. These learned people read the two examinations and assigned grades that ranged all the way from A to E. In a defense of history, these two essays were poorly constructed and the grading criteria were fuzzy. Still, using tests in your classroom can be difficult.

In sampling behavior with tests, you will want to be aware of some of the many difficulties and challenges. As a classroom teacher who is committed to preventing "bad" experiences in the testing situation, you will want to try all of our guidelines for using tests.

 GUIDELINES
FOR
TEACHING

Using Tests Wisely

• *Use more than one test.* As a classroom teacher, you will want to collect several different samples of each student's behavior. You might meet this guideline by using several quizzes and a final examination. On the other hand, you might use one or two formative examinations and a summative observation. In some areas, such as foreign languages and chemistry, you can test students with an examination and with a lab demonstration.

• *Use objective measures.* This guideline is difficult to apply. On some tests, you will not have much difficulty in describing the correct answer. For example, Natalie can demonstrate her skill in a multiple-choice test pretty clearly. However, should you use an essay test, please write out your criteria for scoring before you give the quiz to your students. You will need these criteria when you read their formative or summative performances.

• *Be prepared to give specific performance information.* In preparing to give feedback of test results to students and their parents, you will want to plan specific information and an overall evaluation. Some parents will feel satisfied with "Your daughter is a wonderful person," but others will probe and ask you to provide evidence that their child is indeed such a delight to have in class.

• *Be prepared to communicate the test results clearly.* Over the years, students' test results have become more and more available to parents and students. Fifteen years ago, a few enlightened principals shared test results with parents. Since 1974, the "Buckley amendment" has made test results available to students and their parents. The new law has not been without problems; some specific IQ scores are written into student records. Unfortunately, many people do not understand about overlapping test results—they see a world of difference between 110 and 120. We recommend that you rank individual students' scores as much as possible.

You will probably understand our sensitivity about tests. The benefits are there. Your students will gain valuable information from them. You will learn about yourself and your students. At the same time, tests seem to scare many people. You will want to try to prevent that fear as often as you can. After all, you will use many published and teacher-made tests during your professional career. Appropriately, you will decide that neither teacher-made nor standardized tests can gather all the information you will need about your students' performance.

TEST CONSTRUCTION

In Chapter 9, we talked about the management of learning outcomes. In this chapter, we are discussing the evaluation part of management. You will remember that planning was the first part of good management. You will want to plan your learning experiences, including your evaluations.

In constructing your classroom tests, you will want to be true to your students. "Tell 'em, teach 'em, and test 'em"—the three T's of test construction. Thus, in the "Tell 'em" T, you will want to prepare learning objectives. These learning objectives will take time. They will be shared with students and parents. Objectives are crucial to the construction of tests.

You will try to build a matrix of learning objectives for your course. As a classroom teacher, you will want to start building simple kinds of matrices. Later, you can set up very complex ones for your tests. You might find these activities helpful in matching your instructional goals with your test construction (Popham, 1978a). Let's take a look at four different kinds of learning-objective matrices:

Simple content

Simple content can be tested. You can ask for the atomic numbers of lithium, sodium, potassium, and cobalt or simply the multiplication tables for nines.

Topics versus time

You can examine topics versus time spent on the learning task. You can assign a large value and many test items to the more time-consuming topics and a small value in terms of test items to the brief topics.

Topics versus learning hierarchy

You can make sure that your learning hierarchies relate to the content of the course or textbook. This kind of extended planning would probably help Sally demonstrate whether she has mastered the drivers'-training learning objectives. At this point, you may be beginning to feel that matching learning hierarchies to a course can become rather complex. Indeed, we are guiding you into a new kind of testing which samples some of the skills in a particular domain, for example, those involved in driving a car (Martuza, 1977).

Multiple-source matrix

A multiple-source matrix—such as the content domain versus psychometrics, observations, and interviews—can provide a very comprehensive way to test a person's performance. For example, you might give Dody a multiple-choice test for recognizing Spanish words. Later, you might observe her talking with a Spanish-speaking visitor. Finally, you might conduct your own interview with Dody as if you were the *aduana* (customs agent). From these three sources of testing information, you can make a decision whether she has reached the educational goals that have been set for your course.

As you can anticipate, we prefer a combination of the last two different kinds of learning-objective matrices. You will build your best tests when you plan, task-analyze the learning activity, use the basic teaching model, and evaluate the student's performance. Later in this chapter, we will give you an outline of how tests are professionally developed.

===== **PROBE 10-2** =====

For this particular learning unit, find two friends and work on building a learning-objective matrix. This project will take some time, but we have given you samples in Chapter 8 and in this section. Try to come up with six test items. Share the effort with your instructor.

TEACHER-MADE TESTS

The most common way of gathering information about student knowledge or skills is the teacher-made test. Let us take a look at the way a typical test is constructed:

The working father-teacher staggered home after grading tests in the car pool. After supper, he wrote forty multiple-choice items. He got up early the next morning to open the gates for yard duty. However, his oldest girl had been sick (very seriously) in the middle of the night, the car overheated on the way to school, he was third in line for the ditto machine, and he discovers that he has left the third of four pages at home. Yet—despite the preceding events—he gave the test.

This vignette is somewhat exaggerated, but you get the idea. Teacher-made tests do not benefit from the work of a professional item constructor, from systematic administration and scoring, from an appropriate sample from the learning-objective matrix, or from an adequate norm group. Still, most grades are assigned on the basis of these test results.

As a test maker, you will be limited by only two dimensions—time and your own creative problem-solving skills. As with the working father who needed the system, you might find time closing in on you. Practice the model for the development of self-regulation skills (Chapters 2 and 5) in order to regain control over your time. As a creative problem solver, you will call upon a vast array of different kinds of tests for your learning objectives. In Figure 10-2, you will find a hierarchy for teacher-made tests.

In Figure 10-2, we make the point that you can construct five different kinds of test items for different purposes. For example, you can use matching to measure verbal-chain mastery and fill-in-the-blank to measure mastery of defined or concrete concepts. Let's take a look at these five different kinds of tests.

Essay examinations

Oh, how we have suffered through essay exams. (All the way from "What in the world does she mean by that question?" to "What in the world does he mean by that answer?") Essay examinations have their own

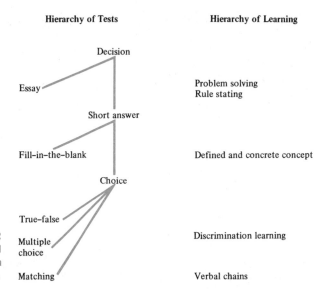

Hierarchy of Tests   Hierarchy of Learning

Figure 10-2 Relating tests and learning in a common hierarchy.

advantages and disadvantages. As far as Sally and Natalie are concerned, essay examinations measure their ability to organize and synthesize information. Students who have mastered problem solving and who write fairly logically seem to benefit from essay examinations. (Are you getting the idea that you will want to facilitate student mastery for answering essay examinations?) You might have a mistaken impression that essay examinations are easy to create. Please don't be fooled. You will want to make sure students know how to "discuss," "compare," "define," and "contrast" before you ask them to perform these skills in an essay examination of American history.

Without preplanning for the students and for yourself, the examination might wind up testing something other than the learning objective. You might find the following ideas helpful in preparing an essay examination.

Limit answer length You might try to limit answer length. In your discussion with Natalie, you might discover that she spent more of her time, almost twenty minutes, on the first essay question. She did not understand that the "(5)" and the "(15)" meant minutes per question. Be clear and precise in communicating this idea to your students.

Give choice of questions Give your students a choice of essay questions to answer. Some students seem to block when they have to answer every question. By giving your students a choice, you are making them more responsible for their own performance.

"Students who have mastered problem solving and who write fairly logically seem to benefit from essay examinations." (Peter Southwick/ Stock, Boston)

Write a model answer Before you hand out the test, write out the several points you want covered for each question. If the answer is worth 10 points, show on your model answer how these points will be distributed. Try your scoring plan on your own sample answer. In this way, you will be fair to yourself and to your students before you are influenced by their answers. Share your model answer with your students during the feedback session following the examination.

Avoid grading bias Please be aware that essay examinations are very difficult to grade. Earlier, we talked about the influence of handwriting on essay grades (Huck & Bounds, 1972). You are going to be further biased in favor of some students, probably the bright, good-looking ones (Finn, 1972). In order to avoid that possibility, we recommend using "secret code numbers" which are sealed in an envelope. Indeed, we have gone so far as to have students use the same yellow legal-size paper and submit each answer separately. We then graded each response separately, recorded the score, and summed the total point count before we opened the envelope containing the secret code numbers. In this way, we have avoided the potential of bias even by names (Harari & McDavid, 1973) and by a student's performance on any particular item. As you can see, there is a lot more work to an essay exam than meets the eye.

Short-answer or fill-in-the-blank examinations

Short-answer examinations—either brief paragraphs or one-word fill-in-the-blank items—do require some different teacher and student behaviors. The short-answer exams seem to require simply stated rules, not elegant answers. Similarly, the fill-in items have a requirement for specific words. Both kinds of exams give you and your students more opportunity to focus your measurement. As far as Dody and Sally are concerned, short-answer items assess their ability to recall specific information. These items require less organizing skill. Indeed, fill-in-the-blank or short-essay answers seem to be a good way to sample some of Sally's new skills. As far as you are concerned, short-answer items are fairly *reliable* and easy to score.

True-false examinations

True-false examinations offer you and your students a grand challenge. You can go way beyond selecting topic sentences from paragraphs and changing one word (you remember those exams!). The statement for true-false items can be written to examine a variety of skills. You can prepare a full paragraph or a single sentence for the student's decision. The tough part will be up to the students, whose chance of being right is 50-50. Indeed, you have doubtlessly noticed that we have not used true-false self-test items precisely because of this possibility of simply guessing. The advantage of true-false testing is really for the teacher. As far as you are concerned, scoring will be simply a matter of ''counting the rights.'' However, you will want some time for feedback. It is extremely important to give students such an opportunity to examine you and your exam. You will have a grand opportunity to respond to these challenges with your best facilitation, mediation, and management skills.

Multiple-choice examinations

A very precise and demanding art is required for the construction of multiple-choice items. In our discussion of standardized tests, we will say a good item writer can prepare eight to ten items per day. As a classroom teacher, you will not have that kind of time for your task.

You will be very busy generating enough multiple-choice items for one test. Each item has two parts: (1) the stem, which describes the content domain for the item, and (2) the several alternatives. As a constructor of items for multiple-choice tests, you will find the following guidelines helpful:

GUIDELINES FOR TEACHING

Constructing Items for Multiple-Choice Tests

Keep choices the same length. You will want to keep your alternative responses about the same length. From your own experience, you will recall that you typically chose the longest answer as the correct one. Before test constructors became aware of that pattern, the longest answer usually *was* the correct answer. Educational psychologists working on this problem have eliminated that cue from their multiple-choice examinations.

* *Equalize answers.* You will want to equalize the position of the correct responses. If you have four alternatives for every item in your test, you will want each alternative (1, 2, 3, or 4) to have an equal chance of being right over the entire exam. In the olden days (middle 1950s), a student's rule was "When in doubt, choose 3 or C." That rule no longer holds much meaning today.

* *Avoid grammatical mistakes.* Keep the stem and the alternatives grammatically correct. Students have blind faith that you will never make a grammatical error. When they spot an error on a multiple-choice test, they tend to eliminate that alternative immediately. You might have to review some basic grammar before you can follow this suggestion.

* *Use logical alternatives.* You will want to use logical and possible choices. The authors have asked students about intelligence tests for adults. The choices were WAIS, ATSF, SBCL, and DRGW—one intelligence test and three railroad names. People still selected the railroads.

* *Avoid "none of the above."* If you use "none of the above," make sure that it is the correct answer. Students get a lot of reinforcement from completing a verbal chain or making a correct discrimination. It is unfair to deny learners this opportunity; we prefer to avoid using "none of the above" as an alternative response in a multiple-choice test.

* *Have one correct answer.* Avoid the absent-minded professor's common problem: two equally correct answers. As far as Natalie or Robert is concerned, multiple-choice items give many opportunities for responding. In addition, they can be written so Sally can demonstrate a wide variety of knowledge and skills about drivers' training. As far as you are concerned, you have worked hard to build the items, and now you will benefit from speedy grading.

* *Measure knowledge and skills.* You will want to measure your students' knowledge about a domain, not their detective skills. In our experience, many multiple-choice tests try to fool or to trick the students with the slightest change of a sentence or a phrase.

Matching examinations

You will be able to use matching examinations to test many of the same cognitive skills you tested with the multiple-choice exams. You can imagine the intensity of problem solving when you give five matching pairs from the single domain of "balance of payments"! Please try to keep this idea in mind when you build a matching examination: you can gain more information from sampling a single domain with five items than you can from using five items for five different domains.

As a classroom teacher, you will be able to choose from the five different kinds of tests that teachers typically construct. Indeed, teacher-made tests can become creative experiences for your students and you. You will be able to focus on your learning objectives. You will sample specific domains. Please do so with a cautious enthusiasm. You will struggle with such questions as "Have I sampled my content-domain-skill matrix?" and "Am I scoring my items consistently?" Struggle, but please do not throw up your hands in frustration and resort to using only standardized tests.

We recommend that you use a mixture of essay questions and well-constructed short-answer questions for your tests. You will want to build your tests from your instructional objectives. You will have gotten our message on test construction if you can assure your students that a consistency exists between your stated objectives and measured ones, between your instructional goals and evaluated ones, and between your instruction and your goals.

STANDARDIZED TESTS

The second most common way for gathering specific information about student knowledge or skills is the STANDARDIZED TEST. A *standardized test* is a professionally developed, standardized procedure for sampling a person's behaviors in order to compare these behaviors with a norm. Standardized tests are typically designed to measure achievement, aptitude, interest, and intelligence. These tests are both *reliable* and *valid* according to the materials provided by the publishers. Let's take a look at the key words which we used above to describe standardized tests.

Professionally developed tests

When we talk about professionally developed tests, we are including many different activities. Publishing tests is a $250-million-per-year business which involves educational psychologists, content-area specialists, item writers, cooperating school districts, and a cast of thousands running such businesses as Science Research Associates (owned by IBM), Psychological Corporation (owned by Harcourt Brace Jovanovich), and the California Test Bureau (owned by McGraw-Hill). The experts in item construction, item selection, and test construction work for long hours in their professional development of standardized tests. In Table 10-1, we give you an outline for test construction. You might use the same activities in constructing your own tests.

Standardized procedure

Standardized procedure covers two major areas: (1) how to administer and score the test and (2) how to interpret the results.

Table 10-1. Sequence in the professional development of a standardized test

Activities	Discussion
1. Define the goals and purposes of the test	In this activity, the important question is: What goals do we want to measure? The answer to this question tells the test constructor about a hierarchy of events: (*a*) goals imply objectives, (*b*) objectives imply task analysis, and (*c*) task analysis implies test items. In standardized tests, the items and the objectives should be closely related.
2. Collect a domain of items related to an objective	*Domain*—a new idea for you in this discussion of tests—means a set, group, or cluster of items related to an objective. In the earlier days of test construction, a panel of "experts" would render judgments on each item. Experts are used today. In addition, test constructors (often called psychometricians) go through a time-consuming task analysis to identify the areas in which test items will be written.
3. Write the best items	Item writing is a new science. A good test-item writer can prepare six to eight items in a working day. A reason why it takes so long is that "good" items (ones that don't give away the answer with grammar cues or silly alternatives) simply have to be created.
4. Try out the items on a small group	Once the items are written, another long phase begins during which the test constructors try to get the bugs out of their tests. They check on item reading level, on scoring the correct answer, on complexity of the instructions, on print size, page color, and a host of other potentially distracting things.
5. Identify the target population for the test	This activity is closely related to the first activity. The purpose of a test must always be checked by asking

**Table 10-1. Sequence in the professional development
of a standardized test (continued)**

Activities	Discussion
	"Good for whom?" The answer lists the characteristics of the norm group. Once the test constructors have found the people who will make up the norm group (you might read about "stratified samples" and "demographics," which are simply fancy terms to describe how you find your norm group), then they give this group the draft test.
6. Rewrite the test	Putting a test together is really creative problem solving! You keep trying out, revising, and tinkering before the creative product is finished. It is quite possible for the test constructor to recycle through activities 1 to 5 several times before this activity is completed.
7. Prepare the test manual	In the preparation of the test manual the guidelines of the American Psychological Association are usually followed. The criteria for a well-developed test are numerous. Included in the guidelines are criteria for adequately describing the administration of the test, for writing the sections on reliability and validity, and for the interpretation of the scores. It takes a great deal of time to write a good manual—one that talks about different norm groups and about alternate ways to interpret the scores. As you gain more and more experience in using standardized tests, you will learn how to recognize well-prepared test manuals.

First, the constructors of standardized tests are careful about decribing every dimension of their test, including how to give it. (Recall your own experiences with the SAT, ACT, or the New York State Regents.) The test publishers describe the seating arrangement, the pencil to be used, time limits for each part, and the wording of the oral instructions. In the test manual which goes with every published test, you will read the carefully prepared instructions for administering and scoring the test. In this way, students take the test under the same conditions and the tests are scored in the same objective manner. Some manuals will even tell you when to pause and for how long before you go on with the administration. As you can anticipate, when you assume the role of "standardized test administrator," you may not laugh, call students by name, or in any way be yourself; you are a part of the standardized procedure.

Second, standardized achievement and aptitude tests provide information for the interpretation of results. This problem of test interpretation remains a gray area for standardized tests. Many arguments, some legal and some ethical, cloud the issue. On the legal side, the new federal laws for student records and for special education say that students have the right and responsibility to see test information. On the ethical side, counselors and teachers seem to be struggling over what is the best kind of information. "What communicates to the student or parent?" seems to be the point of concern for many people. Let's take a brief look at several ways to present the results from a standardized test.

Raw scores Disagreement exists about whether raw scores should be made available to students and parents. On the one hand, the people who are comparing a student with a norm want to keep the scores confidential. On the other hand, the people who are applying mastery learning in their classroom want to keep the student informed about specific mastery of specific learning objectives. No clear answer is available on this issue.

Result profiles When you try to present all the different scale results at the same time, the information can be too much. You can see in Figure 10-3 that Natalie's parents will be quite overwhelmed with the profile of Natalie's performance on seven different tests. We have found that profiles showing the results of standardized tests can be confusing to parents and to students.

Standard scores A standard score converts each student's score into a new value. This new value shows the difference between that student's score and the average score for the test norm group. We like standard scores for reporting the results of tests. Using a standard score, you will have five choices:

• Rank Score. We have a controversy on the use of standard scores. On the one hand, you can tell a student that she is third in a class of forty-

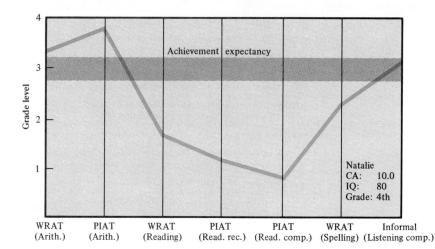

Figure 10-3
Natalie:
Assessment profile.

two students. Being third in a large group is much more meaningful than being third among five classmates. Therefore, you will always want to report rank scores in terms of "out of how many in the group." On the other hand, the entire thrust of mastery learning is away from ranking students in comparison with one another.

• Frequency Distribution. In preparing a frequency distribution, you will list the scores from the highest to the lowest. Simply count the number of people making each score. Use frequency marks to display your information (such as 卌). You can see a frequency distribution in Figure 10-6.

• Percentile Ranks. *Percentile* is another new word for you. Percentiles refer to a percent. For example, Dody made the highest score in Spanish and would be placed in the 99th percentile. This means that 99 percent of the people in the norm group scored lower than she did.

• Standard Deviation Scores. Many standardized tests present the results as standardized scores. For example, the SAT has a mean or average score of 500 and a standard deviation of 100. You might have an SAT score of 510, which means you are performing at about the average for your group.

• Grade-Equivalent Scores. Many publishers' test-scoring services provide the school with a grade-equivalent or grade-level score. Unfortunately, grade-equivalent scores are difficult to interpret. We try to avoid using grade-equivalent scores because some classrooms can be below grade level in comparison with the national norms. At the same time, a particular class can be above grade level for students in the school district. In any case, the best way to use grade equivalents is to know that they are supposed to describe the average score for students at that particular grade level at that particular time of year. For example, Sally's test results suggest that she is at the 7.4 grade level. This grade-equivalent score means that Sally's performance is similar to that of students who are in the seventh grade during that month of the school year, which is January. (You can see that if you start school in September, the fourth month of the school year is January.)

You will want to select the simplest way to present standardized test results. In our view, grade-level scores are too vague and standard scores are too confusing. You will find specific performance results helpful in a mastery classroom and percentiles or rank scores most easily understood by parents.

=== **PROBE 10-3** ===

Think of the times you were told about your standardized test results. When the information was not *all* good, how did your teacher or counselor tell you the not-so-good news? Write a two-paragraph answer. Share your essay with a classmate. How would you two role-play an alternative way to give the feedback?

Sampling behavior

Using standardized tests to sample behavior is a very crucial idea. No published tests can possibly ask everything there is to be known about an educational domain. In building a test, the professionals set aside a small area of the full content domain. For example, Dody's standardized Spanish test will sample a few words, a few verb forms, a few adjectives, and a few paragraphs for comprehension. Not everyone is comfortable with this sampling idea. So people say "I don't know anything about American history" when they fail a test. A better way of putting their dilemma is "I did not know the American history sampled by the standardized test." Young children may say "Daddy, you did not ask me the right question." The point is, tests sample behavior. Standardized tests do not sample all the materials covered in your class. You will want to follow our many guidelines for the management of your learning experiences to prevent mismatch between learning objectives, your instructional materials, and your sample of the test items.

Norm group

The comparison of a student's performance with scores of a norm group is a very controversial area in standardized testing. A norm group is used to obtain a set of scores which are used as a standard. Frequently, student test results are compared with those of a national norm group so that school boards, principals, and teachers can see how their students are performing.

"The scores of a norm group become outdated as a result of changes in curriculum or of advances in socialization." (Owen Franken/ Stock, Boston)

Test constructors use "demographics" to set up the best combination of people for a norm group. They will consider age, grade, gender, ethnic group, socioeconomic level, geographic area, and a host of other characteristics. It is important that the norms be well developed and current. As a user of test results, you will often be tempted to compare your students' performance with that of the norm group. If you compare your students' performance to that of a standardization group, you will encounter at least the four following problems.

Norms change over time   The scores of a norm group become outdated as a result of changes in a curriculum (like new math) or of advances in socialization (such as *Sesame Street*). This is a problem, because some norm groups have never been exposed to base-two counting or to any other innovation you might be using.

Norms may discourage students   Norm-group comparisons can discourage students whose performance is "below the norm." Information that Dody is below almost anything can discourage both Dody and her parents. You will want to plan carefully how you share standardized test results with students and parents.

Local norms are meaningful   One of the special challenges for users of standardized tests is the need for local norms. Over time, a school district can establish how well students perform on a standardized test in comparison with their classmates or their friends in the school district. After all, many students will have to compete with their friends rather than with people in the other parts of the country.

Norms have limited use   In the long run, you will discover that standardized norms have a very limited use. Indeed, we suggest they are best used for selecting students for a program rather than for setting up situations which will lead to discouraging comparisons.

   When you use standardized tests in your classroom, you will want to ask many questions about published norms before you accept the comparisons. For example, you might ask such questions as: What kinds of students were in the groups? Did they use the same version of the test? How old were the members of the norm group? The answers to these questions might give you enough reason to pause before you accept fully the standardized interpretation of the test results.

PROBE 10-4

In a school district near you, visit with the director of testing. Since so many of you will be working on this probe, you might invite him or her to your class. Ask the director of testing to discuss the district's standardized testing program. Does the school district have an assessment-plan matrix? Try to get your visitor to describe the cells in the matrix!

Achievement and aptitude tests

As a classroom teacher, you will probably use standardized achievement and aptitude tests. Achievement tests are prepared in particular areas such as American history, beginning arithmetic, or abnormal psychology. They are designed to help you compare your arithmetic students with a norm group. Sometimes, achievement tests are put together in a battery. For example, rehabilitation counselors, social workers, and counseling psychologists sit for standardized achievement tests in order to become legally licensed in their profession.

   In contrast to achievement tests, aptitude tests are prepared to sample "general abilities" (also substitute "intelligence" and "scholastic aptitude" for general abilities). The aptitude-test scores are used to predict the performance (Chapter 4) of learned intellectual skills. These tests are supposed to sample how much a person has learned in a given area or domain. At present, aptitude tests are being questioned for their appropriateness to the situation. The questions seem to center around whether, for example, performance on a paper-and-pencil exam can predict performance in a law, medical, or dental school. You will be able to watch the resolution of this issue concerning aptitude tests in the 1980s.

Test reliability

In your day-to-day life, you would like to have a consistent alarm clock. This means that if you set it for 7, it will ring day after day at 7 o'clock. In the same way, you want standardized tests to measure reliably what they are supposed to measure. A reliable test produces a stable score. As you can probably guess, no standardized achievement or aptitude test produces the same score time after time. After all, each testing event is different: the students may be tired, errors may occur in scoring, there may be a different administrator, the physical environment may be different, and so on.

Test RELIABILITY can be measured in three typical ways. In talking about standardized tests, you will become familiar with each of these ways. Let's take a look at the three ways to measure reliability.

Test-retest In test-retest reliability, you are simply testing on day 1 and testing again on some other day, day 2. You then compare the scores obtained on day 1 and day 2. Usually, you can get fairly high reliability when the two testing days are close together.

Odd-even In odd-even reliability, you will want to compare the total scores on all the even-numbered test items with the scores on the odd-numbered test items. Thus, you will need only one testing day to complete your information gathering. If your test is reliable, the odd-numbered items will give you about the same total score as the even-numbered items.

Alternate form You will be required to build two forms of the same American history exam and give them to the same students. If your test is reliable, student scores on each form should be very similar. It takes a great deal of time to prepare for this kind of reliability because two forms must be given to students.

Should you have to prepare a reliable test, you can correlate the scores on the first test with the scores on the second test. The correlation that you find is a reliability correlation. (Please don't clutch at this point. You will learn about correlating two scores in your tests and measurement class.) To put the matter simply, you are trying to relate students' performance on two different forms or days. For example, you would expect a dart thrower to practice and hit the bull's-eye most of the time with her right hand. She might do less well with her left hand. However, her two scores would overlap, and that overlap is a correlation. If she threw darts with a blindfold on, she might miss the target completely. Then her blind performance would not be correlated with either her left-hand or her right-hand performance. You will want to use tests that have

"Criterion-referenced measurement typically occurs both during a program to provide corrective feedback to students and at the end of the unit to provide final feedback." (Judy Rosemarin/ E. P. A.)

a fairly high degree of correlation—that seem to hit the same target again and again.

Test validity

You will want to remember two important things about test VALIDITY: (1) you can't have validity without reliability and (2) validity tells you whether the test measures what it is supposed to measure. The first idea about validity makes sense: you want consistency before you go out to measure something. If your tape measure stretches each time you use it, you will never be able to measure anything. The second idea about validity is important because a person can violate the rules used to establish the validity of a test. For example, validity can be deceiving when you ask a deaf person to follow your oral directions or when you ask a blind girl ''Which diagram is the correct one?'' We have actually seen a ''trained'' examiner ask a blind girl that question.

Validity can be described in three ways. You will want to talk about these kinds of validity when you discuss standardized tests.

Content validity In establishing content validity, you will ask a group of experts in the subject area or domain and in educational psychology to examine the test to determine whether it measured the planned learning objectives. In content validity, you are asking whether the test adequately samples the planned subject domain.

Construct validity   You will establish construct validity for a test by giving a standardized test of the construct and your own new test of the same construct to the same group of students. This procedure will help you decide how closely your own test measures the construct or concept (honesty, for example). In construct validity, you are asking how closely your test seems to measure a particular concept, such as honesty.

Criterion-related validity   In criterion-related validity, we are talking about using the standardized test score to predict a future performance (such as using your ACT scores to predict your performance in a liberal arts program).

As a manager of the learning environment, you will want to make sure that you are wisely selecting the better psychometric measures for your particular learning-objective matrix. One way to gather the needed information will be through the use of standardized tests. We believe that in order to make wise selections, you will need the information we have presented in this section.

Issues in the use of standardized tests

The purpose of standardized tests is to give you some information about your students and about yourself. A few tests seem to do a very good job (Salvia & Ysseldyke, 1978). Approach standardized tests cautiously. Please question them whenever you can. In Table 10-2, we have asked some potentially embarrassing questions about standardized tests (the questions are in italics and the reasons for the questions follow). The answers to these five questions will be very important for you and your students. Each time a student like Natalie comes to you in tears, you have to wonder: Am I using the appropriate test for Natalie? Should I use a test? In what other ways can I obtain the same information? You can begin to see that tests do have a limited usefulness. You will want to keep your purposes in mind throughout your selection of standardized tests for your class.

Table 10-2. Critical questions to be asked about any standardized test

1.   *How appropriate is the test for my students?*   In this question you are really trying to get two kinds of information: (*a*) what is the purpose of this test and (*b*) what was the norm group. As far as the first question is concerned, you will want to make sure that the test publisher's purpose(s) for the test and your own educational objectives are very similar. If they are not, then you might find that your students do very poorly on the test. Indeed, choosing an appropriate test for your students is pretty much like selecting a curriculum (we discussed this kind of problem solving in Chapter 7). As far as the second question is concerned, the norm group is decribed in the test manual. You will want to read the description of the norms. Try to select a test with a norm group that is similar to your students in age, boy-girl ratio, grade, socioeconomic level, and geographic region. This choice will be tough to make. Often, the information is not clearly stated in the manual.

Table 10-2. Critical questions to be asked about any standardized test (continued)

---

2. *How ethical will I be in using this test?*   In most instances, you can have faith in the test publishers' good common sense. As you are discovering each day of your life, a code of ethics is a body of rules by which a community can comfortably live. Ethics can vary by region or even by the situation. We are concerned about your ethical use of tests. Without even knowing you are doing it, you might select a test which probes the wrong areas. For example, the test might ask some almost innocent questions about the child's parents ("Do your parents discuss their budget with you?"). Just how probing that kind of question can be cannot really be predicted. Some parents would say it's none of your business. You might discover, for another example, that testing students on the scientific development of the earth can raise questions about a student's fundamental religious beliefs. Usually you can benefit from the publisher's good common sense, but be aware that you can ask the wrong question without even knowing it!

3. *What is the usability of the test?*   You can ask such specific questions as "Can we administer the test to a large group in a short time?" "Can we use the booklets over again?" and "Can the test be manipulated by third-graders?" As a classroom teacher, you will want to base part of your decision to use the test on the answers to these questions. As far as the issues of group size and time are concerned, some of your students might be able to be examined in a large group. Other students in your class might need close supervision. In selecting a standardized test, you will be influenced by its cost. Reusable booklets can represent a savings to the school board. You will be disappointed to discover that some tests are so put together that young students cannot manipulate them: the booklet is too big for the desk, the answer sheet requires too fine motor control to fill in the bubbles, and the print is too small. Usability is a broad area, but it is an important consideration for you and your students.

4. *How presentable are the results?*   Some publishers make a special effort to help present test results. In their efforts, the results are presented in sentences (e.g., You appear to have good study skills) or in phrases (e.g., Strong peer support). Usually the publishers or the state agency provides the school with gummed strips of results. The counselor or an aide then puts the scores into each student's folder. It is these results that can cause problems in presentation when you work with parents or teachers who find true meaning in the scores. We prefer test results which provide short descriptive phrases or sentences about student skills.

5. *How reliable and valid are the tests?*   You will hear a great deal more about reliability and validity. They are very important. Some people will say validity is the most important thing about a test. Therefore, you might wonder why we have not discussed reliability and validity earlier in this table. The answer is simple: You will want to use tests which meet the potential criticisms of our questions 1 to 5. We are sure only a few tests will meet your criteria. Then you can focus on those few and select the better ones.

Standardized test taking can be a pretty threatening experience for some students. You will want to try some of the guidelines suggested below (Hill, 1978; Rudman, 1976) with students like Natalie.

• *Discuss taking a standardized test with your class.* As you are well aware, many students have a fear of tests. You will want to reduce the power of classical learning (Figure 10-1). We recommend that, before the students are required to complete a standardized test, you discuss such topics as time limits, difficult items, narrowing down the choices, guessing, and working quickly.

• *Practice reading the instructions.* Please try to give your students a smooth, calm reading of the instructions. Indeed, we suggest that you practice reading the instructions with a tape recorder. You will want to be aware of the difficult-to-pronounce words before the testing situation. Avoid fumbling through an important series of instructions. You will want to put on a good show for Natalie and her classmates.

• *Promote the proper test-taking attitude.* The earlier in your students' career you can get them ready for standardized tests, the better it will be for them. Many aptitude tests are used in graduate school to select students for specialized programs. Each year, students tell us that they stayed up all night before taking their Graduate Record Examination (GRE) and now they are regretting their very low scores (along with low grade point averages and weak letters of recommendation). You will want students to develop a ''proper respect'' for these tests.

• *Practice getting ready for the test.* Usually, standardized instructions tell how students should fill out the answer sheet, which pencil to use, and where people should sit. These activities can be made into a game or an enjoyable learning activity. The following of instructions can be crucial. (One of the authors seems to have made a career of taking tests like the PSAT, SAT, and GRE. The answers on these tests are usually marked in columns. On one of those test-taking occasions, the answers were to be marked in rows, not columns—contrary to the testee's assumption. He did very poorly on that one!) Indeed, we suggest that *you* practice marking the answers in those little round circles. Some students find that behavior very difficult.

• *Practice with alternate forms of the test.* Sometimes, you will be fortunate enough to find an alternate form of the test. You might find a sample in the guidance counselor's office. Discuss with your students the kinds of skills they will have to demonstrate in working on the test. When Natalie reviews the items, she might discover some tough ones. Remind her to ''pile up'' her best scores. This means that she should not spend too much time on any one item. Indeed, Natalie should mark her best answer and go on. At the end of the test, she can take one or two minutes and try to get the more difficult items correct. (We've found that students often change a correct answer to an incorrect choice. You might urge them to avoid this pattern.)

* *Make sure that your students have the required materials.* It seems that no matter how hard you try, the old Navy rule always applies: "Ten percent never get the word." You will want to bring extra pencils, scratch paper, or whatever else the students are allowed to use during the standardized test.

* *Monitor test-taking.* The standardized instructions will tell you how to monitor the testing session. At the very minimum, pay attention to the students rather than the morning paper or a novel. You will want to be sensitive to student needs (people do sometimes pass out during these exams).

As a classroom manager, you realize that standardized tests are a part of the fabric of education (Barclay, 1968). You will want your students to become self-regulators, and you will also want them to perform effectively on standardized tests.

NORM- AND CRITERION-REFERENCED MEASUREMENT

Until very recently, most of the testing in education was NORM-REFER-ENCED (Popham, 1978a). In this approach to measurement, people's performances on standardized tests were compared with those of a norm group. The norm group was either a national sample or a school-based sample. In the last fifteen years, educational psychologists have raised some serious questions about norm-referenced evaluation (Glaser, 1963; Popham, 1978b). These individuals have suggested that CRITERION-REFERENCED measurement is a more appropriate way to go. In criterion-referenced measurement, students' performance is compared with the criteria in the learning objectives. Thus the measure of achievement becomes mastery of the learning objectives.

As far as Natalie is concerned, scoring below the norm group can be more devastating than failing to reach mastery on a specific learning objective. As far as you are concerned, you will make a delightful discovery: each way of interpreting test results has its better time and place. Indeed, the question is basically this: which is the better way to interpret test scores—comparison with a norm group or with the student's own progress toward an educational goal?

The issue of norm-referenced or criterion-referenced measurement will be a crucial one for you. The arguments seem to be nearly endless. In Table 10-3, we have listed some key phrases related to the several points

Table 10-3. Compare and contrast alternative measurement strategies

Norm-referenced tests	Criterion-referenced tests
1. Also called *summative evaluation*, which places an emphasis on the final product.	Also called *formative evaluation*, which places an emphasis upon the process. Some people want to call it *domain-referenced evaluation*, since the performance in a particular skill area or domain is being evaluated.
2. Useful for communicating with external evaluators, such as the public. Tells how students compare with norm group.	Useful for communicating with people in the program—teachers and students. Tells them how learning materials, learning objectives, teacher and/or student performance interact in learning.
3. Compares a student's scores with those of the rest of the class. Highest performer gets the best grade.	Establishes an absolute criterion for mastery of objectives and sets of objectives. Evaluation reported by objectives mastered.
4. Grades suggest the quality of performance by teacher and/or by students.	A few students will quickly reach mastery. Others will take longer to master the objectives.
5. In a class, only one person can have the best grade.	No competition for grades. However, some students might compete for greater number of objectives mastered.
6. Failure seems to be the student's responsibility.	A "no pass" on a learning activity can arise because of the teacher, the objectives, the evaluation, or the student.
7. Students are obliged to find the objectives and criteria before testing.	Criteria for evaluation are stated in the learning objectives, which are available throughout the learning activity.
8. Better for learning in a fixed time, such as a semester.	Adaptable to learning in a flexible time frame. You will need a flexible school system to adjust to students working on different competency levels.

in contrast. Please be advised that the list of comparisons is by no means complete. You will not have to take sides in this debate. We have said that each kind of measurement is appropriate. You can plan your own classroom management so both kinds of information can be used.

Norm-referenced measurement

The more familiar kind of measurement is norm-referenced. Parents and teachers have experienced norm-referenced ways of doing things, such as (1) time-limited testing in which students must answer within a certain period of time; (2) comparison with a vague but accepted national sample or a norm group; and (3) a hypothetical bell-shaped distribution of success.

In a norm-referenced approach to measuring students' performances, parents and teachers can quickly become discouraged. Millicent, for example, is upset because she did not finish all the items on the test. Natalie has received a standard score of 63 with no interpretation. You can well imagine Natalie's father roaring over the 63; he does not understand that Natalie was actually in the 90th percentile. In this situation, the 63 was a standard deviation score. In norm-referenced measurement, the scores are distributed around the famous bell-shaped curve. In this way, the top sixth of the scores usually earn A's and B's, the middle two-thirds earns C's, and the bottom sixth bring D's or E's. In norm-referenced measurement, students and parents sometimes get a mistaken impression about performance.

You will want to ask yourself whether scores on norm-referenced exams tell you about (1) the quality of your instruction, (2) the appropriateness of the test for your purposes, (3) the slow students who were given the same instruction as the fast students, or (4) the reasons for student failure. When you work with norm-referenced measurement, you will want to try to answer these kinds of questions. For years, the final product evaluation has been the teacher's responsibility. Over the years, teachers have accepted society's charge to make judgments about each student. However, teachers and educators have recently begun to take issue with norm-referenced evaluation as the only way to measure a student's performance.

Criterion-referenced measurement

The greatest challenge to norm-referenced evaluation came from educational psychologists who were involved with learning taxonomies (such as Bloom, 1968) and with comprehensive instructional systems (such as Glaser, 1963). In a potently worded essay, Bloom blasted traditional norm-referenced measurement. At the same time, he argued persuasively in favor of mastery learning.

We believe that criterion-referenced measurement is an idea whose time has come. It awakened the sleeping dragon of traditional evaluation. Controversy has made this kind of evaluation exciting (for example, Ebel,

1978; Popham, 1978b). The old order changeth, yielding place to the new (sorry Shakespeare). It is difficult to pull apart the issues surrounding this controversy. Some of them involve learning objectives, task analysis, comprehensive instructional systems—old friends to you. In addition, parental and community demands for accountability helped to set the stage for criterion-referenced measurement. (Bloom, 1980; Guskey, 1980).

The controversy about measurement focused on the need for a new approach to testing. In criterion-referenced measurement, we have new ways of getting information about students: (1) unlimited time to reach mastery of test items; (2) comparison with learning-objective criteria; and (3) most of the students reaching mastery of the learning objectives. Criterion-referenced measurement typically occurs both during a program to provide corrective feedback to students and at the end of the unit to provide final feedback (Bloom, Hastings, & Madmas, 1971). In a comprehensive program, learning activities have been so ordered that both student and teacher have a fairly good idea of what to do when the student does not master the learning objective. Suppose Natalie asked you for help with her math. In a criterion-referenced learning environment, she would have her objectives, her performance results on specific objectives, and frequent feedback on her performance on homework, classroom activities, and exams. In criterion-referenced measurement, you will have the same information as Natalie. You will be able to recommend corrective learning activities which will be related to not-yet-mastered prerequisite skills. As you can see, an alternative kind of learning environment goes with the criterion-referenced evaluation.

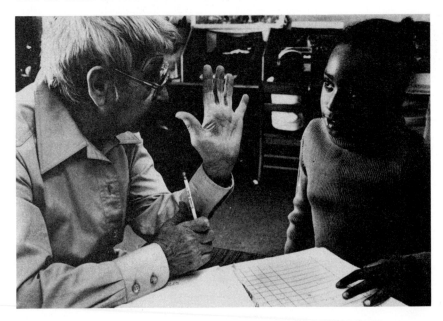

"As a classroom manager, you will want to go beyond test results for gathering information about your students." (Judy Rosemarin/ E. P. A.)

An active approach to using test results

You will want to use your measurement results effectively. Test results contain a great deal of information about your students and your styles of working with selected students. You might be effective with students who need a great deal of support; you might fall flat on your face with students who can learn alone. Test data must be interactive with classroom management. In Figure 10-4, we show how measurement data can help you become a more effective teacher. Too often, overworked teachers collect and file measurement data in their record books or in the students' cumulative records. We call these teachers passive users of test information. You will want to become an active user: discuss test performance with Natalie and Sally; relate your test results to some other information about them; ask some questions or state some hypotheses which you can examine in this present class or in next year's group; use the results from your hypotheses to improve your classroom management techniques.

PRESENTING TEST SCORES

Among the many challenges you will have as a manager of the learning environment is to display your measurement information in a meaningful manner. We have tried to give you some ideas on how to work with a single score, such as the results of Dody's Spanish test. We have talked about comparing these scores with a larger group, such as a norm group. We pointed out a new approach to discussing a student's performance in a mastery learning environment. When you present test scores to students and parents, you will want to consider three ways to display the results: measures of central tendency, pictorial display, and statistical display.

CENTRAL TENDENCY

The most basic idea in ordering data is the normal curve. Many statisticians would have a hard time living without it. Indeed, some statisticians will go to great pains to "normalize" their data so that it fits a normal curve. You should be familiar with the normal curve from your reading about Bryan in Chapter 2. You will recall that many of his characteristics seem to fall along a normal curve of distribution.

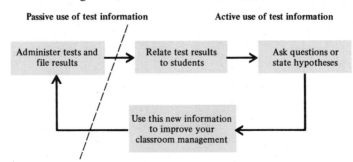

Figure 10-4 Measurement must interact with classroom management.

A normal curve is the way data can be distributed around some middle point. You have seen normal distributions all your life. For example, when you poured sand and it made a cone-shaped pile, you were looking at a normal distribution of sand grains. Let's take a look at Figure 10-5, which shows a normal distribution or bell-shaped curve. Also in Figure 10-5, you will see a not-so-normal curve or a *skewed* distribution, which is very similar to the mastery learning curve discussed in Chapter 2.

As you look at Figure 10-5, you will find that both curves have the same labels, such as *range, mode, median,* and *mean.* For both curves, the range appears to be the same. For the normal curve, however, mode, median, and mean are all on the same line. In the skewed curve, which is found in the mastery learning environment, the mode, median, and mean are in different locations across the range of scores. Let's take a look at these scores, which are called *measures of central tendency.*

Mean scores

You have been using average scores for years to describe your performance in math tests or time for sprinting 60 yards. The idea of adding up all the available information and dividing it by the number of times you gathered it is simply getting the average or mean score.

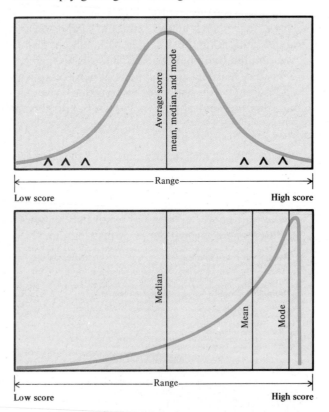

**Figure 10-5
Normal and skewed
curves.**

Median scores

The simplest way to look at a range or distribution of scores is to list each value. When you look at the full distribution and find the middle score, you have also found the median score. In a normal distribution, the median and mean are the same. However, in a mastery learning curve or a skewed distribution, the median and mean are not the same. In mastery learning, you will usually want the median score to be way below the mean score for the distribution.

Mode or modal scores

The most common score in the distribution stands out and is called the mode or modal score. This measure of central tendency is similar to the mean and median in a normal distribution. However, in a mastery learning environment, you will find that the modal score is usually above the mean and way above the median (Figure 10-5).

You will want to try to keep these three terms together when you describe test information. At the same time, you will want to be able to separate them for a discussion of norm-referenced measurement versus criterion-referenced measurement. Each distribution has a place in your monitoring of students' progress. Displaying your data will be a challenge for you.

PICTORIAL DISPLAY

An early educator once said "A picture is worth a thousand words." Ask your colleagues to bear with you while you draw a picture of your data. For examples, you might draw a *frequency table*, a *histogram*, or a *frequency polygon* on the same test results (Figure 10-6). Indeed, looking

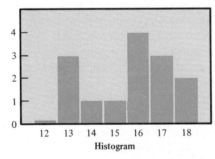

Histogram

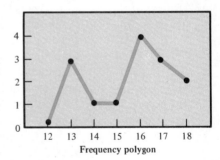

Frequency polygon

Score	Frequency	Cumulative frequency
18	11	14
17	111	12
16	1111	9
15	1	5
14	1	4
13	111	3
12		0

Frequency tables

**Figure 10-6
Three ways to
illustrate the same
information.**

back at the learning activity for Chapter 6, you can see that these three ways of presenting data are very similar to the three methods for graphing student progress.

Frequency table   In the frequency table, you simply count how many people earned each score. The total number of scores is presented under the cumulative frequency column. You can see how the cumulative value increases until you have everyone's scores. This is similar to the cumulative frequency graph in Chapter 6.

Histogram   The histogram simply lays out the data. Each column represents the number of people with that particular score. You can get a good idea of the range of this distribution from the histogram. The bar graph in Chapter 6 is similar to the histogram.

Frequency polygon   The frequency polygon is similar to the line graph in Chapter 6. In Figure 10-6, we have simply used the points and connected them.

Our point is that presenting a pictorial display of data can be informative and is very easily done. You might start your analysis of information by presenting it as a pictorial display.

STATISTICAL DISPLAY

As a committed classroom manager, you will be asked to review a standardized test or to display your data for your principal. In one role, you might be a member of the district test-selection committee. In the other role, you might be chairing the curriculum-evaluation committee. As a recent reader of this book, you will want to demonstrate your own mastery of a few statistical ideas. In Table 10-4, we have presented three statistical ideas and how to compute them. As you practice using these statistics on a set of data, you will find that the ways to compute them are very simple.

We hope that you feel confident about these statistical terms. You will want to use these pictures and these terms in your own classes. You will have fun with test results, watching progress toward goals and trying to understand information. Give statistics a chance.

Table 10-4. A brief discussion of three statistics

Statistic	Discussion
Standard deviation	You will want to be able to locate a student's test score with respect to the middle of the group. You can locate students by how many standard deviations their scores fall above or below the mean. Look back at Figure 10-5. We have put some little arrows on the bottom of the graph. Each arrow is one standard deviation. As you

Table 10-4. A brief discussion of three statistics (continued)

Statistic	Discussion
	can see, in the normal distribution most of the scores fall within one standard deviation above or below the mean. (You will learn to say "Within plus or minus one standard deviation" as you get more experienced.) Indeed, 68 percent of the scores fall within plus or minus one deviation of a normal distribution.
	As a rule of thumb, you can say that a standard deviation is about one-third of the range. For example, in a thirty-student class, you might have boys ranging from 5 feet 2 inches to 6 feet 5 inches. The rule of thumb says that the standard deviation is 5 inches. You will discover that standard deviation has its own symbol: σ. You are now well on your way to using statistical ideas. As you will see in variance and in reliability, both statistics use standard deviations.
Variance	Any kind of information has some variation. For example, line up ten seventh-graders of the same age. You will notice that the children vary in height.
	This variation has a special name—*variance*. Variance is the spread of information around the mean. As a classroom teacher you will observe that any performed behavior is made up of several kinds of variance (like intelligence variance, prior experience variance, teacher variance). You can compute variance very easily. Simply multiply the standard deviation by itself. Variance = σ^2
Reliability	We talked about reliability earlier in this chapter. All measures have at least some reliability; high reliability usually makes a test more useful. For example, you will want a very reliable check of whether any one of your fellow airline passengers is equipped to hijack your plane. As a classroom teacher, you can compute the reliability of your own test by using this formula: $$2\left(\frac{\text{variance of odd scores} + \text{variance of even scores}}{\text{variance of total scores}}\right)$$ You can begin to get an idea on how each statistic seems to build on another. The first statistic we presented in this table was standard deviation. It has been squared for variance and has been used in a formula for odd-even reliability.

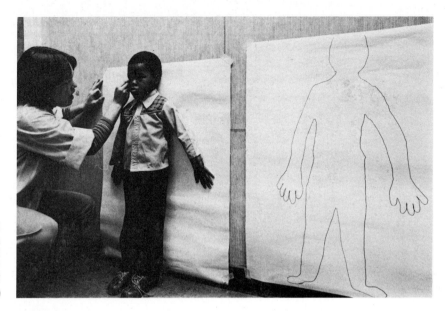

OBSERVING LEARNING OUTCOMES

As a classroom manager, you will want to go beyond test results for gathering information about your students. A test is a sample of behavior. The observation of learning outcomes is another way to sample behavior. You will want to gather observational data which will add to your management information. Indeed, information from a variety of different sources can help you make decisions wisely about your students. You have heard this theme before (Chapters 1, 4, and 8). You can observe behavior in its natural setting or under structured conditions.

NATURAL OBSERVATION

We believe that gathering and using observational data can facilitate your classroom management. Often, you will be asked by your building counselor or a colleague, "How do you know Sally is doing better? So you have given her a higher grade. What's your proof?" This kind of assault can hurt. Your judgment is being questioned. Your professional integrity is at stake. But as an informed manager of the learning environment, you will be able to document your judgments with observational data. Many choices for observing students in their natural environments will be available to you. Let's take a look at several examples in Table 10-5.

As you can see we have arranged these four observational strategies according to a hierarchy: anecdotal records, incident counts, rating scales, and direct observation. The hierarchy is ordered from least complex and least expensive to the most complex and most time-consuming.

Table 10-5. Four strategies of observation

Natural strategies	Comments
Anecdotal records	In an earlier day (before the Buckley amendment), teachers spent hours making entries in the students' cumulative record. These entries were brief summaries of particular, usually aversive experiences in the student's academic year. As you might suspect, the time delay between the event and the actual report often contributed to a distorted description of the event. The story about Sid (of the great thumbtack caper in Chapter 5) might grow between September and June into an account of a violent attack upon the teacher's person. Anecdotal records suffer from three problems: (1) in the time delay you tend to distort the actual events and (2) there are no agreed-upon terms (recall Sid's wild behavior). The lack of agreement encourages further distortion from year to year or from person to person. Finally, (3) bias in favor of pretty girls or against selected ethnic groups can produce yet another distortion. We urge you to use the anecdotal record technique cautiously (Reese, Howard, & Reese, 1977).
Incident counts	This observational strategy is more precise than anectodal records. You will use incident counts for those students who perform a single, specific behavior (e.g., times absent, times failed to submit homework, or times involved in fights). Incident counts are a way to get started in an ABC analysis of a possibly maladaptive behavior. Please note that the antecedents and consequences are not observed in incident counts. Still, these counts are a good starting point for observing a student's or a class's behavior (Sulzer-Azaroff & Mayer, 1977).
Rating scales	Rating scales are a quick way to gather a variety of information about students. You may use a rating scale which lists a variety of skills (many preschool screening techniques are rating scales in which lists of minimum first-grade skills are checked off as either performed or not). Please

Table 10-5. Four strategies of observation (continued)

Natural strategies	Comments
	remember that ratings by only one person (such as you) will probably be biased in some systematic manner. You will find that rating scales completed by more than one person are more valid. Biases seem to be averaged out when more than one teacher rates a student. In our own counselor training program, every faculty member is required to rate every student who is applying for the practicum (fieldwork) experience. We are aware that one faculty member can "get off on the wrong foot" and be biased about a student.
Behavior counts	In our judgment, the best way to collect observational data is by direct behavior counting. First, you will define the specific behavior to be observed and counted. Second, you will want to define the antecedent events which you will record. Third, you will similarly define the consequences which you will record. Finally, you will decide on the unit of behavior you plan to observe. This decision gets to the heart of the economics of observation: can you afford to maintain a continuous observation on Sally's reported progress? Must you sample only a ten-second segment of every minute? Must you fall back and observe Sally only during those few minutes before and after the target behavior (e.g., five minutes before, during, and after the exam)? You will find that behavior counting can be beneficial but expensive.
	Rather than trying to do it all by yourself, we recommend a team approach to this kind of data collection (Stilwell & Santoro, 1976; Mannebach & Stilwell, 1978). You might find two examples helpful in understanding more about direct observation. The examples, shown on page 547 are taken from Worell and Nelson (1974).
	In this figure, the observers noted which behaviors occurred for five seconds. During

Table 10-5. Four strategies of observation (continued)

Natural strategies	Comments
	the next five-second time unit, the observers recorded the behavior. Thus, instead of a continuous record of these two students' behaviors, a time sample was obtained. The observers kept their task simple: blurting out, out of seat, and no score (neither behavior was performed) were the only behaviors recorded for Billy. With a little practice, you can master direct observations.

=== PROBE 10-5 ===

Observing people can become a bit tricky. With a classmate, decide on one of your teacher's behaviors to record. Start five minutes into the class and record the instances of behavior. After class, look over your observations. How often did you agree? When you disagreed, can you figure out why?

STRUCTURED OBSERVATION

As a classroom manager committed to reaching complete judgments about your students' performances, you might also consider three structured kinds of observational strategies for collecting information about learning outcomes. In structured observation, you decide beforehand on the situation, the questions, or the student products.

Self-report

Long ago in the history of psychology, clients were encouraged to reveal their innermost thoughts. These revelations were ordered by the psychologist, who, after some muttering, said something profound. Over time, self-reported data were considered to be fuzzy and very poor form. Today, people are trained to collect their own covert behavioral data (Chapter 5). We have come full circle. You might ask Natalie to record her frequency of feeling depressed—that is, after you have built an operational definition of *depression*. After all, this frequency count is the beginning of the ABCs! You might try other kinds of self-report, such as daily logs about a growth project, personal charts for class participation, and a self-recorded time to complete an assignment.

Work samples

As a classroom teacher, you will frequently collect work samples such as homework submitted to you, in-class projects, notebooks, and the like. Over time, you will discover that work samples can reveal patterns of change. For example, as an office-practices teacher, you will collect typing samples. You can count the erasures: some pages have so many erasures that they look like Swiss cheese. As the semester goes by, you will be able to collect other work samples which will demonstrate student progress toward mastery.

Performance or situational tests

With some planning and management, you can create a standard situation for evaluating a person's performance on a specified task. For example, you can ask Robert in your home-management class to bake a cake, or you can ask your student-teacher to demonstrate an affective education activity with a group of your students. These demonstrations are really situational or performance tests which can be rated or judged by observers who have been given a checklist. From these events, it is possible to collect a wealth of information about your students' performances. Indeed, we like situational testing as a way of providing feedback to students.

As a classroom teacher and a manager of learning experiences, you can quickly get a good idea of what's happening in your classroom from the several different kinds of strategies for observing learning outcomes presented in this section. Use the information to facilitate student behavior change and to improve your own classroom management techniques.

ASSIGNING GRADES

At frequent points in the school year, you will assign grades to your students. At first, you will find this experience difficult—possibly even

"A team of grade-level or domain specialists can get together and build several different checklists from the task analysis." (R. Kalvar/Magnum)

stressful. After all, you too were once a student who was worried or terrified about grades. We believe that grades and grading can be used by the effective classroom manager to provide feedback. Indeed, the process of gathering information for feedback can be informative for both you and your students.

Grading seems to have had a variety of purposes, and many different rules seem to have governed the assignment of grades. Let's take a brief look at the purposes of grades and the methods of their assignment, some of the controversies over grades, and selected alternatives to grading.

PURPOSE OF GRADES

The purpose of grading practices seem to vary. Sometimes, grades are used to communicate about a first-grader's performance (for example, E in reading, E in math, and N in listening. N's are for areas that need improvement). Other times the grades are used to predict performance (for example, ''Given his high school academic performance, his SAT scores, and his commitment to athletics, he will contribute to the bottom 10 percent of his class. However, should he become more intense in his college work, his grades and his SAT scores suggest a potential for the top 8 percent of his graduating class''). A host of other reasons for grades and grading practices can be generated, and this presents us with our challenge.

METHODS OF ASSIGNING GRADES

Grades have been awarded in at least three different ways: by the traditional, halo, and mastery methods. Let's take a look at each of these.

Traditional

A fairly traditional way of assigning grades has been to divide students into some kind of bell-shaped distribution. In this grading pattern, the upper sixth are assigned A's and B's, the middle two-thirds are given C's, and the bottom sixth is failed or barely passed. An improvement upon this traditional method is the upper-division curve, which assigns A's and B's to the students whose standard deviation scores are at or above the mean and C's to students whose scores fall below the mean. Neither traditional option seems to pay much attention to the individual student.

Halo

Somehow, for many unknown reasons, the traditional way for assigning grades was gradually modified. In some selected instances, grades are given according to a halo method: high grades are assigned to communicate pleasure in having a student in class although the work was actually below the top level. In other cases, grades are assigned to signal progress in the last half of the course rather than for the overall performance. In still other instances, we have heard of grades being used to tell students that they were not wanted in a given program. We frown on these halo uses of grades and hope that the readers of this book will employ them more carefully.

Mastery

Mastery learning has required a new approach to assigning grades. Progress in the mastery learning environment can be reported by the number of learning objectives completed. You might want to explain that these completed objectives represent a percentage of the complete domain in the program (for example, objectives equivalent to first-year Spanish).

Each of these three methods of assigning grades can be found in almost every educational environment. Sometimes they become confused, so that an entire class earns A grades yet does not achieve mastery. Other times, an entire class can earn B's because the professor says "This group was below my usual standards." As you can begin to appreciate, grades have unique meanings to faculty, students, and parents.

DEBATE ABOUT GRADES

Since Socrates asked the first probe question, a debate has raged over grading and grading practices. The points of view seem to fall into five groups. Let's take a look at each of these viewpoints.

Grades are motivating

The motivational view seems to be related to the idea of winners and losers. Dody, who receives straight A's for her work in Spanish, is certainly reinforced. Natalie or Sally, who get unexpectedly low grades, find the entire practice of grading obnoxious. Page (1958) suggested some ways to make grades motivating. In Chapter 5, we described his study in which a personalized message that offered encouragement was found to be more powerful than a grade.

Grades are subject to error

The "error prone" argument seems at times to be a valid one. You will be human. You will add or divide and create a new way of counting. We recommend that when you make a mistake in grading, you admit it. You will save a great deal of energy. In fact, you will be surprised to find some students pointing out how you gave them the wrong grade—a C instead of the expected D.

Grades interrupt learning

This argument is very similar to the view that testing interrupts the teacher-student relationship. Feedback is essential to learning. Presented correctly, grades can be very facilitative in the learning environment. Indeed, we recommend that you take frequent samples of your students' performance. Share your judgments with your students. They will appreciate the time you spend with them.

Grades are administratively useful

Grades can be a powerful tool for the administrator. They do predict subsequent performance in the same kinds of situations—for example, high school performance and college work. You can use the ninth-grade averages to predict twelfth-grade overall grade point averages and then build instructional materials based upon these predictions of subsequent performance (Yabroff, 1969).

Grades are biased   The bias argument arouses the strongest feelings among teachers and educational psychologists. Page (1966) has tried to avoid that possibility by developing a computer scoring method for essay examinations. Page's computer program uses cues such as uncommon words, prepositions, commas, and length of answers. He found that students who do more of these things in an essay answer seem to be assigned the higher grade by the classroom teachers. Please read Study 10-1 and see the different ways in which grades can be assigned. Think about Wilson's (1963) findings and apply them to your own hometown.

As a classroom manager committed to facilitating mastery, you will frequently hear arguments about grading. If you decide to use our cognitive social learning theory approach, you will choose different

---

STUDY 10-1: A STUDY OF GRADING THAT HELPED TO CHANGE THE SYSTEM

Wilson (1963) studied sixth-graders in the fourteen elementary schools in California's Berkeley Unified School District. These schools conveniently fell into three groups: (1) Berkeley Hills, with fathers mostly in professional and/or executive roles; (2) "the Flats," with mostly black families who were living in "working class" homes; and (3) "the Foothills," which was a mixture of both groups. Wilson studied standardized intelligence, reading, and achievement results as well as grading practices for the fourteen schools. Wilson found many unexpected results, for example:

1. Among Berkeley Hills girls, 63 percent received A or B in reading while only 35 percent of the Flats girls received these grades.

2. Among Berkeley Hills boys, 56 percent received A or B in math while only 19 percent of the Flats boys received the same grades.

3. Teachers' reading evaluations (A and B grades) were higher than expected for girls, for Oriental students, and for professionals' or executives' children.

Students are sorted out, to some extent, through grades. Indeed, Wilson reported that Berkeley Hills students seem to go into academic streams in high school while Flats students are assigned to the vocational curriculum.

Today, the Berkeley Unified School District offers many models for the in-service training of teachers on grading procedures and for reducing the Foothills and Flats "effects" upon students.

Adapted from: Wilson, A. B. Social stratification and academic achievement. In A. H. Passow (Ed.), *Education in Depressed Areas.* New York: Teachers College Press, 1963.

grading methods for different subject areas. Indeed, in grading, you will try to meet the needs of your students, their parents, and yourself. In a way, you will try to learn what kinds of grading procedures best serve the unique needs of your students. This is another real challenge. Many alternative grading procedures do exist. Let's take a look at several of them.

ALTERNATIVES TO GRADES

Once more, you will be challenged to come up with alternative ways to give feedback to your students and to their parents. Creative problem solving takes time; you cannot quickly develop your own ways of providing these useful kinds of information. You might prefer to select an alternative strategy from this list.

Dual grading system

In the dual grading system, you will be reporting both on Natalie's achievements in her subjects and on her effort. Probably you would use such letters as E, A, N, I, and U (for excellent, satisfactory, needs improvement, improving, and unsatisfactory, respectively).

Checklist

The masterable skills on a checklist can be taken from your task analysis of a learning objective. You will want to take some time to prepare your checklists. Probably a team of grade-level or domain specialists can get together and build several different checklists from the task analysis. You will find that a checklist completed by more than one teacher is more meaningful and more valid than a checklist completed by only one person.

Learning contract

In the last ten to fifteen years, learning contracts have been written by students, teachers, and parents. These contracts contain the learning objectives, performance schedule, monitoring responsibility, and learning resources (Chapter 11). The contract alternative for grading fits in with the thrust of our cognitive social learning theory for promoting self-regulation skills.

Learning narrative

You might find that parents want to know what is happening on a daily basis. If *you* are the one who does the reporting, you will find this procedure time-consuming; however, when the *students* keep their parents informed, learning narratives can be valuable. Indeed, we have watched the "desired performance"—such as spending time on the study of history—actually increase when students keep track of their own learning efforts.

Parent-teacher conference

For a parent-teacher conference about Natalie, you will want to plan your presentation. We suggest that you try to answer these questions about Natalie's performance: (1) What is the pattern of her scores? (2) What is the range of her scores? and (3) How is Natalie progressing?

"You will want to use tests that have a fairly high degree of correlation." (Raimondo Borea/E. P. A.)

From our experiences, many parents in their own way ask for these kinds of information. You might find it helpful to role-play your parent-teacher conference with a roommate. Indeed, you might try to anticipate the thrust of the parent-teacher conference by role-playing with Natalie as each of her parents. Last, in planning your presentation, we recommend that you start with the glum news and end with the happy news. Parents and students, in our experience, seem to enjoy leaving a conference with the good news rather than being discouraged by the not-so-good news. You will read more about how to conduct parent-teacher conferences in Chapter 12.

Pass-fail system

For a while in the 1960s, school administrators, teachers, and students seemed to favor the pass-fail grading system. However, admissions administrators and employers did not seem to understand transcripts with many P's. When properly managed, the pass-fail grading system is effective and useful. Unfortunately, many pass-fail grading notions were transferred to the traditional A, B, C practices. Indeed, in this time of grade inflation, we find courses in which all the students get A's and there are no formative or no summative evaluations. The pass-fail approach has been so badly abused that it is now discredited.

=== PROBE 10-6 ===

In your learning career, have you been given some of these alternative grades? What were they? How did they help you improve your learning? Would you use them? Discuss these ideas with your classmates.

In our judgment, grading time is a good time for giving helpful feedback to students, parents, and yourself. Every one of us has strengths and weaknesses in almost every undertaking. With specific feedback, tactfully given, each of us can use this information to master new skills. As a classroom teacher, you will be asked to grade students, test them, and make evaluations. Unfortunately, you will be consulted by people who believe that grading, measuring, and evaluating are synonymous. You will be able to sort out the differences from your careful reading of this chapter.

EVALUATING LEARNING OUTCOMES

Evaluation is an old friend. In evaluating a learning activity, a class, or a program you will relate information from two or more sources to render a judgment. It is applied problem solving all over again. You have been doing evaluation for years. As a child yourself, you may have tried some rather simple evaluation techniques the first time you saw the child next door: (1) observing him ride the Big Wheel; (2) asking him "How old are you?" and maybe (3) racing him down to the fire hydrant. Given these three sets of information, you made a judgment ("You wanna play with my toys?"). As you got older, your evaluation techniques became more sophisticated. You watched the way he walked; you asked him, "What county are you from?" and "What's your major?" before you made a judgment. As a manager of the learning environment, you will want to improve your data-collection skills so that you can improve your evaluation strategies.

In evaluation, you will want to use many different sources of data. This idea is a fairly old one by now. You will want to collect "good" data. That is, you will want to collect data related to the course, the curriculum, or the program goals. You will want to collect some paper-and-pencil, some observational, and some interview data. Since you have done a good job of planning, these different data will go together like the music on an eight-track stereo. A good tape and good evaluation have high fidelity.

You will be able to choose from a large variety of evaluation models. Indeed, the 1960s were a time of many new evaluation models. The funding agencies and taxpayers wanted someone to show whether programs were accountable or not. Our approach to evaluation involves a familiar group of activities (Table 10-6). As you can see, we have put together the ABC model and our basic management model. Really, we are talking about accountability in our management model for education.

In the long run, the evaluation information will help many people: (1) students can use the information to become more self-regulated; (2) parents can get more involved in their children's education (Kifer, 1975); (3) professional colleagues within a district (Stilwell & Santoro, 1976) or within a building (Mannebach & Stilwell, 1978) can work together as a team; and (4) the community can use the reports in making its judgment on whether to raise salaries or to make program improvements. Indeed, these evaluation reports make up the lifeblood of the program on a continuous monitoring and a final evaluation basis.

Table 10-6. Model for evaluation

Activities	Discussion
1. Generate program objectives	From our experience, we have discovered that many programs get under way with some fuzzy objectives. One of your first activities in helping to evaluate a program is to develop a set of objectives. You will want to apply your best human relations, communications, and listening skills. After some effort, you will be able to specify clear objectives (Scriven, 1967; Stufflebeam, 1971).
2. Specify antecedents to these objectives	Sound familiar? In evaluation, you will want to specify the learning activities which seem to be most related to the objectives. The people running the program might not have completed a task analysis. You will find that listing the performance objectives, the people who are responsible for students performing those activities, and how or when people reached the objectives can become very important in your evaluation (Stake, 1975).
3. List consequences	Here we go on the C of the ABCs! In this activity, you are beginning to organize your information on "what's happening" in the program. For example, you might collect information on the number of people who have mastered knowledge

Table 10-6. Model for evaluation (continued)

Activities	Discussion
	objectives. For another example, you might look at the job placement of graduates from special career education programs (Cegelka & Phillips, 1978). For a third example, you might try to pin down the program's impact in the affective social domain (Cole & Musser, 1977). The consequences which you list possibly will not be related to the objectives which you listed in the first activity. This difference or discrepancy will be important in performing your program evaluation (Provus, 1971).
4. Apply problem-solving skills	Given the potential for a discrepancy between what *is* going on and what *should be* going on, you will want to make several recommendations. You might want to change what is going on. In your classroom, you might change the physical environment, for example. On the other hand, you might want to change the program objectives or the program's schedule. As an educational evaluator who is also a classroom teacher, you will want to apply your problem-solving skills.
5. Revise or maintain "what's happening now"	Your evaluation of the learning activity or instructional program will contain some encouragement and some recommendations. Essentially, you will recommend either that the program be continued without changes (this is unlikely) or that the program be carefully revised. Should you recommend that the program be revised, you might try to comment on its financial, physical, or human resources (Stilwell, 1976).

LEARNING ACTIVITY: RECORDING AND GRAPHING PERFORMANCE

Throughout this book we have emphasized the need for observational information. All too often, observational data will be discarded because they are difficult to understand (for example, a narrative or an anecdotal record), not valid, or not reliable. You are familiar with validity and reliability from the discussion of testing in this chapter.

In observations, you may collect valid data. For example, you can carefully work with Sally or Natalie to specify what she means by "really changed" or "failing grades." In this specification, you are building a hierarchy from your student's label in order to select specific behaviors. You are working with your student in this kind of task analysis, so both of you can agree on the validity of the observation.

Remember our discussion of the ABCs. You might want Natalie to specify under what conditions she has earned failing grades or has really changed. These conditions will be the same as antecedents and consequences in your ABCs.

You will want to collect reliable observational data. In this case, we mean that two people observing the same series of events record the same frequency or variety of behaviors. For example, in the diagram below, we present two sets of frequency counts on Billy's classroom behavior, yours and that of a friend. You can see that the patterns of X and O look very different.

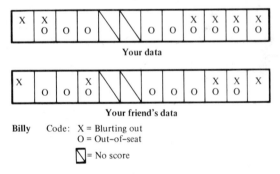

Your data

Your friend's data

Billy   Code: X = Blurting out
O = Out-of-seat
◨ = No score

Supposedly you were both watching the same Billy at the same time! You can compute an observer reliability by using this formula:

$$\frac{\text{Agreements}}{\text{Agreements} + \text{disagreements}} = \text{reliability}$$

or

$$\frac{11}{11 + 4} = 0.73$$

In our own classes, we have tried this recording and graphing project. When a person records and graphs, the behavior often begins to change in the desired direction. What will happen to you?

We give out this form to our students.

CLASS PARTICIPATION RECORD

Date _____ Name _____

Number of times spoke in class _____

Number of times asked questions _____

Number of times answered questions _____

Each behavior is fairly well defined. Sometimes we have to discuss the importance of being sensitive to your own behaviors, particularly in class.

After about two or three classes in which the college sophomores or graduate students practice with this recording form, we go for real! The students record their frequency of performance in each category. At the end of the day, they plot their performance on this kind of display:

Class participation record

Name	Date 6/27	6/30	7/2	7/16
Vickie B.				
Spoke in class	A/0	2/2	5/7	6/13
Asked questions	A/0	0/0	4/4	1/5
Answered questions	A/0	0/0	0/0	2/2
Sue G.				
Spoke in class	2/2	1/3	5/8	A/8
Asked questions	3/3	0/3	8/11	A/11
Answered questions	0/0	0/0	0/0	A/0
Yung L.				
Spoke in class	0/0	0/0	0/0	1/1
Asked questions	0/0	1/1	0/1	1/2
Answered questions	0/0	0/0	0/0	0/0

As you can see, we are maintaining a cumulative frequency distribution for each kind of behavior. In our experience, students have graphed their own performance and have increased their class participation. We have found that increased participation is related to more rapid mastery of learning objectives.

TASK 10-1

For this learning activity, record your own class participation. Graph the results for seven class sessions. Share your results with your instructor: write a brief summary about self-observation and about your own graphing experience.

SUMMARY

1. Testing means obtaining a sample of behavior. No test can cover the full domain. Usually, tests cover only a part of the domain defined by the learning objectives.

2. Teacher-made tests are a common way to assess learning. They are challenges for the hard-working teacher. You can build fair examinations from a learning-objective matrix. In these matrices, you can (a) test the materials in a domain; (b) assign items in terms of time spent on the topics; (c) use subject topics versus a learning-skills hierarchy; and/or (d) evaluate the data from observations, interviews, and tests in terms of the objectives. We prefer a combination of the third and fourth categories.

3. As a classroom teacher, you will often prepare your own exams. You may use essay, short-answer or fill-in-the-blank, true-false, multiple-choice, and matching questions. No one type of exam is easier to construct than any other. Plan on taking plenty of time to build a fair teacher-made test.

4. STANDARDIZED TESTS are one of the two most common ways to gather information about learning. They have (a) been professionally developed; (b) involve a systematic procedure for administration, scoring, and interpretation; and (c) provide results that are usually compared with norm scores. They also offer RELIABILITY and VALIDITY. A reliable test measures almost the same thing time after time. A valid test measures what it is supposed to measure. A test cannot have very high validity without fairly high reliability.

5. You will be able to use alternative ways to present standard scores: (a) a rank score tells the student where he or she stands out of the entire group; (b) a frequency distribution tells how many students earned each score; (c) percentile rank tells how many students out of 100 scored below that percentile rank; (d) standard scores tell how far from the mean a score is; and (e) grade-equivalent scores try to tell how a student compares with grade level norms.

6. Statistics are really procedures for organizing and comparing information. When people use statistical procedures, they hope the scores have been normally distributed. In a normal distribution, the average or mean, the mode or most common score, and the median or halfway point in the range of scores are all in the same place—in the middle of the bell-shaped curve.

7. As a manager of learning outcomes, you will choose between NORM-REFERENCED and CRITERION-REFERENCED TESTS. You will be able to use each kind of evaluation, depending on the learning objectives and upon the purposes of evaluation.

8. Grades and grading have long been debated. Usually the letter or number assigned to a student is subject to misinterpretation. We like alternatives such as a checklist of skills mastered, performance on a learning contract, and parent-teacher conferences.

9. You will want to use more than test results in evaluating students' performance. You might try self-report, work samples, or performance tests. These strategies have unique strengths and weaknesses. You might also consider anecdotal records, incidence counts, and rating scales. Of all the different observational strategies available, we prefer direct observation. Should you elect to use direct observation, we recommend you find a colleague who will help you with this undertaking.

10. Evaluation involves another set of masterable skills. Evaluation is more than paper-and-pencil tests, more than measuring with observations and interviews. It uses these different kinds of information in a problem-solving way to comment on progress and to recommend changes.

 KEY TERMS

CRITERION-REFERENCED TESTS: Tests that measure a student's performance against criteria stated in the learning objectives.

FORMATIVE EVALUATION: Examinations that ask students to demonstrate mastery of items related to learning objectives during the program of study.

NORM-REFERENCED TESTS: Standardized measures whose results are compared with those of a norm group.

RELIABILITY: The degree to which a test or any other measure produces a consistent or stable score.

STANDARDIZED TESTS: Professionally developed, standardized procedures for sampling a person's behaviors in order to compare these behaviors with a norm.

SUMMATIVE EVALUATION: Examinations that ask students to demonstrate mastery of given objectives at the end of the program.

VALIDITY: The degree to which a test measures what it is supposed to measure.

SELF-TEST

1. Testing can have a purpose depending on its timing. Match the terms in column A with the correct choices in column B

Column A	Column B
a. end of program	e. preprogram
b. formative	f. in program
c. diagnostic	g. intelligence
d. standardized	h. summative

2. Tests can have costs and benefits for you. Select the three better examples of benefits for you:
   a. inexpensive to use
   b. familiar to students
   c. useful in diagnosis and prescription
   d. useful in measuring mastery
   e. easy to grade
   f. discriminates among students

3. Measurement and evaluation use which one of the following combinations:
   a. judgment and tests
   b. observation and judgment
   c. tests, observations, and interviews
   d. tests and interviews
   e. judgment, tests, interviews, and observations

4. Teacher-made tests can be used to sample different skills. For example, essay exams seem to sample _____ and matching tests sample _____.

5. Match the standard scores on the left with the ratings on the right. An average score is 500.

a. 400	d. way above average
b. 520	e. below average
c. 640	f. above average

6. Several kinds of reliability can be reported for a standardized test. Which of the following is a kind of reliability?
   a. concurrent
   b. construct
   c. split half
   d. predictive

7. Criterion-referenced measurement appears to be an innovation for education. For example, it allows
   a. comparison with a norm
   b. assignment of a standard score
   c. quick scoring
   d. comparison with learning objectives

8. Curves can be skewed. In mastery learning, the hoped for distribution of student performance is skewed so that the order is
   a. mode, median, mean
   b. median, mean, mode
   c. median, mode, mean
   d. mode, mean, median

9. Observing students is a supplement to collecting test data. You will want to have reliable observations. A formula for reliablity is:

$$\frac{\text{Agreements}}{(\qquad) + (\qquad)}$$

10. Selected grading practices can be one of the following sets:
    a. observations, anecdotal accounts, and testing
    b. feedback, formative tests, and continuous observation
    c. parent-teacher conferences, valid means, and formative tests
    d. dual grading, checklist, and narrative accounts

SELF-TEST KEY

1. a–h
   b–f
   c–e
   d–g
2. c, d, f
3. e
4. Problem-solving, rule-stating verbal chains
5. a–e
   b–f
   c–d
6. c
7. d
8. b
9. agreements, disagreements
10. d

CHAPTER 11
Managing the Learning Environment

LEARNING OBJECTIVES

After reading Chapter 11, answering the self-monitoring questions, completing the laboratory activity, and reading any further references of your choice, you will be able to:

1. Define and give examples of key terms.

2. Specify examples of the three kinds of resources that influence the learning environment.

3. Discuss and contrast teacher and peer influence on the individual learner.

4. Compare how three leadership styles differ for teacher and student behaviors.

5. Compare three behavior management strategies (you choose).

6. Demonstrate how to identify selected reinforcers.

What do you need to know about planning and using strategies to promote an effective classroom environment? How can you choose an alternative management strategy for a particular learning outcome? As a teacher, you will be using your knowledge and skill to find solutions for these problems. Students will ask you for help: Daniel wants help in getting his homework done on time; Anne needs guidelines for completing her math on time; Dorsey whistles in the hall, throws paper wads, and daydreams almost every day.

Students will seek your help. You will want to use your problem-solving skills to facilitate each student's mastery of unique goals. Some students will benefit from your one-to-one support; others will reach their goals with the help of a classmate. Still other student needs can be met by the way in which you manage the whole class in a learning activity. Management, you will recall (from Chapter 9), is a set of learned skills. In management, you will plan, organize, coordinate and direct students and yourself in a productive enterprise. It will be quite a challenge.

How you will perform in these management situations will be related to the ABC analysis, our basic teaching model, and cognitive social learning theory. An ABC analysis of Dorsey's patterns of behavior will help you plan a program for change. The basic teaching model can help you consider the many alternative strategies. Indeed, cognitive social learning theory will suggest guidelines for distributing social power in your learning environment. Thus, the present chapter uses the ideas found earlier in this book and prepares you for the next chapter on working with students who have special needs.

FOCUS ON THE LEARNING ENVIRONMENT

In the 1980s, the environment will become a popular topic. For example, your students may talk about the valve job needed on your car; they might be concerned about water pollution; and a few will come up with creative suggestions for preserving our environment. You will want to introduce your students to their learning environment.

RESOURCES FOR LEARNING

Learning environments are made up of three kinds of resources: (1) economic, (2) physical, and (3) human. By *economic resources* we mean such simple things as the number of dollars available to your classroom for materials and your salary. Such resources often involve complex, value-laden school board decisions on innovative education. You will find economic resources very difficult to manage. By *physical resources* we mean space for learning. We have visited renovated schools in which each room was about the same size. Some rooms appeared crowded and littered while others seemed spacious and warm. You will have better luck managing physical resources. Still, you can begin to see that economic resources influence physical resources. By *human resources* we mean students, parents, administrators, community people, and yourself, all of whom must work together toward common learning goals. Bringing such cooperation about will be your greatest management challenge.

You will want to learn about physical and economic resources available for education. Some colleges have courses on the impact of buildings upon people. You might have to ask your instructor to bring a guest speaker to your class to talk about the economics of education and about designing educational environments. In this book, we are most interested in the human resources within the learning environment.

PROBE 11-1

Think back to your own high school. What were the available economic, physical, and human resources? Try to describe them on one page. Share your ideas with a classmate who completed high school in a very different kind of school. How did these resources meet the needs or fall short in any area? How did these resources help you reach your educational goals?

HUMAN RESOURCES

Several educational psychologists have been looking at classroom environments (Barker, 1968; Moos, 1974). In Chapter 2, we defined the learning environment in terms of four factors: stimulation, models, consequences for behavior, and structure. These factors seem to remain stable in the learning environment, while the human resources change.

A model for organizing human resources

Barclay (1978) has developed a model for organizing human resources in the classroom. We like the simplicity of this model for looking at the student in a classroom, understanding a child in a family, and appreciating your place in your own school. Let's look at how the model for organizing human resources works in a classroom, at home, and for you.

Human resources in classrooms In Figure 11-1, each arrow shows an influence upon a single student. The peer influences and your own influence will mix with the individual students' previous experiences. How these forces interact can be seen in the student's performance. You can get an idea of how these influences interact when you watch Dorsey for a few minutes: he has gotten off on the wrong foot in class—the paint was spilled and he slipped in it! The students laughed at Dorsey's rainbow and you began to worry about the next act. Since students do very well at applying behavioral science, Dorsey and his friends decide to try out a hypothesis: Will the teacher turn quickly at a new sound? Indeed, the teacher does have a fast turn-around time! You will observe that all of you (the students, Dorsey, and the teacher) are working together to produce a unique pattern of behavior. You will want to keep track of these various influences in your own classroom.

Human resources at home This simple model can be made more like the real world and therefore more complex. When you rewrite the model for a family, parents become the teacher, siblings become the peer group, and the child is influenced by these forces. On some days, you can predict that Daniel will not have his homework done (Dad is an avid football fan and schoolwork comes second).

Human resources and you The same kinds of changes can be made in Figure 11-1 to depict *your* relationships. In this new situation, your

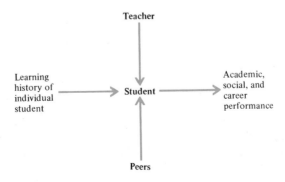

**Figure 11-1
Model for organizing human resources in the classroom.**

"The peer influences and your own influence will mix with the individual student's previous experiences." (Lejeune/Stock, Boston)

fellow teachers become the peers, the principal replaces "teacher," and you are influenced by these forces. On grim days, the principal might have growled at you or your peers questioned too strongly your commitment to mastery learning. This simple starlike model can become complex when you try to diagram the environmental influences on students before they come to school, on students in school, and on you.

You will have an important contribution to make in organizing resources in the classroom. Sometimes the resource picture can become too complex for you to manage. When you get overloaded, call for help. At the same time, try to know your counselor, school social worker, and school psychologist. They may be able to help you untangle very complex human resources. At times, students like Daniel, Anne, and Dorsey can present too many affective and academic challenges. Keep your purpose in mind: you are preparing people to deal with resource allocations in their daily lives.

MANAGING PEER GROUPS

In your classroom, you will want to manage students in small and large groups. Some of these groups will be "natural" ones, such as those that are found when girls get together or the football team swaggers into the room. Other groups will be developed by you for particular learning management purposes. You will want to learn how to work with both kinds of groups.

TYPES OF PEER GROUPS

In our experience, a group is made up of people who are working together in pursuit of a common goal. This definition is quite broad and could fit both a political party and an army! We try to limit ourselves to small groups—at least two people and sometimes more. In these classroom groups, the members are cooperative, not competing or working alone (Johnson & Johnson, 1975). These groups are usually productive and working toward a common goal. They are cohesive (Chapter 8). When a group or some of its members is not productive, you will want to practice your mediation skills. You will want to apply the ABCs and the basic management model to facilitate the mastery of cooperative skills. Using groups in your classroom will be an important management strategy.

Group assignments: Three kinds

You will want to recall your own experiences with groups. Student choices for group membership are not made by chance. They are reached by a mutual choice on one or more dimensions. In your own learning history, you can recall the athlete leaders or the musicians who seemed to make natural groups. Probably one or more groups in your school shared common goals that were not also shared by your principal and teacher. Still other groups are created for special purposes. As a manager of the learning environment, you might consider one of three kinds of group assignments.

Homogeneous groups You might create *homogeneous* groups for some specific academic purpose. When you use homogeneous groups, please remember that the peer models are demonstrating a common way to solve problems. For example, a group of inept problem solvers will learn very little from each other. In some schools, the homogeneous group is used for "low-track students." Research (Wilson, 1959, 1963) and your own appreciation of cognitive social learning theory suggests that these homogeneous groups should have a short life span.

Heterogeneous groups You might use *heterogeneous* groups to help students learn basic skills. In these groups, a balanced mixture of high-, middle-, and low-status students can be merged for a common purpose. In heterogeneous groups, competent students have more opportunities to model skills for peer observers. You will want to make sure that the heterogeneous group will be effective for its members.

Structured groups Last, you might *structure* the group so an isolate and a friend can work together or a fair reader can cooperate with a strong reader in peer modeling experiences. Be careful, plan ahead, before you assign students to one of these three different kinds of groups.

Group size: No simple answer

In making your group assignments, you will want to think about the size of the group. We prefer small groups. We prefer to work with six to twelve students. However, for some classes we lecture to forty or more people. Unfortunately, no clear answers on "best" group sizes seem to be available (Davies, 1973). Instead, group size depends upon learning objectives, the skills of the students, subject area, your own skills, and many unknowns.

Numerous views have been expressed concerning group size. On the one side, larger groups seem to entail smaller amounts of individual productivity and less group cohesiveness. In larger learning groups, you will have students with a wide range of skills. However, in many groups the teacher seems to "teach" to the lowest skill level (Lundgren, 1972). You will want to be very sensitive to this pattern. On the side of the small groups, you will have more time to work with each student, and each student, in turn, will interact with his or her peers. Small groups can help classmates such as Daniel and Anne master skills to reach their goals. You will have more opportunities in a small group to get feedback from your students (Gazda, 1975). We find that students are more willing to ask questions and to seek clarification in small groups. We encourage our students to probe until they are satisfied.

As you can see, the argument is fairly subjective and not too violent. You will want to use small groups to teach problem-solving skills. You will probably use larger groups for drilling students on some basic skills. In either case, you will want to be sensitive to the idea that in large groups, if things are going wrong, the chances are good that they will also go poorly in smaller classes. However, if things are going fairly well in a large class, they will probably be even better in a smaller class (Olson, 1971). The focus is on the manager of the learning environment. Plan ahead; organize the human resources in your classroom carefully.

DEVELOPING A GROUP

In your classroom, you will try to develop special-purpose groups. On the elementary level, you will use groups for reading and for math study skills. In junior high, you will use groups to help Daniel and Anne get their work done. During high school, you will increasingly use groups to help teenagers master new interpersonal skills, such as asking a friend for a date, working on a class committee, or volunteering to help a retired person.

While each of these classroom groups has a unique purpose, they all seem to go through similar stages. Let's take a look at the five stages of group development: developing security, developing influence patterns, developing common purpose, supporting individual creativity, and ending the group.

**Developing
security**

In this first stage, the group members are very cautious or tentative. Each member seems to be trying to find a place in the group. You will notice much silence. You have seen a "group" in an elevator: as soon as the elevator stops between floors, the riders start talking. They have a common bond, since they all face the risk of being stuck for a long while. They want to find a building engineer fast!

In your classroom, you will not be able to count on a broken elevator to bring people together. We have used the following nonverbal strategy several times: we ask the class to "count off" so that they fall into groups of about five people each. They are not permitted to talk to each other. They are told that they must, in a quick series of activities and without speaking, (1) introduce themselves to one another, (2) tell something about themselves, (3) describe something having value, and (4) communicate an emotion. In a small group, each one of these activities takes about two minutes. We have watched students begin to carry on "nonverbal communications" with other group members. When we talked about what happened in the group, these students said they felt accepted, at least by this group of strangers.

PROBE 11-2

Under what crisis conditions have you suddenly become a member of a very cohesive group? Share with a small group how you interacted in this emergency situation.

**Developing
influence patterns**

As people talk with each other in a group, they make judgments about one another. Each one of us seems to have some rules of thumb for making a judgment. We ask questions like "How many acres is your farm?"; "Where do you live?"; "What does your father do for a living?"; "Does your mother work?" These answers help group members make judgments about one another. Those members who are powerful or who have some status are "allowed" to talk more than those who do not have much status. (Watch a group of teachers become quiet when the principal walks into the teachers' lounge!)

**Developing
common purpose**

As each member begins to work as a part of the group, good things happen. For example, togetherness seems to arise when values and norms are similar. Group members seem to become responsible for performances and accountable to each other. These common bonds produce a group spirit or pride which is related to learning. This sense of common purpose in a group is important; without group cohesiveness, management will be a greater challenge (Bany & Johnson, 1975).

"Getting group members to work out responsibilities seems to be related to the common-purpose stage." (Sybil Shelton/Peter Arnold)

Getting group members to work out responsibilities seems to be related to this common-purpose stage. You can talk about common goals and members will struggle with the ideas. We like some simple activities to alert people to a sense of cohesiveness. You can get many good ideas from such small-group activity books as Lyons (1971) and Hawley and Hawley (1972).

Let's look at two example activities for developing common purpose. "Cooperative squares" is a silent exercise which requires group members to put together some pieces of paper. The difficulty is that the pieces have a special order. Some people have a hard time cooperating on this task (Lyons, 1971). Another group activity is a jigsaw story (Aronson et al., 1975). In this small-group exercise, a short story is written and broken up into short segments so that each group member knows only one paragraph. Together, they must put together the whole story. In these two activities, group members seem to become involved with one another. You will want to use similar kinds of activities to promote commitment to the group.

Motivating members of the group to be accountable seems related to this common-purpose stage. We have talked about negotiating goals in Chapter 8. You will want to encourage the same kinds of activities among group members: agree upon goals, set up checkpoints on the way to goals, assign tasks to group members, and try to develop ways to handle disagreements. By now, you may be getting the idea that starting groups in a learning environment calls for some planning and organization. If you do not plan ahead for these groups, you may encounter real problems.

We have had a group made up of four quiet people and one high-status person who showed up for one session and then quit. Another group had five low-status students who had never practiced group management skills. Since then, needless to say, we have improved our strategies for setting up learning groups.

Supporting individual creativity

Groups can help some students "do their own thing." In a way, the common purpose of the group supports the development of individual skills among group members. For example, Anne might form a study group. Members of her group might develop a plan to help her work harder on her math. One group member might offer to tutor her and another might offer to check her homework. Still a third member might call her name softly when she begins to daydream. You will be happy to find that students really do care about one another's progress.

Ending the group

We are suggesting that groups have their own "sunset law." A group in a class does not have to go on for the whole year. We recommend that as soon as the group's learning goals are reached, the group be disbanded. In this way, classmates will have the opportunity to work with several different sets of peers.

You will have a special challenge. Not everyone in the group will be ready to disband. You might have to deal with tears! You will want to prepare your students for the end of one thing and the start of something new. You will have worked hard to build some of these groups. Indeed, your students will also have worked very hard. You can try to explain that the "sunset law" is a way for students to prepare for new situations after they leave school.

In reviewing these five stages of group development, you can see that groups have a life of their own. Groups can start naturally or they can be assigned. Should you assign students to a group, you will want to prepare each student for this experience. It can be fun. It can be frustrating. You will want to organize this human resource so that it is cohesive and productive and its members can take pride in it.

GROUP NORMS

Within any group, a kind of structure begins to develop based on the members' views of standard or acceptable behavior. For many formal groups, the standards are written in a code of ethics. In other groups with long histories, the ideas about group expectations are passed along by word of mouth. In classrooms and in schools, some group norms last for several generations: for example, bobby socks and short haircuts. In other cases, norms have a short life span, perhaps only as long as a given program is on TV. Other norms—such as a pressure to succeed in a college prep program—become a part of the culture. Indeed, group norms are sets of standards or rules accepted by the group (Chapter 3). The members of the group help create the norms. They share attitudes and expectations. The norms seem like a magnet pulling each member toward a common goal.

Group pressure maintains group norms

The enforcer of group norms is group pressure (Chapter 3). In various ways, individuals who stray from the accepted range of behaviors "get the message." In a classic study, Wilson (1959) examined academic performance in several high schools. He found that sons of manual workers are more likely to have middle-class goals if they attend a predominately middle-class school. These middle-class students seem to be modeling and reinforcing group-accepted behaviors (such as completing assignments, participating in class, and so on). Wilson also found that the aspirations of sons of professional workers were lower if these boys attended a predominantly working-class school. It seems that the boys conform to the group norm by modeling behaviors, communication styles, and values. Think about Wilson's findings when you set up your next group.

You will want to use this powerful peer force in managing learning activities. For example, you can use the power of peers to encourage a student to complete an assignment. Arrange to make group rewards correspond to how well Anne and Daniel complete their homework assignments (recall group contingencies in Chapter 6). Group pressure can be used in another way, as when a group is held responsible for any one member's violation of a rule. Barrish, Saunders, and Wolf (1969), for example, developed the "good behavior game." In this cooperative learning activity, they found that misbehavior can be reduced by denying privileges to the entire group when an individual breaks a rule. In the long run, you will use group norms and group pressures many times in a gentle, artful, and skillful manner.

GROUP INTERACTION PATTERNS

As a committed classroom manager, you will want to make certain that group members are participating. As long as they are interacting, they are probably learning from one another.

In a classroom or a group, various patterns of communication will develop. You will want to use some of these patterns for specific learning purposes. You will prefer other patterns for general kinds of interaction. In Figure 11-2, we have presented four typical patterns of communciation among members of a group. They are the "telegraph line," lecture, "wheel," and network. You can see that each pattern has differing advantages and outcomes for effective communication. In planning your group projects, you will want to match each pattern with a better style for learning. Please remember that you have to adjust your management strategy to your material and your students' skills.

Communication pattern

Discussion

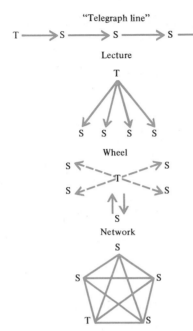

"Telegraph line"

Lecture

Wheel

Network

**Figure 11-2
Four patterns of
group interaction.**

1. In the "telegraph line," the content of the communication has a good chance of being altered. You can quickly recognize the cost of this kind of communication. However, in a discipline situation, you will find that a soft reprimand can go a long way. (O'Leary et al, 1970).

2. In lecture communications, all the students "get the word" at the same time. In Chapter 8, we noted that not all students are ready at the same time for "standard instruction."

3. In this wheel pattern, each student must communicate through you. You will use this pattern for drills on math tables or for reading groups. You will want to hold the attention of the students who are not communicating directly with you. By paying attention, these other students might benefit from observing peer models and your shaping of their behavior.

4. In the network pattern of group communication, each member of the group has an equal opportunity to participate. Each person must remain alert to what is being said. In the network, the opportunities for individual satisfaction and for learning are the greatest.

**Measuring group
interaction
patterns**

For nearly fifty years, psychologists have studied patterns in small groups. They have tried to measure *social distances* between people. They have spent energy and time mapping patterns of interactions in groups. For example, psychologists and classroom teachers have asked "Who is your best friend?"; "Who would you like to come to your birthday party?"; and "Who is a good student?" After hours of plotting reciprocal choices, one-way choices, and no choices, the teacher or psychologist had a map of the group. This technique was *sociometry* and the map was called a *sociogram*. The entire operation took much time. The benefit came only to a few people who knew how to work with isolates (few-choice students) or with leaders in a classroom.

Peer assessment is an alternative approach to measuring group inter-action patterns. Rather than looking at how classmates feel about each other, peers can be asked to judge each other's skills (Kane & Lawler, 1978). Barclay (1978) has urged educational psychologists to use a new approach to the measurement of peer support. He developed an inventory which asked "Who can run fast?" or "Who is a leader?" or "Who uses big words?" Barclay believes that peers are good judges of one another's specific skills. These are several of the questions which make up the peer-support portion of the *Barclay Classroom Climate Inventory* (BCCI). You will want to look closely at the peer support of each student as you plan a small group project or a parent conference.

By now, you are probably feeling quite comfortable with the idea that there is no one way to reach a goal. The same warning applies to group assignments that depend on the particular learning objectives, the students' skills, and the curricular materials. We want to suggest some guidelines for arranging groups in your classroom:

• *Set up groups so you can see the entire room.* As an aware classroom manager, you will want to be able to look at each student. You will want this opportunity because simple eye contact can send "big messages" (a smile to Anne who finishes her assignment, a wink to Dorsey to let him know you know). You will want to see what happens in the classroom for safety reasons as well. Try to follow this guideline by limiting your contact with a particular student to less than about thirty seconds. You *can* do it, but it takes practice!

• *Be aware that you will establish an "action zone."* Adams and Biddle (1970) identified an area in the classroom which they called the "action zone." Think back to your own high school days: some of your teachers stood in a certain part of the room and called on certain students. One of your authors has a diagonal action zone which stretches from one corner near the left side of the blackboard to the far right corner of the room. He calls on people who sit in his action line. Other teachers have T-shaped action lines. The T includes the students in the front row and

"Be aware that you will establish an 'action zone.'" (Owen Franken/Stock, Boston)

those down the middle of the room. Still other teachers seem to have small discussions with the front half of the room while they avoid the back half. An action zone cannot be found in every classroom, but it occurs often enough that you will want to avoid it in your classroom.

* *Consider how students form groups.* Earlier, we talked about natural and assigned groups. You will discover that the bright students seem to sit together in classrooms. Sometimes such a cluster can become a dominant influence. Other times, such a group's competition can disrupt your class. By contrast, the students who are usually less attentive will find seats in the back of the classroom (Schwebel & Cherlin, 1972). You can anticipate this problem by finding your Dorseys and Sids and putting them in your action zone as well as in the front row. When you assign classroom groups, you will want to anticipate another kind of situation. Rist (1970) tracked, from kindergarten to second grade, students who had been grouped by high, middle, and low socioeconomic status by their kindergarten teacher. Two years later, the students were in the same groups! You will want to prevent your groups from becoming permanent social systems.

* *Reassign or mix up the group assignments once in a while.* In following this guideline, you will want to combine your art and skill as a classroom manager. On the one hand, too much flexibility can hurt cohesiveness. Peer dyads are not built when students have little consistent contact. Similarly, too little movement produces few new interactions with other classmates. We do not have a rule of thumb for movement, but we are fairly sure the same group arrangement for the whole year can become dull for everyone. Make some adjustments every semester or every six weeks for young students. (Put the Worells in the front for once!)

As a classroom manager, you will want to adapt these guidelines to the particular goals of your classroom. Grouping by itself can promote cooperative, individual, or even competitive learning activities. Groups can help organize your human resources. You can select group members for cooperative projects. You can choose to assign Daniel or Anne to study carrels for very independent, uninterrupted work. The point is this: each group assignment is an important part of each carefully planned management strategy.

In Figure 11-1, we have diagrammed the relationships among peers in classroom and playground learning. You will want to capture this peer enthusiasm. Conserve this energy. Guide it toward the mastery of academic, social, and career skills. You will find this part of classroom management challenging and satisfying. You can apply the ABCs, the basic teaching model, and a pinch of cognitive social learning theory to create a good mix of this human resource.

MANAGING TEACHER BEHAVIOR

In each chapter of this book, we have tried to talk with you. We have tried to share our knowledge and experiences with you. Our purpose has been to model those skills which we find to be effective. At the same time, we have offered guidelines to help you perform three roles in your classroom: to be a facilitator of human development, a mediator of small groups, and a manager of the learning environment. We believe that you can learn how to manage your own behavior by performing these three roles. You will want to try to master the skills of effective and successful teachers while you learn how to perform these roles.

TEACHER CHARACTERISTICS

In deciding how to manage your own behavior, you might ask "What does a good teacher do?" The search for teacher characteristics and "best teacher behaviors" has gone on for years. Apparently, the characteristics or skills of the "best" teacher have been debated for ages. We can say that selected patterns of interaction will shift depending on such influences as the subject area, the socioeconomic level of students, the gender of the teacher, and the level of student performance. We can also say that certain other patterns of teacher behavior seem to extend over grade levels and over time. In Table 11-1, we have shown the relationships reported by Ryans (1960) in his six-year study of teacher characteristics.

Each of these six characteristics takes a different form at different grade levels. As an elementary-level teacher, you will want to be planful, well organized, enthusiastic, and involved. You will want to be especially

Table 11-1. Characteristics of effective teachers

Characteristic	Typical grade level	Sample skills
Warm and exciting	Elementary	Touching girls and boys Sitting on the floor Wearing costumes
Enthusiastic and involved	Middle school	Working on projects with students Attending sports events and school plays Taking many field trips
Planful and well organized	High school	Using multimedia talks Bringing in outside speakers Relating knowledge or experience in science to the teaching of English

warm and exciting. As a middle-school teacher, you will find that students seem to seek different styles of interaction (Chapter 3). You will want to be warm and planful but also especially involved and enthusiastic. You might sponsor extracurricular activities or show up for all sporting events. However warm and gentle you might be with elementary-age students, high school students seem to prefer a different style of interaction. You might go for a walk or take a moment after class to visit and thereby show your concern. Above all, as a successful secondary-school teacher you will want to be planful and well organized. We have shown these characteristics in Figure 11-3. In the center of these three overlapping circles is a common core—you.

DEVELOPING SELECTED SKILLS

As a person who will become a manager of a learning environment, you will want to perform skills related to effective teaching. Research to date suggests that it will help you to be warm, enthusiastic, just, patient, well-organized, knowledgeable, and reinforcing. Each of these characteristics or learnable skills is discussed in Table 11-2. In our judgment, these teacher management skills will be important to you. A few of you will find this list too long and too threatening. Please feel confident. Each of these teacher characteristics or clusters of skills can be mastered.

Strategies for mastering selected skills

The strategy for mastering a single skill uses our ideas on developing self-regulation (Chapters 2 and 5). You will want to make sure that you (1) apply the ABCs to your learning situation (for example, you might want to show more enthusiasm by smiling frequently, calling students by their correct names, or trying something new once a week); (2) select a behavior or a set of behaviors to be changed; (3) collect base-rate

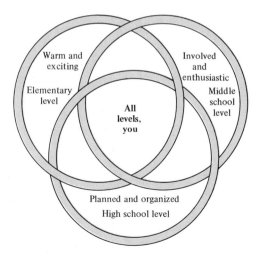

Figure 11-3 Relationships among efective teacher characteristics.

Table 11-2. A closer look at selected teacher characteristics

Characteristic	Comment
1. Warmth	1. Being "warm" or demonstrating warm behavior is very important for any teacher at any grade level (Rosenshine, 1970). We said earlier that the way you show warmth can shift with grade levels (for example, bending down to talk in elementary school, smiling or talking informally with older students). We believe that it will be important for you to master this set of skills.
2. Enthusiasm	2. Enthusiasm must be approached cautiously. You will want to enjoy your students, to accept student challenges, to transmit positive expectations, and to use gestures and voice shifts (Rosenshine & Furst, 1973) *within some limits*. We have used the adjectives from the Barclay Classroom Climate Inventory and found that the ideal teacher is neither extroverted nor introverted but extremely stable. Try to send "I am enthusiastic" messages to your students: they will get the message.
3. Justice	3. Justice is an old idea but it is sometimes not sufficiently practiced in classrooms. You will have a *few* rules. Treat your students fairly and consistently. Be so just that your class *knows* you do not wake the sleeping dragon. You can be just without terrifying the population! Try it.
4. Patience	4. Please be aware that all your students will not be working at the same level of mastery. Keep cool. In showing your students that you are patient, explain rules often, discussing possible alternative ideas and interpretations. You will want your students to perform, even with mistakes! Patient people tolerate small errors. We have found that modeling patience is important. If you are intolerant of errors, you may produce terrorized students (one of us can recall missed translations of Cicero and completely blowing a "proof" in solid geometry). On the other hand, you may be tolerant and produce cohesiveness in the classroom by encouraging peer tutoring or by using a team project. Your students will thrive on your patience—they will learn to enjoy learning.

Table 11-2. A closer look at selected teacher characteristics (continued)

Characteristics	Comment
5. Well organized	5. Rosenshine and Furst (1973) emphasize the need for this skill cluster. We agree. You will want to master objective writing, using advanced organizers and transitional comments between learning tasks, and offering alternative instructional strategies. Without these skills, we believe, you will be so distracting that students will look for your mistakes rather than attending to what you have to offer.
6. Knowledgeable	6. You will not want to stumble over your subject matter, but there will be days when the formula will *not* balance or when the wrong general is fighting in the Civil War. Vague statements starting with "maybe," "sometimes," and "almost" will distract from your presentation (Hiller, 1971). The well-planned use of filmstrips, movies, alternative texts, and a bit of peer tutoring can help students fill in the gaps.
7. Reinforcing	7. You will want to master as many different reinforcing skills as you can. Each child and each subject area involves its own set of better reinforcers. You have your own "best" set of reinforcers—those that are comfortable for you. Stallings (1978) found that positive feedback, few negative interactions, and plenty of student participation supported student mastery of reading skills, for example. It is individual, planned reinforcement that works.

information on these behaviors; and (4) make a determination on which way to go. For example, does the base-rate pattern show a performance excess or does it involve a performance deficit? If the behavior rate is high, you need to decide whether the behavior is disruptive. In the same way, you can decide whether the low behavior rate prevents effective classroom participation. These are important questions for you and your students to answer. Let's see how one skill deficit could be changed.

Carrying out a strategy in the classroom

The third-period class is dull. The students are flat and so are you. It is just before lunch. Nothing seems to go well. You are giving a monologue. It is an unrewarding experience for all of you.

After some thought, you decide to inject some excitement into this class period. Upon observing your own behavior for about five days, you discover that you are lecturing and that several students are trying to ask questions.

You decide to increase student participation and to reduce your lecturing. These are related behavior changes. One can occur if the other happens.

You plan to schedule yourself so that you ask three questions per class period. In order to keep track of the questions, you place a 3 by 5 card on your desk top. After each question, you put a mark on the card.

Because this behavior is fairly new for you and your third-period science class, you set up some cues. Place some signs (such as "Questions can be fun" and "Ask before you leap") in the room for your students. In your text, keep a page marker that says, in large red letters, "Ask questions *now.*"

These several very simple steps have worked. We have used the strategy with friends who have asked us for help (former students in introductory educational psychology) and experienced teachers whom we have visited. Try it and you will like it.

In this section on teacher characteristics, we have talked about some skills for you to master. These skills can be task analyzed and you can master each level. We hope that you already have many of the skills. By applying problem-solving strategies guided by cognitive social learning theory, you will be able to master your needed skills. Later, we will talk about specific strategies for working with students.

PROBE 11-3

Recall your most influential teacher or teachers. How did they follow the model described by Ryans (1960)? Write a short essay (150 words) on how these people resembled or did *not* resemble Ryans's effective teachers.

Monitoring teacher behaviors

As you work to improve your teacher-student interaction skills, you will want to monitor carefully your biased responses to selected students. We talked about this idea earlier (Chapters 2, 3, and 4). Why should you be concerned about teacher bias?

Day after day people, including you, act purposively—not at random. We are talking about little things. Each person acts on those little things to produce a unique set of biases. As a classroom teacher, you will want to assess your own patterns. Do you:

Sit on the left or right side of the classroom?

Sit in the front or the back of the classroom?

Like the more competent or the less competent students in each class? In different classes?

Like to be with minority or with nonminority friends?

Like boys or girls?

The answers to these questions can begin to make you aware of your own biased responses toward particular students. You might go so far as observe friends or a teacher and try to detect their unique preferences for people or for places. What you find out about yourself will become important to your students: you will be repeating a particular pattern with them. Please understand that these little incidents add up. After a while, someone might get hurt by your calling on only boys, by your asking only the brighter students to answer questions, or by your rarely talking to white students.

PROBE 11-4

You have studied students and yourself throughout this book. Can you describe three of your biases? Apply the ABCs to one of them. What can you do? Should you want help in working on this bias, ask your teacher or a friend to work with you.

MANAGING THE ENVIRONMENT

In Figure 11-1, there is a point where the three arrows come together. This point shows that peer support, each student's learning history, and you will interact to produce different kinds of learning experiences. The fourth arrow coming out of this point shows each individual student's unique performance. You will want to focus on effective management styles to facilitate this unique student performance.

EFFECTIVE MANAGEMENT

Nearly a decade ago, Jacob Kounin (1970) tried to get some answers about classroom management. He videotaped some "excellent" class-room managers and some "so-so" managers. Kounin thought that these two groups would be different. At first look, however, they were similar. For example, when a crisis occurred, both groups handled the situation in almost the same way. An educational psychologist may find the lack of difference between groups both meaningful *and* very discouraging. Kounin looked again at the videotapes. Now he found a difference in teachers who prevented classroom problems: the effective teachers kept students on task, so that no one got bored. We can show you Kounin's results in Table 11-3. You will want to master several of these crucial management skills. Reaching mastery on being aware may take a bit longer than learning to prepare exciting seat work. Then again, you might be able to order some unique strengths and skills in this area.

In much of this chapter, we will talk about what goes on inside the center point in Figure 11-3. You will see that management styles are

Table 11-3. Differences between effective and not-so-effective managers

Effective managers	Teachers with problems
Are well-organized and prepared. These people take the time and effort to plan ahead.	Enough said!
Use short transition times. You will have different activities in your classroom. Try to let each event "pour over" into the next.	Long time lapses produce long silences. Both students and teacher can become distracted by long transitions.
Keep a fast-paced learning schedule. You can be lively and active without pushing your students beyond their mastered level of behavior.	Slow-paced learning seems to result in distraction. You have had teachers who frequently checked their notes or lesson plans. They appear to be confused.
Keep students aroused. Berlyne (1960) talks about arousal and curiosity. You will want students to become involved in each learning activity.	Unaroused students seem to get their cues from the most powerful model in the classroom. Please don't be a Mr. Magoo!
Prepare exciting seat work. Effective seat work takes time to prepare. You will want work which challenges students' speed and skill.	Nonconstructive seat work can become boring. It is easy to assign ten boring problems; you can do better than that.
Are aware. A third eye in the back of your head will help!	Many teachers fall short on this skill. They seem to lose focus in the classroom (seeing only one student rather than the entire class). When something develops, these teachers often make errors in timing: they accuse the wrong student, they overreact, they produce a negative effect, and they lose credibility.
Prepare overlapping learning activities. You will want each learning activity to include some ideas from the previous one.	Choppy management of learning activities frequently distracts students from their focus on learning. You might try to determine whether a given student needs help in making a smooth transition from one homework assignment to the next.

closely related to leadership patterns. Leadership or management patterns in your classroom, management guidelines, and actual strategies for change relate to this point of interaction and to student's performances. In a sense, we will be bringing together ideas presented throughout this book for your use in the classroom.

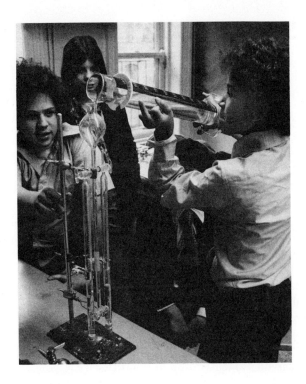

"Effective teachers keep students on task so that no one gets bored." (Brinzac/Stock, Boston)

LEADERSHIP PATTERNS

Many different forces will be coming together in your management pattern. What you will become as a manager will be a product of your own experiences, the skills of your students, and your jointly agreed-upon learning goals. We try to avoid imposing a management pattern on you. It is likely that, at first, you will be either an authoritarian, a democratic, or a laissez faire manager. Later, you may develop your own style—a combination of these leadership patterns.

The classic study of leadership was conducted by Lewin, Lippitt, and White (1939). Essentially, these psychologists studied three groups of 10-year-old boys. In the *authoritarian* group, the "teacher" gave orders, offered little explanation, and made no attempt at promoting group cohesion. In the *democratic* group, the leader worked on developing group cohesion, trying to gather opinions about goals and ways to reach the goals. In the third group, designated *laissez faire*, the adult offered no leadership, gave vague directions, and offered only brisk answers. The results are shown in Table 11-4. Essentially these findings have not been modified in the last forty years! Indeed, in your own learning history, you have probably worked with people who have chosen one of these leadership or management styles. Again, leadership style is an individual choice.

Table 11-4. Results of a classic study of three leadership styles

Leadership style	Rank of production or reaching goals	Enjoyment of the group
Authoritarian	Better than other two groups	Tense and fearful members
Democratic	Almost as well as authoritarian	Most enjoyable experience
Laissez faire	Least productive	Least enjoyable

As a classroom teacher, you will want to develop your own style of leadership. No one style is best for all learning activities and for all students. In our experience, teachers who try to become only democratic or only authoritarian are later forced to adjust, often dramatically. We urge our students to negotiate learning goals and to involve their own students in participatory management. At the same time, we recognize the need for authoritarian leadership under certain conditions such as fire drills, drivers' training, and first-aid procedures. On rare days, we have even recommended small amounts of laissez faire management. You will want to try each style and build your own personalized leadership style.

Sometimes, you will create student-led groups in your class learning activities. Please keep in mind that very young people as well as adults can become authoritarian, democratic, or laissez faire leaders. Plan your activities around these leadership styles. Try to take advantage of the potential human resources in your classroom: let students lead purposeful groups. You will be excited by the great human resources in your classroom.

MANAGEMENT DECISIONS

In the next several years, you will want to work on your own personalized management style. Take advantage of each learning situation, such as student teaching or committee work. Try out your style in role-play situations with a roommate. Get practice wherever you can—work at McDonalds, volunteer at a day camp, observe people managing others. You will want to find answers to these five questions:

1. Will you be rigid or flexible on rules, especially those regarding disruptive behaviors? Often you will hear "Come down hard early. You can always let up." We are not really sure that you have to come down hard. We do know that you will want rules and that you will want to enforce them fairly and promptly.

2. Will you promote a competitive or a cooperative learning environment? Usually, classroom teachers try to promote competition by the use of grades. In contrast, mastery learning seems to encourage cooperation. Johnson and Johnson (1975) report that more learning

seems to occur with cooperation. Are you getting the idea that no clear answer is available?

3. Will your decision making be permissive, directive, or participatory? Again, we have no clear answer to our question. Shaw (1976) reports that teacher-directed groups (read "authoritarian leaders") may be more productive. Yet we know that participatory ("democratic") groups have higher morale and more cohesiveness. Let's compare the way these three groups would be managed (Table 11-5). As you can see, the directive and participatory styles require more work than the permissive. In a sense, you are applying different management styles to promote selected students' skills. In our judgment, participatory decision making allows you to push your students gently into self-regulation.

4. Will you communicate goals and norms to your students? Throughout this book, we have talked about objectives, negotiated common goals, communicating expectations through feedback, and modeling appropriate behaviors. Therefore, the answer to this question will, we believe, be a resounding yes.

5. Will the academic work be self-directed or structured by the students? In Chapter 9, we tried to give you some ideas for this question. Approach the problem carefully. Not all students are able to plan their own learning strategies.

Again we say that no one management style is best for all situations. Remember, we are trying to facilitate mastery of self-regulated behaviors. A balance is needed between too much self-regulation (which might lead to withdrawal) and too little self-regulation (which might lead to disruptive behaviors). Either extreme choice produces a barrier to learning. Ask a familiar question: Which management style is better for these particular students with their unique learning objectives? You will want to find a match between your values, experiences, and strengths and your students' needs, patterns of behavior, and goals (Domino, 1971).

Table 11-5. Your choice in management styles (key words only)

Teacher activities	Your behavior by group type		
Goals	You state them	You solicit ideas	You keep quiet
Role	You justify yours	You clarify	You keep out of it
Direction	Be directive	Enlarge ideas	Watch
Reward	Anticipate correct action	Praise and encourage	Let students give rewards to each other

You will want rules for your classroom. Of course, you don't want just rules for rules' sake. You want rules that will provide structure for the learning environment. Please try to prepare rules having these three characteristics: (1) definable in measurable, specifiable, and observable terms; (2) reasonable to your students and to parents who might visit in your classroom; and (3) enforceable. These three characteristics of rules are very similar to the characteristics of learning outcomes. In a way, rules are learning conditions for your classroom. We have some guidelines which can help you in developing rules that are definable, reasonable, and enforceable.

GUIDELINES
FOR
TEACHING

Using Rules

• *Use very few rules.* We believe that a few rules can be enforced. A large number of rules can come across to students as if you are nagging. Indeed, you might try to post two or three rules at the beginning of the school year such as "Raise your hand when you want help," "Keep your hands to yourself," or "Walk in this room and in the halls." We

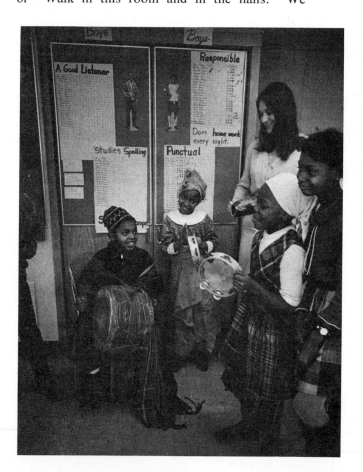

"You will want rules that will provide structure for the learning environment." (Eve Arnold/Magnum)

recommend practicing these rules at the beginning of each day. You can capture the energy of the classmates to help one another observe these simple rules.

• *Get the class involved in making simple rules.* This guideline will be important, especially for those students who need help in following rules. They can try to state rules that are reasonable.

• *Start with reachable rules.* "Silence for all day" is not really reasonable or even reachable. You want rules which can be followed. Should you not have reachable rules, you will find your time lost to enforcement rather than facilitating, mediating, and managing learning.

• *State rules positively.* People always seem to know what they do not like. You will want your students to state what they do like. The whole idea is very different from what goes on today. (Whoever heard of giving a safe-driving ticket?) You can apply these guidelines in your classroom. They will help you and your students to become involved in the learning environment.

STUDY 11-1: HOW STUDENTS CAN TURN ON AN ADULT

Donna Gelfand and her colleagues at the University of Utah have been studying many of the questions which are suggested by cognitive social learning theory. Recently, Cantor and Gelfand (1977) examined how adult women react to responsive or unresponsive children. The study is important because the results suggest some ways to facilitate a shy, withdrawn child's social development.

Cantor and Gelfand carefully trained six boys and six girls to be "responsive" and also to be "unresponsive." In the responsive condition the children were trained to ask for help, to ask for feedback, to give long verbalizations, and to smile. This pattern of behavior might be similar to an outgoing student. For the unresponsive condition these same children were asked to avoid looking at, smiling at, or talking to the adult woman. This behavior pattern might be similar to that of a shy, withdrawn student. The average age of these twelve children was 9. In this study each child performed twice in a responsive condition and twice in an unresponsive condition.

Each adult woman worked with the same child for two fifteen-minute sessions. "Work" involved helping the child with a Tinkertoy construction set and later with an Etch-A-Sketch screen. At the end of the two sessions the adult was asked to rate the child for such things as likability, adeptness, and intelligence.

The results from the study show some very interesting patterns, especially relevant for classroom teachers. The adult women provided more verbal and nonverbal helping and more attention to the responsive condition children than they did to the unresponsive children. At the same time the adults rated the responsive children to be more likable, easy to work with, attractive, adept, natural, and intelligent than the unresponsive children. The responsive children helped to create a more dynamic dyad for learning than did the unresponsive children.

Cantor and Gelfand also found that adult women treated unresponsive and responsive boys and girls very differently. Responsive girls were found to receive more helping and attention behaviors than did unresponsive girls. In contrast, the responsive boys received only more attention than did the unresponsive boys. The adults were unable to differentiate their praise for either boys or girls in any condition. It seems that no matter how hard the researchers tried to eliminate the effects of differences between boys and girls, the women behaved differently.

As a classroom teacher, you will want to use this study in facilitating individual development. It appears that helping a child master smiling, giving long verbalizations, asking for feedback and help can really influence judgments about the child's intelligence, likability, and adeptness. The time and effort spent with a shy, withdrawn student can have a great benefit to you and to the person.

Source: Adapted from Cantor, N. L., & Gelfand, D.M. Effects of responsiveness and sex of children on adults' behavior. *Child Development,* 1977, *48,* 232–238.

MANAGING STUDENT BEHAVIOR

As a classroom teacher, you will want to become aware of the many different classroom strategies. Your choices are really limitless. You can be overwhelmed by the materials on classroom management. We recommend that you study our cognitive social learning theory approach to classroom management. You can study some of the techniques. You will want to adopt some materials found in management "cook books." Later you will adapt a strategy for your special situation. Indeed, adapting strategies makes much more sense than searching through books until you say "That's the one!" (The situation can get out of hand by then.) In rare situations you will create a new behavior management technique. Should you try to create a new technique, drop us a line. Tell us how it worked. We like to learn about new strategies for change. Remember you and your students interact in learning (see Study 11-1).

MANAGING FOR PREVENTION

As a manager of learning experiences you will try to prevent problems. You will spend hours anticipating consequences, role-playing, preparing better materials and thinking about Dorsey:

One day Dorsey walks around your room snapping his fingers. It is a typical Dorsey trick. You have a quick debate: Do you call on him or wait? Dorsey has stopped some of his behaviors. Twenty minutes later he is still snapping—Dorsey wins. You ask a pleasant, democratic manager's question, "Dorsey, what are you doing?" He answers, "Keeping the elephants away." "Dorsey, there are no elephants in this city!" "Pretty effective." Snap! Snap!

Our point is that prevention, to be effective, is rarely seen.

We believe that practicing these guidelines will have a positive effect on your management procedures. By following these guidelines, you can reduce your need for the highly specific, very powerful management techniques which we will discuss later in this chapter. For preventive management, you might try any of the following:

• *Plan ahead.* We cannot overemphasize the importance of planning any activities.
• *Create sensible rules.* You will want to make school inviting (Purkey, 1978). Reasonable, definable, enforceable, and positive rules can have this effect. Be patient with your students. Make sure they can perform the skills needed to follow your rules. (Barth, 1980).
• *Be warm.* Students of all ages seem to like a warm teacher (Ryans, 1960). You will want to practice this set of skills whenever possible. Take time to show your students that you are interested in them as very unique people.
• *Model the appropriate behaviors.* In Chapters 2, 3, 4, and 5, we talked about the growth,that can occur in observers who watch a model perform a skill. You will often be the model for your students. Please show your students what you want them to do, not what you want them to avoid. This guideline will be hard to follow in the middle of a crisis.
• *"Praise in public."* Students like to be told they are doing something well. Indeed, classmates like to hear "good, warm sentences." Students will try to get their own rewarding statements. The converse of this guideline is important for you. In full, the quotation we refer to for this guideline is "Praise in public and censure in private." The second part reminds you to keep the trust of a student who does misbehave. Try to keep the aversive consequences between the student and yourself.
• *Catch the student on task.* Frequently, a reward is presented long after the fact. You will want to move about your classroom. On the one hand, your presence can help remind students to stay on task. On the other hand, you can catch a student on task. For example, you may give Daniel a smile, a token, or a star. In the long run, you won't catch Daniel every time he is on task, but your few reinforcers will help him stay with his class activities.
• *Scan the classroom.* Sometimes you will need a "third eye," but try to see every child in your classroom. A simple glance can go a long way to remind Anne of her agreement with you. In this way, you can pay attention to more than one activity.

Unfortunately, prevention does not always work. Dorsey will continue to poke Anne. Some students perfect a set of skills which may be consistently irritating to you!

When prevention
fails

When prevention does not work, you have at least four options. You may (1) Tolerate no misbehavior. In this option, you might send the offender to the principal. This first option can backfire. Think of the most exciting place in the school—the principal's office where everything happens. We don't like this option. (2) Try to live each day. Hope that no one is harmed. Apply to graduate school before the deadline. (3) Build a wall of behavior-management books (for example, Gelfand & Hartman, 1975; Glavin, 1974; O'Leary & O'Leary, 1977; Sulzer-Azaroff & Mayer, 1977; Walker & Shea, 1976; Worell & Nelson, 1974) on what to do when prevention fails. (4) Get on with your planned program of change. We prefer reading the books and acting on our fourth option. Indeed, throughout this book, we have talked about ways to use strategies that seem to work.

STRATEGIES THAT WORK

Let's list in a brief review the ten steps usually found in an effective behavior-change strategy. All these steps are familiar to you: (1) identify the behavior to be changed, (2) collect the baseline information, (3) decide whether there is an excess rate of behavior (such as pushing, chattering, attention seeking) or a deficit of behavior (such as too little on-task activity, independence, or interaction), (4) examine the antecedents and consequences of the specified behavior, (5) identify—with the student's assistance—particular goals for the change strategy, (6) consider alternative change strategies, (7) select the simplest change strategy for this unique goal, (8) do it, (9) record or monitor the results, and (10) fade out your behavior-management strategy. In the remainder of this chapter, we will describe selected management strategies that seem to work.

Reinforcement

The work of B. F. Skinner (presented in Chapter 5) heads our list of powerful techniques. Keep in mind that systematically applied, well-selected, and carefully used reinforcers shaped many of your present behaviors. You can apply Skinner's principles of reinforcement to increase and to maintain the frequency of many important academic, affective, and life-career behaviors.

Contingency
contracting

Closely related to the reinforcement model is contingency contracting (Homme et al., 1969). Homme applied Premack's principle (Premack, 1965) to education. Essentially, this principle says that a more preferred activity can be used to reinforce a less preferred activity. For example, elementary-level students may read the alphabet (a low-preference activity) and then run across the playground (a high-preference activity). For

Photo 11-6

"The Premack principle says that a more preferred activity can be used to reinforce a less preferred activity." (Juan Massar/Black Star)

an example at the senior-high level, Anne might complete her math homework and then telephone Daniel for fifteen minutes. Your father was also a contingency contractor (''Finish your vegetables and then eat your ice cream''). You can apply this parental rule in your classroom. Let's see how the Premack principle works.

Contingency contracting can be used in the classroom when students need help in reaching goals (Chapter 6). You will want to study the suggestions for a self-management contract in Table 11-6 before you work with an individual or a group. Indeed, you will be able to use contingency contracting with one or more students (Hayes, 1976).

You will want to help your students select reachable goals. For those who have complex goals, try to help them make task analyses of their objectives. You might have to agree on successive approximations as a partial goal. Provide a specific contract for each step. For example, Anne might be able to work for ten minutes without fidgeting. You will want to set the goal for twelve minutes. Make sure you reward her approximation of the desired behavior. For example, in the self-contained elementary classroom, you might have a ''rewarding event area'' (REA). In the REA, the student may play for five minutes upon reaching some contracted goal.

Table 11-6. Suggestions for a self-management contract

Contract conditions
1. Contract is fair: equalize work load and payoff.
2. Contract terms are clear and specific.
3. Contract is positive.
4. Procedures are systematic and consistent.
5. At least one other person participates in contract.

Consequent conditions
1. Self-reward is immediate and contingent on student behaviors.
2. Small steps are self-rewarded.
3. Self-reward is given frequently and in small amounts.
4. Self-reward occurs after performance.
5. Self-reward is individualized to fit the student.

Adapted from: Homme et al., 1969, as cited in Mahoney & Thoreson, 1974.

In order to show the relationship between performance and goal, you and Anne can draw up a "contract." In this document, you will require Anne to (1) complete a certain amount of work (2) at an agreed-upon level of proficiency (3) to obtain her desired reward. Let's look at a sample learning contract (Figure 11-4).

In Anne's contract, you will want to follow the guidelines suggested in Table 11-6. For example, you will want to (1) relate Anne's behavior both to her immediate schoolwork and her sister's birthday present; (2) list Anne's and your responsibilities in this contract; (3) get Anne's father involved in this homework contract. You will want parental support whenever possible (Kifer, 1975); and (4) agree on an expiration date for the contract. You will want to fade out each behavior-management strategy as soon as the goal behavior is maintained.

Token economies Closely related to reinforcement and contingency contracting are token economies (Ayllon & Azrin, 1968; Kazdin, 1977). This reinforcement system is similar to the common adult version of token economies (such as the paycheck and sales commissions). For students, a token economy can be set up differently. Instead of money, you can use painted stones, pieces of old Christmas cards, bulk-purchased canceled stamps, or smiling faces. These tokens are collected by the participants and traded for desirable activities.

You will want to work carefully with the students involved in a token economy. As with the other behavior-management strategies, you may

---

Homework contract for Bryar Cliff School

Anne agrees to:

    1. Complete ten of the assigned math problems each day
       (worth 5 points).

    2. Submit homework problems on time (1 point).

    3. Earn 1 bonus point for each two additional problems
       completed.

You agree to:

    1. Check the homework each night.

    2. Write a positive comment on each homework assignment.

    3. Refrain from nagging about uncompleted work.

Anne may exchange:

    1. Points for time in the REA (1 point per minute).

    2. Points for credits toward her sister's birthday present.

This contract will be renegotiated in six weeks.

_Anne C. Rent_____ Student

_Mr E. L. Lee_____ You

_P. A. Rent_____ Father

**Figure 11-4
Sample homework
contract.**

---

work with groups or with single students. To establish such an economy, you would specify the behaviors to be performed, post the list in several conspicuous places, and reward successive approximations. Further, the participants in a token economy (like Daniel and Dorsey) can agree on how the tokens should be redeemed. For example, five minutes of free time might cost five tokens, two tokens might buy Dorsey a comic book for one day, or three people might pool their tokens and play Parcheesi for ten minutes. In your token economy, you might want to make sure that the following conditions are met.

Reward early   For the first few days, you will want to reward students lavishly. After all, tokens are a new part of their learning environment. You will want to help students value the colored stone or smiling face that is the token in your economy.

Provide tokens immediately   You will want to walk about your room as much as possible. Reward the students on a variable interval–variable ratio schedule.

Combine tokens and social rewards   Couple each token presentation with a smile, touch, or positive comment. We have found that some token-economy participants have rarely received a warm touch or a gentle comment. Indeed, we have found some teachers who need a reason to smile at their students!

Deduct future earnings   When a student like Dorsey violates a rule or a part of the economy, let him keep his earned tokens. Instead, you will want to deduct tokens from his future earnings.

Be alert   Be aware of the "token topplers" who seem to build an illegal trade in tokens! "Protection rings," "trading for dead snakes," and simply snitching tokens seem to create an illegal trade in tokens.

Keep records   You will want to keep records of tokens earned by individual students. You can use these records to plot the patterns of behavior change on a graph.

Fade token economy Fade your token economy in favor of self-managed behaviors. After all, self-regulation is a goal of education.

Pros and cons of token economies

A token economy in many schools is a controversial behavior-management strategy. Those parents and teachers who are opposed to token economies seem to feel that (1) expected performance should not be rewarded; (2) schoolwork should not be rewarded; and (3) "teachers are not gumball dispensers" (we are human beings). Of course, these teachers are quick to point out that the school board is not paying them enough! In contrast, the advocates of token economies generally feel that (1) economics seem to work with people who do not respond to grades or social rewards; (2) tokens minimize disruptions (candy and grades do cause some ripples); (3) tokens take a longer time to satiate than do other reinforcers (see Chapter 5); and (4) the earning of tokens can be generalized to money in the world of work. You will want to balance these arguments when you start to teach. You will find that for some specific purposes, the token economy can be a very powerful behavior-management strategy.

Modeling

Modeling is another very potent strategy. You will try to find models who have an influence upon peer observers (Bandura, 1977). Please recall that observers will try to imitate the rewarded behaviors of models. You can model simple behaviors (such as holding a hot flask in chemistry class), or you can model complex behaviors (such as upholding a value). Remember that the model's characteristics—such as competence, expertise, sex, social power, and ethnic group—seem to influence whether the observer pays attention to the model or not. You will want to pay careful attention to your model's characteristics, the behaviors performed by the model, the consequences assigned to the model's behavior, and your students' goals. For many classroom activities, you will use modeling to help students acquire needed skills.

Role-playing

This important behavior-management technique requires careful planning before it is used. Role-playing is not play-acting. Instead, it is a planned learning activity in which students such as Dorsey can act out situations and ideas. A complete role play can follow the sequence of events shown in Table 11-7.

Of course, your enthusiasm must be tempered by the costs and benefits of role play. You will need support from your colleagues and your principal. (After all, some colleagues might say, "Role-playing is one of those newfangled ideas taught up there at the university.") You can earn this support by pointing out that role-playing can help students develop new skills, stimulate creativity, and improve communications in your classroom.

Table 11-7. A model for conducting a role-play enactment

Activity	Description
1. Warmup	1. In this first activity you will want students to get involved in role-playing. A warmup activity might be to get Dorsey to act out silently a "gruff" interviewer. He can try "talking nonverbally" to get involved. You want each participant to try out a new role during this warmup period.
2. Determine objectives	2. The objectives of role-playing are limitless. You might suggest that Dorsey try playing the role of a person applying for a job. Anne might benefit from being a class representative in student government. And Daniel might want to try acting out the way he would introduce Anne to his parents.
3. Select players	3. A major part of your preparation for role-playing will involve getting selected students "ready." Think of role-playing as a set of skills which are very near the top of a learning hierarchy. Make sure that the prerequisite skills are mastered before role-playing is tried.
4. Set the scene	4. In this step you are preparing the players for their roles *and* getting the audience involved in the learning activity. For very novel role plays such as a drama or Tom Sawyer talking with Alexander the Great, the audience becomes very important.
5. Start the enactment	5. Go ahead and do it.
6. Discuss/evaluate/share	6. When the enactment is finished, the players and the audience will have many ideas and suggestions. This can be a very creative moment. Promote the enthusiasm with all your energy! Be prepared for surprises; quiet students seem to get "turned on" by the role-playing experience.

Peer tutors

The power of peers has been known for years. Until recently, few teachers have systematically used peers as agents of change or "teachers" (Nelson, Polsgrove, & Worell, 1973). For example, junior high students can serve as tutors for elementary-level students (Willis, Morris, & Crowder, 1972). For another example, fifth-grade peers can help you monitor the on-task performance of selected classmates (Surratt, Ulrich, & Hawkins, 1969). The use of peer tutors has become a very positive movement, especially in this period of reduced monies for education. You might consider the costs and benefits listed in Table 11-8 before you start a peer tutoring program.

Ripple effect

Ripple effect refers to the quick communications network among students (Kounin, 1970). Suppose Dorsey really did something awful and you let him know that he "had had it." The word would spread quickly, like a ripple across a pond. Dorsey's peers would get the message that the particular behavior (writing on the walls) was not going to be tolerated.

You will want to anticipate some of these ripple experiences. Suppose you were not using your third eye and Anne wrote on the walls. Before you knew it, the entire class would be imitating Anne's successful and inappropriate behavior. You will want to catch the ripple before it starts by (1) not yelling, (2) whispering quietly, (3) touching Anne gently, (4) asking her a question, or (5) turning off the classroom lights.

Table 11-8. Benefits and costs from a peer tutoring program

Benefits	Costs
1. The *tutor* appears to get a sense of purpose, increased self-competency, an opportunity to try out ideas, and improved grades (Feldman & Devin-Sheehan, 1976).	1. The tutor has to overcome two fears—failure and rejection. Both of these fears can be very destructive. You will want to select your peer tutors very carefully (Varenhorst, 1976). In addition, you will want to gain the support of the teacher who is providing the tutor. (Some teachers believe their class is the most important experience of the day!)
2. The *tutee* benefits from very intense individualized instruction. The younger child typically makes some progress, but not as much as the tutor (Paolitto, 1976).	2. A teacher may mistakenly believe that a given youngster is reaching mastery with a tutor. Remember to monitor this learning activity as closely as you would monitor your own performance.
3. Teachers benefit from expert help from a knowleddeable tutor. This person can help you meet an objective for a student or a classroom goal.	3. It is important to train the tutor in many areas—how to present the materials, how to reinforce, how to correct errors, how to monitor his or her own behavior, and so on. Varenhorst (1976) suggests that tutors be carefully screened and later trained in small groups.

Trigger effect

Sometimes you will have to model the desired behavior. For example, around our house Daddy picks up a lot of toys, and sometimes this unusual adult behavior does trigger a similar behavior by daughter and son. As soon as observers begin to imitate your behavior, reinforce them. Triggering usually does work in the classroom and on the playground.

Don't hesitate: Ask for help

As you can begin to appreciate, behavior-management strategies are great in number and in detail. Please try to learn the principles supporting each technique. Many strategies are extremely powerful when they are correctly used. You can turn to special texts for specific strategies which are adaptable to your particular situation.

You will not be able to do it all. Managing the learning environment can become a nearly overwhelming challenge. In your school, you might be fortunate enough to have a guidance counselor, school social workers, or school psychologist. Ask them for help. You have another usually untapped resource in your students' parents. Invite their support through parent-teacher conferences, home visits, and ''good news'' notes. Parents often do want to get involved in classroom activities. Invite them to work with you (Purkey, 1978). A third source is only recently being discovered: retired people can really help you run small groups, keep records, and conduct special projects. In Chapter 12, you will get further exposure to working with outside people. For the moment, we want you to consider other people for the manager role.

"Retired people can really help you run small groups." (Berndt/Stock, Boston)

Management ruts   Class after class, year after year, can become a very routine experience for some people. We have watched creative, exciting teachers fall into ruts: they ask the same kinds of questions, stand in the same positions, stick to the same action zone, have a favorite kind of student, and practically become living statues. Please practice the ABCs and the basic teaching model in your own classroom behaviors. Indeed, you might build a monitoring matrix in which you carefully plan a wide variety of management strategies. Please try to keep yourself open to new ideas. Plan them, try them, and evaluate them. You and your students will benefit.

LEARNING ACTIVITY: SELECTING REINFORCERS

Reading this chapter might leave you, first, with the impression that behavior management works and, second, with the challenge "Try it; you'll like it." Both the impression and the challenge are easy to write and a little harder to carry out. As a classroom teacher, you will frequently be presented with situations in which behavior management *will* work. We hope that you will take the next step and try it. Our experience has been that you will observe changes in the frequency, intensity, or strength of the behavior and that probably you will like the change. Of course, sometimes everything won't go according to Worell and Stilwell, but you do have the ABC model to help you modify your learning-management plan!

A classroom teacher faces many challenges. These events will not occur weekly but, instead, almost every moment. By planning ahead, you will manage to create the best learning environments. A particular challenge will be selecting the best reinforcers. Essentially, you will answer this question: What is the "best" (most powerful) reinforcer for this particular individual with that distinctive educational goal in this unique environment? (This question should sound familiar because it is also the question to ask when you are selecting a learning management strategy.) This planning of reinforcement can start at the beginning of the school year or as a part of a program for helping a given student change his or her behavior.

To give you a broad idea about selecting reinforcers, let us look at the human social systems involved in the classroom. The most obvious actor is the student. Most of what we have talked about in this book has focused on the student. A second obvious actor in the classroom will be you. Whether you like it or not, you will exert a profound influence on the student's thoughts, feelings, and actions in school and on the playground. A less obvious influence upon the child's performance in school is the parent or parents. A family that supports a student's participation in school is worth almost half a letter grade. These three sets of actors—

students, teachers, and parents—interact, communicate, and relate to influence a child's survival in school and after school. Each set of actors has a best or preferred group of reinforcers. Further, each individual within a set has his or her own answer to our question about best reinforcers. Our point is this: when you start to select reinforcers, you will think about the three actors in the school's human social system.

Selecting the better reinforcers can be a time-consuming process, or it can be done quickly. In either case, you will want to select reinforcers (1) which will be desired by the student, (2) which will be powerful, and (3) which will not satiate over a long period of time. Our basic question about reinforcers suggests that individual differences, learning tasks, and environments appear to interact and influence the better reinforcers. For example, some students might want five minutes of quiet independence after finishing a math assignment while others might want five minutes of ping-pong and still others might want the papers graded immediately! You will have to consider the different ways of finding each student's better reinforcers.

At least three different assessment methods will be available to you. These three techniques will be observation, interview, and paper-and-pencil inventory. Let's see how you might use each of these to build a list of effective reinforcers.

OBSERVATION

This method of identifying the better reinforcers probably will be the most time-consuming. You can make up a list of activities which are usually available in your classroom. This list should probably contain fifteen to twenty activities such as "Looking out the window," "Playing with a puzzle," "Talking with a friend," and so on.

To collect your observations, you will want to create an observation schedule for the students in your group. After five days, the observation schedule for Alice will probably look like this:

Alice	10/2	10/3	10/4	10/5	10/6	Total
Looking out the window	I	II		I	I	5
Drawing	I					1
Sitting alone	I		II			3
Drinking water		I			I	2
Running			I			1
Playing with a puzzle				I	I	2
Talking with a friend				I		1

At least three times each day you will observe Alice for one minute and put a mark by the activity which she is doing. (Sometimes you won't put a mark for that minute because she is not doing anything on your list.

That is OK. You might have an "other" category for these observations.) At the end of the week, count the marks and use the most frequently observed activity as the "best" reinforcer. In your observation week recorded for Alice, it appears that the best reinforcer for Alice is "Looking out the window." The next best reinforcer is "Sitting alone." After a few weeks of observing each student in your class, you will be able to list the reinforcing activities for each one. At appropriate times you can contract with individual students or with groups and use their unique, "best" reinforcers.

INTERVIEWS

This method for collecting information about students' better reinforcers can be quick, simple, and accurate: Simply ask each student to list his or her three favorite activities. You might say, "Suppose you have worked hard on your assignment. When it is finished, what would you like to do?" Each student then would write three activities on a piece of paper. From these thirty or so short lists, you will quickly build your own class menu of reinforcing activities. These new reinforcing events can be individually contracted by you and your students. Of course, you might create a class poster of each classmate's reinforcing activities so that pairs or small groups of students can contract for five minutes of a shared activity (for example, Parcheesi).

PAPER-AND-PENCIL QUESTIONNAIRES

A third way to identify the better reinforcers for students is to use an inventory or a questionnaire. Usually these "instruments" take some patient planning, but they are worth the effort. Essentially, you have to think about what is reasonable for students, to try to state those activities as clearly as possible, and to put the statements together in some logical order.

A classroom teacher can build a questionnaire by listing many of the possible reinforcing activities that are available to the students. This list can become long and cumbersome, so you will want to plan on several revisions before you build the final version. Let's suggest some different reinforcers for students (you already have some ideas from Alice's observation schedule):

Get a friendly note on your homework.

Get a letter grade on your homework.

Get a number grade on your homework.

Be listed with all the people who passed.

Be listed with the five best students.

Be listed as the best student.

Play with lots of friends.

Play with a few friends.

Play with one friend.

Play alone.

Be praised for your clothes.

Be praised for an answer.

Be praised for being "you."

Listen to a musical.

Listen to records.

Listen to strange sounds.

As you can see, it is fairly easy to develop an idea and then make several versions of the same idea for your questionnaire. It takes a great deal of effort to build a meaningful set of questions whose answers can be useful to student, teacher, and parents. You can build a meaningful set of questions only with much effort.

Throughout this discussion of selecting reinforcers we have focused only on the student. A problem can develop if only the student is asked about preferred reinforcers. The problem is that teachers and parents may have their own preferred reinforcers which do not meet the student's needs. Our own work with undergraduates in teacher education revealed that those men and women often have to learn which reinforcers are better for which students in what kind of learning situation.

TASK 11-1

In selecting reinforcers for a particular group of students of any age, you will complete three separate steps:

1. Choose to work with two of the three groups—students, teachers, and/or parents—and identify each groups's list of best reinforcers. You may use observeration, interview, or pencil-and-paper methods to develop your list. For students, your task will be to find out which reinforcers they would want to receive in a social setting or in a classroom. For teachers and for parents, you can find out which reinforcing activities they would be willing to provide. Our experience has been that you will find students wanting one set or list of reinforcers and teachers or parents willing to use a different set of reinforcers.

2. Prepare a table for your data. On the left side, list the reinforcers by name. Then make two columns: one for the rank of the student-preferred reinforcers and the other for the rank of parent or teacher willingness to use a particular reinforcer. Let's take a look at an example:

	Students	Parents/Teachers
Play with a few friends	2	5.5
Be praised for clothes	8	5.5
Listen to music	6	4
Be listed as best student	9	1
Eat candy	4	9
Play Monopoly	3	7
(And so on)		

We suggest that you collect data on twenty to thirty students and five to ten parents or teachers.

You will have an opportunity to be creative in this learning activity. You might choose to use observation and find out which reinforcers students seem to prefer and which reinforcers teachers usually administer. You might interview students and teachers. For example, instead of asking students, "When you finish an assignment, do you like to play with a few friends?" you can ask the adult, "When a student finishes an assignment, do you let the boy or girl play with a few friends?" From the data you collect, you will be able to list "preferred" and "willing to use" reinforcers.

3. Explain the differences between the two lists, using the developmental materials from Chapters 2, 3, and 4 and your own judgment. Sometimes teachers try to give young children very adult reinforcers (such as time alone or peer-related activities) when the students really want twenty seconds with you! Other times the parent is unwilling to praise a son or daughter for completing a learning task. You will think about reasons for the differences and similarities in these two lists.

SUMMARY

1. A learning environment is made up of three kinds of resources: (*a*) economic, (*b*) physical, and (*c*) human. Economic resources include dollars available for decisions affecting your classroom. Physical resources are the ways space is used in a school. Human resources are people working together for common learning goals.

2. Human resources in the learning environment are the interactions among peer groups, teachers and the student's entering behaviors. You will manage this interaction to promote mastery of academic, social or career related performances.

3. The star-like figure proposed by Barclay emphasizes the interaction among peer groups, you, and the student's past and present to produce academic, social and career related performances.

4. Peer groups can be managed to improve each student's learning. You will try to create groups for special purposes and for given lengths of time. You will try to develop the "better" size group for each learning outcome. Guidelines are available for organizing groups for special purposes.

5. Within peer groups you will want to facilitate, mediate, and manage (a) group norms by encouraging appropriate models, (b) group interactions by using different communications patterns and (c) group seating by adapting to your students' and to your own needs.

6. Ryans (1960) tried to study the characteristics of effective teachers and/or productive teacher behaviors. He identified six nearly invariate teacher characteristics (warm, exciting, enthusiastic, involved, planned and organized). Productive teacher behaviors include such things as probing student knowledge, offering students choices for activities, using few negative interactions.

7. Three major styles of leadership have been identified, authoritarian or directive, democratic or participatory, and laissez faire or permissive. Each style can be helpful to promote achievement in academic and/or social skills. Participatory leadership which involves the students in planning and management appears to have a good combination of academic and social skill achievement.

8. Classroom managers can try to be preventive. Catch skill deficits before they become handicaps. However, prevention sometimes fails. You will want to use reinforcement, contingency contracting, token economies, modeling, role play, and peer tutors. Be aware of the ripple and trigger effects.

9. Please be aware that you cannot do it all. Learn who your helpers (counselors, school psychologists, school social workers, parents, and retired people) really are. Meet with them. Build a careful relationship with them. The ABCs will help you communicate with these people. In turn, they will call on you for assistance with unique students.

KEY
TERMS

SURPRISE: NO NEW KEY TERMS. You have read an entire chapter with no new terms! We have talked about many ideas which are based on the preceding chapters. If you need help in mastering some of the ideas discussed in Chapter 11, go back to the previous chapters for key terms.

SELF-TEST

1. Three learning environment resources are:

   _____
   _____
   _____

2. Who are the three contributors to the human resources in your classroom? Draw and label the model.

3. Students can be assigned to one of three kinds of groups. The three groups are:
   _____ ,   _____ ,
   and _____ .

4. A carefully planned, purposeful group has five stages of development. The five stages are
   _____ ,   _____ ,
   _____ ,   _____ ,
   and _____ .

5. Communications patterns in small groups can be labeled as one of four kinds:
   a. free form, fixed form, bent form, and free/fixed form
   b. telegraph line, wheel, lecture, and network
   c. authoritarian, directive, modified, and permissive
   d. interpersonal, cooperative, cohesive, and independent

6. In sociometry, group members receive various patterns of nominations. Which statement is correct?
   a. Isolates are usually powerful people.
   b. A few people receive all the nominations.
   c. Leaders are appreciated by other leaders.
   d. Stars receive many nominations.

7. You will want to be _____ and _____ , depending upon the grade level you are teaching (elementary, middle school, secondary). Fill in the answers which will be appropriate for your grade level.

8. Contingency contracting was an educational application of _____ .

9. Token economies can be helpful with every age group. Tokens for children of elementary school age are _____ ; for high school students, _____ ; and for employed adults, _____ .

10. The identification of reinforcers can involve information from three sources:
    _____
    _____
    _____

SELF-TEST KEY

1. human, physical, economic
2. See Figure 1-1.
3. homogeneous, heterogeneous, structured
4. develop security
   develop influence patterns
   develop common purpose
   support individual creativity
   end the group
5. b
6. d
7. refer to Table 11-1
8. Premack principle
9. smiling faces
   grades
   pay checks
10. observation
    interviews
    paper-and-pencil inventory

CHAPTER 12

Reaching Special Students

LEARNING OBJECTIVES

After reading Chapter 12, answering the self-monitoring questions, completing the learning activity, and reading any other materials of your choice, you will be able to:

1. Define and give examples of key terms.

2. State advantages and objections to the labeling of special students.

3. Compare traditional classification categories with an excess-deficit model.

4. List major causes of differences in learning and behavior.

5. List the provisions of the Education for All Handicapped Children Act.

6. Develop a model for mainstreaming students in one school district. Include cascade services, consulting personnel, and parent conferencing formats.

7. Support or reject the following statement: The same basic principles, procedures, and teaching strategies apply to all students.

8. Develop an individualized educational plan (IEP) for yourself.

WHO ARE THE SPECIAL STUDENTS?

Each of your students is a unique individual. Each student is therefore *special*. We have seen throughout this book that students come to school with differing patterns of experience and skill development. These differences include physical growth, community and home experiences, expectations of self and parent, entering skills for basic subjects, academic survival skills for classroom coping, interpersonal skills for obtaining peer and teacher support, and self-regulated motivation. Despite a wide range of individual differences, most students will show satisfactory progress in your classroom. You will also welcome the variety and interest that these differences contribute to your teaching environment. Wouldn't it be dull if all students were alike?

Some SPECIAL STUDENTS, however, have certain learning and behavioral characteristics that interfere significantly with their educational and social development. In other instances, the entering skills required for your classroom may be unevenly developed. Some areas will be advanced and other areas may be retarded. A few students will present physical and sensory handicaps that require individualized attention. When placed in a typical learning environment, most of these students will not meet the expectations of teachers and parents for achievement and behavior.

If these students are to reach their full potential of academic and social development, special educational strategies will be helpful. Let's consider the following examples:

- Sally is two years behind her fourth-grade class in math and reading. She seldom completes assignments. During independent seat work, she fidgets, plays with her pencil, and doodles. When sent to the board to complete a problem, she says, "I can't." Her teacher is considering holding her back a grade.
- Paula stares at the window during class assignments. She seldom talks to her classmates, remains alone at lunch and recess, and hangs her head low when you ask her a question in class. She never volunteers to talk in class discussions and answers questions in a barely audible whisper.
- Elton frequently skips school. When he does appear, he gets into fights with other students in the halls and is often found smoking in the basement. He is failing all his tenth-grade classes and talks about dropping out.
- Carla never seems to sit still. She is out of her seat during most of the class periods. She seldom attends to her work for more than a few

minutes and disrupts other students by talking to them during work periods. When she does settle down, she drops her books, makes loud noises, and talks to herself while she works.

• Ike is the class clown. He talks out in class discussions by making "smart" remarks. He will pass notes down the row, tie Sally's belt to her chair, and put his foot out to trip Paula when she passes his desk. He is the first one to complain about new procedures and the last one to fall into line.

• Alvin seems to be slow at everything he does. He is always the last one in his seat and the last to complete assignments. He still can't tie his shoes, button his sweater, or jump rope without tripping. He seems very sensitive to criticism and cries when the teacher corrects his behavior or tries to hurry him along.

• Lenny is doing college work in the ninth grade. He has already mastered differential calculus and is constructing a model of a solar-energized system for a senior citizens' residence.

PROBE 12-1

Take any two of these special students and try to point out in what ways they are similar and how they are different. What information do you lack?

What do all these students have in common? We can point to one similarity among them. You and the learning environment must make special adjustments to meet their learning needs. In this chapter, we will be talking about students who have special learning requirements. We will cover classification systems, typical learning and behavior patterns, and alternative teaching strategies. We will also discuss the important role that parents should play in planning individualized programs for special students. We don't expect you to become expert in diagnosing and dealing with all these learning distinctions. However, we want you to become aware of the wide range of behaviors you may encounter in your career. We also want to share with you one important conviction: all children can learn. All your special students can learn new behaviors to replace ineffective ones. All your students can learn to set goals that realistically match their capabilities. All your students can be moving toward mastery of their goals. Each student can find some pleasure and excitement, some challenge and satisfaction in learning activities. In facilitating the academic and social development of these students, you, too, will find a special satisfaction and challenge.

⌐⌐ CLASSIFICATION
⌐⌐ SYSTEMS

When children like Sally and Ike fail to meet the expectancies of school, their parents and teachers want to know why. In trying to answer this important question, you will first use your ABC analysis. You want to know what factors in your classroom may be contributing to the problems you observe. You and the parents may also decide to refer Sally and Ike for diagnostic testing, to have them see a physician for a medical checkup, or to call in the school counselor or psychologist. All of these referrals will be directed first at figuring out the cause of the learning problems. The usual result of the quest for a cause is the attachment of a label to the student. This label classifies the student into a diagnostic category and frequently results in the assignment of this student to a special education setting (Sabatino, 1971). Let's take a look at some traditional ways of classifying special students.

TRADITIONAL CLASSIFICATION

Students who have difficulties in regular class settings are most commonly called EXCEPTIONAL CHILDREN (Cruikshank & Johnson, 1975; Dunn, 1973; Haring, 1974; Hewett & Forness, 1974; Kirk, 1972; Telford & Sawry, 1972). Here is one typical description of such students:

The exceptional child is defined as the child who deviates from the average or normal child in (1) mental characteristics, (2) sensory abilities, (3) neuromuscular or physical characteristics, (4) social or emotional behavior, (5) communication abilities, or (6) multiple handicaps to such an extent that he requires a modification of school practices, or special educational services, in order to develop to his maximum capacity. (Kirk, 1972, p. 4)

This definition of *exceptional* is very broad and inclusive. On some days, it might apply to almost anyone. Surely, on some days you feel brilliant. However, on the day you have just seen the dentist, you can't feel a thing. You may have a day like the one when Ike poured ink into the classroom fish tank; you really lost your cool, became very red in the face, and raised your voice to a scream. At times, you may have been at a loss for words or stammered a little—when giving a speech to the entire PTA, for instance. Each part of the general definition of exceptionality given above is too inclusive to describe any one student accurately. Be careful when you use these general descriptions.

Common labels for special students

How about labels that appear to be more specific? Are they more helpful and appropriate for the individual student? Once it is decided that Sally and Ike deviate sufficiently from the normal expectancies for their grade, they may be classified with a more specific label. This label will frequently determine their educational placement and programming. Consider some of the labels that are currently being applied to these exceptional children. The list in Table 12-1 is only a partial summary of some labels that have appeared in the professional journals in recent years. If this list seems confusing to you now, imagine how you might feel about picking out just one term to attach to Sally and another to describe Ike. Clearly, the specific labels tell us little more about each student than does the broad definition above. Indeed, some of these lists become so comprehensive that the average or "normal" person will be an exception. Think before you label.

Current classification systems

You probably had some difficulty in picking out just one of the descriptive labels in Table 12-1 for Ike and Sally. One source of your confusion may be ignorance; you don't know what specific behaviors are included in each CLASSIFICATION. Also, it seems that some of these labels overlap

Table 12-1. Some common labels for exceptional children

Academically handicapped	Mentally defective
Acting out	Mentally handicapped
Aggressive	Minimal brain dysfunction
Antisocial	Neglected
Aphasic	Neurologic impairment
Autistic	Neurotic
Behavior-disordered	Orthopedically handicapped
Below-average learner	Perceptually handicapped
Brain-damaged	Physically handicapped
Cerebral dysfunction	Psycholinguistically disabled
Communication disorder	Psychopath
Culturally deprived	Psychotic
Delinquent	Retarded development
Dyslexic	Schizophrenic
Educable mentally retarded	Slow learner
Educationally disabled	Socially deprived
Ego deficiency	Socially handicapped
Emotionally disturbed	Socially disruptive
Emotionally handicapped	Socially maladjusted
Emotionally maladjusted	Speech disorder
Gifted	Superior cognitive abilities
Hyperactive	Symbiotic disorder
Hyperkinetic	Trainable mentally retarded
Impulse-ridden	Underachiever
Intellectually superior	Visually handicapped
Learning disabled	Withdrawn
Low IQ	

and do not fit together in a logical manner. Just one quick look at this list tells us that there is no one standard classification system presently in use within special education. However, as you move into a particular school district, you may find that one classification system has been adopted. You will want to become familiar with this system and the types of behaviors that are included in each category. To help you order your thinking in this confusing area, we have prepared a table which summarizes some of the information you will need (Table 12-2).

Here we have taken the major learning and behavior categories and divided them into (1) incidence, or how frequently you may expect this label to appear, and (2) descriptive behaviors or skills which help to define the category. These descriptions are taken from several major sources in special education. A particular school district may decide to use some categories and not others or to include certain behaviors within each category while excluding others. We have tried to list the characteristics which are most frequently used as the basis for classifying students like Sally and Ike. These behavioral descriptions may be helpful to you in decoding some of the labels that you will encounter in your teaching practice.

LABELING PRACTICES IN PERSPECTIVE

A note of caution is in order here. Please be aware that no student ever shows all the behaviors listed in any one category in Table 12-2. Indeed, some students are placed into a category on the basis of only one of these characteristics. Now, whether you decide to use any of these labels in your teaching career may require some hard thinking and decision making on your part. Consider carefully the disadvantages, and then the advantages, of labeling special children before you make this decision.

=== **PROBE 12-2** ===

Look at Table 12-2. Try to fit Paula and Carla into just one category. What information are you lacking? What does this category tell you about Paula and Carla?

Traditional labels can be harmful

In the past ten years, dramatic changes have taken place in the assessment, classification, and instruction of students with learning and behavioral differences. Educators are becoming more aware of the possibilities for teaching new behavior. There is more emphasis on encouraging each student toward optimal use of his or her capabilities. As changes occur in our knowledge, new approaches to labeling and classification are gradually replacing former categories. Some teachers work with students

Table 12-2. Some typical characteristics of current classification systems

Category	Incidence	Descriptive Behaviors
Mild behavior disorders	About 5% to 15% of students in regular and special classes	INTEREREFES WITH OTHERS: Hostile, defiant, quarrels, is disobedient, breaks rules, talks out, destroys property, breaks things. *Excessive attention seeking:* is boisterous, antisocial. *Illegal acts:* Steals. *Hyperactive:* Out of seat, moves, touches. *Aggressive:* Hits, kicks, pushes. INTERFERES WITH SELF: Is withdrawn, fearful, shy, anxious, unhappy, cries, looks sad. *Unresponsive to environment:* Daydreams. *Inattentive in class:* Has short attention span, is academically retarded, has learning deficits.
Severe behavior disorders	About 1% of school-age children; seldom seen in regular classrooms	SEVERE DEFICITS IN RELATION TO SELF AND OTHERS: Difficulties with feeding, dressing, toileting, communication. *Disturbed interpersonal relationships:* Lack of interest in others, refusal to touch them or talk to them. *Distortions in contact with reality:* May believe they are animals or other people, may use strange language. *Communication difficulties:* Refusal to talk, uses bizarre language, repeats what others say. *Severe emotional outbursts:* Screams, cries, yells, vomits, kicks, thrashes. *Self-destructive:* Hits self, bangs head. *Few social skills:* Does not play or laugh.

Table 12-2. Some typical characteristics of current classification systems (continued)

Category	Incidence	Descriptive Behaviors
		Academic deficits: Does not work at same level as peers. *Disorganized thought:* Seems confused, incoherent, perplexed.
Learning disability	About 1% to 2% of students in regular and special classes	DISCREPANCY BETWEEN ABILITY AND ACADEMIC PERFORMANCE: Specific learning impairment in math, reading, spelling, etc. *Perceptual difficulties:* Letter reversal, backward reading, writing problems. *Discrimination problems:* Left-right or up-down. *Motor performance impaired:* Clumsy, writing uneven, inaccurate geometric figure drawing, uncoordinated. *Language deficits:* Difficulties in recall and comprehension of spoken words, self-expression, memory and recall problems. BEHAVIORS THAT INTERFERE WITH SELF AND OTHERS: Hyperactive, distractible, impulsive, acts quickly, makes errors, has emotional outbursts, has attention deficits, does not concentrate.
Mild mental retardation	About 2% of students in the school population	ACADEMIC AND INTELLECTUAL DEFICITS: IQ range 50–55 to 75–80. Acquires basic skills late: between ages 8 and 11. Maximum academic achievement between third- and seventh-grade levels. Significantly behind grade level in basic skills—progress is between half and four-fifths that of the average student. ADAPTIVE AND SOCIAL DEFICITS: Delayed or deficient self-help skills. *Defective communication skills:*

Table 12-2. Some typical characteristics of current classification systems (continued)

Category	Incidence	Descriptive Behaviors
		Language and speech problems. Interpersonal skills may be deficient. Occupational readiness deficits, but can function independently with training and guidance.
Moderate or severe mental retardation	About 0.05% of the school population	INTELLECTUAL AND ADAPTIVE DEFICITS THAT LIMIT INDEPENDENT FUNCTIONING: IQ below 50. Develops at one-half to one-fifth the average rate. Communication deficits. May learn simple rote tasks. Some learn simple math and reading. Will be semidependent throughout life. Physical, motor, and sensory impairments. May learn simple self-care skills.
Intellectually gifted	Upper 2% to 3% of school populations	INTELLECTUAL SKILLS: IQ above 130. Develop basic skills two to four years early. *Talents:* specific advanced skills, as in math. Significantly above grade level in most or all subjects. High vocational success—above average for professional and creative output in later life. SOCIAL AND ADAPTIVE SKILLS: Above average in peer acceptance and interpersonal skills. High in self-competency. Wide range of interests and extracurricular activities.

who demonstrate highly visible excess or deficit behaviors. These teachers are particularly concerned about placing such visibly different students into categorical groups. Consider five of the most common objections to the use of traditional category labels for special students.

Educational irrelevance Labels are educationally irrelevant. That is, labels are seldom related to effective instruction. Having been told that Alvin is educably mentally retarded (EMR), you still know little about his specific skills, deficits, and strategies of learning (Smith & Neisworth, 1975). You do not know his level of reading, writing, or motor development. The label tells you little about how to teach Alvin to be more successful with books, ideas, and people.

With a few exceptions, such as the use of special materials for students with impaired vision or hearing, teaching strategies will be similar across traditional categories. Regardless of whether you call Carla hyperactive or conduct-disordered, she will require the same remediation for her reading deficits, her low motivation in class, and her out-of-seat behavior. For all categories, your attention will still focus on entering skills, classroom survival behaviors, and degree of self-regulated motivation. The differences in teaching strategies should vary across children and not across categories (Hallahan & Kauffman, 1976; Smith & Neisworth, 1975).

Misclassification Labels classify dissimilar students into a single category. Calling both Paula and Ike "emotionally disturbed" erases the important differences between these two students in problem behaviors and academic difficulties. The label here reveals nothing new about either student. Further, such labels may suggest an intervention program that is not equally appropriate for both children (Gardner, 1977; O'Grady, 1974).

Many students have problem behaviors that fit appropriately into several categories. A teacher we know described a student named Paula in her fifth-grade class. We want to share with you a brief learning history of this child. When our friend finished telling us the following facts, she ended by asking: "What is the matter with Paula?"

Since before she began kindergarten, Paula's parents have been concerned about her behavior. Paula has always appeared withdrawn, unresponsive to affection, uncommunicative, and slow in learning. Paula has been seen by many specialists: physicians, psychologists, neurologists, and speech pathologists. No specific physical disability has been found; therefore hearing, vision, and brain-injury problems have been ruled out. Paula was referred for psychological testing in the first, third, and fifth grades. Each time, she received an IQ score between 80 and 90. Mental retardation was thus ruled out as well. However, at various times in this diagnostic procedure, Paula was given the following labels: minimal brain dysfunction, autistic, slow learner, aphasic, *and* emotionally disturbed. *Paula's parents were concerned enough in the first grade to take her kindergarten teacher's advice and hold her back one year. By the time Paula appeared in my fifth-grade class, she was almost 12 and was reading at only the second-grade level. What is the matter with Paula?*

Considerable time was also wasted in trying to decide whether Paula was emotionally disturbed or mentally retarded. Better use of professional time and effort could have been directed toward an ABC analysis of Paula in her natural learning environment and an intervention strategy appropriate to this functional analysis.

Blaming students Labels place the blame on the student. If we conclude that Sally has a learning disability, we are surely ignoring environmental contributions to her present academic problems (Haring, 1974; Hobbs, 1975). Among these are inappropriate earlier instruction, inadequate motivation in the classroom, and material unsuited to her present learning requirements. Our cognitive social learning view certainly tells us that Sally's present performance results from an interaction between her characteristics and what the learning environment has to offer.

Explaining behavior Labels do not "explain" the student's performance or behavior. Having discovered through testing that Sally is two years behind in reading, you might refer her for psychological testing. If her IQ is below 70, she might be labeled "mildly retarded." If Sally's mother then asks you why she is so behind in her reading, you might say "You can't expect Sally to keep up with the other students because she is mentally retarded." We talked earlier in this book about such circular reasoning (Chapter 5). You have used Sally's poor performance to explain her poor performance.

Negative expectations Frequently labels lead to negative expectations. Notice that most of our common labels emphasize deficits: *handicapped, retarded, disabled, deficient, disturbed.* What is the effect of pinning such terms on a child? Research tells us that negative labels result in (1) less teacher effort to stimulate, teach, and reinforce (Brophy & Good, 1970; Rowe, 1969); (2) less favorable personality and behavior ratings by students and teachers (Parish, Ohlsen, & Parish, 1978; Parish et al., 1977); (3) lower self-esteem in the students so labeled (Meyerowitz, 1962; Richmond & Dalton, 1973); and (4) lower teacher expectations for academic achievement (Gaullung & Rucker, 1977). Further, it is common for such labels to "follow" the student by means of school records, class placements, and later employment information. For example, Paula may have improved her behavior and remedied her deficits by the time she reaches tenth grade. However, a label of *emotionally disabled* in her records will certainly affect her chances for part-time employment after school. Study 12-1 is a good example of how IQ labels can influence teacher expectations, teacher behavior, and student achievement (Beez, 1970).

"Most of our
common labels
emphasize deficits."
(Hanna Schreiber/
Photo Researchers)

For the five good reasons outlined above, we suggest that you use labels sparingly, carefully, and reluctantly. When in doubt, avoid them.

STUDY 12-1: LABELS INFLUENCE TEACHING STYLES

How can labels and teacher expectancies influence the way that students perform in class? In a novel study to examine this important question, Beez (1970) proposed that negative information about a student may directly affect the teaching activities of the instructor. As a result of these altered teaching strategies, students may perform less efficiently. In order to

test these hypotheses, Beez gave two different sets of information about Head Start boys and girls to sixty teachers in training. Each teacher, working individually with one child, was given a folder describing the child as either "high-ability" or "low-ability." All reports were identical for the children in each of the two groups. Children in the high-ability group were described as within the normal range of intelligence, highly motivated, and with "very good potential for school-related tasks." Children in the low-ability group were described as having low average intelligence, coming from a culturally disadvantaged home, having low motivation for school, and unlikely to "profit from average learning tasks."

Each teacher was given a set of twenty signs printed on cards and was to teach as many of these signs as possible within ten minutes. Teachers were also to rate the child on ability and motivation for the task. The results gave very positive support for Beez's predictions. When teachers believed they were dealing with a low-ability child, they (1) tried to teach fewer signs, (2) spent more time on each sign and explained more, (3) spent more time on nonteaching activities, and (4) rated the child lower on achievement, social competency, and ability! In addition, 63 percent of

these teachers rated the task as too difficult for the child—as compared with only *one* teacher who felt the task was too hard for the high-ability child.

How did the students respond to these teaching strategies? Children arbitrarily assigned to the "high-ability" group learned almost twice as many signs as did children in the "low-ability" group! These results clearly suggest that negative labels and information about students may interfere with productive student learning. Positive information about students, however, may well encourage teachers to provide a more stimulating learning environment.

Source: Adapted from Beez, W. V., Influence of biased psychological reports on teacher behavior and pupil performance. In M. B. Miles and W. W. Charters, Jr. (Eds.), *Learning in social settings.* Boston: Allyn and Bacon, 1970.

Some labels can be helpful

How can we describe special children if we reject the traditional categories? Many contemporary writers in the field of special education agree that labels can be useful for certain educational purposes (MacMillan & Meyers, 1979; Gardner, 1977; Quay, 1968; Smith & Neisworth, 1975). You might want to adopt a useful set of terms that will help you to accomplish the following goals:

1. To group students for instruction. (You wish to teach the students with reading-skills deficits together.)

2. To describe the student to other teachers, parents, or referral sources. (Ike's talking out and clowning are frequently disruptive to the class.)

3. To develop instructional materials, procedures and programs. ("I want to find some visual aids to maintain Carla's attention to tasks.")

4. To organize research hypotheses and to evaluate the outcome of your instruction. (Are individual study carrels as useful for students with reading deficits as they are for students with high activity levels?)

5. To anticipate problems through early intervention. (Can I prevent later reading problems by using a peer tutor for Alvin's first-grade reading deficits?)

6. To plan for later education, training, and employment. (Since 12-year-old Roy is still reading at the preprimer level, should we consider a sheltered workshop program for him next year?)

ALTERNATIVES TO CLASSIFICATION

For each of these teaching goals, we have been able to describe students in particular ways that do not lock them into a static category. We have used terms or labels that are descriptive of the behaviors that the student presents in the classroom. You can use descriptive labels that summarize the range of behaviors that you have decided require special intervention in your classroom. How can you decide on what labels to use? How can you describe students without categorizing?

DEVELOPING USEFUL LABELS

The primary consideration for any descriptive label is that it should be educationally relevant (Hallahan & Kauffman, 1976). This means that the ways in which you describe students like Paula, Carla, and Ike should focus on three factors: (1) the observable and measurable characteristics of each student; (2) descriptive categories of behavior rather than fixed classifications of children; and (3) the discrepancy between student behavior and environmental expectations (Gardner, 1977). Let's look at each of these factors separately.

Look at observable behaviors

You will need to consider the observable and measurable characteristics of each child. What do you want to change? What does Ike do in class that can be remedied with educational procedures? If you accept a diagnosis of minimal brain dysfunction, does that help you to teach Ike to stay on task and complete his arithmetic problems?

Use descriptive categories

Second, you will use descriptive categories of behaviors that are directly observable in your classroom. What does Carla do? It will be useful for you to know that Carla and Alvin have a short attention span in math computation. You could call them "hyperkinetic," but what does that communicate to parents and other teachers? Similarly, you will find it more helpful to say that Sally reversed p and g than to call her "dyslexic." You can develop a plan for remediating short attention spans and letter reversal more easily than you can cure hyperkinesis or dyslexia.

**Look at student-
environment
discrepancies**

Finally, you will need to develop a DISCREPANCY STATEMENT between what the environment expects and the child's present performance. If Sybil's teacher uses verbal instruction and Sybil is functionally deaf, then Sybil and her learning environment are mismatched. A useful description of Sybil should include her special learning requirements as they are related to functional loss of hearing in a verbal world. Alvin is likewise mismatched with his second-grade class, where he is expected to tie his shoes and read the alphabet. Therefore, your descriptions of student behavior should include the setting or environment in which the child is expected to perform: grade level, teacher, and peer requirements or school regulations.

Indeed, so great is the contribution of the student-environnment match that one author suggests we talk about exceptional situations instead of exceptional students (Lilly, 1970). Here the definition of exceptionality becomes very different than the traditional one we encountered earlier:

An exceptional school situation is one in which interaction between student and teacher has been limited to such an extent that external intervention is deemed necessary by the teacher to cope with the problem.

We like this approach to teacher-student interaction because it places responsibility for learning outcomes on the student-environment match rather than on the deviant student alone.

Frequently, a child's behavior is acceptable in home and neighborhood but is viewed as disruptive, aggressive, or deficient in particular school settings (Hobbs, 1975). We would like to use a descriptive system that integrates all three of these educationally relevant factors. We want to talk about our students in a way that emphasizes and maintains the uniqueness of each individual person. We shall propose a system of describing special students that focuses on observable behaviors and therefore allows maximum flexibility in instructional programming and planning.

EVALUATING BEHAVIOR SITUATIONALLY

What behaviors do you observe in Sally, Paul, and Alvin that might require special educational interventions? Your first decision should involve a judgment about how different these behaviors appear from those of the other students in your classroom. This judgment will answer the following question: *How do the behavior and learning skills of this student match the requirements of my classroom?* In making this judgment, recall that you will focus on observable behaviors that are potentially changeable.

**Criteria for
situational
evaluation**

You can use three criteria for making a judgment about special learning requirements in any particular situation. Figure 12-1 displays these three criteria and shows how they might relate to intervention.

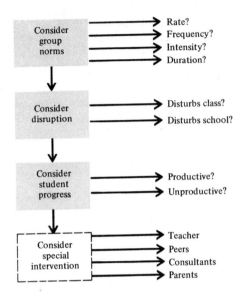

**Figure 12-1
Evaluating behavior
situationally.**

Consider group norms   Here, you will consider the frequency, intensity, duration, and rate of the behavior in relation to that of other students. Does Carla talk too much, too loudly, and too long during quiet work time? It will be helpful first to make a judgment based on the normal curve. The further away your observations are from the average range in your class, the more likely you are to need special adjustments in educational planning. You will tend to focus your attention on students who exhibit certain behaviors at unusually high or low frequencies and who learn at an unusually fast or slow pace.

Consider disruption   At another level, you will want to consider how much the behavior disrupts or interferes with the smooth flow of class activities. Does Carla's talking bother the other students? Here, you are making a judgment about an optimal learning environment for all. You are certainly tolerant of small disruptions. However, continual noise and distraction by one student may lead you to decide that additional programming is required. Remember, however, that what disturbs and annoys you in your classroom may not be a problem for another teacher. Some teachers can tolerate twice as much out-of-seat behavior as others (Worell & Nelson, 1974).

Consider student progress   You should always consider how this student's progress might be facilitated by a change in instructional programming. Here, you are concerned with the optimal learning environment for each individual. You will be looking at behavior as either productive or unproductive. Remember that productive behavior helps the student to reach mastery goals. Alvin has fallen behind in all his academic subjects and turns in uncompleted assignments. Lenny finishes his work quickly and sits around doodling much of the time. Neither student is meeting personal goals for learning. Is something more needed to keep both these boys learning at a productive rate? If you can answer a definite yes to all of these questions for any student, then you can feel comfortable and justified in arranging for special educational planning.

Applying situational criteria

Let's see how your evaluation of the situation would apply to Carla. You can review the vignette on Carla at the opening of this chapter to apply these three criteria to her behavior. First, Carla clearly appears to be at the high end of the curve for frequency of out-of-seat behavior, talking, making noise, and moving around the room. Second, her activity seems to disrupt both class discussions and in-seat assignments. While Carla is making noise and talking to her peers and to herself, you cannot talk and others cannot listen. You judge that Carla's activities prevent the rest of the class from learning effectively. Finally, you feel that Carla cannot possibly be learning very much when she is seldom in her seat, seldom listens to class discussions, and seldom follows instructions.

We have said throughout this book that one kind of information is not enough for problem solving. You will want to find good backup data for all your first impressions. For example, you will back up your casual observations with a frequency count of Carla's conversations with herself and others. In this case, you find that Carla talks five times as much as Mark, who sits next to her. You may also check her workbook and find that she is thirty pages behind and has never turned in an assignment with 90 percent mastery. "Well," you say, "it is really time to make some hard decisions about Carla. How can I describe Carla's behavior in ways that will be helpful to my teaching? How can my description of Carla be useful in dealing with her behavior in my class, on the playground, and perhaps even at home?"

PROBE 12-3

Take the three ways to evaluate behavior situationally and apply them to Lenny (see chapter opening). Should you plan for special educational services for him? Why or why not?

LOOKING AT EXCESS AND DEFICIT BEHAVIORS

We suggest an alternative to traditional classification that is both simple and educationally relevant. By "educationally relevant" we mean useful to you in teaching new behaviors. Since our approach is consistent with the ABC skills you have already mastered, you should have no difficulty in applying these ideas to students like Carla, Alvin, and Ike.

Developing discrepancy statements

You can describe all special behavior according to a discrepancy statement between what the student does and what the situation calls for (Gardner, 1977; Mager & Pipe, 1970). The difference between Carla's performance in your class and what you expect of her represents the basis of your intervention program. You will recognize here that your expectations can be stated in terms of objectives or goals for learning and behavior. These objectives will help you, the student, parents, and other teachers to compare Carla's present behaviors with realistic goals for improvement. You may also notice that this discrepancy forms the basis for moving into the first part of our basic teaching model.

Classifying excess and deficit skills

Your first step in this new approach to classification will be to decide whether the behaviors you observe represent excesses or deficits in meeting your expectancies. EXCESS BEHAVIORS are well above your expectations for frequency, duration, intensity, and rate of occurrence. Excess behaviors represent too much of something in relation to your classroom and school environment. DEFICIT BEHAVIORS are well below your expectancies. Deficit behaviors represent inappropriate, too few, or none at all of the behaviors you require for effective and productive classroom participation. Figure 12-2 shows you how Carla's present social and academic behavior can be described in terms of either excesses or deficits.

The classification of special behaviors into excesses and deficits points to clear ways in which you can intervene. There are two major adjustments you can make: (1) You can develop a program for changing the behavior of the student directly, so that it more closely matches the expectations of your teaching environment, or (2) you can rearrange your teaching environment to accommodate the special skills of this student. Most of

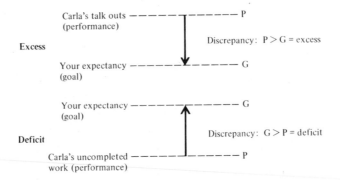

Figure 12-2 Excess and deficit behaviors: Discrepancy between performance and expectations.

the time you will want to make both adjustments: in the behavior of student and in the arrangement of the learning environment. At all times, your intervention strategy will aim at a closer match between the behavior of the student and the expectations of your classroom and school.

Comparing expectations with performance

How do you determine learning and behavioral expectations for your classroom and school environment? For this particular student? In addition to the situational evaluation (Figure 12-1), you will take into account seven factors about a student like Carla:

1. Age: is her behavior age-appropriate?
2. Educational history: does her present behavior fit with how she performed last year?
3. Other behaviors: does she perform this way in other classes or at home?
4. Physical problems: do these prevent or interfere with learning?
5. Cultural differences: is there a language or cultural difference?
6. Learning potential: what do IQ and other measures suggest about Carla's probable performance?
7. Present academic skills: is Carla more than one year behind the average for the class on math or reading?

We know that actual learning potential is impossible to measure accurately. We also know that achievement tests do not always give us a reliable picture of what a given student can do. On the other hand, you will be in a position to put all these seven factors together to make a rough estimate of what to expect from each student in your class.

Using descriptive categories

As you work with many special children, you will find that their excess and deficit behaviors seem to fall into observable patterns and *response classes*. You will find it useful to describe Carla's and Paula's behaviors in terms of the most frequent response patterns you observe. Table 12-3 gives you a range of special behaviors organized first by excesses or deficits, then by major response class, and finally by more discrete behavior patterns. The sample behaviors in Table 12-3 give you ways to be specific about Carla. For example, when you are planning Carla's academic program or discussing her progress with parents or other teachers, you can be quite specific about her particular learning and behavior patterns. You can describe specific behavior patterns, give some examples, and talk about the situations in which these behaviors appear. In this scheme, we have provided you with just a few examples in each descriptive category. You will doubtless come across many more in your teaching experiences.

Table 12-3. Excess—deficit classification

Primary	Secondary	Sample behavior classes
1. Excessive behaviors	*Disruptive* Interpersonal	Interpersonal aggression, noncompliance, negativism, temper tantrums, screaming, high activity, truancy.
	Illegal, harmful	Firesetting, stealing, property damage, sexual assault.
	Unproductive Self-stimulation	Self-mutilation, excessive eating, fantasy, daydreaming, masturbation, impulsivity.
	Affective reactions	Phobias, anxiety, sensitivity to criticism, overreaction to failure, expressions of sadness, inadequacy, worthlessness.
	Avoidance	Tardiness, absenteeism.
2. Deficit behaviors	*Learning difficulties* Academic deficits	General and specific deficits in reading, math, spelling, etc.
	Cognitive and language deficits	Short- and long-term retention, problem solving, concept formation, generalizing, applying principles, mediation skills, attention, task persistence, expressive and receptive speech.
	Sensorimotor deficits	Auditory and visual discrimination, locomotion and manual skills, fine motor coordination (writing).
	Social and personal deficits	Self-care: Dressing, toileting, feeding, traveling. Self-regulation: Self-management of academic and social behavior. Social interaction: Avoidance of adults or peers, inappropriate social responses.
3. Acceleration in learning and creativity	Academic	General and specific skills in academic subjects, special accelerated interests and skills.
	Creative	Unusual skill in art, music, performing arts, mechanics, electronics, etc.

Adapted and condensed from: Gardner, 1977, pp. 106–109.

Using categories to plan interventions

From this point on, your interventions will be organized around the special behaviors and not the exceptional child. In Table 12-4, we suggest how planned interventions can be organized around a system using these descriptive categories. This table shows how you can move from descriptive category to assessment to intervention. Notice that we have included accelerated and creative performance in a separate category in Table 12-3. While these can be seen as excess behaviors according to our definition, it seems useful to separate them out in order to indicate the direction of intervention. For disruptive and unproductive excess behaviors, you will probably design a program to reduce or eliminate them. For accelerated and creative productions, you will, of course, want to develop programs to encourage and nourish them.

You are now familiar with the traditional definitions and characteristics of special students. You can use the standard labels for students like Carla and Paula or you can develop descriptive categories to match the excess and deficit model. Keep in mind that you should aim for a close match between categories of behavior and intervention alternatives. In the remainder of this chapter, we will discuss possible causes, assessment, and intervention strategies for students with special learning patterns.

SEEKING CAUSES FOR PRESENT PERFORMANCE

Figuring out why Carla behaves as she does is like asking what causes a loaf of bread! Many ingredients go into the development of each student. You know from earlier chapters that development is complex and multidetermined. This means that few if any characteristics can be traced to a single cause. For each of our special students, you can probably take some guesses about what developmental factors might have been important for the present behaviors. For each student, many factors have contributed to the behaviors you are now trying to manage. What makes it even harder to untangle is the interaction of all of these factors with each new situation. Each time Carla and Paula play with peers, talk with adults, or try to solve an arithmetic problem, new experiences will certainly have diluted the effects of any "original cause." Right now you are dealing with an active person who is doing her best to cope with her present environment with her present skills. It is probably useless to think about whether Sally's "emotional problems" were the original cause of her learning retardation. Perhaps it was the other way around: did Sally's learning problems cause her to be insecure and fearful? Possibly both hypotheses are true. You will certainly want to look at Sally's reactions to challenge and failure as well as her academic skills.

Table 12-4. Assessment and intervention based on behavioral classification

Exceptional characteristic	What child does	What child is expected to do	Possible correlates	Learner assets	Program implications
Deficits in academic behavior.	When reads aloud in grade-level reading materials, exhibits omissions, sound-blending errors, hesitations, substitutions, and poor use of context cues. Comprehends only 25% of reading material.	Read with fluency and 85% comprehension.	Inadequate instruction, inadequate incentive conditions, excessive negative emotionality, hearing loss.	Normal range cognitive skills, relates well to adults, likes school.	Task analysis of reading materials, training in sound blending, use token reinforcement procedure, use easier materials, provide frequent reinforcement and social approval. Model a relaxed, pleasant manner of reading.
Deficits in prerequisite skills.	Attends to reading instruction for 2 to 3 minutes.	Attend to reading instruction for ten to fifteen minutes.	Excessive failure in attending to reading tasks viewed as avoidance behavior.	Attends for long period when presented easy materials.	Gradually shape attending skills by providing easy and structured performance tasks, use high-value reinforcers initially, label and praise increase in attending skills.
Excessive disruptive interpersonal behavior.	Fights with peers three to four times weekly, disruptive comments during class study period on average of four to five times daily.	No fighting, no disruptive comments.	Isolated by peer group, teased by peer group over being fat, poor self-concept behaviors.	States desire to have friends, responsive to tangible reinforcers.	Develop contingency program for appropriate classroom behavior, encourage peer-group activities.

Source: Gardner, 1977, p. 111.

When you are ready to plan a program for Sally, both these areas may be targets for your intervention.

There may be times when it will be useful for you to consider some of the relevant antecedents and the maintaining consequences of Sally's and Carla's behavior. In the following sections, we will discuss two major factors: the *medical-physical* and the *psychosocial*. Medical-physical factors include events that have occurred before, during, or after birth. Psychosocial factors include those past and present environmental events that have a significant impact on the developing child.

MEDICAL-PHYSICAL FACTORS

There are some events that produce a lasting impact on a child's physical structure. The results of certain changes in physical structure can increase the probability of learning and behavioral difficulties. Most of these changes in structure impose limits on what the developing child can learn. Some structural deviations limit the range of available behaviors the child can use.

Prenatal conditions

Prenatal factors include heredity, condition of the mother during pregnancy, and certain chemical or metabolic changes (Smith & Neisworth, 1975). Only a very few known conditions can be traced to heredity (faulty information carried in the genes). One of these conditions is phenylketonuria (PKU), which results in moderate to severe mental retardation if not corrected by proper diet. Other conditions present in the mother during pregnancy are associated with varying degrees of mental retardation and/or physical deviations in the child: exposure to radiation, inadequate nutrition, diabetes, anemia, a variety of drugs (thalidomide was an infamous one), virus and bacteria present in disease (syphilis, tuberculosis, and German measles or rubella, for example), and certain substances such as alcohol and tobacco. This list of possibilities is lengthy.

Postnatal conditions

A number of abnormal conditions during and after birth can also affect the permanent functioning of the developing child. Premature and difficult births may result in oxygen deprivation and possible damage to the brain. Excessive anaesthesia can have the same oxygen-depriving effects. After birth, the most common causes of developmental problems are disease and physical injury. Did you know that accidents to young children are the commonest cause of permanent disabilities? Medical knowledge is being applied to prevent many of the prenatal conditions that result in mental and physical damage to children. However, children with special learning needs will still come to the attention of teachers because of the continuing possibility of damage and injury to the young, developing child.

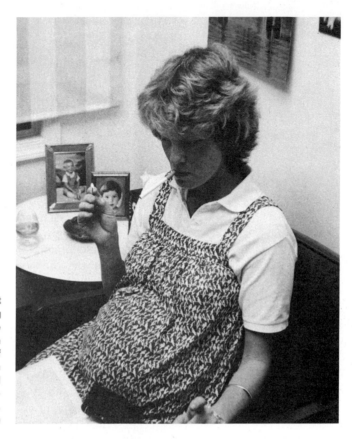

"Conditions present in the mother during pregnancy are associated with varying degrees of mental retardation and/or physical deviations in the child." (Dixie M. Walker)

Neurological impairment

Brain injury and neurological impairment are often used to explain learning problems. Children with known organic brain damage frequently show signs of hyperactivity, distractibility, and problems in motor coordination (Strauss & Kephart, 1955). Now, when a child like Carla shows some of these same behaviors, some people might conclude that she is indeed brain-damaged. Children with high activity levels and learning problems are frequently referred for medical examination. Even if there is no direct physical evidence of brain damage, Carla may be labeled as having MBD, or minimal brain dysfunction (Clements, 1966). We caution you to be very careful with these labels. With some highly active children, brain dysfunction may be a factor. For other children, a high level of activity may be a developmental characteristic or a response to environmental stress (Ross, 1976; Stewart et al., 1966). It is usually very difficult to determine whether or not a child is a victim of such neurological damage (Werry, 1979). Further, this diagnosis seldom has any relationship to the interventions you may plan.

Medical intervention

Regardless of your intervention plans, Carla's physician may have prescribed medication to "quiet down" her behavior during school hours. You may be in the position of administering or supervising such a drug therapy program. You will want to be knowledgeable about the effects of drug therapy on Carla's behavior in your class.

The drugs most frequently used with hyperactive children are dextroamphetamine (Dexedrine) and methylphenidate (Ritalin). Results with these drugs vary; some children improve dramatically, some improve acceptably, and many show no effects at all or even get worse (Omenn, 1973). For those children in whom improvement can be seen, the drugs appear to decrease the high activity level as well as to reduce impulsive, highly aggressive behaviors (Whalen et al., 1979). Once the child is quieted down, there may be some improvement in learning skills. Obviously, a drug cannot increase Carla's abilities, but it may increase her attention to her tasks. If any of your students are taking either of these drugs in school, we would like to suggest three cautions.

Maintain good management   Do not expect the drugs to substitute for good classroom management and effective teaching. Researchers have shown that behavioral management can sometimes be as effective as drugs in decreasing hyperactivity and increasing attention (O'Leary et al., 1976).

Monitor medication   Take care to monitor the administration of medication carefully. Don't double the dose on the day that Carla acts up. Be sure that her parents check on the dosage frequently. Watch for signs of excessive dosage (drowsiness, for example) and report this to the parents or the school nurse.

Deemphasize medication   Underplay the importance of the medication for the student. You do not want Carla to depend on drugs to make her behave. This dependence on external factors can lower her self-control and possibly lead to further drug dependence (Ross, 1976). You can implement this by seeing that Carla takes her medication at a certain time, independently of her good or poor behavior.

The possible abuse of drug therapy makes us very wary. Keep in mind that the effectiveness of drug therapy for any given child does not imply that brain damage is the cause of the hyperactive behavior. Keep in mind also that you can develop effective programs for students like Carla without the use of medication. We prefer management to medication.

"You can develop effective programs for students without the use of medication." (Hrynewych/Stock, Boston)

PSYCHOSOCIAL FACTORS

Consistent with our approach to classification, we can look at two contributing environmental sources of problems: those that produce deficits and those that encourage excess behaviors.

Environments that encourage deficits

A major source of environmental deficit is a restriction on sensory and interpersonal stimulation. Recall from Chapters 2 and 4 that a primary factor contributing to intellectual and behavioral competence is the richness of stimulation. Children who are deprived of opportunities to move about freely, manipulate objects, and explore their environments are handicapped from the start. Early stimulation is thought to be critical to the normal development of many parts of the sensory and nervous systems (Harlow & Zimmerman, 1959; Hunt, 1961). Later restrictions on verbal and cognitive stimulation may prevent the development of adequate discrimination and conceptual skills. For example, Sally may have lived in a cognitively limited situation with few toys or books and few stimulating things to look at, listen to, or touch. Other students with physical impairments will have sensory limitations imposed on them: long periods in bed, confinement to wheelchairs, or restrictions on normal visual and auditory stimulation.

Less obvious types of deprivation are contributed by parents who continually tell the child to "shut up," who do not adequately reinforce competent behaviors, or who largely ignore their children and leave them on their own. Parents who use overly punitive methods with their children may restrict and inhibit the range of developing behaviors. Children will learn not only to avoid the behaviors that were punished but also the people and situations associated with the punishment (Bijou & Baer, 1967). The result may be a fearful, inhibited child with deficits in adaptive social behavior. Thus, lack of opportunity to learn and inappropriate learning experiences may both contribute to learning and behavioral deficits (Gardner & Boyd, 1980; Worell & Nelson, 1974).

Environments that encourage excesses

The origins of excess behavior patterns are frequently puzzling. It seems to you that Ike certainly gets punished and reprimanded enough for his clowning. Why does he continue such nonproductive behavior? Consider three likely factors.

First, Ike has probably been reinforced on an intermittent schedule. At times he is punished, at times his behavior is ignored, and frequently he is applauded heartily by his buddies. You know by now that intermittent reinforcement and punishment both produce behaviors that are highly resistant to extinction.

Second, Ike may have few other appropriate behaviors to use. He may never have learned appropriate ways of interacting with his peers. What else can he do that brings immediate approval and loud guffaws from Alvin and Joe? Further, Ike may be receiving very little approval from you because his academic skills are low and he goofs off so frequently. When students are in an environment that is deficient in total reinforcement, they may (1) develop deviant behaviors to obtain whatever attention is available or (2) do whatever is possible to avoid the failure they experience. Elton's truant behavior might not occur if school were a reinforcing place where he received lots of peer and teacher approval for his excellent schoolwork. These observations remind you that whenever you move to reduce excess response patterns, you will want to start a careful program for reinforcing more productive behaviors. Ike needs to learn more cooperative peer interactions and Elton needs to experience some major success in school.

Finally, you know that any persistent behavior is getting paid off. Ike gets his laughs, Sally gets out of doing very much work, and Elton gets to hang around the local pool halls. If these excess behaviors are to be reduced, you will want to develop reinforcing situations that are stronger than those presently maintaining the excess behaviors. Punishment and school suspension, for example, will hardly be sufficient to encourage Sally, Ike, and Elton to work hard and cooperate with school programs.

INTERACTION AMONG FACTORS

Most of your special students will exhibit both excess and deficit behavior. Alvin is obviously deficient in many academic skills. He also cries too much and asks for help with everything he does. Carla is so busy running

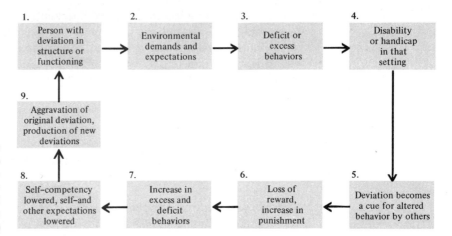

Figure 12-3
The relationship
among causative
factors. (*Source:*
Adapted and
modified from Smith
& Neisworth, 1975.)

around that she hardly pays attention to her class assignments. Elton and Sally have received so much rejection from their teachers and so little social acceptance from their peers that you hardly wonder that they both appear low in self-competency. The factors that produce these behaviors feed into one another. Physical and behavioral deviations produce negative reactions in others. These reactions, in turn, produce lowered expectations, avoidance, and self-depreciation in the student. The circular relationship among causative factors is shown in Figure 12-3. By the time you meet students like Sally and Alvin, the pattern has been set. You can no longer discriminate cause and effect in their behavioral adjustment. Trying to unravel to the original, "real" causes of these puzzling behaviors will be a waste of our professional time. You will make better use of your skills by applying them to a detailed ABC analysis and planning a serious program for each special student.

FACTORS IN ACCELERATED LEARNING

In contrast to students with learning and behavioral difficulties, you can expect to find that students such as Lenny have quite a different background. Lenny's parents are likely to be professional, well-educated, middle-class people who have provided Lenny with a stimulating environment (Hunt, 1961; Martinson, 1973; Payne, 1974). Of course, talent and creativity can appear in any cultural or socioeconomic group. However, an enriched environment is more likely to exist where parents are educated and economically secure. One report on a sample of creative architects found the following trends: high parental respect for and confidence in their children; an atmosphere of autonomy and freedom to explore and make decisions; early encouragement of artistic interests; consistent and predictable discipline with little physical punishment; high values placed on work, ethical values, success, and cultural activities (MacKinnon, 1962). It is clear that these are no ordinary families, just as Lenny is not an ordinary student. As a function of the early development of skills and generous parental encouragement, students like Lenny generally have well-developed self-competency and self-regulation skills. Nevertheless, special educational planning is desirable if Lenny is to develop his maximum range of skills and spend less time doodling at his desk (House, 1980).

EDUCATION FOR ALL CHILDREN

Not so very long ago, students like Alvin, Carla, and Sally might have been diagnosed as mentally retarded or hyperkinetic and placed in special classrooms. They might even have been sent to special schools. Frequently, their treatment would have been simple maintenance: caring for their needs and helping them to adjust to their disabilities. Learning expectancies for these students were often very low, so that efforts were minimal to teach new skills and competencies. More recently, the approach to educating special students has been undergoing rapid change. Learning theories have emphasized the importance of the environment in teaching and supporting new behaviors. The special student is no longer seen as a victim of an unchangeable affliction. There is increasing recognition that all children have some potential for learning adaptive behaviors; they all have the right to a full educational opportunity.

NEW PUBLIC POLICY

The most dramatic outcome of this movement toward recognizing the rights of special students was the formulation of new public policy. Federal legislation to enact this new policy was finally completed in 1975, with the now famous law referred to as PL 94-142. Let us look at what PL 94-142 provides for our special students and how this law is changing the face of special education in the United States.

The Education for All Handicapped Children Act: PL 94-142

This new public policy is represented by The Education for All Handicapped Children Act, or PL 94-142. This law asserts that all handicapped children have the right to full public educational services in the "LEAST RESTRICTIVE ENVIRONMENT." In addition to legislating public education for all children, the law also provides for careful procedures in identification, assessment, and individualized educational planning. Further, parents become new partners as they join the student and schools in determining the most appropriate educational programming. The requirements for a least restrictive environment, for individualized educational planning, and for participation by parents have revolutionized the special

education system. Most importantly for you as a prospective classroom teacher is the concept of MAINSTREAMING. As the requirements for a NORMALIZED ENVIRONMENT are implemented, special classrooms and hospitals are being disbanded. Children with many types of disabilities are now being served by unified schools sysems and frequently attend regular classrooms.

Major provisions of PL 94-142

The implications of this revolution are extremely important for your career. As a teacher in the normal educational stream, you may expect to have several of these students with special learning requirements in your class at any one time. These new procedures for mainstreaming special students put new demands on both regular teachers and on the total school system. Let's take a look at the major provisions of PL 94-142 and how they may affect your interactions with students like Sally, Alvin, and Carla.

Special students are defined   The revised definition of *special students* includes "the mentally retarded, hard of hearing, deaf, speech-impaired, visually handicapped, seriously emotionally disturbed, orthopedically impaired, or children with specific learning disabilities, who, by reason thereof, require special education and related services" (sec. 602). This definition specifically defines these students as "handicapped" and therefore excludes those with accelerated learning patterns.

Special education services are required   Expanded special education services will include individually designed instruction in whatever setting is least restrictive for that child. This may include regular classrooms as well as home-bound or hospital instruction. Related services must be provided, such as transportation, corrective devices, consultation by speech and hearing specialists, psychological and counseling services, recreational and occupational services, and medical diagnosis. This provision will mean that children can receive specialized consultation. Regular teachers will be provided with support personnel. All these services will be at full public expense, with no cost to parents.

Assessment is essential   Now, extensive identification and assessment procedures are assured for all special students before educational planning takes place. Several test or assessment procedures must be used. Tests should be as free as possible of cultural bias. Prevention is encouraged through special incentives to states for early identification of problems in preschoolers from 3 to 5 years of age.

IEPs are required   Individualized educational plans (IEPs) must be written for each student. The IEP must include assessment, long- and short-term goals, objectives to meet these goals, instructional methods for teaching this particular student, and procedures for evaluating whether or not these goals have been met. The IEP is written by a committee and is reviewed at least annually for update and revision. The learning activity for this chapter is one example of an IEP. Can you detect the similarity between the IEP and our basic teaching model?

Parents become partners   Parents must be consulted in all phases of identification, evaluation, and educational placement. Parents are guaranteed DUE PROCESS under this law. Here (sec. 615), due process enables the parents to participate in planning, to agree with or object to placement, and to review school records related to their child. The inclusion of parents will place greater demands on you to develop skills in parent conferencing.

You can certainly see that these five provisions will establish major innovations in your school and your classrooms. Below, we will discuss more fully just three parts of this program: mainstreaming, consultation, and working with parents.

MODELS FOR MAINSTREAMING

The goal of MAINSTREAMING is to normalize the environment for all students. This means that students like Carla and Alvin are more likely to develop age- and situation-appropriate behaviors when they are integrated with their "normal" peers (Brenton, 1974; Wolfensberger,

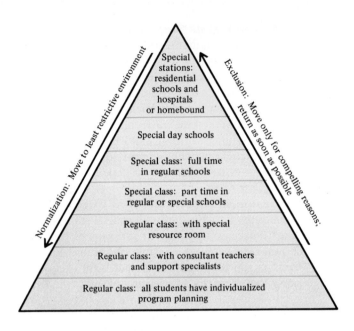

Special
stations:
residential
schools and
hospitals
or homebound

Special day schools

Special class: full time
in regular schools

Special class: part time in
regular or special schools

Regular class: with special
resource room

Regular class: with consultant teachers
and support specialists

Regular class: all students have individualized
program planning

Normalization: Move to least restrictive environment

Exclusion: Move only for compelling reasons; return as soon as possible.

Figure 12-4
A cascade of full educational services. The cascade allows a variety of educational models to coexist within a mainstreaming principle. The cascade assumes that the greatest number of students can be absorbed into regular schools and classes. Consultation and special-education support can be integrated into any level of the cascade. The fewest numbers of students are serviced at the highest and most expensive level.

1972). Maintaining a diverse group of students in a unified setting requires new approaches to planning, management, and instruction (Dunn, 1968; 1973). Rather than opting to isolate students from the mainstream of education, new strategies are being devised to support the inclusion of these students wherever possible. There are many mainstreaming models which can be graded on a continuum in terms of a normalization principle. Within a single school district, you might find some or all of these models in operation at the same time.

A cascade of services for normalization

Ideally, our models will resemble the cascade in Figure 12-4. The largest numbers of students are served by regular classrooms, with or without support services and special instruction. Removal of students from regular mainstream placement is done for limited periods of time. Segregated students are returned to the normal environment as soon as possible (Reynolds & Birch, 1977). At all levels of the CASCADE OF SERVICES, consultation and special instructional services are available. These special services are designed to give both temporary and long-range support to regular teachers who are dealing with a wide range of student skills.

Pros and cons of mainstreaming

Aside from the legal imperative to integrate Alvin and Carla with their peers, supporters of mainstreaming provide some compelling arguments in favor of integration. On the other hand, some experts in the field of special education feel strongly that many special students still need separate classrooms; these individuals have proposed a number of arguments against placing special students in regular classrooms. Let's take a look at both sides of the controversy.

For mainstreaming   On this side of the argument are those who are in favor of reducing segregated classrooms and integrating special students. They seem to focus on three major points:

- Integration of students within regular classrooms is the single best way to ensure normalization of response patterns and living privileges (Smith & Neisworth, 1975). Students with special behavior patterns can better learn and practice acceptable behavior that they observe in their peers. Peers, in turn, can learn to tolerate a range of differences as they live with and adjust to them (Peterson, Peterson, & Scriven, 1977).
- Students with learning problems accomplish as much over time in regular classrooms as they do in segregated classes (Carter, 1976).
- Self-esteem and a sense of personal control are higher in special students with regular class placements (Budoff & Gottlieb, 1976; Calhoun & Elliott, 1977; Parish & Copeland, 1978).

Against mainstreaming   On the other side, three major arguments against mainstreaming and in favor of homogeneous groupings for special students are frequently proposed:

- Special education teachers can give more attention to special learning problems than can the regular classroom teacher.
- Students with visible physical, behavioral, and learning disabilities are rejected by both their teachers and peers and will thus suffer from low self-esteem (Feitler, 1978; Parish, 1977; Siperstein & Gottlieb, 1977).
- Problem students in regular classrooms will still need considerable remedial help if they are to succeed (Barclay & Kehle, 1979; Gottlieb et al., 1976; Samuel, Gottlieb, & Robinson, 1979).

═══ **PROBE 12-4** ═══

Look back at your school experiences. Did you have any students in your classes who could be called "special"? What was your reaction, if any? Do you remember how other students reacted? Would you have preferred to have those special students elsewhere?

Bringing the pros and cons together

It will clearly take time and increased knowledge to make these mainstreaming models work effectively. We suggest that many of the problems which now appear can be helped by three services: First, more consultation and support services to regular teachers in the schools (Cantrell & Cantrell, 1976) and, second, resource rooms with specially trained teachers within regular schools (see Figure 12-5). The resource room provides a place where student learning and behavior difficulties can be dealt with immediately and temporarily (Anderson, 1973; Reger & Koppman, 1971). Finally and most importantly, these models call for the special preparation and training of all regular school personnel (Keough, 1976). Be prepared for special situations when you go out into the world to teach; you may need all three of these special services for your own education if you are to deal effectively with Carla and Alvin in your regular class setting.

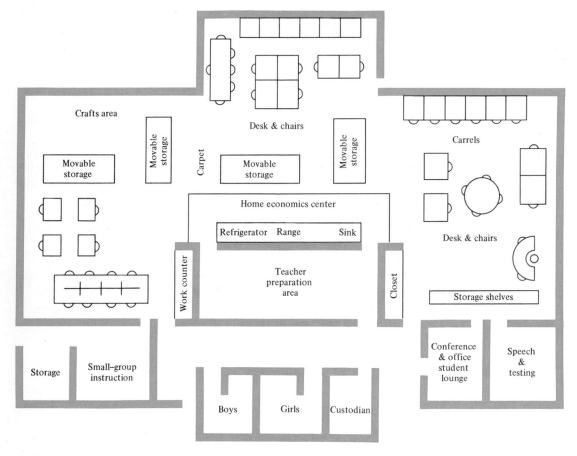

Figure 12-5
Sample plan for a resource room. (*Source:* Affleck, Lehning, & Brow, 1973.)

CONSULTATION SERVICES

As you integrate more students with special learning and behavior patterns into your domain, you will be asking for help more frequently. In the ideal school setting, specialist and *consultation* help will be highly visible and frequently available. Larger school systems can probably afford to maintain a larger staff of specialists and a more intense program of in-service training. Regardless of the current personnel practices in the schools where you will be teaching, you should know the answers to two basic questions: (1) What kinds of support and consultation personnel are available to me in this system? and (2) How can I best work within a consultancy model?

Special consultation skills

The range of potential specialist consultation is wide. Although these highly trained people may be given different titles, there are certain standard services you can expect them to provide. Currently, there are specialists for every aspect of the academic program, from arranging the physical layout of classrooms so as to accomodate all students to devising appropriate assessment and evaluation procedures. The following list gives only a sampling of the consultants available and the kinds of aid you may expect to obtain from them.

Speech pathologist: Speech, language, and hearing problems

School nurse: Health and nutrition questions

School counselor: Problems of personal and vocational adjustment

School psychologist: Decisions in classroom evaluation and management

School social worker: Contact with parents and community

Vocational rehabilitation counselor: Entry into world of work

Diagnostic-prescriptive teacher: Takes over class temporarily to demonstrate techniques

Resource teacher: Manages resource center, offers diagnostic and prescriptive help; may also remediate academic and behavioral problems

Consulting teacher: Consults with classroom or resource teachers

Principal: Wide range of skills depending on background

Learning development teams: Multiple skills in assessment, management, curriculum

The skills that each of these professionals can bring to your classroom teaching is barely touched by our brief description. Many of these individuals have skills which overlap and coordinate. Whichever of these specialists you work with, you will want to prepare yourself to use their time and expertise efficiently. Some of the following suggestions have been helpful to teachers in using consultation (Reynolds & Birch, 1977).

• *Decide who will be the client.* If you want help on management alternatives for Sally and Carla, then you are the client and your targets are the two students. Figure 12-6 shows the relationship between you and the consultant here.

• *Remember that you, as the teacher, remain responsible and in charge.* In calling in a consultant, some teachers hope to ''get rid of'' the student. We hope this will not be your goal. Ultimately, you may decide that an alternative class placement would be better for Alvin. However, this should not be the purpose of your referral to a consultant.

• *Be specific about your observations of the student.* We probably do not need to say this by now. Instead of commenting that ''Paula does not belong in this class; she may be autistic,'' you will list and describe Paula's observable problem behaviors.

• *Ask clear questions.* The consultant needs to know what you want from the referral contact. Do you want educational evaluation for academic programming or suggestions on behavioral management for Ike's out-of-seat activity?

• *Develop agreement on goals and procedures.* If you want the student removed from your class and the consultant believes you want the parents to come in for a conference, miscommunication may occur. You can work best with a consultant when you both agree on the procedures to be followed and the way in which the results of the consultation will be used. This point is especially important in determining whether the consultant works directly with you, with the child, or with other agents such as parents, principal, and community agencies.

• *Keep your consulting time objective and professional.* Indeed, you may have many administrative problems which interfere with the effectiveness of your teaching. You may have too few curriculum resources and too many students in your class. However, if these problems are not relevant to the consulting time for Carla, then you are wasting both your own and the consultant's time and skills in complaining about them.

• *Seek alternative suggestions.* Don't expect to get one plan that will invariably work.

• *Use the consultation as a learning experience.* Use your time constructively to learn more about future consultation skills and future intervention procedures with all your students.

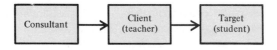

Figure 12-6
Consultation triad.
(*Source:* Reynolds &
Birch, 1977.)

PARENTS AS PARTNERS

Parents can be a valuable resource to you. Parents are an important link in the educational process. We saw in Chapters 2 through 4 that parents play a vital role in stimulation, motivation, and continued support for students. If you are not already convinced that parents provide valuable resources, let us take you one step further.

Parent power: Reasons to include parents

There are at least three good reasons why you will want to work closely with the parents of all your students.

Parents have influence   You know that Paula's parents have been the most influential people in her life. They model behavior, reinforce, and have been Paula's first and most continuing teachers (Patterson & Gullion, 1976). You can use parent power to help you in all aspects of Paula's educational planning. Parents can be encouraging at home and active in cooperating in a tutoring program or in carrying out many of your joint management plans (Brown et al., 1980).

"Parents can be a
valuable resource."
(Sybil Shelton/Peter
Arnold)

Parents provide information   Have you considered parents as a valuable source of information? You can ask Paula's parents about their goals for her school progress and what they expect from the school. This information will help keep your home-school communications clear. Paula's parents can also offer information about her behavior in home and community—what she can do successfully and when problem behaviors appear. You may find out that Paula has one friend to whom she relates well. You can then use this information to plan a program for increasing Paula's social skills. You may also find out what is reinforcing to Paula that can be used in your teaching approach.

Parents are required   According to new public policies, parents are required to be participants in educational planning for all your special students. We believe that this is an important step in bridging the gap between home and school. We hope that the parent-child-teacher conferences we are going to discuss will be useful to you with the parents of all your students. When you are planning a program for Carla and Paula, you will have little choice; parents must be included. This fact alone should motivate you to increase your skills in establishing a working relationship with parents.

Parent interaction skills: From contact to conferences

What kinds of skills will you need to deal effectively with Paula's parents? We suggest two important sets of skills that will be useful to you: (1) *relationship skills* such as establishing contact, demonstrating acceptance and respect, listening actively, and communicating your ideas effectively (Stewart, 1978) and (2) *conferencing skills* such as planning a format, gathering and giving information, developing mutual goals, obtaining agreement on implementation, and following up (Kroth, 1978; McAleer, 1978).

Relationship skills   These interpersonal skills are like many of the social interaction behaviors you probably use every day. You telephone and write to friends with whom you wish to keep in touch. When you meet your friends, you ask questions about how they are feeling, and you certainly don't blame them when they moan "I'm really feeling terrible today." You also look at them closely when they talk; you smile and nod your head, making small comments like "um-humm" to let them know you are listening. You try not to interrupt while they are talking; you wait until they are finished before you have your say. And you certainly do not hog the whole conversation; you give your friends a chance to talk also.

All these small social behaviors are skills which, you have probably learned, will tell your friends that you respect and accept them. These same skills will tell the same thing to the parents of your special students.

Use these skills generously. Why is it so important to let Paula's parents know that you accept and respect them? Parents can be your allies, your adversaries, or an unknown factor. Parents can support, reject, or ignore much of what you are trying to accomplish in school. This is especially true for parents of students with special behaviors.

Parents of special students may have had a history of frustration, anxiety, guilt, despondency, helplessness, and despair about their child. When they come to you, they may be hostile and suspicious of your motives and doubt your good intentions. Other teachers may have placed a label on Paula, for example, ignored her in their classroom, or let her parents know that they went wrong with her somewhere. We want to caution you especially to be sensitive to the feelings of parents. You may need to be particularly tolerant and accepting when parents carry over their bad experiences from other school contacts. You might want to watch your own reactions also. Are you returning their feelings of discomfort and inadequacy with similar responses? Try to keep your good sense of balance and objectivity as you deal with Paula's and Carla's parents. A poignant example of one famous couple's reaction to their son's disability is that of James and Gertrude Gallagher, both professional educators (Figure 12-7).

Conferencing skills   Effective conferencing with all parents will be an important part of your management package. Until recently, teachers had little or no training in how to develop and conduct a parent conference. We hope that you will have more intense practice in parent conferencing later in your educational career. At this point, you will want to know what procedures are involved and how you can implement them in your school setting. Later on, you may have an opportunity to role-play these skills with another student.

**Figure 12-7
Parents versus
professionals.
(*Source:* Gallagher,
J. J., & Gallagher,
G. C. "Family
Adaptation to a
Handicapped Child
and Assorted
Professionals," In A.
P. Turnbull and H. R.
Turnbull, III, (Eds.),
*Parents Speak Out:
Views from the Other
Side of the Two-Way
Mirror.* Columbus,
Ohio: Charles E.
Merrill, 1978.)**

One of the unfortunate components of the era in which our child was growing up was that one of the predominant theories about bronchial asthma was that the parents could be the cause of the condition, rather than being part of the victims of it. We spent many hours being interviewed and questioned, with the obvious purpose of seeing if we were, in some fashion, precipitating the attacks of our child through our own anxieties and problems. Since, we in our other roles, were used to interviewing people, it was transparent in many cases what the intent of the questioning was, but that did not make it any less frustrating.

It is obvious that the parents are under tension when they have a handicapped child or a child who is subject to acute illnesses. Our feeling, which remains constant to this day, is that to accuse parents of creating the problem, whether the problem is asthma or autism or whatever, is akin to accusing the thunder of causing the storm. Our own tensions were clearly evident, though we tried to be casual upon hearing our child begin to wheeze, which signified the onset of an attack. We probably did contribute somewhat to the intensity of the attack, but that is quite different from being held responsible for the basic condition in the first place.

Such an attitude of "blame the parent," which was not uncommon among the professionals at that time, did create a distance in the relationship between the parents and the professionals and probably caused other unfavorable consequences as well.

As you read through the suggestions we will provide for parent conferences, notice that we suggest including the child. This is indeed a new idea for most teachers. Why not include Paula and Carla in their own conferences? They certainly have the greatest investment in the outcomes (Hogan, 1975)! Students become very suspicious when parents and teachers talk about them. They are certain that no good will come of it. Probably, Carla believes that you are listing all of her bad behaviors. Two advantages can be achieved when you include students in their own parent-teacher-child conferences: (1) students can have an active role in developing objectives and setting goals they can meet and (2) students can see firsthand that parents and teachers are indeed interested in being constructive and helpful rather than critical and punitive (Hogan, 1975). Both these factors should work to your long-range advantage with youngsters like Carla and Paula in school.

Before you sit down at the conference table with students and parents, be certain to plan ahead (Kroth, 1978; McAleer, 1978; Reynolds & Birch, 1977). The plan for an effective parent conference follows our basic teaching model:

GUIDELINES FOR TEACHING

Productive Parent Conferencing

- *Plan a format.* You will find that advance planning of personnel and procedures will pay off. A planned format will keep you on task each time and will help prevent time-consuming digressions. The format should include who will be present, how frequently the conferences are to occur, and what broad topics are to be covered. You can even take a checklist with you and keep track of your progress from beginning to end. If your school has a counselor, resource teacher, or other special personnel, it might be helpful to include this person in the format.
- *Define parent and teacher (and student) concerns.* What concerns each of you about the student's progress? Here, you can discuss progress last week, last month, or for the entire year. This should be an exploratory step in which everyone has a voice in clarifying concerns. You will find that this step serves as a good communications bridge between you, the parents, and the student. Watch out that premature decisions are not made at this point. If parents or student are especially hostile or uncommunicative here, you might want to let the counselor/consultant take an active role as mediator.
- *Consider positive accomplishments.* Having listed some problems, you will want to balance them with strengths and assets. What positive gains has the student made in the area of concern? In other areas? Here you are concerned with keeping a positive view of the student. You may also uncover assets that will work to your advantage.
- *List strategies that work.* Now you want to explore what methods have been particularly successful with this student. Each person should be encouraged to make a positive contribution. In this manner, you can

develop a useful list of adaptive strategies that have worked in the past with this student. You can include here any of the ABC management components: curriculum, learning environment, teacher behavior, and reinforcing events. (We hope someone is taking notes at this point; otherwise you will never remember it all.)

• *Consider all alternatives.* Here you can bring in your skills in problem solving. Give parents the chance to be informed about the possibilities for their child. Then they can be more helpful in making decisions. If parents suggest alternatives that appear unworkable, be calm about looking at the pros and cons. You can help them to make informed decisions if they can anticipate probable outcomes.

• *Set specific goals.* Now you are in a position to set short-term goals. We advise you to set goals for the next week or the next month. In that way, goals can be specific and you, the parents, and the student can determine early if they have been met. Then, if goals are not met, you can examine what steps in your strategy need to be changed. Where possible, you will want to be sure to include the student in setting these goals. The success of your planning will depend on student cooperation and participation.

• *Follow-up for checking and evaluation.* You should expect to have more than one conference with each set of parents. It is helpful to plan for the next meeting before you close each conference. The follow-up conference evaluates progress and plans for necessary changes in goals or strategies. It will also be a favorable format for mutual support and the sharing of success. If follow-up conferences use the same format, you will be certain to cover positive outcomes as well as new problems.

STEPS TO EFFECTIVE TEACHING

Finally, you have worked your way through this book. We would like to leave you here with some closing suggestions on how you can be most effective with each special student in your class. We would like to be helpful in providing you with lists of strategies that will work for students like Paula, Carla, and Lenny. If you have mastered all the preceding chapters, we believe you have the basic information you will need to deal with all your students. If we were to develop sets of strategies for each of the special students here, you would recognize a theme and variations.

A TEACHING MODEL FOR ALL STUDENTS

At the base of each of our programs would be the basic teaching model, an ABC analysis for each student, and a review of the principles of learning theories. The same principles apply to all students. The broad outline of procedures will apply to all students. Many similar strategies will work with all students. However, you have seen from this chapter that a mainstream model places many special teaching demands on you. You will need special skills in dealing with the range of students you will meet. How can our general plan of approach to teaching work for all your unique students?

Mainstreaming variations

We will expand the basic teaching model to include the additional demands of a mainstream approach. The major additions are in increased individualization, consultation with parents and specialists, and consideration of alternative class, curriculum, and equipment arrangements. These additions will become relevant in each phase of your teaching procedures. For all your students, you will still want to develop goals and objectives, assess student entry skills, create instructional plans to meet student needs, and evaluate your procedures with formative and summative data. At each step in the model, you may want to consult with parents and professionals. This consultation will help you to make decisions about individualizing your instruction. At this point, the process may seem overwhelming to you. Relax. Remember that you are not alone. The mainstream model suggests that you will have lots of help. In contrast to our earlier comment, you, the teacher, will no longer be "the lone arranger." You will be a member of a team of experts working together. Many times, of course, the team members will be as perplexed as you are. You are all breaking new ground and charting new territory. The positive payoff for this uncertain state of affairs should appeal to your creative side: novelty, uncertainty, and challenge.

GUIDELINES FOR TEACHING

A Teaching Model for All Students

In a recent publication from the Council for Exceptional Children, Reynolds and Birch (1977) proposed a range of teaching strategies that they believe are appropriate for all students. These authors are in essential agreement with the position we have outlined above. They go even further and list a set of teaching approaches that bridge all special categories. Their ideas are exciting and very controversial. We would like to leave you with a sample of the suggestions they provide for teaching all students—slow, accelerated, handicapped, different, and typical. Many of these ideas are still untested and in need of validation. Nevertheless, they will suggest to you some of the many possibilities for creative approaches to problem solving. From their many suggestions, we have sampled a set of fifteen ideas. As you review these, decide how many are really new to you.

* *Get to know your students.* Observe them, interview them, talk to them as people. Accept what they bring to your classroom and respect their individuality. You can make your classroom an equal opportunity class.

• *Help the student to set the pace of learning.* Instead of saying ''This is due by tomorrow noon,'' you might say: ''How long shall we plan for you to spend on this activity?'' In this manner, each student can learn to assess his or her own resources for meeting goals. Students can learn to set realistic goals and to plan strategies for meeting them. You can see how this plan can be useful to students who work at both fast and slow rates.

• *Give the student choices.* Allow some self-scheduling of activities. Students can make decisions on what to do, how to do it, when, where, with whom, and even whether or not to do it at all. An effective way to implement this strategy is by means of contingency contracting. We have seen that contracting approaches can work with students at all ages and skill levels. Of course, judicious teacher monitoring is suggested for all contract agreements.

• *Use direct experience.* Engage all students in ''hands on'' experiences. These authors suggest things like dramatic play, group reading, pupil-led discussions, discovery, and independent study; all these are aimed at developing problem-solving skills. For example, they suggest engaging students in a project to modify the lunchroom for students with special requirements and then monitoring the effectiveness of the project

• *Use peer instruction.* Here you can harness pupil power. Students can be helpful to each other in many ways: tutoring; flipping flash cards; acting as lab, physical education, or dance assistants; or serving as theme readers in advanced English. As students take on the teacher role, they develop increased interpersonal skills and empathy for both the role of

"Use peer instruction." (Bruce Roberts/Photo Researchers)

the teacher and the problems of the learner. Students at all levels of skill can teach something useful to students with lesser skills in some area.

• *Give chances for leadership.* All students can learn to lead small group projects and discussions. Decision-making skills lead to increased self-confidence and a sense of personal control. Students can practice skills in parliamentary procedures, organization, control, and brainstorming. These activities are not only for your accelerated Lenny but also for Carla and Paula.

• *Use undercutting to insure success.* Start below the student's present level of performance in order to insure success, mastery, and confidence. Then move up the ladder of difficulty, but drop back occasionally. The authors suggest that you "seed" frequently with easy spots to insure continued positive expectancy. Although, on the surface, this suggestion seems more appropriate for slow learners, consider it also for students like Lenny. Frequently, students who learn at a fast rate are pushed and pressured too hard to excel at all times.

• *Help students to learn how they learn.* What a novel suggestion! Teach all students some principles of psychology and learning. In this manner, they can look at their own learning and behavior strategies. They might even learn how to be more effective mediators. They might learn to be more self-regulating. Principles of psychology that are typically taught at the college level can be introduced at the earliest grades.

• *Use pupil feedback.* Help students to monitor their progress through the frequent use of tests, charts, programs, and criterion-referenced procedures. The authors suggest an interesting behavioral assessment: place a small group of pregnant teenagers together to discuss their own language skills and how they want their babies to talk; then practice these skills. In this situation, the teacher observes skill development in action; students observe each other.

• *Use reinforcement frequently.* Develop schedules and reinforcement menus that are appropriate for each student. Use the *Premack principle* to reinforce activities that are natural to the school environment. Even accelerated students who appear to be good at everything need encouragement, attention, and opportunities for pleasurable activities.

• *Encourage divergent thinking.* Every day, plan a "what if" that will challenge all your students. What if there were no colors? What if everyone were boys and there were no girls?

• *Use reviews meaningfully.* Here you will build up feelings of accomplishment by reviewing what you have already mastered. Some students like Alvin need a great deal of this activity; others students need less. All students need some. Preferably, you will emphasize recent learning. You can encourage students to teach what they have learned to others. They can incorporate this learning into games, activities, projects, publications. (How about a school newspaper where everyone contributes?)

● *Move from the familiar to the unfamiliar.* Interview your students. Find out about their backgrounds, interests, and experiences. Draw these facts into the learning situations. Have students apply these to their present school activities.

● *Invoke the interest/difficulty principle.* Keep interest level high for all and adjust difficulty to skill level. Here you will be finding interesting materials for Elton, who is turned off by third-grade readers, as well as for Lenny, who is taking a class in college Russian.

● *Model the behavior you want your students to use.* Does this sound familiar?

All these suggestions should sound familiar to you. This sample list of special strategies tells you that good teaching techniques bridge across students, skills, and situations.

LEARNING ACTIVITY: DEVELOPING AN IEP

We want you to have some firsthand experience with an IEP. Since you may not now be working with children, let us suggest that you work on yourself. Use the following format for developing your own IEP.

Assessment team Who would you select to evaluate your present learning and behavioral skills? List them and indicate their positions.

Description of needs What skills in your learning and behavioral repertoire could benefit from intervention? You might apply the three criteria on page 612 here. You might apply a personal criterion: I really want to do something about my sloppy study habits, my inability to talk in class, my tendency to block before I take exams, my excess eating habits, my inadequate social skills every time I meet a person of the opposite sex, my inaccurate math computation skills, my unassertive behavior with my principal and dean, etc.

Learning style Observe how you learn best. Can you listen in class without taking notes? Do you need visuals to help you remember? Do you leave notes around because you need that stimulus cue to remember what you are supposed to do today? Do you need to repeat and rehearse before you try out a new behavior? Have you ever tried a programmed learning book? Survey your learning style and list the conditions under which you learn most effectively.

Statement of services needed What will be helpful to you in your program of change? Do you need a peer to count and record your participation in class? Do you need a quieter place to study? Do you need a good book on developing assertive behavior or reducing test anxiety? Do you think a counselor might help you in your program? State materials, conditions, and personnel who could help you with your IEP. Perhaps a speed-reading course will mend your study skills deficit.

Annual goals   In twelve months, you will be able to demonstrate the following gains:

1. Grades at least one quality point higher.
2. Dating at least once a week.
3. Fitting into a size 10 dress.
4. Etcetera. List all goals that fit with your target behavior. What would you like to be doing about this in a year? How do you want to see yourself?

Short-term goals   With criteria for attainment (first three months):

1. By June 30, I will be studying at least one hour per day.
2. By July 30, I will have asked two people for a date.
3. By August 30, I will have lost 5 pounds.
4. Etcetera—for each of your goals.

Long-term objectives   With criteria for attainment:

1. Objectives 1, 2, and 3 will be reevaluated and upgraded at the end of three months.
2. By the end of six months, I will have found one person that I want to date more than once a month.
3. By the end of nine months, I will have lost 15 pounds.
4. Etcetera—for all your goals.

Special instructional materials   What will you need to help you here? A book on dieting, a calorie chart? A wrist counter to record the number of times you speak up in class? A book in which to record the names and dates of all the people you call up? A scale on which to weigh yourself?

Other specific modifications   How will you need to modify the environment? A separate place in which to study because now you fall asleep on your bed? A lock on the refrigerator door that can be opened only by your roommate?

Specific means of coordinating with other programs   You will meet once a week with two other students in your class to review progress and exchange helpful suggestions. You will meet once monthly with your instructor to monitor your progress and evaluate the effectiveness of your strategies.

Personnel responsible for providing service   Names of your assessment team, student partners, instructor. Telephone numbers in the event that you need to call them for support or advice.

Location to carry out plan   Home, school, car, bar, restaurant, counselor's office.

Describe transportation   Do you need a ride?

Program will begin and end   Write in date, number of days it will continue, total duration.

Method and frequency   Record method and frequency of initial and periodic reviews. Give dates. Consider assessment team review data. Perhaps retest on target behaviors. Ongoing monitoring of progress at least once monthly with your instructor or class team members.

Description of integrated educational activities   This must be given if your intervention is all in a special place—for example, if you have been studying only at your desk or eating only in the kitchen. How can you normalize your learning environment? Do you want to segregate yourself all the time?

I consent to the individual educational plan described above.

SIGNATURE ———————————————————— DATE ——————

TASK 12-1

After reading this chapter and reviewing the IEP form above, you will be able to develop an IEP for one or more of your target behaviors. Further, you will carry out this intervention plan for the remainder of this semester.

TASK 12-2

You will serve as an assessment team member or monitor for another student in your class. Here, you will help the person to assess needs, monitor progress, and evaluate outcome.

SUMMARY

1. SPECIAL STUDENTS are those who have special learning requirements. Both teachers and learning environments must adjust to their learning needs. All special students can learn in a teaching environment that accommodates to their learning characteristics.

2. CLASSIFICATION of special students is traditionally done according to diagnostic categories. These categories separate students by degree of disability, rate of learning, or visible characteristics. Standard categories for exceptional children include mild and severe behavior disorders; learning disabilities; mild, moderate, and severe mental retardation; and intellectually gifted.

3. Labeling special students by traditional categories has at least five harmful effects: they are educationally irrelevant, they classify different students into a single category, they place the blame on the student, they do not explain the student's behavior, and they result in negative expectations. They seldom result in effective instruction. Labeling can be helpful if it is developed to meet your educational goals. Helpful labels have three characteristics: they use observable and measurable characteristics of each student, they use descriptive categories of behavior, and they highlight discrepancies between student skills and environmental expectancies.

4. CLASSIFICATION requires judgment. Three criteria for deciding to label excess or deficit behavior are (1) the frequency, intensity, duration, and rate of the behavior; (2) disruptive effects of the behaviors in the school; and (3) degree to which the behaviors interfere with the student's own progress. All three considerations should play a role before a student is referred for special education intervention.

5. Classification by EXCESS and DEFICIT BEHAVIOR is educationally relevant. It describes the behaviors instead of categorizing students. It is observable and measurable. It points the way for constructive intervention. Further description of response classes and specific situational behaviors is essential for effective educational planning.

6. The original causes of exceptional behaviors are usually unknown or difficult to determine. Major sources of problems that might contribute to special learning requirements are *medical-physical* and *psychosocial*. Medical and physical problems can occur before, during, and after birth. They frequently result in structural changes that influence the learning and behavioral capabilities of the developing child. "Minimal brain dysfunction" is a common diagnosis for children who show hyperactive behavior in school. Many of these students will be on drug therapy. Teachers need to know how to deal with students who are on medication in school. Three

cautions are suggested here. Psychosocial causes of behavioral differences include both environmental deprivations leading to deficits and ineffective reinforcement conditions that support excess behavior. Students with accelerated learning patterns come from family backgrounds that encourage exploration and high achievement and that offer consistent discipline as well as warm support.

7. The Education for All Handicapped Children Act is known as PL 94-142. This federal legislation mandates that all students have the right to a full and free public education. The legislation requires the LEAST RESTRICTIVE ENVIRONMENT for special students. This requirement has placed emphasis on MAINSTREAMING and a NORMALIZED ENVIRONMENT for all students. PL 94-142 also requires an INDIVIDUAL EDUCATIONAL PLAN (IEP) for each student. The IEP includes student needs, long- and short-term goals, objectives, intervention strategies, and frequent evaluation. Parents are to be included in planning the IEP and have the right to DUE PROCESS if they are dissatisfied with any part of the procedure. The IEP procedure requires that all students undergo extensive assessment and evaluation with bias-free tests.

8. MAINSTREAMING can be accomplished with a wide variety of models and procedures. The normalization principle suggests that all students, where possible, be placed in regular classes and moved to special class and special schools only for compelling educational reasons. The CASCADE OF SERVICES provides for a continuum of arrangements from least to most restrictive. Students are always moved or maintained in the least restrictive setting. Common objections to and arguments for placement of special children in regular classrooms are outlined.

9. Consultation by special and skilled support personnel becomes essential in all mainstream models. The consultant works directly with teachers or with students and parents. Regular classroom teachers will need to learn special skills in using consultant time. Suggestions for working with consultants are provided.

10. Parents have a new role to play in educational planning for their children. Teachers have new roles to play in dealing with parents. Teachers need to know how to develop working relationships with parents for the mutual benefit of both parents and students. Teachers and parents both need to develop useful formats for educational planning conferences. A parent conferencing format is suggested. We also suggest including the student in conferences as an important part of the teacher-parent-student relationship.

11. Finally, we suggest that all good teaching strategies are special. We proposed a basic set of instructional skills as the foundation of all

good teaching. The chapter closes with a set of fifteen teacher strategies for special students. We hope you recognize that these strategies will apply equally to all your students.

12. Developing an IEP on yourself teaches you the steps that must be followed. These steps include assessment, description of needs, learning styles, statement of services needed, annual goals, short-term goals, long-term objectives, special instructional materials, coordination with other programs, personnel responsible for providing services, location, transportation, dates of entry and closing, and a description of mainstreaming efforts.

 KEY TERMS

CASCADE OF SERVICES: A system of student academic placement which provides for a continuum of service, from least to most restrictive, for all students.

CLASSIFICATION: Placement of children into categories on the basis of one or more similar characteristics.

DEFICIT BEHAVIOR: Behavior that is well below performance expectancies for a particular student. Deficit behaviors may represent inappropriate, too few, or none at all of the competencies required for effective classroom participation.

DISCREPANCY STATEMENT: A description of the present performance of the child in relation to the expectations of the present environment.

DUE PROCESS: Procedures guaranteed to parents and children referred for assessment under PL 94–142. Due process enables parents to participate in planning, placement, and development of the IEP.

EXCEPTIONAL CHILDREN: Broad term to describe children who deviate significantly from the norms of expected behavior in particular academic situations.

EXCESS BEHAVIOR: Behaviors that are well above performance expectancies for frequency, duration, intensity, and rate of occurrence for a particular student.

IEPS: Individualized educational plans for special students. The IEP is required by PL 94–142 and must include assessment, long- and short-term goals, instructional methods for reaching goals, and procedures for evaluating goal attainment.

LEAST RESTRICTIVE ENVIRONMENT: A learning environment which allows the child access to educational opportunities as similar to the regular classroom as is feasible for that child. See NORMALIZED ENVIRONMENT.

MAINSTREAMING: Placement of special students in the least restrictive educational environment for the majority of their school experiences. The goal of mainstreaming is to normalize the learning environment for all students.

NORMALIZED ENVIRONMENT: A learning environment which closely approximates the academic and social learning opportunities of the average child.

PL 94–142: The Education for All Handicapped Children Act, which provides for the right to full public educational services for all handicapped children in the LEAST RESTRICTIVE ENVIRONMENT.

SPECIAL STUDENTS: Students with learning and behavioral characteristics that do not meet parent and teacher expectations in typical learning environments.

SELF-TEST

1. Students labeled as exceptional
   a. have special learning needs
   b. are best off in special classrooms
   c. are retarded in learning
   d. are accelerated in learning
   e. are handicapped
2. Traditional classification categories
   a. are used in all school systems
   b. are educationally irrelevant
   c. are clearly defined
   d. are never used any more
   e. predict future behavior
3. A discrepancy statement states the difference between _____ and _____.
4. Three criteria for making a judgment about the need for special education intervention are:
   a. _____
   b. _____
   c. _____
5. Deficit behaviors are _____.
6. Children with known brain injury frequently show signs of _____, _____, and _____.
7. Drug therapy for hyperactive behavior
   a. is the single best treatment
   b. is never used in public schools
   c. is only used when direct brain injury is diagnosed
   d. can increase, decrease, or have no effect on behavior
   e. is only used for short periods of time
8. The causes of exceptional learning and behavior patterns are
   a. usually medical-physical
   b. genetic and inherited
   c. due to brain injury or neurological damage
   d. usually complex and unknown
   e. due to poor parental practices
9. PL 94–124 provides that
   a. parents shall be consulted in educational planning
   b. special classrooms shall be increased
   c. gifted students shall receive extra resources
   d. parents have no say about the placement of their children
10. Six steps in a mainstreaming cascade are as follows:
    a. _____
    b. _____
    c. _____
    d. _____
    e. _____
    f. _____

SELF-TEST KEY

1. a
2. b
3. expectations and performance
4. See page 612.
5. See Key Terms.
6. hyperactivity, distractibility, problems in motor coordination.
7. d
8. d
9. a
10. See Figure 12-4.

BIBLIOGRAPHY

Adams, R., & Biddle, R. *Realities of teaching: Explorations with videotape.* New York: Holt, 1970.

Ainsworth, M., Blehar, M., Waters, E., & Wall, S. *Patterns of attachment: Observations in strange situations and at home.* Hillsdale, N.J.: Erlbaum, 1977.

Almy, M., Chittendon, E., & Miller, P. *Young children's thinking.* New York: Teachers College Press, 1966.

Alschuler, A. S., Tabor, D., & McIntyre, J. *Teaching achievement motivation: Theory and practice in psychological education.* Middletown, Conn.: Educational Ventures, Inc., 1970.

American Personnel and Guidance Association. *Sex equality in guidance opportunities: Resources for counselors, teachers and administrators.* Washington, D.C., 1975.

American Personnel and Guidance Association. *A handbook for workshops in sex equality.* Washington, D.C., 1976.

Anastasi, A. *Individual differences* (2d ed). New York: Wiley, 1978.

Anderson, E. M. *The disabled school child: A study of integration in the primary schools.* London: Methuen, 1973.

Anderson, R. C., Kulhavy, R. W., & Andre, T. Conditions under which feedback facilitates learning from a programmed text. *Journal of Educational Psychology,* 1972, *42,* 391–394.

Anderson, R. H., & Shane, H. G. *As the twig is bent: Readings in early childhood education.* Boston: Houghton Mifflin, 1971.

Aronfreed, A. *Conduct and conscience: The socialization of internalized control over behavior.* New York: Academic Press, 1968.

Aronson, E., Blaney, N., Sikes, J., Stephen, C., & Snapp, N. Busing and racial tension: The jigsaw route to learning and liking. *Psychology Today,* 1975, *8*(9), 43–50.

Atkinson, J. W. Toward experimental analysis of human motivation in terms of motives, expectancies and incentives. In J. W. Atkinson (Ed.), *Motives in fantasy, action, and society.* New York: Van Nostrand, 1958.

Atkinson, J. W. *An introduction to motivation.* New York: Van Nostrand, 1965.

Atkinson, R. C., & Shiffrin, R. M. The control of short-term memory. *Scientific American,* 1971, *224,* 82–90.

Ault, R. Problem-solving strategies of reflective, impulsive, fast accurate, and slow inaccurate children. *Child Development*, 1973, *44*, 259–266.

Ausubel, D. P. *The psychology of meaningful verbal learning*. New York: Grune & Stratton, 1963.

Ausubel, D. P. The use of advanced organizers in the learning and retention of meaningful verbal learning. *Journal of Educational Psychology*, 1969, *51*, 267–272.

Ausubel, D. P. The facilitation of meaningful verbal learning in the classroom. *Educational Psychologist*, 1978, *12*, 162–178.

Ayllon, T., & Azrin, N. H. *The token economy*. New York: Appleton-Century-Crofts, 1968.

Azrin, N. H., & Powers, M. A. Eliminating classroom disturbances of emotionally disturbed children by positive practice procedures. *Behavior Therapy*, 1975, *6*, 525–534.

Baer, D. M. Age-irrelevant concept of development. *Merrill-Palmer Quarterly*, 1970, *16*, 238–245.

Baird, L. Teaching styles: An exploratory study of dimensions and effects. *Journal of Educational Psychology*, 1973, *64*, 15–21.

Baldwin, T., Johnson, T., & Wiley, S. *The teacher's perception and attribution of causation*. Paper presented at the American Educational Research Associaton, Minneapolis, Minn., 1970.

Bandura, A. Vicarious processes: A case of no-trial learning. In L. Berkowitz (Ed.), *Advances in experimental social psychology*, Vol. 2. New York: Academic Press, 1965.

Bandura, A. *Principles of behavior modification*. New York: Holt, 1969.

Bandura, A. (Ed.), *Psychological modeling: Conflicting theories*. Chicago: Aldine-Atherton, 1971.

Bandura, A. *Aggression: A social learning analysis*. Englewood Cliffs, N.J.: Prentice-Hall, 1973.

Bandura, A. Self-reinforcement processes. In M. J. Mahoney & C. E. Thoreson (Eds.), *Self-control: Power to the person*. Monterey, Calif.: Brooks/Cole, 1974.

Bandura, A. Social learning theory. In J. T. Spence, R. Carson, & J. Thibaut (Eds.), *Behavioral approaches to therapy*. Morristown, N.J.: Silver Burdett, 1976(a).

Bandura, A. Effecting change through participant modeling. In J. D. Krumboltz & C. E. Thoreson (Eds.), *Counseling methods*. New York: Holt, 1976(b).

Bandura, A. *Social learning theory*. Englewood Cliffs, N.J.: Prentice-Hall, 1977.

Bandura, A., Grusec, J. E., & Menlove, F. L. Some determinants of self-reinforcement monitoring systems. *Journal of Personality and Social Psychology*, 1967, *5*, 499–555.

Bandura, A., & Kupers, C. J. Transmission of patterns of self-reinforcement through modeling, *Journal of Abnormal and Social Psychology*, 1964, *69*, 1–9.

Bandura, A., & McDonald, F. J. The influence of social reinforcement and the behavior of models in shaping children's moral judgments. *Journal of Abnormal and Social Psychology*, 1963, *67*, 274–281.

Bandura, A., Ross, D., & Ross, S. A. Transmission of aggression through imitation of aggressive models. *Journal of Abnormal and Social Psychology*, 1961, *63*, 575–582.

Bandura, A., & Walters, R. H. *Social learning and personality development.* New York: Holt, 1963.

Banks, C. W., McQuater, G. V., & Hubbard, J. L. Toward a reconceptualization of the social-cognitive basis of achievement orientation in Blacks. *Review of Educational Research,* 1978, *48,* 381–397.

Bany, M. A., & Johnson, L. V. *Educational social psychology.* New York: Macmillan, 1975.

Baratz, J. The relationship of black English to reading. In J. L. Laffey & R. Shuy (Eds.), *Language differences: Do they interfere?* Newark, Del.: International Reading Association, 1973.

Baratz, J., & Shuy, R. *Teaching black children to read.* Washington, D.C.: Center for Applied Linguistics, 1969.

Barclay, J. R. *Controversial issues in testing.* Boston: Houghton Mifflin, 1968.

Barclay, J. R. System-wide analysis of social interaction and affective problems in schools. In P. O. Davidson, F. W. Clark, & L. A. Hamerlyack (Eds.), *Evaluation of behavioral programs in community, residential and school settings.* Champaign, Ill.: Research Press, 1974.

Barclay, J. R. *Manual of the Barclay Classroom Climate Inventory.* Lexington, Ky.: Educational Skills Development, Inc., 1978.

Barclay, J. R., Covert, R. M., Scott, T. W., & Stilwell, W. E. Some effects of schooling: A three-year follow-up project report. Prepared for Vigo County School Corporation, Terre Haute, Ind., 1978.

Barclay, J. R., & Kehle, T. J. The impact of handicapped students on other students in the classroom. *Journal of Research and Development in Education,* 1979, *12*(4), 80–92.

Barclay, J. R., Stilwell, W. E., Santoro, D. A., & Clarke, C. M. Correlates of behavioral observations and academic achievement with elementary patterns of social interaction, 1972. (ERIC Documentation Reproduction Service ED 062 394.)

Barker, R. G. *Ecological psychology.* Stanford, Calif.: Stanford University Press, 1968.

Barringer, C., & Gholson, G. Effects of type and combination of feedback upon conceptual learning by children: Implications of research in academic learning. *Review of Educational Research,* 1979, *49,* 459–478.

Barrish, H. H., Saunders, M., & Wolf, M. M. Good behavior game: Effects of individual contingencies for group consequences on disruptive behavior in a classroom. *Journal of Applied Behavior Analysis,* 1969, *2,* 119–124.

Barry, H. B., III, Bacon, M. K., & Child, I. L. A cross-cultural survey of some sex differences in socialization. *Journal of Abnormal and Social Psychology,* 1957, *55,* 327–332.

Barth, R. S. Discipline: If you do that again ———————————. *Phi Delta Kappan,* 1980, *61,* 398–400.

Bash, M., & Camp, B. *Think aloud programs group manual.* Unpublished manuscript, University of Colorado Medical School, 1975. (As cited in D. Meichenbaum, *Cognitive-behavior modification: An integrative approach.* New York: Plenum, 1977.)

Battle, E. S. Motivational determinants and academic task persistence. *Journal of Personality and Social Psychology,* 1965, *2,* 209–218.

Battle, E. S., & Rotter, J. B. Children's feelings of personal control as related to social class and ethnic group. *Journal of Personality,* 1968, *31,* 482–490.

Baumrind, D. Current patterns of parental authority. *Developmental Psychology Monographs,* 1971, *36,* 4 (whole).

Baumrind, D. The development of instrumental competence through socialization. *Minnesota Symposium on Child Psychology,* Vol. 7. Minneapolis: University of Minnesota Press, 1973.

Baumrind, D. *Early socialization and the discipline controversy.* Morristown, N.J.: General Learning Press, 1975.

Bayley, N. Development of mental abilities. In P. H. Mussen (Ed.), *Carmichael's manual of child psychology.* New York: Wiley, 1970.

Becker, W. C. The consequences of different kinds of parental discipline. In M. L. Hoffman & L. W. Hoffman (Eds.), *Review of child development research,* Vol. 1. New York: Russell Sage Foundation, 1964.

Becker, W. C. *Parents are teachers: A child management program.* Champaign, Ill.: Research Press, 1978.

Becker, W. C., & Engelmann, S. *Technical report 1976-1.* Eugene, Ore.: University of Oregon, 1976.

Becker, W. C., Engelmann, S., & Thomas, D. R. *Teaching 1: Classroom management.* Palo Alto, Calif.: Science Research Associates, 1975(a).

Becker, W. C., Engelmann, S., & Thomas, D. R. *Teaching 2: Cognitive learning and instruction.* Chicago: Science Research Associates, 1975(b).

Bee, H. L., Van Egeran, L. F., Streissguth, A. P., Nyman, B. A., & Leckie, M. S. Social class differences in maternal teaching strategies and speech patterns. *Developmental Psychology,* 1969, *1,* 726–734.

Beery, K. *Models for mainstreaming.* Palo Alto, Calif.: Dimension Publishing Co., 1972.

Beez, W. V. Influence of biased psychological reports on teacher behavior and pupil performance. In M. B. Miles & W. W. Charters, Jr. (Eds.), *Learning in social settings.* Boston: Allyn and Bacon, 1970.

Bell, R. Q. A reinterpretation of the direction of effects in studies of socialization. *Psychological Review,* 1970, *41,* 291–311.

Bem, S. L. Probing the promise of androgyny. In A. G. Kaplan & J. P. Bean (Eds.), *Beyond sex-role stereotyping: Readings toward a psychology of androgyny.* Boston: Little, Brown, 1976.

Bereiter, C., & Engelmann, S. *Teaching disadvantaged children in the preschool.* Englewood Cliffs, N.J.: Prentice-Hall, 1966.

Berenda, R. *The influence of the group on the judgments of children.* New York: King's Crown Press, 1950.

Bergan, J. R., & Dunn, J. A. *Psychology and education: A science for instruction.* New York: Wiley, 1976.

Berkowitz, L. The control of aggression. In B. M. Caldwell (Ed.), *Review of child development research,* Vol. 3. Chicago: University of Chicago Press, 1973.

Berlyne, D. E. *Conflict, arousal and curiosity.* New York: McGraw-Hill, 1960.

Berlyne, D. E. Curiosity and education. In J. D. Krumboltz (Ed.), *Learning and the educational process.* Chicago: Rand McNally, 1965, pp. 67–89.

Bernstein, B. Social class and linguistic development: A theory of social learning.

In A. H. Halsey, F. Floud, & C. A. Anderson (Eds.), *Education, economy, and society*. Glencoe, Ill.: Free Press, 1961.

Bernstein, B. *Class, codes and control*. London, Routledge, 1974.

Bernstein, E. What does a Summerhill old school tie look like? *Psychology Today*, 1968, *2*, 37–70.

Bijou, S. W. What psychology has to offer education now. In W. C. Becker (Ed.), *An empirical basis for change in education*. Chicago: Science Research Associates, 1971.

Bijou, S. W., & Baer, D. M. *Child development: Readings in experimental analysis*. New York: Appleton-Century-Crofts, 1967.

Blank, M., & Solomon, F. A tutorial language program to develop abstract thinking in socially disadvantaged preschool children. *Child Development*, 1968, *39*, 379–390.

Block, J. H. (Ed.). *Mastery learning: Theory and practice*. New York: Holt, 1971.

Bloom, B. S. Learning for mastery. *Evaluation comment*, Vol. 1, No. 2. Los Angeles: Center for the Study of the Evaluation of Instructional Programs, University of California, 1968.

Bloom, B. S. *Human characteristics and school learning*. McGraw-Hill, 1976.

Bloom, B. S., Engelhart, M. B., Furst, E. J., Hill, W. H., & Krathwohl, D. R. *Taxonomy of educational objectives, the classification of educational goals, cognitive domain*. New York: Longmans Green, 1956.

Bloom, B. S., Hastings, J. T., & Maduas, G. F. *Handbook on formative and summative evaluation of student learning*. New York: McGraw-Hill, 1971.

Bloom, B. S. The new direction in educational research: Alterable variables. *Phi Delta Kappan*, 1980, *61*, 382–385.

Bloom, L. Language development. In F. D. Horowitz (Ed.), *Review of child development research*, Vol. 4. Chicago: University of Chicago Press, 1975.

Bourne, L. E., Jr., Ekstrand, B. R., & Dominowski, R. L. *The psychology of thinking*. Englewood Cliffs, N.J.: Prentice-Hall, 1971.

Bowlby, J. *Maternal care and mental health*. Geneva: World Health Organization, 1951.

Bowlby, J. *Attachment and loss*, Vol. 1. *Attachment*. New York: Basic Books, 1969.

Brackbill, Y. Extinction of the smiling response in infants as a function of reinforcement schedule. *Child Development*, 1958, *29*, 115–124.

Bradfield, R. H., Brown, J., Kaplan, P., Richert, E., & Stannard, R. The special child in the regular classroom. *Exceptional Children*, 1973, *39*, 384–390.

Brainerd, C. J. Structures of the whole and elementary education. *American Educational Research Journal*, 1975, *12*, 369–378.

Brainerd, C. J. Cognitive development and concept learning: An interpretive review. *Psychological Bulletin*, 1977, *84*, 919–939.

Bramble, W. J., Hensley, C. E., & Goldstein, D. Follow-up report on the Appalachian Education Satellite Project. *Journal of Educational Technology Systems*, 1976, *5*(2), 81–94.

Brenton, M. Mainstreaming the handicapped. *Today's Education*, 1974, *63*, 20–24.

Broden, M., Hall, R. V., & Mitts, B. The effects of self-recording on the classroom behavior of two eighth grade students. *Journal of Applied Behavior Analysis*, 1971, *4*, 191–199.

Brody, G. H. *A social learning explanation of moral development.* Paper presented at the annual convention of the American Educational Research Association, New York, 1977.

Bronfenbrenner, U. *Influences on human behavior.* Hinsdale, Ill.: Dryden, 1972.

Brookover, W. B., Erickson, L. E., & Joiner, L. M. *Self-concept of ability and school achievement, III: Relationship of self-concept to achievement in high school.* U.S. Office of Education, Cooperative Research Project No. 2831. East Lansing, Mich.: Office of Research and Publications, Michigan State University, 1967.

Brophy, J. E., & Good, T. L. Teachers communications of differential expectations for children's classroom performance: Some behavioral data. *Journal of Educational Psychology,* 1970, *61,* 365–374.

Brophy, J. E., & Good, T. L. *Teacher-student relationships: Causes and consequences.* New York: Holt, 1974.

Brown, A. L., & DeLoache, J. S. Skills, plans and self-regulation. In R. Siegler (Ed.), *Children's thinking: What develops.* Hillsdale, N.J.: Erlbaum, 1978.

Brown, A. L., Smiley, S. S., & Lawton, S. Q. C. The effects of experience on the selection of suitable retrieval cues for studying tests. *Child Development,* 1978, *49,* 829–835.

Brown, D., Wyne, M. D., Blackburn, J. E., & Powell, W. C. *Consultation: A Strategy for Improving Education.* Rockleigh, N. J.: Allyn and Bacon, 1980.

Brown, J. L. Effects of logical and scrambled sequences in mathematical materials on learning with programmed instructional materials. *Journal of Educational Psychology,* 1970, *61,* 41–45.

Brown, P., & Elliott, R. Control of aggression in a nursery school class. *Journal of Experimental Child Psychology,* 1965, *2,* 103–107.

Brown, R. *Social psychology.* New York: Free Press, 1965.

Bruner, J. S. The act of discovery. *Harvard Educational Review,* 1961, *31,* 21–32.

Bruner, J. S. The course of cognitive growth. *American Psychologist,* 1964, *19,* 1–15.

Bruner, J. S. *Toward a theory of instruction.* New York: Norton, 1966.

Bruner, J. S. *The relevance of education.* New York: Norton, 1971.

Bryan, J. H. Children's cooperative and helping behaviors. In E. M. Hetherington (Ed.), *Review of Child Development Research.* Chicago: University of Chicago Press, 1975.

Bryan, J. H. Prosocial behavior. In H. L. Ham, Jr., & P. A. Robinson (Eds.), *Psychological processes in early education.* New York: Academic Press, 1977.

Buck, M. R., & Austin, H. R. *Factors affecting the socioeconomically disadvantaged child in an educational setting.* Final report. U.S. Office of Education, Bureau of Research, July 1970.

Budoff, M., & Gottlieb, J. Special class EMR mainstreaming: A study of an aptitude (learning potential) × treatment interaction. *American Journal of Mental Deficiency,* 1976, *80,* 1–11.

Burton, G. *Sex-role stereotyping in elementary school primers.* Pittsburg: KNOW, 1974.

Burton, R. V. Correspondence between behavioral and doll-play measures of conscience. *Developmental Psychology,* 1970, *5,* 320–332.

Burton, R. V. Honesty and dishonesty. In T. Lickona (Ed.), *Moral development and behavior.* Holt, 1976.

Burton, R. V., Maccoby, E. E., & Allinsmith, W. Antecedents of resistance to temptation in four-year-old children. *Child Development,* 1961, *32,* 689–710.

Buss, A. H., & Plomin, R. A. *Temperament theory of personality development.* New York: Wiley, 1975.

Calhoun, G., & Elliott, R. N. Self-concept and academic achievement of educable, retarded and emotionally disturbed pupils. *Exceptional Children,* 1977, *43,* 379–380.

Camp, B. W., Blom, G. E., Hebert, F., & Van Doorwick, W. J. "Think aloud": A program for developing self control in young aggressive boys. *Journal of Abnormal Child Psychology,* 1977, *5,* 157–169.

Campbell, P. *Sex stereotyping in education.* U.S. Department of Health, Education, and Welfare, 1978.

Campbell, R. E., Walz, G. R., Miller, J. V., & Krieger, S. F. *Career guidance: A handbook of methods.* Columbus, Ohio: Merrill, 1973.

Cantor, N. L., & Gelfand, D. M. Effects of responsiveness and sex of children on adults' behavior. *Child Development,* 1977, *48,* 232–238.

Cantrell, R. P., & Cantrell, M. L. Preventative mainstreaming: Impact of a supportive service program. *Exceptional Children,* 1976, *42,* 381–385.

Carpenter, C. J. *Relation of children's sex-typed behavior to classroom and activity structure.* Paper presented at the meeting of the Society for Research in Child Development, San Francisco, March 1979.

Carter, J. L. Intelligence and reading achievement of EMR children in three educational settings. *Mental Retardation,* 1976, *42,* 381–385.

Cartledge, G., & Milburn, J. F. The case for teaching social skills in the classroom: A review. *Review of Educational Research,* 1978, *48,* 133–156.

Cattell, R. B. *The culture-free intelligence test.* Champaign, Ill.: Institute for Personality and Ability, 1949.

Cegelka, P. T., & Phillips, M. W. Individualized education programming at the secondary level. *Teaching Exceptional Children,* 1978, *10,* 84–87.

Cervantes, L. F. *The dropout: Causes and cures.* Ann Arbor, Mich.: University of Michigan Press, 1965.

Charbonneau, C., Robert, M., Bourassa, G., & Gladu-Bissonnette, S. Observational learning of quantity conservation and Piagetian generalization tasks. *Developmental Psychology,* 1976, *12,* 211–217.

Cherry-Peisach, E. Children's comprehension of teacher and peer speech. *Child Development,* 1965, *30,* 467–480.

Child, I. L., Potter, E. H., & Levine, E. M. Children's textbooks and personality development: An exploration in the social psychology of education. *Psychological Monographs,* 1957, *60,* Whole No. 279.

Chomsky, C. *The acquisition of syntax in children from 5 to 10.* Cambridge, Mass.: MIT Press, 1969.

Chomsky, N. *Language and mind.* Harcourt, Brace, Jovanovitch, 1968.

Clarizio, H. F., & McCoy, G. F. *Behavior disorders in children.* New York: Crowell, 1976.

Clark, A. D., & Richards, C. J. Auditory discrimination among economically disadvantaged and non-disadvantaged preshool children. *Exceptional Children,* 1969, *33,* 252–262.

Clements, S. D. *Minimal brain dysfunction in children.* NINDS Monograph #3, Public Health Service Bulletin #1415. Washington, D.C., U.S. Department of Health, Education, and Welfare, 1966.

Clifford, M. M., & Walster, E. The effect of physical attractiveness on teacher expectations. *Sociology of Education,* 1973, *46,* 248–258.

Cobb, J. A. *Survival skills and first-grade academic achievement.* CORBEH: Report No. 1, University of Oregon, 1970.

Cole, H. P. Process curricula and creativity development. *Journal of Creative Behavior,* 1969, *3,* 244–259.

Cole, H. P., & Musser, L. S. Process approaches to the teaching of educational psychology. In D. J. Treffinger, J. K. Davis, & R. E. Ripple (Eds.), *Handbook on teaching educational psychology.* New York: Academic Press, 1977, pp. 263–286.

Coleman, J. S., Campbell, E., Hobson, C., McPartland, J., Mood, A., Weinfield, F., & York, R. *Equality of educational opportunity.* Washington, D.C.: U.S. Department of Health, Education, and Welfare, Office of Education, 1966.

Coleman, J. S., Livingston, S. A., Fennessey, G. M., Edwards, R. J., & Kidder, S. J. The Hopkins game program: Conclusions from seven years of research. *Educational Researcher,* 1973, *2*(8), 3–7.

Condry, J., & Dyer, S. Fear of success: Attribution of cause to the victim. *Journal of Social Issues,* 1976, *32,* 63–83.

Cook, H., & Stingle, S. Cooperative behavior in children. *Psychological Bulletin,* 1974, *81,* 918–935.

Coolidge, J. L., Brodie, R. D., & Feeney, B. A. A ten-year follow-up study of sixty-six school-phobic children. *American Journal of Orthopsychiatry,* 1964, *34,* 673–684.

Cooper, J. O., & Edge, D. *Parenting: Strategies in education and method.* Columbus, Ohio: Merrill, 1978.

Coopersmith, S. *The antecedents of self-esteem.* San Francisco: Freeman, 1967.

Corbin, C. B. (Ed.). *A textbook of motor development.* Dubuque, Iowa: Brown, 1973.

Costanzo, P. R., & Shaw, M. E. Conformity as a function of age level. *Child Development,* 1966, *37,* 967–975.

Coyne, P. D. The effects of peer tutoring with group contingencies on the academic performance of college students. *Journal of Applied Behavior Analysis,* 1978, *11,* 305–307.

Crandall, V. C. Achievement behavior in young children. In *The young child: Reviews of research.* Washington, D.C.: National Association for the Education of Young Children, 1967.

Crandall, V. C. Sex differences in expectancy of intellectual and academic reinforcement. In C. P. Smith (Ed.), *Achievement-related motives in children.* New York: Russell-Sage Foundation, 1969.

Crandall, V. C., & Battle, E. S. The antecedents and adult correlates of academic and intellectual achievement. In J. P. Hill (Ed.), *Minnesota symposium on child psychology.* Minneapolis: University of Minnesota Press, 1970.

Crandall, V. C., & McGhee, P. E. Expectancy of reinforcement and academic competence. *Journal of Personality,* 1968, *36,* 635–648.

Crandall, V. J., Katkovsky, W., & Preston, A. A conceptual formulation for some research on children's achievement development. *Child Development,* 1960, *31,* 787–797.

Crandall, V. J., Preston, A., & Rabson, A. Maternal reactions and the development of independence and achievement behavior in young children. *Child Development,* 1960, *31,* 243–251.

Cratty, B. J. *Perceptual and motor development in infants and children.* New York: Macmillan, 1970.

Crinella, F. M., Beck, F. W., & Robinson, J. W. Unilateral dominance is not related to neuropsychological integrity. *Child Development,* 1971, *43,* 2033–2055.

Cronbach, L. J., & Snow, R. E. *Aptitudes and instructional methods.* New York: Irvington Press, 1977.

Crowder, N. A. On the difference between linear and intrinsic programming. *Phi Delta Kappan,* 1963, *44,* 250–254.

Cruikshank, W. M., & Johnson, G. O. (Eds.). *Education of exceptional children and youth.* Englewood Cliffs, N.J.: Prentice-Hall, 1975.

Crutchfield, R. S. Nurturing the cognitive skills of productive thinking. In L. R. Rubin (Ed.), *Life skills, school and society.* Washington, D.C.: Association of Supervision and Career Development, 1969.

Davies, I. K. *Competency based learning: Technology management and design.* New York: McGraw-Hill, 1973.

Davis, A., & Eells, K. *Davis-Eells games.* Yonkers, N.Y.: World, 1953.

Day, H. I., & Berlyne, D. E. Intrinsic motivation. In G. S. Lesser (Ed.), *Psychology and educational practice.* Glenview, Ill.: Scott, Foresman, 1971.

deCharms, R. From pawns to origins: Toward self-motivation. In G. L. Lesser (Ed.), *Psychology and educational practice.* Glenview, Ill.: Scott, Foresman, 1971.

Deese, J. *The structure of associations in language and thought.* Baltimore, Md.: Johns Hopkins Press, 1966.

Deutsch, C. P. Social class and child development. In B. M. Caldwell & H. N. Riccuiti (Eds.), *Review of child development research,* Vol. 3. Chicago: University of Chicago Press, 1973.

Deutsch, M. Facilitating development in the preschool child: Social and psychological perspectives. *Merrill-Palmer Quarterly,* 1964, *10,* 249–263.

Deutsch, M., & Brown, R. Social influences in Negro-white intelligence differences. *Journal of Social Issues,* 1964, *20,* 24–35.

Deaux, K. *The behavior of women and men.* Monterey, Calif.: Brooks-Cole, 1976.

Dewey, J. *How we think.* Boston: Heath, 1910.

Dick, W., & Carey, L. *The systematic design of instruction.* Glenview, Ill.: Scott, Foresman, 1978.

Dinkmeyer, D. *Developing understanding of self and others* (DUSO-I). Circle Pines, Minn.: American Guidance Service, 1970.

Dinkmeyer, D. *Developing understanding of self and others* (DUSO-II). Circle Pines, Minn.: American Guidance Service, 1973.

Dinkmeyer, D., & McKay, G. D. *Systematic training for effective parenting* (STEP). Circle Pines, Minn.: American Guidance Service, 1976.

Domino, G. Interactive effects of achievement orientation and teaching style on academic achievement. *Journal of Educational Psychology,* 1971, *62,* 427–431.

Dorr, D., & Fry, S. Relative power of symbolic and adult and peer models in modification of children's moral choices. *Journal of Personality and Social Psychology,* 1974, *29,* 335–341.

Drabman, R. S., Spitalnik, R., & O'Leary, K. D. Teaching self-control to disruptive children. *Journal of Applied Behavior Analysis,* 1973, *6,* 241–250.

Dreger, R. M., & Miller, K. S. Comparative psychological studies of Negroes and whites in the United States. *Psychological Bulletin,* 1960, *57,* 361–402.

Dreger, R. M., & Miller, K. S. Comparative psychological studies of Negroes and whites in the United States; 1959–1965. *Psychological Bulletin,* Monograph Supplement, 1968, *70,* 1–58.

Duell, O. K. Effect of type of objective, level of test questions, and the judged importance of tested materials upon posttested performance. *Journal of Educational Psychology,* 1974, *66,* 225–232.

Dunn, L. M. Special education for the mildly retarded: Is much of it justifiable? *Exceptional Children,* 1968, *35,* 5–22.

Dunn, L. M. *Exceptional children in the schools* (2d ed.). New York: Holt, 1973.

DuPont, H., Gardner, O. S., & Brody, D. S. *Toward affective development.* Circle Pines, Minn: American Guidance Service, 1974.

Ebel, R. L. The case for norm-referenced measurement. *Educational Researcher,* 1978, *7*(11), 3–5.

Egeland, B. Training impulsive children in the use of more efficient scanning techniques. *Child Development,* 1974, *45,* 165–171.

Eisner, E. W. Instructional and expressive objectives: Their formation and use in curriculum. In W. J. Popham, Jr., E. W. Eisner, H. J. Sullivan, & L. L. Tyler (Eds.), *Instructional objectives.* Chicago: Rand McNally, 1969.

Elder, G. H., Jr. Adolescent socialization and development. In E. F. Borgatta & W. W. Lambert (Eds.), *Handbook of personality theory and research.* Chicago: Rand McNally, 1968, pp. 239–364.

Emmer, E. T. *The first weeks . . . and the rest of the year.* Paper presented at American Educational Research Association, San Francisco, 1979.

Engelmann, S., & Bruner, E. *Distar reading level I.* Chicago: Science Research Associates, 1974.

Erickson, J. R., & Jones, M. R. Thinking. *Annual Review of Psychology,* Palo Alto, Calif.: 1978, pp. 61–90.

Erikson, E. H. *Childhood and society.* New York: Norton, 1963.

Fagot, B. I. Sex differences in toddlers' behavior and parental reaction. *Developmental Psychology,* 1974, *10,* 554–558.

Fantini, M. D., & Weinstein, G. *The disadvantaged: Challenge to education.* New York: Harper & Row, 1968.

Faust, M. S. Developmental maturity as a determinant in prestige of adolescent girls. *Child Development,* 1960, *31,* 178–184.

Feather, N. T. Effects of prior success and failure on expectations of success and subsequent performance. *Journal of Personality and Social Psychology,* 1966, *3,* 287–298.

Fein, G., Johnson, D., Kosson, N., Stork, L., & Wasserman, L. M. Sex stereotypes and preferences in the toy choices of 20-month-old boys and girls. *Developmental Psychology,* 1975, *11,* 527–528.

Feitler, F. C. *Attitudes of regular classroom teachers toward EMR students.* Paper presented at the annual convention of the American Educational Research Association, Toronto, Canada, March 1978.

Feld, S. C., & Lewis, J. The assessment of achievement anxieties in children. In C. P. Smith (Ed.), *Achievement-related motives in children.* New York: Russell Sage Foundation, 1969.

Feldman, R. S., & Devin-Sheehan, L. Children tutoring children: A critical review of research. In V. L. Allen (Ed.), *Children as teachers.* New York: Academic Press, 1976.

Finn, J. D. Expectations and the educational environment. *Review of Educational Research,* 1972, *42,* 387–410.

Fischer, C. *Dimensions of personality.* Dayton, Ohio: Pflaum/Standard, 1972.

Flanagan, J. C. Individualizing education. *Education,* 1970, *90,* 191–206.

Flanagan, J. C. The PLAN system for individualizing education. *Measurement in Education,* 1971, *2*(2), 1–8.

Flanagan, J. C., Davis, F. B., Dailey, J. T., Shaycoft, M. F., Orr, D. B., Goldberg, I., & Neyman, C. A., Jr. *The American high school student.* Pittsburgh: Project TALENT, University of Pittsburgh (USOE, CRP No. 635), 1964.

Flanagan, J. C., Mager, R. F., & Shanner, W. M. *Social studies behavioral objectives: A guide to individualizing learning.* Palo Alto, Calif.: Westinghouse Learning Press, 1977.

Flanders, N., & Havumaki, S. The effect of teacher-pupil contacts involving praise on the sociometric choices of students. *Journal of Educational Psychology,* 1960, *51,* 65–68.

Flavell, J. *The developmental psychology of Jean Piaget.* New York: Van Nostrand, 1963.

Foxx, R. M., & Azrin, N. H. Restitution: A method of eliminating aggressive-disruptive behavior of retarded and brain-damaged patients. *Behavior Research and Therapy,* 1972, *10,* 15–27.

Frazier, N., & Sadker, M. *Sexism in school and society.* New York: Harper & Row, 1973.

Friedrich, L. K., & Stein, A. H. Aggressive and prosocial television programs and the natural behavior of preschool children. *Monographs of the Society for Research in Child Development,* 1973, *38*(4), Serial No. 151.

Gagné, R. M. *Conditions of learning.* New York: Holt, 1965.

Gagné, R. M. Contributions of learning to human development. *Psychological Review,* 1968, *75,* 177–191.

Gagné, R. M. *Conditions of learning* (2d ed.). New York: Holt, 1970.

Gagné, R. M. *Essentials of learning for instruction.* Hinsdale, Ill.: Dryden, 1974.

Gagné, R. M. *Conditions of learning* (3rd ed.). New York: Holt, 1977.

Gagné, R. M., & Briggs, L. J. *Principles of instructional design* (2d ed.). New York: Holt, 1979.

Gagné, R. M., & White, R. T. Memory structures and learning outcomes. *Review of Educational Research,* 1978, *48,* 187–222.

Gallagher, J. J., & Gallagher, G. C. Family adaptation to a handicapped child and assorted professionals. In A. P. Turnbull & H. R. Turnbull III (Eds.), *Parents speak out: Views from the other side of the two-way mirror.* Columbus, Ohio: Merrill, 1978.

Gardner, W. I. *Children with learning and behavior problems: A behavior management approach.* Boston: Allyn and Bacon, 1977.

Gardner, W. I., & Boyd, R. In J. Worell (Ed.), *Psychological Development in the Elementary Years.* New York: Academic Press, 1980.

Gaudry, E., & Spielberger, C. *Anxiety and educational achievement.* New York: Wiley, 1971.

Gay, J., & Tweney, R. D. Comprehension and production of standard and Black English by lower-class Black children. *Developmental Psychology,* 1976, *12,* 262–268.

Gazda, G. M. (Ed.). *Basic approaches to group psychotherapy and group counseling.* Springfield, Ill.: Thomas, 1975.

Gelfand, D. M., & Hartmann, D. P. *Child behavior analysis and therapy.* New York: Pergamon, 1975.

Gelman, R. Conservation acquisition: A problem of learning to attend to relevant attributes. *Journal of Experimental Child Psychology,* 1969, *7,* 167–187.

Gerbner, G. Violence in television drama: Trends and symbolic functions. In G. A. Comstock & E. A. Rubenstein (Eds.), *Television and social behavior,* Vol. 1. Washington, D.C.: Media Content and Control, U.S. Government Printing Office, 1972.

Gesell, A. L., Ames, L. B., & Ilg, F. L. *The child from five to ten.* New York: Harper & Row, 1976.

Gesell, A. L., & Armatruda, C. S. *Developmental diagnosis: Normal and abnormal child development.* New York: Harper & Row, 1947.

Gewirtz, J. L. Mechanisms of social learning. In D. A. Goslin (Ed.), *Handbook of socialization theory and research.* Chicago: Rand McNally, 1969.

Gibby, R. G., Sr., & Gibby, R. G., Jr. The effects of stress resulting from academic failure. *Journal of Clinical Psychology,* 1967, *23,* 35–37.

Gibson, E. J. *Principles of perceptual learning and development.* New York: Appleton-Century-Crofts, 1969.

Gifford, E. M., & Marston, A. R. Test anxiety, reading ratio and task experience. *Journal of Educational Research,* 1966, *59,* 303–306.

Ginsburg, H., & Opper, S. *Piaget's theory of intellectual development: An introduction* (2d ed.). Englewood Cliffs, N.J.: Prentice-Hall, 1979.

Ginzburg, E. Toward a theory of occupational choice. *Occupations,* 1952, *30,* 491–494.

Glaser, R. Psychology and instructional technology. In R. Glaser (Ed.), *Training research and education.* Pittsburgh, Pa.: University of Pittsburgh Press, 1962, pp. 1–30.

Glaser, R. Instructional technology and the measurement of learning outcomes: Some questions. *American Psychologist,* 1963, *18,* 519–521.

Glaser, R. *Adaptive education: Individual diversity and learning.* New York: Holt, 1977.

Glavin, J. P. *Behavioral strategies for classroom management.* Columbus, Ohio: Merrill, 1974.

Glover, J., & Gary, A. L. Procedures to increase some aspects of creativity. *Journal of Applied Behavior Analysis,* 1976, *9,* 79–84.

Glucksberg, S., Krauss, R., & Higgins, E. T. The development of referential communication skills. In F. D. Horowitz, (Ed.), *Review of Child Development Research,* Vol. 4. Chicago: University of Chicago Press, 1975.

Gold, D., & Berger, C. Problem-solving performance of young boys and girls as a function of task appropriateness and sex identity. *Sex Roles,* 1978, *4,* 183–194.

Goldberg, S., & Lewis, M. Play behavior in the year old infant. Early sex differences. *Child Development,* 1969, *40,* 21–31.

Good, T. Which pupils do teachers call on? *Elementary School Journal,* 1970, *70,* 190–198.

Goodman, J. *Impulsive and reflective: A developmental analysis of attentional and cognitive strategies.* Unpublished doctoral dissertation. University of Waterloo, Ontario, 1973. (As cited in D. Meichenbaum, *Cognitive-behavior modification.* New York: Plenum, 1977.)

Goodwin, D. L., & Coates, T. J. *Helping students help themselves.* Englewood Cliffs, N.J.: Prentice-Hall, 1976.

Gordon, A. K. *Games for growth.* Palo Alto, Calif.: Science Research Associates, 1970.

Gottlieb, J., Agard, J., Kauffman, N., & Semmel, M. Retarded children mainstreamed: Practices as they affect minority group children. In R. L. Jones (Ed.), *Mainstreaming and the minority child.* Reston, Va.: Council for Exceptional Children, 1976.

Gouze, K. *Children's initial aggression level and the effectiveness of intervention strategies in moderating TV effects on aggression.* Paper presented at the Society for Research in Child Development, San Francisco, California, March 1979.

Gray, S. W., & Klaus, R. A. The early training project: A seventh-year report. *Child Development,* 1970, *41,* 909–924.

Grimes, J. W., & Allinsmith, W. Compulsivity, anxiety and school achievement. *Merrill-Palmer Quarterly,* 1961, *7,* 247–271.

Gronlund, N. E. *Stating objectives for classroom instruction* (2d ed.). New York: Macmillan, 1978.

Grove, C. L. Nonverbal behavior, crosscultural contact, and the urban classroom teacher. *Equal opportunity review.* New York: ERIC Clearinghouse on Urban Education, Institute for Urban and Minority Education, Teachers College, Columbia University, 1976.

Grusec, J. E., & Kuczynski, L. Teaching children to punish themselves and effects on subsequent compliance. *Child Development,* 1977, *48,* 1296–1300.

Guilford, J. P. *The nature of human intelligence.* New York: McGraw-Hill, 1967.

Guilford, J. P., & Hoepfner, R. *The analysis of intelligence.* New York: McGraw-Hill, 1971.

Gullung, T. B., & Rucker, C. N. Labels and teacher expectations. *Exceptional Children,* 1977, *43,* 464–465.

Guskey, T. Mastery learning: Applying the theory. *Theory into Practice,* 1980, *19* (in press).

Hagen, J. W., & Kail, G. H. The development of attention in children. In A. D. Pick (Ed.), *Minnesota symposium on child development,* Vol. 7. Minneapolis: University of Minnesota, 1973.

Hall, E. T. Listening behavior: Some cultural differences. In R. H. Anderson & H. G. Shane (Eds.), *As the twig is bent: Readings in early childhood education.* Boston: Houghton Mifflin, 1971.

Hallahan, D. P., & Kauffman, J. M. *Introduction to learning disabilities: A psycho-behavioral approach.* Englewood Cliffs, N.J.: Prentice-Hall, 1976.

Hamblin, R. L., Hathaway, C., & Wodarski, J. S. Group contingencies, peer tutoring and accelerating academic achievement. In E. Ramp & W. Hopkins (Eds.), *A new direction for education: Behavior analysis.* Lawrence, Kans.: The University of Kansas, 1971, pp. 41–53.

Harari, H., & McDavid, J. W. Name stereotypes and teachers' expectations. *Journal of Educational Psychology,* 1973, *65,* 222–225.

Harbor, J. R., & Beatty, J. N. *Reading and the black English-speaking child.* Newark, Del.: International Reading Association, 1978.

Haring, N. G. (Ed.). *Behavior of exceptional children: An introduction to special education.* Columbus, Ohio: Merrill, 1974.

Harlow, H. F., & Zimmerman, R. R. Affectional responses in the infant monkey. *Science,* 1959, *130,* 421–432.

Harteshorne, H., & May, M. A. *Studies in the nature of character,* Vol. 1. *Studies in deceit.* New York: Macmillan, 1928.

Hartup, W. W. Nurturance and nurturance withdrawal in relation to the dependency behavior of preschool children. *Child Development,* 1958, *29,* 291–309.

Hartup, W. W. Peer interaction and social organization. In P. H. Mussen (Ed.), *Carmichael's manual of child psychology* (3d ed.), Vol. 2. New York: Wiley, 1970.

Harvey, O. H., Prather, M., White, B. J., & Hoffmeister, J. K. Teacher's beliefs, classroom atmosphere and student behavior. *American Educational Research Journal,* 1968, *5,* 151–166.

Harway, M., & Astin, H. S. *Sex discrimination in career counseling and education.* New York: Praeger, 1977.

Hawley, R. C., & Hawley, I. *A handbook of personal growth activities for classroom use.* Amherst, Mass.: Educational Research Associates, 1972.

Hayes, L. A. The use of group contingencies for behavioral control: A review. *Psychological Bulletin,* 1976, *83,* 628–648.

Hebb, D. O. *A textbook of psychology.* Philadelphia, Pa.: Saunders, 1966.

Heber, R., Garber, H., Harrington, S., Hoffman, C., & Falender, C. *Rehabilitation of families at risk for mental retardation: Progress report.* Madison, Wis.: Rehabilitation and Training Center in Mental Retardation, University of Wisconsin, 1972.

Helfer, R. E., & Kempe, C. H. *The battered child.* University of Chicago Press, 1974.

Henderson, R. W. Personnel and social causation in the school context. In J. Worell (Ed.), *Psychological development in the elementary years.* New York: Academic Press, 1980.

Hennig, M. M. Family dynamics and the successful woman executive. In R. B. Kundsin (Ed.), *Women and success: The anatomy of achievement.* New York: Morrow, 1974.

Hentoff, N. Making schools accountable. *Phi Delta Kappan,* 1967, *48,* 332.

Herrick, V. E., & Okada, N. Teaching handwriting in the United States. In V. E. Herrick (Ed.), *New horizons for research in handwriting.* Madison, Wis.: University of Wisconsin Press, 1963.

Hess, R. D. Social class and ethnic differences in socialization. In P. H. Mussen (Ed.), *Carmichael's manual of child psychology* (3d ed.), Vol. 2. New York: Wiley, 1970.

Hetherington, E. M., & Parke, R. D. *Child psychology: A contemporary viewpoint.* New York: McGraw-Hill, 1975.

Hetherington, E. M. *The aftermaths of divorce.* Paper presented at American Psychological Association annual meeting, Washington, D.C., September 1976.

Hewett, F. M. *The emotionally disturbed child in the classroom.* Boston: Allyn and Bacon, 1968.

Hewett, F. M., & Forness, S. *Education of exceptional learners.* Boston: Allyn and Bacon, 1974.

Hildreth, G. Manual dominance in nursery school children. *Journal of Genetic Psychology,* 1948, *73,* 29–45.

Hill, K. T. *Evaluative feedback in a broader perspective.* Paper presented at the annual meeting of the American Educational Research Association, Toronto, March 1978.

Hiller, J. H. Verbal response indicators of conceptual vagueness. *American Educational Research Journal,* 1971, *8,* 151–161.

Hobbs, N. *The futures of children.* San Francisco: Jossey-Bass, 1975.

Hoffman, M. L. Moral development. In P. H. Mussen (Ed.), *Carmichael's handbook of child psychology* (3d ed.), Vol. 2. New York: Wiley, 1970.

Hoffman, M. L. Personality and social development. In M. R. Rosenzweig & L. W. Porter (Eds.), *Annual Review of Psychology,* 1977, *28,* 295–322.

Hogan, J. R. The three-way conference: Parent-teacher-child. *The Elementary School Journal,* 1975, *75*(5).

Holland, J. L. *The psychology of vocational choice.* Waltham, Mass.: Blaisdell, 1966.

Hollander, E. P. Competence and conformity in the acceptance of influence. *Journal of Abnormal and Social Psychology,* 1960, *61,* 365–369.

Hollingshead, A. B., & Redlich, C. F. *Social class and mental illness: A community study.* New York: Wiley, 1958.

Homme, L., Csanyi, A. P., Gonzales, M. A., & Rechs, J. R. *How to use contingency contracting in the classroom.* Champaign, Ill.: Research Press, 1969.

Horner, M. S. Toward an understanding of achievement-related conflicts in women. *Journal of Social Issues,* 1972, *28*(2), 157–175.

House, C. Do you need a differentiated program for your gifted students. *Phi Delta Kappan,* 1980, *61,* 412–413.

Hoyenga, K. B., & Hoyenga, K. T. *The question of sex differences: Psychological, cultural, and biological issues.* Boston: Little, Brown, 1979.

Huck, S., & Bounds, W. Essay grades: An interaction between graders' handwriting clarity and the neatness of examination papers. *American Educational Research Journal,* 1972, *9,* 279–283.

Hunt, J. McV. *Intelligence and experience.* New York: Ronald Press, 1961.

Hunt, J. McV. The role of experience in the development of competence. In J. McV. Hunt (Ed.), *Human intelligence.* Brunswick, N.J.: Transaction Books, 1972.

Jacklyn, C. N., & Mischel, H. N. As the twig is bent: Sex-role stereotyping in early readers. *The School Psychology Digest,* Summer 1973, pp. 30–38.

Jamison, D., Suppes, P., & Wells, S. The effectiveness of alternative instructional media: A survey. *Review of Educational Research,* 1974, *44,* 1–68.

Janda, L. H., O'Grady, K. E., & Capps, C. F. Fear of success in males and females in sex-linked occupations. *Sex Roles,* 1978, *4,* 43–50.

Jensen, A. R. How much can we boost I.Q. and scholastic achievement? *Harvard Educational Review,* 1969, *39,* 1–123.

Jensen, A. R. *Educability and group differences.* New York: Harper & Row, 1973.

Johnson, D. W., & Johnson, R. T. Instructional goal structure: Cooperative, competitive or individualistic. *Review of Educational Research,* 1974, *44,* 213–240.

Johnson, D. W., & Johnson, R. T. *Learning together and alone: Cooperation, competition and individualization.* Englewood Cliffs, N.J.: Prentice-Hall, 1975.

Johnson, K. R. *Teaching the culturally disadvantaged.* Palo Alto, Calif.: Science Research Associates, 1970.

Jones, M. C. The later career of boys who were early or late maturing. *Child Development,* 1957, *28,* 113–128.

Jones, M. C., & Mussen, P. H. Self conceptions, motivations and interpersonal attitudes of early and late maturing girls. *Child Development,* 1958, *29,* 491–501.

Kagan, J. Impulsive and reflective children: Significance of conceptual tempo. In J. D. Krumboltz (Ed.), *Learning and the educational process.* Chicago: Rand McNally, 1965.

Kagan, J. Reflection-impulsivity: The generality and dynamics of conceptual tempo. *Journal of Abnormal Psychology,* 1966, *71,* 17–24.

Kagan, J., & Moss, H. A. *Birth to maturity: A study in psychological development.* New York: Wiley, 1962.

Kagan, J., Pearson, L., & Welsch, L. The modifiability of an impulsive tempo. *Journal of Educational Psychology,* 1966, *57,* 359–365.

Kahn, W. J. Self-management: Learning to be your own counselor. *Personnel and Guidance Journal,* 1976, *55,* 176–180.

Kamin, L. J. *The science and politics of I.Q.* Potomac, Md.: Erlbaum Associates, 1974.

Kampelman, M. *K-12 education kit.* Washington, D.C.: Women's Equity Action League, 1973.

Kane, J. S., & Lawler, E. E. Methods of peer assessment. *Psychological Bulletin,* 1978, *85,* 555–586.

Kanfer, F. H. Behavior modification: An overview. In C. E. Thoreson (Ed.), *Behavior Modification in Education.* Chicago: National Society for the Study of Education, 1972.

Kanfer, F. H., & Grimm, L. G. Freedom of choice and behavioral change. *Journal of Consulting and Clinical Psychology,* 1978, *46,* 873–878.

Kaplan, A. G., & Bean, J. P. *Beyond sex-role stereotypes: Readings toward a psychology of androgyny.* Boston: Little, Brown, 1976.

Karnes, M. B., Hodgins, A. S., Stoneburner, R. L., Studley, W. M., & Teska, J. A. Effects of a highly structured program of language development on intellectual functioning and psycholinguistic development of culturally disadvantaged three-year-olds. *Journal of Special Education,* 1968, *2,* 405–412.

Kazdin, A. E. Effects of covert modeling and model reinforcement on assertive behavior. *Journal of Abnormal Psychology,* 1974, *83,* 240–252.

Kazdin, A. E. *The token economy: A review and evaluation.* New York: Plenum, 1977.

Kazdin, A. E., & Bootzin, R. R. The token economy: An evaluative review. *Journal of Applied Behavior Analysis,* 1972, *5,* 343–372.

Keating, D. P. Precocious cognitive development at the level of formal operations. *Child Development,* 1975, *46,* 276–280.

Keller, F. S. Good-bye, teacher. *Journal of Applied Behavior Analysis,* 1968, *1,* 79–89.

Kelly, J. A., & Worell, J. New formulations of sex roles and androgyny: A critical review. *Journal of Consulting and Clinical Psychology,* 1977, *45,* 1101–1115.

Kelly, J. A., & Worell, L. Parent behaviors related to masculine, feminine and androgynous sex role orientations. *Journal of Consulting and Clinical Psychology,* 1976, *44,* 843–851.

Kendler, H. H. Environmental and cognitive control of behavior. In N. S. Endler, L. R. Boulter, & H. Osser (Eds.), *Contemporary issues in developmental psychology.* New York: Holt, 1976.

Kendler, H. H., & Kendler, T. S. Vertical and horizontal processes in problem-solving. *Psychological Review,* 1962, *69,* 1–16.

Kennedy, W. A. A follow-up normative study of Negro intelligence and achievement. *Monographs of the Society for Research in Child Development,* 1969, *34*(2), No. 126.

Kennedy, W. A., Van De Riet, V., & White, J. C., Jr. A normative sample of intelligence and achievement of Negro elementary school children in the southeastern United States. *Monographs of the Society for Research in Child Development,* 1963, *28*(6), No. 90.

Keogh, B. What research tells us about mainstreaming. In P. O'Donnell & R. Bradfield (Eds.), *Mainstreaming: Controversy and consensus.* San Rafael, Calif.: Academic Therapy, 1976, pp. 25–38.

Kibler, R. J., Barker, L. L., & Mills, D. T. *Behavioral objectives and instruction.* Boston: Allyn and Bacon, 1970.

Kifer, E. W. Relationship between academic achievement and personality characteristics: A quasi-longitudinal study. *American Educational Research Journal,* 1975, *12,* 191–210.

Kirby, F. D., & Shields, F. Modification of arithmetic response rate and attending behavior in a seventh-grade student. *Journal of Applied Behavior Analysis,* 1972, *5,* 79–84.

Kirk, S. A. *Educating exceptional children* (2d ed.). Boston: Houghton Mifflin, 1972.

Klaus, R. A., & Gray, S. W. The early training project for disadvantaged children: A report after five years. *Monographs of the Society for Research in Child Development,* 1968, *33*(4), Whole No. 120.

Klausmeier, H. J., Rossmiller, R. A., & Saily, M. *Individually guided elementary education.* New York: Academic Press, 1977.

Kohlberg, L. Development of moral character and moral idealogy. In M. L. Hoffman & L. W. Hoffman (Eds.), *Review of child development research,* Vol. 1. New York: Russell-Sage, 1964.

Kohlberg, L. Moral states and moralization: The cognitive developmental approach. In T. Lickona (Ed.), *Moral development and behavior.* Holt, 1976.

Kohlberg, L., & Mayer, R. Development as the aim of education. *Harvard Educational Review,* 1972, *42,* 449–496.

Kolb, D. A. Achievement motivation training for underachieving high school boys. *Journal of Personality and Social Psychology,* 1965, *2,* 783–792.

Kounin, J. *Discipline and group management in classrooms.* New York: Holt, 1970.

Krathwohl, D. R., Bloom, B. S., & Masia, B. B. *Taxonomy of educational objectives: The classification of educational goals, affective domain.* New York: McKay, 1964.

Krauss, R. M., & Rotter, G. S. Communication abilities of children as a function of status and age. *Merrill-Palmer Quarterly,* 1968, *14,* 161–173.

Kroth, R. Parents—powerful and necessary allies. *Teaching Exceptional Children,* 1978, *10,* 88–91.

Krumboltz, J. D. The nature and importance of the required response in programmed instruction. *American Educational Research Journal,* 1964, *1,* 203–209.

Krumboltz, J. D. Promoting adaptive behavior: New answers to familiar questions. In J. D. Krumboltz (Ed.), *Revolution in counseling: Implications of behavioral science.* Boston: Houghton Mifflin, 1966.

Krumboltz, J. D., & Baker, R. D. Behavioral counseling for vocational decisions. In H. Borrow (Ed.), *Career guidance for a new age.* Boston: Houghton Mifflin, 1973, pp. 235–284.

Kulhavy, R. W. Feedback in written instruction. *Review of Educational Research,* 1977, *47,* 211–232.

Kulhavy, R. W., & Parsons, J. A. Learning-criterion error perseveration in text materials. *Journal of Educational Psychology,* 1972, *63,* 81–86.

Kulih, J. A., Kulih, C. L., & Carmichael, K. The Keller plan in science teaching. *Science,* 1974, *183,* 379–383.

Kurtines, W., & Grief, E. B. The development of moral thought: Review and evaluation of Kohlberg's approach. *Psychological Bulletin,* 1974, *81,* 453–470.

Labov, W. *The study of non-standard English.* Champaign, Ill.: National Council of Teachers of English, 1970(a).

Labov, W. The logic of non-standard English. In F. Williams (Ed.), *Language and poverty.* Chicago: Markham, 1970(b).

Landsbaum, J. B., & Willis, R. H. Conformity in early and late adolescence. *Developmental Psychology,* 1971, *4,* 334–337.

Lange, J. A., & Jakubowski, P. *Responsible assertive behavior.* Champaign, Ill.: Research Press, 1976.

Langer, J. H. The disadvantaged, the three R's and individual differences. In W. W. Brickman & S. Lehrer (Eds.), *Education and the many faces of the disadvantaged.* New York: Wiley, 1972.

Lavin, D. E. *The prediction of academic performance.* New York: Wiley, 1965.

Leaverton, L. Dialectal readers: Rationale, use and value. In J. L. Laffey & R. Shuy (Eds.), *Language differences: Do they interfere?* Newark, Del.: International Reading Association, 1973.

Lee, P. C., & Kedar-Voiradas, F. Sex-role and pupil role in early childhood education. In L. A. Katz (Ed.), *Current topics in early childhood education,* Vol. 1. Norwood, N.Y.: Ables Publishing Corp., 1976.

Lefkowitz, M. M., Eron, L. D., Walder, L. O., & Huesmann, L. R. Television violence and child aggression: A follow-up study. In G. A. Comstock & E. A. Rubenstein (Eds.), *Television and social behavior: Television and adolescent aggressiveness.* Washington, D.C.: U.S. Government Printing Office, 1972.

Lenneberg, E. H. *Biological foundations of language.* New York: Wiley, 1967.

Lenney, E. Women's self-confidence in achievement settings. *Psychological Bulletin,* 1977, *84,* 1–13.

Lepper, M. R., & Green, D. Turning play into work: Effects of adult surveillance and extrinsic rewards on children's intrinsic motivation. *Journal of Personality and Social Psychology,* 1975, *31,* 479–486.

Lepper, M. R., Green, D., & Nisbett, R. E. Undermining children's intrinsic interest with extrinsic rewards: A test of the "overjustification" hypothesis. *Journal of Personality and Social Psychology,* 1973, *28,* 129–137.

Lessing, E. E. Racial differences in indices of ego-functioning relevant to academic achievement. *Journal of Genetic Psychology,* 1969, *115,* 153–167.

Leton, D. A. Assessment of school phobia. *Mental Hygiene,* 1962, *46,* 256–264.

Lewin, K., Lippitt, R., & White, R. K. Patterns of aggressive behavior in experimentally created social climates. *Journal of Social Psychology,* 1939, *10,* 271–299.

Lewis, M. *Origins of intelligence: Infancy and early childhood.* New York: Plenum, 1976.

Lewis, M., & Rosenblum, L. A. *The effect of the infant on its caregiver.* New York: Wiley, 1974.

Liebert, R. M., Neale, J. M., & Davidson, E. S. *The early window: Effects of television on children and youth.* New York: Pergamon, 1973.

Liebert, R. M., Poulos, R. W., & Strauss, G. D. *Developmental psychology.* Englewood Cliffs, N.J.: Prentice-Hall, 1974.

Lilly, M. S. Special education: A teapot in a tempest. *Exceptional Children,* 1970, *37,* 43–59.

Locke, E. A., Cartledge, N., & Koeppel, J. Motivating effect of knowledge of results. *Psychological Bulletin,* 1968, *70,* 474–485.

Lockhart, A. The motor learning of children. In C. B. Corbin (Ed.), *A textbook of motor development.* Dubuque, Iowa: Brown, 1973.

Lockheed, M. E., & Ekstrom, R. G. *Sex discrimination in education: A literature review and bibliography (ETS RB-77-5).* Princeton, N.J.: Educational Testing Service, May 1977.

Loehlin, J. C., Lindzey, L. G., & Spuhler, J. N. *Race differences in intelligence.* San Francisco: Freeman, 1975.

Lott, A. J., & Lott, B. E. Group cohesiveness and individual learning. *Journal of Educational Psychology,* 1966, *57,* 61–73.

Lundgren, V. *Frame factors and the teaching process.* Stockholm: Almquist and Wiksell, 1972.

Luria, A. R. *The role of speech in the regulation of normal and abnormal behavior.* New York: Pergamon, 1961.

Lyle, J., & Hoffman, H. Children's use of television and other media. In E. A. Rubenstein, G. A. Comstock, & J. P. Murray (Eds.), *Television and social behavior,* Vol. 4. *Television in day-to-day life: Patterns of use.* Washington, D.C.: U.S. Government Printing Office, 1972.

Lynn, D. B. *The father: His role in child development.* Monterey, Calif.: Brooks-Cole, 1974.

Lyons, H. *Learning to feel: Feeling to learn.* Columbus, Ohio: Merrill, 1971.

Maccoby, E. E. *The development of sex differences.* Stanford, Calif.: Stanford University Press, 1966.

Maccoby, E. E., & Jacklyn, C. N. *The psychology of sex differences.* Stanford, Calif.: Stanford University Press, 1974.

Maccoby, E. E., & Wilson, W. C. Identification and observational learning from films. *Journal of Personality,* 1957, *26,* 259–267.

MacKinnon, D. W. The nature and nurture of creative talent. *American Psychologist,* 1962, *17,* 484–493.

MacMillan, D. L., Forness, S. R., & Trumbull, B. M. The role of punishment in the classroom. *Exceptional Children,* 1973, *40,* 85–96.

MacMillan, D. L., & Meyers, C. E. Educational labeling of handicapped learners. In D. C. Berliner (Ed.), *Review of Research in Education: 7.* Washington, D.C.: American Educational Research Association, 1979.

Mager, R. F. *Preparing objectives for instruction.* Belmont, Calif.: Fearon, 1962.

Mager, R. F. *Developing attitude toward learning.* Belmont, Calif.: Fearon, 1968.

Mager, R. F., & Pipe, P. *Analyzing performance problems, or "You really oughta wanna."* Belmont, Calif.: Fearon, 1970.

Maher, B. A. *Principles of psychopathology: An experimental approach.* New York: McGraw-Hill, 1966.

Mahoney, M. J. Research issues in self-management. *Behavior Therapy,* 1972, *3,* 46–63.

Mahoney, M. J. *Cognition and behavior modification.* Cambridge, Mass.: Ballinger, 1974.

Mahoney, M. J., & Thoresen, C. E. *Self-control: Power to the person.* Monterey, Calif.: Brooks/Cole, 1974.

Maier, N. R. F. Reasoning in humans. I. ON direction. *Journal of Comparative Psychology.* 1930, *10,* 115–143.

Malik, S. R., & McCandless, B. R. A study of the catharsis of aggression. *Journal of Personality and Social Psychology,* 1966, *4,* 591–596.

Mannebach, A. J., & Stilwell, W. E. Installing career education: A systems approach. *Vocational Guidance Quarterly,* 1974, *22,* 180–188.

Mannebach, A. J., & Stilwell, W. E. Developing career education: A team approach. *Vocational Guidance Quarterly,* 1978, *26,* 308–317.

Markle, S. M., & Tiemann, P. W. Some principles of instructional design at higher cognitive levels. In R. Ulrich, T. Stachnik, & J. Mabry (Eds.), *Control of human behavior,* Vol. 3. Glenview, Ill.: Scott, Foresman, 1974.

Marland, S. P., Jr. *Career education now.* Paper delivered at the convention of the National Association of Secondary School Principals. Houston, Texas, 1971.

Marston, A. R. Imitation, self-reinforcement, and reinforcement of another person. *Journal of Personality and Social Psychology,* 1965, *2,* 255–261.

Martinson, R. A. Children with superior cognitive abilities. In L. M. Dunn (Ed.), *Exceptional children in the schools* (rev. ed.). New York: Holt, 1973.

Martorano, S. A developmental analysis of performance on Piaget's formal operations tasks. *Developmental Psychology,* 1977, *13,* 666–672.

Martuza, V. R. *Applying norm-referenced and criterion-referenced measurement in education.* Boston: Allyn and Bacon, 1977.

Maslow, A. H. A theory of human motivation. *Psychological Review,* 1943, *50,* 370–396.

Masters, J. C., Furman, W., & Barden, R. C. Effects of achievement standards, tangible rewards and self-dispensed achievement evaluations on children's task mastery. *Child Development,* 1977, *48,* 217–224.

Matteson, D. R. *Adolescence today: Sex roles and the search for identity.* Homewood, Ill.: Dorsey, 1975.

McAleer, I. M. The parent, teacher, and child as conference partners. *Teaching Exceptional Children,* 1978, *10,* 103–105.

McCall, R. B., Applebaum, M. I., & Hogarty, P. S. Developmental changes in mental performance. *Monographs of the Society for Research in Child Development*, 1973, *38*(3), Whole No. 150.

McCandless, B. R., & Evans, E. D. *Children and youth: Psychological development*. Hinsdale, Ill.: Dryden, 1973.

McClelland, D. C., Atkinson, J. W., Clark, R. A., & Lowell, E. L. *The achievement motive*. New York: Appleton-Century-Crofts, 1953.

McGee, C. S., Kauffman, J. M., & Nussen, J. L. Children as therapeutic change agents: Reinforcement intervention paradigms. *Review of Educational Research*, 1977, *47*, 451–477.

McGinnies, E. *Social behavior: A functional analysis*. Boston: Houghton Mifflin, 1970.

McLachlan, J. F. C., & Hunt, D. E. Differential effects of discovery learning as a function of student conceptual level. *Canadian Journal of Behavioural Science*, 1973, *5*, 152–160.

McLaughlin, T. F. Self-control in the classroom. *Review of Educational Research*, 1976, *46*, 631–663.

McLeish, J. *The lecture method*. Cambridge, England: Cambridge Institute of Education, 1968.

McMillan, J. H. The social psychology of education: New field of study or just educational psychology. *Educational Psychologist*, 1978, *12*, 345–354.

McNeill, D. *The acquisition of language*. New York: Harper & Row, 1970.

Mednick, M., Tangri, S. S., & Hoffman, L. W. *Women and achievement: Social and motivational analysis*. New York: Halstead, 1975.

Meichenbaum, D. *The nature and modification of impulsive children*. Paper presented at the meeting of the Society for Research in Child Development, 1971. (As cited in D. Meichenbaum, *Cognitive-behavior modification*. New York: Plenum, 1977.

Meichenbaum, D. *Cognitive behavior modification: An integrative approach*. New York: Plenum, 1977.

Meichenbaum, D., & Goodman, J. Reflection-impulsivity and verbal control of motor behavior. *Child Development*, 1969, *40*, 785–797.

Melton, A. W., & Martin, E. (Eds.), *Coding processes in human memory*. Washington, D.C.: Winston, 1972.

Melton, R. F. Resolution of conflicting claims concerning the effects of behavioral objectives on student learning. *Review of Educational Research*, 1978, *48*, 291–302.

Mercer, J. Psychological assessment and the rights of children. In N. Hobbs (Ed.), *Issues in the classification of children*, Vol. 1. San Francisco: Jossey Bass, 1975, pp. 130–158.

Mercer, J. *System of multicultural pluralistic assessment (SOMPA)*. New York: Psychological Corporation, 1977.

Messer, S. B. The relation of internal-external control to academic performance. *Child Development*, 1972, *43*, 1456–1462.

Meyerowitz, J. H. Self-derogation in young retardates and special class placement. *Child Development*, 1962, *33*, 443–451.

Michaels, J. W. Classroom reward structure and academic performance. *Review of Educational Research*, 1977, *47*, 89–98.

Miller, D. R., & Swanson, G. E. *Inner conflict and defense.* New York: Holt, 1960.

Miller, G. A. The magical number seven; plus or minus two: Some limits on our capacity for processing information. *Psychological Review,* 1956, *63,* 81–97.

Miller, G. A. Some psychological studies of grammar. *American Psychologist,* 1962, *17,* 748–762.

Miller, J. A. *Humanizing the classroom.* New York: Praeger, 1976.

Miller, L. B., & Dyer, J. L. Four preschool programs: Their dimensions and effects. *Monographs of the Society for Research in Child Development,* 1975, *40* (Serial No. 162).

Minuchin, P., Biber, B., Shapiro, E., & Zimiles, H. *The psychological impact of school experience: A comparative study of nine-year-old children in contrasting schools.* New York: Basic Books, 1969.

Mischel, W. *Personality and assessment.* New York: Wiley, 1968.

Mischel, W. Toward a cognitive social learning reconceptualization of personality. *Psychological Review,* 1973, *80,* 252–283.

Mischel, W. *Introduction to personality.* Holt, 1976.

Mischel, W. On the future of personality and measurement. *American Psychologist,* 1977, *32,* 246–254.

Mischel, W., & Liebert, R. Effects of discrepancies between observed and imposed reward criteria on their acquisition and transmission. *Journal of Personality and Social Psychology,* 1966, *3,* 45–53.

Mischel, W., & Mischel, H. N. A cognitive social learning approach to morality and self-regulation. In T. Lickona (Ed.), *Moral development and behavior: Theory, research and social issues.* New York: Holt, 1976.

Mitchell, A. M., Jones, G. B., & Krumboltz, J. D. *Social learning and career decision making.* Cranston, R.I.: Carroll, 1979.

Moos, R. H. *Evaluating treatment environments: A social ecological approach.* New York: Wiley, 1974.

Mowrer, O. H. *Learning theory and the symbolic processes.* New York: Wiley, 1960.

Murray, H. *Explorations in personality: A clinical and experimental study of fifty men of college age.* New York: Oxford, 1938.

Murray, J. P. Television and violence: Implications of the Surgeon General's research program. *American Psychologist,* 1973, *28,* 474–478.

Mussen, P. H., & Jones, M. C. Self-conceptions, motivations, and interpersonal attitudes of late and early maturing boys. *Child Development,* 1957, *28,* 243–256.

Mussen, P. H., & Jones, M. C. The behavior inferred motivations of late and early maturing boys. *Child Development,* 1958, *29,* 61–67.

National Education Association. *Combatting discrimination in the schools: Legal remedies and guidelines,* Washington, D.C., 1973.

National Education Association. *Today's changing roles: An approach to non-sexist teaching,* Washington, D.C., 1974.

National Organization for Women, Education Task Force Report, NOW, 1976.

Nelson, C. M., & Gast, D. L. Legal and ethical considerations for the use of time out in special education settings. *Journal of Special Education.* 1978, *11,* 457–467.

Nelson, C. M., Polsgrove, L., & Worell, J. Behaviorally disordered peers as contingency managers. *Behavior Therapy,* 1973, *4,* 270–276.

Notz, W. W. Work motivation and the negative effects of extrinsic rewards. *American Psychologist,* 1975, *30,* 884–891.

O'Grady, D. J. Psycholinguistic abilities in learning-disabled, emotionally disturbed, and normal children. *Journal of Special Education,* 1974, *8,* 157–165.

O'Leary, K. D., & Drabman, R. Token reinforcement in the classroom: A review. *Psychological Bulletin,* 1971, *75,* 379–398.

O'Leary, K. D., Kaufman, K., Kess, R., & Drabman, R. The effects of loud and soft reprimands on the behavior of disruptive students. *Exceptional Children,* 1970, *36,* 145–155.

O'Leary, K. D., & O'Leary, S. G. *Classroom management: The successful use of behavior modification.* New York: Pergamon, 1977.

O'Leary, K. D., Pelham, W. E., Rosenbaum, A., & Price, G. H. Behavioral treatment of hyperkinetic children. *Clinical Pediatrics,* 1976, *15,* 510–515.

O'Leary, S. G., Dubey, D. R. Applications of self-control procedures by children: A review. *Journal of Applied Behavior Analysis,* 1979, *12,* 449–465.

Olson, M. Ways to achieve quality in school classrooms: Some definitive answers. *Phi Delta Kappan,* 1971, *53,* 63–65.

Omenn, G. S. Genetic issues in the syndrome of minimal brain dysfunction. In S. Walzer & P. H. Wolff (Eds.), *Minimal cerebral dysfunction in children.* New York: Grune & Stratton, 1973.

Otto, W., & Rarick, G. L. Effect of time of transition from manuscript to cursive writing upon subsequent performance in handwriting, spelling and reading. *Journal of Educational Research,* 1969, *62,* 211–216.

Page, E. B. Teacher comments and student performance: A seventy-four classroom experiment in school motivation. *Journal of Educational Psychology,* 1958, *49,* 173–181.

Page, E. B. The imminence of grading essays by computer. *Phi Delta Kappan,* 1966, *47,* 238–243.

Palermo, D., & Malfese, D. K. Language acquisition from five onwards. *Psychological Bulletin,* 1972, *78,* 409–428.

Palkes, H., Stewart, M., & Kahana, B. Porteus maze performance after training in self-directed verbal commands. *Child Development,* 1968, *39,* 817–826.

Paolitto, D. P. The effect of cross-age tutoring on adolescence: An inquiry into theoretical assumptions. *Review of Educational Research,* 1976, *46,* 215–237.

Parish, T. S., & Copeland, T. F. Teacher's and student's attitudes in mainstreamed classrooms. *Psychological Reports,* 1978, *43,* 54.

Parish, T. S., Eads, G. M., Reece, N. R., & Piscitello, M. A. Assessment and attempted modification of future teacher's attitudes toward handicapped children. *Perceptual and Motor Skills,* 1977, *44,* 540–542.

Parish, T. S., Ohlsen, R. L., & Parish, J. G. A look at mainstreaming in the light of children's attitudes toward the handicapped. *Perceptual and Motor Skills,* 1979, *46,* 1019–1021.

Parke, R. D. *Readings in social development.* New York: Holt, 1969.

Parke, R. D., & Collmer, C. W. Child abuse: An interdisciplinary analysis. In E. M. Hetherington (Ed.), *Review of child development research,* Vol. 5. Chicago: University of Chicago Press, 1975.

Parsons, J. E. *The development of attributions, expectancies and persistence.*

Paper presented at annual meeting of American Educational Research Association, March 1978.

Parsons, J. E., & Ruble, D. N. The development of achievement-related expectancies. *Child Development*, 1977, *48*, 1075–1079.

Passow, A. H., & Elliott, D. L. The nature and needs of the educationally disadvantaged. In A. H. Passow (Ed.), *Developing programs for the disadvantaged*. New York: Teachers College Press, 1968.

Patterson, G. R., & Cobb, J. A. A dyadic analysis of aggressive behavior. In J. P. Hill (Ed.), *Minnesota symposium on child psychology,* vol. 5. Minneapolis: University of Minnesota Press, 1971.

Patterson, G. R., & Gullion, M. E. *Living with children: New methods for parents and teachers*. Research Press, 1976.

Payne, J. The gifted. In N. G. Haring (Ed.), *Behavior of exceptional children: An introduction to special education*. Columbus, Ohio: Merrill, 1974.

Penk, W. E. Age changes and correlates of internal-external locus of control scale. *Psychological Reports*, 1969, *25,* 856.

Peplau, L. A. Impact of fear of success and sex-role attitudes on women's competitive achievement. *Journal of Personality and Social Psychology,* 1976, *34,* 561–568.

Peterson, C., Peterson, J. H., & Scriven, G. Peer imitation by non-handicapped and handicapped preschoolers. *Exceptional Children,* 1977, *43,* 223–224.

Phares, E. J. *Locus of control in personality*. Morristown, N.J.: Silver Burdett, 1976.

Phillips, B. N., Martin, R. P., & Meyers, J. Interventions in relation to anxiety in school. In C. D. Spielberger (Ed.), *Anxiety: Current trends in theory and research*. New York: Academic Press, 1972.

Piaget, J. *The origins of intelligence*. New York: International Universities Press, 1952.

Piaget, J. Piaget's theory. In P. H. Mussen (Ed.), *Carmichael's manual of child psychology* (3d ed.), Vol. I. New York: Wiley, 1970.

Piaget, J. *Science of education and the psychology of the child*. New York: Viking, 1971.

Piaget, J. *The child and reality*. New York: Viking, 1973.

Piaget, J., & Inhelder, B. *The psychology of the child*. New York: Basic Books, 1969.

Pietrofesa, J. J., & Schlossberg, N. K. Counselor bias and the female occupational role. In J. Pottker & A. Fishel (Eds.), *Sex bias in the schools*. Rutherford, N.J.: Fairleigh Dickinson University Press, 1977.

Popham, W. J. Instructional objectives exchange: New support for criterion-referenced instruction. *Phi Delta Kappan*, 1970, *52,* 174–175.

Popham, W. J. Teaching skill under scrutiny. *Phi Delta Kappan*, 1971, *52,* 199–201.

Popham, W. J. *Criterion-referenced measurement*. Englewood Cliffs, N.J.: Prentice-Hall, 1978(a).

Popham, W. J. The case for criterion-referenced measurement. *Educational Researcher,* 1978b, 7(11), 6–10.

Popham, W. J., & Baker, E. L. *Systematic instruction*. Englewood Cliffs, N.J.: Prentice-Hall, 1970.

Pottker, J. Psychological and occupational sex stereotypes in elementary school readers. In J. Pottker & A. Fishel (Eds.), *Sex bias in the schools*. Rutherford, N.J.: Fairleigh Dickinson University Press, 1977.

Pottker, J., & Fishel, A. *Sex bias in the schools*. Rutherford, N.J.: Fairleigh Dickinson University Press, 1977.

Premack, D. Toward empirical behavioral laws: I. Positive reinforcement. *Psychological Review,* 1959, *69,* 219–233.

Premack, D. Reinforcement theory. In D. Levine (Ed.), *Nebraska symposium on motivation,* Vol. 13. Lincoln, Nebr.: University of Nebraska Press, 1965.

Pressley, M. Increasing children's self-control through cognitive interventions. *Review of Educational Research,* 1979, *49,* 319–370.

Provus, M. *Discrepancy model for educational program improvement and assessment.* Berkeley, Calif.: McCutchen, 1971.

Purkey, W. W. *Self-concept and school achievement.* Englewood Cliffs, N.J.: Prentice-Hall, 1976.

Purkey, W. W. *Inviting school success: A self-concept approach to teaching and learning.* Belmont, Calif.: Wadsworth, 1978.

Quay, H. C. The facets of educational exceptionality: A conceptual framework for assessment, grouping and instruction. *Exceptional Children,* 1968, *35,* 25–31.

Rafferty, M. An analysis of Summerhill—continued. In H. H. Hart (Ed.), *Summerhill: For and against.* New York: Hart, 1970.

Raths, L. E., Harmin, M., & Simon, S. B. *Values and teaching.* Columbus, Ohio: Merrill, 1966.

Rees, A. H., & Palmer, F. H. Factors related to change in mental test performance. *Developmental Psychology Monograph,* 1970, *3*(2).

Reese, E. P., Howard, J. S., & Reese, T. W. *Human behavior: An experimental analysis and its applications.* Dubuque, Iowa: Brown, 1977.

Reese, H. W., & Lipsett, L. P. *Experimental child psychology.* New York: Academic Press, 1970.

Reger, R., & Koppman, M. The child-oriented resource room program. *Exceptional Children,* 1971, *37,* 460–462.

Reigeluth, C. M., & Merrill, M. D. A knowledge base for improving our methods of instruction. *Educational Psychologist,* 1978, *13,* 57–70.

Reynolds, M. C., & Birch, J. W. *Teaching exceptional children in all America's schools: A first course for teachers and principals.* Reston, Va.: Council for Exceptional Children, 1977.

Rheingold, H. L. The development of social behavior in human infants. In H. W. Stevenson (Ed.), Concepts of development. *Monographs of the Society for Research in Child Development,* 1966, *3,* No. 107, 2–17.

Richmond, B. O., & Dalton, J. L. Teacher ratings and self-concept reports of retarded pupils. *Exceptional Children,* 1973, *40,* 178–183.

Rist, R. Student social class and teacher expectations: The self-fulfilling prophecy in ghetto education. *Harvard Educational Review,* 1970, *40,* 411–451.

Robertson, D., & Keeley, S. *Evaluation of a mediational training program for impulsive children by a multiple case study design.* Paper presented at the meeting of the American Psychological Association, 1974. (As cited in D. Meichenbaum, *Cognitive-behavior modification: An integrative approach.* New York: Plenum, 1977.)

Robinson, H. B., & Robinson, N. M. Longitudinal development of very young children in a comprehensive day care program: The first two years. *Child Development*, 1971, *42*, 1673–1683.

Rosen, B. C., & D'Andrade, R. The psychological origins of achievement motivation. *Sociometry*, 1959, *22*, 185–218.

Rosenbaum, M. S., & Drabman, R. S. Self-control training in the classroom: A review and critique. *Journal of Applied Behavior Analysis*, 1979, *12*, 467–485.

Rosenkrantz, P., Vogel, S., Bee, H., Broverman, I., & Broverman, D. Sex-role stereotypes and self-concepts in college students. *Journal of Consulting and Clinical Psychology*, 1968, *32*, 287–295.

Rosenshine, B. Enthusiastic teaching: A research review. *School Review*, 1970, *78*, 499–514.

Rosenshine, B., & Furst, N. The use of direct observations to study teaching. In R. M. W. Travers (Ed.), *Second handbook of research on teaching*. Chicago: Rand McNally, 1973.

Rosenthal, T. L., & Zimmerman, B. J. Modeling by exemplification and instruction in training conservation. *Developmental Psychology*, 1972, *6*, 392–401.

Rosenthal, T. L., & Zimmerman, B. J. *Social learning and cognition*. New York: Academic Press, 1978.

Ross, A. O. *Psychological aspects of learning disabilities and reading disorders*. New York: McGraw-Hill, 1976.

Ross, M. The self-perception of intrinsic motivation. In J. H. Harvey, W. J. Ickes, & R. F. Kidd (Eds.), *New directions in attribution research*. Hillsdale, N.J.: Erlbaum, 1976.

Rotter, J. B. *Social learning and clinical psychology*. Englewood Cliffs, N.J.: Prentice-Hall, 1954.

Rotter, J. B. Generalized expectancies for internal versus external control of reinforcement. *Psychological Monographs*, 1966, *80* (Whole No. 609).

Rowe, M. B. Science, silence, and sanctions. *Science and Children*, 1969, *6*, 11–13.

Rowe, M. B. Wait-time and rewards as instructional variables, their influence on language, logic, and fate of control: Part one—wait time. *Journal of Research in Science Teaching*, 1974, *11*, 81–91.

Rudman, M. K. Standardized test taking: Your students can do better. *Learning*, 1976, *4*(6), 76–82.

Ryans, D. G. *Characteristics of teachers*. Washington, D.C.: American Council on Education, 1960.

Sabatino, D. A. A scientific approach toward a discipline of special education. *Journal of Special Education*, 1971, *5*, 15–22.

Sadker, D., & Sadker, M. Nonsexist teaching: Strategies and practical applications. In J. D. Grambs (Ed.), *Teaching about women in the social studies: Concepts, methods and materials*. National Council for the Social Studies, 1976, No. 48.

Salvia, J., & Ysseldyke, J. E. *Assessment in special and remedial education*. Boston: Houghton Mifflin, 1978.

Salzburg, C. L. Freedom and responsibility in an elementary school. In G. Semb (Ed.), *Behavior analysis and education*. Lawrence: University of Kansas, Department of Human Development, 1972.

Sarason, S. B., Davidson, K. S., Lighthall, F. F., Waite, R. R., & Ruebush, B. K. *Anxiety in elementary school children.* New York: Wiley, 1960.

Sarason, S. B., Hill, K. T., & Zimbardo, P. G. A longitudinal study of the relationship of test anxiety to performance on intelligence and achievement tests. *Monographs of the Society for Research in Child Development,* 1964, *29,* Whole No. 7.

Sassenrath, J. M. Theory and results on feedback and retention. *Journal of Educational Psychology,* 1975, *67,* 894–899.

Scandura, J. M. Structural approach to instructional problems. *American Psychologist,* 1977, *32,* 33–53.

Scanlon, R. G., & Brown, M. V. Individualizing instruction. In D. S. Bushnell & D. Rappaport (Eds.), *Planned change in education.* New York: Harcourt, Brace, Jovanovich, 1971.

Schacter, S. Deviation, rejection, and communication. *Journal of Abnormal and Social Psychology,* 1951, *46,* 190–207.

Scharf, P. *Readings in moral education.* Minneapolis: Winston, 1978.

Schwebel, A., & Cherlin, D. Physical and social distancing in teacher-pupil relationships. *Journal of Educational Psychology,* 1972, *63,* 543–550.

Schwebel, M. Formal operations in college freshmen. *Journal of Psychology,* 1975, *91,* 133–141.

Schwitzgebel, R., & Kolb, D. A. Inducing behavior change in adolescent delinquents. *Behavior Research and Therapy,* 1964, *1,* 297–304.

Scriven, M. The methodology of evaluation. In R. W. Tyler, R. M. Gagné, & M. Scriven (Eds.), *Perspectives of curriculum evaluation: AERA monograph series on curriculum evaluation.* Chicago: Rand McNally, 1967, *1,* 39–83.

Sears, R. R. Identification as a form of behavior development. In D. B. Harris (Ed.), *The concept of development.* Minneapolis: Jones Press, 1957.

Sears, R. R. Relation of early socialization experiences to aggression in middle childhood. *Journal of Abnormal and Social Psychology,* 1961, *63,* 466–492.

Sears, R. R., Maccoby, E. E., & Levin, H. *Patterns of child rearing.* New York: Harper & Row, 1957.

Sears, R. R., Rau, L., & Alpert, R. *Identification and child rearing.* Stanford Calif.: Stanford University Press, 1965.

Seavy, C. A., Katz, P. A., & Zalk, S. R. Baby X: The effect of gender labels on adult responses to infants. *Sex Roles,* 1975, *1,* 103–110.

Semmel, M. I., Gottlieb, J., & Robinson, N. M. Mainstreaming: Perspectives on educating handicapped children in the public schools. In D. C. Berliner (Ed.), *Review of Research in Education: 7.* Washington, D.C.: American Educational Research Association, 1979.

Serbin, L. A., & Connor, J. M. Environmental control of sex-related behaviors in the preschool. Paper presented at the Society for Research in Child Development. San Francisco, March 1979.

Serbin, L. A., O'Leary, D. K., Kent, R. N., & Tonik, J. J. A comparison of teacher response to the preacademic and problem behavior of boys and girls. *Child Development,* 1973, *44,* 796–804.

Sexton, P. *The feminized male.* New York: Vintage, 1969.

Sexton, P. *Women in education.* Bloomington, Ind.: Phi Delta Kappa, Educational Foundation, 1976.

Shatz, M., & Gelman, R. The development of communication skills: Modifications of the speech of young children as a function of listener. *Monographs of the Society for Research in Child Development,* 1973, *38,* No. 5.

Shaw, M. E. *Group dynamics—The psychology of small group behavior,* 2d ed. New York: McGraw-Hill, 1976.

Shuy, R. Non-standard dialect problems. In J. L. Laffey & R. Shuy (Eds.), *Language differences: Do they interfere?* Newark, Del.: International Reading Association, 1973.

Sigel, I. E., & Cocking, R. R. *Cognitive development from childhood to adolescence: A constructivist perspective.* New York: Holt, 1977.

Simon, S., Howe, H., & Kirschenbaum, H. *Values clarification: A handbook of practical strategies.* New York: Hart, 1972.

Singer, R. D., & Singer, A. *Psychological development in children.* Philadelphia: Saunders, 1969.

Siperstein, G., & Gottlieb, J. Physical stigma and academic performance as factors affecting children's first impressions of handicapped peers. *American Journal of Mental Deficiency,* 1977, *81,* 455–462.

Skinner, B. F. *Science and human behavior.* New York: Macmillan, 1953.

Skinner, B. F. The science and the art of teaching. *Harvard Educational Review,* 1954, *24,* 86–97.

Skinner, B. F. *Verbal behavior.* New York: Appleton-Century-Crofts, 1957.

Skinner, B. F. *The technology of teaching.* New York: Appleton-Century-Crofts, 1968.

Slaby, R. G., & Frey, K. S. Development of gender constancy and selective attention to same-sex models. *Child Development,* 1975, *46,* 848–856.

Slavin, R. E. Classroom reward structure: An analytical and practical review. *Review of Educational Research,* 1977, *47,* 633–650.

Smith, M. F. *The valuing approach to career education.* Waco, Texas: Educational Achievement Corporation, 1972.

Smith, R. M. *Teacher diagnosis of educational difficulties.* Columbus, Ohio: Merrill, 1969.

Smith, R. M., & Neisworth, J. T. *The exceptional child: A functional approach.* New York: McGraw-Hill, 1975.

Smith, S. F., & Worell, J. The screening test of educational prerequisite skills. *Journal of Educational Measurement,* 1980 (in press).

Soloman, D., & Kendall, A. J. *Individual characteristics and children's performance in varied educational settings.* Chicago: Spencer Foundation, Final Report, 1976.

Soloman, D., & Kendall, A. J. *Children in classrooms: An investigation of person-environment interaction.* New York: Praeger, 1979.

Sontag, L. W., Baker, C. T., & Nelson, V. L. Mental growth and personality: A longitudinal study. *Monographs of the Society for Research in Child Development,* 1958, *23,* 1–143.

Spearman, C. *The abilities of man: Their nature and measurement.* New York: Macmillan, 1927.

Spence, K. A theory of emotionally-based drive (D) and its relation to performance in simple learning situations. *American Psychologist,* 1958, *13,* 131–141.

Spielberger, C. (Ed.), *Anxiety and behavior.* New York: Academic Press, 1966.

Sroufe, A. L., & Waters, E. Attachment as an organizational construct. *Child Development,* 1977, *48,* 1184–1199.

Staats, A. W. *Child learning, intelligence, and personality.* New York: Harper & Row, 1971.

Staats, A. W. *Social behaviorism.* Homewood, Ill.: Dorsey, 1975.

Staffieri, R. J. A study of social stereotypes and body image in children. *Journal of Personality and Social Psychology,* 1967, *7,* 101–104.

Stake, R. E. *Evaluating the arts in education: A responsive approach.* Columbus, Ohio: Merrill, 1975.

Stallings, J. A. Implementation and child effects of teaching practices in Follow-Through classrooms. *Monographs of the Society for Research in Child Development,* 1975, *40* (No. 163).

Stallings, J. A. *Teaching basic reading skills in secondary schools.* Paper presented at the Annual Meeting of the American Educational Research Association, Toronto, March, 1978.

Starch, D., & Elliot, E. C. Reliability of the grading of high school work in English. *School Review,* 1912, *20,* 442–445.

Stein, A. H., & Bailey, M. M. The socialization of achievement orientation in females. *Psychological Bulletin,* 1973, *80,* 345–366.

Stein, A. H., & Friedrich, L. K. Television content and young children's behavior. In J. P. Murray, E. A. Rubenstein, & G. A. Comstock (Eds.), *Television and social behavior,* Vol. 2. *Television and social learning.* Washington, D.C.: U.S. Government Printing Office, 1972.

Stein, A. H., & Friedrich, L. K. The impact of television on children and youth. In E. M. Hetherington (Ed.), *Review of child development research,* Vol. 5. Chicago: University of Chicago Press, 1975.

Stewart, J. C. *Counseling parents of exceptional children.* Columbus, Ohio: Merrill, 1978.

Stewart, M. A., Pitts, F. N., Craig, A. G., & Dieruf, W. The hyperactive child syndrome. *American Journal of Orthopsychiatry,* 1966, *36,* 861–867.

Stilwell, W. E. A systems approach for social, educational, and institutional change. In L. C. Silvern (Ed.), *Application of systems thinking to the administration of instruction.* Los Angeles, Calif.: Educational and Training Consultants, 1976, 79–88.

Stilwell, W. E. *A comprehensive affective-social educational system (CASES),* 1977. (ERIC Document Reproduction Service ED 136 176.)

Stilwell, W. E., & Barclay, J. R. Effects of an affective-social education program over two years, 1978. (ERIC Documentation Reproduction Service ED 143 425.)

Stilwell, W. E., & Barclay, J. R. Effects of affective education interventions in the elementary schools. *Psychology in the Schools,* 1979, *16,* 80–87.

Stilwell, W. E., & Santoro, D. A. A training model for the 80's. *Personnel and Guidance Journal,* 1976, *54,* 322–326.

Stilwell, W. E., & Thoresen, C. E. Social modeling and vocational behaviors in Mexican American and non-Mexican American adolescents. *Vocational Guidance Quarterly,* 1972, *20,* 279–286.

Strauss, A., & Kephart, N. *Psychopathology and education of the brain-injured child.* New York: Grune & Stratton, 1955.

Stufflebeam, D. L. The use of experimental design in educational evaluation. *Journal of Educational Measurement, 1971, 4,* 267–274.

Stukat, K. G. *Suggestibility: A factorial and experimental analysis.* Stockholm: Almquist and Wiksell, 1958.

Sullivan, H. S. *The interpersonal theory of psychiatry.* New York: Norton, 1953.

Sulzer-Azaroff, B., & Mayer, G. R. *Applying behavioral analysis procedures with children and youth.* New York: Holt, 1977.

Super, D. E. *The psychology of careers.* New York: Harper & Row, 1957.

Surratt, P. R., Ulrich, R. E., & Hawkins, R. P. An elementary student as a behavioral engineer. *Journal of Applied Behavior Analysis, 1969, 2,* 85–92.

Tanner, J. M. *Growth at adolescence.* Oxford: Blackwell Science Publishers, 1955.

Tanner, J. M. Physical growth. In P. H. Mussen (Ed.), *Carmichael's handbook of child psychology* (3d ed.), Vol. 1. New York: Wiley, 1970.

Telford, C. W., & Sawry, J. M. *The exceptional individual* (2d ed.). Englewood Cliffs, N.J.: Prentice-Hall, 1972.

Terman, L. M. *The measurement of intelligence.* Boston: Houghton Mifflin, 1916.

Terman, L. M., & Merrill, M. A. *Measuring intelligence.* Boston: Houghton Mifflin, 1937.

Terman, L. M., & Oden, M. *Genetic studies of genius,* Vol. 1. *The mental and physical traits of a thousand gifted children.* Stanford: Stanford University Press, 1925.

Terman, L. M., & Oden, M. *Genetic studies of genius: The gifted group at mid-life. Thirty-five years' follow-up of the superior child.* Stanford, Calif.: Stanford University Press, 1954.

Thayer, L., & Beeler, K. D. (Eds.), *Affective innovations for learning.* Ypsilanti, Mich.: Eastern Michigan University, 1977.

Thomas, A., Chess, S., & Birch, H. G. *Temperament and behavior disorders in children.* New York: University Press, 1968.

Thoresen, C. E. Constructs don't speak for themselves. *Counselor Education and Supervision, 1977, 16,* 296–303.

Thoresen, C. E., & Mahoney, M. J. *Behavioral self-control: Power to the person.* Monterey, Calif.: Brooks/Cole, 1974.

Thurstone, L. L. *Primary mental abilities.* Psychometric Monographs, No. 1. Chicago: University of Chicago Press, 1938.

Thurstone, L. L., & Thurstone, T. G. *SRA primary abilities.* Chicago: Science Research Associates, 1963.

Torrance, E. P. *Torrance tests of creative thinking.* Princeton, N.J.: Personnel Press, 1966.

Torrance, E. P. *Encouraging creativity in the classroom.* Dubuque, Iowa: Brown, 1970.

Trabasso, T. R. Stimulus emphasis and all-or-none learning in concept identification. *Journal of Experimental Psychology, 1963, 65,* 398–406.

Tracy, J., & Cross, R. Antecedents of shift in moral judgement. *Journal of Personality and Social Psychology, 1973, 26,* 238–244.

Trap, J. J., Milner-Davis, P., Joseph, S., & Cooper, J. O. The effects of feedback and consequences on traditional cursive letter formation, *Journal of Applied Behavior Analysis, 1978, 11,* 381–393.

Travers, R. M., Van Wagenen, R. K., Haygood, D. H., & McCormick, M. Learning as a consequence of the learner's task involvement under different conditions of feedback. *Journal of Educational Psychology,* 1964, *55,* 167–173.

Tulin, S. R. Race, class, family and school achievement. *Journal of Personality and Social Psychology,* 1968, *9,* 31–37.

Tulving, E., & Donaldson, W. (Eds.), *Organization of memory.* New York: Academic Press, 1972.

Turkewitz, H., O'Leary, K. D., & Ironsmith, M. Generalization and maintenance of appropriate behavior through self-control. *Journal of Consulting and Clinical Psychology,* 1975, *43,* 577–583.

Tyler, B. Peers as social agents. In J. Worell (Ed.), *Psychological development in the elementary years.* New York: Academic Press, 1980.

Underwood, B. J. Interference and forgetting. *Psychological Review,* 1957, *64,* 49–60.

Underwood, B. J., & Schultz, R. W. *Meaningfulness and verbal learning.* Philadelphia: Lippincott, 1960.

Varenhorst, B. B. Peer counseling: A guidance program and a behavioral intervention. In J. D. Krumboltz & C. E. Thoresen (Eds.), *Counseling methods.* New York: Holt, 1976, 541–556.

Walker, J. E., & Shea, T. M. *Behavior modification: A practical approach for educators.* St. Louis, Mo.: Mosby, 1976.

Walker, R. N. Body build and behavior in young children: Body build and nursery school teacher's ratings. *Monographs of the Society for Research in Child Development,* 1962, *27*(3), No. 84.

Walters, G. C., & Grusec, J. E. *Punishment.* San Francisco: Freeman, 1977.

Weatherly, D. Self-perceived rate of physical maturation and personality in late adolescence. *Child Development,* 1964, *35,* 1197–1210.

Wechsler, D. *The measurement and appraisal of adult intelligence.* Baltimore: Williams & Wilkins, 1958.

Wechsler, D. *Manual for the Wechsler intelligence scale for children, revised.* New York: Psychological Corporation, 1974.

Weikert, D. P. Relationship of curriculum, teaching, and learning in preschool education. In J. C. Stanley (Ed.), *Preschool programs for the disadvantaged.* Baltimore: Johns Hopkins University Press, 1972.

Weiner, B. Attribution theory, achievement motivation and the education process. *Review of Educational Research,* 1972, *42,* 203–205.

Weiner, B., Frieze, I., Kukla, A., Reed, L., Rest, S., & Rosenbaum, R. M. *Perceiving the causes of success and failure.* Morristown, N.J.: General Learning Press, 1971.

Weiner, B., Heckhausen, H., Meyer, W. U., & Cook, R. E. Causal ascriptions and achievement motivation: A conceptual analysis of effort and reanalysis of locus of control. *Journal of Personality and Social Psychology,* 1972, *21,* 239–248.

Weiner, G., Rider, R. V., & Opel, W. Some correlates of I.Q. changes in children. *Child Development,* 1963, *34,* 61–67.

Weinraub, M., & Lewis, M. The determinants of children's responses to separation. *Monographs of the Society for Research in Child Development,* 1977, Serial No. 172, Vol. 42, No. 4.

Weisgerber, R. A. *Developmental efforts in individualized instruction.* Itasca, Ill.: Peacock, 1971.

Weitzman, L. J. Sex-role socialization. In J. Freeman (Ed.), *Women: A feminist perspective*. Palo Alto, Calif.: Mayfield Publishing, 1979.

Weitzman, L. J., & Rizzo, D. *Biased textbooks: A research perspective. Action steps you can take*. The Resource Center on Sex Roles in Education. National Foundation for the Improvement of Education, Washington, D.C., 1974.

Werry, J. S. Organic factors in childhood psychopathology. In H. C. Quay & J. S. Werry (Eds.), *Psychopathological disorders of childhood* (2d ed.), New York: Wiley, 1979.

Whalen, C. K., Henker, B., Collin, B. E., Finck, D., & Dotemoto, S. A social ecology of hyperactive boys' medication effects in structured classroom environments. *Journal of Applied Behavior Analysis*, 1979, *12*, 65–82.

White, R. W. Motivation reconsidered: The concept of competence. *Psychological Review*, 1959, *66*, 297–333.

White, S. H. Evidence for the hierarchical arrangement of learning processes. In L. P. Lipsett & C. C. Spiker (Eds.), *Advances in child development and behavior*, Vol. 2. New York: Academic Press, 1965.

Whitehurst, G. J. *The contributions of social learning theory to language acquisition*. Paper presented at the annual meeting of the American Educational Research Association. New York City, April, 1977.

Whiteman, M., Brown, B. R., & Deutsch, M. Some effects of social class and race on children's language and intellectual abilities. In M. Deutsch, et al. (Eds.), *The disadvantaged child*. New York: Basic Books, 1967.

Willis, J. W., Morris, B., & Crowder, J. A remedial reading technique for disabled readers that employs students as behavioral engineers. *Psychology in the Schools*, 1972, *9*, 67–70.

Wilson, A. B. Residential segregation of social classes and aspirations of high school boys. *American Sociological Review*, 1959, *24*, 836–845.

Wilson, A. B. Social stratification and academic achievement. In A. H. Passow (Ed.), *Education in depressed areas*. New York: Teachers College Press, 1963.

Winnet, R. A., & Winkler, R. C. Current behavior modification in the classroom: Be still, be quiet, be docile. *Journal of Applied Behavior Analysis*, 1972, *5*, 499–504.

Winterbottom, M. R. The relation of need for achievement to learning experiences in independence and mastery. In J. Atkinson (Ed.), *Motives in fantasy, action and society*. Princeton, N.J.: Van Nostrand, 1958, pp. 453–478.

Wittig, M. L. Culturally disadvantaged children and reading achievement. In *Combining research results and good practice*. Newark, Del.: International Reading Association, 1966, 2 (part 2), pp. 29–34.

Wittrock, M. C. The cognitive movement in instruction. *Educational Psychologist*, 1978, *13*, 15–29.

Wolfensberger, W. *The principle of normalization in human service*. Toronto: National Institute for Mental Retardation, 1972.

Wolff, R. The measurement of environments. In A. Anastasi (Ed.), *Testing problems in perspective*. Washington, D.C.: American Council on Education, 1966.

Worell, J. Child values inventory. In *Children and their relationship to public agencies*. Lexington, Ky.: Kentucky Humanities Council, 1976.

Worell, J. Sex roles and psychological well-being: Perspectives on methodology. *Journal of Consulting and Clinical Psychology*, 1978, *46*, 777–791.

Worell, J. Psychological sex roles: Significance and change. In J. Worell (Ed.),

Psychological development in the elementary years. New York: Academic Press, 1980.

Worell, J., & Nelson, C. M. *Managing instructional problems.* New York: McGraw-Hill, 1974.

Worell, L., & Worell, J. A theoretical and experimental note on "Conscious and pre-conscious influences on recall." *Journal of Personality and Social Psychology,* 1966, *3,* 119–123.

Wright, H. F. *Recording and analyzing child behavior.* New York: Harper & Row, 1967.

Wrightsman, L. S. *Social psychology.* Belmont, California: Wadsworth, 1977.

Yabroff, W. Learning decision making. In J. D. Krumboltz & C. E. Thoresen (Eds.), *Behavioral counseling: Cases and techniques.* New York: Holt, 1969.

Yarrow, M. R., Waxler, C. Z., & Scott, P. M. Child effects on adult behavior. *Developmental Psychology,* 1971, *5,* 300–311.

Zigler, E. Social class and the socialization process. *Review of Educational Research,* 1970, *40,* 87–110.

Zigler, E. The effectiveness of Head Start: Another look. *Educational Psychologist,* 1978, *13,* 71–78.

Zimmerman, B. J. *A social learning explanation for age-related changes in children's conceptual behavior.* Paper presented at a symposium titled "A social learning alternative to structured theories for explaining developmental changes in children's behavior." Annual meeting of the American Educational Research Association, New York City, April 1977(a).

Zimmerman, B. J. Modeling. In H. L. Hom, Jr., & P. A. Robinson (Eds.), *Psychological processes in early education.* New York: Academic Press, 1977(b).

Zimmerman, B. J., & Lanaro, P. Acquiring and retaining conservation of length through modeling and reversibility cues. *Merrill-Palmer Quarterly,* 1974, *20,* 145–161.

Zimmerman, B. J., & Rosenthal, T. L. Conserving and retaining equalities and inequalities through observation and correction. *Developmental Psychology,* 1974, *10,* 269–276.

Zimmerman, B. J., & Rosenthal, T. L. Observational learning of rule-governed behavior by children. *Psychological Bulletin,* 1974, *81,* 29–42.

Zubek, J. P. *Sensory deprivation: Fifteen years of research.* New York: Appleton-Century-Crofts, 1969.

INDEXES

NAME INDEX

Adams, R., 564
Agard, J., 629
Ainsworth, M., 109
Allinsmith, W., 16, 132, 321
Almy, M., 205
Alpert, R., 110
Alschuler, A. S., 122, 292, 294
American Personnel and Guidance
    Association, 108
Ames, L. B., 50
Anastasi, A., 53, 193
Anderson, E. M., 630
Anderson, R. C., 308
Andre, T., 308
Applebaum, M. I., 200, 201
Armatruda, C. S., 50
Aronfreed, J., 132, 133
Aronson, E., 560
Atkinson, J. W., 119, 120
Atkinson, R. C., 349
Ault, R., 188
Austin, H. R., 105, 294
Ausubel, D. P., 371, 379, 401
Ayllon, T., 582
Azrin, N. H., 128, 582

Bacon, M. K., 102
Baer, D. M., 52, 623
Bailey, M. M., 121, 290
Baird, L., 116
Baker, C. T., 200
Baker, E. L., 22
Baker, R. D., 431
Baldwin, T., 374
Bandura, A., 52, 55, 57, 113, 114,
    123, 126, 130, 135, 136, 185,
    266, 268, 269, 296, 306, 318,
    426, 471, 585

Banks, C. W., 290
Bany, M. A., 305, 559
Baratz, J., 181, 182
Barclay, L. K., 71, 429
Barclay, J. R., 39, 61, 71, 105, 115,
    138, 415, 425, 428, 462, 465,
    525, 555, 563, 629
Barden, R. C., 119, 121
Barker, L. L., 452
Barker, R. G., 554
Barringer, C., 349
Barrish, H. H., 562
Barry, H. B., 102
Barth, R. S., 579
Bash, M., 190
Battle, E. S., 76, 118, 119, 290
Baumrind, D., 80, 97, 132
Bayley, N., 200
Bean, J. P., 100–102
Beatty, J. N., 182, 183
Beck, F. W., 69
Becker, W. C., 78, 133, 141, 347,
    348, 361, 493
Bee, H. D., 64, 73
Beeler, K. D., 415
Beez, W., 607–609
Bell, R. Q., 55
Bem, S. L., 100, 107
Bereiter, C., 182, 202
Berenda, R., 113
Bergan, J. R., 359
Berger, C., 290
Berkowitz, L., 125, 127
Berlyne, D. E., 303, 464, 572
Bernstein, B. S., 74, 181
Bernstein, E., 304
Biber, B., 100
Bijou, S. W., 29, 623
Birch, H. G., 80

Birch, J. W., 228, 628, 630, 636, 638
Blackburn, J. E., 633
Blaney, N., 560
Blank, M., 202
Blehar, M., 109
Block, J. H., 481
Bloom, B. S., 48, 452, 527, 528
Bloom, L., 177
Bootzin, R. R., 312
Bounds, W., 504, 509
Bourassa, G., 164
Bourne, L. E., Jr., 365
Bowlby, J., 109
Boyd, R., 615, 623
Brackbill, Y., 225
Brainerd, C. J., 165, 166
Bramble, W. J., 488
Brenton, M., 627
Briggs, L. J., 52, 169, 205
Broden, M., 297, 298
Brodie, R. D., 324
Brody, D. S., 415, 427, 494
Brody, G. H., 135
Bronfenbrenner, U., 202
Brookover, W. B., 140
Brophy, J., 464, 607
Broverman, D., 64
Broverman, I., 64
Brown, A. L., 152, 155, 185, 378
Brown, B. R., 74
Brown, D., 633
Brown, J. L., 468
Brown, M. V., 490
Brown, P., 129
Brown, R., 74, 177
Bruner, E., 493
Bruner, J. S., 155, 166, 414, 473
Bryan, J. H., 84
Buck, M. R., 294

SUBJECT INDEX

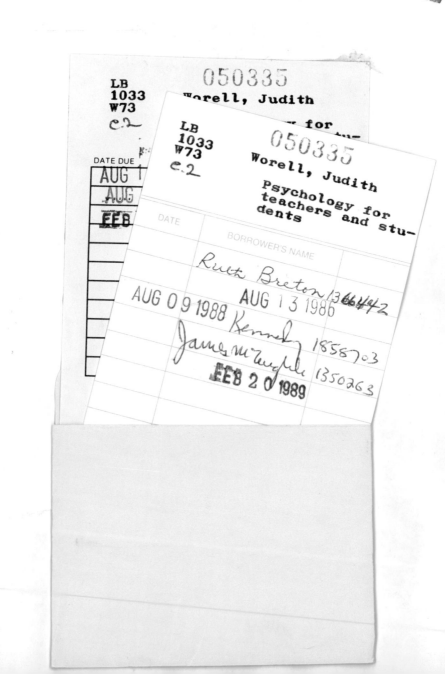